TALES
of the
CANADIAN
NORTH

Compiled by Frank Oppel

CASTLE

CONTENTS

1

Friends

LAWRENCE MOTT

"Detanges had Andres' knife haft, and the hand that held
it in a convulsive grasp could not be shaken off."

FRIENDS

By LAWRENCE MOTT

DRAWING BY FRANK E. SCHOONOVER

"HOLLA, Niko!" André La Farge shouted lustily as his canoe approached the other.

"Eh, la bas, where go?" answered a powerful voice.

The two canoes drifted together and were the only specks that marred the placid surface of Lac du Mirage. The still waters reached away on every side to the distant green shores. Each dawdling cloud was mirrored faithfully and the heat was great. Here and there the swirls of trout broke the flatness and little bubbles floated, round and iridescent.

"Phu-i-i!" Niko Detanges mopped his face with a large red handkerchief that seemed to intensify the temperature of the torpid air.

"Ah go ovaire to de store for buy som'-ting for to mak' de trap baim by; where go toi?"

"Tak' de grub to dose mans what mak' feesh and la chasse up dere on Portage du Rat." La Farge pointed to several bundles that lay in the bottom of his canoe.

"You got tabac', André? Ah leeve dat leet' piece Ah had at de camp las' night."

"Certainement," the other answered, and pulled out a dirty half plug of black tobacco. He passed it across and watched Detanges idly as he laid his paddle over his knees and filled his pipe.

"Là!" the latter exclaimed as he lighted the stubby bowl and inhaled great breaths of the harsh smoke. "Ve go togedder leet' taim!"

The two took up their paddles again and the canoes moved forward silently over the calm waters, scarce creating ripples. The sun shone with hot northern summer brilliancy, piercing the green depths with long rayonnings; the air was breathless, humid and still. Ahead of the two far-off mountains loomed hazy and indistinct, dark colored at their bases, their peaks gray and overhung with mists.

"Ah goin' be marrié dam' queeck," Detanges announced abruptly. La Farge looked at him and chuckled.

"You be marrié! Dat fine. Who de girrl?"

"Ol' Batiste Victeur, hees girrl."

La Farge started violently; his big hands clutched the paddle till the muscles stood out in knots on his bare forearms. The gray eyes narrowed and snapped and the square underjaw advanced aggressively.

"Ah—goin'—be—marrié—too!" his voice quivered, and he looked straight ahead.

"By gar, dat magnifique! Ve be marrié, you an' moi, de sam' taim, hein? Vhat fille you got?"

"Ol'—Batiste—Victeur—hees—girrl!" André's tones were of deep emotion barely suppressed. Niko's face contorted into an ugly snarl.

"Bon Dieu, how you tell dat?" he asked through his teeth.

"Ah goin' be marrié to dat girrl," La Farge answered stolidly.

The two let their canoes drift. Then Detanges controlled himself sufficiently to articulate, though his breathing was deep and his nostrils contracted and expanded.

"André, you an' me ben fren's dis long taim; ve have mak' chasse togedder, ve have sleep togedder, h'eat, drink togedder. Tell to moi v'at you talk dis 'vay h'about?"

"Ah no talk notting onlee dat Ah goin' be marrié to dat ol' Victeur hees girrl," the broad-shouldered man in the other canoe answered quietly. "She tell to me dat she loove moi an' dat she goin' to marrié moi, das all!"

He looked his friend squarely in the face and met the flashing eyes steadily.

"Ah goin' h'ave dat leet' girrl, André! She tell to me dat she loove Niko de-bessis!" Detanges shrugged his massive frame as if his answer left no room for doubt on the other's part.

"An' by diable Ah tell to you dat she no can h'ave us deux! She *mus'* marrié you or me; no can do dat for two; v'at mans have dat girrl?"

The canoes were side by side now, their

occupants sitting immovable on the last thwart. A light breeze grew on the lake, fanning its waters into faint undulations that dimpled along noiselessly. The clouds overhead swung on, at first slowly, creating dark shadows that scurried over the surface ghostlike and slow, then vanished into the distance. The canoes turned with the wind that grew.

"Ah no know how feex," Niko whispered. André thought for an instant.

"Fight?" he inquired tentatively. The other stared at him.

"Mak' fight wid toi, André?"

La Farge nodded. "Weed knife," he added solemnly.

"Ah mak' fighd den; ve go to de shore an' feenesh dees by dam queeck!" Detanges decided.

They started for the nearest shore silently. The light draught had grown into a steady breeze; this in turn grew to a strong wind. Long wavelets curled about the men, breaking liquidly into foam. The sun was gone. Dull and dark gray clouds gathered in swiftly moving masses across the heavens, and over in the southwestern horizon huge banks of black thunder heads grouped themselves and advanced deliberately.

When Niko and André grounded their canoes, a muffled rumbling sounded. The beach they were on was a small one, fringed by tall pine and hemlock. The underbrush was thick and waved in the wind that now whistled and shrilled through the forest.

"Mak' feex for fight!"

Detanges drew his long knife and tore off his shirt, showing the powerful chest and solid muscled arms. La Farge took off his shirt more slowly, disclosing a gigantic pair of biceps muscles that stretched the skin over them to the semblance of brown marble. His shoulders were smaller than those of his friend, but they were more wiry and supple. The knife he pulled from its sheath was shorter than that of Detanges, but thicker at the haft and double edged.

"Prêt?" Niko shouted.

"Prêt!" and the two watched each other warily.

"Vait min'te," Detanges said; they faced each other grave and silent.

"André, Ah no h'ave enemie for toi, but by diable deux ol' fren's no can marrié sam' girrl! You say you goin' h'ave dat fille?" La Farge drew his forehead down till the skin wrinkled like brown leather.

"Certaine, Ah marrié Elise ef le bon Dieu mak' eet so dat Ah keel you; ef Hee no vant me for to have dat fille, den you keel me, je suppose," he answered thickly.

"Bien! tout prêt?" Detanges asked.

"Prêt!" the other answered and they circled about each other.

The atmosphere was thick and heavy; crashings and rumblings of thunder sounded near by, while jagged tines of lightning ripped and tore the southern skies. Dark it became, and darker, as the two edged about; then of a sudden they rushed in and grappled fiercely.

"Elise!" one grunted, trying to wrest his knife hand from the other's grip.

"Elise!" and the other hung on grimly. They fell, rolling over and over, fighting and dodging each other's thrusts.

The heavens opened, and the rain poured down in sheets and torrents, soaking the two that struggled mutely. The thunder crackled with sharp detonations and rolling vibrations after each flash of lightning had zigzagged its steel-blue way to the earth.

Niko, his body slippery from water and sweat, wrenched his knife arm free.

"Ha, Elise!" he gasped and struck downward viciously, but André caught his hand in time and the sharp steel barely scratched La Farge's side. The two rolled and grunted, each striving to get in the death blow.

The wind shrieked through the underbrush and lifted the wave heads, driving them in damp spray over the beach.

Boom! Boom! Cr-a-a-ack! The thunder peals echoed and re-echoed from the mountains that lent themselves as sounding-boards to the violent crashings of the skies.

La Farge held Niko's wrist in a grip of iron, and Detanges had André's knife haft and the hand that held it in a convulsive grasp that could not be shaken off. Thus they lay, glaring at each other, breathing in hoarse gasps, while the rain beat on them and the wind droned through the trees.

Waves broke on the beach near them with cold furlings; then the thunder passed on and faded gradually away to the westward.

André jerked tremendously, but Niko hung on with teeth clenched and fingers set like bands of metal on the other's wrist.

"No good!" he grunted after more of the silent struggle.

"Ve try som'ting h'else."

La Farge moved his head affirmatively. Each relaxed his hold and they rose. The storm itself had gone; the rain had ceased, but the wind blew strongly yet as peeping rays of the afternoon sun broke through the thinning thunder clouds.

The men dressed in silence.

"Eh bien?" André asked.

"Ah goin' marrié dat girrl!" Niko answered.

His friend laughed wildly.

"You no keel me, Ah no keel you; vhat ve do maintenant?"

"Leesten à moi; you know de rapides h'at de Grande Rivière?" Detanges looked keenly at La Farge; the latter nodded.

"Ve go ovaire dere an' run dose rapides; ve mak' de chance for see who go en avant; de man vat h'alive marrié Elise. V'at say?"

"Bon," the other answered.

They pushed off their canoes and paddled toward the other shore. The wind died away slowly till the waters were almost as calm as they had been. Above the two the skies were azure blue again, and the sinking sun shot streaks of warm softened light over everything.

When near the forest line again the mellow roar of quick water came to them softly, and in a short time the current of the lake outlet pushed on their paddles.

"Go 'shore an' mak' see who go en avant."

They shoved the canoes ashore almost at the brink of the white water. Hungry and fierce it looked, rolling and dashing away in great reef breaks and tumbling rock waves. The two stood up and gazed silently at the downward rush.

"Vone mans go troo dere sauf, fif'ten year gon'; dat was d'Indien Ma-na-le-to; he go troo."

"Mabbe ve bot' go sauf; 'ow dat?" Detanges asked from the shore. André swung on his heel in the canoe.

"Ef bot' go sauf, den fighd avec gun at de store."

"Ah'm content," and Niko picked up a bit of dried stick that had a forked end.

"Ef de crook'd end she pointe to d'Est ou Nord w'en de leet' steeck he fall, you go en avant; ef Sout ou Ouest, Ah go."

"Certaine!"

The piece of dead branch whirled rapidly in the air under the impulse of Niko's strong twirl, struck the ground, bounced and fell. The forked end pointed fairly toward the sun that shone hot yellow in the west.

"Eet for me to go," Niko said gently. He emptied his canoe of the rain water, started to push out, thought a moment and came back.

"Aur'voir, André, mon gar, mabbe Ah no see you h'again. Ef Ah'm feenesh la bas," he nodded toward the snarling rapids, "you geef promesse for to come h'affaire me an' try get troo?"

La Farge drew himself up proudly, and held out his hand.

"Ah geef promesse, Niko, ve ol' fren's, dat a' 'nough; de mans dat laif' in half heure have Elise. Aur'voir, mabbe adieu!"

Detanges rolled up his sleeves, grasped his paddle firmly and shoved out into the whirling current. La Farge stood up on a high rock at the river edge.

"Bonne chance!" he called, as his friend struck the first crests. Niko's canoe bobbed up and down, cleared gulch after gulch of tumbling white-toothed waters, staggered for a moment, steadied and kept on, then reached the worst of the heavy water. André held his breath and watched. Niko was standing now and pushed hard on his paddle. Suddenly his canoe swayed, twisted round, fluttered on a sea and overturned in an instant, disappearing like magic from La Farge's straining eyes. Many minutes André watched; nothing was to be seen but the foaming current.

"Bien," he whispered to himself. "Ah geef promesse to Niko dat Ah try. He dead; Ah try jus' sam'!"

He looked all around before he stepped from the high rock. The sun had gone and the evening skies were tinted purple, yellow and dark blue. To the eastward the evening star twinkled brightly.

"Elise, Ah loove you; Niko he dead, he loove you aussi; le bon Dieu be goin' say ef Ah marrié you. Niko he no can h'ave you maintenant!"

Before pushing out from the shore André carefully piled the provisions that were in the bottom of his canoe on the bank under a thick spruce, and tied his yellow handkerchief to one of its piney branches.

"Dey see dat an' come look for see v'at

ees," he muttered, went to the canoe again, knelt solidly in it, bracing his knees and back.

"Bonne chance à moi!" he shouted loudly, pushing out. He struck the first rapids skillfully, edging his light craft now to the right, then to the left and dodging the harsh rocks cleverly.

The hardest was still to come, and he knew it. His face was drawn with pain, haggard and gray as he rushed on, nearly helpless, toward the frightful breakers on the steepest pitch of all.

"Elise!" he screamed as he struck them; then he felt the canoe sag and lurch sickeningly; he tried frantically to keep control of it, but the paddle was torn from his hands.

"Adieu, Elise, chérie, Ah loove toi," he mumbled.

Wssht-t-swa-a-sh—br-m-oom—! and it was over.

The thousand stars peeped glittering from the dark vaults and shone on a desolate wild stretch of hurtling waters. Nothing living anywhere; only the silent forest that loomed black and forbidding over the furious rushing river.

2

New Year's Day at a Hudson's Bay Fur Post

WILLIAM BLEASDELL CAMERON

Painted for OUTING by Albert Hencke.

THE TWO-HUNDREDTH NEW-YEAR'S RECEPTION.

NEW YEAR'S DAY AT A HUDSON'S BAY FUR POST.

BY WILLIAM BLEASDELL CAMERON.

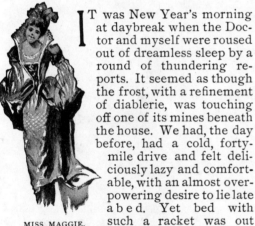

MISS MAGGIE.

IT was New Year's morning at daybreak when the Doctor and myself were roused out of dreamless sleep by a round of thundering reports. It seemed as though the frost, with a refinement of diablerie, was touching off one of its mines beneath the house. We had, the day before, had a cold, forty-mile drive and felt deliciously lazy and comfortable, with an almost overpowering desire to lie late a b e d. Yet bed with such a racket was out of the question, so, hurrying on some essential part of our wardrobe and snatching up our guns, we rushed to the front door. Here we came upon Uncle Joe and the source of our demoralization. He and his son were emptying their breechloaders into the air as quickly as the attendant interpreter could remove the exploded shells and replace them with full ones. Of course we joined in the fun and helped to swell the din, which continued until the barrels grew so hot that we could hardly hold them. It was the signal to the Indians that the "master" at the fort was ready to receive them, as Hudson's Bay Company officers had, for two hundred New Year mornings before this one, made it their custom to do in each of the isolated posts of the company scattered over all British North America.

Uncle Joe was simply one of those blessed, whole-souled old boys who put so much into all that they do that ordinary terms fail entirely to convey an adequate idea of the energy with which they do it. Thus, when the salute had ended and he caught our hands in a grip that made us wince, as he wished us the happiness of the day, his face expanded into such an exotic glow of heartiness that he might only be said to have grinned.

"And now, my boys," said he, at length releasing our crying fingers, "let's get back into the house. Mrs. Mac will have finished overlooking the breakfast and we'll be none of us the worse for a bite. The air is nipping and favors strong appetites. And we'll have to dispose of the greetings first."

Answering reports began to reach us through the skirt of bare, snow-footed poplars before the post as we went inside. When we had made ourselves something more presentable and came again into the hall, Miss Maggie, a vision of loveliness in a gallant costume, a veritable fascinating Queen of Scots, with here and there a dash of bright color, stood at the foot of the stair, and with her the principal ceremony of the day in the North began. It was very simple, and one into which the Doctor and myself entered with spirit and celerity. Miss Maggie was unquestionably a pretty girl. Later, we kissed Mrs. Mac and her younger daughters, the half-breed domestic, and all the Indian women in the settlement; but, without meaning disrespect to anybody, I think it may be safely stated that neither the Doctor nor myself would have murmured had each of the names upon our kissing list that day been Miss Maggie.

We had barely disposed of the broiled venison and partridges and returned to the hall, when the Indians, headed by their chief, came into view on the trail through the poplars. Lining up before the fort, they fired a round salute. Many of them had their faces painted.

Chief Atimoosis (Little Dog), when later he was robed in his vestments of state and abundant dignity, was a character. He had by that time put on a long scarlet cloth coat, resplendent with gold lace and brass buttons ; trousers of blue broadcloth, with wide yellow stripes

which in his younger days had been keen and bright, were dimmed by time and his face was seared and wrinkled.

"How! How! Wachee! Wachee! (What cheer! What cheer!)" he exclaimed pleasantly, as he passed through the hall, shaking hands with Uncle Joe and the other men and solemnly kissing the ladies. When he came to Miss Maggie, either the Doctor or myself would have been glad to relieve the old man of his engagement, but he seemed nowise loath to finish it for himself. And who had a better title to kiss Miss Maggie than the aged chief? He had called upon Uncle Joe on every New Year

THE POST.

down the side ; a big white felt hat with a gilt band, topped by two jet-tipped eagle plumes, and beaded moccasins. Upon his ample breast rested the great silver medal given him in token of the compact made at "The Treaty" with the Great Mother, with a picture of the Great Mother, Queen Victoria, herself, on the one side, and on the other one of his own race in a hand-clasp of friendship with a man who, like himself, wore a red coat and who was the representative of the law of the Great Mother in the land—a Northwest mounted policeman. Chief Little Dog's long, plaited hair, where it had once been all a raven black, was streaked with white, for many snows had fallen upon it. His eyes,

since she was a wee chit, and had religiously kissed the young lady each time, as she grew step by step to womanhood with the years that passed.

The dining table was piled high with cake, pie, cold meats and bread, and large kettles of tea steamed upon the damper of the stove. Chief Atimoosis began the day, which is one of continued feasting with the Indians, by hiding away under his brass buttons liberal helpings of almost everything provided. After him came the others of the band —the minor chiefs, the bucks, and the squaws and children. They passed in at the front door and out at the back. For four hours the procession kept up, and many of the guests who had

assembled from various parts of the country to spend the day with hospitable Uncle Joe and his family, including the Doctor and I, probably did more kissing than we had done during a whole decade before.

There were old Indian women with faces which resembled nothing so much as smoked parchment, but we had to close our eyes and go through the form or be forever regarded by the "Four Hundred" of Shell River settlement with haughty disdain, as ignorant of the first law of etiquette and politeness. All were decked in holiday attire. They wore no caps, but simply shawls, which were drawn about their heads like hoods. Some had fine tartan dresses and others were clothed in velvet and like expensive goods, mostly of bright colors, as blue, maroon, purple,

pink, lilac and orange, but with a predominance of red. Some of the girls were really pretty, with their olive, oval faces and handsome black hair and eyes. They wore soft mooseskin moccasins of a rich, golden smoketan, beautifully embroidered with silk of many shades in gay floral designs, broad sashes of brave ribbon about their waists, and narrower bows of the same composing their plaited, shining tresses.

By the time dinner was announced, all the Indians had paid their respects at the fort. From here they would go to visit one another, the missionaries, the school teacher, and at each place they would drink tea and eat cake and pie, moose tongue, beaver tail, bear steak and other delicacies.

After dinner Uncle Joe had the interpreter harness his horses, and he and I

started to pay the return calls upon the Indians, as befitted good manners. At the chief's were two fiddles at work and a brisk dance was in movement. The Indians of this band, as a matter of fact, were but half-breeds who had learned something of the white man's arts, including a facility for drawing the bow over the catgut and tripping to its lively measures. I think Uncle Joe must have forgotten that he had already seen the women in the morning, for he kissed all the pretty ones over again, while everybody looked on and laughed.

Upon our homeward road we lit on a covey of white ptarmigan in a bunch of willows along the trail and succeeded in bringing down a half dozen with our guns. These beautiful birds, which are not unlike a pigeon, though larger, are usually to be found only in the extreme north and seldom come so far south even as the Saskatchewan River, except in the severest winters and then only during the most snapping cold. During the summer they frequent the Barren Grounds of the north with the caribou, or reindeer, and the musk ox, and are then said to be brown in color. After

our arrival at the house, I understood why the Doctor had pleaded laziness as an excuse for not accompanying Uncle Joe and myself on our outing. He and Miss Maggie appeared to have been improving their acquaintance of the morning, and were now very good friends indeed.

During the morning a half-breed trader, accompanied by a Chippewayan Indian, had arrived at the fort from Isle à la Crosse with two dog trains. His cap was a whole foxskin, looped round like a cuff, with the top open and the bushy tail hanging down his back. In place of a coat he wore a beaded and fringed buckskin shirt, caught at the waist with a *L'Assompcion* belt, leggins of blue stroud, and moccasins. The Chippewayan was as great a stranger to the Shell River Indians as were the Doctor and I, the languages of the two tribes being entirely different, and he was certainly much more shy than either of us. The trader had a violin and could play it as well, so that we were all provided with the requisites to make of the inevitable dance to follow at the fort in the evening a memorable success.

The train dogs greatly engaged the

attention of the guests. They were huge, sneaking creatures of the "Huskie" or Esquimaux breed, with small, pointed ears and eyes and a general wolfish appearance. They snarled and fought savagely over the delicate whitefish thrown to them as food—such whitefish as one might wish in vain to have served up to one at Delmonico's—fresh, firm and fat, from the cold, untainted waters of northland lakes. They were pitched frozen to the dogs, torn apart by them with their teeth as they held the fish under their fore paws, and devoured ravenously. The stronger dogs finished their meal first and were only prevented from robbing their weaker brothers by the lash of the Chippewayan Indian.

As dusk drew on, preparations were making for the great event of the day, or rather the night—the annual feast and dance at the fort. By six o'clock the guests began to arrive; the young half-breed and Indian women in their finest dresses and the young men in black, with fancy silk handkerchiefs about their throats and *L'Assomption* belts. These so-called French belts are really scarfs, wrought of the finest wool in mixed bright colors and are truly very pretty. They cost the Indians at least five dollars each and are the envy of all those who have not the means to purchase them, for the French belt is the *ne plus ultra* of fashionable Indian dress; there are imitations, but they "do not count."

At seven o'clock we all filed into the long dining-room, the table of which was fairly freighted with a burden of good things to eat and drink. There were two great roasts of moose meat, baked young beaver and salted wild goose, broiled hare, partridges and ptarmigan, boiled beaver tail, caribou tongues, cold moose muffle, mashed potatoes, vegetables, plum puddings, mince pies, cranberry and strawberry tarts, black tea, coffee, chocolate, raspberry vinegar and lime juice, with reindeer-berry pemmican asking homage of everyone as the chief and rare titbit upon the board.

And what a feast was there, my countrymen, when Uncle Joe had said grace and looked down the long table with one of the broadest of his comprehensive, all-embracing grins, and the knives began to flash and the forks to play! And the chat and the laughter, in a strange babel of tongues—French, English, Cree and Salteaux! It was bewildering altogether, and it was amazing a half-hour later to look upon the wreck that had been made of that wondrous spread of eatables.

And then came the ball. Clear the hall, fling wide all the doors, tuck the seats into the corners, and all who are not nimble on their pins pack themselves into the nooks and crannies out of the way, for the night and the place belong to the devotees of Terpsichore, and they have no patience for laggard feet! The fiddles squeak and ring and cry, the wooden walls are attuned to the strains and vibrate with sound, while moccasined soles thump time on the polished boards in jig, reel and *cotillon*, whilst the French half-breed interpreter sings out the changes in his broken English drawl. Truly, it is a dance the like of which may be seen only in the Northland and which *must* be seen to be appreciated —especially the Red River jig. Let me try to give an idea of it:

A young Indian led out a coy, dark-skinned little native to the centre of the floor. The music screeched, he bowed, and still, with joined hands, they danced up the middle and back again. Then he dropped her hand and away they went jigging separately up and down the room again, opposite one another, she with her eyes watching his feet—I was going to say invisible feet, for they moved so fast they could hardly be seen —wheeling and circling round one another, here and there, and scarce seeming to touch the floor, in a "one-two-three" time, like a horse at a full gallop or the click of a passenger car over steel rails. In a few moments a second pair took the place of the first, "cutting them out" with a neat courtesy. And after a time the fiddler stopped from sheer exhaustion and the delighted onlookers yelled: "*Apeeta! Apeeta!* (*Half! Half!*)" and the jig struck up again, as fast and furious as ever, and lasted as long as the first "half."

The dancing was something into which the Doctor and I threw ourselves with enthusiasm. In the "*Reel de huit*" we were among the first to take partners. This is an exceedingly informal procedure amongst the natives in the Northland. It consists in making a more or less indefinite motion with one's hand in the direction of the lady whom one has chosen for one's partner. One does not go, necessarily, near her; he does not say: "May I have the pleasure of this dance?" or anything else, nor does he write her name on a card. After a hurried consultation with her nearest neighbors, to determine that it was really she and not one of them who had been honored, she follows him to the position he has taken up on the floor and takes her place beside him.

EN ROUTE.

The Doctor was wearing slippers, and as we were wheeling through the eighth-hand reel in "Elbow swing as you go," he had the luck to step out of one of them. The crowd around the walls instantly broke into a howl of ecstasy, but this failed at all to ruffle the genial Doctor. He kept right on around the circle, and when he came to the recreant shoe smilingly stepped into it again, amid the cheers of the natives and cries of "Bravo! Bravo!" from the whites, and so preserved the harmony of the reel.

It was destined, however, to come incontinently to a close, for Uncle Joe just then tossed a pound of candies into the air, and a moment later all the dancers were scrambling for them on the floor.

Later in the evening the Doctor and Miss Maggie bewitched the Indians by dancing "the beautiful English dance" —a schottische—while Uncle Joe (who had no *real* nephews) played the violin. I think, too, that it must have been during our visit to Shell River Post that Miss Maggie lost her heart to the Doctor, because, not many months later, she married another man.

3

Camp Life in Arctic America

ANDREW J. STONE

Whaler in winter quarters.

CAMP LIFE IN ARCTIC AMERICA

By Andrew J. Stone

ILLUSTRATIONS FROM PHOTOGRAPHS BY THE AUTHOR

ARCTIC AMERICA is anything but a merry playground for campers-out who have tastes only for luxurious things, but even its most forbidding regions hold fascinations for some men. I can hardly believe that most men who go into the Arctics are attracted there through any particular phase of life to be found there, but rather by some particular thing they hope to accomplish.

I found no charm in enduring cold and fatigue and suffering hunger and the many other deprivations one must experience within this atmosphere of desolation and gloom. I found pleasure only in the acquisition of a more perfect knowledge of the physical features of those regions, the people and the animal life, and to know these by personal observation I en-

dured willingly all the attendant evils of travel in such a country. To know it one must travel it, and to know its people and its animals one must see them as they live at all times of the year. To do this brings one to face a great variety of conditions and often compels one to endure many things seemingly impossible to human beings.

In the winter of 1898–99 I sledged twice across the most northerly reaches of the Rockies, three times through the entire length of the Mackenzie delta, twice along the coast west of the delta to Herschel Island, and twice along the coast east of the delta as far as Dolphin and Union straits, making important corrections in our charts of the coast country to the east and travelling with sledge in the one winter over 3,000 miles. I spent six of the

17

Some choice Polar bear skins.

winter months in camp and travelled 155 days. Blizzards are frequent during the winter months and the traveller must fully understand how to protect himself against the force of their awful fury. I experienced many of them. While crossing the Rockies, myself and two men, with our dogs and sleds, were almost carried away, on the very summit of the range, in a storm so blinding that we could scarcely see even a few feet. On the head of Copeland Hutchinson Bay on the Arctic coast we were compelled to remain in camp through a forty-eight-hour blow, that buried our dogs so deep in snow that we were compelled to almost dig them out when we fed them. We prevented our tent from blowing away by building around it a heavy wall of the solidly packed snow. We were fortunate in having fuel and did not suffer, but the life inside such narrow walls was so monotonous that we resorted to every conceivable thing possible to us to counteract the depressing effect, even to stripping off our footwear, rolling up our trousers, and running three times around the camp in the howling cold, before coming in. It was a severe ordeal, but a splendid way of keeping up life and courage.

It was on Cape Brown that I experienced the most fearful blizzard possible to imagine. With me was one white companion and a Loucheaux Indian. The coast country of all this region is very low and level and we had travelled hard all day in an effort to cross Cape Brown to Russell Inlet, knowing our only chance for fuel was in reaching the coast, where we might possibly find some drift-wood. Fortune smiled upon us most graciously, for we reached the coast and found an abundance of wood near a little level plateau convenient for camp. Men and dogs were in good spirits and the evening, though very cold, was calm, promising an ideal Arctic night. I had no thought of storm, but was delighted with the abundance of wood and the prospects of a hot cup of tea, for no climate in the world can provide a greater thirst than an Arctic night. Our little tent was soon up, the small sheet-iron stove in place, my big caribou skin spread down as a rug on the smooth floor of snow, and our sleeping-bags put in on top of that, and

In camp with the Eskimo on Allen Channel the last of May.—The end of sledding.

camp was complete. Then we ate our supper of pemmican (dried moose meat pounded to a pulp and filled with the fat) and hard biscuits. We could have only an allowance of these, as we were living on a ration of slightly less than thirty-two ounces per day, but we had all the tea we wanted. After supper I fed the poor hungry dogs their ration of whale blubber and dogfish, and then I thawed the ice off of their moccasins and dried them and darned them by the light of a candle and made them all ready for the next day, then made my notes of the day's work, and crawled into my sleeping-bag quite tired enough to go to sleep. For all this camp duty always added several hours to the day's work, and it was late before I could get to bed. I awoke the following morning almost suffocated. The tent had blown down on top of us and the snow was drifting hard upon top of that, and a storm was raging with a fury beyond description. Arousing my companions we managed, with difficulty, to get out of our bags and from beneath the heavy mass of snow and canvas. We always slept in our deerskin suits, and this was very for-tunate, for we only had to slip on our big fur mittens, which we kept inside our sleeping-bags to keep them from freezing, and we were ready for the worst. The wind struck us with a force that made it difficult for us to stand, the atmosphere was so full of flying snow that we could scarcely see, and the roar of the storm was so great we could not hear each other speak. The sound of it was exactly that of the wind and water during a heavy storm at sea.

The only sign I could find of my sled-dogs would be when I would stumble over a mound of snow and discover there was a dog inside of it. At such a time a practical knowledge of how to do things saves many a life. The snow of these regions is always hard, packed by the winds, and we set to work with axes cut-ting and carrying huge blocks of it and building walls with them around our camp. For three hours we worked with all our might, building heavy walls on three sides until they were almost as high as our heads. Then we cleaned the snow off of the top of the tent and once more erected that and made it fast. Then we dragged out our bedding and deerskin rug and shook the snow out of them and rearranged the camp inside. Luckily we had prepared a lot of wood the evening before, and the stove was soon again in place and a fire going.

Never was anything quite so welcome as our hot tea after that fearful awakening. Not only was such work of the most laborious kind, but the severity of the storm was beyond the endurance of any but the strongest of men accustomed to the elements of an Arctic winter; but I had experienced months in camping and travelling this coast, and had learned to face every sort of thing that came to it.

Just seventy-two hours of monotonous inactivity, with a growing scarcity of food, was experienced in this camp before the storm ceased, and during the whole time the dogs never stirred except when we shovelled them out to feed them. Our provisions had become so low that we were compelled to share a part of the dogs' dry fish, which we would boil three times a day with a little rice. This I regretted very much, for they were thin and very much worn out from long, hard travel on scant food.

Leaving camp in the morning after the storm had passed, we travelled all day across Russell Inlet in the face of a fearfully strong, cold wind, reaching Cape Dalhousie just at night. Not a particle of wood could be found, and tired and thirsty and hungry, we dug a deep pit in the snow, in which to sleep protected from the wind, put our sled to windward and fastened our tent above us, and then kicked our way into our frozen sleeping-bags. At nine o'clock the next morning we found a little wood, and stopped to make tea, after which we crossed Liverpool Bay to Nicholson Island, a distance of forty-five miles, a long day's run. Two days later we found a whaling ship frozen in at Cape Bathurst, where we took a short rest and, securing food, continued east.

I left camp one day to the east of Darnley Bay and followed the general course of a stream in hunt of musk-ox. In the afternoon I grew fearfully thirsty. I did not have so much as a cup in which to melt snow or ice, even though I could find

A beauty, and the first food of any kind we had for forty-four hours of travel.

Male caribou of a new species, discovered by author.

fuel. The case seemed hopeless, but it was not, for I was determined to have a drink if I could find anything that would burn. On a high gravel bar I found some little broken pieces of willows that had at some time drifted down stream and lodged there, and with these I set to work to secure a drink. I went on to the level river ice and with my jack-knife cut a little trench in the surface of the ice about fifteen inches long. At one end of it I chipped out a basin the size of a saucer, at the other end I placed a small block of ice that I had secured from a broken-up jam, and against this block of ice I stacked my bits of dead willow and set them afire. My little saucer-like basin at the other end soon supplied my wants.

To travel such countries successfully, one must be strong, self-reliant, practical and resourceful. With these qualifications only can a man bring his work within the bounds of a possibility. It was in these very latitudes and only a short distance from my furthest point east that the entire Franklin expedition of 129 souls perished, leaving not a single individual to tell the story. Such a fearful tragedy is almost beyond the conception of the experienced Arctic traveller, and yet circumstances must have woven around them a net-work of difficulties through which none of them was strong enough to break. Had the blizzard caught me in the snow-pit at Cape Dalhousie without fuel, instead of at Cape Smith, where we had plenty of it, my fate might have been very different.

There is abundant animal life in Arctic America and it is all of the greatest interest, but is in every way very different from that found in temperate zones. The attitude of birds and animals in temperate regions, when undisturbed, is a happy one —the reflection of the sunshine and the warmth they absorb from their surroundings. In the Arctics solitude has spread her wings over the great, limitless expanse of frozen waste, and every kind of life is affected by their depressing shadows. The birds and animals have not the same merry voices or playful manner possessed by

21

their southern relatives. Though life is everywhere, it is a quiet, stolid, almost monotonous life, and throughout almost the entire year a stillness that is painful to contemplate pervades land and sea. The few exceptions are the roar of an occasional storm, the grinding of the ice-fields, and the arrival of our feathered friends in spring. Aside from these, one hears only the occasional weird sounds produced by the croaking of a lone raven or the howl of a wolf, and yet the whole of the animal life is as much at home as animals in any other part of the world. They are fitted to their environments, content to know only such things as these afford.

The one great break in the monotony of the whole year along the Arctic coast is the coming of the birds in the spring— the nature of it is almost violent. The last of May they begin to arrive. The notes of the first few comers are musical, and buoy one with a feeling of messages from home and friends. But the stream of birds rapidly grows, and the few first joyous notes merge into a ceaseless, hideous, distracting din, that robs one of his rest, and for a few days becomes unbearable. Swans, cranes, geese, brant, ducks, gulls, and terns swoop down upon the coast by thousands. The old birds are delighted at the sight of the old family nesting-ground and the young ones at reaching once more their birth-place, and the thousands of them are all talking and screaming at the same time. The contrast of the now endless days of sunshine and abundant and animated life, with that of the still Arctic night, is very great.

In a few days, however, each happy family has settled down in its own little home, and quietude reigns supreme through the short summer, and then again sets in the long solitudinous night.

Many interesting things may be learned of the birds that annually visit the Arctic coast for the purpose of bringing up their families; of their reasons for going there, and of the intelligence displayed by them in many ways. They have not the enemies there they have further south. The fox is very nearly their only foe, and they find so many ways of avoiding it, that it would surely go very hungry were it dependent on birds for food. Little islands in lakes and streams that are free from foxes become great nesting-places, and the birds swarm to them until, on many of them, every available space suitable for nesting is pre-empted.

When nesting on the mainland or where exposed to the depredations of the cunning little fox (though really the white fox is not at all cunning when compared with the red one) the weaker birds seek the protection of the stronger ones in the most interesting manner. The Canada goose has but little fear of the white fox and makes its own defence if disturbed, and the swans delight in driving it from the field by pelting it with their great, strong wings. Large numbers of the great snowy owl nest in the same regions, and they too are more than a match for the fox. The timid little snowy goose, and many others of the weaker varieties of birds, find protection by nesting alongside the swan and the owl, leaving them to do the battles of the neighborhood. It is the quiet peace and mutual protection birds find in bringing up their broods that cause them to travel yearly to these far-off lands, and it is upon the mating-grounds one is afforded the best opportunity of studying them.

Both sea and land furnish interesting studies in animal life. During the few weeks of the short summer the monster bow-head whale finds a congenial playground among the vast fields of broken ice, and pays its annual dues to the commerce of the world by contributing baleen (whalebone) to the value of millions of dollars.

In July and August of each year, the beluga or white whale visits Allen Channel and its many small inlets in great schools, and the Eskimo gather there from hundreds of miles along the coast to join in the capture of it. These white beauties of the sea, often weighing a ton each, are the base of the food supply of the primitive people who live upon these desolate shores. From it they put away each year great stores of meat and fat that serve as food for themselves and dogs and provide oil for their lamps, while from the skins they cover the frames of their comiaks (family boats), make their dog-harness, sled-lashings, and every kind of lines and toggle they require.

It is difficult for one to conceive how,

in this land of ice and gloom and solitude, so many beautiful animals live out their existence in perfect content.

The little harbor seal lives most of the year beneath the ice. As winter approaches and the new ice forms above its feeding-ground, it will make a hole in the ice for a breathing-place and visit it daily. As the ice grows deeper and deeper, often reaching a depth of ten to fifteen feet, it

down the edges of these open lanes of water, watching for seal, never hesitating to plunge into the icy depths at the sight of their prey. Dragging their helpless victims upon the solid ice, they will enjoy their dinner in the midst of storm and frost, with their long shaggy coats of tawny white hair soaked and dripping, with not the slightest thought of inconvenience. A human being subjected to such an ex-

In camp in a storm near Darnley Bay, on the Arctic coast.
In a basin between two hills, with the tent in a three-foot excavation in the snow and snow walls built higher to protect the tent.

will keep this hole open large enough to admit the passing of the body, and in the very midst of the relentless Arctic night it will climb out daily through this aperture to the surface of the ice, leaving for a short time its subterranean life for a breathing-spell in the open air, it matters not how cold the air. In doing this it will often experience a sudden change in temperature of seventy to ninety degrees with no evident discomfort.

Far out to sea the winds and currents cause the mighty fields of ice to break and separate, and the Polar bears (the ice bear of the Eskimo) wander up and

perience would freeze almost instantly. I never heard of one of these animals playing, or in any way indicating a happy disposition, but the severest cold of an Arctic night is to them a matter of perfect unconcern. Down into the water they go, and then out across the fields of ice, in temperature so low that one fails to see how they escape turning to solid ice.

Just inland, on the open plains, the timid caribou live throughout sunless winters, digging through the snow with their broad, flat hoofs to find their daily food of moss and lichens, little heeding the relentless cold of the long, cheerless night.

In the most northerly reaches of the mighty Rockies, as they trend west along the Arctic coast, the beautiful white sheep (the Ovis Dalli) find a home. Who can fail to admire the magnificent ram who proudly walks the highest storm-swept and barren rocky ridges in midwinter, where no sun has shed its warming light for weeks? They cannot so well dig through the deep snow for their food, for their hoofs are not large enough, and they must therefore seek the crest of the highest ridges, where the wind keeps the little plateaus swept clean of snows and the single tiny blades of dry grass that peer out from between the rocks are left exposed to furnish them the food that gives them warmth and strength with which to defy the elements. Magnificent, proud, beautiful animals; white as the snow that furnishes their only bed—timid in the presence of man, but grandly courageous in the face of that which is beyond his endurance—content with their lot as the little deer that roams the tropical forest!

Here and there, across the spotless fields of white, trips the little Arctic fox, so nearly the color of the snow as to often give it the appearance of a ghost-like shadow travelling before the wind.

The splendid long, heavy coat of the musk-ox, unequalled by that of any other animal on the American continent, with its soft silky lining, insures it perfect protection in the highest latitudes, and it has been found almost as far north as man has gone, living in northern Greenland and in Grant Land upon vegetation that would seem inadequate to sustain any sort of life. In color it shades from brown to black, a striking contrast to that of all the rest of the animal life of such regions. The Polar bear, Arctic fox, and Arctic hare, all found in the same latitudes, are white.

The wolverine has honestly won the reputation of being the greatest thief in the Arctics, and the wolf, that of being the most depraved character. A pack of wolves when pressed by hunger does not hesitate to fall upon one of their own number and sacrifice it to their beastly cravings. They are utterly lacking in conscience, and the young or weak of every class of land animals suffer from their wanton lack of mercy.

Winter on the Liard River.

4

The Current of Fear

LAWRENCE MOTT

THE CURRENT OF FEAR

BY LAWRENCE MOTT

HO says the dogs in this blamed country is savage?" Black Dan waited, glowering drunkenly, revolver in hand, at the crowd in the bar.

"Who says it?" he roared again, cursing. "Yur a passel o' cowards, yu dassent shout!"

One man's hand reached toward his hip. A spit of flame from Black Dan's weapon, and a lifeless thing twitched on the floor. The Indians stared, expressionless; then Tim Samson, with a sweeping throw, hurled his whiskey in Black Dan's face. The crowd were on him as he staggered, and got his gun.

The huge man stood up slowly, his face twisted into a frightful snarl. "That's whut yu call a fair show, is't? Yur wuss cowards than I thunk, damn yu!"

"He's drunk, boys, and Jake did try fer to draw on him, so that's fair 'nuff, but by G—— we won't stand fur no cheap skate from Simpson a-comin' up hyar and callin' us cowards, whut?" English Jack sprang on a chair as he spoke.

"No!" the crowd thundered.

"Well, then, let's make the skunk take ıy team, they're the wust I knows of hyar-.-bouts, bein' part wolf ev'ry one of 'em, and drive to Skagway!"

Black Dan's eye glittered. "Yu dassent! I'll take yur dogs clear to Yukon an' back!"

"You take that bunch to Skagway, an' yu kin have 'em; if yu don't get 'em there we'll fix yu next trip!" Whispers passed round. "What's Jack up to?

Ought to ride the cuss!" "He knows his biz."

"Neow yur talkin', Jack." Dan's face lightened. "I'll——"

"Hol' on, hol' on, I ain't done yit! We'll give yu some grub, a pair of snow-shoes, but no knife nor gun."

Black Dan hesitated, the crowd jeered.

"Who's a coward now, yu big bully? Yu kin drop a man, I'll admit, when his weepon's in his holster, but yur a-scared to take eight dogs to Skagway!" English Jack snapped his long fingers in derision.

"I'll go," the big man said sullenly, "s'posin' Hell freezes over. Gimme a drop o' whiskey ter take erlong?"

"Shall we, boys?"

"Sure, an' a good drop; he'll need it with yur team," and the men roared with laughter; why, Black Dan did not understand. So it was arranged.

"They'll tear him ter bits ef he falls down," Long Anderson whispered to Jack.

"Sssh! Thet's whut I'm countin' on," the other answered; "we cyant shoot him in 'cause Jake reached fer his gun, but by the etarnel, this 'll fix him good. I'm a-goin' ter foller him so's not ter lose my team; they'll have a good feed for onct!" English Jack chuckled. "Lend me yur outfit, Andy?"

"Cert! Jiminy blazes, but yu've got a imagination!" Dirty Dick, the bartender, furnished the whiskey; he shook his head solemnly as he did so, but it was no affair of his. The gang tramped out to see Black Dan start.

The afternoon was cold, freezing with bitter sting, and the wind yowled mournfully across the wild country. The skies were low and drear; the clouds moving with imperceptible slide. To the right, mountains loomed gray-dark and hazy, reaching beyond the foot-hills in vanishing heights. The lonely wind came in nasty gusts, whirling the snow in biting masses. In the stables dogs howled sadly; one yelping, the others taking up the weird cadence. English Jack brought out his team; eight ugly brutes with drooling mouths and wolf-like coats. They snapped and bit at him as he curled the long whip about their heads.

"Get in there, Swift!" The leader showed his teeth and took his place before the team. Jack slung the last straps over them, then fastened the light sledge. The food, a small blanket and the whiskey were all tied down.

"Now then, Dan, come on ef yur not afeared!" All this time the man had been watching, liquor courage in his heart; he grabbed the whip, "Psh-sht-Marrse!" and away.

The crowd gazed after him, out of sight on the plains, going like mad.

"He'll get there, Jack, by G—— he will!"

"Don't yu fuss yurself 'bout it; he'll git skeared purty soon, and then—" They all went back to the bar.

English Jack took a drink. "I'll start in an hour or so, catch him 'bout on Crooked Plains."

"Them fools," Black Dan muttered as the dogs coursed on, "a-thinkin' I cyant run this hyar team ter Skagway! I'll git my crowd thar, come back, wait fur night and wipe out the hull shebang!" He sat comfortably on the sledge, its whirring sound lulling him almost to sleep. Then the snow began to fall as he climbed into the uplands. Straight and damp the flakes came, clinging to his face, coating his clothes with prismatic myriads. The north wind blew mercilessly, and the dogs whined as they sped on. Deeper and deeper the layers of white became until the team could pull no more, even though the man lashed them hard, bringing away bits of fur at every stroke.

"Marse, damn yu, Marse, go on!" The softness reached the bottom of the sledge, impeded its way heavily and the eight stopped, gasping in loud pantings, audible above the weird whistlings of the storm.

Black Dan got off the sledge and put on the snowshoes; tied a bit of rope to the runners. "Ah-hai, Marse!" The brutes struggled on.

"I'll show them cusses back thar," he swore. On and on till the snow was more firm on the hills. The whiskey began to lose its effect, and he remembered all that he had ever heard of "wolf" teams. Strangely a fear grew within him, like a stream that swept him along, powerless, and he watched the dogs furtively.

No sign yet. They plodded ahead sullenly, heads low, tongues streaming. He pulled out the flask and took a drink. "That's better," he whispered as the hot liquid ran down his throat. "Hai-a, Marse!" The animals pulled away sluggishly. Thicker and thicker came the snow, deadening the click of his snowshoes as he strode, clogging his way. He took another drink soon, and the way seemed easy, the world a glorious thing, success within his grasp. "I'll bust that crowd!" he muttered.

Drink after drink, hour after hour was passed, till the bottle was empty. "Hell!" he threw it away. The whip thong was red with blood from the vicious blows. All night he kept on, the alcohol stirring his blood, urging his mind to false action, forcing his muscles to work. Daylight found him over the hills, heading for the Crooked Plains and keeping his course fairly well for Skagway; the dogs bleeding at every step, snarling at every curl of the whip, snapping at each other in their distress. Little by little the fumes wore away, and the hints, whisperings, of the savagery of the "wolf" teams came to him stronger than before.

"They're a-lookin' at me now!" he said uneasily as Swift, the shaggy leader, turned his dripping jaws toward him from time to time. Still the team kept on obediently, and the snow softness grew into a crust as he came down toward Taku River. He tried to sit on the sledge, but his weight was just enough to force the runners through, and the dogs would stop, eying him. He had to walk. The whiskey was past stimulation; he felt no hunger, the team did; their pulls became weaker and weaker, then they stopped again.

"They're a-watchin' me!" he grumbled, and tried to beat them into movement. No use. At each whine of the lash and snap of its tip they huddled closer together and growled. As it was hopeless to attempt more, Black Dan got some food and squatted on the snow. Swift came forward with sneaking step, eyes aflame. "God!" the man screamed, leaping to his feet; he lashed the brute; it retreated, mane stiff, fangs showing. He had to eat standing, the dogs watching him the while with starving eyes; then he tossed them the remains, and they fought for it, tangling the harness. When Black Dan was ready he tried to undo the mess; Swift foamed and crouched when he approached.

"D——n yu, I ain't afeard!" But there was a quaver in the tones. By dint of kicks and beatings he got the harness straight. He slipped as he started.

"No fallin' down!" The whispered words of a friendly Indian as he left the night before forced themselves on him, grew in his ears till the very wind seemed to shriek them. Was it his fancy, or did the dogs keep their eyes on him continually? Did they wait for him to fall?

"I ain't a-goin' ter fall," he shouted in answer to his thoughts and lashed away.

Then the sun burst forth, dazzling his eyes with its violent glare. Spots of blue appeared between the rifts in the snow clouds and the wind came less harshly. "My God, fur some whiskey!" Dan whimpered as he felt the current of fear sweeping, sweeping him on, his body and mind too tired to resist. Again he attempted to sit down; Swift turned each time; the seven others waited, watching. The man now was the one to struggle, and the fight was hard against nature, against the fear that was slowly maddening him.

"I killed Jake, mu fust mu'der!" he whispered again and again; the dogs swung their heads studying him, almost as though they were wondering how much longer he would last, so it seemed to Dan.

"No fallin' down!" The words seared his mind, crazed him by their suggestion. Hour after hour he stuck to it, picking each step with assiduous care. The face of the man he had killed, with the shadow of agony on it, stood before him often and frightened him still more.

"No fallin' down!" Yet he began to slip and totter on his snowshoes. "Curse the luck," he mumbled, "cyant I stand up?" Ha! he almost fell. The dogs saw and turned. "Marse!" as he recovered

himself; the whip sang again and again in the bitter air.

"I'll show yu!" Then he swore till his voice was gone. His powerlessness struck him like a blow. The team seemed to realize and hesitated in their traces. Often now he slipped, caught the toes of the shoes and stumbled badly. The harder he tried the worse he became. Night grew slowly, darkening the distances, hiding the long plains in misty gloom. Tears in his eyes, the man crawled along, the dogs barely moving. "That's it," as he fell on one knee. "No, by heaven, not yet!" as he picked himself up. Swift saw, but kept on when the thong cut a bit of fur from him. At last Black Dan knew that he could do no more. One final attempt to lie down, but the team crowded as close as they dared, snarling. He went on a few paces. "The whip, my whip!" he groaned. In his fear he had lost it, and dared not turn his back to the dogs. Overhead the cold, glittering stars of a mid-winter night shone strangely far away, twinkling with eery effect. The wind had gone, everything was silent save for the panting of the dogs and the liquid lap-lap of their tongues. The man's knees refused to carry his huge bulk.

"No fallin' down!" He saw the words in letters of fire, and understood their full meaning as the brutes sat about him, waiting—waiting.

"If I fall, they'll tear me ter bits," he whispered; then "Shan't do it, s' help me!"

Wearily, slowly, he undid the knots in the rope that fastened the blanket to the sledge, wrangled off the harness, lifted the long thing, and by dint of many poundings drove it into the snow, not very far, because he was weak, but far enough for his purpose. The dogs edged closer in a half circle; he kicked at them. With his back to the support, he managed to lash himself securely, so that when he relaxed, the upright sledge held him.

"Thar, yu cowards, ye dassent touch me! I'll rest awhile, and git ye into Skagway yit!" Then all was still. The night became freezing cold at the approach of dawn. A drowsiness came over Dan. "This is great!" he stuttered, feeling himself warm and comfortable. His head sank on his chest and he was quiet, the team still waiting.

They did not know.

5

The Canada Lynx

WILLIAM DAVENPORT HULBERT

THE CANADA LYNX.

By William Davenport Hulbert,

Author of "The Deer," "The Beaver," etc.

IN the darkest corner of a hollow tree lay two small balls of reddish fur, which turned over once in a while and murred for their dinner. Outside, not far away, a widowed lynx stood upon the carcass of a deer looking at a man. Some hunter had wounded the deer, and the hungry cat found it before the wolves. She finished the kill. It was hers. Trappers will tell you that the lynx is a fool and a coward that will run from man or dog, but this gray cat took her stand on the flank of that deer, her eyes flamed yellow at the landlooker, she spit and growled and snarled, her ears were laid back, her white teeth gleamed. The man had no weapon; he went round.

Those kittens in the tree were the finest the lynx had ever had, and she had had many. At first, of course, they were rather insignificant.

Imagine, if you can, what their first impressions were like. And remember that they were blind, like all other kittens, and that if their ears heard sounds, they certainly did not comprehend them. Sometimes they were cold, and hungry, and lonesome. They didn't know what cold was, or hunger, or loneliness; but they knew that something was wrong, and they cried about it, like other babies. Then would come a great, warm, comforting presence, and all would be right again. I don't suppose they knew exactly what had been done to them. Probably they were not definitely aware that their empty stomachs had been filled, or that

their shrinking, shivering little bodies were snuggled down in somebody's thick fur coat, or that somebody's warm red tongue was licking and stroking and caressing them. But they knew that all was well, and that they were at peace.

By and by they began to look about for impressions, and were no longer content with lying still and taking what came to them. They seemed to acquire a mental appetite for impressions that was almost as ravenous as their stomachs' appetite for milk, and their weak little legs were forced to lift their squat little bodies and carry them on exploring expeditions around the inside of the tree, where they bumped their heads against the walls, and stumbled and fell down over the inequalities in the floor. Sometimes they explored their mother, and went scrambling and sprawling all over her from her head to her tail. But as their eyes were still closed, they must have known her only as a big, kind, loving, furry thing, that fed them and warmed them and licked them, and made them feel good. Now try to imagine what their sensations were when they first beheld the light of day shining in—rather dimly, perhaps— through a hole in the side of the tree. And

Baby lynxes eating.

imagine that hole being darkened, and a round, hairy face looking in—a face with big, unwinking eyes, pointed, tufted ears, and a thick whisker brushed back from under its chin. Do you suppose they recognized their mother the first time she came home after their eyes were opened? I don't believe they did. But when she jumped in beside them, then they knew her, and another wonderful impression wrote itself on the fresh pages of their lives.

In looks the babies were not so very different from ordinary kittens, except that they were bigger and perhaps a little clumsier, and that their paws were very large, and their tails very short and stubby. They grew stronger as the days went on, and their legs did not wobble quite so much when they went traveling around the inside of the tree. And they were learning to use their ears as well as their eyes. They knew what their mother's step meant at the entrance, and they liked to hear her purr. Other sounds there were which they did not understand so well, and to most of which they gave little heed—the scream of the rabbit when the lynx leaps upon him from the shadow of a bush; the scolding of the red squirrel, disturbed and angry at the sight, and fearful that he himself will be the next victim; the bark of the fox, the rasping of the porcupine's teeth, and oftenest of all, the pleasant rustling and whispering of the trees; for by this time the south wind had come back and had done its work, and the voice of the leaves was heard in the land; all the noises of the woods, and many others besides, that came to them from outside the walls of the tree, from a vast, mysterious region of which they knew nothing except that their mother often went there. But one day she led them out of the hole, and for the first time they saw the sunshine,

"And imagine that hole being darkened, and a round, hairy face looking in."

and the blue of the sky, and the green of the trees, and the whiteness of the sailing clouds, and the beauty of the Glimmerglass. But I don't think that they paid as much attention to it as they ought. They were too much interested in making their legs work properly. It was a hard task, and they were more than pleased when their mother took them back to the hollow tree, gave them their supper, and told them to lie down and take a nap while she went after another rabbit. But they had really done very well, considering that it was their first day out. One of them in particular was very smart and precocious, and she had taken much pleasure in watching the independent way in which he went staggering about for impressions.

She was in the habit of bringing things home for the children to play with, part of a rabbit, or a woodmouse, or a red squirrel, or a chipmunk. And the children played with them with a vengeance, shaking and worrying them, and spitting and growling and snarling over them. You should have seen them the first time they saw their mother catch a rabbit. They didn't try to help her, for she had told them not to, but they watched her with all their might. As she crept up behind him, very quietly and stealthily, until she was within leaping distance, the kittens' eyes grew bigger and bigger, and rounder and rounder. They nearly jumped out of their skins with excitement when at last they saw her give a bound and land with both forepaws on the middle of his back. They seemed to understand it perfectly. A few days later they had another experience. Their mother happened to see two little wood-mice running under a half-decayed log. She put her paws against it and rolled it half-way over, and while she held it there the larger kitten rushed in and seized one of the mice. The other got away, but no matter, this was glory enough for one day. They had made their first kill.

From wood-mice the kittens progressed to chipmunks, and from chipmunks to larger game; and in time they learned to take care of themselves, and were no longer absolutely dependent on their mother. It was well that they were not, for one day she was taken from them in a strange, sad way, and there was nothing they could do but cry, and try to follow her, and at last see her pass out of sight still looking back and calling to them pitifully. It began with a steel trap, as so many forest tragedies do. This one was down by the edge of the water, a branch of the Tahquamenon River. When the lynx first stepped into it she screamed and yelled and spit and clawed, and made such a demonstration that the kittens were astonished. But after a while she grew weary, and quieted down. Before long it began to rain. She was soon soaking wet, and as the hours dragged on every ounce of courage and gumption seemed to ooze out of her. If the trapper had come then he would have found her very meek and limp.

It rained very hard, and it rained very long. In fact, it had been raining most of the time for several days before she found the trap, and it needed only a few more hours to fill the Great Tahquamenon Swamp as full of water as a soaked sponge. The river was rising rapidly, and the lynx was soon lying in a puddle. The other end of the chain which held her trap was fast to a saw-log, and presently she climbed upon it and stretched herself out on the wet, brown bark. By and by the log began to stir in its bed, and at last it quietly swung out into the current and drifted away down the stream. The lynx was a very good swimmer, and she promptly jumped overboard and tried to reach the shore, but of course the chain put a stop to that. She was very near drowning before she could scramble up again over the end of the log and seat herself amidships.

The kittens had been foraging, but she called to them in a tone which told plainly enough that some new trouble had befallen her, and they hurried down the bank and stood at the water's edge, mewing piteously. She implored them to follow her, and finally the bigger and bolder of the two screwed up his courage and plunged bravely in. He didn't get far. It was very cold and very wet, and he wasn't used to swimming. Besides, the water got into his nose and made him sneeze, distracting his attention so that for a moment he forgot all about his mother, and just turned around and hustled back to the shore as fast as he could go. After that he contented himself with following along the bank. Before either of them really knew what had happened, the little tributary emptied itself into the main stream of the Tahquamenon, and they suddenly realized that they were much farther apart than they had been at any time before. This new river was several times broader than the one on which the voyage had begun, and the wind was steadily carrying her away from the shore, while the current bore her resistlessly onward in its long, slow journey to Lake Superior. She was still calling to him, but her voice was growing fainter and

" They hurried down the bank . . . mewing piteously."

" They both stood still and looked at each other."

fainter in the distance, and so, at last, she passed out of his sight and hearing forever.

And then, for the first time, he missed his brother. The other kitten had always been the slower of the two, and in some way he had dropped behind. The young lynx was alone in the world.

But the same river that had carried his mother away brought him a little comfort in his desolation, for down by the water's edge, cast up on the sand by a circling eddy, he found a dead sucker. He ate it, and felt better in spite of himself. It made a very large meal for so small a lynx, and by the time it was finished he began to feel drowsy, so he chose the driest spot he could find, under the thick branches of a large hemlock, and curled himself up on the brown needles and went to sleep.

The next day he had to hustle for a living, and the next it was the same, and the next, and the next. As the weeks and the months went by there was every indication that life would be little else than one long hustle— or perhaps a short one,—and in spite of all he could do there were times when he seemed very near the end of the chapter. But he was well armed for the chase, and his mother's lessons stood him in good stead. His teeth were wonderful implements. In front, on both the upper and lower jaws, were the incisors—chisel-shaped, for cutting. Flanking them were the canines— very long and slender, and very sharply-pointed, thrusting themselves into the meat

like the tines of a carving-fork, and tearing it away in great shreds. And back of the canines were other teeth that were still larger, but shorter and broader, and more like notched knife-blades. Those of the lower jaw worked inside those of the upper, like shears, and they were very handy for cutting the large chunks into pieces small enough to pass down his throat. His claws, too, were admirably suited to pulling things to bits, for they were very long and very wickedly curved; and he kept them sharp by scratching tree-trunks with them, just as your house-cat sharpens hers on the leg of the kitchen table. When he wasn't using them he kept them hidden between his toes, so that they wouldn't be constantly catching and breaking on roots and things, but all he had to do when he wanted them was to pull certain muscles, and out they came, ready to scratch and claw and tear to his heart's content. By the time he got through with a partridge there was not much left of it but a puddle of brown feathers.

But the rabbits were his mainstay, as they had been his mother's. With them and the other small fry of the woods, and an occasional bird, he pulled through the winter in fairly good shape, although he was pretty thin by the time spring came round again. Summer was easier, for he didn't have to use up any of his vitality in keeping warm. Several times during his first year or two he caught sight of a man—a landlooker, or a trapper, or a lumberman—but none ever saw him, and none was destined ever to see

" He was a goodly lynx."

him. He was sly—more sly than intelligent, perhaps—and he learned to keep out of the way. He was fond of frequenting such secluded places as old burnings and wind-falls, where dead trees and half-burned logs lay thrown together in the wildest confusion, places which were almost impassable to men, and which even the landlooker avoided whenever he could, but which a cat could tread as readily as the locomotive follows the rails. And in those secret places of the woods, hidden away from all his most dangerous enemies, he grew out of his kitten-hood and became an adult lynx.

Once in a while he visited the Glimmer-glass, and one autumn afternoon he might have been seen trotting briskly down the deer runway that follows the brink of the high bank along the northern shore of the lake. It was Indian summer, and the sun-shine was warm and yellow, the south wind was just loafing around and pretending to be busy, and all the world was full of that delicious laziness that comes when the year's work is finished, and there is nothing more for us to do but have a good time till the snow begins to fly. Suddenly he stopped short, for coming up the path straight to-ward him he saw another lynx, enough like him to be his twin-sister. She saw him, too, and they both stood still and looked at each other as if they had just discovered that, after all, life was something more than hustling for meat and drink. Yet even then the instinct of the chase asserted itself. A faint sound came up from the lake—" Quack, quack, quack "—and the two big cats stole to the edge of the bank and looked down.

Above them the tall trees stood dreamily motionless in the Indian summer sunshine; below was a steep slope of ten or fifteen feet, beyond that a tiny strip of beach, and then the quiet water. A flock of wild ducks, on their way from Canada to the Gulf, had taken stop-over checks for the Glimmerglass, and now they were loitering through the dead bulrushes, pausing occasionally to thrust their heads under and dabble in the mud for some choice morsel of food, and murmuring placidly in soft, mild voices that sounded as if they were talking of nice little minnows and snails and all sorts of delicious things to eat. The lynxes crouched on the brink, side by side, and waited. Their eyes were fairly blazing with excitement, and their long, narrow pupils grew still narrower; their short, stubby tails twitched nervously, and their paws fumbled about among the dry pine-needles, feeling for the very best footing from which to make the flying leap. The ducks came on, still prattling pleasantly over their own private affairs. Closer and closer they swam, without a thought of death waiting for them at the top of the bank, and suddenly four splendid sets of muscles jerked like bow-strings, four long, powerful hind legs straightened with a spring, and two great, furry creatures shot out from the brink and came sailing down through the air like twin angels of fury, with their heads up, their eyes blazing, their tails on end, and their forepaws stretched out to grasp an unhappy duck. They struck the water with a mighty splash, and the flock broke up with frightened cries and a won-derful whirring of wings. In another mo-

ment it was far away and going like the very
wind, but two of its number stayed behind,
and presently the lynxes waded out upon the
beach and settled down to eat their supper
together. They talked as much over that
meal as the ducks had over theirs, but the
lynx's language is very different from that
of the water-fowl. Instead of soft, gentle
murmuring, there were low, fierce growls
and snarls as the long white claws scattered
the feathers, and the long white teeth tore
the warm, sweet, red flesh from the bones.
So they talked on in angry, threatening tones
that sounded like quarreling, but that really
meant only a certain wild, savage kind of
pleasure; and when the meal was ended,
and the very last shred of duck-flesh had
disappeared, they washed their faces, and

purred, and lay still a while to visit and
get acquainted.

There were many other meetings during
the weeks that followed, and at last they
took to living in the same hollow tree, and
their matrimonial career was fairly begun.

In the years that followed, the lynx's principal occupation continued to be hunting, but
most of the time he hunted for the sake of
his mate and his kittens, as well as for his
own benefit. Of course they were not always
the same kittens, and I regret to say that
it wasn't always the same mate either.
But he never had any difficulty in finding
some one to share his lot with him. Perhaps
this was not to be wondered at, for he was
always a goodly lynx, even after his years had
begun to tell on him. He was a trifle larger

"*And two great furry creatures shot out from the brink.*"

than any of his mates—something over three feet in length, and twenty-odd inches in height—and his long hind legs, heavy buttocks, thick fore limbs, and big, clumsy-looking paws, told of a magnificent array of muscles pulling and sliding and hauling under his coat. And the coat itself—steel-colored, with darker trimmings — was so soft and fine; his claws were so long—a good two inches — and so sharp and white; his teeth were so big and cruel; the tassels of stiff dark hair that stood up from the tips of his ears had such an uncommonly jaunty effect; his mustachios were so becoming, and the thick bunch of grizzled whiskers that hung from each side of his jaw gave him such an imposing and distinguished appearance—not handsome, according to human standards, but decidedly fierce and warlike.

" Fairly trembled with eagerness and excitement as they passed, all unconscious, beneath his perch."

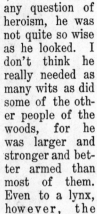

The last winter of his life was a hard one. The cold was intense, the snow was very deep, and the storms came often. Spruce-hens and partridges were scarce; even rabbits were hard to find; and sometimes it seemed to the two lynxes that they were the only living creatures left in all the woods. It was well for them that they had each other, for when one failed in the hunt the other sometimes succeeded. Yet I cannot help thinking that he might have been of more assistance to his mate if he had not confined his hunting operations so entirely to animals that were smaller and weaker than himself. There were plenty of deer down in the cedar swamp, and their tracks were as plain as a lumberman's logging road; but although he sometimes watched them from a treetop, and fairly trembled with eagerness and excitement as they passed, all unconscious, beneath his perch, he never could quite make up his mind to attack them. And yet, such were the contradictions of his nature, that one night he trotted half a mile in pursuit of a shanty-boy who was going home with a haunch of venison over his shoulder. He was just about to spring on him from behind when another man appeared. Two against one were too many,

and he gave it up and beat a retreat without either of them seeing him. He had had a pretty close call, for the shanty-boy had a revolver in his pocket.

Perhaps you have guessed, that aside from any question of heroism, he was not quite so wise as he looked. I don't think he really needed as many wits as did some of the other people of the woods, for he was larger and stronger and better armed than most of them. Even to a lynx, however, the time is pretty sure to come, sooner or later, when he needs them in his business. Your fellow-citizens of the woods may leave you respectfully alone, but the trapper-man will get you if you don't watch out.

Early in March he found some more snow-shoe tracks. He wasn't particularly hungry this time, and there was absolutely no excuse for his following them. It certainly wasn't bravery that inspired him, for he had not the least idea of attacking any one. He simply wanted to see where the trail led. So he took a course parallel to it, and at a recklessly slight distance to one side, and went plowing his way through the soft drifts, wallowing heavily and working hard, for eight or ten inches of light, fluffy snow had fallen the day before, and even his big, broad, furry paws could not bear him up.

" Didn't really look as if it were good to eat, and yet it might be."

" He saw several others still farther away, slinking from bush to bush, and gradually drawing nearer."

Presently he caught sight of a little piece of scarlet cloth fastened to a stick that stood upright in the snow a few feet from the trail. It ought to have been a warning to him, but it only roused his foolish curiosity to a still higher pitch, as the trapper knew it would. Instead of running away, as he should have done, he sat down in the snow and considered. The thing didn't really look as if it were good to eat, and yet it might be. The only way to find out would be to taste it, and, anyhow, eatable or not, such a bit of bright color was very attractive to the eye. He got up and walked slowly toward it, and the first thing he knew a steel trap had him by the right foreleg.

He suddenly lost all interest in pieces of red flannel, and for the next few minutes he was the very maddest cat in all the Great Tahquamenon Swamp. The woods rang and rang again with his screaming, and the rabbits heard it and trembled, and the partridges, hidden away among the thick branches of the spruces and cedars, glanced furtively over their shoulders, and were glad that he was no nearer.

But after a while he began to realize that this sort of thing did him no good. Luckily he was not bound to a tree. A heavy wooden clog was fastened to the trap by a short chain, and he found that by pulling with all his might he could drag it at a snail's pace through the snow. The strain on his foot hurt him cruelly, and the blood oozed out around the steel jaws, and left a line of bright crimson stains behind him; but he pushed on, for a great fear was in his heart, and he knew that he must go away or die. How he growled and snarled with fear and rage and pain, and how his eyes flamed as he looked ahead to see what was before him, or back along the trail to know if the trapper was coming! It was a terrible journey that he made that night.

The hours dragged by, slow as his pace and heavy as his clog. Far away in the east the sky began to brighten ever so little, though to the lynx, down among the shadows of the deep woods, it seemed as dark as ever. The day was coming, and he was hardly half-way home. His strength was almost gone, he was faint from loss of blood, and he looked thinner and smaller than fifteen hours before. And now he suddenly discovered that he was not alone. Off to the right, in among some thick bushes, he caught sight of the lurking form of a timber wolf. He looked to the left, and there was another. Behind him was a third, and he thought he saw several others still farther away, slinking from bush to bush, and gradually drawing nearer. Ordinarily they would hardly have thought of tackling him, and if they had really screwed up their courage and tried to overpower him by sheer force of numbers, he would simply have climbed a tree. But now it was different. The lynx trembled, and seemed to shrink to half his normal size; and then, as all the horror and the hopelessness of it burst upon him, he lifted up his voice in such a cry of abject fear, such a wail of utter agony and despair, as even the Great Tahquamenon Swamp had very seldom heard.

And yet when the last moment came, he braced up and gave a good account of himself. At least that was what the trapper decided when he came a few hours later and looked the ground over. The lynx was gone— not even a broken bone of him was left—but in the trodden, red-stained snow there was the record of an awful struggle. There was something heroic about him, after all.

Once more, in the same old hollow tree by the Glimmerglass, a big gray cat lay down in a lonely bed, and rose again to take up a double burden of toil and care. For such is the way of the woods.

" Growled and snarled with fear and rage and pain."

6

Salmon Fishing on the Forteau, Labrador

LAWRENCE MOTT

SALMON FISHING ON THE FORTEAU, LABRADOR

BY LAWRENCE MOTT

WELL, Jack, here's for the first fish on the Labrador!" I stood on the bank of the river, whose clear waters rushed foaming and tumbling at my feet. Just below me was what we had named the "Sea Pool"; an ideal bit of water. At its head a long, even rapid sparkled in the sunlight, very quick water at the top, slowing down to a deeper and heavier current below. There was plenty of room for the back cast, and a level bottom to wade out on. I breathed the crisp air with a sense of exhilaration, and lingered, enjoying my anticipation to the utmost.

"There's a fish, sir, and a good one!" Dawson pointed to a widening lot of ripples. I looked my flies over; the air was clear and the bottom light-colored. "About a No. 10 Jock this morning, Jack?" "That will do, I think, sir," my head guide, philosopher and friend replied. I looped the small fly on a medium weight gray leader and waded out. Ye fishermen that love the casting of a fly, that glory in the first cast of the season, can appreciate my feelings and my thoughts. I lengthened the line to thirty feet and cast obliquely across the fast water; the fly circled beautifully and I kept my tip in slight motion.

"There he is!" Dawson whispered as a flash of silvered sides and the flirt of a wide black tail showed that our friend was watching. I drew the fly in slowly.

"Better rest him a minute; a twenty-pounder if an ounce!" quoth I, and holding a few feet of line in my hand I made a short cast directly below me, twitching the fly gently as it hung in the bubbles of a big eddy.

"Got one!" I shouted as I felt a surge on the rod; the fish had taken the Jock under water, making no swirl on the surface. "Curious fish, Dawson!" The line cut back and forth across the current with an audible humming, and the fish hugged the deep water close; not a run, not a jump even, only this peculiar zigzag motion, and it was continued for several minutes.

"He's got to get out of that!" I walked down as far as I could and tried to swing the fish up stream. No use! I could not steer him, nor influence him in the least. This may be thought strange; I should have told you that I am a great believer in the use of the lightest tackle possible. The rod I had in hand was an eight-ounce Leonard, ten feet long; the line was next to the smallest waxed taper that I could get, and the reel a medium-sized Vom Hofe (trout). Therefore, it will be understood when I say that I was powerless with my criss-crossing friend.

"Heave a rock at him, Jack, move him somehow!" I called back to Dawson, who was leaning on the gaff and watching this new continuous performance with interest.

He threw a stone accurately.

"That fixed him!" Indeed it did! *Whir-r-r-r! Z-i-i-i-pp!* a wild rush and a beautiful curving leap way up above me.

"A buster!" I yelled at the sight of the deep shoulder and gleaming length. By this time the salmon was almost at the foot of the pool, and still going; I checked him a little, but he kept on down.

"Got to get after him now," Dawson advised. I waited a moment longer, hoping to turn the fish, then I splashed my way ashore, slipping and stumbling in my mad haste, and footed it at a good pace.

Time I did so! I only had a little line left, and His Majesty never hesitated or swerved in his course. "He's bound for the sea!" Dawson chuckled, and I commenced to worry; the salt water was but two hundred yards below us. Once there I was snubbed, as a steep rock shelf blocked the way for farther chasing. "Now or never," I thought, and held hard. The light line sung with the strain, and I had to straighten the rod or run the risk of getting a cast in it; I gritted my teeth and prepared for the sickening snap that I dreaded at each second—but the gods were kind. The pull was too much for the big fellow; he turned like a flash and came at me furiously; I reeled in like mad, running backward up the beach as I did so, and more by good luck than good management, kept a tight line on him. Up, up, up and still up stream he went at a great rate, I after him. Then he began to jump! And such jumps they were! Worth going ten thousand miles for! Long leaps, short ones, then a skating effect along the surface with the spray and foam glistening, and drops flying high in the sunlight and shining like globules of mercury. Back somersaults, forward twists, everything that a fish could do this one did. I have never experienced any salmon play equal to it either on the Restigouche or any other famous salmon waters. This fish seemed imbued with a doggedness and deviltry that was superb; I had fought him hard for fifty minutes, in heavy water, keeping below him most of the fight, and yet he did not show any signs of tiring.

Once I thought that the end was near; the fish was lying out in the quickest water, cleverly playing the current against me; I picked up a pebble and started him, as I imagined, for Dawson and the gaff. Nearer and nearer I led him. "A cracker-jack," Dawson announced, peering through the stream. I could see the long, dark shape, and a vision of the first salmon of the season lying at my feet rose before me—and nearly cost me the fish! I hurried him a bit too much, and tried to drag him within reach of the gaff; instantly that he felt the extra pressure, and realized that he was in shoal water, he gave a mighty surge, a quick lunge, and there he was out in the pool again, but, misery of miseries, behind a sharp ledge that projected black and ugly

over the surface; the line led directly on it, and I dared not try to work it off for fear of fraying it, in which case, good-by to His Majesty. I sized up the situation and saw that the only thing to do was to get across the stream—but how? The water was very swift and deep unless I went up to the top, and that would entail a sure necessity of sawing the line. No, I must wade it here!

"Come and get my fly boxes, Jack; it may be a case of swimming," I shouted. Dawson relieved me of those, also of my broad hat and sweater, and I started. The water was very cold, and the bottom slippery as the mischief; a few yards and I was in to my armpits, and the bottom fast receding from my face! I had gone in below the fish and slackened up on the line so as not to disturb him. "Now for swim!" and swim I did as best I could with one hand, holding the rod up with the other. It wasn't far to go and I paddled on desperately and struck bottom twenty-five yards below where I had gone in. I dripped ashore, shivering.

"Ah, there, friend, it's up to you again!" Unconsciously I spoke aloud to the fish, and Dawson laughed. "Go above and come across!" I shouted, which he did.

Very carefully this time I coaxed the salmon away from his rock and got him into clear water. He took two short runs and another "skitter," then came in tamely. "Now, Jack!" A flutter of foam, a lift, and he was on the beach! I laid the rod down and knelt over him, lingering on the glorious colors and scintillating scales, and dreaming, yet realizing the joy of it all.

"A fine fish, sir." Dawson's voice "woke" me.

"Weigh him." Jack brought out the dear old instrument that had recorded many, many pounds of the king of fish in varied and widespread waters.

"Twenty-two and a half, sir."

Ah, that *was* a fish! A nervy fighter, a schemer with a will that only gave out when its shell could do no more; superb in life, beautiful in death.

"That's enough for the morning. I am going to take a walk and a look at the river above. Tell the others that I will be back in an hour or so, and ask Mr. —— to come out on this pool; he is sure of fish," I said.

Dawson looked reproachfully at me. Dear Jack! Ever since I was a wee bit of a chap he has looked after me on our trips after the salmon. Aye, more than looked after me, but he did love to see lots of fish on the beach! That is when he and I had tiffs.

"I know what is on your mind, lad," I teased. "Never mind, we have three months on this coast and are going to try every river worth trying, and there will be plenty of fish."

"Humph!" he grunted, "come way up here on this trip, and now that fish are fairly leapin' for the fly you stop at one!" and he walked off, still muttering.

I went up to the top of the pool, and climbed the bank on to the moss and tundra barren. The Forteau River comes to the sea from a system of lakes in the interior, and for fifteen miles its lower reaches lie in a valley or cleft in the barrens. The day was glorious, and I breathed the very breath of immortality as I wandered slowly onward, following the river. Series of quick waters, with long, fascinating and delightfully tempting pools between them, met my eager eye at every turn. The water was so limpid and wondrous clear that I could see the dark outlines of salmon lying behind their rocks; I tossed little stones into the pools and watched the big fish and the grilse scurry about, then settle quietly back to their places. Overhead, great billowy masses of white clouds bellied and rolled across the heavens, their tops dazzling in the sun, their under sides gray and deep blue in the shadows; their outlines mirrored on the river and turning its water dark-colored—sometimes in the deepest pools it seemed quite black. It was only for a few moments, though; then the sun streamed out again and six feet of water seemed but a scant foot. The light north wind blew from over the distant blue-hazed mountains with a suggestion of far-off snows, and it waved the heather pines on the banks with gentle whisperings.

"Hello, you!" I called to J. K. H., as I came on to the bank below which he was casting industriously. "How's the luck?"

"Rotten, d—n it! I've lost four fish, one after the other; can't seem to keep 'em above that cussed rapid," he shouted, pointing to the stiffish white water below him. As he spoke, I saw a fish gleam as it

took his fly and I heard the merry song of the reel. With that freedom of fishermen, I yelled sundry advices to him such as: "Keep him up! Work him upstream!" and then, because I saw that the fish—a good one it was—inclined strongly toward "that cussed rapid," I tumbled down the bank beside him.

"Hold as hard as you dare, and swing your rod out stream," I suggested. He did so, and the salmon turned back.

"Thanks," he called, and I sat on a bowlder to see the fun. Round and round, up and down, over and across, out of water and in—another devil such as mine had been. Although my pal had never killed a salmon, he handled this one exceedingly well. I ventured a word now and then, but not often. At last the big fish tired, and the gaffer did a pretty job. We danced a miniature fling and then I left and continued up river.

In an hour I came to the first of the lakes. It shone blue and dancing before me, and stretched away a mile or more to the northeast. There I stopped and gazed with scenic-saturated eyes toward the looming mountains of the Labrador that raised their tall heads above the level barrens. A fine pool lay at the foot of the rapid out of the lake, and as I watched, salmon after salmon rose in sportiveness, creating wide swirls and bulging ripples that flowed away to the pebbled shores. Among these big rises were many of the heavy sea trout, of which thousands wend their way up river to the spawning grounds.

When I returned I found that the rest of the party had had fine sport, and a number of large fish reposed in the little stonebound fish-pond that we had made for this purpose. Several big trout were among the lot; one of six and three-quarters was especially to be admired. The "crowd" were happy, I was happy, we were all happy but poor old Jack, who still murmured that "the Captain" (my nickname) "didn't fish as he should ought to!"

The camp was situated on the river at the top of the Sea Pool rapid, and the roar of the quick water sounded lullingly in our ears.

"Give us an idea of your theories of this kind of salmon fishing," the crowd asked, so I proceeded to tell them what little I knew of the salmon lures of the far North.

"The first and great thing to learn is to reconcile yourselves to using *small* flies. It is very true that you lose many fish by so doing, *but* it is worthy of remembering that you will hook far more fish by using small flies than you will in adorning your leader with No. 6's and 4's. Also burden your minds with the fact that it is always well to approach a pool with due caution. Don't blunder on to its very edge and then cuss because you do not get a rise; the fish often lie close to the banks, especially in the early morning when the sun warms the shallows a bit, and if you will curb your impatience to reach the more tempting water you will find, I think, that many fish will rise to you much nearer the shore than you would suppose. Always cast athwart the current, say at an angle of forty-five degrees; let your fly swing with the stream, and move the tip of your rod up and down with a slight and always regular motion. Don't try to reach all over the pool from one spot. A forty to fifty foot cast is plenty; then when you have covered that water carefully (*never* hurry over your water) move down the length of your last cast and begin over again. Above all, never let yourself become restless and impatient, and cast over a fish that you have risen at once!

"You will find by disappointing experience, as I have, that nine times out of ten a fish that is of any weight at all will not rise again if he sees the fly he missed but a second before float over him in so short a time. In all my fishing of these northern waters I have found that the Jock Scott is the first choice, be the day bright or dark. Next comes the Silver Doctor. On some rivers, especially in Newfoundland, the Silver Doctor is a most killing fly; indeed on the Upper Humber, the Little and Grand Codroy, Fischell's, and the Barrachois rivers in Newfoundland, this fly is preferable even to the Jock. Farther down the list of preferences come the Durham Ranger, Brown Fairy and Black Dose; always remembering that sizes eight to twelve are by *far* the greatest takers. Another thing: you fellows have great heavy Forest rods; you can see for yourselves that they are not necessary, can't you? Use light rods, anywhere from seven to twelve ounces. They are plenty powerful enough, and will give you far more *sport* than the fourteen

to sixteen foot rods that you have. The rivers like this one we are on, up in this country and in Newfoundland, average small, and you can reach all over with a Leonard such as I am using. It's all very well to say that I am prejudiced toward light rods, but the fact remains that I am *not*. What I want is the sport that is obtained in using light tackle. It is more sportsmanlike, and gives your fish a decent chance to fight you. That, to me, is the whole pleasure; to know, unless one is very careful, and handles his fish with a glove, so to speak, that the fish is very liable to carry away everything and leave one minus the whole outfit. This is the sort of feeling I crave. Just one more suggestion: Don't kill fish for the sake of killing! There is no use in slaughtering them just because they rise plentifully to your fly; in using these small flies it is only one fish in a hundred that is hooked in the tongue. Look at that fish-pond! There are enough salmon there to feed an army, and what earthly good are they to us? Would it not have been better to have had your sport with them, and then instead of gaffing the poor devils that afforded you that sport to have beached them and let them go? I shall not gaff another fish this season!" (Growls from Jack in the background.) I waited.

"We're with you," they shouted; "no more salmon gaffed or killed unless we need them to eat!" I bowed my acknowledgments.

It was time for supper. Behind the camp the sunset colors were glorious, and changed with shifting hues as we watched them. The first night in the wilderness is always the acme of delight and comfort that one longs for during the tedious winter months. And as we sat by the fire that shone ruddy and warm in our faces, and watched the guides' shadows lengthen and shorten as they moved about the flames, we were truly indescribably happy. There were no sand flies to bother us, and we sat there till long into the night talking, singing and counting the falling stars that flashed and trailed across the twinkling heavens. Then, one by one, the crowd turned in, and one by one the fires went out, leaving but the star darkness shining mystically on our five-tent camp on Forteau River, Labrador.

7

Adventures on the Ice-Floes

P.T. McGRATH

THE COSMOPOLITAN.

From every man according to his ability : to every one according to his needs.

NOVEMBER, 1903.

SEALMEN PUSHING BACK THE SHIP BY MAIN STRENGTH TO PREVENT HER BEING N   "ED.

ADVENTURES ON THE ICE-FLOES.

By P. T. McGrath.

NEWFOUNDLAND is the greatest fishing country in the world. Two-thirds of its people are engaged in the business of harvesting the ocean's wealth. But this involves a dreadful annual waste of human life. The seaboard is exposed to nature's fiercest rages, and the perils of the region are varied and stupendous. The annual roster of the victims in this never-ending warfare runs into hundreds; there are more widows and orphans in the island than in any other country. One-tenth of its yearly revenue goes for asylums, orphanages, hospitals and "poor" relief (with a fine chivalry, the word "pauper" is tabooed), and the distressed are "God's people" the whole coast over.

Among all the branches of this maritime

HURRYING BACK TO THE SHIP IN FEAR OF A FOG.

A CAPTURED PET.

winter's final fury is then spending itself, fierce blizzards sweep the north
Atlantic, the icy masses are sent crashing against one another, or rafted into
chaotic heaps, and no situation could
be worse than that of the ships and
crews enmeshed therein. The inset of
the currents usually carries the floes
against the shore, and the coast-folk
can venture out on foot or in boats to
stalk the wary seals, though the main
fishery is now conducted by steamers
in the outer waters. The steam fleet
consists of twenty ships, specially built
of oak and greenheart, neither attractive nor speedy, but unequaled for ice
navigation.

They carry about four thousand men,
each ship being literally packed with
human beings, for the idea is to kill a
load of seals as rapidly as possible and
then return. There are but scant living-
room, no sanitation and wretched fare
aboard these crafts, and a man cannot
possibly earn more than sixty dollars for
the cruise, which under most favorable
circumstances means a month's work—
a week preparing, a fortnight in the voyage and a week "settling up" after
the return. The ships are not allowed
to kill seals after April 30th, so that
the unlucky are usually out eight weeks.

The Newfoundland seals are hunted for
their skin and fat. They do not possess
the furry covering of their Alaskan con-
gener. The skin is used to make patent-
leather and "kid" gloves; the fat is con-
verted into oil as a base for high-class
soaps, or, with the stearin removed, becomes a substitute for olive oil. The seals

industry, the most dangerous is the seal-
hunt. None other faces such appalling
risks as the sealman, or sees the grim Reaper
in such ghastly guise. Though you search
the world, among all the employments
which tempt men abroad upon the ocean
you will find no counterpart of the pathos
in the drama of bread-winning that this
conquest of the frozen plains involves.
Apart from the mischances which attach
to the ships that carry the men among the
seal-herds, there are the perils which en-
compass the men when they venture forth
on the vast gleaming fields of ice where
they pursue their prey.

This seal-fishery, or seal-hunt, takes
place in March and April each year, among
the floes which cover the ocean off Labrador and northern Newfoundland. The

SKINNING SEALS.

mount the ice-floes off Labrador in February, to deposit their young. These weigh but a few pounds at first, but grow so rapidly that within a fortnight they scale forty-five to fifty pounds. They are then fit to kill, but to prevent the slaughter of immature ones the steamers are held in port until March 10th. The young seals, known as "whitecoats," are the most valuable and the easiest got. They lie helpless on the floes and are killed by a blow on the head with an iron-shod pole called a gaff. The parents are more difficult to handle, and often give battle, having to be despatched with a bullet.

It takes mature experience and profound sagacity to strike the "whelping ice"

accounted for fourteen thousand. As the victims are slain they are gathered into a number of heaps, each on a separate "pan," or islet of ice, and the ship's flag is displayed above every pan, so that as she comes along in the wake of her men she takes those seals aboard, the crew falling back to her at sundown.

But a fog often closes over the floes, and hundreds of men from different ships are isolated by it, cut off from their vessels and rendered incapable of movement because of the dangers they may stray into in this blinding mist. In 1900, nearly a thousand men were adrift for two days and nights owing to fog, scantily clad, poorly rationed, and having to burn their

From an old drawing.

KILLING THE SEALS.

whereon the young are bedded, in a mighty expanse of floating crystal covering the ocean for thousands of miles. The extent of the arctic floe driven south each year is at least three or four times as large as New York state.

The killing of seals is a ruthless outbreak of the human passion for slaughter. The thousands of men rush onto the ice with clubs and knives, and as the "whitecoats" are stunned with the former they are disemboweled with the latter. An idea of the ease and extent of this butchery can be obtained from the fact that the crew of one steamer, two hundred and seventy men, totaled more than nineteen thousand in a day, and the crew of another

clubs and ropes to keep warm and eat seal carcasses to avoid starving. Fortunately, the weather kept mild, without snowstorms or severe frosts, and a dire disaster was averted.

When blinding snow-storms arise while the men are away on the ice, the peril is extreme. They go lightly clad, and carry little or no food, that they may all the more easily traverse the floes; and they aim, in leaving the ship at daylight, to return by nightfall. When such a danger threatens, they make for the nearest ship, and sometimes a single steamer shelters seven hundred men.

The disaster to the crew of the "Greenland," in the season of 1898, by which

SEALMEN STARTING AT DAYBREAK.

forty-eight men lost their lives and sixty-five were frostbitten, exceeded in harrowing interest any other connected with the industry. In all its appalling details of privation and suffering, this exemplified the terrible hardships which are incurred by the sealmen and the hazardous character of the enterprise itself. When a catastrophe involving large loss of life occurs ashore, the victims are usually hurled into eternity without a moment's notice, but in this instance they suffered unspeakable torments from exposure and hunger before they perished on the pitiless ice-floe.

The "Greenland" had one hundred and eighty men out on the ice, when a blizzard arose, driving her seaward and leaving these unfortunates helpless, many of them looking their last upon the ship that represented home and friends and safety to them. The plight of those on board was nothing compared with the awful position of the castaways exposed to the piercing gale and bitter arctic frost. They had no food, no shelter, no extra clothing —nothing to help them in battling against the terrible fate which they knew beset them. They maintained some order at first, collected fragments of ice to improvise shelters, and sought the lee of hummocks or small bergs. Some tried to keep warm by circling about, but the effort, after their hard day's work,

was too great. Weak and dispirited, they gave up and huddled together for warmth. Others wandered off in search of the ship, only to fall benumbed and perish as they lay. A few went crazy, and others fell into seal blowholes and were drowned.

As the night wore on, the shrieks of the frost-bitten, the moans of the dying and the ravings of the insane added to the horror. The pitiless storm lashed them all through the night and the next day. The salt spray cut like whips and the snowy particles struck to the skin and made the clothing clinging wet. The living stripped the dead of their outer garb to protect themselves. The stronger helped their weaker comrades, and if a man lay down he was kicked till he staggered upright again, all knowing that inaction meant the coming of the stupor which locks the lids with the everlasting sleep.

When the gale abated, the ship steamed back into the floe, where, dead and dying, the starved and frostbitten sealmen lay. The survivors were gathered in as rapidly as could be, and the ship then bore up for home, her waist piled with the dead, and sixty suffering, frostbitten seamen berthed below in foul-smelling, ill-lighted quarters.

HAULING SEALS.

SEALING-STEAMERS LEAVING ST. JOHNS.

A recent shipwreck recalls another famous ice-floe horror, the loss of the schooner "Huntsman," in 1872, off Battle Harbor, Labrador. She and the "Rescue," a sister ship, both seal-hunting, got gripped in the ice in a storm, and were swept south by the current. Shortly after dark on Sunday evening, April 9th, she struck Bird Rock, an outlying islet, and was flung over on her beam-ends by the ice and waves. The waves, sweeping over her, jerked out her spars and flung a mass of struggling wretches into the surf, where the jagged

tween the writhing fragments, and the hapless occupants sank or scrambled onto a tossing pan. For two days the gale raged, and at its close there was not a vestige of the little flotilla to be seen. Two more days were spent by the schooner in cruising about, and part of one boat was sighted, and upon its being overhauled two starving and frostbitten sealmen were found beneath it, who died soon after being rescued. They were the only ones of the whole number ever heard from.

The St. Mary's Bay disaster occurred in

HOISTING SEALS ABOARD SHIP IN ICE-FLOE.

chunks of ice battered the life out of them. Others climbed over the weather bulwark to the floe, only to be caught and crushed to death by this as it rafted up against her side. Within an hour forty-two out of the sixty-two men she carried were dead.

The very next year, 1873, the schooner "Deerhound" lost twenty-four men out of fifty-six. They had been sent off in boats among the "open," or scattered, ice to cruise in the watery lanes and thus conduct the hunt impossible on foot. A storm arose and the boats were crushed be-

1875, and stout and stalwart men to-day, who figured in it as boys, have never forgotten the dreadful experience. The ice drove in during March and brought with it a derelict French schooner, the "Violette," from St. Pierre, which had become enmeshed in the floe. Her crew had got ashore, and the coastfolk swarmed off to her to strip her of her fittings. An offshore gale struck them as they went. Many returned, but the ice opened and cut off forty-five from succor. They made toward the brig as a means of shelter, but many

SEALING-STEAMERS FROZEN IN ICE-FLOE.

never reached her. Blinded by the whirling snow in the darkness and the cold, they toiled on only to fall as their strength gave out, and perish by the way. Thirty died on the chilling floes; some were frozen, many smothered, others drowned. Fifteen reached the ship, and drifted about on her for fourteen days before being rescued by a vessel off the Banks. During that time, their only food consisted of "flapjacks" made out of half a barrel of flour which they scraped up in the hold.

Some years the fleet escapes without disaster, but other years witness a whole series of mishaps. In 1897, within a week of sailing, news was received that the "Wolf," one of the finest of the ships, had been crushed in the floes and sunk, her two hundred and seventy-five men making their way over the ice to the shore, with their season's fruits thus snatched from them at the very outset. The ships are built to withstand ordinary pressure, but sometimes conditions are encountered that human agency cannot contend against.

Before the shock of the "Wolf's" mishap had passed, the steamer "Newfoundland" arrived, with half a catch, leaking badly. She had barely escaped foundering in a fearful gale. She reported the "Hope" with a broken shaft, the "Vanguard" with her bows stove, the "Ranger" nipped and leaking badly, and the "Walrus" also damaged by the grinding floes. The next day the tale of disaster was augmented when the "Labrador" followed her into port, bringing the crew of the "Windsor," which ship had had her stokeholds stove in and was in a sinking condition when her crew were taken off, while the "Iceland" had rammed a berg in a fog and narrowly escaped going to the bottom with her one hundred and ninety-five men.

SEAL-SHIP IN THE FLOE.

"PRESSING" OUT THE SHIP TO PREVENT HER GETTING NIPPED.

Almost every spring, a succession of easterly winds will drive the "whelping ice" against the shore. The coastfolk hail its advent joyfully, as it means a rich if risky harvest for them. Every man who can walk, all the boys over twelve years old, and oftentimes the women too, hurry forth on the floes to glean the spoil that lies there. They start at midnight, so as to be among the herds at daybreak, and as soon as the light permits the slaughter begins. While the floes are "jammed"

SEALMEN ADRIFT ON A PAN.

against the coast, the settlers know neither rest nor sleep, for every "tow" of seals they bring to land means a few hard dollars, and while the harvest may continue for a fortnight it may, on the other hand, last only a day.

The stronger the landward breezes have been, the tighter the ice is packed against the shore. This closes the blowholes and islets, and the seals, to mount and leave the pans with ease, must go farther out, among the looser ice. Thither the hunters follow, and when the shift of wind comes this ice is the first driven to sea, for the inner sections, being so closely packed, are not as readily moved. The men are usually so absorbed in their work that they give no thought to the veering breeze.

But by and by it freshens, and they awake to their danger. It then becomes a wild scramble for life. Dropping everything, they hurry for the shore. Wide lanes of water cut them off from safety, the pack is opening and its separate fragments are dispersing over the face of the ocean. If there is an extensive unbroken area, they may reach it and get near enough to land to be rescued by boats; but if the pans are smaller, there is little hope for

AT BAY.

them. Sometimes a group will gather on a pan, propel it as near a floe as possible with their gaffs, and then one man will strip, plunge into the water and swim to the floe, towing a line composed of their ropes, by means of which he will drag across to him that pan with its living freight. This operation will be repeated by man after man until they get to the "standing" ice and so reach the shore.

telegrams to St. Johns for tugs, and a call for volunteer schooners from the bights and inlets which breast the wide Atlantic. Heroic efforts toward rescue were made, but all in vain. Men from every hamlet within even remote reach of the scene were recklessly risking their lives to reach the doomed ones, but none could traverse the floes and lanes which barred the passage. For two days the keen-eyed mariners watched the big floes with their long telescopes; for two nights the twinkling of fires amid the wintry darkness told that the driftaways were burning their gaffs, ropes and seal carcasses to keep alive. Then the wild fury of a blizzard swept the bay, and blotted out the whole grim tab-

AN ICEBERG.

One of the most harrowing of all these catastrophes was the Trinity Bay disaster in 1891. The ice had closed along the shore and the coastfolk sallied out for seals. Suddenly, the wind changed and hundreds were driven seaward before a sharp breeze, incapable of helping themselves. Then the alarm spread and the rush for safety began. Some landed near their homes, others many miles away. Scores were driven right across the estuary, forty miles beyond, and effected a lodgment there; but thirty-six fishermen of English Harbor were swept toward the ocean, trapped among the outer floes and doomed beyond salvation. Then there were hurrying and signaling along the shore, the firing of alarm-guns and the lighting of beacons,

leau of this fateful struggle for existence.

Transcending all, however, in thrilling intensity, was the horror off the Funks, in 1862. These are a group of barren islets forty miles from the mainland, in the midst of the seal-herding area. One trader equipped a crew of fifteen men, which he placed there in November, to remain until April and hunt the seals as they came. The men built a hut and lived comfortably the winter

SEALMEN IN BOAT AMONG THE FLOES ("DEERHOUND" INCIDENT).

CANADIAN CRUISERS FAST IN THE ICE.

through, and on February 17, 1862, seals were espied in the offing. All hands started away over the floes, except James Reid, aged seventeen, who was cook for the party. The wind changed, the ice broke up, and as the gale increased the hapless wretches perished one by one, in sight of the lonely watcher on the rocks. He saw them hurrying shoreward, saw the great waves beat up the pans and engulf the men or crush them between the grinding fragments, and saw the last survivor get so near the shore that Reid threw him a rope, but he was sucked under before he could knot it around his waist.

Slowly the horror of it framed itself in Reid's mind. All were gone and he was left alone, unknowing of what the future had in store for him. Six long weeks elapsed before he was rescued. The seals came in thousands, crooning and gamboling around him. Blizzards and tempests raged, and he heard the calls of his dead companions. He cowered in the hut by night, and by day watched in vain from the summit of the rock for the gleam of a welcome sail. The party had erected a flagstaff there, and from it he displayed a distress signal. Later his mind became deranged, and when the sealer "Coquette," on March 30th, sighted his flag and sent a boat ashore, he fled from the rescuers,

believing them the wraiths of his unfortunate friends. They had to surround and capture him, and as the debarking was dangerous they tied a rope about him and sent him off through the surf. The line slipped down on his legs and he was dragged into the boat feet foremost. It was months before he recovered from his dreadful experience, and so far-reaching was the effect of this disaster that there has never been a renewal of the experiment from that day to this.

Every Newfoundland fisherboy has to face the perils of the rescuer at an age when lads in other lands are at school, and it is this hardy upbringing which makes a brave man of him, for the rescuers face the same risk of death as those to whose aid they go.

In Newfoundland these sealing horrors are epochal events, and people as frequently use such phrases as "the spring of the 'Greenland,'" or "the 'Huntsman' year," as they do the regular names of particular seasons. And these tales of daring and heroism, of adventure and escape, of disaster and death, are told at every fireside, while the wintry gales lash the rugged seaboard, and the little hamlets are clad with snow, and the ice-pack sweeps south with its freight of seals to tempt newer generations to repeat these somber episodes of the northern seas.

8

The Sledge Dogs of the North

TAPPAN ADNEY

THE SLEDGE DOGS OF THE NORTH

By Tappan Adney

A LITTLE while ago, a dog harnessed to a boy's rude wagon, passed my door at a lively trot, followed by a troop of roystering children. He was doing all the work, yet he appeared to be having as much fun as his human companions. I never contemplate a dog in the society of mankind, whether sharing his work or play, without marveling at the close bond between two animals separated so widely in the scale of nature. With civilized man the dog lives a life of comparative idleness. Even the hunting dogs, which exert themselves more than any other in the service of civilized man, can hardly be called workers, since they are but obeying the natural wolf instinct. The watch dog's rôle, too, is largely passive. The lap dog and the mere pet, although the most utterly useless of dogs, doubtless have a place in our complex civilization. So, to my mind, we rarely see the dog in his noblest relation to mankind—that is, when brute and human, reduced to the first principles of existence, work and suffer together.

The use of dogs for drawing loads and carrying burdens is less general in this country now than formerly. A generation ago in New York city dogs, in teams of three and four, drawing peddler's little carts, were a common sight. In the streets of a modern city dogs, particularly if driven in teams, would be sadly out of place; though in Holland the inconvenience attending the driving of a long-drawn-out affair is obviated by hitching a single dog directly under the axle of the vehicle. Except in children's play, civilization is ceasing to have use for the true working dog. But there are still parts of our country where the dog is not only a constant, but most picturesque feature of the daily life. One may say that the line between the United States and Canada marks the two parts of our continent where, on the one hand, dogs are chiefly companions, and, on the other, important factors in the economy of the country. Endurance and ability to draw small loads with great speed peculiarly fit the dog for a wilderness where neither roads nor railways have to any considerable extent made their appearance. Then, again, as in this northern wilderness, peopled only along its southern border, where the rivers and lakes are the highways of travel in summer, it follows that in winter, when the tangled forest trails have been made smooth by their deep covering of snow, the dog enters upon his real usefulness. Long before white men set foot upon the western shore of the Atlantic, the Indian hunter and trapper drove his string of hardy wolf dogs over the frozen watercourses. The Hudson's Bay Company, pushing westward even to the Pacific coast, northward as far as the mouth of the arctic McKenzie, and thence still farther west into the Yukon Valley of Alaska, adopted the native dog and toboggan as the sole means of winter travel; and to-day, as far as one may go, even to the shores of Behring Sea, white men are driving the dog as the aborigine did before them. Before the advance of civilization these characteristic features of the life are disappearing. The old Hudson's Bay posts of the border are no longer stations for the exchange of furs, and the locomotive's whistle drowns the tinkle of sleighbells on the gaily caparisoned back of the sledge dog; one must travel beyond, where the dog is still the only, or almost only, domestic animal, and white men live scarcely better than savages, in order to realize the true worth of the best friend of man. The Klondike excitement and the consequent demand for sledge dogs, introduced for the first time, to thousands of persons, this characteristic and necessary adjunct of northern life, and of all that number, including not only those who plodded along the weary trail behind the patient, faithful brutes, but also those who merely read of it, I am sure there was not one who did not come to love the dog as never before. If there was one such, he was without a soul, and the dog was the better of the two.

The range of the true sledge dog may almost be spoken of as circumpolar. The finest specimens are still found within the Arctic Circle, and although locally known

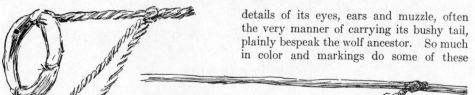

ESKIMO DOG HARNESS.
A. Bearskin. B. Ropes.

by various names, as
Eskimo, husky, mala-
moot, siwash, etc., and
regarded by some as
being so many distinct breeds, they possess
in common many characteristics distinguishing them from civilized dogs. In
Klondike and Alaska, where I have seen side
by side the native dog of Siberia, the malamoot from Behring Sea, the husky from the
valley of the McKenzie River, and the ordinary siwash dog of the Indian, there was
observable much variety in size, color and
markings, yet their differences seemed more
individual than otherwise. There were
malamoots which could not be told from
huskies, and Indian dogs that could not be
told from those that came from the Eskimo.
They were all wolf dogs. The name Eskimo is perhaps the best to represent the
uniform type of extreme northern dog.
The name husky, given in the Hudson's
Bay country, is derived from the Eskimo
of that name on the coast at the mouth of
the McKenzie River; while in the Yukon
Valley, including Klondike, the name malamoot is similarly given, from a tribe of
Eskimo of that name dwelling on the eastern shore of Behring Sea, from whence the
first, and for a long time only, dogs for sledge
purposes were brought into that country.
Siwash, being merely Chinook, or Hudson's
Bay Company's trade-language, for Indian (French *sauvage*), that name is applied
to all native dogs by people from the west
coast, where the aforesaid jargon is still in
general use.

The typical Eskimo dog has a thick,
short neck; a sharp, wolf-like muzzle; slanting eyes, but without the wild wolf's hard,
sinister expression; short and generally
erect pointed ears, and it is protected from
the severe cold by a coat of the warmest
and thickest hair. Its general form, the

details of its eyes, ears and muzzle, often
the very manner of carrying its bushy tail,
plainly bespeak the wolf ancestor. So much
in color and markings do some of these
native dogs re-
semble the gray
wolf which inhabits
the wooded parts of the
Northwest that at a little
distance it is frequently impossible to distinguish them, and miners
in the Yukon have more than once refrained from shooting at a solitary wolf
until they were able, by some sign, to make
certain that it was not a stray dog. In
color the purest strain runs from solid black
through black and white, to white all over,
while these colors may be modified by a
grizzled-gray quality in the fur more or less
completely replacing the positive markings, and so closely resembling the gray
wolf, that one is irresistibly impelled to
believe the reports which are current in
all parts of the Northwest, of the native
dogs breeding with wolves. The dogs of
the Indian villages in the interior of Alaska,
are often of the meanest description, undersized, lean, and in proportion as they are
starved and stunted do they seem vicious
and cowardly in disposition. It is now rare,
in the length and breadth of the Yukon
Valley, to find a good dog in the possession
of either Indian or Eskimo. The best have
been bought up by the miners and traders,
who have been willing to pay almost any
price. Moreover, in order to supply the
extraordinary demand for sledge dogs re-
sulting from the Klondike excitement, the
Canadian Northwest was raked and scraped
for dogs by intending miners and others
bound for the scene of the great gold strike.
Some notion of how thoroughly all available dogs were snatched up at the beginning of the excitement is shown by the
experience of the Canadian government,
when getting together a set of dog teams
to send in with mail to Dawson. A hundred
huskies were expected, but when the teams
arrived at Dawson, there were only forty
dogs, and half of that number were not
native dogs, but setters and Newfoundlands.
Thousands of "outside dogs" (so called by
the miners to distinguish them from the

"inside" or native dog) were carried to Klondike; a few trained to sledwork, but the majority unused to harness. Besides Newfoundlands, and Gordon, English and Llewellyn setters, there were long and short-haired St. Bernards, spaniels and collies; that is to say, any large, solidly built dog with a full covering of hair. Numbering nearly as many as the native dogs, on the upper Yukon, and about Dawson, these have begun intermingling with the natives, until now the native breed is fast losing its identity, and it can be but a short time when, as a well-marked breed, it will disappear from all but the more remote re-

of his forequarters, standing square and solid, with head and ears up and with tail tightly curled over his back, he is the embodiment of strength, energy and an independence that is fairly aggressive. As he stands thus he craves favor of neither man nor dog. Derived from generations of sledge dogs, having no other example nor precept than that of pulling, in a state where the sledge or toboggan is next in importance only to the implements of hunting, he knows his place and is conscious of his worth. In the sledge train he carries himself as if proud of his work. With some of the newcomers it has been quite different.

A TWO THOUSAND DOLLAR TEAM OF "HUSKIES."

gions, like Greenland and Siberia. The outside dog has proven well fitted for his work. Without the extreme hardiness of the native dog, or his indifference to cold, and ability to work for days at a time without food, when necessity demands; nevertheless he soon becomes acclimated. The second winter an outside dog carries a much heavier coat of fur, and long before that probably he has learned his work, and accustomed himself to the drudgery of the trail, like a native.

The Eskimo is distinctly the dog of the North. Broad chested and with powerful shoulders, almost hyena-like in the tallness

Especially to the hunting dog, it was a very sad come-down, when the miserable hoop of stuffed moosehide was first thrust over his tender ears, and he was shoved into a train of four or five other dogs and compelled to pull.

Dogs are driven in a variety of ways. The voyageurs in the region south of Hudson's Bay employ a collar with two short traces which meet on the dog's back, and to these is attached a single trace to the toboggan, and if four or five dogs are driven together, there are as many separate traces as dogs. The Eskimo tribes around Behring Sea adopt a somewhat different method.

The harness itself is not greatly dissimilar. Sometimes built of leather or pieces of rope, the traces, instead of leading directly over the back, first pass under the foreleg. This style of harness in its original form, I was told by Edwin Inglestad, at St. Michael, was simply a piece of fresh bearskin, through which three long slits were made lengthwise. The middle slit was pulled over the dog's head and served as a collar, and the forelegs were thrust through the remaining slits. To the other end, resting upon the back, was attached the trace. This trace, in the Eskimo style of harness, is a strand of raw seal hide about three feet in length. It is made fast to a long single trace—a thong of walrus hide—and the dogs are hitched generally in pairs, at intervals of about six feet, with a single dog as leader. The small trace joins the main trace with a bone swivel. Thus, if the dogs become entangled, as happens when two rival teams meet and start to settle a feud, or when the sledge takes the notion of going down some steep hill faster than the dogs, it is easy to straighten them out afterwards. Although the advantages of this arrangement of dogs are obvious, it is not so convenient in a wooded country, where two dogs may try to pass upon opposite sides of one tree. The harness almost universally used by white men throughout Alaska and Klondike consists of collar and side traces, backband and belly string—like an ordinary horse harness. In this style the Indians harness their dogs to their light hunting toboggans. The collar is simply a round affair about two inches in thickness, of moosehide stuffed with moose hair. The traces, two inches wide, are of the same material. The back-band, supporting the traces, is a band of leather four to ten inches wide, often highly ornamented with bright chenille patterns and surmounted by a string of small sleighbells.

If a dog is driven alone the traces attach directly to the sledge or toboggan, and when two or more are hitched together, the traces of the forward dog are tied into a slit in the trace of the hinder dog, between the collar and back-band. Between each dog is a space of two or three feet. Thus harnessed a string of dogs is easily kept in a narrow trail, but it is a style of harness that is constantly becoming tangled. Often the leather of the traces and back band is replaced by strips of drill or canvas. Fine harnesses, made by white men out of regular harness leather, the collar being stiffened with a stiff wire which serves as hames, and with regular iron snaps on the traces, are now made expressly for the Yukon trade.

Two distinct kinds of sleds are used by the native tribes of the North and Northwest. One is the familiar toboggan, made of thin white birch with the front part bent upwards and backward. It skims lightly over the snow in the trail of the snowshoe and is the universal hunting sledge of the Indian, and is exactly the same both in the Hudson's Bay country and in the Yukon Valley. The Eskimo, who inhabit the sea coast and short distances up into the mouths of the large rivers, do not employ the toboggan, but use instead a sledge made of driftwood, setting well up on runners shod frequently with walrus ivory, and having a superstructure consisting of uprights of wood filled in with thongs of rawhide, for containing the load, or occupants, of the sledge. They are further fitted with two plow-like handles behind, by means of which the sledge, when passing over the rough, hummocky ice of the sea, is kept from overturning. Those seen at St. Michael and at Nome are very strong and heavy. As one goes up the Yukon toward Klondike, this sledge becomes much lighter in build and is constructed of the best available wood—white birch—and is known as the "basket sleigh."

Both Indians and Eskimo use the "basket sleigh," just as their snowshoes are similar, but as one goes farther up the river the toboggan altogether replaces it among the Indians. The min-

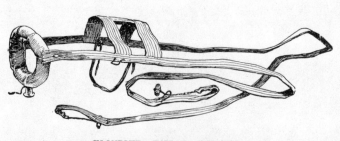

KLONDIKE INDIAN HARNESS.
Moosehide with canvas traces.

ers have adopted the "basket sleigh," but never use the low, flat toboggan, for the reason that the constantly used trails along the creeks and river bottoms are frequently overflowed with water, even in the coldest winters, and their goods would become wet. The miner's "basket sleigh" is eight to twelve feet in length, with a with a rope strung along each side, by means of which the load is lashed fast to the sled. A distinguishing peculiarity of the "Yukon sleigh" is a stout pole, known as the gee-pole, six or seven feet long, securely lashed to the fore part of the right-hand runner and extending forward, so that as a man stands in front of

FITTING OUT A PACK-TRAIN.

floor about eight inches from the ground, runners unshod with metal, and a "tread" of twenty to twenty-two inches. Originally all made by natives, they can now be purchased in the Puget Sound cities, as well as in Dawson, where they are constructed by white men of hickory and ash. The regular price for such a sleigh of hickory in Dawson, in the winter of 1898, was $75; very much more, of course, than their cost outside. The miner's sled, pre-eminently, however, is the "Yukon sleigh," formerly known as the "Cassiar sleigh," because the first miners who went into the Yukon fifteen or twenty years ago came from the Cassiar mining region, south of the headwaters of the Yukon. This sled was invented there, and has since undergone no material modification. It is seven feet in length, with a tread of about sixteen inches, and a hight of six inches. It is strongly built of hickory, the sleigh his hand, as it falls naturally to his side, may reach and grasp it.

The gee-pole is invaluable for steering, as well as for holding back upon grades not steep enough for the "rough lock"—a rope or dog-chain dragging under the runners. The "Yukon sleigh" is shod with steel. Sometimes, but rarely, handles are placed behind, as on the basket sleigh. As the driver of the "Yukon sleigh" must travel in front where he can hold the gee-pole, a rope long enough to clear the gee-pole is fastened to the front cross-bar, and to the front of this is a short singletree to which the traces of the team are fastened. As one can imagine, when the trail is very crooked the driver is obliged to jump with considerable liveliness to keep from being tripped as the rope swings from side to side. The driver further assists his team with a rope around his neck and shoulders. Thus rigged and on a smooth trail a strong malamoot, or an outside dog, like a St. Bernard or Newfoundland, will draw three to four hundred pounds, which is more than a man will care to pull for even a short distance. Indeed, it is well known that a man will hardly pull all day a weight much greater than his own. Much of the man's strength is lost by the upward lift and by the insecurity of his foothold, while the dog pulling horizontally and digging in with its toes, utilizes its full strength. The sleigh used by freighters is larger than the usual, and generally a second sleigh, known as the "trail sleigh," is hooked on behind.

A limit is sometimes reached to the number of dogs that can be driven together, tandem; so when say two teams of five to seven dogs are doubled-up they may be hitched in pairs, with a single dog as leader. A good leader is all important. Without one that obeys quickly the words of command it is nearly impossible to drive a dog team, for the ordinary dog naturally prefers to follow rather than lead, for which reason when making rapid journeys it is nearly always necessary, in order to get the most out of the team, for one man to run ahead. The leader is taught to respond to "Gee," "Haw" and "Whoa." There is another word which every dog comes to learn, if only at the cost of much sorrow, the meaning of which, apart from its derivation, is apparent from the expression with which it is uttered by the driver. It is the word, "*Mahsh*," a Chinook word known wherever the Hudson's Bay Company's trade-language is heard. Obviously a corruption of the French *marche*, it means "get-up"—"Git." To the majority of late newcomers into the Yukon the word was unknown, and, as uttered by the dog drivers there, it sounded more like mush, so mush the word forthwith became, until now that pronunciation is nearly universal. There has also been introduced into the English language as now spoken on the Pacific coast, not only a new verb "to mush," but also the noun, "musher." Originally a musher was a traveler by dog team, then from meaning a person who pulls his own sled, it has come to signify simply a traveler afoot. The word calls up to a Klondiker, not the horrors of the trail, but rather its humorous side.

The cost of getting together a dog team in Alaska varies so much at different times and places that it is impossible to give figures that will serve as a guide. Extraordinarily high prices prevailed at Dawson in the winter of 1897–8, as for nearly everything else. The demand was far in excess of the supply at hand, and the wealth of the miners, together with the high prices that they were willing to pay for freighting, ran the prices of dogs up to a fabulous figure. Fares of six hundred to fifteen hundred dollars were paid for single passage from Dawson to Skagway with a dog team, with no other privilege than that of sleeping under the teamster's robe and eating his food. If a person preferred to take his own team, it would have cost him more than that to have fitted out one. The best dogs were not for sale at any price, while the best that were for sale brought three to four hundred dollars each, and any kind of dog large enough for sled work, brought one hundred dollars and upwards. The highest price I positively know of was paid by the agent of the Alaska Commercial Company at Fort Yukon, for a team of five magnificent huskies from Rampart House on the Porcupine River—two being bought from an Indian for $500 the pair, the other three for $400 apiece from old John Shuman, chief of the Indians at that place. "Yukon sleighs," worth seven dollars outside, sold for forty-two dollars—thirty dollars for the wood-work, and twelve dollars for the iron runners. Before the discovery of Klondike and the stampede to Dawson good native dogs could be had for from five to ten dollars each. While dogs were so high at Dawson they could be bought at St. Michaels and the lower Yukon for twenty-five to thirty dollars. When the spring came in 1898, dogs suddenly dropped in value. Incoming dog teams, sold at public auction, brought from ninety dollars to as low as twenty to thirty dollars per dog. All these were nearly worn out by their hard work during the winter. Prices again advanced the following winter.

The usual food of the sledge dog consists of dried salmon, cooked rice, cornmeal and oatmeal with bacon. By the most experienced drivers the dogs are fed but once a day, and that at night, after the day's journey; although when the travelers upon a long journey stop for their noonday rest and a hot cup of tea, they may give them out of their own larder a doughnut apiece. Upon long journeys, such as from Dawson and Circle City to Skagway, before road-houses were built at forty and fifty-mile intervals along the route, it was necessary to measure the time and weigh out before-hand with utmost care each article carried on the sleigh. The cooking of the dog feed was as important as making camp. Some drivers invented a large boiler of heavy tin that fitted around the sheet iron Yukon stove. They would set up their tent, place the stove inside for their own warmth, and then cook the rice or bacon for the dogs in the boiler over a blazing fire outside. The native dog cheerfully lies outdoors in the coldest weather, but the more careful dog-drivers bring their dogs inside their cabin or tent at night, if only one or two at a time, as they start in on their work next morn-ing in much better spirits.

The distance a dog can travel in a day and draw a load is astonishing. With a light load of one hundred to one hundred and fifty pounds he will make easily forty

his natural powers of vehement expression and vigorous epithets, conspicuous among which are references to the particular dog's ancestry on the mother's side. When threats, as well as words of encouragement, fail and the dog sulks or will not mahsh, the driver betakes himself to his big mittened fists, with which he thumps the refractory one about the ears or ribs, occasionally laying on with a light dog-chain, a mode of pun-ishment not so liable to cause injury as a hard stick would be. The good dog-puncher is sparing of blows and everything that will rattle or discourage his dog, but when all other measures fail and the dog thinks he has found an easy boss, he then whips him soundly, or to use his own pic-turesque expression, "bastes hell out of him." A sound thrashing when needed, with consistently kind treatment constantly at all other times makes a good dog; while nagging soon spoils the best.

In summer the sledge dog formerly had, as

HOW THEY PEDDLED WATER AT NOME.

miles a day, while the best teams under favorable conditions will make sixty miles for day after day. This is the rate at which the six hundred and odd miles between Daw-son and the coast has been covered by a single team, while, by relays, a single sled has covered the distance in even less time. No whip is necessary in driving dogs, but drivers sometimes carry a thick plaited one seven or eight feet long, having a short wood handle and the butt of the leather part weighted inside with a slender bag of shot. The driver usually has recourse only to

a rule, nothing to do but bask in the sunshine of the long days. But now in the new mining camps of Alaska and the Yukon Territory, there is much summer work which dogs can do. At Dawson and Nome horses have been imported for heavy freighting, but the dogs continue to perform much light work. At Dawson a pack-train of eighteen dogs made daily trips from Dawson to the mines on Eldorado, a distance of sixteen miles. Each dog was fitted with a pack-saddle made of a small canvas flour-sack with the end sewed up and a slit made across the middle, and when this was fastened over the dog's back the two pouches each side could be filled with cans of provisions or small sacks of gold dust. The weight carried by each dog was twenty to thirty-five pounds. One day as the train was returning to Dawson with a load of gold dust, one of the dogs in crossing a foot-log over Bonanza Creek fell into the water. Fortunately for the dog, the pack fell off, with about six thousand dollars' worth of gold dust, and the dog swam out, the precious dust being recovered afterwards.

At Nome, during the summer of 1900, there was great demand for the service of dogs for hauling up and down the beach upon which the city stood. Teams of two to half a dozen dogs hitched to small carts were a constant feature of the crowded streets; but more noticeable than the dogs

a team of five black Newfoundlands used a cask fitted with a sort of axle by which it could be hauled over the ground like a roller. Still another man conducted an express business, delivering anything from a can of milk to a ton of coal, employing five slender undersized boarhounds—a team altogether unique. Dogs are often used by the miners along the shores of Behring Sea, when the weather is fine and the sea is still, for towing their skiffs. The towline being attached a third or a quarter of the way back from the bow, the driver sits in the stern with a paddle, while his team of perhaps seven dogs carries him along faster than a man can walk.

It has been said that the Eskimo dog does not show affection for man. Doubtless there are instances of vicious dogs, but in all my experience, both at Dawson and at Nome,

WHEN THE DRIVER LENDS A HAND.

themselves were some of the vehicles that were used. One young man used to haul water from one of the wells from which drinking water was obtained, and distribute it to his customers in a low, rude wagon with four small discs sawed off a log for wheels; the water being transported in old five-gallon oil cans. Another water carrier with

where more dogs of that kind were gathered together than ever at one place before, I never saw a native dog attack a man, nor even snap at him, excepting one half-starved Indian dog which had never learned to expect anything but a blow from an outstretched hand, and this same dog afterwards became friendly. Independence of a certain sort characterizes the native dog, and if to display affection is to grovel and fawn and go into hysterics because a man pats him on the head, then the native dog may be said to lack affection. A wonder it has been to me that, under the abuse constantly piled upon their poor bodies by their native owners, they do not turn. Some outlet for suppressed feeling must be, and I think the native dog, for every blow and harsh word he receives from human-kind, holds a bite or a snarl for each of his fellows. In an Indian dog community every dog's lip is raised against his neighbor, so fierce is the struggle for existence. Snow, wind, cold and curses, the native dog accepts with a show of stolid indifference, but he also possesses a trait hard to reconcile with the former. I should call the Eskimo dog the bravest, yet the greatest coward among dogs. When in the mood he yelps at the upraising of a hand. I have seen a stick shaken at an Indian's dog, and though the dog was well out of reach, every time the stick was waved, the dog let a yelp. It is apparently a part of the game. At times, when receiving only moderate chastisement, a malamoot will yell as if being murdered by inches. This disposition to make much outcry causes their frequent battles with each other to sound much worse than they really are. They seem to know perfectly that their thick coat of hair protects them. No matter how furious the onslaught, or vicious the shakings, a dog is rarely hurt in a single-handed fight. Consequently he is a great bluffer, and when in anger his row of hideous fangs and the expression of eyes and whole attitude is the most ferocious that I ever observed in man or beast.

Conspicuous as his good traits are, it must be acknowledged however that as regards rights of property—edible property—the malamoot approaches the lowest depths of turpitude. In this respect he is without moral sense. A born thief, he glories in the fact. To steal is as natural to him as to eat. I knew only one native dog that would not touch his owner's provisions when in reach and only that on hearsay. That dog, strangely enough, had lived the first year of his life in an Indian's lodge, but he had been taken by a kind, intelligent white man, who had trained him. It was at Teller City I saw the dog, a fine black fellow who had hauled

his master from Klondike. His present master then made the assertion that he would on the spot test the dog with a piece of bacon, and he offered fifty dollars to back up what he said. Everyone present was incredulous, but no one covered the bet. At Circle City the men freighting supplies to the mines on Birch Creek, used to make an extra charge for hauling bacon, as a sort of insurance precaution. Indians when camping for the night in winter raise their tobóggans upon stakes some distance off the snow and cache their supplies of meat or fish in little log houses raised eight or ten feet from the ground upon posts. The miners do the same, or else enclose the overhanging fronts of their cabins, where they store meats and such supplies that would spoil inside the warm cabins. These elevated caches are a conspicuous feature of the northern mining camps.

The Eskimo dog does not bark, or bay, like the civilized dog. His only note for expressing deep emotion is a long-drawn howl. It is the wolf cry—a sound that seems to me the most mournful, the most dismal in nature. When fifty or a hundred dogs raise their voices in unison (or dissonance) the effect is impossible to describe. At Dawson, in the summer of 1898, four or five thousand dogs were assembled, about equally divided between native and outside dogs. Whenever a steamboat hove into sight from down-river, the malamoots would begin, in the same key as the steamboat's whistle, and the other dogs, not knowing the cause of the outbreak, would join in, and the concert would be kept up for several minutes, the deep baying of the outside dogs keeping up for some time after the malamoots had subsided.

At present there is no person breeding the native sledge dog with a view to preserving it distinct. It would be difficult under the conditions. It might be worth while to do, as has been done along the coast of Alaska with blue and black foxes, set apart an island for breeding purposes. There will always be a demand for good native dogs and trained sled dogs of any breed but it would not be profitable to import them to the gold-fields, if, as was done last summer, some of the steamers bound for Nome should make a charge of twenty-five dollars per dog for freight.

9

Père Lacombe,
A Wilderness Apostle of the North

AGNES C. LAUT

O U T I N G

APRIL, 1905

PÈRE LACOMBE, A WILDERNESS
APOSTLE OF THE NORTH

By AGNES C. LAUT

I

IN the month of September, there passed through Montreal, on the way from France to the foothills of the Rockies, a distinguished figure unique for the last three-quarters of a century in the annals of the great Northwest.

Doers of big things—men who have made history—we still have with us; but not every maker of history has by the mere lifting of a hand prevented massacres that might have wiped out the frontier of half a continent. Few leaders have rallied half a hundred men to victory against a thousand through pitchy darkness, in the confusion of what was worse than darkness,—panic. And not every hero of victory can be the hero of defeat, a hero—for instance—to the extent of standing siege by scourge, with three thousand dying and dead of the plague, men fleeing from camp pursued by a phantom death, wolves skulking past the wind-blown tent-flaps unmolested, none remaining to bury the dead but the one man whose hands are over-busy with the dying.

And not every hero is as unaware of the world's blare as a child; and as indifferent to it. Such is Père Lacombe, known to all old timers from the Mackenzie River to the Missouri.

To call him simply a priest is misleading; for in these days of sentimental religion, with the abolition of the devil and a pious turning up of the whites of one's eyes to an attenuated Deity, priesthood is sometimes associated with a sort of anæmic goodness —the man who sits in a cushioned study-chair. But Father Lacombe's goodness is of the red-blood type, that knows how to deal with men who think in terms of the clenched fist.

Two kinds of men make desolating failures in a new land. There is the one who sits moused up in a house, measuring every thing in the new country by the standards of the old; and there is the book-full man, who essays the wilds with city theories of how to do everything from handling a bucking broncho to converting a savage, only to learn that he can't keep up with the procession for the simple reason—as the French say—that one has to learn much in the woods not contained in "le curé's pet-ee cat-ee-cheesm."

To neither of these classes did Father Lacombe belong. He realized that one is up against facts in the wilderness, not theories; that to clothe those facts in our Eastern ideas of proprieties, is about as incongruous as to dress an Indian in the cast-off garments of the white man. Instead of expecting the Indian to adopt the white

75

man's mode of life, Father Lacombe adopted the Indian's. He rode to their buffalo
hunts with them half a century ago, when
the herds roamed from the Missouri to the
Saskatchewan in millions; or he broke the
way for the dog train over the trackless
leagues of snow between the Saskatchewan
and Athabasca. Twice he was a peace-
maker with the great Confederacy of Blackfeet, Bloods and Piegans. Yet when honorable peace could not be won, he won
another kind of peace—the peace that is a
victory.

II

It was in the region of what is known as
Old Man's River, south of the Saskatchewan. Here the Blackfeet Indians could
pasture their numerous bands of ponies for
the winter, sheltered from the north wind
by the bluffs and deep ravines that cut
athwart the prairie in trenches. Here, too,
the buffalo herds were likely to be found
browsing below the cliffs, or on the lee side
of the poplar groves along the banks of
rivers.

"Were the buffalo as plentiful as old
timers say; or is this more of the old timer's
yarns?" I asked Father Lacombe.

"Plentiful!" he repeated derisively.
"When I first went to the West and joined
the hunt of the buffalo, they were literally
in millions. I should think at least a million a year must have been slaughtered
by the Indians of the Northwest. Why,
I have heard the old Cree and Blackfeet
chiefs say that at fording time, the rush of
the herds almost stopped the current of the
Saskatchewan and Missouri.''

But camping ground that offered such
ideal conditions of shelter, ford and food,
had its dangers. From days immemorial,
war existed between Blackfeet and Cree.
The tribe with best horses had greatest success at the buffalo hunt; and that meant
security against want. From the time that
Spanish horses spread north of the Missouri,
the Indians of this region had only two oc-
cupations—hunting the buffalo, and raiding
other tribes for horses. The Blackfeet, like
the Sioux, were tigerish fighters. They were
even bolder; for after sweeping down on
Cree or Assiniboine or Sautaux to the east,
they could drive their booty back up Old
Man's River to the passes of the Rockies,
where no alien tribes could follow. When

leagued with their confederates, the Bloods
and Piegans, they were invincible.

All through the winters of '68, '69 and '70
it was well known that an alliance of a thousand Cree, Assiniboine and Sautaux were on
the war-path against the Blackfeet; but no
one dreamed of the enemy invading the very
center of the Blackfeet's hunting ground.
The circumstances were not unlike the dangers that threatened the French settlements
two hundred years before, when the Iroquois invaded the land of the Algonquins
and Hurons. The different missions of the
half dozen Oblates who were in the Northwest, were scattered two, three, four hundred miles apart. In case of attack, they
were farther away from help than Quebec
had been from France. It took six months
to go from Eastern Canada to the missions
west of Edmonton, two months to go from
Ft. Garry (Winnipeg), where a handful of
fur traders lived inside a walled fort, to the
foothills of the Rockies, and three months
to send word to the outside world by way
of the Missouri-Benton trail to St. Paul.

Father Lacombe had already won the
respect of the Blackfeet by his heroism during the small-pox scourge. He had taken
up winter quarters in the lodge of the great
Sun Chief of the tribe. Some forty tepees
with sixty men, and their women and children were in the camp; and a short distance
away were two other encampments of fifty
or sixty tents. The prairie traveler learns
to read the signs of the snow as an open
page; and alien footprints distinctly fore-
warned the presence of an enemy. Father
Lacombe urged Sun Chief to call all the encampments together for the general safety;
but his caution was perhaps mistaken for
fear; and the camps not only remained
apart, but half the warriors in Sun Chief's
encampment went off to hunt.

It was a bitterly cold day in December
with the early dark and woolly, surcharged
atmosphere that precedes storm. Tent
thongs were braced taut against the howling wind. Extra wood was carried in
from the bluffs and heaped on the fire in the
centers of the tepees; and the four or five-
hundred horses were carefully picketed in
shelter, so they could not drive before the
wind. Supper consisted of pemmican and
tea without sugar; and those were nights
when tin cup and fork almost stuck to the
lips in a burn from intensity of frost. In

Pere Lacombe.

such weather, as one venerable Oblate, who has been forty years on the Mackenzie, said: "The hatchet was our Cross; for we did nothing but chop down saplings for firewood to keep from freezing to death."

The hatchet was to be another kind of Cross to Father Lacombe that night.

It must have been a unique scene—one that will never again be enacted in America, the wind howling like a demon pack of loup-garou, outside; the tawny faces crouching round the center fire inside the big tepee of Sun Chief; the leap of lambent flame to the suck of the wind at the hole in the top of the tepee; the blue smoke blinding the eyesight the minute one stood erect in the tent; the shadows on the skin walls of the tepee; the whining of the dogs to gain entrance; the whinnying of the picketed ponies, and upright in the crowded tepee above the Blackfeet stretched on buffalo robes round the fire, the figure of the weather-worn, stalwart priest leading the chant of evensong to the Great Spirit that is as much God of red man as of white.

Sun Chief and the priest must have talked late, heaping wood on the fire; for it was midnight before fires were out and Father Lacombe rolled himself in a buffalo robe with outer clothing folded as pillow. Outside, raged the storm, "the forty below and a blizzard" that Westerners know, wrenching at the tent poles, heaping drifts, lifting and falling in the shrill, whistling cry that seems to die away in the wail of a lost soul. One does not sleep on such nights. It is the same instinct that makes animals restless in storm; something primordial, below consciousness, that pricks the senses to alertness for danger. You may have reduced the whole cosmography of existence to a scientific formula, proved that "winds are currents of air in violent activity," that ghosts don't course the earth disembodied, and that fiends are only the myths of human fear; but you can't lie awake all night listening to the corsairs of northern storms screaming, hissing, shouting venomous glee with the undertone of a deathless wail, and not think a good many thoughts you don't talk out.

Suddenly, Sun Chief leaped into the air with a yell: "Assinaw! Assinaw! The Cree! The Cree!"

Nearly a thousand warriors had swooped down on the camp of half-armed Blackfeet.

III

The late fire had marked out the chief's tent for special attack. The only safety was the darkness of storm outside; but before Sun Chief could grasp his gun and slash open the tight-laced tent-flap, bullets were whizzing through the tepee walls. Two balls bounded with a spit of fire through the dark at the priest's feet. Then, the Indian chief had hurled his family out to the safety of darkness away from the marked tent; and Father Lacombe was the target for a thousand shots, one musket charge splintering two of the tent poles, bullets whistling about his head with the sing—*zizzz*—*sip*, that one never forgets.

It took but a trice to jerk his soutane from the pillow and slip it over his shoulders. Seizing the little metal cross in his right hand, he muttered a prayer, dashed out and was in the thick of it, shouting at the top of his voice——

"Fight! Fight! Don't run! Don't run! They'll cut you to pieces if you run! Hooray! Hooray! Fight, *mes enfants! En avant, mes braves!* Fight for your wives and children!"

*   *   *   *   *   *

Up to the time Father Lacombe came to talk of that famous fight, he had worn rather a wearied air. He had just landed from the Atlantic steamer and was tired. He couldn't understand why the world should wish to know about the little things he had been able to do. Other men would have done the same. Many men had done more. But as the memory of that night came back, the eyes took on a new light, the light of the war-horse that smells powder.

"Ah," he said, unconsciously falling into that picturesque medley half English, half French, "t'at night—it was hell! It was hell! T'ere is no light but the sinister blaze of the muskets, when some one drop with the death-cry. We hear the Cree shouting the war whoop, the Blackfeet women and children lost in the dark, screaming for each other, not knowing which way to hide; the horses whinny and stampede through camp among the howling dogs; and the blaze—blaze—blaze of the guns, with the bullets spitting through the snow like hot iron!"

As Father Lacombe dashed from the tent a squaw staggered forward, shot through the upper part of her body; and the blaze of a musket showed a child in her arms. Before he knew it, his feet were bathed in her blood. Barely could he administer the last rites to the dying woman, when the enemy had burst into the encampment and torn the scalp from her head. Twenty-five tents were scattered to the winds; but the Blackfeet never ceased to fight nor the priest to hurrah them on! A hostile Assiniboine was in the very act of plundering Father Lacombe's possessions when a ball stretched the miscreant dead on the bed which the priest had just left. As if in instant punishment of the squaw's death, a Blackfoot sprang upon the corpse, and the Assiniboine's scalp was ripped away before the body was cold. Of all Lacombe's belongings, everything was taken but the soutane he had slipped over his shoulders, the Cross he held in his hand, and a little book of prayers—not much for a man exposed to a forty-degree-below blizzard, a thousand miles from help.

"If I failed now," he said, "I felt everything would be lost—all the years with the Blackfeet and Cree gone for nothing."

More than that, if the thousand hostiles had succeeded in exterminating the Blackfeet camp, including the priest, every mission and fur post and frontier settlement between the Missouri and Mackenzie would have been exposed to attack. It does not take much success to turn a white man's head; and it takes less to intoxicate a thousand warriors on the ramp.

The one hope was to let the assailants know the priest was among the Blackfeet; for he had befriended the Cree, too, in the small-pox scourge.

Uplifting the Cross in his right hand, with a flag flourished in the left, he rushed forward shouting: "It is I—Lacombe, your friend!" But in the confusion of storm and musketry, he could make himself neither seen nor heard.

Three times the fury of assault was driven back and assuaged, the besieged, of whom more than half already lay dead or wounded, huddling together, exposed to the storm, not knowing which way they dare retreat, when with a roar like the boom of a tidal wave, the Cree war whoop rose and they attempted to rush the camp. And three times Father Lacombe's "Hooray! Hooray! On, *mes braves!* Fight! Fight! Defend your children!"—rallied the dispirited little band to keep their stand and hurl back the assailants.

The storm that had prevented the Crees from seeing the priest, also prevented them from learning the weakness of the Blackfeet.

All night the firing never ceased; and all night the little band of Blackfeet gave way never an inch.

Then morning came—sun dawn over a bloody field with the tempest lulling like a thing tired out and the enemy's musketry spitting over the drifts from the hiding of the wooded bluffs.

A clearer atmosphere gave Lacombe his chance. Bidding the Blackfeet stop firing and hide where the Cree shots could not reach them, Father Lacombe raised his Cross in his right hand, a flag of truce in his left, and marched straight out in the face of the firing line, shouting on the Cree to come out and parley. The Blackfeet could hardly believe their eyes when they realized what he was doing—marching straight in the face of certain death. They called to him to come back. They would fight to the end and die together; but he marched right on. Bullets fell at his feet. Two or three balls *siffed* past his ears, singeing his hair. Again the Blackfeet shouted for him to come back; but he was beyond call, and the bullets were raining around him like hail.

If the sun that rises over northern snowfields ever witnessed a more human piece of unconscious heroism than this solitary figure advancing against the firing line—I do not know of it.

Suddenly, he was seen to reel and fall, drenched in blood. A bullet had bounced from the ground, striking him in the shoulder, and glancing up grazed across his forehead. Demons could not have restrained the Blackfeet then. To the triumphant yell of the Crees, they sent back countershout that set the ravine ringing. They were no longer on the defensive. A whirlwind rush of rage carried them past all bounds of fear. They only waited to see the priest on his feet—for the force of the bullet had been broken by the shoulder wound—when, with yells of fury, they poured volley after volley into the Cree bluffs, running from hiding of snowdrift to brushwood, pressing the hostiles back and back till, before midday, the fighters were in talking distance and a Blackfoot snarled

Fort Gary (Winnipeg), as it was when Father Lacombe went West sixty years ago.

The habitants where Father Lacombe passed his childhood, who make everything for themselves from ovens to boats.

Habitant woman of Lower St. Lawrence, weaving homespun cloth.

out—"You have wounded your priest! Canaille! Have you not done enough?"

Wounded the man who had nursed them, too, through the small-pox scourge? The Crees were dumbfounded. Besides, they were beaten; and they probably reasoned that if a handful of men taken by surprise put up this kind of a fight, the same men on the aggressive with daylight to aid them and couriers scurrying to bring back the absent hunters, could coop the Cree company up in one of these ravines and exterminate the entire band. Besides, thirty of their braves were dead, fifty wounded; and retreat on horseback over deep snow with fifty wounded to carry could not be made with as great speed as the return of Blackfeet warriors might warrant.

A Cree advanced to parley.

They had not known the priest had been among the Blackfeet. The smoke had hidden the face of the man, who had advanced alone! It was enough—the Cree would retire; and retire they did with all the speed they could put into their horses.

When the battle was over, the Blackfeet turned to Lacombe. A more haughty tribe never existed among North American Indians. They had no words now to express their pent up feelings. They threw their arms about him like children, sobbing out gratitude. They prostrated themselves at his feet. They declared that he was divine, or the bullets that rained round him would surely have killed him; but he only told them that that was the way his God took care of men who would risk their lives for His sake; and no doubt the Blackfeet did what the Indians call some "long thinking."

But the heroism of real life has no time for stage effects. It was the kind of Northwest cold that doesn't just chill you. It takes hold of you with nippers. What was to be done? Two hundred of the horses had been stampeded and were even now on the way to the Cree land. Not much was left of the encampment but the tent poles, skins blown away by the wind, and the horses running wild over the prairie.

The famous Chateau de Ramezay, Montreal.   This is a typical interior of a habitant's house.

"I was never in all my life so completely a pauper, as after that fight with the Cree," said Father Lacombe.

Some of the Blackfeet from the other camps arrived. They gave him buffalo robes to keep him from freezing; and the next day, in spite of the cold, all set out for a camp twenty miles distant. Needless to say that when he left this camp for a six days' journey to a fort of the mountains, in all the dangers of cold and storm he was escorted by three Blackfeet.

The most of men would have rested satisfied with that battle as one good winter's work; but Lacombe followed up his forcible object lesson in muscular goodness by going straight to the Cree encampments and teaching what it was—in Indian language —"that made a man's heart strong."

IV

One can't help wondering if the many martyrs to persecuted faith had used a little of Lacombe's muscular methods whether results would not have totaled up better.

The Oblates have been in the West only three-quarters of a century; and they have civilized fifty thousand Indians. The Jesuits sacrificed life and means for two centuries among the Iroquois; and nothing remains of it. But the wilderness leader is born, not made. For a man of the purely studious temperament—no matter how zealous—to attempt running rapids, fording rivers, riding tricky bronchos, mingling in the melée of the buffalo hunt or warriors' foray—is to make himself ridiculous. To succeed in these things a man has to be born with a strain of adventure in his blood. And Father Lacombe's youth prepared him for such a life.

He was born of habitant parents on the banks of the St. Lawrence. Now, it is safe to say that there is not a single French family in the province of Quebec, seignior or peasant, that has not some strain of an ancestor who took to the woods in the early days and lived the free life of the wilderness hunter, camping under the stars. Where the English colonist farmed, the French colonist hunted, gay of heart, careless of to-morrow; and that hunter strain is in the blood yet. Seventy years ago, wildwood tales were in the very air that a Quebec boy breathed. There was not a hamlet on the banks of the St. Lawrence that had not sent out its hero to hunt, to explore, to fight. The French-Canadian took to the rapids like a duck to water. Nothing daunted him. He courted dangerous adventure for the fun of it. He didn't care for trade. What he liked was *la gloire;* and I'm inclined to think that men live bigger, broader lives for the sake of the huzzy who is called "La Gloire," than for dollars and cents.

In this atmosphere Father Lacombe passed his youth. Besides, the French-Canadian habitant is taught to do everything for himself. He weaves the cloth for his own clothes, he makes his own hats, he spins his own wool, he tans the leather for his boots. He even disdains a bought stove. He builds a clay or brick oven. He grows his own tobacco. He catches the fish required for his table; and fifty years ago, above the white-washed stone wall of the hearthside fireplace, on an iron rack, hung the musket that supplied the family table with fresh meat from the woods.

What better environment to prepare for the wilderness life? The city man, who essays the wilds, has had his mind fed by the college factory and his stomach by a machine-regulated market. You pay your money and men will think your thoughts for you, and put clothing on your back. The place where such a man fails is where he is suddenly and nakedly thrown on his own resources. Stripped of the adventitious, his own resources are nil; and he lies down to die. If ammunition fails the true wilderness hunter, he has the dead-fall, or some other trap. If the trap fails him, he tries snares for birds. If birds fail him, he will fish with home-made net, or home-made hook. It is only when bird, beast, and fish fail that he is at the end of his tether. And not the least important part of his equipment is that almost animal instinct of alertness to danger.

These were the things that fitted Father Lacombe for his wilderness life; but it was a kind act, whose author little foresaw the consequences, that set him on the path of his after-life. The parish priest gave him money to go on with his education. All the return asked by the priest was that the boy "be good;" and young Lacombe began casting about in his mind the best way to be practically good, not sentimentally, or as the street says, "dishwater," good. He was as muscular, strong and athletic as a young Indian. Why not consecrate his muscularity to goodness? Where would such muscularity tell best? Manifestly, the Church is not a boxing-school, though it aims to give hard knocks to the Devil; but there was the Pays d'en Haut, the Up-Country where so many young Frenchmen sought "la gloire." There was a field uninvaded by any but the fur trader from Missouri to the North Pole; and there was a field for iron strength and muscular goodness.

He at once went to the House of the Oblates, Montreal. The Oblates were preparing to capture this field. A curious old pile of unpretentious gray stone is this house of dreams, that has sent out so many brave men to heroism and death in the Northwest! It is a house of poverty and ideals as well as dreams. Perhaps they go together. Vespers were ringing as I drove up to the door; and I could not but think as I listened to the lilt of the chimes how many young mystics had dreamed of white-robed victory to the sound of those bells, only to go forth to life-long exile, to death by famine or cold, or the assassin hand, like young Fafard and Marchand at Frog Lake.

Success is such a white-robed thing to young dreamers full of ideals to their necks, and such a bloody, cruel thing all tattered at the edges and worm-eaten to the middle in real life, and yet if young mystics had not dreamed what the world calls "moonshine" to the lilt of those chimes, could Lacombe have won the Crees from a war that would have deluged the West with blood as the Sioux deluged Minnesota?

An inscription tells me that I am to ring the bell and open the door. I do so, to find myself in a chairless anteroom, with a tiny frosted window in the wall. I rap on the wicket as we are told a certain mythical pilgrim rapped at the gates of Paradise. The window swings open, and a priest-porter, with shrewd enough eyes to have been a relative of Peter's, asks me what I want. I tell him in French, that would have made anyone but that porter laugh, that I want to find out about the delayed boat that is bringing Father Lacombe from the last trip he will ever make to the East. At the name "Lacombe," the porter's antiquity falls from him like rags. He goes off at such speed that I catch only every second word and guess the others, but gather that if I will "please to walk *au parloir*" someone will come who will tell me everything, things that Father Lacombe does not tell about himself. So I pass through another door, *au parloir*, beyond which are sacred precincts where no outsider goes. Here, Father Corneillier comes, and we talk of the long line of French-Canadian path-makers who have won the West, of Provencher, and Taché, and Grandin. Here, I presently meet Husson, who has been up on the Mackenzie for forty years, and tells me of seeing American whalers who have rounded the Horn, passed through Bering Strait and summered at Pt. Barrow, in the Arctic. Here, too, I meet Father Lacombe himself, the next day, a muscularly built, close-knit man, who looks more as if he were in the sixties than in the seventies, with hands that could take a bulldog grasp of difficulties, shoulders broad to carry the heaviest weights unbent, and on his face a kindness inexpressible.

V

Fifty years ago the Up-Country was entered either by way of the Ottawa across the Great Lakes, or up the Mississippi to St. Paul, whence the journey was continued by ox-cart and boat to Ft. Garry, now Winnipeg. Just at the international boundary westward of Red River from Pembina was the great hunting ground of the buffalo. Into the rough-and-tumble hunting camps went young Lacombe to learn the language of the Indians, and what was more important than the language—the things not taught in the curé's "pet-ee cat-ee-cheesm." The story of these buffalo hunts I have told elsewhere and shall not repeat here, except to add that the implacable hatred between the Sioux and Cree—of which this was the border land—turned many a buffalo hunt into a bloody foray. These fights are a story in themselves.

Westward of Red River, the journey was continued either by boat up the Saskatchewan, or "the plains across" for a thousand miles by horseback, ox-cart or dog-train. The Saskatchewan boats were the famous

Mackinaw flat-bottom barges propelled by eight oarsmen. Boxes, bales, hardware, mattresses, heterogeneously pitched on board, loaded these craft to the water line; and anywhere he could find handhold or foothold or pillow for his head, the traveler stowed himself. Except in cases of great urgency, stop was made at night to camp *a la belle etoile*. Here, the priest held his earliest services in a temple as old as time —the vault of heaven.

Half way westward at Portage La Loche, the Red River flotilla of boats met the men of the Athabasca and Mackenzie and Saskatchewan coming out with the annual loads of furs. Cargoes were exchanged. The crews paused to rest, and one can guess that a good deal went on among the rollicking French voyageurs and Scotch clerks not according to the curé's catechism.

For some reason, there was always good-natured rivalry and chaffing between the Scotch and the French employées of the fur company. The French were most mercurial—could do big things at a rush; but the Scotch were credited with better staying powers. Among the French was one giant packer from Sorel, Quebec, who could pick any two Scotchmen up under his arms and bundle them head first through the parchment windows before their comrades could come to the rescue. One day, the Scotch clerk in the fort thought to put up a trick on Jo Paul, that would take the brag out of the French voyageurs. Barrels of sugar stood piled in one corner of the store. In one barrel, apart from the rest, the sugar had been replaced by lead.

"Jo Paul," ordered the clerk, with a wink to the men, "I wish you'd put that barrel on the counter."

Jo Paul went at the barrel as if it had been a ball of down; but, behold, "the sugar" did not budge; and Jo Paul "caught on." Mustering all his strength, with clenched teeth, he seized the barrel of lead and hurled it bang, with giant impetus, slap on the top of the counter. The clerks held their breath, then there was no laughter. The lead crashed through counter, through planks, through floor beams and all, clear to the bottom of the cellar.

"*Voila, mon petit*," says Jo Paul, "you can go ga'der up y' own lead."

When the journeys were by dog-train, one significant fact was often noticed of the

The Blackfeet Indian Camp.

A Dance of the Blackfeet Indians.

dog driver. Spite of danger, hunger, cold, the Indian runner would keep his courage unless one thing happened. All Westerners know that the whiskey-jack or scolding jay will follow travelers for miles to pick up the crumbs of the camp. So will wolves; but a poisoned fish settles them. But sometimes, on a long journey, when food runs short, and a driver is half blind from snow glare, sick to the very pit of his stomach from snow nausea, and dizzy from snow staggers, there will be observed following the lone courser across the snow glaze of spring thaw, black shadows—the carrion crows. When that happens, the very marrow of an Indian's courage melts.

VI

Once, on such a journey southward over interminable snows, Father Lacombe had camped with his guide on the edge of a small woods. Both men were dead tired. Their snow-shoes dragged heavily. Supper over, they spread their snow-logged garments to dry before the fire, prepared beds of spruce branches, and sat listening to that strange, unearthly silence of the snow-padded plains. The dogs crouched round asleep. The night grew black as ink, foreboding storm. An uncanny muteness fell over the two. They knew they were eighty miles from a living soul; and the cold was terrific. There was no sound but the crackle of the fire, and an occasional splinter of frost-split trees outside. Suddenly the guide pricked up his ears, with dilated eyes intent. Faint, more like a breath of storm than a voice, came a muffled wail. Then, silence again, of very death. The men looked at each other, but didn't say anything. It was the kind of silence where you can hear your breath. Half an hour passed. There is no use pretending. The ozone of northern latitudes at midnight, eighty miles from a living soul, can prick your nerves and send tickles down your spine. You become aware that solitude is positively palpable. It's like a ghost-hand touching you out of Nowhere. You feel as if your own nothingness got drowned in an Infinite Almightiness. And it came again, out of the frost-muffled woods—the long, sighing wail.

"Alex, do you hear?"

"Yes," but he didn't want to.

"What is that?"

"Hare seized by owl."

"You think—that?"

"Yes," but he thought it weakly.

"Your hare has a human voice, Alex."

But Alex, who was visibly chattering, became voluble. Of course, it was a hare. He'd often remarked the resemb——But the words died in a gulp of fright: and the guide got himself to bed in haste with the blanket robe over his head.

"Alex, your hare has a long life, *hein?* Listen! Do you hear? Get up! Some one has need of us! I'm going to see."

In vain Alex explained to the priest that the voice would only lead him to death in the woods, that it came from the body of some brave buried among the branches of the trees in there, who was calling for the things his relatives had forgotten to place with the corpse.

"Then, I'll go alone," said Lacombe, "but you keep your gun ready; and if there is danger, I'll call you!"

And surely, from a prudent point of view, it was rash to follow a vague voice into unknown woods blanketed black with the thickness of intense frost. He would catch the sound, follow it; find nothing—wait; hear it again; again follow it; and again lose it. What was terrifying was that the groans seemed nearer than his own hands and feet—yet he could find nothing! Suddenly, he was aware of the warmth of cinders under his moccasins; and stooping, felt a voice in his very face. A human form lay wrapped in a buffalo robe across the dying camp fire.

"Speak! What are you?" he demanded.

"A woman with her child—lost. I could tramp no longer—my feet are frozen."

Calling the guide, the two men carried woman and infant to their tepee. She was little more than a child herself, and had evidently been outrageously beaten. Both feet required amputation. The priest learned that she had been cast off by her Cree husband, and had gone forth from the camp to kill both herself and the child; but at the sound of its cry, her courage failed her. She could not do the act, and marched on and on, day after day, till the frozen feet could march no farther. Then, wrapping the child in her warmest clothing, she had gathered it close in her arms, spread the buffalo robe over herself, and lain down to die. But to this Hagar of the wilderness came also a visitant of mercy. When Father Lacombe wakened in the morning, he found that the guide had plied the woman with restoratives all night, wrapped her in robes and placed her on the dog sleigh. The guide then hitched himself with the dogs to pull. Father Lacombe fastened the steering pole behind to push; and so they took her to the mission house, hundreds of miles distant. On the way they came up with the Cree husband who had abandoned her. The man was dumb-founded at the apparition.

"What," he blustered. "I don't want this wife! You'd have done much better to have minded your own business and left her alone where she was, to die."

For just a second, the Man in Father Lacombe got the better of the Priest. I think if that Cree had waited, he would have received all he needed.

"You miserable beast!" thundered Lacombe. "You don't think as much of your child as a dog of its pups! Get into that tent this minute and hide your dishonorable head, or—! I'll find someone to take care of her!"

VII

Space fails to tell of the days when the West held its breath lest the Blackfeet snould join Riel in the Metis rebellion, and Father Lacombe had the fate of the frontier in the hollow of his hand; or of the old Indian sage, who sent his son to Lacombe to learn if there were no Better Way than the Wolf Code of Brute Existence.

All night the two men sat talking, the wise man of the Indians and the wise man of the whites; comparing the wisdom of all that each knew, about a Better Way; and when the fevered eyes of the dying Indian turned to watch his last sunrise, there was on his faces the light that is neither of land nor sea. What his mystic visions had told him might betrue, the white man had confirmed.

These are but a few episodes in the life of a man whom the West venerates and the Indians almost worship. A secular friend has built for him a home called "The Hermitage" among the foothills of the Rockies; and, in the shadow of the mountains of the setting sun, he has decided to pass the evening of his life.

10

Love in the Wilderness

LAWRENCE MOTT

"A rounded shape on a little hillside
caught his eyes."

Drawing for "Love in the Wilderness" by N. C. Wyeth.

LOVE IN THE WILDERNESS

BY LAWRENCE MOTT

DRAWING BY N. C. WYETH

I

"HERE *is* Chictou?" Constable Clyde, of the R. N. W. M. Police, asked the girl for the third time.

She was quick-witted and clever, this half-breed woman of the North. Tossing her small head derisively—"Gon' mabbe somew'ere, Ah tol' to you!"

The constable seated himself on the edge of the rough table, one leg swinging, the drip of the snow-water falling from the moccasin in a little stream to the floor. "Come, come, Nanon; there's no use in lying about it. He's been here *to-day!*"

"How you—?" she began.

"A—ah!" He leaned forward quickly. "He *has* been here, then!" He chuckled softly.

The girl's eyes flamed, but she controlled herself, humming a French-Canadian voyageur's song. Her voice was soft, and the cadence filled the interior of the log cabin with gentle, lulling effect.

Clyde listened, his body tired from long miles by snowshoes on the trail of Chictou Bènard, "wanted" for robbing the Hudson Bay Company's Store at Spirit River. The track had led straight to the cabin, fresh made that morning; Clyde knew it; now he sought further information. "Do you remember when we used to dance together at Dunvegan?"

She looked at him sharply: "Si, Ah 'membaire."

Silence then, broken only by the snow that fell slowly through the pine and fir outside, dropping with a faint, almost inaudible seething.

The half light showed a clean, square room with a big bunk of boughs in one corner, triangular fireplace in the other; old clothes, traps, unfinished snowshoes, caribou hides and a few bearskins filling up the rest of the floor-space under the low eaves. Clyde's leg swung on, the water dropping now. "Look here, Nanon," and he went toward her, "it doesn't mean much to Chictou—six months at the most, and I've *got* to find him. I *will* too!" he added.

"Seex mois! An' who goin' tak' care de me dose taimes, hein?"

"You can get somebody to come up with you; any of the boys would be glad to," he answered unthinkingly.

"*Beas'! Diable!*" she screamed at him, quivering.

Clyde was startled for an instant. "I'm sorry, Nanon; I didn't know you cared so much for him."

The girl drew herself up in her tanned caribou shirt and skirt, till her black hair mingled with the gloom overhead, so it seemed to the constable. "Et no for you, Poleec', to mak' t'ink 't all 'bout Chictou an' me! Ve très good liv' wid'out *you* t'ink!"

Night settled slowly on the vast forests, causing shapes to vanish, outlines that were against the sky only remaining. Snow drifted more slowly from the heavens, the flakes great, white and damp, heavy with the moisture of the lower air.

"Since you won't save him a long hard trail trying to dodge *me*, I'll have to——"

"Bo' jou', petite! De Poleec' no fin'—" The great gaunt figure in the doorway stopped, seeing the constable.

Clyde recognized his man. The girl tried to hold him, but he tore from her, drawing his revolver. "Halt!" The flitting shadow of a form vanishing among the trees answered him. He fired two shots.

The girl laughed hysterically as the constable rushed into the night. She leaned against the doorway, her hands clenched tightly. "Allez, Chic'! *Allez*—queeck! Ah, mon Dieu!" The tones, loud and piercing because of her fear, vibrated in the dark mass of branches, as though the forest grudgingly permitted them a tortuous path in its labyrinth of needles.

Solemn and still was the night; the lonely, far-away *hoo-hoo-hooo* of an owl floated with indescribable suggestion of the absolute wilderness; and from the barren beyond the shrill yelping of foxes at play came sharply. The snowfall ceased as she waited, the flakes diminishing in numbers till but a few pirouetted to earth. No more came then; and the breathless silence of a midwinter snow-night was over everything.

"*Cr-ang!*"

She shivered when the faint report struck on her ears. Very distant it was, but it brought visions of what might be, and she began to cry. Softly at first the tears draggled down her face. Then, as no further sound came, she cried bitterly, her sobs waking vague echoes among the trees.

"Chic', *Chic'!* you keel, Ah'm know!" she muttered brokenly, and staggered to the bunk, throwing herself on it, her body racked with sadness. A long time she lay there, whispering, moaning to herself, while the hours fled on in silence and cold.

The crunching of snow aroused her. She sat up.

"Lost him, Nanon, at the top of Moose Hill; he got his snowshoes on there before I could reach him!"

She stared at Clyde, her eyes heavy and puffed with tears. He lighted a candle, and looked at her in the yellow flare. "I'm sorry, girl; but I *must* get him; it's my *duty!*" He spoke regretfully.

"You *no* get!" she murmured.

"I *will!*" His voice was strong. "By daylight I'll find his snowshoe trail and follow it, even if it leads me to Eskimo House!" He turned to close the door—and missed the flash that crossed her face.

"Mabbe," she breathed softly, standing up. "Mabbe, Cly'!"

She gathered chips from the little wood pile by the hearth, and knelt, blowing on the tiny blaze. He watched her graceful figure as, in lithe abandonment, it was bent in rounded lines. The fire grew rapidly, showing her features as if they were carved in light-brown marble. The shadows danced over her limbs, striking a bold outline of her on the logs behind. Her black eyes were big, reflecting the leaping flames as would tiny mirrors.

"Do you mind if I sleep here, Nanon?"

"Non!" She stirred the fire thoughtfully. "Non: you Poleec', Cly', an' beeg Engleesh homme; you sle'p een cabane, s'posen' you like!"

He sat on the edge of the bunk. "There's many an English woman that wouldn't have the confidence and trust in me that you have!" he whispered.

She heard him, but did not understand. "You say som'ting?"

"No—nothing, Nanon."

A curious tense look in her eyes, she got some food for him, because the Police can commandeer sustenance and shelter anywhere when on duty.

The meal finished, he signed a slip from his record-book. She tucked it in her shirt.

"Merci."

He lighted his pipe and went to the door. "It'll be daylight in four hours, Nanon. Have you a spare blanket? I'll take a nap by the fire."

The girl tossed him a rabbit-skin covering.

He shoved his pipe in his pocket, took off the wet moccasins, and rolled up in the deliciously warm fur, his arm for a pillow. She blew out the candle, and crept on the bunk, drawing the rough coverings over her.

The fire crackled sharply, myriads of sparks ascending the crooked flue. The embers cast a dull red glow over his figure at rest near the hearth.

No wind, no whisper of breeze disturbed the stillness outside. The gigantic trees loomed tall and graven as images against the dull skies, their branches blurred into a hazy denseness of silent black. The snow-clouds, far up in the heavens, moved on sluggishly, but the wind that pushed them did not reach the wilderness of the North.

The constable snored then, his grunts and indrawings of breath sounding sleepily in the stillness of the cabin.

The girl pushed her coverings aside, inch by inch. She got to the floor without a sound, listening to the breathings of the man stretched at her feet. She looked down at him in the dying firelight, a gleam of triumph in her eyes. "You tell too mooch, Cly'! You mooch beeg fool!"

She stole to where an extra pair of her husband's snowshoes hung on a peg; got them down, opened the door with but few light creakings that did not waken the man, and slipped out, closing the aperture with the greatest care. The thonged hoops under her arm, she sped away into the gloom of the forest, vanishing instantly in the silent darkness.

Slowly the snow began to fall when she had been gone but a short time, and with it daylight grew apace. Faint, and as a thread of reflection, the pale lights of a gray dawn, tinged with scarlet, appeared through the trees toward the east, across the Big Barrens. The red of the rising sun, glowing for several moments through the quiet, thick veils of snow, was peculiarly angry and foreboding, showing the flakes ruddily for an instant. Clouds drifted then, and the dreary dullness of day followed.

Clyde stirred, muttered in half-sleep, turned over; remembering his work then, he sprang up. "Nanon!" seeing the light filtering in the forest round the cabin. He looked at the bunk. "Gone for wood!" stretching and yawning.

"D—— it all!" as he pulled on the damp moccasins. "The devil of a job having to travel after that poor trapper again!" He yanked viciously at the thongs. "And all for that dashed Company! It 'll be hard on the girl for six months, but "—he sighed, staring at the cold hearthstones—"it's none of my business; I've got to get him, and that's all there is to it!" He laced the thongs, grumbling. "She trusted me!" he murmured, watching the few bits of white snow that dropped from above.

He was hungry.

"Where'd she go?" he asked himself aloud finally, when an hour passed and no sound of the girl.

The snow had ceased entirely; a vague, desultory wind whined in the tree tops with mournful sound. The loneliness of it all moved him deeply.

"Home," he murmured, "home—and so far, so very far away!" His eyes became moist as he stood in the sullen, chill light. "And *she*—ha!" he laughed harshly, the grim sound ugly under the forest. "*She* in England, and I—where, and what?"

The bitterness of his position sank further than ever before in his mind.

"A policeman whose work is to track, to trail, to hound down wretched beggars, who only ask to be allowed to exist!" A dry sob came from his throat. "A little love from *her*, just a little confidence—far less than this half-breed showed," he snarled, his anger growing—"far less, and I should have been— *Rot!*" he said quietly. "Duty, duty, DUTY for me now! *Here's at it!*"

He belted his side arms a hole tighter, picked up his snowshoes by the door, and swung away to the north. He turned when the cabin was barely visible among the massive trunks: "Good-by, Nanon; when you get back you will know that I'm after him!" His voice echoed dully. "And sorry to have to do it, because you love him!"

Unerringly he traveled through the dense timberlands, startling foxes and sables from their meanderings in search of food, frightening the ptarmigan that scratched for pine-bark lustily. They broke from his path with thrumming wings and disappeared into a somewhere beyond.

In an hour he reached the little valley at the foot of Moose Hill. "Last night's flurry won't hide his trail much!" he muttered, working his way up the steep side. He stopped when nearly at the top.

Plainly visible through a light cover of white a snowshoe trail crossed his course.

"I thought it was farther on!" He followed it for several yards. "No; this is it! I know Chictou's make of shoe!"

He got out his pipe, lighted it and puffed, resting.

The gray North was still, save for the spasmodic wind. Below him, stretching out in a vastness of trees, the forest dwindled away to the horizon. The fir under which he stood murmured sibilantly.

"Off again!" He strode on, snowshoes on his feet now, that he might travel the faster. Over hills and through valleys, across frozen streams, and along their snow-crowded banks, in and out of the forest—when it fringed long barrens; across them sometimes, he traveled on, his snowshoes clacking in the silence.

The wind came in his face. "D——curious the breeze should change so suddenly!" He strode on, tireless, following the trail that grew clearer and clearer. "I've got him!"

After hours of work, and sticking close to the snowshoe marks, he saw the cabin in front of him. "The man's a fool," he whispered, stealing on, "to leave a trail like that—or he must think me one!"

He got to the door noiselessly. "My prisoner, Bènard!" he shouted, revolver in hand.

"Me?" the girl asked, taking off her wet socks, eyes open wide in surprise. "Me?"

He searched the interior rapidly with his eyes—no one there but the girl, and no possible place for a man to hide. He went outside, studying the scarcely disturbed snow of the little clearing—no moccasin track, no trail of any kind. "And yet his shoes led to the door!"

He went in.

"Where did—" He stopped. The girl was watching him quizzically, a lurking smile round her lips, her black eyes dancing. Slowly suspicion came on him.

"How in the world—" he whispered, looking about. "*Ah!* that's it!"

Chictou's extra pair of snowshoes stood dripping in the darkest corner; *her* heavy wet stockings were spread on a stool by the fire. Her hair was damp on her forehead, with exertion.

He holstered his weapon slowly, the snap of the hammer, as he half-cocked it, sounding sharply.

Nanon squatted before the blaze, her long tapering hands spread to the heat. He stood over her, arms folded.

"You got me that time, Nanon!"

There was no anger in his voice, and his eyes were kind. The girl, with a woman's quick instinct, felt the attitude of his mind.

"Ah do eet onlee for sauf Chic'—da's all; you no much angree weet Nanon?"

"Not angry, Nanon; I suppose I ought to be, having traveled a good many hard miles on *your* trail!"

The cleverness of her scheme made him laugh, and the sound filled the small spaces pleasantly.

"No, not angry. You saved him this time by the use of your wits, by the hardest kind of work in your body; but I'll get him some day, when *you* are not watching!"

"Eet hav' to be lak' dat! W'en me dere, no catch Chic', Cly'!"

He stared at her moodily then, the fire snapping and glowing, she sitting at his feet, looking up at him. "You love him *very* much, Nanon? He's kind to you? Takes care of you?"

She nodded vehemently. "Me love—si! He good to Nanon—*si!*"

She leaped to her feet, one hand on his arm, face close to his, her hair falling in great luxurious quantities about her shoulders. In her excitement she spoke in the Ojibway language; now and then he could understand a few words, and from them gathered the girl's fierce devotion for her husband.

"It's all right, Nanon; ——*sssh*," as tears came; "it's all right, but I'll have to get him just the same!"

She pushed him away. "You Engleesh," she said, with slow precision, "no know w'at de Canadienne love, she ees! Bah—allez!"

"No!" taking up his snowshoes and mits; "no, we don't, Nanon. Bo'jou—bo'jou!" He started away to the south.

She watched him out of sight in the forest. "Ah sauf Chic', jus' same!"

II

On a wild, stormy night, Clyde pushed ahead against a driving, biting snow, that stung his face and clogged his way, bound for the Police shanty at Spirit River. The distances were but yards, and each one had to be fought for in the howling fury of the wind. It tugged and lashed at his form, creeping up his sleeves, chilling and strong. He stopped to rest, and turned his back that he might open his eyes fully and breathe more easily.

"This *is* a bad one!" He tried to light his pipe, but the tobacco was damp with the sweat of his body, and would not draw.

He went on slowly, head bent, snowshoes lifting hard. Over Moose Hill and down Long Gulch he traveled. The storm abated; the gusts grew weaker, and the snow ceased of a sudden. Daylight came little by little; with it a breeze—stillness He swung on fast now, hungry for the food and heat that awaited him beyond. "What——?"

A rounded shape on a little hillside

caught his eyes. It was not quite covered with snow, being sheltered by a group of young birches.

"A caribou dead, maybe!" and he kept on, looking at the gray-brown thing as he passed it.

A strange feeling came over him—that he *must* go and see what it was.

He swerved from his course, laboring up the hill, and brushed the snow from the figure.

"It's a woman, by God!" He slipped off his snowshoes that he might kneel beside her, and turned the body over. "Nanon!"

The girl's heart beat faintly, as with trembling fingers he felt under her shirt. Working desperately now, he chafed her hands, slapping them with all his strength. He breathed his warm breath into her mouth, and lifted the eyelids for signs of returning consciousness. An hour he toiled, sweat pouring from him. He gathered the hot drops from his face and put them over her heart, on her skin.

"Thank God!" he groaned, as the girl moved, opening her eyes.

"Chic', Chic'," she called faintly. Then, seeing the constable, she shivered. "He gon' 'way!" her first thought to hide the whereabouts of Bènard from "de Poleec'."

"Are you frozen anywhere, Nanon? *Answer me!*"

She looked at him dazedly. "De feet mabbe, Ah t'ink!"

He ripped off his capote, put it under her head, gathered wood as fast as he could find it dry enough, and lighted the little heap. When it flamed, he drew off her moccasins and stockings. The small feet were marble white, and hard to his fingers.

"Good God!" he moaned, rubbing them powerfully with snow. As it melted in his hands he gathered more, and rubbed till his arms ached from wrist to shoulder. The sensation roused the girl thoroughly; she lifted her head, watching him at work.

"You Engleesh—good mans!"

"Never mind that, girl; can you feel?" pinching her foot sharply.

She drew it up. "Ai—dat hurt!"

"Ah-h-h! Saved then!" He pinched the other; she flinched. He rubbed on till he could see the veins purple and swell with the rush of liberated blood. Then he gathered her in his arms and shook her up

and down till her cheeks were flushed and her breath came audibly. Exhausted, he laid her on the capote, and wrung her stockings damp-dry.

"What were you doing out here?"

"Ah go see trap fo' Chic'!"

"Where is he?"

"No tell you!" Her eyes glittered. "Ah die een snow bee-for' Ah tell!"

The doggedness of her bravery in her suffering awed Clyde.

"Why doesn't he look after you better than this? Hell!" he cursed; "to let you tend a line when a storm was coming!"

"Ah los' w'en de win' she come so bad."

"Does he know where you are?"

"Si!" Her head moved up and down.

"Why doesn't he come then, when you didn't get home last night?"

"Ah don' know!"

Silence between the two, as the shifting breeze whispered about them, fanning the fire by spurts.

"Can you walk, Nanon?" He lifted her to her feet.

"Oh—h—h!" she cried, when her weight came on them. She sagged in his arms. "No can!"

"I'll have to carry you home, then!"

"Non—non!" She fought him.

"Why not?"

She was silent, writhing slightly as the throbs of returning life in her feet tortured her.

Clyde knew why, but he said nothing. He laced on his snowshoes, and picked her up, one arm under her knees and the other under her shoulders, and plodded to the north, her weight dragging his body forward.

"Non! non!" she screamed, struggling and twisting. He held her close, his great strength overcoming her. Her endeavors grew less and less; the heat of his body soothing her mentally and physically.

She slept in his arms.

The miles passed very slowly; his body ached from her weight, but he pushed on, teeth clenched, legs working automatically.

"*Arrête!*"

He swung on his shoes at the voice behind him.

Chictou Bènard, face drawn out of shape with anxiety, came straight to him!

"Nanon, chérie!" he mumbled, kissing the sleeping girl passionately—paying no attention to the constable. He knelt, and covered the little brown hands with his face, Clyde still holding. her.

"Ah'm readee go weet you, Poleec', w'en you say so. Par Dieu, Ah t'ink ma leetle girrl los' an' die, an' follo' de track."

She awoke, hearing the last words.

"Ah be'n dead aussi, only Cly', he come! Ah—ai—!" as she remembered; "go queeck, Chic'—allez!"

The gaunt trapper stood up, huge on his snowshoes.

"Non—Ah *no* go; dat Poleec' homme he sauf yo'r laif! Ah go weet heem, s'posen' he want me."

She trembled in Clyde's arms and sobbed. "Chic', w'at Ah do seex mont' wid'out you?" She writhed out of the constable's arms, regardless of the pain in her feet. "Chic'!" kissing him, her arms about his swarthy neck—"Chic', oh—h, Chic'!"

Thus they stood, the three, in the stillness of the forests, the snow as a sharp background against their figures.

Clyde coughed harshly—making up his mind. "You, Bènard, take her home, and don't let her tend a trap line in a storm!"

The girl was the first to realize what he meant. She flung herself at his knees, clutching them.

He lifted her till her face was on a level with his own. "Remember, Nanon, that an Englishman well enough knows *love* when he sees it!"

Her eyes burned into his for an instant. "Ah 'membaire!" she whispered.

"Take her home, Bènard, and keep out of my way—unless you want six months!"

The trapper took off his fur cap. "Le Bon Dieu w'el t'ank you for dees, Poleec', an' Chictou Bènard, he mak' beeg merci!"

The giant figure, before Clyde could resist, kissed his hand. The constable helped him to get the girl firmly on his back.

"Au r'voir, Chictou!—bo'jou—bo'jou!"

"Bo'jou—bo'jou!" the girl answered, a deep gratitude in her eyes.

Bènard turned. "Ah no forg-et dees!" he said, and plodded away, the girl clinging to his shoulders.

Clyde saw them out of sight among the sear black trunks of the forest.

"That's *Love!*" he muttered sadly, striking off for home.

11

Adolph, A Faithful Fool

THÉRÈSE GUÉRIN RANDALL

ADOLPH.

A FAITHFUL FOOL.

By Thérèse Guérin Randall.

THE old Curé laid his pipe aside, and drew his chair closer to the box-like wood stove. He gathered his long *soutane* well about his thin legs and prepared to be sociable this stormy wintry night.

"Yes, I, like you say, I have seen strange t'ings since I have been *missionaire*. It make me much *honeur*, dat you desire I say you a lil' *histoire* what I know am true. Ver' well, I tell you 'bout Adolph.

"When I was de young priest, dere was not so many messenger of God in dis part of Canada as dere is now. We have on'y one mission house in de wes' of Ontario den.

"Dere was no railroad, an' it was ver' hard fer de emigrant to make hees way so far as dis. But see how it have change in t'irty year. Here have I de lil' chapel in a village of near t'ree hundred peoples where once was on'y dis lil' tavern on de edge of de tamaracks wood. We has de school an' de *docteur*, an' de store for all t'ing, an' de blacksmith shop—dat is grow much, eh, in so lil' time ?

"But in dose day long past it was diff'rent. We know not de luxury den. I mus' travel from settlement to settlement for many hundred miles ever' year. I visit de white mans an' de Indian in deir home, 'cause it was too far for dem to come to our lil' mission to practice deir religion an' take de sacrements.

"On'y a few farms have been cut out of de wildness of bush den. Dey was ver' small farm, an' scatter 'way down de river ver' far 'part. In dose time I can on'y come where we is now once in de year, in de winter. You see, I mus' work on de farm at de mission in summer to make de vegetable grow so we won't starve. In de autumn I begin travel, an' here I arrive generally in December.

"I mus' drive t'rough all kind of wedder, an' meet many danger, but I don't mind dat 'cause de heart was young an' full of fire. Ah, my parish was ver' big in dose past day, but dere was on'y few peoples in it.

"I can't never forget dat night when I was drive along dis road in my sleigh an' see Adolph. It was jus' before he go be trapper for de ver' las' time. De snow was deep on de groun', an' de moon was make it glis'en wit' lil' stars all over it. De big pines an' tamaracks look so black beside it. I t'ink dose bare tree seem like de brown knotted finger of de airth what try reach heaven.

"I was begin sing de hymn to make de lonliness not seem so big when I hear de large voice make music in dose mile an' mile of silence so thick an' broad.

"It was not de hymn I hear, no, it was de boatman's song, but it make my heart glad. No more did I feel I was 'way far off in de waves of stillness, de solemn, awful *éternité* where I seem so lil' an' so los'. Ah, sometimes even de priest forget dat God hol' us ever in Hees breas'; his heart is what we call by dat word *éternité*.

"Well, ver' soon I see de mans come out from de tamaracks, an' spring into de road, far 'bove where I was. I know who it mus' be firs' by dat loud, happy voice, an' den by de fine, high figure, but mos' by de fastness he have on de snow shoe.

"I laugh wit' glad to hear de song an' see de human in dis wild place. More often have I hear de howl of de hungered wolf, and see de sabage creatures, but God have ever save me to do Hees work.

"Well, as I lis'en to dat loud voice I say :

"'Ah, I know where goes my Adolph. He run to jus' de same place as me. Both go to Mère Dertrain's lil' tavern ; he to see hees sweetheart, *la belle* Elfride, an' me to attend to my duty so holy.'

"It t'aint no use for me to call dat happy Adolph, he don't hear, 'cause he was make such noise. He can go more fas' on de snow shoe dan my poor tire horse, can dat fine young mans, an' soon he disappear far down de road where it bend 'round de river.

"Dat was great favorite, dat Adolph. He was so full of speerits, ever gay, an' he have de energy an' courage what is need in dis place.

"I have hear many wild stories 'bout him, but I can't believe dem all. Sometimes he take too much *veille Jamaique* I know, but I don't t'ink it is true dat he ride in '*la chasse galerie*.' People b'lieve dis 'cause he can walk so ver' fas' on de snow shoes, it is *incredible* how fas'.

"Ah, you don't know what is '*la chasse galerie?*' Well, de mans when dey wish go many hundred miles in few hours take de paddle an' step in de canoe an' call on de debbil. Den dey promise sell deir soul to him while dey ride, an' while dey steer clear of all church steeple, crosses, an' such t'ing, de evil one make dem fly t'rough de sky. But dey mus' never say one holy word, or touch one holy t'ing, 'cause if dey do dey drop to de airth at once. Dat is what peoples say Adolph have travel in to see hees sweetheart when he was 'way in de nort'wes'.

"'Well,' say I dat night, as I try hurry a ver' lil' my poor horse, 'I hope Adolph will make de confession to me to-night, for he go way, now dat de winter is begin, to de nort'wes' to get de skins. I mus' ask hees *belle* Elfride to talk de serious word wit' him.'

"In dose day I was de young *enthusiast*. Always my thought have been for de good of my peoples. While my horse make hees way t'rough de deep sof' snow I t'ink of many t'ing, but mos' of all I t'ink of Elfride an' her Adolph. Dey was so han'some, dose two, so happy an' so well match. 'Ah, God have will it,' I say ; 'He have made de love for each odder to be born in deir heart.'

"Soon after I was come to de tavern of Mère Dertrain. I was stiff wit' de col' and ver' tired, but soon de nice hot *galette*, eat by de big stove wit' so much fire in him, make me feel all well 'gain.

"Mère Dertrain talk ver' much 'bout her Elfride while she fry de *galettes* for me. She say :

"'It is de ver' good match my girl makes wit' Adolph, eh, M'sieu' le Curé He is ver' strong young mans, an' de face, how fine he have! Den when hees ol' fadder die he will own also de farm ; dere is no odder child, as M'sieu' know. He is de good son ; he work always wit' hees fadder on de farm in summer, an' den he mus' get much money from de skins he sell in de winter.'

"Dat night when I go to my room some one make de knock at my door. When I open it dere was Adolph lookin' ver' shame :

"'M'sieu',' he say, 'I would like ver' much to confess de sins to you. Elfride she give me no moment of peace till I do. She tell me to come now, an' if you is not too tire—'

"'No, my Adolph,' I say, 'never too tire to help one soul to be pure ;' an' I put on my stole, an' he—dat fine Adolph—kneel at my side and tell hees sin.

"Oh, I was ver' happy mans when, after I give him de lil' advice, I lif' my hands over him to give him de *absolution* from all hees sin.

"Nex' morning I was up ver' early, 'cause de peoples begin to confess jus' so soon as possible, an' till after ten I was busy dis way. Den we have de mass, an' I was ver' glad to see all take de sacrement, an' 'mong dem Adolph and Elfride.

"Ah, how beautiful de holiness make all t'ings! It is dis what govern de stars, an' what make de blind lil' seed toil t'rough de airth an' grow an' bloom when he hour has come. Holiness is jus' de embroidered name for obedience.

"De lil' tavern was ever full of peoples when I was dere, an' when de mass is over we mus' have de dinner all togedder. After dis begin de games.

"I mus' watch all de snow-shoe race an' whatever dey do, but dis time it was, as it ever was, Adolph who win whenever dey run. He leave de starting place like de swish of de rapids coming to de falls. He win so easy I mus' laugh.

"Ever' one was happy dose day; Mère Dertrain mos' of all, cause she do such good business.

"An' Elfride! Ah, how shall I tell somet'ing 'bout dat girl? She was ever help de modder, an' she can sing all de time she work. Me, I like dat, it show de heart content. She have many lonely day an' ver' much hard work, but ever she have de laugh in de eye.

"Well, de peoples, go way before it was get ver' dark, but Adolph he stay till it was night. When he come say *adieu* to me he laugh an' say: "'Nex' time you will come here, M'sieu' le Curé, you mus' marry Elfride an' me. Den I go no more 'way from dis place.

"While I was talk to de Widow Dertrain in de kitchen, I can see dos two young peoples in de bar. Elfride she help Adolph put on hees blanket coat an' tie de red woolen sash so nice 'roun' hees waist. He put hees tocque on hees head, an' de big wool sock on hees feet an' den he kiss Elfride. She box hees ear wit' de tassel of hees tocque which hang over de side. Dey have much hap'ness, dose two young people.

"When he was outside an' put on hees snow-shoes I hear him call out:

"'Adieu, ma belle Elfride, when I come back no more we be separate.'

"Elfride stan' so long at de door an' watch dat fine Adolph dat her modder call to her:

"'Come in, ma fille, and make de door shut. Thy lil' sister wait thee for go to de bed.'

"Den dat gay young girl she laugh an' come to us dancing all de way. She have no fear of me, de young Curé. Fifine, so was name her sister of fifteen, was 'sleep wit' de head on de lap of her modder. Elfride she wake her wit' a kiss, an' wit' deir arm 'roun' each odder dey go 'way togedder.

"Nex' morning early I mus' start for de nex' station where meet my peoples for take de *sacrement* an' hear de mass. I mus' go 'cross de river an' many 'miles t'rough de wood, an' it is late night when I come dere. Elfride she give me de breakfas' of hot pea soup an' potacks. I don't know den

dat never 'gain shall I hear dat gay, ever happy laugh as I lis'en while I eat.

"In annoder year I come back to de tavern of her modder 'gain. I was much seprise when I met wit' Elfride dat time. She have no more de bright red cheek, so roun' an' wholesome. She was ver' t'in an' white. De big black eyes dat was ever dance wit' laugh now look at me like de sad, far-off eye of one speerit. De fire was all gone; on'y de sof' glow of de embers what have burn out deir quick life was lef'. Dey was so sof' dose eye, jus' like de soul of sorrow have gone dere to stay an' look out to me from hees dwelling.

"Ah, my heart was pain, an' no more can I tease her like I use. I can on'y take both her han's in mine an' say ver' quiet:

"'My poor, poor Elfride.'

"Jus' den her sister, Fifine, now so much de grown up womans I was seprise, come to me and make de lil' cou'tesy:

"Ah, M'sieu' le Curé, you is ever in time; de peoples say dey mus' never have much wait for you. Many has come, as you may see in de bar;' she say while she hang up my buffalo coat.

"'Well I has on'y come dis far for four year,' I make de reply, 'an I have ever de good fortune wit' de roads, but some time I may not be so happy dat way, I may get in de bad snow storm when I can't not find de way, I may meet de snow drifts dat I can't not go t'rough, I might freeze to death, it is all as God wish, not as I make it.'

"As I was look at dat young girls I was feel de shock. She was jus' so like Elfride when I have seen her first. Jus' de same short, lil' figure, so roun' an' plump. Jus' de same long black hair in de braid hang' down her back, de same red cheek, de same black eye. Jus' so gay she was, an' laugh so much an' show de white teeth, an' is so quick in her movements.

"'She is de same,' I t'ink in my mind, 'de same an' yet dif'rent.' De heart, de soul is not much like in dese two. I could see dat while I look at de sisters. One pale an' say lil', de odder talk much, an' is full of life an' hap'ness.'

"When I has take off all my wrap, I

mus follow Fifine to de bar for greet my parish. Dere was many mans sit 'roun' de stove an' smoke an' talk. Peoples what don't often see deir neighbors.

"Dey was all rise an' take off deir ol' tocques from de head but one. He don't stir. I say to him ver' stern when I have shake de han's of my peoples:

"'Why don't you rise? Is you so far '*mauvais sujet*' dat you don't show some respec' to de priest of God?'

"I have step near de man what de odders try make stan' up, and de next minute I was cry out: '*Mon Dieu! Mon Dieu! Mon Dieu!*'

"Dose eyes, once de han'some brown eye, now stare at me wit' no expression —de eyes of one *vrai* fool.

"'Me, I love Elfride, I love Elfride, *la belle Elfride*,' he repeat many time while all de res' is silent. Dey feel my sorrow, dose rough mans, as I fall on my knee beside dat poor fool, an' say:

"'Do you not know me, Adolph? Do you not remember M'sieu' le Curé?'

"But he looked at me wit' eyes so dull an' say: 'Me, I love Elfride, la belle Elfride.'

"'God's will be done,' I mus' sigh, as I make de sign of de cross, an' go 'way. 'My poor, poor Adolph!' I keep t'ink all dat night.

"But I mus' tell you what have happen since de year before. I have say to you dat Adolph was de trapper, also dat he was a lil' wild an' take too much of *veille jamaique* sometime, eh?

"'Bout t'ree week, after he have confess to me at de lil' tavern he find heeself near de lumber camp where he have many friend. He stay 'mong de shanty mans an' pull *de latire*, an' play de games what dey have on New Years night, as it was de first of January. I don't know for sure what have happened to him. De shanty mans have all take too much *veille jamaique*, dat is 'bout all we can b'lieve, dey tell so many dif'rent story. Some say dat when Adolph try jump de barrel', as such mans do on dat night, he have fall on hees head an' was insensible for long time. Odders say dat he wish much to see hees Elfride an' call on de debbil to help him.

Of course he can't not go many hundred mile on de snow shoe in one night an' dey say he have ride in '*la chasse galerie!*'

"As de canoe rise into de air he t'ink how seprise will be Elfride, an' he forget hees compact not to say de holy word. 'Ah, *Sainte Vierge,* he say, 'how seprise will be my—' but he don't never finish dose word. Jus' so soon as he say de holy name of de Bless' Virgin de debbil's power was gone.

"Adolph an' hees canoe drop down t'rough de tamaracks, an' when hees friends pick him up he don't know nothing. It was long time before he open hees eyes 'gain, an' when he do *he was fool!* But he have not forget Elfride, an' so soon as he can get 'way he manage to come back to de lil' tavern.

"An' how hard was all dis for Elfride! De good daughter, de faithful one, de true child of de church, her heart was break.

"Dere was shadder on de lil' log tavern dose days, but Fifine, de *jolie* young Fifine, she was de brightness for all. Jus' so like Elfride have once look. She laugh too de same, an' she sing all day de happy song at de work.

"It was ver' sad to see Elfride go 'bout dat rough lil' kitchen like she can work well, 'cause she have ever work, but de hap'ness in do it was all done.

"She can't not read, she was so far 'way from de school in dose day, an' dere was nothing to do for amusement for such serious mind. She mus' jus' scrub, cook an' knit to morning till night. In de summer dere was de work on de farm, de tavern an' farm too; dat was de on'y change in de year, an' lil' excitement when I mus' come.

"It make de pain in my heart when I see how tire' she look in dose eye where always de sorrow speaks to me. She do not laugh wit' de young mans like she use'; an' dey, dey step ver' sof' an' dey talk ver' sof' when dey are near her, jus' like dey mus' in de chapel.

"Her modder, de widow Dertrain, say to me while I sit by de stove in de kitchen to make myself warm:

"'She will get over love dis poor Adolph. I is sure God ain't goin' let such good daughter, who help de modder, be ever like dis. She will marry some good mans, 'cause I wish have some here. She won't never disobey de modder, me. I have de *rheumatique* and I can't not do de man's work so well as I use' in odder day. It is hard since my good mans die.'

"Den she go put de wood in de fire, an' she say: 'Baugh, dere is need more wood here,' an' she call: 'Adolph, Adolph.'

"De tall foolish fellow, what was once so fine, come to de door.

"'Why has you not fill de wood box?' ask Mère Dertrain ver' cross. 'See you not M'sieu' le Curé,' she say, 'dat you stan' dere wit' de cap on you' head?'

"Adolph he look at her ver' sullen an' walk 'way to hees companions in de bar.

"'Come, my Fifine, you can make him do all t'ing,' she say, ver' coax to her young daughter. 'Go tell Adolph to bring in some wood.'

"Soon I see dat Adolph carry in many armsful from de shed by de kitchen, an' put dem by de fire. All de time he smile hees foolish smile at Fifine.

"'He don't know Elfride no more since she have change so much, an' he won't do nothing for her. He call Fifine hees "Belle Elfride,"' whisper de modder to me, ''cause she look so like her sister in dose happy days.'

"Before I leave de tavern to go on 'round my wide circle of so many, many miles 'way, I see dat what she tell me is true. Adolph is ver' cross to de real Elfride, and when she speak to him so sof' and gentle, he don't never answer. He was ever stubborn an' silent excep' to Fifine.

"De nex' December I have still de good fortune wit' de good roads; and I come to de tavern of de widow Dertrain in de secon' week in December, as I always mus' do ever' year.

"Many of my peoples have gather an' wait for me, an' dere was many young mans. Dis make me glad, till I see dey come more for de games, an' for love of Fifine, den for de religion. Dis gay lil' Fifine have many lover, but none dat love her like dat foolish Adolph.

"On my way here I have stop at de farm of hees fadder, as I mus' always do for rest and food. I hear much dat give me trouble 'bout dis poor young mans.

"'When he was home,' say hees fadder, 'he won't work sometimes for days, but stay in bed and don't eat, but jus' say all de time, "I love my Elfride.' Now he stay ever at de tavern of Mère Dertrain; dere he mus' work.'

"Dis was all true I see when I was at de lil' log tavern. He is, dis poor, poor Adolph, like one slave. He hunt far off for game, he saw and split de wood, he carry de water from de river, or melt de snow, he go wit' de mail once in de month to de village many miles away where de stage go from. Oh, I can't never tell you how much he do, an' Mère Dertrain, de ver' shrewd womans for make money, she don't give him nothing but what he mus' eat.

"Elfride tell me dis, an' she have de tear in de eye.

"'Oh, dey don't have some feeling for de poor Adolph,' she say. 'You can't t'ink how he mus' work, an' he don't even get 'nough to eat.'

"But Adolph t'ink he was ver' well pay, cause always Fifine she smile on him; she do on ever' odder young mans, too.

"My heart was sore wit' pain dat day when I go out on de road. De moon was jus' rise behin' de trees as I walk up an' down. I was say my office, an' de priest mus' be 'lone, 'cause he can't not speak to de human while he talk hees office to God. Jus' as I finish, de tall figure fly pas' me wit' de mail bag on hees back. When he reach de lil' tavern I see dat he stagger—almos' fall. I know by hees fastness on de snow shoe dat it was Adolph.

"I go ver' quick to hees side, but jus' den Fifine she open de door, an' I hear her say to de young mans, 'I tol' you he would run all de way, an' back, if I say him to do it, an' he has. See, he have bring back de mail.'

"Adolph he look in de face of Fifine an' he don't stagger no more wit' being so tire, he walk in proud an' straight.

"I was ver' mad wit' dis foolish girls. She have tell dat poor Adolph to run so many miles when he should take de oxes an' sleigh. She have do dis jus' to show de young mans how he love her.

"'Come to you modder, Fifine,' I say ver' stern, an' she look much 'fraid when she see I have been outside too an' hear what she was tell.

"'Ah, *Méchante*,' say de modder to her when she have lis'en to me, 'you was ver' bad to make dat *pauvre* run so many mile, besides to-morrow he mus' go back an' bring de t'ings I have tol' him to get fer me at de village. He have brought on'y de mail. M'sieu,' she say to me, 'you mus' not be so mad, 'cause Fifine she don't mean some harm, she is on'y like de fun——'

"'Fun, modder,' broke in Elfride wit' much of passion in de voice, 'how can you call it dat, *ma mère*? You mus' know it is cruel, it is—,' but de big sob break her voice an' she can't say no more.

"It was 'bout nine o'clock dat I was go to bed. I mus' pass de kitchen, 'cause my room is on de odder side of de house, an' I can see Fifine wit' some young mans. One of dem, Henri Gauchert, was hol' both her han's an' say while he was laugh so loud:

"'You mus' marry de man what win de snow shoe race, eh, Fifine? Promise you do, 'cause dat will be me. I do not let you go till you say yes.'

"Fifine an' all de odders was laugh much, all but Adolph. He have jus' come in de door wit' some wood for de stove, an' hees eyes look cunning and ver' strange as he lis'en.

"'Yes,' say Fifine, 'I promise what you is ask, if you let me go now,' an' Henri loose de han's.

"De next day was de games like dey have always when I come. I mus' go see dem to please my peoples. I was not surprise when as I stan' on de river bank I see Adolph go pas' wit' hees snow shoes throw over de shoulder. He was goin' in de race.

"Dey was all laugh when he put on hees snow shoes, but him he don't mind if dey make de fun, he say nothing.

"As dey was stan' side to side ready for start, I t'ink how fine was Adolph, so tall 'bove de odders, so straight an' light, *un vrai* figure for run. When dey have de word to go he can make such fas' time that I mus' laugh. Yet have I de pain in de heart to t'ink he was fool, dis fine fellow, who can keep so far 'way from dose odders in dat race.

Down de river, so deep in snow, he fly to de pole wit' de red flag. He turn roun' it an' come back so swift widout trouble it seem, an' win de race. De bes' of de odders have gone lil' more den tree quarter way.

"'You mus' marry me, Elfride,' cry dat foolish Adolph, as he run to Fifine widout stop, 'You have promise marry de winner,' an' he was ver' grave.

"'But I have say dat on'y for make fun, you *pauvre* Adolph, don't you know dat?' she say.

"He on'y look at her wit' dat foolish look of love he always do when he is near her. Me, I see dat he do not take de meaning of her word, he don't know what it is 'to make fun.'

"When we was all back in de tavern after de games I call him to me an 'say:

"'My poor Adolph, you mus' not love dat girl; she is not you' good Elfride. She is on'y thoughtless lil' Fifine, who has not discover she has one heart of her own, an' how can she know dat you have one, to make suffer?'

"He lis'en, but me, I see it was no use talk, he can't never un'erstand.

"Ah, I was feel ver' bad, an my heart was as lead when once more I mus' go from dat poor Elfride, who fight 'gainst dis treatment of her Adolph, all for nothing. I mus' t'ink of what her modder have say to me de night after de games:

"'M'sieu', I want you do de goodness to say some advice to Elfride. You mus' tell her she mus' no more love dat Adolph. She owe de duty to her modder, an' me I want her marry de good mans. I need one here on de farm to manage t'ings for me. She is disobedient, is Elfride, 'cause I have tell her she mus' on'y talk to Adolph to make him work, but she speak to him like he was you, M'sieu', or some odder great mans. Dat won't not do, I don't like have her fry de hot *galettes* for him, an' knit him de warm stocking an' sew de button on hees ol' flannel shirt. He aint no good to marry wit'—he is on'y fool.'

"'Elfride will never marry some one now, Mère Dertrain,' I say," "You mus' let her 'lone. She is one strange girl to find here in dis wil' country. Her great heart is more noble, her feelings more refine' den peoples here can ever un'erstand. Fifine will marry jus' as you wish, she is de lil' *Canadienne* in ever' way. She will not make de foolish marriage, nor be carry away by love.

"De modder was comfort by dis; she do not know my meaning no more den she can read de soul of Elfride.

"De nex' year when I was come I mus' marry some one. Fifine was de bride, and her mans was Henri Gauchert, the young mans what have ask her to marry wit' de winner of de snowshoe race.

"Adolph was kep' busy in de bar while I was make de marriage; but when de fiddlers begin play, an' ever' one was dance in de kitchen, he come in.

"Henri Gauchert was try drag Elfride out to dance wit' him, an' ever' one cry out:

"'Oh, she mus' take off her shoes! She mus' take off her shoes! Her sister, what is younger den she is, is marry first.'

"Dey begin try to pull off de shoes of Elfride as she sit near me by de door. Adolph stan' by an' watch, an' when he see de shoes off, an' Elfride dragged 'long de floor in de stocking feet, he say to her:

"'Why must you take off you' shoes? No one else has do it.'

"Elfride look at him wit' eyes so full of pity, and say :

"'Oh, you *pauvre* Adolph, don't you know not dat' ——

"'I am marry firs',' break in Fifine, laughing at hees queer look, 'an' I am de younges'. Dis is my weddin',' an' she mus' in de stockin' feet dance. Here is my mans,' she say, taking de han' of Henri Gauchert.

"'Oh, no, you is not marry,' laugh Adolph in hees foolish way. 'You is goin' marry wit' me.'

"Ever' one was shout, an' de bridegroom say, as he take de chin of dat lil' Fifine in hees han': "You is de *vraie* coquette, an' have break many heart;' and he kiss her.

"De eyes of Adolph grow big wit' anger when he see dis, an' before some one know what he mean he have struck dat bridegroom on de forehead so hard, an' Henri fall to de floor, like a tree dat is dead.

"Adolph stan' an' look at him wit' hees lips drawn back over hees teeth like de wil' animal.

"Ever' one was run at him, dis *pauvre ;* while Fifine kneel by her husban' and call, 'Henri! Henri!' I t'ink mus' Adolph have been kill if Elfride had not throw herself on hees neck.

"'He do not know what he do,' she cry, 'an' he has been treat ver' cruel. Fifine have deceive him; she can make him un'erstan' dat she is going be marry, but she won't never tell him. Me, I have try to let him know how it was, but it ain't no use, he never lis'en to me. Oh! M'sieu' le Curé, come save my poor Adolph.'

"But she don't need call me wit' dat voice so full of de terror. I have raise my han' an' de peoples so full of de fury fall 'way from dat Adolph, who don't know hees danger.

"'Adolph,' say I, an' I beg God to let dis foolish one know what I tell him, 'Adolph, lis'en well to what I mus' say. You' Fifine, de girl you call you' Elfride, *is marry to Henri Gauchert ! She can't never be you' Elfride no more !'*

"Dere was such silence you can hear, de heavy breathing of Mère Dertrain who is so fat. Adolph he look at me wit' such strange eye. He get ver' pale an' ver' red. Den he push Elfride 'way an' wit' a mad cry he run into de night.

"'Let him go, de fool is *dangerous*,' say Mère Dertrain, but Elfride have follow; an' me, when I see dat de bridegroom was on his feet 'gain all well, I go after Elfride—out de back of de house.'

"Adolph have trip over de saw-horse what stan' outside de kitchen door, where he have leave it when he was saw de wood de day before. As I step out I see dat Elfride she was kneel at hees side an' was say:

"'Oh, my Adolph, come thou back wit' me. Do not run off far in de col' night where you may freeze. Oh, dey has treat you ver' bad, but you has ever de love of my heart. Won't you not go wit' me in de light an' warm inside? See, you has no coat, on'y de thin flannel shirt all worn an' old. Come my—' But she can't make him do as she wish dese day. Once more he spring 'way from her arms, and disappear down de road into de woods beyond.

"I have snatch de snow shoes from de nail in de wood shed an' when I have pull off my cowhide boots I strap dem on fas'. One pair sock was not ver' warm on de feet, eh, but me I was too much excite to feel dat.

"'Go in an' call de mans, my poor Elfride, we follow Adolph an' bring him back, else he may perish.'

"She stop cry and obey me. Soon I was follow by many mans wit' de pine torch, but we don't see Adolph.

"'He may have climb de tree for hide, or he may have jump in de air hole in de river to get drown,' say some ones. But when we go down de steep bank we can't not tell, 'cause dere is so many track in de snow since we have watch de many games which we have also had dat day.'

"All de time Elfride have follow us 'bout, an' when we shout hees name, she sob, 'Adolph, Adolph.'

"She refuse leave when I ask her to go to de womens in de house, an' me I can't not look on her white face an' be stern. So I call to de mans dat it ain't no use to search dese great woods what cover near de whole country den.

"'Adolph know hees way mong de pines an' tamaracks better den all of us togedder,' I say, 'an' all we can do is to ask God to protect him.'

"I was near freeze, an' my foots was pain ver' much when I was go inside, But I mus' feel 'shamed of my weakness when I look at Elfride. She don't seem cold or tire like de res'. It was on'y de heart what suffer in dat poor girl.

"One day more den two year after dis a tall t'in man walk into de tavern on de snow shoes. When he have take dem off he go to de stove an' look in it to see if it is full, den he go to de woodshed an' bring in some wood. All de time he mutter:

"'I love my Elfride, I love my Elfride.'

"It was Adolph come back from no one knew where.

"Poor Elfride, she would never more be pain by dese foolish word which he mean for her sister. Dat gentle one she was never get well from de night Fifine have marry, an' in lil' more dan one year she was no more on airth. Ah, well, God have right to take her, an' me, I is Hees priest, an' mus' not complain. But ever when I come dose firs' years when I was young, I go to de lonely grave near de edge of de tamarack wood, an' I say de prayer an' when I build de lil' chapel here I have raise it over dat spot where sleep de gentle Elfride.

"An' Fifine?

"Ah, here she comes from de kitchen. Dat rosy, roun' lil' widow what own de tavern now, was one time de gay lil' Fifine.

"We call her Mère Gauchert now, an' she has been widow many year. She is ver' prosperous, de good business womans like her modder was when she live. Fifine is ver' smart. See how quick she move, an' scol' dat ol' mans what polish de t'ings on de bar all de time.

"Have you notice dis ol' mans how he carry hees head far out like it nearly hang from hees neck? Jus' as one gander it makes him look while he work, work ever' minute, and smile on Mère Gauchert when she is near.

"He is happy, dis poor ol' fellow, 'cause he loves. Ah, me! I know dat love is de green paradise where dwells ever but one Adam and hees Eve. So is he always in joy, dis ragged mans, for he knows not'ing but to love; he feel not'ing on'y dat.

"'Me, I love my Elfride, I love my Elfride,' he mutters all day, dis poor, faithful fool, Adolph."

12

Children of the Bush

LEONIDAS HUBBARD, JR.

OUTING

FEBRUARY, 1903

THE CHILDREN OF THE BUSH

By LEONIDAS HUBBARD, Jr.

PHOTOGRAPHS BY THE AUTHOR

TO THE resident of Lower Canada the whole world is divided into two parts, the "settlements" and the "bush." You go through the settlements on the train until the railway ends. Then you drive until you come to the last house. Here the road ends, and all beyond is the bush. When you stand for the first time on its edge and look away toward the North Star, you suddenly realize that the bush runs all the way to the pole. If it is night and winter, and a wind like fine shot is coming down from Ungava, it seems to you that a wolfish presence hangs over the bush ready to seize any one who ventures beyond the last house, and you understand why the Indians see an evil spirit in the land, and give good furs to the *windago* for that spirit's appeasing.

When winter comes the white wastes are peopled by nomad families, who have left the reserves and missions to tramp over the rocks and snow fields and frozen lakes, pitching and folding their tents more silently than the Arabs, in pursuit of furs—furs which come to the markets for you and me to buy, if we can afford them. I wanted to know something of these men of the bush, to know the motive that inspires their lives, and to see what the forest holds of joy or sorrow for its people. So, one day I rode through the Laurentides to the railroad's end, and from there went northward to the reserve of the Montagnais. There I met La Jeunesse, which was very fortunate for me, since La Jeunesse was everywhere described as a "good Indian." The man at the store told me this first. To prove it, he opened his books and read off the list of skins La Jeunesse had already turned in. Since the value of these more than half covered his indebtedness for supplies and outfit, furnished last fall on credit, there could be no doubt. A bad Indian would get all possible credit, and then, slipping out in the spring, sell to some stray fur buyer, leaving the store in the lurch. This is the trader's view of a good Indian. To the priest, the title applies to him who has forsaken the *windago* and does not go after mass to consult the prophet of the evil one as to the prospects of a good hunt. To the interpreter, who assured me that La Jeunesse was "good Hinjun," it meant "he not git drunk an' raise hell."

He had another name, for when I asked why men called him La Jeunesse, he answered:

"My fadder same name."

He had just come in from his trapping grounds, many miles westward on lakes and streams that the white man had never named. The interpreter said he was the very man to take me to the bush, but when we mentioned the matter, La Jeunesse shook his head. If he stopped to guide white man he would lose fur. The winter was nearly over now, and he still owed fifty dollars at

111

the store. He must get back to the traps. Maybe Kitloogin would go.

We found Kitloogin in front of his little log house. He was big and dark, with the broad face of the typical Montagnais. While the interpreter talked he kept raising his axe and striking it into a green birch log, with the air of a man who wants to end an interview. Finally the interpreter led the way into the house, and pointed to the worn form of a woman on the bed.

"Dat his wife. Got consumption. She not dead in the morning, he go."

But when morning came Kitloogin could not go. He must stay and dig a grave.

Then La Jeunesse and I entered into council. I said I did not want a guide at all. I wanted to go to the bush with a trapper. I wanted to live like an Indian. I would come out of the bush alone. I hinted at outfit and provisions to be discarded when I should return to the settlement, and then I waited, wondering whether or not I had touched a responsive chord. The bronze face never moved, nor did the eyes betray a single feeling. But the head nodded, and La Jeunesse said:

"Yes. Ver' good."

Right there La Jeunesse gained an admirer. He was the first man I had met in the North who did not tell of bogies that lurk in the bush, who did not discover that my snowshoes were frail things, my blanket too thin, or my clothing inadequate. His soul was large enough to grasp the white man's desire to see the bush in winter, and to assume that the white man understood the difficulties.

Two days of stormy driving over drifted roads, and we stood at the last house on the way toward Hudson Bay. It was a log house of one room. From its door came a brawny pioneer of the most kindly French type, to grasp our hands with a heartiness that left no doubt as to our welcome. He threw open the door, and Madame, as large and jolly as her lord, slapped La Jeunesse on the shoulder in an effort to break down the Indian taciturnity. Madame mixed brandy toddy to drive the chill from her guests, seemingly forgetful that who gives brandy to the Indian commits a serious offense against the law. Then we sat down to a supper of pork, rabbit pie, and hot tea. When bed time came Madame took the broom of spruce brush and swept the floor very clean. Monsieur brought in an armful of boughs and threw them down, to be a bed for his guests. Here La Jeunesse and I spread blankets, and, warmed by the glow of the big square stove, lay down for the night.

With the morning came Guilliam, another

Moose Decides to Rest.

"The trail, a narrow opening * * * just wide enough to permit the passage of a toboggan or a man with a pack."

Montagnais, employed by La Jeunesse to help in the bush. With him was Nigger, the black Eskimo dog of La Jeunesse. I hired a dog of our host, also an Eskimo, with a black fur coat as heavy as a bear's. His name was Moose, and I hope no one ever had to drive a lazier animal. Moose was hitched to a little sleigh with steel runners, and Nigger to a toboggan. La Jeunesse and Guilliam also stepped into toboggan harness, and so loaded, we left the clearing and entered the trail, a narrow opening which ran away through the forest, just wide enough to permit the passage between the trees of a toboggan or a man with a pack. It wound along streams whose waters were hidden far beneath a white covering; it mounted hills and descended into valleys; it plunged into

Repairing Broken Snowshoe Webs is as Important as Patching Damaged Canoes in Summer.

Then I had carried a thirty pound sack of pork and caribou meat, and later bent under a sixty pound sack of flour. When La Jeunesse and the good Nigger were far out of sight in the forest Moose had quit for good, while Guilliam, just arrived on the scene, sat down astride his toboggan with an air that said the white man must work out his own salvation. So I had taken a light rope from the sleigh and was pulling tandem with Moose, when, at noon, we came up with La Jeunesse. He stood by the side of the trail, piling little sticks on a fire that leaped and crackled about a pail of tea. When we were ready to start again, he stepped to the sleigh, picked up a sack of meat and placed it on his toboggan, with the remark:

" Moose no good. You git tire', ver' tire."

thickets where silvery birch struggled with thick-limbed spruce for sunlight ; it emerged among the fantastic shadows of the more open forest where, save for the occasional hammering of the woodpecker or screaming of the moose bird, there was the silence of the infinite North. Now we were in the bush. We would have to go to the pole and away down on the other side of the earth before we would find another road in the direction whither we turned our faces.

At noon that day I began to see a difference between Indian and good Indian. It involved the difference between dog and good dog. Early in the day Moose had begun to lag on the hillsides. Then he had lain down again and again, while I shouted, " Marche donc, Moose," and cut whips that promptly broke on the dog's bear-like coat.

During five hours of work on the trail that afternoon, I appreciated at least one of the advantages of having a good Indian for one's host in the forest.

Our trail crossed five lakes—five white openings in the birch and balsam. Then we stood by a sixth, and at a point where a narrow beaver meadow came down to the edge La Jeunesse and Guilliam threw off their harness. The sun was behind the tree tops, and the clear northern twilight was stealing over the forest. A crescent moon hung white and loose in the evening sky. But the bright cheeriness of the day was gone. The breath of the evil spirit was coming out of the woods to pierce coats and sweaters, and cause panic where the little rivers of perspiration had burst forth during the last hours on the trail. This is the woodsman's cheerless hour, the hour when the spirit of the North is snarling at his heels, and his own efforts have not yet raised a barrier against that spirit's strength.

Moose and Nigger had dug round holes in the snow, and were cuddled away safe from the reach of the wind. Guilliam was cutting wood. La Jeunesse was carpeting the snow with balsam boughs. This finished, he took off one snowshoe, and, using it as a shovel, dug into the drift. He stooped and threw out an armful of boughs. After that he pulled up a roll of blankets, a tent, and a light, folding stove of sheet iron. This was his *caché*, one day's march from the last house.

It is easy to pitch a tent in the snow, the stakes drive so readily. This was a small cotton tent, but it had a wide margin at the bottom. When this had been fastened down with poles, and a bank of snow had been thrown around it, the little stove grew red, and the cheerless hour had departed. La Jeunesse took an axe and chipped off enough frozen caribou meat to fill the frying-pan. He put the bread by the stove to thaw. He steeped the tea and poured it into cups. Then he took from its sheath his new bowie knife, handed it to his guest, and therewith the feast began.

The Indian has· been accused of undue fondness for feasting, and what wonder! Who of us all can go to the woods to work at the paddle in summer or in the toboggan straps in winter, without a mighty desire toward the morning and evening meat and tea? Then, too, life in the bush is a struggle for things to eat, and what one

struggles for inevitably assumes undue proportions, whether it be the millions of the millionaire or the bread and meat of the wretch whose battle is ever with starvation.

After supper La Jeunesse made oatmeal mush for the dogs, and clubbed them when they fought. Then he squatted by the stove and said; "Ver' tir'. 'Tink I not make bread till morning." This was comforting, for I knew I was not the only one who felt he could sleep on through eternity and not have enough of sleeping. When I awoke Moose—Moose, the forgiving—lay with his head on my shoulder.

Next morning La Jeunesse heated water in the frying-pan and washed his hands. Then, sitting cross-legged on his blanket, he mixed flour, water, and baking-powder and kneaded it into round cakes of dough, which he baked in the frying-pan. While so engaged, he said:

"'Tink we stay here to-day. Odder Hinjun come, mebbe."

"What other Indian?"

"Hinjun named George. He marry my sister."

"Dere," and he pointed to a blackened stick, one end of which rose above the snow,

Guilliam Cools the Stove.

We Stop for Breath When the Wood Comes Down to a Frozen Lake.

slanting southward. Some one had used it to hang a tea pail over the noonday fire.

" Hinjun put stick dat way. Show he gone dat way. Been gone 'bout week. Time come .back lookin' trap odder way."

We were on the trapping grounds, now, of the brother-in-law, George. I asked how far those grounds might run. La Jeunesse pointed south, saying:

" Four day dat way," and, pointing north, "tree day dat way."

The grounds of La Jeunesse run from

its associations. When we start to look at his traps, the first of which is perhaps a mile from the tent, he points to a hillside, and says :

"Dere kill big moose two year 'go." And later, where a stream empties into another little lake, he pointed to a spruce tree, and said :

"Dere my father shoot carcajou."

It is not a wonderful instinct, so much as long acquaintance, that makes the Indian so thoroughly at home on his trapping grounds.

Our First Camp Stood Where Forest and Beaver Meadow Meet.

here westward about seventy-five miles, to the head waters of the St. Maurice River. Three days' journey to the southwest, and the grounds of his uncle begin on the lakes where the Crooked River takes its head. The rights to territory have descended from father to son since the days of far-off ancestors who dressed their heads in feathers and streaked their faces with war paint. La Jeunesse has tramped these grounds of his every winter since he was big enough to cut wood for his father's camp fire. Every stream, every hollow, and every clump of timber has

On the land of another he is not so infallible. La Jeunesse respects the trapping rights of other Indians, and they respect his, with an instinct of fair play closely akin to something that makes you and me keep off the property of other men. It becomes plain to me, now, how Iroquois, pushing northward to trespass upon Algonquin trapping grounds, brought on battles in which blood flowed and scalps changed owners. And sometimes I wonder how you and I would feel if, while our fellows respected our holdings, men of another color should invade them to make

"A brawny pioneer of the most kindly French type."

houses where our camps had been; to turn deer haunts into factory sights, and beaver-filled streams into sources of water power.

La Jeunesse and Guilliam spent the day digging up steel traps to set above the snow, uncovering snares and dead-falls, to see if they contained fur, and setting new ones for mink, martin, fox, and lynx. There was not a single catch, which fact caused La Jeunesse to shake his head and say:

"Snow make ver' bad luck. Cover traps jus' when set."

And the irony of the trapper's fate was evident when tracks on the snow and scattered rabbit's fur showed that a lynx had eaten his dinner almost directly over a snare, now covered three feet below the drift. I remember how, as a twelve-year-old, I used to lie awake when it rained on the October nights, after I had set half a dozen musk-rat traps in the creek. For the rain would raise the stream, and rats would swim over the traps to eat the bate at leisure. Now, I knew how it must seem to these trappers of the northern bush, whose living depends on their catch, to stay in a tent day after day while snow covers their traps. As is the protracted rain in harvest to the farmer with a mortgaged farm, so is the long-drawn-out snow-storm to the trapper in debt at the store for supplies. When spring comes, more

than one Indian will return to the settlements poorer than he left. He will skulk into the Company store and stand silent till the agent asks about his catch. Then he will look down at the floor and whine out his hard-luck tale of storms and sickness and the carcajou.

When we reached camp another tent stood by our own. The sister of La Jeunesse was a strong, silent squaw, with a face that never told tales. The boy was a quiet little fellow, whose eyes sometimes laughed without any help from his facial muscles. George, the man, was a hollow-cheeked wretch, coughing the cough of the consumptive. He waved his arms and talked in excited tones. Then all entered our tent, and La Jeunesse made tea and handed out chunks of bread.

"Dey have bad luck," he said when the others were eating.

"*Cash* broke. Flour an' tea all stole."

"Carcajou?" I asked.

"No, tink hit odder Hinjun."

"I thought Indians never broke *cash*."

"Hinjuns steal two bags flour from my *cash* once. No bread fur two week."

George must leave his traps, and, coughing at well-nigh every step, make his way to the settlements and to the store and beg a little more credit. The credit extended will be charity, for his luck has been bad all winter, and he is sure to leave the woods in debt. And the agent at the store knows from the cough that he will not pay next winter. Next winter if he continues to keep the fast days and shun the *windago,* and deal fairly with the company, he will be trapping on grounds where the *caché* is never broken, and where the beaver never fail. His widow will inherit his trapping grounds and will be sought in marriage by impecunious young men.

Half the Montagnais, I am told, have consumption. Locally, it is attributed to exposure in the bush. But it is more than that. It is the old, old story, of the savage in contact with civilization. Chief of the curses of the Montagnais is the dreaded "white whiskey," alcohol and water. They get the liquor, in spite of laws to the contrary, and when an Indian has drunk half a pint or thereabouts, he kicks down the stove and goes out to sleep in the snow.

We speak of the passing of the caribou and beaver. But it is the Indian that is passing. The Indian population in all this region, between Hudson Bay and the Atlantic, is decreasing. Mr. Low, who explored it in the interests of the Canadian Geological Survey, found streams in the interior from which the last family had disappeared, dying in a winter, to leave their lodges standing, habitations for their wolfish dogs. There the beaver had been restored to their primeval numbers. So, too, with the disappearance of the old-time Indian trappers of New Brunswick, the caribou increased, until nowadays men go from north of the St. Lawrence southward to hunt. As family after family disappears from its old grounds, the beaver will restore its houses and dams, and the caribou will return from its banishment.

To-night no brightness is visible in this life. There is only the struggle with the wilds for food to eat and clothing to wear. But morning comes, and the sky is bright. When we have moved camp some half dozen miles, and thrown off the ropes to take up the trapper's work, a shade of care has gone from the faces of the red men. When we leave the trail to look at traps set the day before, there is a new elasticity in their steps. This tramping through the zero crispness is a joy in itself; but when we near a

trap, it gives way to the keen expectation of the trapper. After all, looking at one's traps is not so very different from looking at the tape on the ticker. It is all a matter of seeing whether we are richer, or not so rich. At one trap, a dead-fall set in a bunch of spruce at the side of a little stream, the pole has fallen, and a mink is caught. It is only one mink, worth perhaps two dollars, yet it is so much toward success. Then we come to rabbit snares set to help out our larder. Two big white rabbits hang stiff and stark from the bent saplings. Several times we have seen grouse. They sit in the trees, apparently not in the least afraid. We camp early, and Guilliam, taking his light, muzzle loading smooth-bore, brings in a pair to stew with a rabbit for our evening meal. Next day we did not move camp, but worked at the traps. Two more mink were dug up from buried dead-falls. La Jeunesse said:

"Set longer before snow. 'Tink better luck now," while Guilliam grinned a grin of unmistakable pleasure at the catch. I do not wonder, now, that the Indian goes to the bush. True, he makes only a living, but how

La Jeunesse Makes Bread.

much more does the laborer of the outside world make? And how much better this freedom in the endless woods than the dreary grind within factory walls! And how much better the matching of cunning with the forest things, than shoveling coal or digging sewers, while surely the tent is no bad dwelling, contrasted with the ill-smelling tenement!

The exposure of the trapper's life is not so great when all goes well. When we lie down around the little stove at night blankets are almost a superfluity, and I can think of scarcely anything that would add to our

and, in extremity, boil the skins themselves, Or again, he may find himself many days from the settlement when the spring thaws commence. If he remains, the streams will swell until they cannot be crossed, and to a man without a canoe this may mean starvation. La Jeunesse found himself in this predicament once. When I asked how he got out, he said:

"Walk t'ree day an' t'ree night widout sleep."

But while these possibilities haunt those who live in the forest, they are perhaps no worse than the possibilities of wrecks and

" La Jeunesse also slipped into toboggan harness."

comfort. I thought this must be an unusually favorable glimpse at the life, but when I asked La Jeunesse if he never slept away from his tent, he said:

"No. Too col'. Git seek."

It is when the unexpected happens that bad times come. The unexpected happens sooner or later to every one who goes long to the bush. Maybe a *caché* is robbed. Now the trapper will hunt around old camp fires for bones that he may crack them to get the marrow; or he will kill and eat blue jays, or cook an ill-smelling mink from his dead fall. He will scrape the fat from his furs,

explosions, while surely the ravages of the carcajou can not be more troublesome than those of civilization's wolf.

In avoiding exposure, La Jeunesse is more careful than even the average white man who goes to the woods for sport. One day at noon, when we were about to move camp, I told him I was going back to the settlement.

"Too far go to-day," he said.

"Sleep in shanty," said I, for some way one gets to stripping his speech of cloying adjectives when he talks with these children of the bush.

Setting a Lynx Snare.

"Git ver' col'. You stay till mornin'. We not move camp. Den you git to house 'fore night."

This was very unlike the average Indian, but very like La Jeunesse. Guilliam would let the white man take care of himself. But

La Jeunesse was always helpful. Once I was eating snow on the march:

"Don' eat snow. Make you seek," said La Jeunesse.

When I spread my blanket the first night in the woods, he said:

121

"Wait min-ute," and spread one of his own between mine and the boughs. Before we entered the bush I gave him a bowie knife. Whenever we sat down to eat, he drew this from his belt and offered it to me, to be knife and fork and spoon, for the meal. Perhaps it is such little things that make the difference between Indian and good Indian. Or perhaps these are not Indian at all. Maybe they are an inheritance of French politeness from some far-off *coureur du bois*.

In the morning I threw away all but the bare necessaries, packed these upon the sleigh, and put Moose into his harness. By hard going he and I could reach a house that day. When we were starting, La Jeunesse slipped on his round snowshoes.

"T'ink I go part way," he said. "Mebbe git los'."

I said I could follow the old trail, and that even if that failed, I could strike east by compass and in three days reach the Chamouchouan River.

"No," said La Jeunesse. "Chamouchouan too far. Go sout'. Find River Aux Doré. Go down dat, find Frenchman house 'bout one day."

I hope good things will come to La Jeunesse. But when I reached the settlements I learned that a white man went through his trapping grounds not long ago, surveying for a railroad. In the cities I heard men promising each other that within five years a railroad will furnish an outlet for

the minerals and pulp wood between Lake St. John and Hudson Bay. I wonder what La Jeunesse will do then? If he goes south or north or west, he will be on the ground of other Indians.

La Jeunesse has a farm on the reserve, and a house—a three-roomed house—with a red roof. He is very proud of his house, and I thought perhaps he might sometime quit the bush and turn farmer. But once I had asked him that, and he had said no. I had asked him why he liked the bush better than the settlement, but he merely said:

"Don' know. Jus' likum better." The mind of La Jeunesse is not analytical.

"But when you are married," I ventured; "Will you come to the bush then?"

"Yes. Wife come too."

His sisters are all in the bush. His mother went every winter till rheumatism seized her. That was fifteen years ago. Since then she has not walked.

Once I had asked him where his father and brothers trapped.

"Dey dead," he answered. "All die las' spring."

At the mission they told me that the father and two sons came out of the bush a year ago, all coughing, with a newly contracted disease. The tubercular bacillus works rapidly in the Indian's lungs, and within two months all three were dead.

Perhaps, when the railroad is completed, La Jeunesse will not need his hunting grounds.

Philip R. Goodwin -1902

The Last Stand

Drawn by Philip R. Goodwin.

13

The Passing of the Black Whelps

CHARLES G.D. ROBERTS

"A little steep, rocky island, upthrusting itself boldly."

THE PASSING OF THE BLACK WHELPS

By CHARLES G. D. ROBERTS

ILLUSTRATED BY CHARLES LIVINGSTON BULL

I.

A LOPSIDED, waning moon, not long risen, looked over the ragged crest of the ridge, and sent long shadows down the sparsely wooded slope. Though there was no wind, and every tree was as motionless as if carved of ice, these long, intricate shadows seemed to stir and writhe, as if instinct with a kind of sinister, suppressed activity. This confusion of light and dark was increased by the patches of snow that still clung in the dips and on the gentler slopes. The air was cold, yet with a bitter softness in it, the breath of the thaw. The sound of running water was everywhere—the light clamor of rivulets, and the rush of the swollen brooks; while from the bottom of the valley came the deep, pervading voice of the river at freshet, laboring between high banks with its burden of sudden flood.

Over the crest of the ridge, inky black for an instant against the distorted moon, came a leaping deer. He vanished in a patch of young firs. He shot out again into the moonlight. Down the slope he came in mighty bounds, so light of foot and so elastic that he seemed to float through the air; though from his heaving sides and wild eyes it was evident that he was fleeing in desperation from some appalling terror. Straight down the slope he came, to the very brink of the high bluff overlooking the river. There he wheeled, and continued his flight up the valley, his violent shadow every now and then, as he crossed the spaces of moonlight, projecting grotesquely far out upon the swirling flood.

Up along the river bluff he fled for perhaps a mile. Then he stopped suddenly and listened, his sensitive ears and dilating nostrils held high to catch the faintest waft of air. Not a sound came to him, except the calling of the waters; not a scent, save the raw freshness of melting snow and the balsamic tang of buds just beginning to thrill to the first of the rising sap. He bounded on again for perhaps a hundred yards, then with a tremendous leap sprang to one side, a full thirty feet, landing belly deep in a thicket of scrub juniper. Another leap, as if he were propelled by steel springs, carried him yet another thirty feet aside. Then he turned, ran back a couple of hundred yards parallel to his old trail, and lay down in a dense covert of spruces to catch breath and ease his pounding heart. He was a very young buck, not yet seasoned in the craft of the wilderness, and his terror shook him. But he knew enough to take his snatched rest at the very edge of his covert, where his eyes could watch the back trail. For a quarter of an hour, however, nothing appeared along that staring trail. Then he got up nervously and resumed his flight, still ascending the valley, but now slanting away from the river, and gradually climbing

127

back toward the crest of the ridge. He had in mind a wide reach of swales and flooded meadows, still miles away, wherein he might hope to elude the doom that followed him.

Not long after the buck had vanished there arose a strange sound upon the still, wet air. It came in a rising and falling cadence from far behind the ridge, under the low, lopsided moon. It was a high, confused sound, not unmusical, but terrifying—a cry of many voices. It drifted up into the silvery night, wavered and diminished, swelled again, and then died away, leaving a sense of fear upon the quiet that followed. The soft clamor of the waters, when one noticed them again, seemed to have taken a new note from the menace of that cadenced cry.

Presently over the top of the ridge, at the gap wherein had first appeared the form of the leaping buck, a low, dark shape came, moving sinuously and with deadly swiftness. It did not bound into the air and float, as the buck had seemed to do, but slid smoothly, like a small, dense patch of cloud-shadow—a direct, inevitable movement, wasting no force and fairly eating up the trail of the fleeing deer.

As it came down the slope, disappearing in the hemlock groves and emerging upon the bright, snowy hollows, the dread shape resolved itself into a pack of seven wolves. They ran so close, so evenly, with fanged muzzles a little low, and ample, cloudy tails a little high, that one might have almost covered the whole deadly pack with a table cloth. Their tongues were hanging out, and their eyes shot green fire; they were fiercely hungry, for game was scarce and cunning that winter on their much ravaged range, and this chase was already a long

"He was in mid-air, falling to the ice cakes of the swollen river."

one. When the trail of the buck wheeled at the river-brink, the leader of the pack gave one short howl as he turned, barely escaping the abyss. It seemed to him that the buck must have been nearly winded, or he would not, even for an instant, have contemplated taking to such mad water. With the renewed vigor of encouragement, he swept his pack along up the edge of the bluff.

On the pack leader's right flank ran a sturdy wolf of a darker color than his fellows—nearly black, indeed, on the top of his head, over his shoulders, and along his stiff-haired backbone. Not quite so tall or so long-flanked as the leader, he had that greater breadth of skull between the eyes which betokens the stronger intelligence, the more individualized resourcefulness. He had a look in his deep-set, fierce eye which seemed to prophesy that unless the unforeseen should happen he would ere long seize the leadership to himself.

But—the unforeseen did happen, at that moment. The trail, just there, led across a little dip wherein the snow still lingered. Thinly covered by the snow lay a young pine tree, lightning shivered and long dead. Thrust up from the trunk was a slim, sharp pointed stub, keen and hard and preserved by its resin. Upon this hidden dagger-point, as he ran, the dark wolf planted his right fore-foot—planted it fair and with a mighty push. Between the spreading toes, between the fine bones and sinews and the cringing nerves of the foot, and out by the first joint of the leg it thrust its rending way.

At the suddenness of the anguish the dark wolf yelped, falling forward upon his muzzle as he did so, and dropping from his place as the pack sped on. But as he wrenched his foot free and took one stumbling stride forward the pack stopped, and turned. Their long white fangs snapped, and the fire in their eyes took a different hue.

Very well the dark wolf knew the meaning of the halt, the turn, the change in his fellows' eyes. He knew the stern law of the pack—the instant and inevitable doom of its hurt member. The average gray wolf knows how to accept the inevitable. Fate itself—the law of the pack—he does not presume to defy. He will fight—to justify his blood, and, perhaps, to drug his despair and die in the heat of the struggle. But he does not dream of trying to escape.

And in this fashion, fighting in silence, this dark wolf would have died at the brink of the river-bluff, and been·eaten by his fellows ere they continued their chase of the leaping buck—in this fashion would he have died, but for that extra breadth of skull between the eyes, that heightened individualism and resourcefulness. Had there been any chance to escape by fighting, fighting would have been the choice of his fierce and hardy spirit. But what was he against six?

Defying the fiery anguish in his foot, he made a desperate leap which took him to the extreme overhanging edge of the bluff. Already the jaws of the executioners were gnashing at his heels. A second more and they would have been at his throat. But before that second passed he was in mid-air, his legs spread wide like those of a squirrel, falling to the ice-cakes of the swollen river. From the brink above, the grim eyes of the baffled pack flamed down upon him for an instant, and then withdrew. What was a drowned wolf, when there was a winded buck not far ahead?

But the black-shouldered wolf was not drowned. The flood was thick, indeed, with crunching ice-cakes and wallowing logs and slowly-turning islets of uprooted trees and the _débris_ of the winter forest. But fortune so favored the wolf that he fell in a space of clear water, instead of being dashed to a pulp on ice-cake or tree-trunk. He disappeared, came to the surface gasping, struck out hardily through the grim and daunting turmoil, and succeeded in gaining one of those islets of toughly interlaced _débris_ which turned slowly in the flood. Upon this precarious refuge, crouched shivering upon the largest tree root and licking persistently at his wounded paw, he was carried swiftly down stream through the roar of waters.

II.

When the lopsided moon, now hung high over a low, desolate shore of blanched rampikes, was fading to a papery whiteness against a sky of dawn the roar of the river grew louder, and the islet, no longer slowly revolving, plunged forward, through a succession of wallowing waves, over a wild half mile of ledges, and joined itself to a wider and mightier stream; the wolf, drenched, shivering, and appalled by the tumult, clung to his refuge by tooth and claw; and the islet, being well compacted, held together through the wrenching plunges, and carried its burden safely forth upon the quiet current:

For a day and a night and a day the starving wolf voyaged down the flood, till his gaunt sides clung together, and a fierce ache gnawed at his vitals. But with the fasting and the ceaseless soothing of his tongue his wound rapidly healed; and when, after sunset of his second evening on the river, the islet grounded in an eddy under the bank, he sprang ashore with speed little impaired. Only a limp and an ache remained to remind him of the hurt which had so nearly cost him his life and had exiled him to untried hunting grounds.

His feet once more on firm ground, the wolf halted warily. The air that came down the bank carried a strange and warning scent. Noiselessly he crept up the steep, went through a few yards of shrubbery like a ghost, and peered forth upon a rough back-settlement road. To one side he saw a cabin, with a barn beside it, and two long-horned steers (he had seen steers at a lumber camp in his own wild land), thrusting their muzzles over the pasture fence. Down the road toward the cabin came a man in gray homespun and cowhide larrigans, with an axe over his shoulder. It was the man-smell which had made him so cautious.

With savage but curious eyes he watched the man, with no thought of attacking alone so redoubtable a foe. Presently the latter began to whistle, and at the incomprehensible sound the wolf shrank back, fear mingled with his curiosity. But when the man was well past, there came a new scent upon the air, a scent quite unknown to him; and then a small black and white cur trotted into view, nosing along the roadside in quest of chipmunks. The jaws of the starving wolf dripped water at the sight. He gathered himself for a rush. He saw that the man had disappeared. The dog ran across the road, nosing a new chipmunk trail, and halted, in sudden apprehension, not five feet from the hidden wolf. There was a rustle, a leap, a sharp yelp; and the wolf was back into cover with his prey.

Emboldened by the success of this, his first hunting in the unknown land, the wolf slept for a few hours in his bushy retreat, and then, when the misshapen moon was up, went prowling cautiously around the outskirts of the scattered little settlement. Everywhere the man smell kept him on his guard. Once he was careless enough to get between the wind and a farmyard, whereupon a watchful cur started a barking, which was taken up and kept up for an hour by all the dogs of the village. At this the wolf, with snarling, contemptuous jaws apart, withdrew to a knoll, sat quietly erect upon his haunches, and waited for the din to subside. He noted carefully the fact that one or two men were aroused by the alarm, and came out to see what was the matter. When all was quiet again he sought the house of the nearest yelper, took him by surprise, and killed

him in sheer rage, leaving his torn body beside the very doorstep, instead of dragging it away for a later meal. This was a mistake

in hunting craft. Had he been more familiar with the man folk, his wide-skulled intelligence would have taught him better than to leave a clue behind him in this careless fashion.

From the farm-yard he wandered back toward the hills, and came upon a lonely sheep pasture. Here he found killing so easy that he slew in wantonness; and then, about daybreak, gorged and triumphant, withdrew to a rocky hillside, where he found a lair to his taste.

Later in the day, however, he realized his mistake. He had called down upon himself the wrath of the man folk. A din

CHARLES LIVINGSTON BULL

of dogs aroused him, and, mounting a rock, he saw a motley crowd of curs upon his trail, with half a dozen men following far behind them. He bared his fangs disdainfully, then turned and sought the forest at a long gallop, which, for all his limp and his twinge, soon carried him beyond ear-shot of his pursuers.

For hours he pressed on, ever eastward, with a little trend to the south, crossing many a trail of deer, caribou, and moose, passing here and there a beaver village, and realizing that he had come to wonderful hunting grounds. But when he came to the outskirts of another settlement, he halted. His jaws ran water at the thought of finding another sheep-pasture, and he decided to range for a while in this neighborhood. He was quick to realize the disadvantage of man's proximity, but he would dare it for a little before retiring into the untainted wilderness. He had learned his lesson quickly, however. That night he refrained from stirring up the dogs of the settlement; and he killed but one sheep, in a secluded corner of the pasture.

Now, by singular chance, it happened that at this particular settlement there was already a sheep-killer harrying the thick-wooled flocks. A wandering peddler, smitten with a fever while visiting the settlement, had died, and left to pay for his board and burial only his pack and his dog. The dog, so fiercely devoted to him as to have made the funeral difficult, was a long-legged, long-haired, long-jawed bitch, apparently a cross between a collie and a Scotch deerhound. So unusual a beast, making all the other dogs of the settlement look contemptible, was in demand; but she was deaf, for a time, to all overtures. For a week she pined for the dead peddler; and then, with an air of scornful tolerance, consented to take up her abode with the village shopkeeper. Her choice was made not for any distinction in the man, but for a certain association, apparently, with the smell of the contents of her late master's pack. For months she sulked and was admired, making friends with neither man, woman, nor child, and keeping all the village curs at a respectful distance.

A few days, however, before the arrival of the journeying wolf, a new interest had entered into the life of the long-jawed bitch. Her eyes resumed their old bright alertness, and she grew perceptibly less ungracious to the loafers gathered around the stove in the back store. She had entered upon a career which would have ended right speedily with a bullet in her reckless brain, but for an utterly unlooked-for freak of fate. She had discovered that, if every night she could hunt, run down, and kill our sheep, life might again become worth living, and the coarse-clodded grave in the little lonely cemetery might be forgotten. It was not the killing, but the chase, that she craved. The killing was, of course, merely the ecstatic culmination. So she went about the sport with artistic cunning. To disguise her trail she came upon the flocks from the side of the forest, as any wild beast would. Then she would segregate her victim with a skill born of her collie ancestry, set it running, madden it to the topmost delirium of fear and flight, and almost let it escape before darting at its throat and ending the game with the gush of warm blood between her jaws.

Such had been her adventures for three nights; and already the settlement was concerned, and already

" A rush, a leap, a short yelp, and the wolf was back into cover with his prey."

glances of half-formed suspicion had been cast upon the long-legged bitch so innocently asleep by the stove, when the wandering wolf arrived upon the outskirts of the settlement. The newcomer was quick to note and examine the tracks of a peculiarly large dog—a foeman, perhaps, to prove not unworthy of his fangs. And he conducted his reconnoitering with more care. Then he came upon the carcass of a sheep, torn and partly eaten. It was almost like a wolf's work—though less cleanly done—and the smell of the cold trail was unmistakably dog. The black-backed wolf was puzzled. He had a vague notion that dogs were the protectors, not the hunters, of all the four-legged kindred belonging to men. The problem seeming to him an important one, he crouched in an ambush near the carcass to consider it for a time, before setting out upon his own sheep-hunting.

As he crouched, watching, he saw the killer approach. He saw a tall, lean bitch come up, tear carelessly at the dead sheep for a moment or two, in a manner of ownership, and turn to leave. She was as long in leg and flank as himself, and possessed of the like punishing jaws; but she was not so massive in the shoulder. The wolf felt that he could master her in combat; but he felt no disposition for the fight. The dog smell that came to his nostrils did not excite the usual hot aversion. On the contrary, it made him desire to know more of the sheep-killing stranger.

But acquaintance is not made lightly among the wild kindred, who are quick to resent a presumption. The wolf slipped noiselessly back into his covert, emerged upon the further side of the thicket, and at a distance of some twenty paces stood forth in the glimmering light. To attract the tall bitch's attention he made a soft, whining sound.

At the unexpected noise behind her the bitch wheeled like lightning. At sight of the big wolf the hair rose along her back, her fangs bared themselves dangerously, and she growled a deep note of challenge. For some seconds the wolf thought she would fly at him; but he stood motionless, tail drooping humbly, tongue hanging a little way from his lips, a soft light in his eyes. Then he sat back upon his haunches, let his tongue hang out still farther, and drooped his head a little to one side—the picture of conciliation and deference.

The long-jawed bitch had never before seen a wolf, but she recognized him at once as a natural enemy. There was

"Here the wanderers found a dry cave."

something in his attitude of unoffending confidence, however, which made her hesitate to attack, although he was plainly a trespasser. As she eyed him, she felt her anger melting away. How like he was to certain big, strong dogs which she had seen once or twice in her wanderings with the peddler! and how unlike to the diminutive, yelping curs of the settlement! Her bristling hairs smoothed themselves, the skin of her jaws relaxed and set itself about her teeth in a totally different expression; her growling ceased, and she gave an amicable whine. Diffidently the two approached each other, and in a few minutes a perfect understanding was established.

That night they hunted sheep together. In the joy of comradeship and emulation, prudence was scattered to the winds, and they held a riot of slaughter. When day broke a dozen or more sheep lay dead about the pastures. And the wolf, knowing that men and dogs would soon be noisy on their trail, led his new found mate far back into the wilderness.

III.

The tall bitch, hating the settlement and all the folk therein, was glad to be quit of it. And she found the hunting of deer far more thrilling than the tame pursuit of sheep. Slipping with curious ease the inherited sympathies of her kind, she fell into the ways of the wild kindred, save for a brusque open ness that she never suc ceeded in laying off.

For weeks the strangely mated pair drifted southward through the bright New Brunswick spring, to come to a halt at last in a region to their liking between the St. John and the Chiputneticook chain of lakes. It was a land of deer and rabbits and ducks, with settlements small and widely scattered; a land where never a wolf-snout had been seen for half a hundred years. And here, on a thick-wooded hill slope, the wanderers found a dry cave and made it their den.

"A pack which * * * no like number of wolves in all Canada could have matched."

In due course the long-jawed bitch bore a litter of six sturdy whelps, which throve amazingly. As they grew up they showed almost all wolf, harking back to the type— save that in color they were nearly black, with a touch of tan in the gray of their under parts. When they came to maturity, and were accredited hunters all, they were in general larger and more savage than either of their parents, differing more widely, one from another, than would the like number of full-blooded wolves. The eight, when they hunted together, made a pack which, for strength, ferocity, and craft, no like number of full-blooded wolves in all Canada could have matched.

The long-jawed bitch, whose highly de- veloped brain guided, for the most part, the destinies of the pack, for a time kept them far from the settlement and away from contact with men; and the existence of wolves in the Chiputneticook country was not dreamed of among the backwoods settlements. In this policy she was backed by the sagacity and strength of her mate, under whose wide-arched skull was a clear perception of the truth that man is the one master animal. But the hybrid whelps, by some perversion of inherited instinct, hated man savagely, and had the dread of him more than either of their parents. More than once was the authority of the leaders sharply strained to prevent a disastrous attack upon some unsuspecting pair of lumbermen with their ox-team and their axes.

The second winter of the wolves in the Chiputneticook country proved a very hard one—game scarce and hunting difficult; and toward the end of February the pack drew in toward the settlements, in the hope of more abundant foraging. Fate promptly favored the move. Some sheep, and a heifer or two, were easily killed, with no calamitous result; and the authority of the leaders was somewhat discredited. Three of the young wolves even went so far as to besiege a solitary cabin, where a woman and three trembling children awaited the return of the man. For two hideous moonlit hours they prowled and howled about the door, sniffing at the sill, and grinning in through the low window; and when the sound of bells came near they withdrew sullenly, half-minded to attack the man and horse.

A few nights after this, when the pack was following together the discouraging trail of a long-winded and wily buck, they crossed the trail of a man on snowshoes. This trail was fresher, and to the young wolves it seemed to promise easier hunting. The leaders were overruled, and the new trail was taken up with heat.

The trail was that of a gaunt, tan-faced backwoodsman, on his way to a lumber camp a few miles down the other side of the lake. He was packing a supply of light needfuls, of which the lumbermen had unexpectedly run short, and he was pressing forward in haste to avoid a second night on the trail. The pack was carried high on his powerful shoulders, in a manner to interfere as little as possible with his long, snowshoeing stride. In one hand he carried his axe. From under the brim of his coonskin cap his piercing gray eyes kept watch with a quiet alertness—expecting no danger, indeed, and fearing none, but trained to cool readiness for every vicissitude of the wild.

He was traveling through a stretch of heavy timber, where the moonlight came down in such scant streaks that he had trouble in picking a clear path, when his ear was caught by an unwonted sound far behind him. He paused to listen, no unwonted sound being matter of indifference to them who range the wood. It came again, long-drawn and high and cadenced. The big woodsman looked surprised. "I'd 'a' took my oath," said he to himself, "ther' wa'n't a wolf in New Brunswick! But I knowed the deer 'd bring 'em back afore long!" Then, unconcernedly, he resumed his tramp, such experience as he had with wolves in the Far West having convinced him that they would not want to meddle with a man.

In a few minutes, however, the instinct of the woods awoke in him suddenly, and told him that it was not some buck, but himself, whom the hunting pack were trailing. Then the sound came again, perceptibly nearer, though still far off. The woodsman gave a grunt of impatience, angry to think that any four-foot creature of the forest should presume to hunt *him!* But the barest prudence told him that he should make haste for the open. Under protest, as it were, he broke into a long trot, and swerved to the right that he might sooner reach the lake.

As he ran, the novel experience of feeling himself pursued got on his nerves, and filled him with rage. Were there not plenty of deer in the woods? he thought indignantly. He would teach the vermin a lesson. Several times he was on the point of stopping and waiting, to have it out with them as soon as possible. But wisdom prevailed, and he pushed on to the open. On the lake, the moonlit snow was packed hard and the running good. About a mile from shore a little steep, rocky island, upthrusting itself boldly, suggested to the woodsman that if his pursuers were really going to have the audacity to attack him, it might be well to have his back to a rock, that he might not be surrounded. He headed for the island, therefore, though with protest in his heart. And just as he got to it the wolves emerged from cover, and darted out upon the shining level.

"Looks like they really meant it!" growled the big woodsman, loosing his pack strap and setting his jaws for a fight.

When the pack came near he was astonished first at the stature and dark color of its members, and realized with a sudden fury that the outcome was not so assured as he had taken for granted it would be. Perhaps he would never see camp, after all! Then he was further astonished to note that one of the pack-leaders looked like a dog. He shouted, in a voice of angry command; and the onrushing pack hesitated, checked themselves, spread apart. From that dominating voice it was evident that this was a

"At sight of the big wolf the hair rose along her back, * * * and she growled a deep note of challenge."

creature of power—not to be attacked carelessly, but to be surrounded.

That voice of command had thrilled the heart of the long-jawed bitch. Something in it reminded her of the dead peddler, who had been a masterful man. She would have none of this hunting. But she looked at each of her savage whelps, and knew that any attempt to lead them off would be worse than vain. A strange hatred began to stir within her, and her fangs bared toward them as if they, not the man against the rock, were the enemy. She looked again at the man, and saw the pack at his feet! Instantly her heart went out to him. She was no longer a wolf, but a dog; and there was her master—not her old master, but such a one as he had been. At his side, and fighting his foes, was her place. Like a flash she darted away from her companion, stopped a few feet in front of the ready woodsman, turned about, and faced the pack with a savage growl. Her hair was stiffly erect from neck to tail; her long white teeth were bared to the roots; her eyes were narrowed to slits of green flame; she half crouched, ready to spring in mad fury, and tear the throat of any beast which should try to hurt the man.

As for the woodsman, he knew dogs, and was not greatly surprised at his strange ally. At her sudden approach he had swung his axe in readiness, but his cool eye had read her signals aright. "Good dog!" he said, with cheerful confidence. "We'll lick the varmin!"

But the young wolves went wild with rage at this defection and defiance, and rushed in at once. They sprang first upon the bitch, though one, rushing past, leaped venomously at the woodsman's throat, got the axe in his skull, and dropped without a sound. Meanwhile the old wolf, which had been holding back in uncertainty, had made his decision. When he saw his mate attacked his doubts vanished, and a red haze for an instant went over his eyes. These whelps that attacked her—he suddenly saw them not as wolves at all, but as dogs, and hated them with a deadly hate. Silently he fell upon the nearest, and tore him savagely. He was too late, however, to save his mistress. The long-jawed bitch, for all her strength and her valiant spirit, was overwhelmed by her powerful offspring. One she had killed, and for one she had crunched a leg-joint to splinters; but now she lay mangled and still under the struggle. The brute whose leg-joint she had smashed dragged out from the *mêlée;* and her faithful mate, the wide-skulled old wanderer wolf, found himself in the death-grapple with three raging adversaries, each fairly his match for weight and strength. True wolf, he fought in silence; but in his antagonists the mixed breed came out, and they fought with yelps and snarls.

At this juncture, fortunately for the old wolf, the woodsman's understanding eye had penetrated the whole situation. He saw that the black-haired beasts were the common enemy; and he fell upon the three with his axe. His snowshoes he had kicked off when making ready for the struggle. In his mighty grasp, the light axe whirled and smote with the cunning of a rapier; and in a few seconds the old wolf, bleeding but still

"Crouched shivering upon the largest tree root, and licking persistently at his wounded paw."

vigorous, found himself confronting the man across a heap of mangled black bodies. The man, lowering his axe, looked at the bleeding wolf with mingled doubt and approbation. The wolf glared back for an instant—fear, hate, and grief in the green gleam of his eyes—then turned and fled, his pace accelerated by the cheerful yell which the man sent after him.

"He'd got the sand, sure!" muttered the woodsman to himself, wiping his axe. "Glad I did'nt hev to knock him on the head, too!"

Then, turning about, he saw the disabled whelp trying to sneak off, and with unerring aim threw his axe. The black mongrel sank with a kick, and lay still. The woodsman got out his pipe, slowly stuffed it with black-jack, and smoked contemplatively, while he stood and pondered the slain. He turned over the bodies, and patted the fur of the long-jawed bitch which had so splendidly turned back to her traditions in the time of need. As he thought, the main elements of the story unfolded themselves to him. Considerately, he carried the limp body, and securely buried it under a heap of stones on the island. The rest he *cachéd* carelessly, intending to return and skin them on the morrow.

"Them black pelts 'll be worth somethin', I reckon!" he said to himself with satisfaction as he took up his pack.

14

Canadian Winter Pastimes

GEO. W. ORTON, Ph.D.

CANADIAN WINTER PASTIMES

BY GEO. W. ORTON, PH.D.

RUDYARD KIPLING'S poem, "Our Lady of the Snows," was inopportunely published, when the mercury was up in the nineties. Still, we must do Mr. Kipling the justice to observe that in his poem he has struck the one great point of difference which distinguishes Canada from the United States to the south of her ; and especially, as more befitting the particular occasion of the poem, from the remainder of the British colonies.

It is very hot in summer, true ; still Canada lies partly in the Arctic circle, where ice, frost, and snow hold their frozen reign for seven or eight months.

It would be unfair, however, to take this section of the country as an example of Canadian winter weather. It would be better to strike a happy mean by accepting the conditions prevailing in and around Montreal as a fair type. If we go further north the weather is too severe, while, if we were to take such weather as is found in Toronto, the Niagara peninsula, or along the coast of British Columbia, we should err too much in the other direction.

About the middle of November, or perhaps earlier, the Montrealer expects cold weather, and he is very seldom disappointed. The small streams then commence to freeze, and there are occasional flurries of snow. But by December first the ice is strong enough for skating. All through the winter the snow steadily accumulates, until by the middle of January there is a level covering of white in the woods, from three to five feet deep. The ice also becomes thicker and firmer, until every sheet of water, every river, and ordinary lake is covered with a firm sheeting of it. The greater lakes must be excepted. These never freeze over, although every

THE TROTTING TRACK ON THE RIVER.

bay and indentation is covered with ice, and in exceptionally cold winters they have been known to freeze several miles from shore.

If the snow did not drift, all would be well for the countryman; but it does, and at times makes traveling by horse or afoot very difficult. The wind will first drift all the cross-roads full, and then, perchance, the very next week, turning about, it will do the same kind act for the roads running at right angles. Thus, when riding in the country, it is no uncommon thing to meet such a large drift in the road that you must simply turn off, drive right over the fence down into a field and then along the side of the road until the latter becomes passable again.

Another point to be noted in these snow roads is the "pitch-holes," so called because they pitch the occupant of the sleigh forward or nearly out of his seat when one is passed. Through some inequality in the ground, or other natural cause, a furrow is made across the road. This is gradually hollowed out, sometimes to a depth of three feet

ICE PALACE, MONTREAL.

or over. A bob-sleigh will slide through one very easily and smoothly, but a cutter takes a pitch-hole in a very bumpy manner, especially as four horses out of five, when attached to a cutter, will insist on jumping the hole, the cutter consequently hitting the opposite side with considerable force.

The rivers are very frequently used as roads, because, the sweep of the wind being greater, much of the snow is generally blown to the banks or off the ice, leaving a very good, level road-bed.

However, it must not be supposed that traveling is impossible or even unenjoyable. On the contrary, sleighing is considered by every one a very enjoyable feature of winter. To be sure, after every storm the roads are blocked with snow, but they are soon beaten down, and then there is nothing more exhilarating than a drive behind a pair of fleet horses, through the cold, crisp, winter air, over the fields of ice and snow. The horses, decked with gay trappings and sweet-toned bells, seem to feel the effect of such bracing weather, and rush forward unspurred by whip or voice.

The occupants of the sleigh, warmly wrapped in furs, do not fear the cold, but enjoy to the full the strengthening breeze and the winter scenery, the earth being covered with a blanket of virgin whiteness and splendor. Especially is this so if the drive be taken when the moon is full. No night scene can be more brilliant than a Canadian winter sky, after the rising of the moon. The heavens are studded with stars, shining like immense diamonds through the translucent winter air. The sky is a very

UNION AVENUE, MONTREAL.

canopy of beauty, while the moon sheds over the snowy scene her silvery beams, making almost a day-like brightness.

Rather because than in despite of the snow and cold, the Canadian winter is really a very enjoyable season. It is in every way preferable to such mongrel weather as afflicts more southern latitudes, where a little snow, March winds, and just enough ice to tantalize a lover of skating, make up a species of weather which is an uncomfortable compromise.

In and around Montreal, the weather is settled. It is cold, but one gets used to that and even enjoys it; there is plenty of snow, which is the delight of every healthy child's heart, while the ice comes the first of December, and there are three straight months of skating.

The Canadian people, with the exception of those of the Province of Quebec, where the population is mostly of French origin, are greatly devoted to field sports, to out-of-door exercises of all kinds. In the spring, summer, and autumn, rowing, fishing, lacrosse, baseball, football, cricket, hunting, etc., are engaged in to a very great extent. But when winter comes, the Canadian grows even more enthusiastic.

At the first fall of snow the fun begins; the boys and girls get out their coasters, and the hills are black with a merry crowd of rosy-cheeked children. Later on when the hills be in better condition, we see even the papas and mamas out, either on a single sled, or, as is more usual, upon a bob-sleigh, steered by a boy in front, and holding from eight to fourteen passengers. This is grand sport. At Sherbrooke, in the Province of Quebec, there is a succession of hills terminating with a lake. You go down one hill, then along a level stretch, then down another, and so on, until at last you shoot out upon the ice, and finally stop at least one mile and a half from your point of departure.

Skating vies with coasting, and is extremely popular. Our northern neighbors do not trust to the weather, as they know that snow will soon cover the ice. Every town has one or more covered rinks, which are kept in perfect condition, and where good ice is always to be found, and every kind of a skater is to be seen, from little girl to stately matron, and from boys to gray-haired men.

Although the rinks are very popular, every one prefers the open ice, if such is to be found. If it freezes and the snow keeps off, the ice will be covered with skaters, and the rinks almost deserted. When Toronto Bay freezes over, men will leave their business, and boys and girls their schools, to go skating on it before a snowstorm arises and spoils the surface.

The great popularity which skating enjoys has made Canada famous for both its speed and fancy skaters. Last year the speed championships of the world were held at Montreal, and the winner of the majority of events was a Canadian from Winnipeg, a Mr. McCullough.

Almost every rink has its hockey team. Hockey is, to describe it briefly, organized shinny. That is, there are off-side rules, penalties for fouls, etc., just as in football. The game is very popular in Canada, and in the championship contests a degree of expertness and skill has been reached that is simply marvelous. As in all other Canadian sports, there is a governing body. The country is divided into districts, regular championship matches are held, and at the end of the season, after the meeting of the district champions, the champion team of the country is known and recognized. This game is, of course, played by the young men.

Another game, in which older men are principally interested, is curling; and owing undoubtedly to the long season and the widespread popularity of the sport, a great deal of skill has been reached, as our American teams (for this game is played in Northern New York, and in Dakota, Illinois, Wisconsin, and Minnesota) have almost invariably been compelled to admit.

Just as the Canadian national game, lacrosse, has been inherited from the aboriginal inhabitants of Canada, so tobogganing, at one time the national winter pastime, is also an old Indian sport. When the early inhabitants of Canada passed their first winter on this side of the Atlantic, they were doubtless surprised at seeing the little pappooses merrily sliding down the hill-sides on flat pieces of wood strapped together and turned over in front. The more sober Indians used these toboggans, as they called them, to drag their game over the deep winter snow. Doubtless the Canadians, seeing the sport to be gotten out of the toboggan, adopted it and made it popular. The game is not in as much favor now as it was some years ago. Then every town had its toboggan-slide. The slide itself was generally built on the side of a hill, and varied in height from twenty to sixty feet, according to the incline of the hill before the structure. The paths were kept iced not only on the slides, but also along the hill, and great speed was the result. It is a grand and exciting pastime.

The Canadian is indebted to the Indian, too, for snow-shoeing. The shoes are made of thongs of rawhide netted to oval frames of tough, light wood. They are tied to the feet, and keep the wearer from sinking deeply in the snow. Snow-shoes, of course, in some parts of Canada are used by the people not as a luxury, but as a necessity. The hunter, especially, has need of them. In and around Montreal, however, the snow-shoes are used for pleasure, and a regular course over Mount Royal is made by these shoes every year. Snow-shoes are awkward things to manage at first, as the leg must be brought up perpendicularly and then thrown forward, one motion more than in a walk or run. In Montreal, the snow-shoers are very skillful, as is shown by the fact that in their annual races they have a hurdle (two feet, six inches) race as one of the events.

Ice-boating is popular all over Canada; wherever there are frozen lakes, rivers, or bays, these boats are to be seen. It is exciting sport, mainly because of the great speed that can be attained. At Brockville, on the St. Lawrence, a few years ago, a boat sailed a mile in a fraction under one minute. At Toronto and Montreal the sport is very much favored. Toronto Bay, when frozen over, is especially adapted to the sport. Under the leadership of Ned Hanlan, the famous oarsman, races are held every year, and fast and exciting contests take place.

The horsemen of the country take advantage of the level surface the ice presents, and the result is winter racing on the ice. The most important meets are held at Ottawa and Montreal. There, a half-mile track on the ice is laid out yearly, and fenced off, and a regular trotting and pacing meeting is held. All along the St. Lawrence River

spirited, the robes and blankets are numerous, every one is jolly; and with song and laughter, with banter and joke, with sly love-making and flirting, the time flies only too rapidly, and every one reluctantly leaves the sleigh when it draws up before the door on the return journey. Of course, a sleighing party would be a failure without at least one upset, and he is indeed an unskillful driver who cannot manage to land the crowd in some friendly snow-drift in an apparently accidental manner.

In Toronto and Montreal, where sleighing parties are frequent, long sleighs holding between thirty-five and fifty people, can be engaged. Two,

OVER THE MOUNT.

small meetings take place, in which local talent is mainly represented.

One other enjoyable feature of the Canadian winter is the sleighing parties. These correspond to the straw-rides given in Pennsylvania, New Jersey, and New York in the summer. Generally a party of young men and women drive out of town to some country friends'. Provisions are taken along, and the hosts are treated to a surprise-party.

The company make merry until the wee small hours and then depart for their homes, or the party merely goes for a long ride, but generally, in Canada, a stop is made somewhere for refreshments. The horses are always

three, and four teams, covered with bells, are driven, and with merry shouts, the tooting of horns, the blowing of bugles, etc., a very enjoyable outing is taken. These are more ambitious parties than the ordinary trips. To me, the good old-fashioned bob-sleigh and surprise-party, with their unaffected simplicity, are the more enjoyable.

In these ways the Canadians have been able to make of the cold and snow a source of genuine enjoyment and pleasure. In Canada, winter is not held in dread, but by many is looked forward to with keen anticipation. Instead of being a source of colds and disease, it is really the feature which gives to the average Canadian that bright eye and clear complexion, that general appearance of robust hardihood which is so envied by many of his southern brothers, and which is only to be obtained by an outdoor life in a bracing climate.

There is one especial feature of the Canadian winter, which has grown up around these winter sports, viz., the "Carnival." This is held alternately at Montreal, Quebec, and Ottawa. Montreal was the originator of the "Carnival," and to her are mainly due the magnificence and beauty to which this fête has attained. When reading Jas. Russell Lowell's "The Vision of Sir Launfal," lately, I came upon a note which stated that "the Empress of Russia, Catherine II., in a magnificent freak, built a palace of ice, which was a nine days' wonder." The editor need not have gone so far afield for his illustration, as this nine days' wonder is a yearly occurrence at the Canadian Carnival. In fact, the ice palace, a symmetrical and beautiful edifice of crystal, becomes the center of the whole week's festivities. In the daytime it is a glittering and dazzling sight, while at night, when lighted up by electric lights, and by innumerable Chinese lanterns, it becomes a very blaze of glory, and a scene which, in its elfin beauty, baffles description. The fairy-like scene is rendered almost realistic on masquerade night, when fairies, hobgoblins, kings and queens, courtiers and ladies-in-waiting, and countless other characters glide over the glittering surface and pass before our eyes as a disordered but dazzling dream.

Besides the masquerade, there are hockey matches between the champion teams of the country, racing on skates, figure-skating competitions, snowshoe races, curling, and, in fact, every Canadian winter sport. The Carnival generally ends in a blaze of glory by the storming of the palace. This is a scene which is unrivaled in effect. Hundreds of Canadians, dressed in the picturesque toboggan suits, march, with torch in hand, to the storming of the fortress. Others upon the walls repel the attack. The weapons are fireworks. The cracking of these,

MONTREAL TOBOGGAN SLIDE.

their brilliant hues thrown off and reflected in myriad beams by the shining palace, the torches and the Chinese lanterns all go to make up a scene which, through its intrinsic beauty and excitement, forces an involuntary shout from the interested multitude.

Throughout all these amusements the same spirit of sport prevails. The Canadian loves sport for its own sake, and reaps unquestioned benefits from his wintry gambols.

15

With the Canadian Northwest Mounted Police

H. CHRISTIE THOMPSON

With the Canadian Northwest Mounted Police.

BY H. CHRISTIE THOMPSON.

THE mounted police of the Canadian Northwest have, by the trend of circumstances in the farthest extremity of their Alaskan border, become an object of considerable interest across the line.

Eternal vigilance is the price of the control which these silent patrols up to the eternal snows have gained over the natives, and neither the service which individuals will be called upon to perform, nor its extent, can be foretold from hour to hour. The bureau of information moves its atoms, and " Theirs not to make reply ; theirs but to do and [if need be] die."

I recall an instance that will serve, perhaps, as a timely example of this.

I was crossing the barrack square at Battleford, late in the fall, when an order was put into my hand which read as follows : "Inspector M—— and Sergeant L——, with horses, regimental numbers 1242 and 1673, will leave to-morrow morning at 9 A. M. for Pelican Lake, on special duty. They will be accompanied by Constable T——, with horses, regimental numbers 1485 and 1640, and light patrol wagon number 2. Guide and interpreter S—— will go as teamster's off-man. They will take ten days' rations for four men, and ten days' forage for four horses."

The object of our trip was to discover the truthfulness of certain reports concerning the restlessness of the Indians, at Pelican Lake, under a chief called Yellow Sky. They were said to be in an extremely restless and dissatisfied state of mind.

The morning was a busy one for me.

Rising from my cot at the first strains of reveille, I was soon dressed, and at once began making up my roll of bedding. I had been long enough in the country to realize the necessity of sleeping warmly, so three pairs of heavy blankets, a rabbit-skin robe and an oil sheet, with a big, fat, soft feather pillow, a pair of socks, moccasins, towel, soap and toothbrush were placed in the blankets, which were rolled tightly in the oil sheet, and securely strapped.

My next care was for my wagon. I carefully oiled that and saw that oil, wrench, spare bolts, straps, etc., were stowed away in the jockey box, that the tires and wheels were tight and everything in good running order.

Then the bugler sounded " Stables," after which I harnessed my horses and went to the mess-room for breakfast. After that meal, my off-man appeared on the scene, and together we hitched up the team, and carefully overhauled the harness. Then we started around the barracks to collect our load, first visiting the quartermaster's store, where we loaded the large bell tent, with its complement of poles and pins, and obtained cooking kit, pots, pans and kettles, axes, spades, etc., together with the rations and oats. The former consisted of soft bread and hard-tack, pork, potatoes, butter, tea, sugar, salt, matches and candles. The bread and potatoes were packed in gunny-sacks, the remaining rations in the mess-box with our tableware.

We next drove to the sergeant-major's, where we obtained horse-blankets, nose bags, picket-ropes, hobbles, and other articles needed for prairie traveling, not forgetting robes and fur coats for ourselves. Then to the veterinary store for the horse medicines that we never travel without; and putting our bedding on the top of all, our load was complete. Securely lashing it on with a picket-rope, we drove on to the square at 5 minutes to 9 to await the customary inspection before starting. We were here joined by Mr. M—— and the sergeant (mounted, of course), and in a few moments the commanding officer examined the outfit critically, looked the horses over and felt a doubtful fetlock, and finally gave the command: "Transport-right take ground-march!" and we were off. Each of us, as a matter of course, carried his revolver and ammunition; in addition to which I had my Winchester, while the inspector and sergeant each had a shotgun.

A few minutes' drive brought us to the town of Battleford, and we pulled up for a moment at the Hudson Bay Co.'s store to purchase a little *médécine*. We already had colic mixture for our horses and we now laid in a *liti'le colic* mixture for ourselves. It is always well to be prepared for emergencies. A short drive brought us to the bank of the Saskatchewan (great river of the north), which is here crossed by a steam ferry. The boat was on the other side as usual. The crossing took about half an hour, but, finally, we bowled away merrily for our prospective noon camp at Round Hill, eighteen miles away. A fresh team, a good trail, and a perfect day—no wonder we were in the best of spirits.

As we proceeded, the country unrolled itself before us in a constant but varying succession of river, lake, prairie, and woodland. At our feet, between its high wooded banks, flowed the mighty Saskatchewan, stretching away in many varied curves, like a long thread of silver, to the distant northern horizon. Off to the south and west the Eagle Hills reared their blue summits against a bluer sky, while the prairie itself, dotted with its bluffs of poplar and cottonwood, extended before us like a vast park.

The general rate of travel is about six miles per hour. This may not seem very much, but an average of sixty miles a day, up hill and down, across swamps and creeks and rivers, over good trails and bad (or no trail at all), is very good traveling, indeed. The only method of measuring a distance is by the time occupied in traveling it, and a man soon gets to know the exact speed of his team, and can judge distances most accurately. I have heard two old hands coming in off a trip argue whether they had traveled forty-seven or forty-eight miles, and finally agree on a little over forty-seven, so exact does long practice make them.

About two and a half hours after leaving the ferry we came in sight of Round Hill. As its name implies, it is of a rounded outline, and, rising high above the surrounding country, serves as a valuable landmark. It rises a sheer six hundred feet out of the waters of a pretty little lake of the same name, a regular oval in shape, and about a mile long. Here and there upon the shore are Indian tepees, and very picturesque they look nestling down among the trees, the blue smoke curling lazily upward, and the brightly clad natives passing to and fro. The numerous dogs and ponies, without which no Indian encampment is complete, add life and motion to the scene.

A detachment of our men is stationed here during the summer and autumn as a fire patrol, and we could see their white tents upon the farther shore. Skirting the lake we soon pulled into their camp and turned out for dinner. It would surprise the average Eastern camper-out to witness the speed with which an experienced prairie hand will prepare a meal. A very few minutes generally suffice, if wood and water are convenient, though generally our food is of the simplest description. To-day we are going to fare sumptuously.

Dinner disposed of, after a short rest and smoke, we hitched up and pulled out for Jackfish Creek, twenty-two miles away, where we intended camping for the night. Instead of going by the regular freighters' trail, we took a short cut across country. The boys at the detachment told us we would strike a pretty bad hill to go down. We struck it! Where we first approached it, it is a sheer cut-bank, steep as the side of a house, but a little reconnoitering discovered an easier descent—easier by comparison. But we had to descend diagonally, at great risk of upsetting, and to make things worse, there was a wide, boggy creek at the bottom, crossed by a narrow rickety bridge—merely a few poles laid in the bed of the creek. The guide got out and took hold of the wagon behind to steady it, while I got a good grip of the reins, a good foothold on the brake, and started the team. They went down in a succession of bounds and plunges, gaining momentum at every jump. The first jump jarred my foot off the brake, and I was too busy keeping on my seat to recover it, so by the time we reached the bottom we were traveling like a steam engine. Bump—bump — bang — bump — plunk. We missed the bridge, for I had turned straight down the hill to avoid upsetting, and the "plunk" landed us in the soft bed of the creek, with only the backs of the horses showing, and the wagon buried to the hubs. With considerable labor and difficulty, we pried the horses out, and proceeded to extricate the wagon. We hitched the horses to the rear axle by a picket-rope, but they could not budge it, so the riders had to give us a pull, and by their aid we "yanked her out." We crossed the bridge safely, and after a little "scratching" surmounted the opposite hill and were again on the level prairie.

We saw a great many chickens that afternoon, and Mr. M—— shot several brace without going a dozen yards from the wagon, and as we neared the creek we secured some ducks. We were crossing a narrow neck of land between two little lakes, and the birds flying to and fro above our heads. The sergeant dropped behind, and lying on his back in the long slough grass, got a good many shots and soon rejoined us with several ducks. We reached the creek about five o'clock, just in nice time to get our camp fixed up before dark. An hour or so later we were lying before the fire, blissfully inhaling the fragrant weed, and feeling at peace with all the world. As we lie there, under the deep, dark-blue canopy of the northern night, and musingly watch the sparks flying upward into the darkness, the voices of the wilderness come softly and whisper in our ears. The night wind soughing through the prairie grasses, the whirring wings of a passing bird, the plaintive cry of a plover, or the long-drawn quavering howl of a distant wolf, all have a message to convey.

We silently roll our blankets around us and sink to sleep, thinking how much better we are going to live to-morrow than we did to-day. But we wake up cold, sleepy, and cross. Strange how cross and disagreeable most people *are* before breakfast.

A cold bath and a hot meal restore our spirits to their usual tone, and we briskly set about preparation for breaking camp. Constant practice makes this but a few minutes' work, and we were soon on the trail again. We are always particularly solicitous to see that our fire is thoroughly extinguished. Too many prairie fires are caused by the gross carelessness of individuals in leaving their camp fires burning when breaking camp. A puff of wind comes, a spark is blown into a tuft of dry grass, and the result is a prairie fire sweeping over miles and miles of country, and perhaps destroying a dozen settlers' homes. One such fire near Battleford burned from early May until the snow flew in October.

This morning the two mounted men were riding ahead, and as they surmounted a little ridge in front, Mr. M—— threw up his hands as a signal for me to stop. Riding back he told me there was a flock of geese just to the left of the trail, where there is a little lake. Giving the reins to the guide, and getting out my rifle, I proceeded to reconnoiter. On topping the little rise, I found they were about four hundred yards away, with no shelter to stalk them from, save a small bunch of cattle. Carefully getting a cow in a line with the birds, I commenced crawling forward on my hands and knees, hoping if they noticed me at all they would think I was a calf. I might, perhaps, fool the geese, though they are about as cute as any birds that fly, but I could not fool the cow. As I crept nearer she took one startled look at me, bellowed for her calf, and then came for me with head down and horns well to the front. At the first bellow, off went the geese.

We were still traveling through a fairly well-settled country—that is to say, there was a settler's "shack" every ten miles or so, and we stopped at one for dinner. Early in the afternoon, however, we left the last of these behind and passed beyond the limits of civilization. At last we were in "the great lone land," our faces set toward the north, and nothing between us and the pole save a vast tract of primeval wilderness. For hundreds—yes, thousands of miles—there are no inhabitants save the red men, and a mere handful of white trappers and traders.

Our trail had been growing more and more indistinct, until at the last house it finally vanished. We struck across country for an Indian trail that leads from the reservations northward to Turtle Lake, where the "nitchies" (Indians) go every summer to fish. As soon as we got off the trail the horses seemed to get discouraged. This is always the case. No matter how dim the trail may be, a horse will jog along contentedly, for he seems to realize that it must lead somewhere, and to that "somewhere" he is willing to go. But when he gets off a trail altogether, he seems to think that he is not going to any place in particular, and might just as well stop where he is, consequently needing continual urging.

About four o'clock in the afternoon we struck the trail, which turned out to be a mere cart track. As the prairie is open it makes pretty fair traveling, and our horses jogged along merrily. We were now gradually approaching the great timber belt, and for the last few miles had been passing here and there stunted pines and spruce. These gradually attained a more stalwart growth, and toward evening we pulled up in a beautiful grove of pines on the shore of a little lake, and encamped for the night.

We were afoot with the first streaks of dawn, for we had a drive of sixty-five miles to make before night, and we wished to give our horses a good rest at noon. An hour later we were in motion, heading for Turtle Lake, thirty-five miles away, where we intended to camp for dinner. Hitherto all the game shot on the trip had fallen to the guns of the inspector and sergeant, but this morning I got two trophies. A couple of hundred yards ahead of us, just to the right of the trail, a badger was sitting at the mouth of his hole. Now, I very much desired that animal's skin to make a pair of winter mitts. As we approached him he, of course, dived into his hole. Giving the reins to the guide, I got my rifle out, and, without stopping the wagon, dropped quietly to the ground about fifty yards from the hole and waited. As I expected, when the wagon had got past him, the badger popped up his head to have another look. A forty-five caliber bullet through the head procured for me my winter mitts. Tying him underneath the wagon, we had not gone many miles before we saw a skunk crossing the trail ahead of us. A skunk skin is worth a pair of moccasins in trade, so off I got in pursuit. A skunk is never in a hurry, not being built for speed, and will often wait for one most obligingly. This gentleman not only waited for me, but, seeing that I wished to speak to him, most politely came toward me. Letting him get within about thirty yards (for I wanted to be sure of hitting him in the head), I pressed the trigger, and he rolled over with a bullet between the eyes. Picking him up gingerly by the tail, I secured him under the wagon with the badger, and we proceeded on our way. He was with us all day. We had skunk for dinner, and skunk for supper, and would undoubtedly have had him for a bedfellow, if the sergeant (in a thoughtless moment) had not hurled the carcass into the lake.

During the latter part of the morning we were riding through a thick bush, and only left it as, without any previous warning, we suddenly emerged upon the shore of Turtle Lake. The scene is one of the most beautiful it has ever been my good fortune to gaze upon. The lake, of the most intense and vivid blue, stretches away for twenty-five miles. We could just make out a high range of hills upon the farther shore. A brisk, northerly wind blew, cresting the big blue waves with foam and sending the heavy billows tumbling in at our feet. We stood on a beautiful, clear, sandy beach that would make the fortune of a summer hotel, and just behind us was the dark fringe of primeval forest. A fleet of birch canoes was hauled up on the beach, and just within the edge of the timber were scattered the tepees. The white canvas merging into smoke-dried brown, the dark green of the pines and spruces, the snowy whites and yellows of the birches, the waving tassels of the tamarack, the blue lake, the scurrying clouds, the dusky natives—all form a picture that requires the brush of an artist to do it justice.

We obtained a few fine whitefish from the natives in exchange for a little bacon, a welcome addition to our meal. We rested our horses for an hour or two before starting for Birch Lake (our prospective camp), and this interval we spent in studying the aborigines. A few of the children had never seen a white man before, and they peeped out from behind their mothers' blankets at the shemanginis (soldiers) in awe.

We were still sixty miles—two days' travel—from our destination, and had the hardest part of our journey ahead of us. From the camp to Pelican Lake there is no trail other than a mere track made by the occasional passage of an Indian cart, and only one camping place —forty miles from our present camp. Both days' journey would have to be made in single drives, as there is no water for a noon camp, and in the last twenty miles we should have to cross a small range of hills.

We got an early start the following morning, and after some little difficulty found the trail and were again in motion for the north. We reeled off the forty miles in a little over eight hours, and reached our camping ground in the middle of the afternoon. Hitherto we had enjoyed the best of weather, but all this day it had been getting colder and colder, with a promise of snow from the northward, and one by one we donned our fur coats. As we were pitching our tent the first few white flakes fell, and inside of an hour came down thick and fast, accompanied by a furious gale from the northwest.

We were fortunately in a very well-sheltered situation; had we been on open ground, our tent would not have stood a moment against the gale. Each of our camps seemed more beautiful than the last, and this was no exception. We were in a deep hollow on the shore of a small lake, a perfect circle in shape, and surrounded by a larger but no less perfect circle of pine-clad hills. It was exactly like a large amphitheatre. The lake seemed so utterly lonely nestling down among the hills as though to escape observation it seemed such a long way off to civilization, we could almost imagine ours to be the first footprints to mark the shores. The wildness of the tempest added to its apparent loneliness and isolation.

In contrast with the turmoil of the storm, our camp seemed positively comfortable. Nestling cozily down in a grove of firs, with a bright fire in front, on which the frying pans were frizzling merrily and the coffee pot sending up its fragrant steam, it seemed to us—cold, tired and hungry—the very *beau ideal* of contentment.

In the morning the sun shone. Under his genial rays the six inches or so of snow that had fallen during the night rapidly disappeared, in spite of the fact that a pretty cold, raw northwind blew. Everything around was cold and wet and sloppy, and our hands and feet soaking wet in spite of boots and gauntlets. As was to be expected, we had trouble with the horses. They were colder and wetter and crosser than we were. It took the two of us all our time to harness the team, but they were finally hitched up and the guide held them by the heads, while I climbed to my seat and gathered up the reins.

"Let 'em go!" He sprang aside and we were off with a plunge and a jump. As the wagon flew past, the guide grabbed the tailboard and scrambled in behind. In a mile or so the horses quieted down pretty well, and consented to walk and wait for the riders. In a little while they joined us, and I noticed that the sergeant was quite wet down one side of his body, and I asked him if he was thrown.

"Yes," he replied. "The brute reared, and came over backward with me, nearly knocking my brains out against a tree."

We were wet enough in all conscience at starting, but a short time afterward could only be compared to drowned rats. The trail now wended through thick woods, and the trees grew so close together that we were brushing them on either hand. Underbrush growing ten or twelve feet high stood in the very center of the trail, and sitting on our high seat we were being continually swept by overhanging branches. In view of the fact that each branch and leaf and twig carried its burden of wet snow, it will be easy to realize our drenched condition. And a cold north-wind blowing! Every now and then the front wheels would catch in a sapling, which, being released, sprang back with a swish and caught us a stinging blow across the face. One such blow, from a sharp icy twig, cut my ear open badly, while the guide's face was a mass of welts. The two riders fared better, as they proceeded in single file in the center of the trail.

As we rounded a little bend, we found they had halted on the edge of a very nasty hill, and Mr. M—— asked me if I thought I could get down without unloading the wagon. I had not the slightest doubt about getting down, though I had grave doubts about reaching the bottom right-side up. However, as I had no desire to lug sacks of oats, etc., down and up a steep hill, I replied, with the utmost confidence, that I could. Locking the two hind wheels, the sergeant and guide prepared to steady the load, and down we went. All morning I had been blessing the high, narrow springy seat, and now I had additional cause. Half-way down the hill, the front wheel struck one of the bowlders, and I was shot off the seat on to my head like a catapult. Fortunately, I lighted in a low bush, which broke my fall and as I had still firm hold of the reins, we reached the bottom safely.

We had to call on the riders for aid to surmount the opposite hill. Taking two picket ropes, we fastened one end of each securely to the tongue, and they the other ends to their saddles. With this novel four-in-hand we easily surmounted the slope. The trail got worse and worse as we ascended the mountain, until the horses could hardly proceed faster than a walk. The deep cart ruts were too narrow for them to travel in, but wide enough to have one or another foot continually slipping in, which is very tiring on poor brutes. Traveling so very slowly seemed to make the distance longer than it really was, but at last we emerged from the wood on to a stretch of comparatively open prairie. The guide pointed to a range of hills some five or six miles ahead, told us that Pelican Lake lay just at their foot. We had been nearly seven hours doing the odd fifteen miles over the mountain, but now rattled along at a good pace and pulled into the Indian village, cold, wet, tired and ravenous. Our hunger satisfied, our clothes dried, and our bodies warmed, we sallied forth to pay our respects to old Yellow Sky. The village comprises over fifty lodges, mostly laid out in two straight rows on either side of a wide lane. We strolled down this avenue, and were apparently great objects of curiosity, for every doorway was full of dark faces peering out at the shemanginis. The dogs were also greatly interested, and gathered around in their anxiety to find out who we were, and what we wanted in their camp. Having had some previous experience of Indian dogs, we had thoughtfully provided ourselves with clubs, and the animals kept at a respectful distance. Entering the low doorway of the chief's lodge, we received a very friendly greeting: "Haw! Haw! men kirsecaw" (How do you do? Good day, good day), and a long pow-wow ensued. Mr. M—— tells the chief that the oky maw (head man) at Battleford has heard that he (Yellow Sky) is not very friendly to his brothers the whites. This the chief indignantly denied, and declared that the white man never had a better friend than himself. In the end he succeeded in convincing Mr. M—— of his friendliness and honesty, and we were soon on the best of terms.

Two pleasant days were spent in prospecting, hunting and fishing with the natives, and on the third day we pulled out for home. Many were the handshakings, many were the men kirsecaws spoken, and many were the invitations given to come and see them again, as with our wagon, laden with presents of fish and game, we reluctantly turned our backs upon our dusky friends. The trip homeward was but a repetition of the first part of our journey. We encountered no bad weather, and met with no incidents other than the everyday events of travel. We saw some moose and jumping deer, but had not time to stop and hunt. On the evening of the eleventh day we entered the barrack gate, and our trip was over.

It may seem a great deal of trouble to have taken about so small a matter, but a stitch in time saves nine in more things than darning socks.

16

Wild Motherhood

CHARLES G.D. ROBERTS

"I'LL SAVE HIM FOR THE BOY TO PLAY WITH."

OUTING

FEBRUARY, 1901

WILD MOTHERHOOD

By Charles G. D. Roberts

THE deep snow in the moose-yard was trodden down to the moss, and darkly soiled with many days of occupancy. The young spruce and birch trees which dotted the trodden space were cropped of all but their toughest and coarsest branches; and the wall of loftier growth which fenced the yard was stripped of its tenderer twigs to the utmost height of the tall bull's neck. The available provender was all but gone, and the herd was in that restlessness which precedes a move to new pastures.

The herd of moose was a small one—three gaunt, rusty-brown, slouching cows, two ungainly calves of a lighter hue, and one huge, high-shouldered bull, whose sweep of palmated antlers bristled like a forest. Compared with the towering bulk of his forequarters, the massive depth of his rough-maned neck, the weight of the formidable antlers, the length and thickness of his clumsy, hooked muzzle with its prehensile upper lip—his lean and frayed hindquarters looked grotesquely diminutive. Surprised by three days of blinding snowfall, the great bull-moose had been forced to establish the yard for his herd in an unfavorable neighborhood; and now he found himself confronted by the necessity of a long march through snow of such softness and depth as would make swift movement impossible and fetter him in the face of his enemies. In deep snow the moose can neither flee nor fight, at both of which he is adept under fair conditions; and deep snow, as he knew, is the opportunity of the wolf and the hunter. But in this case the herd had no choice. It was simply take the risk or starve.

That same night, when the moon was rising round and white behind the fir-tops, the tall bull breasted and trod down the snowy barrier, and led his herd off northward between the hemlock trunks and the jutting granite boulders. He moved slowly, his immense muzzle stretched straight out before him, the bony array of his antlers laid back level to avoid the hindrance of clinging boughs. Here and there a hollow under the level surface would set him plunging and wallowing for a moment, but in the main his giant strength enabled him to forge his way ahead with a steady majesty of might. Behind him, in dutiful line, came the three cows; and behind these, again, the calves followed at ease in a clear trail, their muzzles not outstretched like that of the leader, but drooping almost to the snow, their high shoulders working awkwardly at every stride. In utter silence, like dark, monstrous spectres, the line of strange shapes moved on; and down the bewildering, ever-rearranging forest corridors the ominous fingers of long moonlight felt curiously after them. When they had journeyed for some hours the herd came out upon a high and somewhat bare plateau, dotted sparsely with clumps of aspen, stunted yellow birch, and spruce. From this table-land the streaming northwest winds had swept the snow almost clean, carrying it off to fill the neighboring valleys. The big bull, who knew where he was going and had no will to linger on the way, halted only for a few minutes' browsing, and then started forward on a long, swinging trot. At every stride his loose-hung, wide-cleft, spreading hooves came sharply together with a flat, clacking noise. The rest of the line swept dutifully into place, and the herd was off.

But not all the herd. One of the calves, tempted a little aside by a thicket of special juiciness and savor, took alarm, and thought he was going to be left behind. He sprang forward, a powerful but clumsy stride, careless of his footing. A treacherous screen of snow-crusted scrub gave way, and he slid sprawling to the bottom of a little narrow falling back with a hoarse bleat from each frightened effort; while the mother, with head down and piteous eyes staring upon him, ran round and round the rim of the trap. At last, when he stopped and stood with palpitating sides and wide nostrils of terror, she, too, halted. Dropping awkwardly upon her knees in the snowy bushes, with loud, blowing breaths, she reached down her head to nose and comfort him with her sensitive muzzle. The calf leaned up as close as possible to her caresses. Under their tenderness the tremblings of his gaunt, pathetic knees presently ceased.

"THAT SAME NIGHT WHEN THE MOON WAS RISING ROUND AND WHITE."

gully or crevice, a natural pitfall. His mother, looking solicitously backward, saw him disappear. With a heave of her shoulders, a sweep of her long, hornless head, an anxious flick of her little naked tail, she swung out of the line and trotted swiftly to the rescue.

There was nothing she could do. The crevice was some ten or twelve feet long and five or six in width, with sides almost perpendicular. The calf could just reach its bushy edges with his up-stretched muzzle, but he could get no foothold by which to clamber out. On every side he essayed it, And in this position the two remained almost motionless for an hour, under the white, unfriendly moon. The herd had gone on without them.

II

In the wolf's cave in the great blue-and-white wall of plaster-rock, miles back beside the rushing of the river, there was famine. The she-wolf, heavy and near her time, lay agonizing in the darkest corner of the cave, licking in grim silence the raw stump of her right foreleg. Caught in a steel trap, she had gnawed off her own paw as the price of freedom. She could not hunt; and the hunting was bad that winter in the forests by the blue-and-white wall. The wapiti deer had migrated to safer ranges, and her gray mate, hunting alone, was hard put to it to keep starvation from the cave.

The gray wolf trotted briskly down the broken face of the plaster-rock, in the full glare of the moon, and stood for a moment to sniff the air that came blowing lightly but keenly over the stiff tops of the forest. The wind was clean. It gave him no tidings of a quarry. Descending hurriedly the last fifty yards of the slope, he plunged into the darkness of the fir-woods. Soft as was the snow in those quiet recesses, it was yet sufficiently packed to support him as he trotted, noiseless and alert, on the broad-spreading pads of his paws. Furtive and fierce, he slipped through the shadow like a ghost. Across the open glades he fleeted more swiftly, a bright and sinister shape, his head swinging a little from side to side, every sense upon the watch. His direction was pretty steadily to the west of north.

He had traveled long, till the direction of the moon-shadows had taken a different angle to his path, when suddenly there came a scent upon the wind. He stopped, one foot up, arrested in his stride. The gray, cloudy brush of his tail stiffened out. His nostrils, held high to catch every waft of the new scent, dilated; and the edges of his upper lip came down over the white fangs, from which they had been snarlingly withdrawn. His pause was but for a breath or two. Yes, there was no mistaking it. The scent was moose—very far off, but moose, without question. He darted forward at a gallop, but with his muzzle still held high, following that scent up the wind.

Presently he struck the trail of the herd. An instant's scrutiny told his trained sense that there were calves and young cows, one or another of which he might hope to stampede by his cunning. The same instant's scrutiny revealed to him that the herd had passed nearly an hour ahead of him. Up went the gray cloud of his tail and down went his nose; and then he straightened himself to his top speed, compared to which the pace wherewith he had followed the scent up the wind was a mere casual sauntering.

When he emerged upon the open plateau and reached the spot where the herd had scattered to browse, he slackened his pace and went warily, peering from side to side. The cow-moose, lying down in the bushes to fondle her imprisoned young, was hidden from his sight for the moment; and so it chanced that before he discovered her he came between her and the wind. That scent—it was the taint of death to her. It went through her frame like an electric shock. With a snort of fear and fury she heaved to her feet and stood, wide-eyed and with lowered brow, facing the menace.

The wolf heard that snorting challenge, and saw the awkward bulk of her shoulders as she rose above the scrub. His jaws wrinkled back tightly, baring the full length of his keen white fangs, and a greenish phosphorescent film seemed to pass suddenly across his narrowed eyeballs. But he did not spring at once to the attack. He was surprised. Moreover, he inferred the calf, from the presence of the cow apart from the rest of the herd. And a full-grown cow-moose, with the mother fury in her heart, he knew to be a dangerous adversary. Though she was hornless, he knew the force of her battering front, the swift, sharp stroke of her hoof, the dauntless intrepidity of her courage. Further, though his own courage and the avid urge of his hunger might have led him under other circumstances to attack forthwith, to-night he knew that he must take no chances. The cave in the blue-and-white rocks was depending on his success. His mate, wounded and heavy with young—if he let himself get disabled in this hunting she must perish miserably. With prudent tactics, therefore, he circled at a safe distance around the hidden pit; and around its rim circled the wary mother, presenting to him ceaselessly the defiance of her huge and sullen front. By this means he easily concluded that the calf was a prisoner in the pit. This being the case, he knew that with patience and his experienced craft the game was safely his. He drew off some half-dozen paces, and sat upon his haunches contemplatively to weigh the situation. Everything had turned out most fortunately for his hunting, and food would no longer be scarce in the cave of the painted rocks.

III

THAT same night, in a cabin of unutterable loneliness some miles to the west of the trail from the moose-yard, a sallow-faced, lean backwoodsman was awakened by the moonlight streaming into his face through the small square window. He glanced at the embers on the open hearth, and knew that for the white maple logs to have so burned down he must have been sleeping a good six hours. And he had turned in soon after the early winter sunset. Rising on his elbow, he threw down the gaudy patchwork quilt of red, yellow, blue and mottled squares which draped the bunk in its corner against the rough log walls. He looked long at the thin face of his wife, whose pale brown hair lay over the bare arm crooked beneath her cheek. Her lips looked pathetically white in the decolorizing rays which streamed through the window. His mouth, stubbled with a week's growth of dark beard, twitched curiously as he looked. Then he got up, very noiselessly. Stepping across the bare, hard room, whose austerity the moon made more austere, he gazed into a trundle-bed where a yellow-haired, round-faced boy slept, with the chubby sprawling legs and arms of perfect security. The lad's face looked pale to his troubled eyes.

"It's fresh meat they want, the both of 'em," he muttered to himself. "They can't live and thrive on pork an' molasses, no-how!"

His big fingers, clumsily gentle, played for a moment with the child's yellow curls. Then he pulled a thick, gray homespun hunting-shirt over his head, hitched his heavy trousers up under his belt, clothed his feet in three pairs of home-knit socks and heavy cowhide moccasins, took down his rifle, cartridge pouch, and snowshoes from their nails on the moss-chinked wall, cast one tender look on the sleepers' faces, and slipped out of the cabin door as silently as a shadow.

"I'll have fresh meat for them before next sundown," he vowed to himself.

Outside, amid the chips of his chopping, with a rough well-sweep on one hand and a rougher barn on the other, he knelt to put on his snowshoes. The cabin stood, a desolate, silver-gray dot in the waste of snow, naked to the steely skies of winter. With the curious improvidence of the backwoodsman, he had cut down every tree in the neighborhood of the cabin, and the thick woods which might so well have sheltered him, stood acres distant on every side. When the woodsman had settled the thongs of his snowshoes over his moccasins quite to his satisfaction, he straightened himself with a deep breath, pulled his cap well down over his ears, slung his rifle over his shoulder, and started out with the white moon in his face.

In the ancient forest, among the silent wilderness folk, things happen with the slow inexorableness of time. For days, for weeks, nothing may befall. Hour may tread noiselessly on hour, apparently working no change; yet all the time the forces are assembling, and at last doom strikes. The violence is swift, and soon done. And then the great, still world looks inscrutable, unhurried, changeless as before.

So, after long tranquillity, the forces of fate were assembling about that high plateau in the wilderness. The backwoodsman could no longer endure to see the woman and boy pining for the tonic, vitalizing juices of fresh meat. He was not a professional hunter. Absorbed in the clearing and securing of a farm in the free forest, he cared not to kill for the killing's sake. For his own part, he was well content with his salt pork, beans and molasses, and corn-meal mush; but when occasion called, he could handle a rifle as backwoodsmen should. On this night he was all hunter, and his quiet, wide-open eye, alert for every woodland sign, had a fire in it that would have looked strange to the wife and child.

His long strides carried him swiftly through the glimmering glades. Journeying to the north of east, as the gray wolf had to the north of west, he too, before long, struck the trail of the moose, but at a point far beyond that at which the wolf had come upon it. So trampled and confused a trail it was, however, that for a time he took no note of the light wolf track among the heavy footprints of the moose. Suddenly it caught his eye—one print on a smooth spread of snow, emphasized in a pour of unobstructed radiance. He stopped, scrutinized the trail minutely to assure himself he had but a single wolf to deal with, then resumed his march with new zest and springier pace. Hunting was not without its relish for him when it admitted some savor of the combat.

"AT THE REPORT THE WOLF SHOT INTO THE AIR."

The cabin stood in the valley lands just back of the high plateau, and so it chanced that the backwoodsman had not far to travel that night. Where the trail broke into the open he stopped, and reconnoitered cautiously through a screen of hemlock boughs. He saw the big gray wolf sitting straight up on his haunches, his tongue hanging out, contemplating securely his intended prey. He saw the dark shape of the cow-moose, obstinately confronting her foe, her hindquarters backed close up to the edge of the gully. He caught the fierce and anxious gleam of her eyes, as she rolled them backward for an instant's reassuring glance at her young one. And though he could not see the calf in its prisoning pit, he understood the whole situation.

Well, there was a bounty on wolf-snouts, and this fellow's pelt was worth considering. As for the moose, he knew that not a broadside of cannon would scare her away from that hole in the rocks so long as the calf was in it. He took careful aim from his covert. At the report the wolf shot into the air, straightened out, and fell upon the snow kicking dumbly, a bullet through his neck. As the light faded from his fierce eyes, with it faded out a vision of the cave in the painted rocks. In half a minute he lay still; and the cow-moose, startled by his convulsive leaps more than by the rifle-shot, blew and snorted, eyeing him with new suspicion. Her spacious flank was toward the hunter. He, with cool but hasty fingers, slipped a fresh cartridge into the breech, and aimed with care at a spot low down behind the fore-shoulder.

Again rang out the thin, vicious report, slapping the great silences in the face. The woodsman's aim was true. With a cough the moose fell forward on her knees. Then, with a mighty, shuddering effort, she got up, turned about, and fell again with her head over the edge of the crevice. Her awkward muzzle touched and twitched against the neck of the frightened calf, and with a heavy sigh she lay still.

The settler stepped out from his hiding place, and examined with deep satisfaction the results of his night's hunting. Already he saw the color coming back into the pale cheeks of the woman and the child. The wolf's pelt and snout, too, he thought to himself, would get them both some little things they'd like, from the cross-roads store, next time he went in for corn-meal. Then, there was the calf—no meat like moose-veal, after all. He drew his knife from its sheath. But no; he hated butchering. He slipped the knife back, reloaded his rifle, stepped to the side of the pit, and stood looking down at the baby captive, where it leaned nosing in piteous bewilderment at the head of its dead mother.

Again the woodsman changed his mind. He bit off a chew of black tobacco, and for some moments stood deliberating, stubbly chin in hand. "I'll save him for the boy to play with and bring up," he at last decided.

17

The Silver Fox

LAWRENCE MOTT

THE SILVER FOX

BY LAWRENCE MOTT

WHEN the days were short and the forest bare of leaves; when autumnal colors had gone, leaving brown trunks and the dark green of pines and firs; when the caribou called hoarsely on the barren lands and the beaver worked to get in their winter supply, then Sebat gathered the few steel traps he had, packed some food, his blanket and two shirts around them, slung the whole on his axe-handle, tossed the bundle to his shoulder, picked up his carbine and started from Fort à la Corne for Lac le Rouge through the wilderness.

The day was dark and a raw wind muttered among the tall tops.

"Hm!" he snorted as he traveled rapidly on. "Dat facteur Daniele he tink he h'ave som'ting for not'ing. Ah goin' see dat Murchee-son h'at le Rouge, mabbe so he mor' honorable."

Around windfalls, down ravines, up the rough river beaches, over low mountain runs, past lakes and the dead water stretches of streams, he plodded on.

Always the wind mourned and the forest was deserted save for a hurrying rabbit now and then and sometimes a fleeting glimpse that he got of a caribou, its thudding feet rustling in the depths of frosted leaves. He camped that night near the Hudson Bay post at Green Lake, but he did not go in there because he knew that the factor was short of trappers and would try to make him stay.

"De troubl' weet dees Compagnie," he whispered as he boiled some tea by the little fire, "ees dat les facteurs dey fighten' too much wan noddaire for mak' beeges' lot monnaie; d'Indians no get 'nough for h'eat an' die. Sacrée," he spoke aloud in his vehemence, "dey no goin' starrve Sebat, dat sure!" and he ate his supper. Tiny snowflakes dropped into the firelight as he finished.

"Snow? she come earlee dees saison,"

and he laid on a few more boughs over his one-man lean-to. Soon he was asleep and the night passed on, cold and dismal. The snow ceased and the wind came stronger and stronger, shrilling in the hemlocks with long-drawn sounds. By the first signs of light Sebat had his fire going again, and when the frugal breakfast was over he shouldered his load and went on. Late in the afternoon of the next day he stopped suddenly, while passing through a musky swamp.

"Silvare fox?" and he got down on his knees by a log that had fallen outward from the timber. He searched the bark keenly.

"Ha!" He carefully drew a long gray hair from the rough edges.

"Ha—ha! by diable, dat wan nombair wan silvaire fox," he muttered. "Dat feller mus' be leeven clos'. S'posin' ovaire dere een dat spleet rock, hein?" Then he answered his own questions.

"Certain! Ah goin' get dat fine animal. leetle mor' late, w'en snow deep!"

At dusk he reached the company's post at Lac le Rouge.

"Bojou—bojou, Michele," he said, pushing open the door of a little log house.

The man looked up startled. "Eh? Ben dat you, Sebat! Ah tink you down à la Corne."

"Jus' so, but Ah no lak de facteur; Ah'm comen' le Rouge for trappen' dees wintare; for mek beeg lot monnaie, go see Annette and dose petits Ah got," and he chuckled. "Par Dieu, you know Ah got seez! T'ree garcons, an' t'ree filles!" The other laughed.

"Dat all ver' bon w'en you got strong han's for worrk; s'posen' you seeck, w'at happen?"

"Ah dun-no," Sebat answered, and his face sank; then brightened, "Ah'm strrong feller manee year yet!"

Michele Poitrin lighted his pipe.

"You get suppaire ef you want, hein?"

They talked long, for they were old friends; then Sebat went to the store.

"Bojou, M'sieu Murcheeson."

The factor, at his desk behind the counter, nodded, and Sebat glanced about the whitewashed and raftered interior.

A few "outside" trappers, one or two Canadians and a lot of Indians squatted and stood round, talking in low, soft voices. The air was thick with the reek of pipes; candles lighted the scene.

Murchison looked up: "What is't ye'r wantin'?"

Sebat gazed at the little Scotchman from his towering height.

"Ah'm tinkin' mak' hunt for you dees wintaire."

"Trap an' welcome," Murchison chuckled; then in a whisper to the clerk, "We'll have the grreatest lot o' skins ever come out the deestrict this year! They're all flockin' to us." His subordinate acquiesced wearily and continued to add rows of small figures that danced before his eyes as the candle in front of him guttered and wavered.

"D'ye want some grub?"

"Ai—hai" (yes). Sebat walked over to the counter and brought his fist down with a crackling thump.

"An' Ah wan' grub at de 'line' cost! Ha—ha! You see Sebat he know w'at de cost ees at de 'line,' an' w'at dey geef for skeens dere aussi."

The factor stared. The store was silent —then Murchison's eyes narrowed, but he turned to his desk without further remark.

"H'm!" Sebat snorted again, and went out. "Dat Murcheeson ees 'fraid h'of me!" he announced proudly, entering Michele's hut.

"You bessis tak' care h'of dat mans! He h'ave wan hearrt lak'—" Michele took up a stone hammer and slammed it on the floor—"dat."

Sebat laughed. "Ah don' tink he goin' hurrt me!" and the two rolled up in their blankets on the little bough beds.

Outside, dogs yowled singly and in unison; the long-drawn wails echoing and re-echoing fainter and fainter in the silent forests. They listened to their own voices, then yelped on.

The waters of the lake rolled noiselessly; sometimes breaking on the shingle with chill whisperings; then curling liquidly, lapping one another. Across from the Post islands stood out black and lonely, only their outlines visible in the darkness.

As the first signs of day came, pale green and scarlet in the east, the Post was awake. After breakfast Sebat went over to the store again.

"Geef me twent' pound flour, t'ree pound tea, ten pound porrk an' wan pound salt!"

The clerk weighed each article and put the amount in his ledger. "Sebat Duval four dollars and twelve cents." The voice was apathetic and dull.

"How dat?"

"Those are our prices! Take it — or leave it!" The big trapper started to push the food back, thought better of it and tucked the packages under his arms.

"You goin' see!" he called over his shoulder, "Ah'm no Indian for mak' starrve, par Dieu!"

The clerk paid no attention, and Sebat went back to Michele's.

"Ah'm goin' by Churcheel Riviere to-day," he said, packing his supplies and outfit.

"W'at for dere?"

Sebat looked about the yard. "Beeg lot fur la bas," he whispered "mabbe Ah get—den h'ave plent' monnaie, go home, see Annette an' de leetle wans."

"B'en, au'woir," Michele called as Sebat started, snowshoes, axe, traps, food, blankets in a firm pack-load on his back, tump line over his forehead. He waved his hand, and disappeared among the hemlock, on the lake trail.

Every two hours or so he would rest, either propping his heavy load on a high-fallen tree, or slipping it to the ground; then he would smoke, his eyes coursing through the forest the while, noting everything. He saw the shuffling, padded track of a bear, and noted that the footprints were far apart.

"He goin' fast, looken' for place sleep wintaire," he muttered. On a ridge he was crossing later he found a moose trail leading to the river beyond; he followed it, and crossed the stream at a shallow ford.

"De moose dey know w'ere good place," he chuckled as he waded to his knees.

At noon the next day he reached the spot he wished to camp on, at Churchill

River, and he soon had a strong lean-to built.

The following weeks were spent in setting traps, and collecting his fur, that was not plentiful as luck seemed against him. Then he had no more cartridges or food and he went back to the Post. Michele was away trapping; so were nearly all the Indians, save for a few decrepit old men and squaws that sewed moccasins and made snowshoes.

He took his fur to the factor. Twelve beaver, seven sable, three red fox, two sable, one marten, five mink and eighteen musk-rat.

"Eighteen dollars," Murchison said abruptly examining the skins.

"Non!" Sebat shouted. "For'-five dollaires!"

The Scotchman looked at him.

"Ye'r crazy, man," he said quietly.

"Mabbe Ah'm crazee, but you no get dose skeens les dan w'at Ah say!"

"Take 'em away then, and get out my store."

"Ah wan' grub!"

"So that's it, is't? Ye want this and that and t'other for naething! Get out, I tell ye!"

Murchison kept three beaver and a marten, the best of the lot.

"That's for the grub ye got afore."

"By diable, down h'at de 'line' dey geef——"

"I don't care what they give at the line! I'm running this place, and what I say stands, d'ye hear?"

Sullenly Sebat took the other skins and went away.

By dint of coaxing and threatening he got a little flour here, some tea there, thus eking out enough food for a two weeks' hunt. It was late; he slept that night in Michele's hut. The next morning the ground was deep with snow; he put on the caribou-thonged snowshoes and started for the silver fox.

The way was long and slow, the traveling hard, and the cold bitter in its strength. The white surfaces were indented by tracks, even and stretching away somberly into the depths of the trees.

Sebat came at last to the muskeg swamp and built his camp. He ate sparingly, then slepts by starts while another winter's night passed, the moon shining mystically

on the white of the north and creating deep, black shadows.

As he slept there came a fox by the lean-to. It stopped, seeing the embers of the fire, and stood there, motionless, head lifted, dainty pointed ears thrown forward inquiringly; its silvered coat reflecting the light rays that crept through the spruce branches above. The fox sniffed high, then low and vanished noiselessly.

"Hah! Fox, by gar!" Sebat said next morning when he started out to set his traps, seeing the track.

All day he worked. Down by the frozen stream he put out three "steels," cunningly hidden by snow that looked as if it had fallen naturally. This he did by gathering it on boughs, and tossing it in the air over the trap; the bait lay tempting on top.

In other places he put dead-falls for marten and sable, and at the last took off the tump line (that he used for a belt), sprung down a sturdy young birch, and fixed a noose on a caribou trail. As he shuffled home, his snowshoes clinking sharply, he talked aloud.

"Dat Murchee-son? Saprée, he wan voleur! He don' get my fur fur h'eighteen dollaires! B'en non!"

The sound of his voice was deadened by the snow-laden branches.

Day after day he went to his traps, and always the same result—nothing.

Sometimes the bait was stolen (this was bad as he did not have any to spare); again the traps were sprung, but no body was between the sharp jaws. His food grew lower and lower; then he ate but once a day, saving his scanty supply.

"Mus' go back to-mor'," he whispered mournfully. A thought came. He took off his fur cap.

"Bon Dieu, dees pauv'r Sebat h'ave not'ing, onlee Annette an' seex child'en! He wan' for go see dem, an' mus' catch dat silvaire fox for to go dere." Satisfied he slept.

The morning dawned red and calm, with the sting of frost and the silence of daylight. As soon as he could see, Sebat went the mile to the musky swamp for the last time. He looked, rubbed his eyes, and stared. A few yards from the timber edge was a dark body; attached to one of its hind legs a steel trap, chain and clog.

"De silvaire fox!" he cried and ran out.

It was stiffened and straight — was the lithe form; glossy and perfect its coat, each hair tipped with silver points, the under mass pure gray and of one tone. The eyes were half closed and glassy, frozen in their sockets. Almost in awe at its beauty, Sebat released the jaws; the trap clinked to the light crust. He picked up the body and ran like mad to camp; sat down, the fox in his arms, crooning like a child.

"Ah goin' see Annette, Ah goin' see Annette; dey geef me hund'er dollaires for dees," he repeated over and over again.

Realizing that he had no food he packed his load and started for the post again, carrying the fox always.

At dark he reached the store, hungry, tired, snowshoe sore, but *so* happy and triumphant.

"How dat, M'sieu Murcheeson?" he asked, carefully putting the silver fox on the counter and smoothing the glorious coat that shone, even in the candle light.

The factor looked carelessly, then a gleam of greed flitted across his face. He examined thoroughly.

"Thirty dollars," he said, and put out his hand to take the fox.

Sebat seemed not to understand; he gazed at the Scotchman in astonishment.

"T'irt' dollaires?" he asked in sing-song voice.

"Aye, mon, and a gude price, too!"

Then the trapper awoke to the bitter disappointment. He struck fiercely at the hand that was drawing the fox, *his* Silver Gray for Annette, from him, and the factor winced. All the fury of the French blood boiled out, and Sebat cursed the company and the factor.

"You steal f'm de Indians, dey starrve an' you get deir monnaie. Ah'm goin' tak' dees to de 'line' an' get hund'er dollaires! You—you—you—Ah—sacrée," he snarled, seized the fox and darted out.

He ran headlong to Michele's. It was dark in the hut; he strode in, and stood there panting, listening to the violent surging of his heart. Silence—stillness everywhere, and he was hungry and tired. He hid the fox under a bunk, wrapping it in his jacket, and went back to the factor.

"Geef me for h'eat, for go to 'line,' Ah geef you all dose skeens Ah have."

Murchison cursed him. "Go to the line

and be dammed to ye, ye French cur! Ye'll get naething here!"

Sebat went.

From tepee to tepee he tried to obtain enough food for the two hundred mile trip, but everywhere there was some excuse. He realized then that the factor had ordered it so among the Indians, and that they dared not disobey.

In Michele's home he found an old crust of bread, hard as wood, but it was food, and he gnawed eagerly.

"Par Dieu, Ah'm goin' 'line' jus' same'! Ah'm strrong 'nough for go t'ree day hongree!"

Fox under his arm, snowshoes on his feet, he started on the trail. The night was black, and snow clouds hung heavy and low.

He traveled on relentlessly, though the thongs wore into his ankles and his body craved nourishment and rest. Daylight came, grew and broadened, as he was crossing a long barren; then it began to snow. Faster and faster, thicker and thicker came the flakes, deadening the sound of his snowshoes, clogging the swing of his stride; but he pushed on, shifting the fox from arm to arm.

Of a sudden he looked up and saw a high ridge before him. "Dees no de way," he muttered and swung to the left.

On and on and on he traveled, head low to the blinding snow that swept across the open in whirling clouds, urged by the strong wind. To the right, then to the left, he struggled. At last he knew that he was lost, and he stood still.

Crisply the snow settled about him, lonely the wind yowled and sirened across the wastes. Daylight was nearly gone. He was weak and trembling. Far in the distance, only intermittently visible through the shifting white, was a hill.

"Ah go dere, mabbe see w'ere Ah goin'," he muttered hoarsely.

Dragging his feet along, he fought his way; stumbling, slipping, he tried to reach the top—and fell. He rose slowly, worked his way a little farther and fell again. Up, more painfully, and on. Another fall, the snow cutting his face and trickling over his throat. On one hand and knees now, the silver-gray fox weakly clasped to his body, he strove to reach the top of the rise.

A sense of warmth, of unutterable comfort, came over him.

"Ah'm tire', ' he whispered, as he felt the drowsiness creep on his giant frame; and he lay still.

"Ah mus' go, Ah *mus'* go!" he gasped, and tried to move; but the peace and luxurious rest his body felt was too great and his brain could enforce no action.

"Ah'm goin' die here—die ici—jus' here alon'!"

He dragged the fox to his face. The fur felt warm and soft.

"Annette—Annette," he murmured, "so manee, manee leetle chil'—den!"

The snow fell seething on the still figure; covering it lightly at first, then blending its shape with the whiteness of everything. Finally the place was level with the rest. The wind shrieked spasmodically and the white clouds tossed and drifted.

18

In Rugged Labrador

R.G. TABER

IN RUGGED LABRADOR.

By R. G. Taber.

THE KYAK.

IT is surprising how little has been written regarding this great and comparatively unknown peninsula of our eastern coast. Excepting the Newfoundland fishermen who visit its shore during the summer months in search of cod and herring; the Hudson Bay Company's officers and the Moravian missionaries, who established their stations as far north as Nain, in latitude 56° 30', over one hundred and twenty years ago, the general public possesses a knowledge of it as vague and indefinite as the Labrador mists.

Even to the earnest seeker for information there is but little of a satisfactory nature to be obtained. The best of such writings as are to be found in print are full of contradictory statements, and the little they contain regarding the northern coast from Cape Harrigan to Cape Chudleigh, a distance of over three hundred miles, is based upon hearsay and not calculated to excite an interest in what is really a country teeming with novelties for the tourist, scientist and sportsman.

Almost the entire eastern coast-line of Labrador is fringed with islands, great and small, and to local pilots, familiar with the channels, it would be possible to take a pleasure yacht from the Straits of Belle Isle to Ungava and return with but a few short encounters with the ocean swell.

The majority of these islands are barren porphyritic rocks, worn smooth and polished by glaciers in the long ago and denuded of all the higher forms of vegetation through the influence of the Arctic stream, which packs the indentations of their shores with giant bergs.

In sheltered places there are surprising growths of reindeer moss and, wherever there is soil enough for it to cling, the hardy plant of the curlewberry furnishes a velvety carpet of brilliant green.

A few dwarf alders, spruce and hackmatack, that aggressive cousin of the western sage, are all the trees these rocky isles afford. Yet they possess a picturesqueness and grandeur which, from a scenic standpoint, must eventually place them among the foremost of America's natural attractions.

One of the most striking features of the coast is the succession of bold, frowning cliffs and headlands, which greet one at every turn. There is such diversity in their rugged outlines, and such noticeable increase in their altitude as the coast is followed to the north, that the sight is never satiated. The cliffs which at Cape Saint Charles are mere slides a few hundred feet in height, become at Harrigan precipices, and from Cape Mugford northward they are sheer perpendicular walls, rising grandly two thousand to three thousand feet above the sea.

These are but tables upon which the mountain ranges rest, and the perpetual

THE TAPEH.

snow upon their summits furnishes each ravine and chasm with a crystal brook which tumbles merrily down the steep incline, until, plunging over the ocean wall, it breaks into clouds of silvery spray and mist.

Where the mountains meet the sea there are many deep inlets, and the arms of these extend far back into the interior. Few but the Indians and Esquimaux know how far, for the survey of the coast to Hamilton Inlet is quite incomplete, and north of that point, the published charts are little more than guess-work.

Into these inlets numerous small streams and many considerable rivers empty, and here the angler, who loves his sport sufficiently to brave the insect pests, will find the brook trout in abundance.

A curious feature of this mountainous land is the presence of innumerable moss-covered bogs, which not only furnish a liberal supply of moisture to the surrounding vegetation during the short, dry, summer months, but also serve as excellent breeding spots for myriads of insects. To the credit of the Labrador flies and mosquitoes, be it said, their period of existence is short. They are rarely troublesome at any time but the first three weeks of August, and do not molest humanity save during periods of calm weather. The slightest breeze clears the air of them, as if by magic. I have tried many patented preparations, advertised as guaranteed to afford absolute protection from their stings, but the only perfectly effective remedy I have found is one easily prepared and no doubt well known to many sportsmen. It consists of a pint of sweet or olive oil,

THE DEVIL'S TABLE.

half a pint of Norwegian pine tar and half an ounce of carbolic acid. The application of this mixture to the hands and face will keep all "neighbors," as the Esquimaux term these pests, at a most comfortable distance. It must be repeated, from time to time, as the strength of the acid evaporates, but it is perfectly harmless, the odor is not unpleasantly noticeable, as in the use of pennyroyal preparations, and all trace of it is easily removed with soap and water after the day's outing.

In these deep bays and inlets, a few hours' journey from the direct influence of the Arctic current, the character of the vegetation and floral growth is delightfully surprising, to one who may have had his expectations colored a dismal gray by reading the hap-hazard descriptions furnished by casual voyagers among the barren outer islands.

The trees are no longer pigmies, to be measured by inches. The spruce and fir are often forty feet in height. One may walk in the shade of mountain ash and poplars, and graceful willows line each rivulet's bank. Sturdy creepers and hackmatack are plentiful; purple flags, blue harebells, yellow daisies and soft, creamy berry-blossoms make the hill-sides gay; and, during the short but kindly visit of the summer sun, it requires a buffet with the floe-ice, among the bergs and outer islands in the Arctic stream, to remind one this is really sub-Arctic Labrador, reputed to be the coldest, most barren portion of the Western Hemisphere.

In spite of latitude and Arctic current, Labrador is the home of much that is delicious in the berry world. Even the out-lying islands furnish the curlew-berry and bake-apple in profusion; and upon the mainland, in the proper month, September, a veritable feast awaits one. Three varieties of blue-berries, huckleberries, wild red currants, having a pungent aromatic flavor, unequaled by the cultivated varieties; marsh-berries, raspberries, tiny white capillaire tea-berries, with a flavor like some rare perfume and having just a faint suggestion of wintergreen; squash-berries, pear-berries and curlew-berries, the latter not so grateful as the others but a prime favorite with the Esquimaux who prefer it to almost any other; and lastly, the typical Labrador fruit, which, excepting a few scattering plants in Canada and Newfoundland, is found, I believe, nowhere outside of the Peninsula,—the gorgeous bake-apple.

These cover the entire coast from the Saint Lawrence to Ungava. Their beautiful geranium-like leaves struggle with the reindeer moss upon the islands, carpet alike the low valleys and the highest hill-tops, and even peep from banks of everlasting snow. Only one berry grows upon each plant, but this one makes a most delicious mouthful. It is the size and form of a large dewberry, but the color is a bright crimson when half ripe and a golden yellow at maturity. Its taste is sweetly acid, it is exceedingly juicy, and so delicate that it might be thought impossible to preserve it. Yet the natives do preserve it with all its freshness and original flavor throughout the entire winter, merely by covering it with fresh water and heading it up tightly in casks or barrels. At Chateau Bay, near the eastern entrance to the Straits of Belle Isle, all these varieties of berries may be found growing upon the same acre.

Considering the shortness of the temperate season, the gardening that is possible in Northern Labrador is remarkable. At Nain, the Moravian missionaries grow a sufficient quantity of potatoes, turnips, carrots, beets, lettuce and other vegetables to supply their modest wants. At Hebron, until recently the most northern missionary station, they exhibited, with some pride, a cucumber fourteen inches long.

The German love of flowers has overcome all obstacles, and it would be difficult to find larger or more beautiful pansies than those grown at the missions, while hyacinths, tuberoses, calla-lilies and other equally delicate flowers, by careful nursing are made to bloom luxuriantly.

The method of caring for the plants pursued at Hebron, 59° north latitude, is as unique as it is laborious, and is an eulogy on German perseverance.

The post is located in an exposed and very barren spot, and the soil used is gathered a little in a place and brought, sometimes from considerable distances, to the mission garden. Fertilizers are a scarce commodity, and all possible substances, from kelp to capelin, are pressed into service to enrich the ground. The plants are sprouted within doors, and when the weather moderates sufficiently to admit of safely transplanting to the outer air, they are carefully placed in tiers of boxes, covered with glass frames and having a southern exposure. When the sun shines these cases are covered with canvas. When the wind blows the canvas is supplemented with wooden frames and these held firmly in place by piling heavy rocks upon them. As the season advances, the hardier plants are transplanted to mother earth.

Strong gales of wind, night frosts, and occasional storms of hail and snow, are not uncommon during the summer months. To provide against the destruction caused by these, the patient missionaries have, for years, carefully husbanded every empty tin can, and one of these is placed over each separate plant and weighted with a piece of stone, when any danger threatens.

Even the coarser vegetables are covered each night; to facilitate which, they are planted in long rows, with walks between. Half barrel hoops are placed across the rows at regular intervals, and over the rib-work thus formed, long strips of canvas are stretched and the edges pinned down with boulders.

But these careful precautions do not always suffice, the unfortunate missionaries being sometimes obliged to gather up their cans and canvas at the distance of a quarter of a mile, and, what is worse, to behold the havoc wrought amongst their garden beds by the relentless wind, which, in a single hour, may have destroyed the product of months of anxious toil.

"A Labrador summer" is a very indefinite term. It might mean twelve, or even fourteen weeks on the southern coast, of weather greatly resembling New England's Indian summer; while at Nachvack the native ice did not leave the bay until August 10th, and the first fall snow-storm turned the landscape white on August 20th. To this should be added the fact that snow fell up to July 1st, and the shortness of the season can be appreciated. Moderate weather usually prevails throughout September, however, and navigation is not closed until December.

The average summer temperature is about fifty-five degrees Fahrenheit at Hamilton Inlet, and five degrees colder at the northern extremity. There are several days each summer when the mercury touches seventy-five degrees, and on two occasions in the last three years eighty in the shade was reached at Nain.

The summer days are generally beautiful. Clear skies and westerly winds prevail, and there is very little rainfall, although there are sometimes heavy dews. The most objectionable feature in the climate is the sudden change in temperature at sunset, a fall of thirty degrees being sometimes experienced. In September, however, for two weeks, I have seen the thermometer stationary at forty degrees Fahrenheit.

A change of wind from westerly to north, or east, will always cause a rapid fall in temperature. With such large bodies of drift ice at all times close inshore, even a slight breeze from the ocean puts every insect fast asleep at once, and sends the cold chills creeping through one's bones, though the hour be midday and the sky without a cloud to screen the sun.

A change of wind is usually heralded, the night before, by some aurora, and these phenomena, so common in these latitudes, are often grandly beautiful; great bands of waving flame, of richly variegated rainbow-like hues, dividing the starry heavens from all the cardinal points and culminating in one glorious burst of light at the zenith.

Owing to the dryness of the rarefied air, the stars seem nearer and more numerous, and the same condition probably aids in furnishing the richest sunsets visible from our continent. The prevailing colors are purple, green and pink, with a greater variety of delicate tints and shades than it would be possible to catalogue. The sunsets are one of the most delightful features of the Labrador summer, and during the long July evenings their glory lasts for hours.

Labrador is not a land of midnight sun; but for a fortnight, or more, the daylight never leaves the sky, and one can read comfortably until ten o'clock at night without artificial light.

Mirage is another common natural phenomenon to which the visitor is treated upon almost every clear summer day, particularly if there are many icebergs in the neighboring sea. The objects reflected are seldom inverted, but are generally elevated and distorted.

For a number of years, Newfoundland has held a nominal jurisdiction over the Labrador coast, from Blanc Sablòn, on the Straits of Belle Isle, to the entrance to Hudson Straits.

The government's acts of sovereignty, thus far, have consisted of an appointment, conferred upon one of the officers of the northern mail steamer, to the position of magistrate, with powers similar to those enjoyed by a justice of the peace; and of a revenue collector, who patrols the coast between Battle Harbor and Hopedale during the months of July and August of each year.

It has never asserted its dominion to the north of Cape Harrigan, and at no time has it exhibited any very active interest in any portion of this large territory, despite the fact that it is the mainstay of Newfoundland fishing interests, and is visited by at least ten per cent. of the island's population each summer, the number probably including over forty per cent. of its able-bodied men.

Over one-half of these Labrador-going fishermen are what are termed "planters, sharesmen and crews." These have their permanent locations on the coast, to which they are carried, early in the season, by the sealing fleet at the close of the seal fishery.

A "planter" may either be the owner of a "plant," speculating on his own account upon credit obtained from the merchants in Newfoundland, or he may be an agent in charge of a merchant's plant, either upon salary, commission or share of profits.

"Sharesmen" obtain their transportation,

AT THE NAIN MISSION.

punts, traps, nets, fishing outfit and bait from the planter free of charge. They are credited with a certain share of what they catch, a third to a half usually going to the planter, and are charged "going prices" for provisions and such other supplies as they obtain from the planter's store. It is customary for a number of sharesmen to club together, forming crews sufficiently large to handle the punts, traps and nets; but, occasionally, a sharesman may ship a crew, in which event he holds the dual position of sharesman to the planter and planter to his crew.

THE ORGANIST.

The crews are men regularly shipped for the voyage, provided with food and lodging and paid a small sum as wages, or, in lieu thereof, allowed a very small share in the planter's catch of fish.

A "plant" usually consists of half-a-dozen stages built of boughs and saplings and extending out over the water, for cleaning and curing fish ; a store-house, in which a general stock of traders' and fishermen's supplies is kept; the "skipper's quarters," a warm and comfortable dwelling, in which the chief planter resides, and containing a commodious kitchen, where the planter's personal crews take their meals and carry on a rough flirtation with the kitchen maids; a barracks, where the crews bunk at night; a warehouse for salt, casks, nets, cables, etc., and half-a-dozen to a score of sharesmen's "tilts"— rude, turf-covered huts, some of which are little better or cleaner than the Esquimaux' habitations.

The remaining fishermen who visit Labrador are designated "green-fishers" or "floaters," though it must not be inferred from this that they are novices, or in any way inferior in skill to the others. On the contrary, they take more chances, undergo greater hardships and privations, and are often more successful, and consequently better paid.

These are the "cruisers," who live on board their craft, shifting about from place to place in search of fish, which, when caught, are cleaned upon the decks, salted "green," and packed away in the holds in bulk.

The fleet numbers over one thousand schooners, the largest being rarely over sixty tons, and many of them not more than thirty·tons burden. Yet a successful season for this fleet would mean a million quintals of fish, having a market value of over three millions of dollars.

The Labrador codfish are small in size, and fifty fish to the quintal is a very low average. It is safe to say that the number of codfish killed during a fair season on the Labrador coast exeeds one hundred and fifty millions!

Owing to the reckless use of trap-nets, which destroy whole schools of fish, old and young alike, the fishing has been growing poorer within the last three years, two of which have resulted in but half a

ESQUIMAUX TYPES.

catch. As a consequence, the "floaters" have gone further and further north each year. In 1890, Cape Harrigan was the northern limit; in 1892, Cape Mugford; in 1893, Sieglick Bay, Ramah and Nachvack were visited by the more adventurous; and in 1894, the majority of the fleet stretched along the coast from Mugford to Eclipse, a few vessels even reaching Cape Chudleigh.

Paradoxical as it may seem, these fishermen do not, as a rule, make good pilots for the coast. The bays and inside runs and channels are almost unknown to them, the fishery being wholly confined to the outlying islands.

The seal fishery along the Labrador Coast is also an important source of revenue. The fleet of sealing steamers fitted out in Newfoundland each spring includes the *Aurora, Algerine, Diana, Hope, Kite, Labrador, Leopard, Neptune, Nimrod, Panther, Ranger, Wolf* and *Walrus* from St. Johns; and the *Greenland, Iceland, Mastiff* and *Vanguard,* from Harbor Grace. Many of these are known to Arctic fame. Their hulls are built of wood strongly fortified with immense crossbeams and timbers, and covered with greenheart sheathing to protect them from ice.

The *Neptune,* of six hundred tons measurement, is the largest of the fleet, and carries from three hundred to three hundred and fifty men in her sealing crew. The *Aurora, Ranger, Wolf* and *Vanguard,* each of about five hundred tons and carrying about two hundred and fifty men, are next in importance. The others average about three hundred tons, and one hundred and fifty men to each crew.

The crews are shipped on shares, dividing the proceeds of one-fourth of the catch, the owners reserving the remainder. The officers receive salaries in addition to their shares, and all are provisioned by the owners, who furnish the ships and equipments.

The lawful sealing season opens March 12th and closes April 20th, a total of forty days; during which, if the fishing prove ordinarily successful, over five hundred thousand seals are brought to market by the steamers. The value of such a catch approximates a million and a half of dollars. To this must be added the value of seals captured by the shore fishermen, which will increase the proceeds of the sealing season to over two millions of dollars.

The seals are sometimes encountered as far south as White Bay, but the best territory usually extends from the latitude of Belle Isle to that of Hamilton Inlet. The Gulf of St. Lawrence and the western portion of the Straits of Belle Isle are also resorted to, and as the ice there is lighter and slacker, progress is more rapid and the results correspondingly satisfactory.

FALLS AND RAPIDS AT BIG BIGHT.

Old seal hunters aver that they can smell the seals at such great distances as fifteen to twenty miles, when the wind is blowing from the right direction. In clear weather the packs may

FALLS OF RAHAMA.

be seen from the topmasts, whilst eight to ten miles distant.

If the ice floe is so closely packed as to prevent the seals from taking to the water, they are rounded up like droves of sheep and slaughtered by clubbing, pieces of dogwood, six to seven feet in length, tipped with iron gaffs, being used for weapons. The seals make desperate efforts to escape when first attacked. They scramble for the narrow cracks between the ice pans, insert their muzzles and, erecting their bodies perpendicularly, bear with all their weight upon the crevices. By concerted action they sometimes succeed in forcing an opening, of sufficient width to permit large numbers to slip through and escape. If their efforts are not quickly successful, however, the harp seals lose all hope, drop their heads upon the ice and tremblingly await the fatal blow.

The harp seals are far more numerous than any other species, and are exceedingly wary when in reach of open water. They post a sentinel, usually a bedlamer or two-year-old harp, on one of the highest pinnacles of the floe. Should the watch perceive anything alarming, he rapidly descends from his post and scurries through the pack, uttering short, sharp, warning barks to awaken all the slumberers, when the whole pack takes to the water and disappears in a twinkling. To capture any number of seals at such a time requires an experienced hunter and a sure rifle shot. The hunter must make his way within easy range, without alarming the sentinel bedlamer; then, taking up a position behind some sheltering hummock, secure from observation, he must select his seal and kill it instantly, with the first shot fired. The seals will raise their heads at the report, but, seeing nothing to alarm them, they will drop asleep again almost immediately, when the hunter repeats the operation. In this way one man may sometimes kill a hundred seals before alarming the pack; but if he wounds a seal, the injured animal will at once roll off the pan, instantly followed by the whole pack.

The hooded seals are not so timid. They are fully twice as large as the harps and will often show fight, particularly if their young are not old enough to swim. As they may be approached

GIANTS OF THE DEEP.

with ease, it is considered a waste of ammunition to shoot them, and they are generally clubbed, or "batted," as it is locally termed. They are found in families of three on a pan, the dog, the female and the pup. The dogs, which sometimes attain a thousand pounds in weight, are quite fierce, and clubbing them is always attended with some danger. In spite of their size, they are exceedingly active, and will travel over the ice much faster than a man can run. If the dog is not killed by the first blow, it sometimes requires a hard fight to finish him.

When wounded or angered, he puffs out his great red hood, which consists of a hard cartilage or membrane secreted inside the nostrils. When extended, this is over a foot in diameter; it is attached to the nose by flexible ligaments and is impervious to even a rifle ball. He uses this to protect himself, swinging it from side to side with such dexterous rapidity as to enable him to ward off every blow, although he may have two or three "batters" to contend with.

The method usually pursued by the hunter is to approach within a dozen feet of the dog and throw a piece of ice, or, preferably, a mitten into the air, so aimed that it will fall a little to one side of the seal, who invariably turns his head to catch it as it descends. At this moment, the hunter must spring forward and deliver a crushing blow upon the animal's exposed ear. Should he hit true, this stroke will prove instantly fatal; but if he fails of his mark, by even a hand's-breadth, he must then look out for himself.

An old hunter once told me that, in crossing a floe off Belle Isle, he saw something moving behind one of the hummocks. He went to investigate and found an old dog hood sitting upright, his strong teeth firmly imbedded in the back of an unfortunate hunter. He was holding the man's body suspended in the air, leisurely swinging it to and fro, with an occasional jounce up and down to vary the monotony. The man was quickly rescued, but died from the injuries he had received.

After the dog is killed, his mate is easily disposed of, as a slight tap on the nose will dispatch her. The

snow-white pup then looks up at the hunter, with its great black eyes full of tears, and, moaning piteously, crouches to receive the finishing stroke. The latter is the game principally aimed at, as its pelt and fat bring far the best prices in the market. When the seals are very plentiful, the orders to the men sometimes are to bring in only the pups. The result is that three seals must be killed for every one that is taken.

An inexperienced hunter, who had received such an order, started out to kill his first seal and in some way managed to steal a hood pup, without alarming its parents. He carried it to another pan and was busily removing the "sculp," as the pelt with the adhering fat is designated, when he felt himself roughly elevated and, as he afterwards expressed it: "Sartenly knowed as 'ow a rat ud feel wens a crackey nipped aholt!"

When rescued by his shipmates, his clothing was torn to shreds and his flesh terribly lacerated.

Accidents are of frequent occurrence, and it is owing to the fact that assistance is usually close at hand that there are so few fatal encounters.

The greatest danger is from drifting away on the pan ice in a storm, which might prevent a rescue, and death would rapidly ensue from freezing.

The "sculp" of the dog hood sometimes weighs six hundredweight, but is usually not more than three; that of the harp and bedlamer will average one hundred and fifty pounds, and the pups fifty to seventy pounds apiece. The values range from $2.75 to $5.50 per quintal, the old hoods bringing the lowest and the pups the highest prices. As the capacity of the steamers is not great, the desirability of loading with young seals is apparent. At the close of the season the steamers are commissioned to northern waters in search of whales; or to the fisheries in Northern Labrador.

OUTING.

NOVEMBER, 1895.

RUGGED LABRADOR.

By R. G. Taber.

ALTHOUGH it is to the sea that Arctic commerce looks for its greatest harvest, it is to the land streams and mountains of rugged Labrador that the sportsman will turn for his. Nor will he turn in vain, for, paradoxical as it may at first appear, whilst the seal and the cod are disappearing before the advent of civilized man, the reindeer is rapidly increasing in number, and generations yet unborn will find on mossy barrens and in snow-chilled waters, falls and rapids abundant sport. At present, of course, it is not very easily accessible, but then on the other hand it is rather time and thought than money that is the bar. Time one must have, but the cost of such an excursion need not be great. Eighteen hundred dollars covered all expenditures for our party of four, which I will roughly itemize for the benefit of those who might desire to make a similar trip: Four round-trip passages, New York to Saint John's, at $60, $240. The *Swallow* charter, four months, at $100 per month, $400; master and engineer's wages, four months, at $32, $128; fireman's wages, four months, at $18, $72; pilot and cook's wages, four months, at $26, $104; coal consumed, forty tons, at $5, principally obtained from coastal steamer, $200; provisions for seven persons for the voyage, purchased at New York, $400; hotel at Saint John's, two weeks, at $6 per day for the party, $84; allowance for sundry other necessary expenditures, $172: total, $1,800.

An average of four hundred and fifty dollars for each person in the party is surely not a heavy expenditure for such a five-months' outing; and the average cost of the trip would have been materially decreased had the party consisted of six persons, instead of four, as the accommodations on board the *Swallow* were quite sufficient for nine men.

If time is not an object, by far the most pleasant and convenient way to visit Labrador would be to charter a small vessel, preferably a steamer, as long calms prevail, and which would make it possible to visit, at will, the inside runs and heads of bays and inlets where the best sport is to be found. Under no circumstances should a vessel

THE KING OF THE FLOE.

with anything but a staunch wooden hull be chartered.

By chartering a small sailing vessel, instead of a steamer, the expense would, of course, be considerably lessened. The usual charter charges for small craft at Saint John's are four dollars per ton measurement for the season. A schooner of thirty-five tons, which could be managed by a crew of three men, would comfortably accommodate eight or nine passengers.

Such an excursion party should not leave Saint John's earlier than July 1st, and should waste no time on the southern Labrador shore. Harborage is easily found at any time, and little is to be gained by sailing at night. The night stops, and delays which may be occasioned by foggy weather, will afford ample opportunity for testing the streams and ponds along the southern portion of the coast.

The mail steamers made their first trip north of Nain in 1894, and it is possible that a route will be established as far as Nachvack. Should this be done it will place the most interesting portions of the coast within easy reach

and at a comparatively small expense. The trip, from Saint John's to Nain and return, is made in twenty-eight days. There are no desirable row-boats, suitable for hunting or fishing, to be obtained in Labrador; but they may be procured in Saint John's and carried north on the mail steamers.

Sportsmen should also provide themselves with light, easily portable camp outfits, and with such provisions and other supplies as they may require, for very little can be procured on the coast, aside from absolute necessaries, and these only at most exorbitant prices.

The first stop of any duration should be made under Altaguyivivik, either at Mannok Island or in Mokkovik or Aillik bays. All three of these may be visited with profit. Eight miles northwest from Cape Aillik are the Turnavik Islands, an important fishing station. During the winter months the "plant" is in charge of Robert Evans, a brawny, fair-haired, good-natured Scot, who has held the trust a number of years.

Nicknames are quite as common in Labrador as they were in the days of '49, in California, and I enjoyed his ac-

A NATIVE MISSIONARY—ZOAR.

quaintance some time before discovering his true title. Evans has quite forfeited his name to the marked peculiarity of his luxuriant, reddish beard, which distinctive feature suggested and earned for him the sobriquet of "the foxy man," contracted to simple "Fox" in familiar intercourse.

Evans' pride is in the ownership of a fine team of Esquimaux dogs; tall, strong-limbed, wolfish creatures, the color of whose shaggy hides and curling tails matches their master's whiskers, by his own selection. With them he has made the trip from Turnavick to Davis Inlet in midwinter, over the frozen sea, in one day's drive, a distance of some eighty miles.

The true home of the reindeer is found in the mountainous

OUR PILOT.

districts about Nain, and extends northward from there a distance of two hundred miles. Some idea of their profuse numbers may be gathered from the extent of the mission's trade for deer skins. The number annually purchased by them from the Esquimaux exceeds five thousand, and this certainly represents much less than half of the number of deer slain. A great many skins are used for making topeks, clothing, bedding and for various other purposes.

The missionaries complain bitterly of the wasteful slaughter committed by the natives. The deer visit the seashore regularly in the months of April, July and October, and during these migrations the Esquimaux often shoot them for the mere love of killing, allowing the carcasses to rot where they fall, without preserving even the hides. There is an Esquimaux at Nain who boasts of having killed one hundred and fifty deer in one day's shooting!

It is probably owing to this barbarous butchery that the deer return to the interior. Thirty or forty miles inland they are comparatively safe. There are but a few, small, wandering tribes of Indians whom they may encounter, and the indolent Esquimaux are too averse to tramping to pursue them.

The deer are to the Indians, what the seals are to the Esquimaux, almost an indispensable necessity. They value them accordingly and are never guilty of such excesses in the chase. The skins both house and cloth them. The sinews answer better than any other possible substitute for thread. The spreading antlers, with their broad brow-branches, ingeniously carved and fashioned, supply a variety of useful implements, and the flesh is their staple, never-failing food.

The game laws of Newfoundland are very stringent and fairly well enforced. They impose both fine and imprisonment for killing deer out of season; and prohibit non-residents from hunting them in season, excepting upon payment to the government of a fee of twenty pounds. Moreover, no one is allowed to kill more than seven deer. These laws do not extend to Labrador, however, and nothing has as yet been done towards the preservation of its game.

It is remarkable that the Labrador deer have survived the terrible destruction which has been carried on for years. Old residents affirm, however, that instead of diminishing, their numbers are steadily increasing; and attribute this to the rapid diminu-

IN THE OIL HOUSE AT THE NAIN MISSION.

tion in the number of Indians and Esquimaux.

The ranks of both these races, deteri-
orating for over a century, have been
sadly thinned within the last two score
of years. War, famine, exposure, in-
termarriage of blood relations, the introduction of European food and frail-
ties, and with these, very likely, the
germs of pestilence and contagious
disease which have made fearful inroads,
have all combined to reduce the number of living descendants of these once
numerous and powerful aborigines to a

few hundred men and women, stunted in stature, blunted in natural intelligence, living in fear of their energetic creditors, the mighty Company or the dominant missionaries, and whose vague understanding of the doctrine of Christian love is hardly encouraged by the strict business methods pursued by the "London Society for the Furtherance of the Gospel," which has the Moravian missions in charge.

An illustration of the apathy with which mortality is regarded by the Esquimaux was afforded by an incident of our cruise. Ten deaths from blood-poisoning had occurred among the natives within ten days, yet there were but few evidences of sorrow or alarm. When I expressed sympathy with a man whom I had employed as a pilot, and who, within a month, had lost his father, wife, child, and wife's brother, he said to me, smilingly:

"At chook! Not so many to feed. Flour dear. No fish. Plenty men hungry. Plenty men die. Ananak! Very good! Byme-bye no more Esquimaux. All sleep, —me—everybody.

So!" Then emphasized his philosophy with a hearty laugh.

The mortality amongst children is very great. The uninformed visitor may manifest some surprise at the inconsiderable number of them to be seen; but when he ventures to inquire, the Esquimaux, for answer, point significantly to the picketed enclosure which occupies a prominent position near every mission, and which guards the dead.

Although the Esquimaux laugh at death and make a jest of sorrow, they are none the less indulgent husbands and affectionate fathers. True communists in both theory and practice; unselfishly sharing their last morsel, with a smile; a simple, kindly, dirty, good-natured, child-like race, possessing no hope of betterment; giving no thought to the future; systematically forgetful of the past; living only in the present and making the heaviest burdens of that present light with irrepressible cheerfulness of heart!

The wit in which they indulge is of a harmless character, practical joking being a thing unknown. Their fine and

ESQUIMAUX TOPEK AT KINAUK.

ready sense of humor is fairly shown by the following episode:

We had in our crew an elderly Irish fisherman who was sometimes conveniently deaf, and whose inherent indolence was only exceeded by his enormous appetite and wonderful capacity for food, both of which had become proverbial among us. We were visiting an encampment of half a dozen "topeks," and, one morning, some of our "Huskie" friends volunteered to go with us in the boats for wood. Arriving at the grove the crowd soon gathered a sufficient quantity, but Mr. Whalen, who had promptly disappeared upon our landing, was nowhere to be found when we were ready to return.

Our loud calls and half a dozen shots from a repeater were only answered by the echoes; whereupon Itavaluk, who had learned a few words of English, jumped upon an elevated log, made of his hands a trumpet and, in attempted imitation of our cook, shouted: "Meester Wheelin! Meester Wheelin! brekfas' ees ready!" in a manner eliciting broad smiles from his companions, who burst into hearty laughter as Mr. Whalen's response reached us, and he was seen making his way rapidly toward us through the trees.

The fishermen hold the Labrador dogs in great fear. They will tell you that "thim bru-its" are savage, ferocious and treacherous, lacking in intelligence and all the noble attributes with which the race is usually accredited. The few which have been carried to Newfoundland were found to be so destructive to domestic animals that the government has prohibited their importation. Yet my own experiences among them have earned for them a warm regard. I have ever found them playful, affectionate and grateful, quick to understand and to obey.

THE PATRIARCH OF THE HERD.

AN OUTING IN LABRADOR.

By R. G. Taber.

WHILE at the Labrador Company's mines I enjoyed a fine September day's outing, the description of which will admirably serve to illustrate the sport Labrador offers.

The camp had been without fresh meat for some time, and although a gill-net, stretched at the mouth of the brook, supplied sea-trout and salmon, the superintendent suggested one evening at mess that a few birds would be greatly appreciated.

I made my arrangements accordingly, and at four o'clock next morning was awakened by Angeuk, a good-natured "Huskie," whom I had selected to row me. It was still quite dark when I came up on deck, as a dense fog obscured the daybreak; but after a cup of hot coffee, we bundled overboard into a punt and pulled down the run toward the islands. Each oar had a heavy wrapping of cloth and the thole-pins were carefully muffled, for our object was rather the pot than the sport, and we counted on making a killing.

Angeuk silently bent to the oars and I puffed at my pipe, without speaking. The morning stillness was on sea and land, not a breath disturbed the water; and the ghostly gray mist enveloped the whole, leaving no marks whatever to guide us.

A heavy black cloud rose out of the fog and we barely escaped a beaching; but a few strokes to port wiped it suddenly out, and we plunged again into the silent gray depths.

Then a startling cry—half a yelp, half a bark—echoed sharply along the precipice; and Angeuk carefully rested his oars and listened. Again the cry; then a kissing sound which Angeuk made on his finger; and then a rattle of small loose stones and the cry was repeated quite near us.

We peered toward the land, but I discerned nothing. Angeuk motioned to hand him my gun and reached back toward me to grasp it; then his wet boot slipped and jostled an oar, and a scramble of paws and rattling of stones told us the chance was over.

"*Oovunga piungituk!*" Angeuk exclaimed, angrily striking his forehead.

"*Chua?*" (What was it?) I asked.

"A wolf—two—three—at chook! More maybe."

Again the oars were silently dipped and we slipped along through the gloaming. Then we heard the fluttering chirp of a bird and noiselessly stole toward it.

A black spot appeared—another—a score, and then I turned loose my Parker; and we had the pleasure of gathering in the first results of the morning. As we were out for a pot, I did not regret the half-dozen ducks I had murdered.

After this the morning grew rapidly light, and the birds became more wary, still we managed another pot shot and obtained four more young eiders.

As the breeze rolled the fog away, long moving strings and spots of black appeared on the water; thousands of birds were waking up and searching about for their breakfasts.

I had no more pot shots, but by noon had secured enough birds for a week's camp rations. There were twenty-eight eiders, which comprised but a third of the number of birds we had taken. The rest were pin-tails, wigeons, black ducks, an auk, some puffins and guillemots.

We hauled up on shore for a meal and a smoke, and a rest in the bright noon sunshine; after which I wandered off for a stroll, to stretch my legs and get rid of the cramp occasioned by eight hours' boating.

I climbed the hill by a well-beaten path, which the reindeer had made in passing. I had no thought of seeing the deer, for it was not their month of migration.

What a thrilling sight is that migrating horde; an almost endless procession of graceful creatures clothed in gray, their heavy white beards waving, with great horns wildly tossing as they bound across the barrens, or laid at rest on their sleek round backs to plunge through strips of timber; pursuing an even, air-line route across the roughest country, swimming the streams and salt water bays, and scaling the highest mountains!

Near the comb of the ridge was a great white mark which resembled a quartz vein's cropping; but on nearer inspection it proved to be a large flock of white grouse feeding. It was easy enough to approach within range, and in fact I was almost upon them before they heavily took to flight, and I emptied my gun at the covey.

Then with a snort a buck sprang out from behind a sheltering boulder, and, followed by a family of doe and fawns, vanished over the crest of the mountain. For a moment his spreading antlers were lined, like dead trees, against the horizon, while I vainly searched for a charge of buck. I had nothing but small shot with me.

On our way back we gathered in a few more ducks and divers; and greatly to Angeuk's delight secured a fine young ranger seal, the Esquimaux's choicest delicacy.

Attention has been somewhat directed to Labrador of late, by the summer expeditions which have recently been made there.

In 1890, Professors Kenaston and Bryant, of Oberlin College, reached the Grand Falls of the Hamilton River, which empties into Lake Melville, the western extremity of Hamilton Inlet, or Grosswater Bay.

A number of students from Bowdoin College, in charge of some of the college faculty, made an ineffectual attempt to visit the same locality the following year. That they failed was undoubtedly due to their lack of forethought and ignorance of woodcraft, for the country presents no very serious obstacles.

In 1892 a party of young Americans, which included two representatives of Harvard University, cruised for three months along the coast, as far as the sixteenth degree of north latitude; and in 1893 the Hudson Bay Company's post at Davis Inlet was visited by two gentlemen from New York City, in search of sport and recreation.

Lieutenant Peary called at several of the Moravian settlements, on his way to the Arctic circle last year, and gave a cursory account in his published letters of what he saw there.

In the summer of 1894, a number of Doctor Cook's OUTING Arctic excursionists deserted the ill-fated steamer, *Miranda*, after her collision with the iceberg off Belle Isle, and passed a few weeks in the vicinity of Cape Saint Charles. They expressed themselves as greatly pleased with the sport they obtained, and talked of returning.

Another party of Americans, of which the writer was a member, left St. John's, Newfoundland, June 30th, 1894, in the *Swallow*, a steam launch of but twenty-two tons gross measurement, on an extended trip of four months' duration.

Going north, the channels along the mainland, inside all the islands, were followed from the Straights of Belle Isle to the fifty-seventh degree of north latitude, which was reached July 26th. The return journey was commenced September 26th, and successfully accomplished, without mishap of any kind, October 28th.

The *Swallow* had a wooden hull forty-eight feet in length, of twelve feet beam and six feet draught; carried mainsail, foresail and staysail, and was fully sheathed with greenheart timber, making her safe to travel through the floes, which were unusually heavy and numerous off the Labrador coast last season.

This battling with the floes is not by any means monotonous, or devoid of interest, especially to one who can appreciate the grandeur and sublimity of a sea of ice. Let those desiring novel sensations test an experience amid the ever-shifting bergs and pans, as they are carried silently along upon the ocean current, now opening a narrow, snake-like passage of blue water, through which the vessel steams at headlong speed, dodging the sunken greenish spurs and crashing over the smaller broken pieces; then suddenly closing down *en-masse* and presenting a close and seemingly impenetrable wall of solid ice, at which the steamer hurls herself, driving her bows high upon some low-lying pan and crushing it with her weight; then with blow upon blow, beating, grinding, crunching, pushing and so violently forcing her way into a crack, which slowly opens across the jamb, into another strip of open water just beyond.

The angler can find ample amusement in any of the bays along the mainland and the streams which feed them. There is an excellent river at Blanc Sablon, in which the brook-trout average above a pound. Another locally well-known stream empties into St. Michael's Bay, and is easily reached from Battle Harbor.

Battle Harbor is the meeting point for the two coasting mail steamers which ply between Saint John's, Newfoundland, and the Moravian missions, making fortnightly voyages. This station is owned by a well-known supply firm of St. John's, and is headquarters for one of the most extensive fishing establishments on the coast. Here, too, is located the head office of the Mission to Deep Sea Fishermen. Through the efforts of Doctor Grenfell, a comfortable hospital has been erected and furnished with every necessity and convenience. The staff includes a resident physician and a trained nurse.

Between Battle Harbor and Hamilton Inlet there are many fine trout streams and ponds, notably at Spear Harbor, Snug Harbor, Porcupine Run and Sandwich Bay. This entire territory is literally over-run with Ptarmigan, the white Arctic grouse, and in the months of September and October half a dozen coveys may be found during an hour's walk over the hill-tops.

The caribou are not so numerous on this portion of the coast as they are a few hundred miles further north. An occasional black bear may be encountered in any of the bays, and a search for them in the neighborhood of Porcupine should be successful. The wild geese, eider ducks and sea fowl which make their summer haunts from Harrigan northward, begin to arrive in this locality about September 15th, and furnish excellent sport throughout October.

A most unique and interesting natural phenomenon is to be found some miles southwest from Nain, upon an island called Nepoktulegatsuk. Extending across the island is a broad vein of opalescent spar, or Labradorite, as it is sometimes called. Its chatoyant, iridescent colors suggest the fancy that it might have had its birth in the crystallization of some magnificent aurora.

Small crystals of this gem-like stone are distributed throughout the felspathic rocks almost everywhere within a radius of twenty miles; but Nature seems to have selected this particular spot for its chief abode, and has supplied it with a lavish and artistic hand.

Blue is the predominating hue, which finds expression in all possible variations, from the lightest of silvery sky tints, through delicate shadings to a deep and richly glowing indigo. Next in order of prominence are the golds and bronzes. Their wavy, flame-like delineations sometimes produce startling, though always harmonious contrasts. In one portion of the deposit may be found broad splashes of brilliant green, also in varying shades from soft ultramarine to vivid emerald.

The colors are the more pleasing in that they are produced by a remarkable refraction of the rays of light. The stone possesses no inherent color of its own, and these prismatic tints come and go, as the position of the observer changes; flashing out unexpectedly at this point, eluding one at that, playing at hide and seek like elfish rainbows, in a multitude of tints and hues.

Nain is the most southern station at which the ivory carvings of the Esquimaux can be procured. The best are to be found at Okkak, and are the handwork of two cripples named Boaz and Nicodemus, by virtue of their Moravian baptisms. The walrus is seldom found south of Kig-la-pait. The tusks are, therefore, difficult to procure at the southern stations, and are considered too valuable to be wasted in whittling trinkets.

Some of the Okkak carvings are really beautiful and are, without doubt, superior to those made by the natives of Alaska or any other portion of the North. The trueness to nature and delicacy of outline and finish with which they are executed, evince decided artistic instincts and natural genius, and enable them to compare favorably with the carvings of the Japanese.

At Nayasivivik I found a cave-like dwelling, and at its entrance the cliffy rock bore traces, here and there, of hieroglyphic carvings. Not far away a monstrous boulder stands alone upon the plain of death, like some grim monument. Upon its level top, so said my guide, the naked bodies of infants were exposed until the birds and beasts came and devoured them.

By far the most interesting ruins on the coast were those we found near the entrance to Nachvack Bay. It was evident from their appearance that they had never been visited by desecrating strangers, and even the natives disclaimed all knowledge of them.

Upon a narrow strip of beach, at the foot of a precipitous ravine cutting the crest of the mountainous cliffs which overhang the sea, half buried in shingle and weighted with a heavy covering of turf and moss, are the well-preserved remains of what was once the residence of a populous tribe.

The main entrance had been formed by setting upon end the lower jawbones of a whale. This led into a broad passageway, from which smaller ones branched at irregular intervals, and which terminated at the various family apartments, or habitations. Whales' bones entered largely into the construction of the whole, no other material having been used for supports. Nachvack is far beyond the northern tree limit of the coast, and these were, doubtless, the best substitute for timbers which could be procured. The vertebræ of whales had been used as stools and for various other purposes; the frameworks of kayaks and komatiks, skin boats and sledges, were of bone and horn; the weapons and implements were of stone, bone, horn and ivory. Enough of these were present to have filled a ship, but not a scrap of iron or other metal could be found.

The population of this village seemed to have been buried at its very doors. Every available spot in the ravine contained a burial cairn.

RUGGED LABRADOR.

By R. G. Taber.

energy, perseverance, a determination to meet hardships with cheerfulness, annoyances with patience, possible dangers with firmness, and with a fair knowledge of how to use his weapons, the merest tyro will be rewarded with gratifying success. Not the least valued among his trophies will be the magnificent head and antlers of his first gray-bearded caribou buck, and the memory of its capture will thrill him in after years when recollections of other incidents, pleasures and vexations have faded from his mind.

The Hudson Bay Company's officers complain that the white water bears are not so plentiful as they were a few years ago. Yet their trader at Davis Inlet procured fourteen skins last year, the largest of which measured thirteen feet and brought fifteen pounds sterling at the Company's annual auction. The Nachvach station obtains the largest number, sometimes securing fifty skins in a single season.

I shall not easily forget my first introduction to one of these North Sea monsters. It was a bright day in August and I had started with a canoe upon a voyage of discovery, along the wild shore of Kaipokok Bay. I took my breech-loader in order to pick up a few water fowl, but a trout brook was the principal object of my search and I carried all my tackle. The boat was a small one with a single thwart and a pair of short oars. The tide runs fiercely into the bay and forms quite a "rattle" in places, so that I made rapid progress, skimming along close to the base of the towering precipices. I had proceeded a couple of miles from our anchorage when, turning to glance ahead, my attention was arrested by the head of an animal swimming. The distance was considerable and the glint of the sunlight was so strong that I could not see the creature distinctly. Concluding that it must be a large, square flipper seal, I shoved two loads of buckshot into my gun and waited for the game to dive. This it presently did, and noting the proper direction I

GAME of all kinds is very plentiful in this northern country at certain seasons of the year, and finer fly-fishing cannot be obtained. While in Nachvach Bay, our friend, the young chief of the Kakkertaksoaks, who glories in the name of Kargegatsuk-Okalishiak-Disiatchiak, brought us a present of the largest seatrout I have ever seen. When cleaned it weighed a trifle over seventeen pounds.

Nevertheless, whoever goes to Labrador with the idea that he has only to provide himself with a rod and gun to win a sportsman's record, will be disappointed. If in pursuit of game, he must be prepared to undergo no small amount of discomfort, labor and fatigue; to make long trips in open boats and afoot; to climb the rugged hills; to ford the mountain streams; to wade through swamp and morass covered with thorny hackmatack; to endure the tormenting stings of insects, dine on hardtack, sleep beneath the stars, or seek the shelter of some natural cave.

With this in mind, and forethought,

pulled away toward it lustily. It rose much sooner than I had expected, and with a crumbling "Gr-r-r-nyah!" shook the water from its head scarcely thirty yards beyond me. I shall never see such a sight again, nor experience such a sensation. Magnified both by its reflection in the sea and my heated imagination, the head appeared fully two feet in breadth; the eyes glowed like coals; the heavy, black upper-lip curled back and displayed the long white incisors. I grasped my gun, took a hurried sight and discharged both the barrels. I had not calculated the recoil from eleven drams of best powder and nearly lost my balance. As the boat "righted" one oar slipped out from between the clumsy thole-pins and drifted away on the current. I did not attempt its recovery, but hastily reloaded in order to be prepared to meet the struggle I feared was coming. The bear had dived and I waited breathlessly, with tensely strung nerves, for its reappearance, each moment expecting that wicked "Gr-r-r-nyah!" to roll out of the water beside me. The moments sped but it never came. I grew anxious, impatient, angry, and finally, cursing my faulty aim, sculled away to recover my oar.

My second encounter, which occurred somewhat later, although not so exciting, was attended with more satisfactory results.

We were three hundred miles further north and bowling along homeward, before a stiff breeze, under a double reefed mainsail. In the open sea, three miles off Sieglick Head, we sighted a bear in the water, which had evidently abandoned the distant floe ice and was making a bee-line landward. We put the helm down and came about, got up the guns and rifles, and soon had a battery formed in the bows large enough to repel a pirate. Bruin felt the gravity of the pursuit and vainly tried to outswim us, but seeing the uselessness of the attempt she finally turned and swam toward us. We wondered why she did not dive, for these creatures are nearly as expert as seals at keeping below the surface; but the reason was obvious, when we made out the heads of two cubs beside her. We reserved our fire until we had them well under the bows,

and then discharged a volley. It was a slaughter which hardly deserved the name of sport, for it lacked the essential elements of a chance for the game or danger. We had secured the prize of the trip. The skins were carefully salted down, and the flesh of the half-grown cubs kept us in meat for a fortnight. It was tender and juicy, and although there was a slight fishy flavor, it was not unpalatable. The change it afforded from tough salt junk was certainly agreeable.

It has been stated that the primitive Esquimaux had no religious ideas, yet evidences, or rather indications of belief in a resurrection are to be found in all their undisturbed graves. Beside the bodies are always placed the hunters' spears, harpoons, bows and arrows, or the housewives' soapstone kettles, lamps and ivory needles. A small compartment at the right of the head contains a bowl or two of seals' meat, ribs or joints; and another, at the left, a jar once filled with water. Not unfrequently a komatik or kayak may be discovered, one on either side the cairn, and in one grave I opened the hunter's dogs had been buried at his feet.

One of our most successful investigations was barely commenced when a violent storm compelled us to put out to sea and abandon the exploration, together with most of the interesting relics we had purposed taking with us, and which possessed great ethnographic value.

From Ramah to Cape Chudleigh, on the eastern slope of the height of land, the Esquimaux number barely three-score persons. These have not been visited by the missionaries, as yet, and they are probably as primitive and uncivilized as any that exist on our continent to-day. They practice polygamy, buying, selling and trading their wives with as little compunction as they would their dogs, and sometimes for a smaller consideration. It would be unjust to them, however, not to mention the affectionate kindness with which they generally treat their consorts; and they consult and follow the wishes and devices of their helpmates with a frequency and fidelity which might be worthy of imitation by the husbands in more fortunate and civilized climes. Yet, if the truth were known, this laudable complaisance might possibly explain the reason for a good many of the marital transactions.

They acknowledge a chieftain, or elder, but his influence is not as powerful as is that of the tribal medicine-man; nor is he treated with such consideration and respect as are bestowed, through superstitious fear, upon the latter.

The remedies employed by the shaman consist of phrensied incantations, charms, amulets and "cure by faith," an occasional resort being had to more direct and vigorous measures, which include the sweat-box and massage. A certain kind of vermin, swallowed alive at stated intervals, is held to be an infallible specific for coughs and colds.

The flesh these people eat is seldom cooked. I have seen them devour a trout, just taken from the water, without even indulging in the formality of using a knife upon it. They are good hunters, as the thirty white bear and ninety silver fox skins, obtained from them last year by the Hudson Bay Company, attest.

"The price those poor Chudleigh people get for their fur is perfectly outrageous," remarked the captain of a Halifax trader, who had once made a trip to the Cape. "Why, when I went trading to Ungava, in 'eighty, the Company was only allowing them a plug of tobacco for an otter skin worth three pounds. Think of *that!*"

"Shameful," I replied; "I presume you secured all the fur that year, by giving them a fairer bargain?"

"Well, yes. I got the fur," he said, with a twinkle in his eyes. "You see, as it didn't cut much of a figure in the

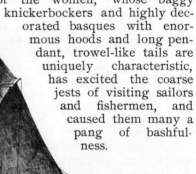

profits to double prices, I gave the Huskies *two* plugs to the Company's *one*."

These Esquimaux have no fixed residence, but are as nomadic as the mountaineers, shifting from place to place in search of game, and dwelling in snow igloos eight or nine months of every year. They are much more healthy and hardy than their southern cousins, and with their robust bodies and clear complexions, they bear an air of boldness, pride and confidence, in all of which the others are sadly lacking. Their language is scarcely intelligible to the men from Nain, and our interpreter made very difficult work of the simple questions we desired him to address to them.

Here the typical Esquimaux attire is worn the whole year round. The deer and seal skins of which the garments are composed are beautifully tanned, and are as soft and white as the finest chamois. An occasional fur cassock may be seen in summer use from Aillik to Harrigan; the people at Nain are all provided with them, and when they are not in attendance at the mission, wear them throughout the warmest weather. But the natives south of Cape Mugford seem somewhat ashamed of their national dress, and wear it as little as possible when in the presence of strangers.

They are very sensitive to ridicule, and their curious apparel, particularly that of the women, whose baggy knickerbockers and highly decorated basques with enormous hoods and long pendant, trowel-like tails are uniquely characteristic, has excited the coarse jests of visiting sailors and fishermen, and caused them many a pang of bashfulness.

RUGGED LABRADOR.

By R. G. Taber.

[CONCLUDED.]

FOR a short mid-summer outing I do not know of any better locality than the country about Altaguyivivik, midway up the coast. The mail steamer calls at Aillik, a conveniently located settlement at the foot of the mountains and formerly a post of the Hudson Bay Company. There are several resident families of Esquimaux here, who speak fairly good English, and any of whom would make acceptable guides, particularly an exceptionally good hunter named Lucy, who was one of the Esquimaux exhibited at the World's Fair.

A small stream falls into Aillik Bay from which, one afternoon in July, I took thirty-seven trout, the smallest of which tipped the scales at two pounds and the largest at three and a quarter.

The Labrador trout are very notional and the only fly that would tempt them that day was a number four "Dark Montreal."

After landing my biggest fish, which cost me half an hour of vigorous work to kill, I made a score of casts without a rise. I had turned away, with the intention of trying the next whirlpool,

and my flies were idly trailing along behind me, when, with a jerk which nearly caused me to lose my balance in the rapid current, a large salmon struck and spun the line out down-stream, the full length of my hundred yards, before I could pull myself together sufficiently to put on an extra drag. There was a momentary shock as the end of the line was reached, and then I wound in my tackle, to find it parted at the knot which spliced the leader.

The pools are half a mile up-stream and are not reached by salt water, yet it is only on a rising tide that good sport can be had there. At the mouth of the stream is an inexhaustible bed of clams, or "cocks and hens," as the fishermen are wont to call them.

The summit of Altaguyivivik, shining white, is distant a dozen miles or thereabouts, and upon the elevated plateaux and in the valleys on its slopes the reindeer may be found, the whole year round. Not in immense droves of thousands, such as visit the shores further north at certain times each year, but in herds, or families, of half a dozen each. It is also good hunting ground for bear, the white fox, and the large Arctic wolf, which is fully twice the size of the timber wolf of Wisconsin.

At Davis Inlet I saw a magnificent wolf pelt of a rich, dark brown color, measuring over nine feet in length. I am indebted to Mr. Swaffield, the company's factor there, for an account of its capture, which illustrates the strength and ferocity of these animals.

He was awakened in the early morning by a commotion among his dog teams, and, thinking they were indulging in one of their customary frays, which sometimes seriously injure a number of the participants, he seized a cudgel and rushed out to put a stop to it.

It was barely light enough for him to make out the struggling mass of growling and yelping canines, which were engaged within a stone's throw of his house, and it was not until he was in the midst of them that he discovered the cause of the disturbance. In the centre of the throng a panting wolf was standing, with crested mane and fiery eyes which showed no sign of fear. Below him lay the prostrate body of one of Swaffield's best out-runners. The Esquimaux dogs are plucky fighters and these returned again and again to the attack; but not one came within reach of the wolf's ivory fangs without leaving a trail of blood upon the snow.

The wolf paid no attention to Swaffield's approach, and, realizing that he must not delay if he would prevent the crippling of his entire pack, he ran back for his Winchester. Although but a few moments elapsed, the wolf had slain another dog before his return. It required considerable clubbing to drive the dogs away and prevent them from tearing the creature into pieces after it had been shot.

Among the varieties of waterfowl which nest upon the islands about Aillik, the most common are the puffins, auks, murres, and guillemots. The razorbill, grebe, loon, s h a g, albatross, gannet, wigeon, pintail and black ducks are also to be found there.

The student of geology will discover much that is worthy of investigation in the stratified Cambrian and Laurentian rocks, the columnar formation of the basaltic dykes, the numerous sulphuret bearing veins, and the shell-strewn beaches raised scores of feet above the level of the sea, for which the coast of Labrador is famous, and which are more perfect in this locality than at any other point.

Among the interesting crystalized mineral forms which have been found there may be mentioned topaz, beryl, amazon - stone, amethystine quartz, chrysolite, gypsum, talc, mica, allanite, cuprite, chalco-pyrite, magnetite, limonite, pyrite and other forms of iron and copper.

The Esquimaux at Aillik are Moravian converts and members of the mission church at Hopedale. They are about the first pure Esquimaux to be met with on the coast, although there are mixed bloods in nearly all the bays beyond Cape North. At Hopedale one sees but a few faces bearing the Caucasian imprint and at Nain the number is still less.

The able-bodied natives at these stations range about, during the summer seasons, among the outer islands in search of the best fishing grounds, but on Sundays there is a gathering, from far and near, to attend the mission services. These are held at nine and eleven in the morning, and at two, four and seven o'clock in the afternoon.

WARM AND HAPPY.

Each service occupies from twenty minutes to half an hour. It usually consists of an opening hymn, a short prayer, another hymn, a verse or two from the Bible, again a hymn, a three minute exhortation, and a closing hymn, all rendered in the Esquimaux tongue.

The majority of the congregation appear in white cotton cassocks, trimmed with blue and red braid, and spotlessly clean for the occasion. The men are seated to the right of the altar and the women and children occupy the left side of the chapel, each entering and departing through separate doorways.

The organist is a native and on church festivals, or other grand occasions, the organ is sometimes supplemented by a mixed orchestra of stringed instruments and horns, also manipulated by natives.

The hymns are opened by some hesitating, tremulous, female voice, which gives the first note or two entirely unsupported. Others gradually take up the refrain, and by the time the last line of the first verse is reached the whole congregation is *en rapport*.

The sacrament of Holy Communion is administered three times a year, on Christmas, Easter Sunday, and a Sunday in August set apart to commemorate the foundation of their church. The ceremony is simple and impressive. The consecrated bread is passed and held in the open palm during the reading of the service, the congregation standing throughout. Upon the completion of the reading, it is partaken of simultaneously, and then each communicant salutes his neighbor, to the right and left, with a hand clasp and a kiss. After this, the wine is passed from hand to hand and all kneel and listen to a short but earnest prayer. The Esquimaux are very fond of music, and, between the services, mingling strains from violins, harmonicas and concertinas, rise from all points.

The mission buildings are roomy, comfortable, warm and scrupulously clean; in striking contrast with the habitations of the natives, grouped about them without any regularity, and consisting of small, low, gloomy, damp, moss-covered huts, superlatively dirty and malodorous.

The missionaries carry on an extensive trade and are brisk competitors with the Hudson Bay Company for the products of the country, fish, fur and oil.

A DOMESTICATED NATIVE.

Their eleemosynary character exempts them from the payment of duties to Newfoundland, and as the prices they obtain in trade are equal to, and in some cases exceed those obtained by the Company for similar goods, their profits are larger in proportion.

I am not well informed as to the prices charged for merchandise, but I have had occasion to purchase a few supplies and quote the following from the bill which was rendered : Salt pork at 30 cents per pound; coarse brown sugar at 17 cents per pound; ship bread at $6.40 per bag of 100 pounds; butter at 50 cents per pound; soap at 50 cents per bar; salt at $3\frac{1}{3}$ cents per pound; nails at 10 cents per pound; candles at 15 cents per pound; kerosene at 50 cents per gallon. I was told that the goods were sold to me at prices considerably below the usual charges to the natives.

The latter's account receives a credit of from $30.00 to $45.00 for a silver fox skin, according to its quality; $5.00 to $8.00 for a crossed fox, and the same for otter; $2.00 for red and $1.50 for Arctic foxes; $12.00 to $15.00 for white and $8.00 to $10.00 for black bear skins; 20 cents each for seal skins; 15 cents for deer skins; $1.10 per pair for first-class water-tight seal-skin boots; $2.40 to $2.80 per quintal for cod-fish; $4.00 to $5.00 per barrel for trout.

The pernicious credit system, which has proved so disastrous in Newfoundland, is encouraged by both the missions and the Company. The Esquimaux in the trade of each are taught that to dispose of any of their fish or fur to the competitor is little less than stealing. A good many natives surreptitiously trade with both, but when a case of this kind comes to light the malefactor is punished by having his credit stopped. This may not appear a very severe penalty, but the serious consequences will be better appreciated when it is understood that these poor people are invariably in debt for nearly a year's supplies, which have been advanced to them; they are never allowed a longer credit than twelve months' time; there are no traders to whom they can dispose of their catch, and a delinquent is condemned to pay what he owes before he can obtain from the only available stores another pound of flour.

During the summer months, existence may be maintained upon the bountiful product of the sea; and, were he not by nature the most improvident of beings, he might, with industry, preserve a sufficient quantity of such food to insure his family against starvation for the winter period. But when the winter comes, burying the sea beneath six to seven feet of solid ice, it drives the game inland in search of food and shelter, and he has no recourse but to follow. With such scant supplies as friends or relatives may be prevailed upon to furnish, he pursues the roving herds of deer, sets his traps for otter, bear and fox, relies for sustenance upon the precarious issues of the chase, and makes his home in hastily constructed igloos built of snow and ice. The "mountaineers," as the Indians of the interior are called, have been his bitter foes for centuries. Although there has been no open warfare between the races since the Battle Island Massacre, the sullen Indians resent any intrusion upon their hunting grounds by their ancient enemies, and, when opportunity offers they "abate the nuisance" in their proverbially radical way. Another danger exists in the vicissitudinous climate. Added to the peril of storms and excessive cold, are the chances of a sudden thaw, which may, in a single day, devour the snow. It is upon the snow he must rely for shelter; but more than this, the snow alone enables him to overtake the game, and also to reach the coast again with his dogs and Komatik.

The Esquimaux will tell you that each fall a number of families go "into the land," and that, be it from starvation, cold, exposure, the Indians, casualties, or a combination of causes, the number of those who return is often less than half of those who go. The missing are seldom, if ever, heard from.

19

Wa-Gush

LAWRENCE MOTT

WA-GUSH

BY LAWRENCE MOTT

THE north wind flung itself wildly, viciously over the gray barrens; shrieking and whistling, it passed into the dark forests beyond.

A lone figure, urging on his dog team, sometimes pushing the sledge behind them when the snow was soft, struggled slowly across the mournful distances.

"Sacrée, Ah no get to de poste dees night," he murmured.

As though in answer to his words the dogs stopped, panting, their feet bleeding, their eyes half closed; worn out with the weight of their load and the killing softness of the snow.

The man, Phiné Poleon, straightened up and looked about, while the wind tore at his clothes, bellowed in his ears and slung the biting drift over him. Everywhere loomed the solitude of the winter barrens; everywhere the snow flew along in tumbling clouds, ever and always the gale shrieked in gusts. The dogs had lain down together, creeping to one another that their warmth might keep off the fury of the storm.

"Ah mus' get to de fores'," Phiné said aloud, took up his whip and curled the thong about the tired brutes.

"Allez! allez! Marse!"

They got to their feet painfully and started on, he helping from the rear.

At last, after hours of fighting against the whirling snow, he came to the forest. Tall, black and grim the hemlock and pine stood before him, their tops pirouetting wildly in the wind.

In their shelter Poleon halted, built a lean-to, gathered some dry wood and lighted his fire. The flames ate their red way speedily, and roared their heat to the coldness of the air.

After supper he fed the dogs, rolled himself in his rabbit-skin blanket and slept.

It was nearly daylight when he woke, his mind roused to action by the feeling of the presence of something. He got up, started to call the dogs, when the gleam of a fire in the forest below arrested his voice.

"Who's dere?" he muttered

In yellow lines of light that flickered and shone, the other fire gleamed warmly. His own had gone out.

"Ah go see!" and he went, stealing from tree to tree, the sound of his feet crunching in the snow covered up by the noises of the angry night.

By the brightly blazing fire were two figures close together, a man and a woman. Her face he could not see for the dancing shadows.

"Dat ees Le Renard," he whispered, recognizing an old comrade in the man. He was about to go forward when the woman rose and passed behind the other figure. Poleon saw the flash of steel, but could not hear the groan. He saw the body roll over and twitch convulsively.

"Bon Dieu, w'at you do?" he shouted, leaping on. The woman saw him coming and darted away in the blackness, seizing a pair of snowshoes that were near as she ran.

"D—n you," he cursed and tried to follow. He stumbled and slipped, then stopped breathless. Only the impenetrable mass of trunks met his eyes, their branches flapping monotonously to and fro.

"No can catch now," and he went back to the wounded man.

"Renard, w'at ees?" he asked frantically, tearing open his friend's capote and shirt. The latter opened his great black eyes for an instant.

"Dat—you—Poleon?"

"Si—si," the latter answered, trying to stop the flow of blood that reddened the snow.

"Ah'm—een—de—Pol—eece—dees—year; catch mans for steal, he—go—Stonee—Montaigne;* dees girl—mak' me t'ink—she—loove—me; she sistaire dat mans!" the voice finished.

"Ah catch her sure!" Poleon screamed, seeing that his friend's death was near. "W'at her name? no could see her, me."

The dying trapper·gasped and gurgled a moment, "W—g——" and died.

The dead man in his arms, the glazing eyes looking unseeing into his, Poleon crouched, dazed, horror-stricken. As in a dream, old scenes, memories of trapping days together, days that were fraught with success sometimes, sometimes burdened with failure, but always hours of companionship and a deep friendliness, passed before his memory eyes.

"An' now," he muttered sadly, "eet all feenesh forevaire." Then he stood up and took off his cap. "Bon Dieu, hear w'en Ah, Phiné Poleon, say dat Ah goin' keel dat girl somtaim!" He looked up at the heavens. They were dull gray and black with the coming light. Clouds sped over in banks and hurrying rifts. Gloomy, forbidding and cold they were.

He picked up the dead man and carried him to where his dogs were waiting, curled up, asleep. On top of the load of fur he fastened the stiffening form. Without breakfast or even a thought of food he crackled his whip.

"Allez—hoop!"

The half light in the forest showed the drifts and piled-up masses of snow, and the dogs worked slowly along. Weaker and weaker their pulls at the load became, then they stopped, powerless to pull more.

"W'at Ah do?" Phiné whispered, wiping the beads of sweat from his face. "Ah mus' leave Renard or my skeens."

He stood long, hesitating between the body of his friend and the fur he had collected from his traps; these meant money and food to him. At last—"Ah buree Renard," and he fell to work.

With his axe he dug through the snow and hacked at the frozen earth beneath, finally sinking a hole big enough for his purpose. Then he undid the lashings, lifted the dead man from the sledge, lowered him carefully, put back the earth, dragged the snow over the spot and stamped it down.

*The penitentiary for the N. W. Provinces.

Gravely he stood on it then, and said his Ave Maria twice, called to the team and turned away, tears in his eyes.

At night he reached the Hudson Bay Company's post at Mistassiny and took his furs to the factor, receiving for them food and some money.

"'Tis a good thing ye got a fair lot this time," the Scotchman said as he examined the skins, "fur ye hae nae doun so well lately, Phin!"

But the big French Canadian said nothing.

For days he fought with himself as to whether he should tell of the murder he had seen committed, because the Post was asking for Le Renard, but he argued, "Ah no know dat w'man; dey no b'lief me; mabbe tink *Ah* keel Renard," and he was silent.

The knife that he had found in his friend's back he kept. It was a peculiar blade, with a moose-horn handle and a blunted haft. He would take it out when he was alone in his tepee and look at it, moisture in his gaunt eyes.

"Ef Ah onlee knew who deed dat!" he would whisper over and over again.

Each night before he slept he solemnly repeated his vow to kill the girl "somtaim," and each day he watched everything and every one about the Post furtively, but learned nothing. The questions about Le Renard faded away.

"He mus' ha' lost hisself," the factor said.

But Poleon knew and he chafed at his own powerlessness. All winter he worked on at his traps, and when spring came he had a good credit account at the store.

"Ah goin' be marry," he announced abruptly one day to the factor.

"Who?" the latter asked.

"Wa-gush." (Little Fox.)

"She is a fox, too," and the Scotchman chuckled, "but I hae nae doubt ye can beat her well enou' to keep her frae foxin'," and he laughed aloud.

"Ah loove her, dat all I know," Poleon answered gravely and went out of the store.

On a glorious June day, when the trees were green with springing life, and the air warm with the luxury of the coming short months of heat, Poleon was married to Wa-gush, the little Indian girl he had grown to love, if a rough mastership with a passionate adoration besides can be called love. All the Post were there, and when the Jesuit father pronounced his blessing, they cheered.

Wa-gush and Phiné took up their home in a large, fine tepee that Poleon had built for the occasion. The girl was slim, but strong in body, muscular and active. Her face was of the Chippewa type, with long, slender nose, aloe eyes, high forehead, straight black hair, tiny feet and hands.

"Dieu, Ah loove you!" Poleon whispered softly to her one night as the little supper fire flamed and spluttered at their feet. She looked at him and her eyes narrowed more than ever.

"An' Ah loove you!" she answered softly, tapping her beaded moccasins with a little stick.

Poleon never beat her; on the contrary he carried the wood, built the fires, hauled the nets on the lake; in short, did everything that is usually done by the squaws —so much so that the Post laughed at him.

"Ye do love her, don't ye, Poleon?" the factor said one day sarcastically.

"Ah-hai" (yes), he answered.

All this time of great happiness with the girl, the old sorrow for his friend was working at his heart. He would sit by his fire, with her on the other side, and somberly dream, sometimes seeing the death picture, sometimes almost feeling Le Renard in his arms.

Often he tried to tell her of his pain, but at each attempt the words stuck in his throat. No, he could not make her unhappy, especially because they both hoped for a child. Unseen he would take out the knife and gloomily handle it, wondering, praying that some time he might have his vengeance.

The days passed on, one by one, each filled with its own particular happiness with Wa-gush, each bringing nearer the longed-for event. In the evenings, when his nets were hauled and the dogs fed, Poleon would take her out on the lake in one of his birch-bark canoes and paddle quietly along the warm, dark shores, startling the deer from their feeding, and listening to the lonely hoot of owls.

One night his sorrow was too great.

"Chérie," he said quietly.

"Ai?" she put her hand on his knee that rested on the canoe bottom.

"Ah have beeg pain!"

"Ai?" she said again, waiting.

He drew out the knife from his bosom.

"Dees kn'fe—" he began, when he heard the startled gasp, felt her shiver run over the canoe and looked up. In the moonlight her dusky face was white, and her eyes burned strangely at him. She controlled herself by a valiant effort.

"Ai?"

A wild thought flashed across him, and he remembered, could hear the dying man's attempt at a name: "W—g——"

She was herself again. "Tell to me?"

And he told her the story, watching, now that the iron was in his heart, with the keenness of a hound, but Wa-gush gave no further sign.

"Dat too bad, Poleon," she said when he finished, "you mus' fin' dat girrl an' keel!" Straight she looked at him and he stared back. No waver of an eyelid met his gaze.

"You t'ink dat?"

"Ai-hai" (yes), she answered steadily, and they went home.

More days passed, but now they were fraught with double pain to Poleon.

"It no can be dat!" he would say to himself when alone.

At supper one night the blanket at the entrance was pushed aside and a great Indian came in.

"Bo' jou', Poleon, bo' jou', sistaire, Ah comme f'om Stonee Montaigne, Ah'm free at las'!" and he sat down.

Poleon turned to the girl; she was watching him with a tense, hunted look.

"Ah-h!" he whispered, and talked on gayly.

She was lulled to carelessness, thinking he did not know, and when he suggested they go on the lake, the next evening, she got into the canoe quietly.

The moon shone in all its glorious splendor, silvering the waters and causing the forest to appear as black lines. When at a distance from the Post, Poleon got out the old knife.

"You keel Le Renard," he said, with no anger in his voice, only an ineffable sorrow.

"Non—non," she answered, seeing the light in his eyes.

"Ah say yes, an' Ah'm goin' keel you!"

She begged for mercy as he put the paddle down.

"T'ink of you' petit," she whispered then; he crawled over the thwart.

"Ah *am* t'inken," he said, and struck! The canoe trembled for an instant, then was quiet on the calm waters.

He looked at her, dead at his feet, her little hands resting over the side. The knife was still in his hands.

"Bon Dieu, Ah have keel lak' Ah say, now Ah keel h'again."

He thrust at his own chest with a powerful, heavy blow. "Adieu, Wa-gush, Ah alway loove you," he gasped as he fell, overturning the canoe by his weight.

The waters rolled away in sullen ripples after the splash; and the upturned canoe floated motionless and dark on the still, moonlit surface.

20

Saga of 54°

HERMAN WHITAKER

Saga of 54°

BY HERMAN WHITAKER

EYOND the parallel of 54°, a hundred miles north of Cumberland House—named after his Grace, the "Butcher"—and two hundred miles from Pelly, lies the country of the Makwas. If you should wish to go there, a team of shaganappy ponies, if they be tough, will run you up from Pelly in five days. The High Commissioner of the Hudson Bay makes it in three, but his horses are then turned out for a year's rest. You cannot afford this. Between this country and the Lake of Amisk lie the pot-hole lands. Here, say the Makwas, the Great Spirit rested from his labors, and, blind to the chaos at his feet, looked forth on his work and called it good. But on arising to go thence, says the legend, he saw the evil of the land, and because it had made him to say the thing which was not, he cursed it forevermore. And so, seamed, rugged, broken, bordered by forests of gloomy spruce, crude, just as it dropped from his hand, it endures to this day.

Over its scarred surface writhe fathomless earth-cracks. Bleak sand-hills lie cheek by jowl with black morasses; and huge pits—the pot-holes of the Makwas— gape amid shaking quagmires and treacherous muskegs. A thousand lakes dot the bush. From their waters petrified trees thrust skeleton limbs. Over the inky depths the loon races his shadow, the hawk shrieks a malediction from the sky, and at night the owl bells anathema in the sleeping woods. Accursed, devil-haunted, peopled by wild beasts, it is avoided of Cree and Sioux and Makwa, and even the trappers of Fort à la Corne give it a wide berth.

The last rays of a blood-red sun flamed over the pot-hole lands, crimsoning the waters and clothing the abomination of desolation with scarlet robes and gold. From the eastern face of a deep pit the rose light glanced on the upturned countenance of a man. He stood at the bottom. All around the rock sloped up and out, so that a stone dropped from the top would have landed ten feet from the base. He was trapped; a cat could not have scaled that overhanging surface.

At the foot of the cliff the wearing hand of time had deposited a loose bank of sand and rubble. On this the man stood, the slack of a lariat coiled in his left hand, his eyes fixed on a storm-riven stump that leaned over the cliff. Slowly at first, but with gradually increasing speed, he swung the noose until it whirled in whistling circles. Suddenly he jerked it up and out. Like a darting cobra it rose, whipping out the coils, hovered for an instant, straight and rigid, then curved easily over the stump.

"Bien!" the man exclaimed, throwing up his arms. He had forgotten his precarious footing. Overbalancing, he rolled, the center of a small landslide, to the bottom of the heap. He sat up, wiped the sweat from his eyes and gazed at the swinging rope.

"Peste!" he muttered. "Two days in this pit of hell. Mère de Dieu! Two days!"

Scrambling up the heap, he began to climb, gripping the rope with knees and feet. Three yards from the top he stopped dead. A grim face looked down from above. The climber's wrists felt as big as buckets, his arms were pulling from the sockets, but, staring defiantly upward, he hung on, swinging in mid-air. A minute passed. Then a big hand slipped by the face and shook the rope. The man dropped, and the next moment the lariat fell from above, coiling across his body.

Stunned, and badly shaken, he lay on the sand while the sun slipped into his dusky blanket and the twilight faded. Up rose the noises of the night. Frogs croaked in the sloughs, a fox barked among the sand-hills, a wolf howled in the bush. A bronze moon peeped at him over the tree-tops, then climbed her silver path.

The man stirred, sat up, and glanced above. The stump stood, solitary, clearly outlined against the moonlit sky. Noiselessly mounting the heap, he tried another cast. It missed. He tried again, and again, and again, and still again, and many more times, until, toward midnight, the tightening rope sent a welcome thrill along his arm. He leaned forward, listening. The soughing night-wind, the myriad-tongued mosquito, the babel of frogs, these were all he heard.

"So!" he breathed. "The weasel sleeps."

He seized the rope, knife between teeth, ready to climb, but, as he reached up, it flew through his hand, rose, and fell about him. Sitting down, he coiled the lariat, then lay over and dozed. Once more, in the gray morning, he lassoed the stump; and this time his head leveled the bank before the silent watcher snapped him from the rope. He fell, turning head over heels, and lay until the rising sun flushed the east with trembling rose and gold.

When the sun arched to the meridian, he crawled into the shade of the overhanging bank. It was hot. The pot-hole glowed like a devil's oven. Waves of heat rolled down from the high cliff, the sand-bank glared, the stones scorched his feet. Toward noon he stripped. Then lively sand-lizards ran over him, and buzzing flies nipped pieces from his body. Hot, hungry and tired, he tried to forget his misery in sleep, but choking thirst kept him wide awake until the sun ran down the western grade. Then he dozed.

The clip of a cutting ax brought him flying into the open. There, against the fiery sunset glow, stood a man, chopping away the stump.

"Devil!"

The man looked down. "What is it, M'sieu The-Factor-That-Is-To-Be?" he sneered. "It is warm down there, eh? I see m'sieu affects negligée since he inhabited the lower regions."

"It is warm, yes." The prisoner's hand was fumbling behind his back. "But, see you, Gène Lascurrettes, it is not so hot as—hell!" The knife flashed from his finger-tips straight at the chopper's back, who just then stepped sidewise to reach farther round the tree. It whizzed between arm and body, and stuck quivering in the stump.

"So!" exclaimed Lascurrettes, swinging slowly round. "The little knife! My own, too, I had forgotten. Careless! An' this was a good throw of the knife. Forty feet if an inch! Excellent! But see you"—he pulled the knife and threw it on the ground—"now is your last bolt spent. An' M'sieu The-Factor-That-Is-To-Be will soon soon have opportunity of comparing this"—he waved his hand airily —"with hell." The prisoner made no reply. He sat on the sand-heap quietly playing with the coils of his lariat. "But m'sieu tires of the play," continued Lascurrettes. "Then, see you, we will finish." He thrust against the stump. "Not yet, eh? More chopping? Behold the white chips showering like the white blossom on the grave of M'sieu The-Factor-That-Is-To-Be. A pretty fancy."

When Gène Lascurrettes gave out his intention of building on the pot-hole lands, Fort à la Corne shrugged its shoulders and commented according to its kind.

"The man's daft!" growled the Scotch factor.

"He is one fool, this Gène!" chorused the French half-breeds. They liked not the prospect of having Gène's wife, the prettiest woman in À la Corne, removed from the sphere of their observation.

The Cree runners expressed their surprise in harsh gutturals eked out by wealth of signs. Few men cared to trap in the "scab lands"; that any should wish to live there was beyond the compass of the Cree imagination. But, indifferent to criticism, Gène continued his preparation.

He was something of a mystery to Fort à la Corne, and mysteries it hated. Experience had taught it that those things which cannot be comprehended are to be feared. Therefore, being incomprehensible, Gène was disliked.

The coldest day of the preceding winter, when the spirit registered sixty and odd below and you could hear the groan of a sled ten miles, a team of lathered ponies had swept through the fort gate. Poking its nose carefully out of doors, À la Corne had watched a sawed-off giant carry a half-frozen woman into the factor's house. And such a woman! When the frozen veil was thawed from off her face, the Fort forgot its manners (inherited from the best blood of France) and stared; and not until she quietly turned her back did they remember. It was Gène and his wife. When they inquired of his journey, he was extremely reticent, answering in general terms.

"He had come from the north?"

"He had."

"Far?"

"Far."

"Then, it was somewhat strange that

*Drawn by
T. de Thulstrup.*

"A GRIM FACE LOOKED DOWN FROM ABOVE."

a man should travel in the heavy frost?"

"Was it?"

"See you, sir, the ponies. They are the brothers of the little team of Pete Despard?"

"Likely."

Long after, they heard that he had traded dogs for ponies at Norquay's road-house, on the Great Slave Trail.

By a curious stroke of fortune, there landed in À la Corne, the next day, the Commissioner of Garry. He was on a quest for ponies, having just killed a team. He came face to face with Gène in the stable.

No one else was around.

"Ph—ew!" whistled the Commissioner. "I thought you were beyond the Arctic Circle."

"I am at À la Corne, m'sieu."

"So I see. And your wife?"

"She also."

The Commissioner thought awhile. "You wish to stay?"

"Why not? A man must eat."

"How much for the ponies?"

"Two hundred."

"I take 'em. Now go and tell the factor to put your name on the books. But say!" Gène stopped. "There's a man looking for you beyond the Great Bear Lake."

"He will not find me there, m'sieu."

The Commissioner watched him crossing the yard. "If that man gets down to À la Corne," he muttered, shaking his head, "there'll be a pretty fight. I'd like to see it"—he licked his lips in sinful anticipation—"but there'd be some dead men round. And dead men," he sighed, "are no use to the Company. Well, we'll get something out of him while he's here." The Commissioner had the knack of getting things out of men, and if there was nothing to be got, he packed them off to some place where killing was easy.

When Gène's name was spread on the book, the factor wondered, the Crees grunted astonishment, and the breeds lost their eyebrows in the roots of their hair. Then they remembered his wife, and grinned. Surely the Commissioner had been looking at himself in those dark eyes, which were as deep black pools edged with willow. But presently they had other cause for wonder. Gène drove a nail with a rifle-shot at fifty yards, he tossed the caber farther than the factor, broke the back of a Sioux wrestler, and his tongue cut like a two-edged sword. There was at first great talk of his wife.

"She's seen sorrow," said the factor's wife. "An' I'm doobtin' if she gaes much on her man."

"La Petite!" exclaimed France Dubois. "Alas! To be married to one bear." Being young and hot in the blood, France would willingly have consoled the mismated woman. For a while he followed hard on her trail. Then, hearing of the matter, Gène pitched him over the Fort wall into a snowbank and left him there to cool. Which he did, quickly, and returned to his forest loves.

Though very much in the minority, the women made most noise at the news of the moving. The breeds' wives cluttered together like a flock of angry mallards, but it fell to the factor's woman to voice the general discontent.

"It's carryin' ye til' that beast hole 'e'll be, is it?" she exclaimed, kissing Lois. "We'll see aboot it."

First she tackled the factor, getting no satisfaction; then she cornered Gène in the store. "What'll be the meanin' o' this?" she demanded. "D'ye think to tak' the puir lassie, an' her wi' a weak heart, till yon desert place amang birds an' beasts an' deils an' Injuns? Tak' shame till ye!"

She paused, winded. Gène's black eye wandered over the stout figure. "Madame," he said, bowing, "is please to be interest in the matter? Yes? Well, if she will know, it is good to trap on the bad lands. Game is plenty. Indians? Bah! They will not go within goose-flight of the pot-holes. Madame know this. The devils, is it? Yes," he mused, "we will take with us the big crucifix, an' Father Francis shall bless the cabin. Then again"—his brows shot up, and a wicked smile twinkled in his eye—"in Quebec, the Lascurrettes were of importance. Yes! An' the associations of À la Corne are scarcely—but I see madame understand. She, perhaps, has visit a good family." Slipping by, he left the woman paralyzed with indignation.

"Weel!" she gasped. "Did—you—ever? Siccan an impudence! An' me once housemaid to a real laird!"

In early springtime, Gène raised a cabin of spruce logs on the bank of a small creek hard by a big pot-hole. It was an honest day's ride from the Fort, which fact he took peculiar pleasure in drawing to the attention of the factor's wife. And when the ground thawed enough to permit the cutting of roof-sod, he loaded his gear on a huge-wheeled Red River cart, and creaked over the prairie and through the bush to his own place. For a month or so he and Lois labored at the house, chinking and plastering, cutting roof-holes and sod to cover them; there was also a fireplace to build and a door to make. But this done and the last shovelful of mud plastered smoothly on the walls, time began to drag heavy on Lois's hands. Gène was away all day, tending his traps or hunting among the pot-holes; so, sitting by the cabin door, hands folded, eyes dreamily fixed on the distant bush, she thought and thought and thought; and through her mind slipped fleeting shadows.

Harking back to her childhood, she saw dimly the face of her mother, faintly beautiful, framed in the cloudy past. Then uprose the log mission of St. Ignace, its silvery chime, the gentle sisters, and the things they had taught her. When she was grown into a tall girl, some things she learned of herself: chief among them, that

Drawn by T. de Thulstrup.

"WITH A CHOKING CRY, SHE FELL AT HIS FEET."

against the Rockies. Shortly after, she followed her father the length of the Great Slave Trail to Fort Confidence beyond the Arctic Circle. There she met Gène Lascurrettes. That was a bitter winter. The sun abdicated and withdrew to the southland, leaving the north to the cold stars and Aurora Borealis. And the Forest King blew on her with his icy breath, and the elements seemed to conspire to chill the warmth at her heart, and the young men of Fort Confidence wondered at her coldness. The next summer came news of his death, and Lois's sun went out. He was killed, in the Rockies, by a grizzly, so said Lascurrettes, who himself had the news from a trapper of Fort York, who got it in Garry. Last of all she thought of the mortal sickness of

in the hands of a maid a man is as wax, though hard as steel to the wedded woman.

She dwelt tenderly on the glory of her first love, when the sun shone brighter and the birds sang sweeter than before. But with this was linked the memory of the black day when, by order of the Company, he mounted and rode away to Fort McCloud

old Pierre Mondot—how he besought her to marry Gène, who stood well to become a factor of the Company, and so let him die in peace.

"Thou art beautiful, child, an' need a strong husband!" These were his words. Then he told of the ruthlessness of men when handsome women were in question, until, half frightened, and to please him, she yielded. Happy? No! She had not been happy. She had done her duty in a mechanical sort of way, but there was no love on her side. And now indifference was turning to dislike. Had he not torn her from her friends at Confidence, and hurried her through frost and snow and ice and shrieking blizzard, the length of the Great North Trail? Made her a stranger in a strange land? And, on top of all, isolated her in this barren spot? Here was small cause of love.

She sat thus one afternoon in the late spring. It was the time of flowers. Harlot-like, the pot-hole lands had clothed their barrenness with robes of spangled green. In the thick grass, brazen tiger-lilies flaunted before humble ox-eye daisies, yellow buttercups shouldered Scotch bluebells, and trembling golden-rod bowed over seas of dandelion. Through the floral ocean nimble gophers chased their loves. A dozen prairie-cocks strutted on a knoll before the hens, a quacking mallard steered her brood over a prairie slough, while high overhead a pair of sand-hill cranes circled up in the eye of the sun.

Gène was among the sand-hills trying for a shot at a sneaking wolverine; yet, far down the Fort trail, the girl spied a black spot moving over the prairie. It grew larger and larger, presently resolving into the figure of a mounted man.

Suddenly she sprang up, hands to brow, eyes strained. "Mère de Dieu!" she whispered. She sank back, white and trembling, one hand pressed against her heart. The man hobbled his pony and stood before her. He was tall, heavy-jawed, aquiline of feature, and massively handsome; a strong man, earnest in good or evil.

" 'I will wait for thee, Jehan le Balt,' " he began, surveying her with questioning eyes, " 'until the everlasting prairies shrivel in the fire of the last day.' These were the words of Lois Mondot. These were the words I told to my starved heart over there"—he waved to the west—"at Fort McCloud against the Rockies. Now am I a factor of the Company an' return for my bride, to find——"

Every speck of color had vanished from her face. Her mouth stood open entreating breath; she swayed, recovered, then fell forward. He caught her, and pulled a flask from his pocket.

"Drink!" he commanded.

"It—it—is over!" she gasped.

"Drink!" He spoke with authority. The spirit sent the blood flushing to her cheek. "You are better?" She nodded. "An' when I come to Garry," he continued, doggedly, "I find——"

"Stop, Jehan!" She held up a staying hand. "You know I love—loved you. But they tell me, my father an' Gène, that you are dead—kill by a bear. Mère de Dieu!" she wailed. "How wretched I am! I do not care. 'Marry,' say my father, an'—an'—I did." She hung her head.

"For this he——"

"Ah, no, Jehan!" she anticipated. "For then would there be blood between us. It must not be. No, Jehan, no!"

"Then you will——" He drew her close, whispering. She shook her head, repeating again and again a faint "No, Jehan"; but, indifferent to yea or nay, he talked on, rapidly, authoritatively, laying his plan. The strong will prevailed. Soon she ceased, and nestled in, warm flushes chasing one another over her face and neck.

"To-morrow," she answered to a question, "he goes to the Fort, an' will not be back till midnight. But oh, Jehan, Father Francis?"

"Bah! little one! The fat priest, is it? The good father know that love is greater than law, an' he has a fine eye for a pretty maid. See you, there will be absolution when we are old and gray!"

She smiled, and nestled closer. The afternoon slipped by and the flickering shadows moved round a quarter circle while they were still in talk. Suddenly the girl sprang from his arms; a passing cloud had obscured the sun, bringing on the evening twilight.

"Go, dear!" she exclaimed. "It is near sundown! He will soon be here!"

"Then," he said, kissing her on the mouth, "to-morrow, little one! Before moonrise. It is a long trail, the Fort McCloud, but love lies by the way an' happiness at the end."

She followed him among the pot-holes with her eyes and down the trail to the distant bush, and while she was still gazing, Gène turned the corner. He leaned his rifle against the wall.

"This devil-beast," he growled, throwing down the wolverine, "will no more rob the traps. An' this was a fine shot. By the Christ! Yes. Two hund—— What is that?" His eye had caught the moving speck.

"I know not," she faltered. "This half-hour have I watched it, wishing for thy coming. Just now I had another stroke of the heart. One more such an' I am done."

"Pouf!" He laid a caressing hand on her shoulder. "What foolish talk is this? No Cree would venture among the potholes. Afraid? Of a stray pony? See you, I will mount an' bring it to thee, an' we shall have the great laugh."

"No! No!" she exclaimed, shrinking from his hand. "Do not leave me. An' you are hungry? It was wrong of me to be afraid an' neglect the meal."

After he had eaten, she moved outdoors. He lay on their bed, smoking and telling, between puffs, of a silver fox he had tracked in the sand-hills. Fifty dollars was its hide worth at À la Corne! Of this she should have ten, to buy her a dress fit for a queen. She should have brave gear, yes, as became a pretty woman, wife to a good hunter. Thus he rambled on. She answered in monosyllables. Twice he called her to come to bed, but not until he slept did she enter the cabin.

She was up betimes, and fried the breakfast bannock while Gène hitched his pony to the cart. After he was gone, she harkened to the huge wheels creaking over the prairie and drew a long, full breath. Just as he turned into the bush, the night-wind sank to rest, the air chilled, and the sky blacks paled to dullest drab. Trembling flushes of red and yellow shot through the grays of dawn. Easily the drabs faded into the blue of the zenith, the yellows deepened and blushed into rosy reds, while fleecy clouds drew dusky lines across the eastern sky. As the sun raised a golden rim, a robin perched on the roof-tree and piped his melodious note. Blackbirds in a near-by bluff broke into liquid music, a snipe chirped a cheerful pee-wee from a slough, and a pair of jays quarreled in the joy of the morning. The hush, the glow, the throaty music of the birds, the infinite peace and freshness of the new-born day, filled her starved soul. Kneeling, like some fire-worshiper of old, she watched the great red sun lift and roll up his burnished plane.

All day she burned with a fever of impatience. Time and again, though she knew he would not come till night, her gaze traveled down the trail to the distant bush. Once, on turning from the door, her eyes fell on the crucifix against the wall. She shrank back. The church had no blessing for an enterprise like hers; and, beneath Christ's cross, Gène had nailed a colored mission print of the "broad and easy way" leading down to Tophet. Toward evening the excitement brought on another palpitation of the heart which left her, blanched and trembling, on the bed. At last the unwelcome sun dropped below the horizon. Rising, she lit an oil fire, and by its light got ready for the trail. She had but little gear. Her few things were soon rolled into a small bundle; then, throwing a shawl about her, she sat shivering with expectation. With dusk came the thud of a horse's hoofs. A hasty foot stumbled on the threshold.

"Jehan!"

She threw wide the door, and the yellow flare shone full on her husband's face. With a choking cry, she fell at his feet. He stepped within. He had heard the name; her bundle lay on the floor.

"So, so," he whispered, gently, "it was to be the rider of the stray pony, was it?" The tone was quiet, but the veins on his forehead ridged black, the skin drew tight over his heavy jaw, and his hand played with his knife. "Rise!" he roared with sudden passion. "Rise an' speak!" He struck his heel heavily into her side. "The stray pony!" he laughed. "That was not to be caught! The heavy pony! Whose hoofs bit deep in the soft places!"

She lay still. A minute passed. She had not yet moved. Stooping, he turned up her face. It was marble-white. Falling on his knees, he tore her dress from the neck and laid his rough head to the white breast.

Night fell as Jehan le Balt spurred from

the bush. He was late. A led horse had persistently taken the wrong side of many trees, wherefore Jehan swore softly but with eloquence and variety.

"O son of the devil!" he muttered, "may you burn in one thousand hells! This is your fault. Black night an' a new trail." Dismounting, he followed the faint white line of dead grass around yawning pits and between bottomless earth-cracks, while his anxious eye scanned a distant light. Half an hour's fast walking brought him to the big pot-hole, and here he tied the horses at a poplar bluff.

The oil flare cast a broad stream of light through the cabin door, punching a yellow hole in the blackness. "Ho, petite!" he called. "Here am I!" The steep sides of the pot-holes threw back a hollow echo. All was strangely silent. A sudden fear chilled him. High overhead, with rush of beating wings, a shape swept by.

He started. "Bah!" he exclaimed. "Jehan le Balt, you are become as one chicken. Ma foi! To jump at a passing goose!"

Standing on the threshold, he laughed softly. "La pauvre," he whispered. "So? She is tired, an' sleeps. Good! She will travel the better."

She lay on the rude bed, the torn dress revealing the ivory bust gleaming round and full in the yellow flare. Love and passion surged with the hot blood through his veins. Quietly tip-toeing, he stooped and kissed her full on the mouth. Instantly he straightened. Her lips were icy-cold.

"M'sieu salutes his love!"

Jehan whirled about. In the doorway, broad body touching either post, stood Lascurrettes. He was smiling; his hand played gently with his knife.

"You—did—this—thing?"

The man shrugged his shoulders. "It was not my fortune, m'sieu. The good God avenges the outraged husband. So say the holy fathers. She died of a stroke of the heart."

"Of a broken heart!"

"As you please. What matter? She is dead. An' you, M'sieu The-Factor-That-Is-To-Be, pay for her death. But not now. Presently. There is work to do."

Taking ax and shovel, Gène led the way to the bluff where the horses were tied.

The moon had just peeked over the trees; the black darkness had withdrawn to the pits.

"Here is a good place." Lascurrettes buried the ax in the sod. "Soon there will be more light."

They worked by spells, preserving the silence of good haters, one picking and the other shoveling. After an hour's digging, Gène looked down on the grave. "It will do," he said.

At the door Jehan le Balt drew to one side. "M'sieu will wish to make his adieus?"

He waited patiently. No need for hurry, though the northern moon silvered plain and forest, and he could see the faint white trail winding over a mile of prairie. Yet, time and again, he caught himself thinking of Lois as waiting, waiting, waiting; waiting to start on the long journey which ended at Fort McCloud.

"It is her spirit," he whispered.

"M'sieu?" Lascurrettes stood by the open door. He entered, closed the door and knelt by the dead. Raising the small hand, he placed it on his head. Softly, like a caress, it settled among his curls, quieting, with cool touch, the pain at his heart. He arose soothed and calm, and called the husband.

"M'sieu," he said, "this was good, an' I would repay in kind. As I hope to presently kill you, I swear she was innocent of wrong. Her heart was always mine. This you knew when you lied away her body."

Lascurrettes's lips drew into a wicked snarl. "Innocent!" he growled. "This is the talk of a boy. Does the hand hold from the ripe fruit when the belly says pluck? This will not save you."

In her blankets they buried Lois, shoveling by turns until the grave was filled and mounded. When the last sod was turned, they stood for a space with bowed heads; then, retiring a few yards, they faced together.

Between the grave and the pot-hole stretched a level sward. Over this they began to circle, backward, forward, sidewise, tricking for an opening, knives scintillating sparks of blue moonlight.

Suddenly Jehan let drive a circular cut from face to waist. It fell short. The return flashed straight at his breast, and Lascurrettes drove in thrust upon thrust,

Drawn by T. de Thulstrup.

"JEHAN WHIRLED ABOUT. IN THE DOORWAY . . . STOOD LASCURRETTES."

bearing him back toward the pot-hole. A quick side-leap reversed the position, and Jehan slashed at the side, and missed. Steel sawed steel. The knives flashed in and out for a breathless minute, weaving a fiery pattern; then, bleeding, they drew apart and circled.

The next rush brought them together, free hand to knife hand, and Jehan felt the power of his foe. Slowly he was forced back to the pit. He felt the knife hand tearing from his grip, while the grasp tightened on his wrist. He must do something, and do it quick.

"Courage!" the voice of Lascurrettes sounded in his ear; "it will soon be over, an' m'sieu in hell."

Raising his knee, he jammed it with desperate energy into the other's stomach, at the same time throwing back. The grapple broke. He fell, head and shoulders over the pit. For one moment he hung in the balance, then Lascurrettes's knife flashed straight at his face. He saw it coming, dodged, overbalanced, clutched at the grass, and toppled back.

Lascurettes crawled to the edge and looked down. He could see nothing, but presently a groaning curse ascended to him through the blackness. Jehan had fallen in the loose sand. Quietly withdrawing, he walked to the grave and lay down to chew the bitter cud of sorrow and thwarted purpose.

He was the child of iron forces and rigorous conditions; the last link of a chain every length of which was hot-forged by nature and chosen from a thousand. Strong, obstinate, acute, he had shouldered through life, bending man and woman to his will. But his wife's weakness had proved her strength. She was gone beyond recall. To be robbed of his love!—even by death? Springing up, he shook a threatening fist skyward, and cursed the power which had leveled him in the dust. He waited, almost expectant. The stars looked coldly down, the moon shed her pale light as before, the murmuring night-wind plucked a dead leaf and cast it in his hot face. The mote in the sunbeam had defied the infinite and received its answer.

Smarting under a vague sense of futility and failure, he turned his gaze to the black pot-hole. "Peste!" he muttered, "this is fool work, this challenging the stars, but over there"—he shook his big fist— "is one that shall pay."

For two days he kept secret watch and ward, awaiting the torment of thirst and hunger. But on the second day he observed the prisoner cutting his mooseskin coat into strips, and saw him twist them into a long lasso. When it was ready for the cast, he crawled to the stump and waited. For a night and day he feasted fat, then, glutted, turned to destroy the last hope of the doomed man.

"See you," he called below, "how great is my solicitude. Presently the tree will fall, an' I would not spoil a factor of the Company. Stand from under!" The stump cracked. "Now," he laughed, raising for the last blow, "to hell with you, Jehan le Balt!"

Unseen, noiseless, the lasso shot up from below, hovered, curved over, and fell around his shoulders. He grasped the tottering tree. It cracked smartly, toppled over, and man and stump crashed into the yawning pit.

21

The White Darkness

LAWRENCE MOTT

THE WHITE DARKNESS

BY LAWRENCE MOTT

THE afternoon light faded gradually
till the tall pines cast no shadows,
and the white landscape was gray.
Whistling faintly, the wind swayed the
forest branches to and ·fro, now in long
sweeps with strong puffs, then in short
bowings. The leaden sky was dark and
low, cold and repellant.

Laflin filled his pipe slowly at the door
of the N.W.M.P. post, Onion Lake, his
home. "Looks like snow," he muttered,
his eyes roaming over the long distances
beyond the forests. Little by little the
pipe was filled; he lighted a match. Puff-
puff, "I don't suppose (puff) that Jake
will (puff) get back to-night (puff-puff-
puff). Anyhow, I'll have supper by'n'by
and take a run over to the Store." He
stood there smoking quietly. Then the
flakes of white came; dropping one by one
at first, then falling in silent quantities,
finally coming down in eddying and pirouetting myriads. As he watched, they
piled themselves on the wood heap, hid the
bright bit of the axe, settled on its handle,
and clung damply to the shingles and logs
of the cabin. "Wonder how far they
come?" He looked up. Out of pale gray
nothingness the big spots of white came
in noiseless masses; appearing like magic
from the oneness of the heavens, and, as
he followed them, disappearing into the
cold gray oneness that lay on the north.
Always tumbling, always blending, the
particles dropped in clouds. The wind had
gone entirely; only the crisp, settling,
seething sound of the flakes could be heard.
He went into the cabin. A bright fire sent
forth cheery snappings from a little stove,
whose red-hot cover cast a sheen on the
log ceiling. He lifted the cover from a
pot; a burst of steam rose, billowed about
the small interior, and vanished. Laflin

stirred the contents. "Those beans are
the hardest I ever saw!" The water boiled
and bubbled with liquid hissings. He took
down a frying-pan from its nail behind the
stovepipe oven, put bacon and sliced potatoes in it and a bit of butter; it began
to sizzle and cook at once. He was making
his tea when the door opened and a tall,
strong figure came in, snow-shoes in hand.

"Bo' jou, bo' jou, Lafleen!"

"Hello, LaGrange; where are you
bound?"

The trapper unwound his muffler, stuck
the snow-shoes in a corner and sat on the
rough bench. "Me? Ah'm goin' longue
way baim'by; wan' talk leetle firs'!"

"Anything wrong?" Laflin asked, noting
the sullen voice and the gleam of the deep-
set blue-gray eyes.

"Mabbe ye-es, mabbe non," the French
Canadian answered hesitatingly.

The constable waited for him to go on,
stirring and turning the bacon and potatoes
the while.

"You know dat Gros Gorge an' ma femme
gon' way?"

Laflin turned quickly. "No! When was
this?"

Steadily and impassively the other answered: "Mabbe t'ree day h'ago, mabbe
two day. Ah come f'om de trap lignes
dees aftaire-noon, fin' de cabane emptee,
no'tin dere, onlee dees pair ol' snow-shoe!"
He pointed to them contemptuously.

"But your wife maybe went to Tomah's,
or to her father's house?"

The other laughed bitterly. "Ah mak'
fin' h'out ev'w'ere *een post;* no dere! Som'
de boy dey say dat she gon' weet Gros
Gorge, dat sacre Metis!" The voice thrilled
and shook with fury, but the huge body
was quiet.

"I'm very sorry for you, LaGrange, but

she's not worth having if that's the sort of thing she has done; and——"

The trapper leaped to his feet. "Ah no come for h'ask you eef she good for have or no! LaGrange he wan' you say w'at 'appen eef he shoote dose two!"

The constable stared at the powerful square face, the ominous flash of the eyes, and saw the clenched fists, whose muscles stood out like tautened ropes. "You can't do that, LaGrange, or I should have to arrest you, and murder's a bad charge."

The trapper stared at the other, still, save for the quick trembling of his nostrils. "An' ef you no can catch . . . me?"

Laflin chuckled. "Then you'd be safe; but we *would* get you, LaGrange, and you know it!"

The bacon was done; he put out a tin plate, cup and saucer on the tiny table, and began to eat, the Canadian watching him stolidly.

"Have a bite? Come on, now—forget that killing plan. I know it's damned hard, but you'll have to do it, LaGrange, that's sure!"

"No wan' for h'eat. Ah go! Bo' jou!" He took up the snowshoes, slung the woolen muffler about his massive throat and went out into the snow without another word.

"He's hit hard," Laflin said aloud. "I always felt that he was too good for her." He ate on comfortably. When his meal was finished he cleaned away the remains, lighted the pipe again and took a look outside.

The night was clammy and raw, the air still laden with the tumbling snow that showed white in the candle-light that came from the open door. Down in a hollow the lights of the Hudson Bay Company's Post twinkled brightly through the trunks; now and then the sound of voices was wafted to him by the light draught. The heavens were black and forbidding.

"An ugly night by the look of it now," Laflin whispered, and turned. As he did so he heard the short, sharp breathing of dogs, and in an instant a sledge drew up in the circle of yellow light.

"Ah'm goin' fin' dose two," the muffled figure said that crouched on it, "an' Ah'm goin' keel w'en Ah fin': you no catch . . . me! Allez-Marse!"

A few yelps, the whine of a whip thong,

and the circle of light was empty. The constable stared, and listened to the fast fading swi-i-ish of the sledge-runners through the snow. They were gone!

"He won't find them, and if he does he won't dare anything beyond a fight. My, but it's cold!" and he went in.

He tried to read some old magazines that furnished the only literature the cabin boasted of, but somehow he could not focus his attention on the pages. Then he put out the candles, took off his heavy service boots, stretched himself comfortably between the long blankets and tried to sleep. No use. The more he tried the more wide awake he became.

"Why did that fool come and tell me his story? I feel that—that . . . . damn it, I don't know what I feel," and he lighted up again.

He went to the door and listened. Nothing but the wind that crooned softly through the pine needles answered his unacknowledged quest for sound and lurking dread of something.

All night he sat up, troubled and wondering. He waited impatiently for daylight, going to the door often, then throwing himself on the bunk again.

"There's something wrong, and I know it!" he muttered, tossing restlessly. "Poor old LaGrange; it's pretty hard lines on a man when his eyes are nearly gone snow-blind working for that girl, and she plays this sort of a game."

He got up and walked the floor, sometimes throwing bits of wood into the stove. "What's the matter with me?" he asked himself angrily. "I suppose it's just sympathy, but it's uncomfortable."

"At last," he said, as, opening the door for the manyeth time, he saw the first faint streaks of daylight through the shrouds of drifting flakes. He watched the lightness grow. In solid mass the trunks stood, dark and shapeless; then, bit by bit, outline by outline, they stood away from each other, growing in breadth and depth till each was clear and defined. The branches crept into silhouette against the brightening sky, gray as ever, and ever belching snow. He boiled some tea, fried some caribou meat, warmed some bread and ate slowly. As he was finishing, a ray of pallid sunlight stole timidly athwart the floor.

"A fine day after all!" Having

quenched the fire, he took down his snow-shoes, and buckled on his side arms. "I'll have a look round toward Battleford: Father Lesbauts said that two hours in the bright sun would blind him for months!"

The snow was deep and heavy, clinging to his snowshoes with soggy weight and strength as he pushed on among the trees. Higher and higher the now open sun climbed, shedding warm rays that instilled in him a sense of power. The white surface offered a dazzling glare to his eyes; they cringed and squinted. At the end of the strip of woods began the Long Barren. Straight away it stretched before him, pale blue-white and chilling gray in the sun. Billions of frost points shimmered on the surface, all burning his eyes with their power and gleam. He pulled his fur cap well down. "Very bad glare to-day!" he muttered, and started across the apparently endless distance.

Click-clack, click-clack, sounded his snowshoes as they struck together, the noise muffled by the impeding snow. Hour after hour passed, Laflin swinging in a great circle toward Battleford. Of a sudden he stopped. Far off, a mere speck against the whiteness of everything, was a figure—at least, he thought it so. He worked his way toward it, and at last distinguished a man, standing alone and motionless. He kept his eyes on him, fearing to lose the dark form if he looked away, so bright and strong was the glare. He drew closer.

"LaGrange! but where's his team?" he asked aloud.

The man was standing quiet, snowshoes on his feet, dog lash in his hand, his face turned toward the west. Unconsciously Laflin looked there too, and saw a larger spot, apparently motionless, in the near distance.

"L——" he started to call, but did not, and edged nearer. When he was quite close he understood. LaGrange was absolutely snow-blind. The tall figure stood, straining the sightless eyes to the west; the snow was disturbed about, as though in a struggle.

"I wonder if—? Yes, by h——l, it must be! I'll see pretty quick." Laflin decided, and worked his way noiselessly past the blind man, keeping at some distance from him, so as to be sure that he should not be heard. He hurried along then toward the far black spot, that was in the same place; striding on, he kept under the brow of a snow rise until he was close to the place; then he crept forward. Just over the top was a sledge and two people beside it—a man and a woman. The man was busily at work demolishing the remains of a sledge, whose bone runners lay on the snow by him; the woman stood waiting. A double team of dogs sat about, their tongues lolling and drool streaming to the softening snow under their feet.

"The devils! they've got his sledge and team away from him, and now they are going to leave him to die! Not if I know it, even if I can't arrest any one!" He drew his revolver, sneaked to the very top of the rise, then—"Árrête!" he ordered.

The girl screamed, the man, Gros Gorge flinching at the sight of the gun. Laflin scrambled to them. "I'll give you just one minute to start away from here; and if I ever see you again in Onion Lake post I'll have you sent to Stony Mountain * for stealing a sledge: you understand?"

The half-breed (Metis) mumbled his willingness to do anything for "de Polees."

"Take your own dogs and sledge. GO!" Gros Gorge went, the dogs' feet stirring up clouds of snow-dust that sparkled in the sunlight. Laflin watched him out of sight to the westward. He turned to the girl. "How did you get your husband's sledge?"

She began to cry.

"None of that! Speak up, or I arrest you!"

She looked at him with tear-dimmed brown eyes. "He fallen h'off w'en sledde turn ovaire een hole la bas."

"What were you doing there?"

She stammered and hesitated.

"Come, speak up!"

"Gros Gorge he loove me," she whimpered. "We no wan' for to keel La-Grange." She leaned forward. "Onlee tak' hees sledde."

"And leave him to die, you fiend! You know that LaGrange is snow-blind, and blind for your sake, working like a dog for the Company to give you a home and food!"

She whined and cried softly.

"I am going to take you to him: he

* The penitentiary for the Northwest Provinces.

loves you more than his life; and listen well to what I say. I am going to tell him—never mind *what* I tell him, only obey me, or I will take you to Barracks. You know what that means?"

The girl nodded.

"And if I ever see anything like this again, I——"

"Non, non!" she pleaded; and the two started back for the lone figure. It came in sight soon, but not quite as it was when Laflin passed it. LaGrange was stumbling slowly about, wandering aimlessly over the dazzling Barren; groping weirdly with his hands, and muttering to himself.

"Holla, LaGrange!"

Hearing Laflin's voice, he stiffened and stood still.

"I've found your wife!"

"W'ere? w'ere?" he asked thickly.

"Why, she got lost out here on that long trap line of yours; I always told you it was too long for her to look after!"

"Go to him," Laflin whispered fiercely. She went.

He put his great arms about her lithe figure. "Dieu merci! Dieu merci!" he groaned. "Ah'm loss' de team een dat hole down dere; dey gon' ouest. Ah was comen'," he stuttered a moment—"Ah was comen' for lock de line, but my eye'hes dey go bad. Ah no can see now! Ah, Nanette, your ol' mari he h'ave sooch terri-ble drream 'bout you, but eet no trrue. Dieu merci! no trrue!" He wrapped his long, gaunt arms about her, and the tears came from the temporarily sightless eyes. "You tak' me home, Nanette, hein?"

Laflin nodded, glowering at her.

"Certaine, mon pauvre."

The three started, LaGrange holding tightly to the girl's hand, Laflin following. They came to the police cabin.

"What in the devil—?" began a figure in the doorway.

"It's all right, Jake. Nanette got lost, and LaGrange has gone snow-blind, just as Father Lesbauts said he would if he didn't take care."

The girl, leading the tall, helpless figure, moved on toward the group of houses in the valley

"Don't forget," Laflin whispered as she passed; and she nodded slowly.

The two mounted police watched them down the path, the sun in its afternoon glory softening the outlines of the forest, and throwing the two departing figures into strong relief.

"She's young—may be all right yet," Laflin muttered as they disappeared.

"Who's young? what's young?" the other asked.

"Oh, nothing, nothing; I was thinking, that's all." And the two went into the cabin.

22

Musk-ox Hunting Among the Iwilics

A. HYATT VERRILL

LONE MONARCH OF A LONE LAND.

MUSK-OX HUNTING AMONG THE IWILICS

By A. Hyatt Verrill

SIX long and dreary months our little whaling schooner had been locked fast in the ice of northern Hudson's Bay with naught to break the monotony of our existence save the impromptu dances in the deck-house and the modest festivities called forth by Thanksgiving and Christmas. Although to a stranger the land appeared still in the grip of midwinter, yet to the natives and whalers many signs gave warning of the approach of Arctic spring. Daily the black edge of water beyond the floe grew nearer and the flocks of eider and "old squaws" grew more restless; daily, too, the ptarmigan increased in numbers and added brown feathers to their spotless winter costume. Then one dull and gloomy day a flock of snowbirds, chattering gaily, overran the vessel and all hands knew and rejoiced that winter had flown and spring had come. A day or two later the Iwilics, whose low, domed houses of frozen snow had nestled in the lee of the schooner all winter, began to move ashore and build new igloos on a firm foundation. Interesting, indeed, was it to watch these Arctic nomads construct their queer homes. By the aid of long, curved, snow-knives, made from the tusks of the walrus, the sturdy fellows cut squarish blocks of snow of just the right dimensions, while

others piled them up in an ever-narrowing circle, until at last the home was complete. Their moving, once the igloo was finished, took but a short time, for their furnishings are of the simplest. A soapstone lamp, an old tin or iron pot or two, quantities of skins and furs all chewed soft (and also evil smelling), extra clothes, guns, horn dippers, seal spears, bunches of sinew, bone needles and sewing gear, and numerous odds and ends of bright calico, flannel, beads, etc., completes the inventory of the average hut. To a white the chief drawback to one of these interiors is the smell, which at first seems overpowering. One becomes accustomed to it after a time, however, and really gets to like the simple folk. They are ever moving from place to place, for it seems easier to build a new house than to clean an old one. Then again, they are very superstitious and among other beliefs is that of the two twin-sister goddesses, one of whom has charge of all the land animals, while her sister looks after those of the sea. According to the Iwilics it would offend the land goddess to work on skins or clothes made of skins of land animals while living on the ice, or vice versa. As a result, whenever a garment made of deerskin needs repairing during the winter, the seamstress is obliged to move to a tem-

GOING OUT TO THE HUNT.

porary house on shore. As a consequence of all these peregrinations the ice and shore, at the beginning of spring, looked as if a small army of Iwilics had lived there, so numerous were the abandoned igloos, whereas, in reality, the families did not exceed a dozen at any time.

A few days after moving into their new quarters, Harry, our head Eskimo, came aboard and invited me to accompany him

ptarmigan filled our tiny dwelling. As we sat about in our heavy deerskin garments and picked the bones, the boy called his father's attention to the stiff leg tendons and asked him how they came there. Now the Iwilics have a fable or fairy tale to account for everything, and are never tired of relating them, so, although I have no doubt that the little fellow had heard the tale hundreds of times, his father smiled and nar-

DEERSKIN (SUMMER) HOUSE.

on a sled journey to Yellow Bluff, where he had cachéd some whales' bones which he wished to use for sled runners. Early the following day we started off with Harry's little boy riding on the sled, while his father and I ran alongside to keep warm; for although balmy spring had arrived, the mercury stood twenty-eight below zero. On the way our dogs chased and brought to bay a large bear, which we secured. We arrived at Yellow Bluff in due time, but although thoroughly tired out and half famished, before we could eat, drink or sleep, it was necessary to build a small igloo, light a stone lamp and melt ice for water. By the time this was accomplished I was glad to munch some frozen meat and crawl into a sleeping bag. I awoke hungry and refreshed and found Harry and his son already up, while the savory odor of stewing

rated it again. "Many years ago," said Harry, "there was an old woman who lived in a small igloo with her granddaughter. The little girl was very fond of stories and teased the old woman to tell them to her. One night the grandmother was cross and when the child asked for a story she said, 'Don't want to tell story, little girl go to sleep.' But the little girl said, 'please tell me a story, Annanating (grandmother).' Then the grandmother grew angry and said very quick, 'Huh, I see mouse!' Now the little girl, like all Eskimos, was very much afraid of mice and hid her face and cried and cried, until her eyes were red and Nudliauk took pity on her and changed her to a bird, and she flew away from the cruel old woman, and ever since the ptarmigans have had red eyes and stiff tendons in their legs, where the child carried her needles in her boots.'' At the conclusion of the story we packed up our goods and started on our return. We reached the schooner about 10 p. m., and I was very glad to doff fur underclothing and turn into a decently warm bunk. A few days later the Iwilics reported a wolf about, but although we set numerous traps, we failed to secure him that night. The next day when I returned from a short tramp on the floe, I found the wolf had come skulking about the vessel during my absence and had been shot from the deck by our first mate. The poor creature was almost starved to death, but was exceedingly large and almost pure white.

To the sportsman hardy enough to spend a winter in this desolate land, it would prove a rich hunting ground, for game is plenty and generally fairly tame. Throughout the whole region polar bears and caribou are numerous, although the former are not seen during midwinter and the latter are more abundant in spring and autumn, when they travel across country in immense herds. Wolves are not common, but the Eskimos manage to get them regularly, as well as wolverines. White foxes are very abundant and readily secured, as are also ptarmigan, eider and other ducks. On the wide, rocky plains further inland, musk oxen roam, and, if you are guided by experienced Iwilic hunters, are fairly easy to obtain. The bay itself furnishes four species of seal, as well as the walrus. The largest of these seals, known as the " oogjug,'' is used mainly for boat bottoms and is so highly prized that the Eskimos celebrate the capture of one by a three days' round of gayeties, during which time the men can do no work and the women are not allowed to comb their hair; a custom which none of the natives seem able to explain, although doubtless it originally had some mystic significance. During these celebrations the " anticoots,'' or magicians, take a prominent part, as in fact they do at all times. These fellows are clever, intelligent chaps, who claim to be able to visit the spirit land at will, as well as to drive off evil spirits and cure disease. They certainly do have more or less hypnotic power and are really capable of throwing themselves into a trance. At these times, also, games of strength take place, and some of these are very odd and original. In one two lusty young Eskimos tie their heads together by means of stout

sinews around the neck and then try to see who can pull the other along—a sort of tug-of-war. Then there are wrestling matches, races, etc., and last, but by no means least, in the estimation of the Iwilics, the gambling. All the tribe, women as well as men, are inveterate gamblers and never miss a chance to risk their property in gaming. One of the favorite gambling devices is to try and jab a spear through a perforated piece of ivory hung immovably in the center of an igloo. This seems quite a simple thing to do, but when a dozen or more excited natives are all jumping about and jabbing away at the same time, it is literally a game of chance, and the fortunate winner takes the pot. Another game, particularly among the women, is played by means of a dipper made from the base of a musk-ox horn and fitted with a short brass or wooden handle. The women sit in a circle and each stakes something, then one of them spins the dipper rapidly around and when the revolutions finally cease the one towards whom the handle points is declared the winner and must start the betting for the next round and also spin the dipper.

Often during the festivities occasioned by the capture of one " oogjug,'' the men kill another (for they do not consider hunting in the light of work), and thus one fiesta crowds on the tail of another. The men are born hunters and spend most of their time hunting, in fact, their lives depend upon it. The mainstay of their existence is the Barren Ground caribou. After the caribou in importance, come the seals, while musk oxen are used for comparatively few purposes. Of course the whales and salmon furnish them with a great deal of food and other materials, but since they have come in contact with the whites they save the bone and oil for the whalers, having discovered that it furnishes more comforts in trade than they could secure from it direct. Above everything else they prize matches, and so precious are these to them that when wishing to light a fire the Iwilics, instead of striking a match, carefully split one into small pieces, keeping this up until one is accidentally ignited. As they are quite skilful at this, it is frequently some time before the fire is started and the Eskimo has by that time trebled his supply of matches. This same careful economy of civilized articles is observed in other ways. The stems of their pipes, after being smoked for some time, are whittled up and smoked over with a very little fresh tobacco added. Cartridge shells are saved carefully and after being cut up with files, are hammered out and used in a number of ways. In hunting, economy of ammunition is their main effort and they seldom take chances on a long shot. In hunting caribou they usually go in companies of four or five, and when the game is sighted, two or three of the party lie hidden to leeward, while the others, making a detour, approach down the wind. As soon as the

sledges, about thirty dogs, six squaws and three men, Billy, Stonewall Jackson, and John L., besides Harry and myself. It was quite warm, five above, when we started, and the exercise making our heavy fur garments uncomfortable, they were removed and piled on the sleds. A few hours later, however, it clouded over, the wind increased and we were glad to don the sealskin clothing. That night we camped in a little hollow, while a blizzard raged outside. We minded it little, however, for the Iwilics are a jovial people and always make the best of things and thoroughly believe in

IWILIC SQUAWS.

deer scent these they of course travel in the opposite direction and fall easy prey to the hidden hunters. After being shot at they turn about and dash off, forgetting all caution, and still more are brought down by the other party. In this way it not infrequently happens that an entire herd is killed off in a few minutes.

All during the winter we had hunters in the musk-ox country, and although I greatly desired to kill one of the creatures, no opportunity presented itself for me to go until well along in the spring. At last the promised day arrived and we started off. Our party consisted of three large

having a good time wherever they may be. We spent the evening sitting about the stone lamp, smoking and telling stories, and when we awoke the following morning found the weather clear and cold, with the new-fallen snow just right for tracking. Late in the afternoon we ran across our first game, a herd of eight caribou, from which, after a little stalking and manœuvering, we secured four. For the two following days we met with little game, two wolves and three or four foxes comprising our bag. On the third day we entered an entirely different sort of country, rough and rocky, with numerous hills, and small ledges jut-

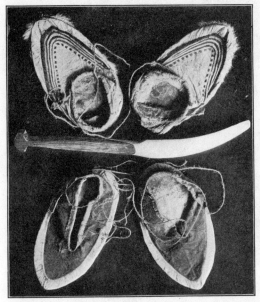

MOCCASINS AND SNOW-KNIFE.

ting out from the surface. This was the musk-ox country, and although we saw no signs of game during the first day, all proceeded with caution, stopping and peering ahead as each rise was ascended. About noon of the second day we struck a trail and after following it a short distance unleashed the dogs, who at once started off on the fresh scent. Very soon their yelping and howling told us the game was in sight and as we reached the crest of the next ridge we caught sight of them, four dark-brown, shapeless bodies, galloping over the snow, a half mile away, with the dogs in hot pursuit. Over a ridge they dashed and over the ridges we followed, across a flat and rocky plain and over another ridge, until it seemed as if we would d op from sheer exhaustion but the sturdy Iwilics never slowed up, trotting rapidly along on their sho t legs; knowing full well that ere long the oxen would be brought to bay. At last the shaggy, wild-eyed creatures turned and faced the yelping curs; and truly a fine picture of defiance they presented, as with lowered heads, steaming nostrils and foaming mouths they stood shoulder to shoulder, im-

patiently pawing the ground and awaiting the onslaught of their savage enemies. For a moment the dogs hesitated, and then the leader, a big, tawny brute, sprang forward with a snarl. There was a sickening thud as the massive horns caught him squarely in the breast and flung him backward for a dozen yards, crippled and bleeding. Profiting by the fate of their leader, the other curs held off, now and again dashing in to snap at the oxen's heels, but keeping well out of reach of the long, wicked horns. So intent were the musk oxen watching their four-footed foes, that they failed to note our approach until we were within fifty yards, when suddenly they caught sight of the new enemy and, whirling about, dashed out of sight over the ledge before we could raise rifle to shoulder. The oxen were now thoroughly frightened and although we followed them for several miles they refused to come to bay and we abandoned the chase, returning tired and disgusted to camp.

The following morning, after several hours of hard tramping and patient trailing, we again sighted the herd. They had evidently recovered from their fright of the day preceding, for they ran barely half a mile before making a stand. Taught by our former experience, we approached cautiously with rifles ready for instant service. When

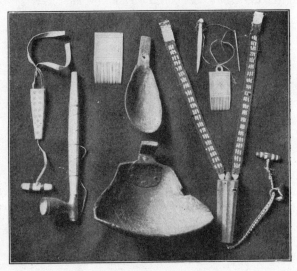

IWILIC PIPE, COMBS, DIPPERS, NEEDLE CASES, PIN AND NEEDLE.

seventy-five yards distant they caught our
wind and started to run, but this time we
were prepared, and dropping on one knee,
I took a quick shot at the leading bull
just as he reached the top of a ridge.
The big fellow leaped from the ground
and disappeared on the farther side. At
the same instant the Iwilics let drive, but
the rest of us busied ourselves skinning the
ox; and a truly noble fellow he was, his
great horns curving in a grand sweep downward and outward with massive shield
over his shaggy forehead. We spent a fortnight in the musk-ox country and secured
in all seven of the wild Arctic cattle, returning to the schooner with fully laden

"RETURNING TO THE SCHOONER WITH FULLY LADEN SLEDGES."

aside from little spurts of frozen snow, I
could see no results from their shots. We
rushed forward, thinking to get another
shot at the retreating creatures, and as we
reached the top of the little hill almost
stumbled over the body of the bull. One
of the men started at once for camp, while
sledges. Upon reaching the Bay we found
the vessel had come up from the ice and all
hands were making ready for whaling. A
few days later the spring thaws were on in
earnest, with squalls and rain, which rapidly
broke up the ice and permitted us to once
more spread our well-patched sails.

23
Moosuk

FITZHERBERT LEATHER

MOOSUK

A WHITE AND RED CHRISTMAS OF THE DEBATABLE GROUND

By FITZHERBERT LEATHER

DRAWINGS BY THE AUTHOR

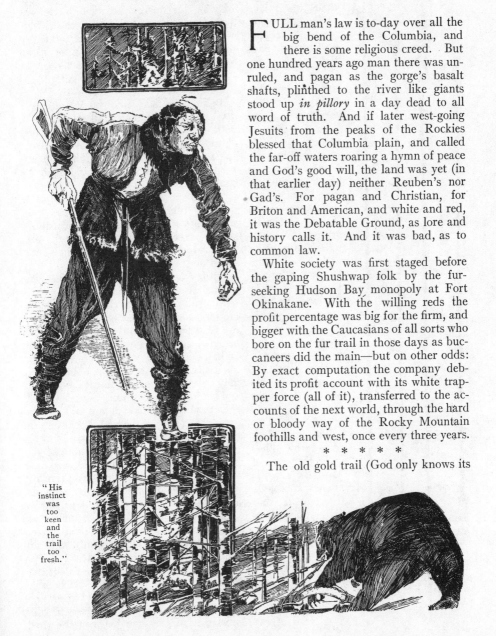

"His instinct was too keen and the trail too fresh."

FULL man's law is to-day over all the big bend of the Columbia, and there is some religious creed. But one hundred years ago man there was unruled, and pagan as the gorge's basalt shafts, plinthed to the river like giants stood up *in pillory* in a day dead to all word of truth. And if later west-going Jesuits from the peaks of the Rockies blessed that Columbia plain, and called the far-off waters roaring a hymn of peace and God's good will, the land was yet (in that earlier day) neither Reuben's nor Gad's. For pagan and Christian, for Briton and American, and white and red, it was the Debatable Ground, as lore and history calls it. And it was bad, as to common law.

White society was first staged before the gaping Shushwap folk by the fur-seeking Hudson Bay monopoly at Fort Okinakane. With the willing reds the profit percentage was big for the firm, and bigger with the Caucasians of all sorts who bore on the fur trail in those days as buccaneers did the main—but on other odds: By exact computation the company debited its profit account with its white trapper force (all of it), transferred to the accounts of the next world, through the hard or bloody way of the Rocky Mountain foothills and west, once every three years.

* * * * *

The old gold trail (God only knows its

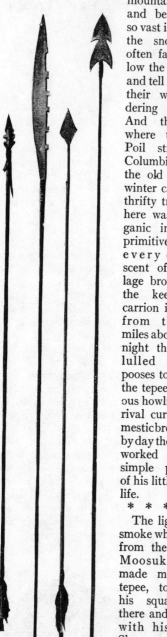

length) from Cariboo to California, sights the timber along the valley of the Sans Poil. The land rolls and tumbles to mountains above and below; and so vast is the plain the snow peaks often fall far below the hem of it, and tell nothing of their world-wondering grandeur. And that spot where the Sans Poil strikes the Columbia was in the old days the winter camp of a thrifty tribe; and here was life organic in all its primitive fulness; every day the scent of the village brought out the keen - nosed carrion in the air from the hills miles about; every night the coyote lulled the papooses to sleep in the tepee by envious howling at his rival curs of domestic breeds; day by day the redman worked out the simple problems of his little-taught life.

* * * * *

The light alder smoke which blew from the cone of Moosuk's well-made moosehide tepee, told that his squaw was there and waiting with his mess. She watched the warm smoke run to the funnel, and harked for the moccasin *boof-boof* tread of her

buck coming back over the snow; the while she uselessly dreamed of Blackfoot bogies too afraid or too lazy to raid in snowtime. Moosuk was not held by Blackfoot; and his toes pointed to his camp. But he did not just then kick the snow in front of him: Moosuk had shuffled up to his swamp, set his few traps (hard enough earned last winter at the fort), and hugging himself, and again blowing his fingers for warmth, he was swinging happy but hungry to the village, when he suddenly stopped; he jerked up on his heels, his quiet face turned to an astonished mask, and from his throat came the best guttural of his gamut:

"*Oogh-k!*"

Before the surprised buck the snow was red. A new made trail was there—a wide trail as if a mad moose had pushed sideways through the thick growth. Moosuk's mouth slowly shut. His lips pouted, then drew back to a smile, and again he spoke:

"Big bear!" His Indian mind easily deduced the fancy of a bleeding bruin wrestling with some gripping steel; and a small forest of entanglement with him. Then Moosuk's face looked serious, and again he spoke:

"Jules' bear!" Jules was the fur company's Sans Poil *voyageur*.

Moosuk put his face closer to the snow. He forgot his hungry stomach as his keen eye read the trail; and again there was a satisfied Shushwap guttural as the young Indian decided Jules had not yet followed his game. Jules' track was not there; it may have been too early in the day.

The soul of the simple Sans Poil had been mightily changed of late years by the new questions in the red book on the rights of man. Moosuk's gift was of an easy, honest sort, but the coming of the pirating Caucasians (they took his food from his mouth) had undone his primitive sense, and the old fine dealing between red and red did not in those days apply. Moosuk's little-wise mind had known no rest since he first saw a Sans Poil beaver biting the steel of Jules' skilfully laid trap the winter gone.

But the Indian had no time to sift this immediate question of the Debatable Ground. His instinct was too keen, and the trail too fresh. The fever in him pressed, and the race between the tired

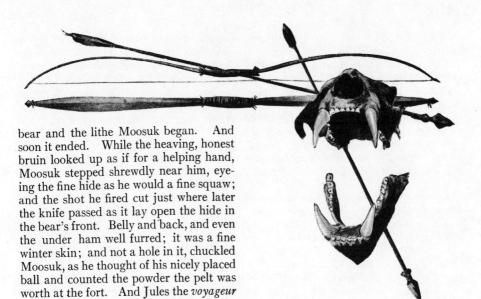

bear and the lithe Moosuk began. And soon it ended. While the heaving, honest bruin looked up as if for a helping hand, Moosuk stepped shrewdly near him, eyeing the fine hide as he would a fine squaw; and the shot he fired cut just where later the knife passed as it lay open the hide in the bear's front. Belly and back, and even the under ham well furred; it was a fine winter skin; and not a hole in it, chuckled Moosuk, as he thought of his nicely placed ball and counted the powder the pelt was worth at the fort. And Jules the *voyageur* made only a misty atom of guilt in the Indian's happy mind.

* * * * *

Jules Perrin sat on a pine log outside his cabin, his mink-peaked beaver back on his head, and his face pointed to catch all the winter sun's meager ration. Jules took off his gloves and cut an end of black twist with a mighty pleasure to the length of a smoke, thinking of his profitable winter campaign and the Christmas feast at the fort nearly due, when he would meet the rest (spared by the grace of God) of the over-Rocky Mountain brotherhood. Jules rolled and pressed the weed in his palm in a time-wasting loafer's way, as he thought of his little sweetheart in Montreal. Finally he felt for his pipe and his tinder; and he wondered if his bear trap ten miles south had results. He lifted a leg off the log; put a glove on; fixed his cap snug to his head, and, satisfied with his morning preparatory, started south over the snow. Jules kept by the river, trailing in the timber near the bank. The maple's wiry lacework, the white alder, the low berry brush, all showed the mark of Jules' industrious axe above the beaten path where first (and ages before his time) the salmon-seeking bear ran; or where bruin listened as he heard the kingfisher crying down the stream at game in the water too big for little birds; where the skunk ran sniffing tremblingly the heavy odor of his bigger friend, or the wild cat's dangerous musk. The trapper's trail often led on a log swaying across the frothing creek, and again angled inland to the beaver and otter slides. When dipping into the timber Jules left his pipe in the trail, lest the smell of it prove too strong for the suspicious fur ahead. Shortly Jules put away his pipe altogether. He stopped, too, to rub his cold nose. Then he fixed his cap firmly again to his head, and tied again his moccasin strings; he took up a hole in his belt, and looked to the lock of his gun. Jules thought he was near bear ground.

"This must be about where I fixed that trap," said Jules.

He worked more cautiously forward, bearing by slight new axe blazes on the bottom's timber.

"It's too quiet for real business," thought Jules. "Ah!" Jules opened his eyes. "He has come and gone," he added. "With the trap!" he appendixed.

Before Jules was a space well cleared of small brush, and finely thrashed about. The trees were barked as if something there had been kicking mad. Jules picked up the trail, more earnest in the business of getting bear; and his lively footing became livelier as sign more and more proved it sure his bear needed only the fine finishing touches of powder and shot.

Soon, however, the trapper slackened his pace. His well-posted hunter's sense told him his quarry had not struggled beyond a certain brush knoll above him. He primed his gun afresh, and cautiously he entered the arena of a bear's death struggle. But for Jules it was not to be. When Jules Perrin saw the fine carcass of the late bruin, the skeleton jaw openly grinning at him, his attitude doubled Moosuk's when that innocent, thrown back on his heels, first guessed the nearness of Jules in the valley. Jules a moment after danced a mad reel about his well-skinned trophy, and loud patois oaths traveled over those Okinakane wilds as his strong voice sent everything rouge rapidly to purgatory and other perdition.

Jules felt as severely involved in the rights of man on the Debatable Ground as Moosuk. But Jules had no scruples. His mind read the guilt of the Indian by his moccasin marks, and his conscience said at once, "an eye for an eye"—a Mosaic pattern unknown in that exact way to the ignorant red. And later Jules swung over the tracks of Moosuk to where the untaught red fellow had worked all that raw day in the swamps with his miserable half-score traps. Jules was soon the mortgagee of all Moosuk's winter capital stock. Then he took the trail for home, satisfied with his financial deal and any developments Sans Poil red men might excite from it.

* * * * *

The first ceremony of another act on the Debatable Ground was now over. Moosuk's squaw next day feared a paleface bogie instead of a Blackfoot as she listened for the *boof-boof* tread in the snow coming back.

Moosuk on the trail in the first gray of the day noted Jules' track. Soon he noted Jules' work. Every trap in the beaver swamp was gone. The young Sans Poil let his jaw drop as if he were sick. Then his eyes showed his blind madness, while his mouth roughed out the picture of a redman's hate. Soon he turned sick again with the whole effect of it; thinking hard of the work those traps had caused him. Moosuk yesterday had thrown up his face and sniffed the heavy beaver taint in the air, as he thought of more tobacco and a new blanket for his wife at the fort, that now he could not buy. Moosuk grew sicker. He counted the beaver he should have found in the drift with the white whittled pole marking the steel below. A Blackfoot could not have done worse, he thought. The Indian saw again the moccasin track of the alien, and turned home to nurse his rights in primitive common law.

* * * * *

Moosuk's squaw after that was worried about Moosuk. The buck slipped out of his tepee in the morning only to come back early without a hair of fur, and to mope the rest of the day. Fur did not seem to be his business. She did not see, nor did Jules see, the swift Moosuk lope up the Sans Poil each day, and at the end of an hour climb a high alder. If Jules had had the eyes of a hawk he would have caught the intent gaze of Moosuk, as he perched high in the limbs of a tree not far below the *voyageur's* cabin. But the morning came when Moosuk did not back trail to the tepee. Far out on the snow-covered plain a black speck moved west. Moosuk saw it from his perch. His mouth opened, and his face smiled as he said:

"Jules—fort!" Jules was, in fact, tramping at a good gait for the Christmas feast at Fort Okinakane, four days away on the Cariboo trail.

There were soon two black dots on the plain that led to the Columbia—two specks on the great snow plateau, moving over low hills and among bits of winter-dead timber and brush. Moosuk trod lightly in the trail of Jules. Jules crunched the new snow that had had no man's foot on it that winter; the wide highway to him was his alone, and Jules looked only forward. The brilliant glare of the sun gave him his only distraction, but that worried him as much, perhaps, as if he had known that his murderous enemy Moosuk was behind him: Now

" The Indian watched Jules open-mouthed."

and again Jules put his hand nervously to his eyes, and he swore a little at a pain that shot back in his head. Moosuk at times saw Jules' peculiar action, and wondered humorously what flies could bother him in dead of winter and on the desert snow.

Moosuk was following steadily the trail of Jules on the second day, and he was closer. Once Moosuk climbed a higher hill, and looked west to where the Columbia tore its way through the earth; and that spot, if Moosuk's mind could have been so skilfully divined from his well-written facial expression, had intensest interest for him. It was there Jules would have to ford the river; and it was there that Moosuk might find the opportunity fitted to his cautious Indian idea.

The roar of the river reached up as it plunged through its canyon, the only voice to the two moving objects on the snow world above. There was little distraction in Moosuk's desperate game. But it was odd, thought Moosuk, that Jules now goes north. In fact, Jules' trail now bore away from the true course. Moosuk could not understand it. He sat down to figure the matter. Then he followed more swiftly. North, then south, then north again, and east and west, Jules wandered indifferently. He might have been crazed.

Moosuk was mightily puzzled. He could not account for Jules, and as his enemy continued his erratic movements the Indian could only utter a guttural "That's queer!" The Indian now came nearer, and now Jules bore back on his trail. "That is queerer still!" Moosuk must have thought. Moosuk was within a few yards of his enemy. He dropped into a clump of brush. Hidden, the Indian watched Jules open-mouthed. The trapper strode aimlessly in every direction.

"What is the matter with him?" Moosuk was asking himself. No answer was suggested by the trapper's strange bearing; though often he clasped his hands to his head, and a round patois oath would soar above the plain; nor even when Jules at last sat down on his furs and buried his face in his hands. Moosuk then muttered the equivalent for "terribly sick," as the best solution of the mystery. Jules put his hand to his head; rubbed his eyes. Moosuk involuntarily did the same, but

the mystery remained. "*Oogh-k!*" exclaimed Moosuk. It was his first hearty guttural since he saw the blood-covered trail of Jules' troublesome bear. "Him not lost trail. Trail clear!" he further thought. The Indian was completely foiled by the manner of Jules. He now lay down to await developments. Nothing like this had happened in his life before.

Jules did not sit silent long. He astonished the Indian by sudden activity. The trapper shook a little powder into the pan of his gun; he blazed away, and the Okinakane wilds awakened to a rifle shot, while Moosuk, with peculiar adroitness and suddenness, flung himself flat on the snow. Again and again Jules fired, but no shot replied. Moosuk only heard, trembling. Then the trapper tossed his rifle from him, as if in despair.

Jules half disarmed, Moosuk felt freer. He peeped out of his hiding place for a better view, his curiosity as much as his hate tempting him. The Indian stole now to the rear, softly crawling in the snow. He understood the silent art of moving on his belly—Moosuk had raided his neighbor Blackfoot in his day. The rear, however, taught Moosuk nothing, and he stole past a hummock to the front, his knife anxiously clenched in his hand. Soon he raised his head. Yet Jules did not move. Moosuk's face was cut in bronze against the faultless background. There seemed no passion in the mask that propped itself on the snow, but a child's absorbing curiosity and wonderment. From the tendons of his neck to the ligaments of his heels he was tense and rigid as the salmon he smoked in his tepee and chewed in the winter time. That was from physical anxiousness. Moosuk's nature was under a new trial, and it was tempted with new emotions. There was no creed to apply here, and as his muzzle pitched over the snow the Indian blinked and blinked again to unfathom the helplessness of his enemy. Soon he once more asked himself:

"Is Jules sick?" Just then Jules moved. The Indian gopher disappeared in the snow, and Jules was alone. Slowly, however, the apparition showed again on the snow. Then more slowly above the confident head came the shoulders, and Moosuk, with his elbows and his chin

"Jules was not dead but strong yet in that wild, desert plain."

resting on his hands, kicked his toes into his soft bed, still waiting patiently. Jules fronted Moosuk square, but he saw no more of him than Montreal; but with his face pushed in his hands he seemed absorbed. At last Jules lifted his face and seemed to look earnestly over the snow. Moosuk diplomatically slipped, as it were, into the earth. Jules still stared as Moosuk lifted himself cautiously again. As the mask appeared and it saw Jules' face, it opened its mouth. There could be but one answer, and Moosuk breathed:

"*Oogh-k!*—Jules no see." The practical Indian did not pinch himself to know if he were in a dream. He could under-

stand now that the keen-eyed trapper had lost one of his senses.

"Him no see, him no hear; him mebbe half dead," might have been the expressed jargon of the Sans Poil's collected thought, and from it sprang an original idea. The Indian's mouth took a flat oval form, and his face muscles became rigid, while from his throat tore a yell that Blackfoot over the Rockies might have heard. The effect was all that could have been desired. If Moosuk was astonished at Jules' rifle shot, Jules was thrilled by the Shushwap war whoop. Jules was transformed. Straight up he stood, holding his knife in his hand. He was not dead, but strong yet in that wild, desert plain, and brave

"His quiet face turned to an astonished mask."

among his enemies; and if Jules ever cursed things rouge he cursed them then. His desperate patois oration in synopsis simply meant:

"Come on, ye devils, if ye dare!" No further Moosuk yells greeted Jules, however. Moosuk simply kept silent in front of the unintelligent jargon, and as the minutes ran by without a sound the *voyageur* sat down and cursed himself for a dreamer and a madman.

Moosuk was a cautious, calculating brave; but not a coward. He would bring this odd circumstance to a climax. With another yell he was now within two steps of the trapper, who jumped upright and defiant before him.

But Moosuk went no further. Jules' face was clear, and the Indian dropped his hands: the complete solution of the mystery was his. He uttered one word. It meant this:

"Snowblind." In his Shushwap lingo

Moosuk repeated: "Snowblind." And he knew what it meant. The tall, strong trapper was less dangerous than a cub bear, and his head was racked as if fire had been plunged in his eyes. Moosuk repeated:

"Snowblind!" His hands dropped, and his face lines again moved to new and sudden emotions. Moosuk again repeated the momentous word. His face showed he had forgotten the devil that was in him all day, and the temptation to send Jules to eternity was strangely weak in him.

"Come on, ye varmint, and fight," roared the trapper. "Fight a blind man. Stick yer knife in a blind man!"

But Moosuk was not ready. He rummaged his mind for ideas. He held a council of war with himself, as he and his tribesmen had together before the slumbering lodge of Blackfoot. There was Kyak, thought Moosuk, if his thoughts could be so freely translated; he killed everything, like a cougar and he stuck his knife into his dead for simple ugliness. There was more good in Moosuk than in Kyak; though there was less in Kyak than in the ordinary coyote. But there was Feather-at-His-Back. He killed Two-Horse because Two-Horse tortured that Utah when Feather-at-His-Back said "Enough." Over such and other domestic knowledge Moosuk lingered to find a cue to that problem standing blind and defiant on the snow.

Then there was the temptation of Jules' fine furs; the danger of discovery of a killing; the Columbia could carry Jules' corpse to eternal silence, but the bloody snow plain might tell the tale. But Moosuk was not a professional murderer. That was not in his red heart. And he did not know enough of the white to hate him deep forever. So ran the complex data of thought and emotion through the strategic, half-soulful Indian mind—a mind capable enough, as his council talks had proved. And he knew no creed but his simple inspiration and the rough training of his utilitarian Indian life. And Moosuk had cried like a child when his sister died. And once he traveled forty days with a ransom to the Cayuses for his brother. And Moosuk often had grown sick of the torture tricks of the old women when Blackfoot were tied to the stakes of his tribe. And there was in this situation something akin, and that touched his human strings. He did not know that as he stood alone with his worst enemy, doubting, he had already worked out a little of the detail of the true love of a Christ; and he did not know as at last the nature in him took pity on Jules, and he sulkily put back his knife, and came to terms, that that was Christian. And Moosuk's red soul knew nothing, as he led Jules over the Columbia (the roaring voice of it a hymn to Jules) ford, of other men's creeds. Nor until he led the trapper by a string through the stockade of the fort on that Christmas day had he ever heard: "Peace on earth, and good will toward all men."

24

Beaver Ways

FRANK H. RISTEEN

BEAVER WAYS.

By FRANK H. RISTEEN.

IT is early in April, in the heart of the still New Brunswick wilderness. From the outer world of sunshine and open fields the snow has departed for the most part, and spring's balmy air is vocal with the rush and murmur of little hillside streams, while the big ones in the valleys fret and fume to be relieved of their icy fetters. But how is it here in the shadowed depths of the virgin woods, where the siren voices are the last to be heard ? The snow is still five or six feet deep on the level ; the nights are nearly as cold as in mid-winter, promptly undoing the feeble efforts put forth each day by the northward marching sun. The latter has only sent out his skirmishers as yet ; soon there will come the earnest shock of battle when the chill battalions of the Frost King will yield the field sullenly to the ardent attack of his ancient foe.

Up the sunken snowshoe-path that leads to a homely trapper's shanty two men walk wearily. They are laden with furs they have taken that day from a line of traps about eight miles in length, and are leg-weary from their long struggle with the cloying drifts. One of these men is Henry Braithwaite, the famous woodsman, who has spent all his days in the forest ; the other, a young amateur sportsman, whose love for the woods is sufficient to induce him, as a matter of friendship and recreation, to share with the professional the toils and trials of the trapping season. That evening, as the camp-fire roars cheerily, telling with a thousand fiery tongues its tale of triumph to the surrounding chill and gloom, the elder man, in response to his companion's questioning, discusses freely the subject of beaver ways.

" Beavers are not as numerous over the province generally as they were twenty years ago, but on my own ground they are about as plentiful as ever, for the reason that I have always made it a point to leave a sufficient number every year on the different streams to keep the stock replenished. The trapper who finds a beaver family and never lets up until he has wiped them all out is pursuing a very short-sighted policy. A female beaver will bring forth from two to five kittens each spring, and I have known them to have six, and in one case seven, in a litter. In this country the kittens are born the latter part of May or the first of June. The animals are now more numerous in Northumberland and Restigouche than any of the other counties. They would be numerous in Gloucester, Madawaska, and Victoria, but are followed up too closely by the Frenchmen, who never give them a chance to breed. In the southern and western counties few are now to be found. The pelts at present are worth about nine shillings a pound. They vary from half a pound to two pounds in weight, the average being about one and a quarter. I generally bring in from thirty to sixty skins in a season. Most of these go to the London market ; some of them to Montreal. The age of the beaver makes very little difference with regard to the quality of the fur. Three and four year olds are about the best, as the skins are more pliable. The drop in Alaska seal has brought down the value of beaver, because the latter is used to counterfeit the former. After the beaver skin has been plucked and dyed to resemble seal it takes an expert to tell the difference.

"A good many stories are told about beavers by people who are not well informed. For instance, it is claimed that they use their broad, scaly tails as trowels to plaster their houses or dams. As a matter of fact, they simply keep lugging up mud and tramping over it, and that is all the plastering that is done. Then, again, it is stated that they only work at night. I have often seen them working in the daytime, especially in the spring of the year, when it freezes too hard at night for them to cut their wood. I have known them to come out of their houses at eleven o'clock in the forenoon, but it is usual for them to appear at three o'clock and work till dark. The Indians, and some white men, take advantage of this and lie in wait to shoot them when they show up. On warm nights in the early autumn they are not apt to be seen in the daytime. For shooting a beaver in the water the shot-gun is preferable to the rifle. Only about half of the animal's head shows above the surface, and as he is nearly always under full head of steam, it is hard to stop him with the rifle. If you miss your beaver, he up-ends and dives like a shot, his broad tail striking the water like a side of sole leather. I believe his object in spanking the water is to put the other beavers on their guard.

"In some respects the cleverness of the beaver is overrated. He is certainly a very good, clean workman in the mason and carpenter line, but is far easier to trap than a fox or a fisher. When you are lying for him with a gun, all you have to do is to keep perfectly still, and he will swim right up to you, but the slightest whiff of human scent will send him to the bottom.

"Beaver dams are not always built of sticks and mud. I have seen four of them built entirely of stone. At Beaver Brook Lake there is an old stone dam about forty rods long. When this dam was first made, it probably was cemented with leaves and mud; but this soft material washed out after a while without materially lowering the dam, and when a new family of beavers fell heir to it, they had water enough there without having to raise the dam. The beaver is a great worker, but he likes to loaf as much as anyone else when he has a chance. For instance, when he can find an old lumberman's dam, it is a regular windfall for him. He goes right to work and plugs up the old gateway, and soon has a splendid fit-out. It makes him fairly grin to strike such a snap as that. But I have seen beavers that didn't seem to have good horse sense. They will undertake to build a dam in a place where it will be carried away with every freshet, while within ten rods of it there is a good, safe site. Sometimes they

"Swimming down the canal with a tree five times his own weight in tow."

"If he can get hold of you with his teeth, he will almost take a leg off."

will pick out very mean places for food and will nearly starve in the winter, though there is plenty of good poplar and birch not a quarter of a mile away.

"Some people who write stories for the papers say that what are called bank beavers are lazy old males that have been forced out of the house by the rest of the family because they wouldn't work. I wonder what kind of a spy-glass the man had who saw this taking place. Perhaps he was a mind-reader, who could figure out what the beavers were thinking about. Bank beavers are not always males, by any means. I have trapped female bank beavers with their kittens. The fact is that when beavers take to the bank, it is because there is so much water there that they don't need a dam, or because there is no chance to build a dam. That is why you find the bank beavers mostly on lakes or large rivers, which they are unable to dam.

"A full-grown beaver will weigh from thirty to forty pounds. I have caught a good many scaling over forty pounds, and have been told by very reliable people that sixty pounders have been taken. I think the beaver, if he could only keep out of the trap, would live to a ripe old age. His growth is very slow, yet he sometimes reaches a remarkable size, with every sign of extreme

age. I feel safe in saying that he is liable to live to be twenty-five or thirty years of age. The fur of the beaver is at its best in the winter and early spring. The outer and longer coating is coarse and glossy, almost black in colour; the under coat is very thick and silky, nearly black on top and silver-grey underneath.

"The beaver is really a sort of automatic pulp-mill, grinding up almost any kind of bark that comes his way. I once measured a white birch tree, twenty-two inches through, cut down by a beaver. A single beaver generally, if not always, cuts the tree; and when it comes down, the whole family fall to and have a regular frolic with the bark and branches. A big beaver will bring down a fair-sized sapling, say three inches through, in about two minutes, and a large tree in about an hour. The favourite food of the animal is the poplar; next comes the cherry, then the balm of Gilead. They are fond of all kinds of maples, and will eat cedar, hemlock, or spruce. In some places they feed principally on alders. They also eat the roots of many kinds of water plants. When food is scarce, they will consume the bark of the largest trees.

"They commence to build their houses and yard up wood for the winter in September; sometimes, however, as early as August, and sometimes as late as October. They drag in the wood from all directions to the pond, and float it up as near as they can to the front of the lodge. There are usually two doors to a beaver house, and a favourite place for them to pile their wood is between these openings. A large quantity, however, is left out in the open pond, very little of which is available for consumption, because when the shallow pond freezes up, the beavers are only able to reach what is below the ice. The size of the house, as well as of the wood-pile stored in the pond, depends on the size of the family. An average house, which is circular in shape, will measure about twelve feet in diameter, and stand from three to six feet above the surface of the water. I have known them to be as large as sixteen and as small as six feet in diameter. The walls are about two feet thick, and even without the aid of winter's masonry are strong enough to support the weight of a full-grown moose. After the rains and frosts of early winter have cemented the mass, the house is well-nigh impregnable. It is perfectly air-tight, and being steam-heated by the beavers, must be very warm and cosy in the coldest weather. Old beavers build large houses, work systematically, and go in for comfort generally.

"Each beaver places his bed neatly against the inner surface of the wall. His bedding is composed usually of wood fibres stripped fine, like an Indian's broom. In the case of lake beaver, with whom wood is scarce, blue joint-grass is used for bedding. This is taken out frequently and a fresh supply brought in, for the beaver is a most cleanly animal, and his couch is soon fouled by his muddy occupation. Occasionally a beaver house is found with a root or stump running up through the centre, around which the beds are ranged.

"The two outlets from the lodge are built on an incline to the bottom of the pond. I think the intention is that if an enemy comes in at one door, the beavers can leave by the other. The mud with which the roof is plastered is mostly taken from the bottom of the pond close to the house, sometimes leaving quite a ditch there, which is handy, as giving the beavers room to move about when the ice gets thick. As the ice freezes down to the bottom, the beavers extend a trench from this ditch out farther into the pond, to enable them to reach their food. This trench is sometimes ten rods in length. They will often cut a canal about three feet wide from one lake to another, if the intervening ground is barren and the surface level. Sometimes they will excavate an underground canal between the lakes. If the house is on a lake and there is a wide strip of barren between the house and the edge of the woods, they will cut a canal clear up to the edge of the

woods, so that they can float their stuff down. To see a beaver swimming down the canal with a tree five times his own weight in tow is an amusing sight. He has a good deal the same look of mingled triumph and responsibility on his face as the man who is lugging home his Thanksgiving turkey.

"It is very seldom that the house is located on or near the dam. Beaver dams vary a good deal in height, according to the shape of the bank and the depth of water, seldom, however, measuring over seven feet. They are often eight or ten feet wide at the base, sloping up to a width of from one to three feet on top, and are usually water-tight. They are very firmly constructed and will last for years, as a rule, after the beavers have left them. Where beavers have seldom been disturbed, they can be captured by making a small break in the dam and setting a trap for them when they come to repair the leak. But where they have been much hunted—and they are mostly all pretty well posted nowadays—this plan is a poor one. The beavers will promenade on top of the dam and smell around the trap to see what is the matter; and when you visit the trap, you are liable to find in it nothing but a bunch of sticks. A beaver colony may use the same dam for a number of years, especially when it is at the outlet or inlet of a lake, but they will usually build a new house every year. I think they do this on the ground of cleanliness, on which point they are very particular.

"As compared with the otter or mink, the beaver is a very slow swimmer. His front legs hang by his sides, and he uses only his webbed hind-feet. It is easy to capture him with a canoe if you can find him in shallow water. He is a most determined fighter, but clumsy and easy to handle. If he can get hold of you with his teeth, he will almost take a leg off—so you want to watch him sharply. The proper place to grab him, with safety to yourself, is by the tail.

"The only enemy the beaver really has to fear is man. The bear and the lynx still hunt him sometimes, but not with much success. I have known a bear to go down into four feet of water and haul a beaver out of a trap. The lynx occasionally catches a small beaver on the bank, or in a shallow brook, but a full-grown specimen is too much for him to handle. The intelligence of wild animals in some respects is superior to that of men. They never have a swelled head; never bite off more than they can comfortably digest. Each fellow knows what he is able to tackle and get away with without injuring his health. The bear has too much sense to tackle the porcupine, and all hands line up to give the skunk the right of way.

"As soon as the lakes and streams open in the spring, the old males, and all the two and three year olds, start off on a regular excursion and ramble over the brooks and lakes for miles around, the old females remaining at home to rear their young.

very human. If the trapper comes along, and her mate is taken, she goes skirmishing as soon as possible for another husband.

"Near the root of the beaver's tail are glands which hold a thick, musty substance called the castoreum, which is used by trappers to scent their bait. When I want to shoot a beaver, I get out my bottle of castoreum and pull the cork. The beaver will swim right up within range as soon as he catches the scent. When trapping in the autumn, which I seldom do, I generally daub

"They can be captured by making a small break in the dam and setting a trap for them when they come to repair the leak."

In fact, the mother beavers remain at home all summer, while the rest of the tribe range about until September, when they commence to club together again. The kittens generally remain with the mother for two years. When they are three years old, they mate and start off on their own hook. You can only tell the newly wedded couple by the small, snug house they build. They seem to be very devoted to each other, but I have noticed one point about the young she beaver that is

a little of the substance on a dry stub a few yards away from the shore. The trap is set about three inches under water, where the beaver climbs up on the bank, a bunch of poplar being generally used for bait. When trapping in the winter, you cannot use the castoreum, as the trap must be set under the ice, where the scent has no effect.

"Some old trappers, when setting traps under the ice, cut four stakes, three of green poplar and the other of some kind of dry wood. These are driven down through the hole in the ice close to the house, solidly into the bottom, forming a square about a foot each way. The trap is set and lowered carefully to the bottom by means of two hooked sticks, the ring on the chain being slipped over the dry stake. This is not a sure plan at all. There is nothing to prevent the beaver from cutting off the poplars above the trap and carrying them away. In fact, if the beaver gets in the trap, he is simply playing in hard luck. The best way is to shove down a small, dry tree, with three or four branches sticking out, on which the trap can be set, and place the bait above it in such a fashion that the beaver will have to step on the trap to reach it. But if the water is shallow enough, the safest way is to place your trap on the bottom. It is, of course, all important that the beaver should drown soon after he is caught; otherwise you are very apt to get nothing but a claw, especially if he is caught by the fore-foot, which can be twisted off very easily.

" The cutting of a hole in the ice and other disturbances caused by setting the trap, of course, scare the beavers in the house, and you are not likely to catch any for two or three nights. But the beavers cannot escape, are very hungry for fresh food, and after they get over their panic will readily walk into the trap.

" The ability of a beaver to remain under water for a long time is really not so hard a problem as it looks. When the lake or pond is frozen over, a beaver will come to the under surface of the ice and expel his breath so that it forms a wide, flat bubble. The air coming in contact with the ice and water, is purified, and the beaver breathes it in again. This operation he can repeat several times. The otter and musk-rat do the same thing. When the ice is thin and clear, I have often seen the musk-rat attached to his bubble, and by pounding on the ice have driven him away from it, whereupon he drowns in a very short time.

" It almost takes a burglar-proof safe to hold a newly captured beaver. I once caught an old one and two kittens up the north branch of the Sou'west Miramichi, put them in a barrel, and brought them down to Miramichi Lake. That night the old beaver gnawed a hole through the barrel and escaped, leaving her kittens behind. They were so young that I had no way of feeding them, so released them in the hope that the mother might find them. Soon afterwards I caught a very large male beaver. I made a log pen for him of dry spruce, but the second night he cut a log out and disappeared. Beavers, when alarmed, generally make up stream, so I went up the brook to where a little branch came in, and thought I would give that a look, and I hadn't gone more than ten rods before I came across my old friend sitting up in the bed of the brook, having a lunch on a stick he had cut. He actually looked as if he knew he was playing truant when he caught sight of me out of the side of his eye. I picked him up by the tail, brought him back, put him in the pen, supplied him with plenty of fresh poplar, and he never gave me any more trouble."

25
Paddling in the Winnipeg Country

PADDLING IN THE WINNIPEG COUNTRY.[1]

As we paddled nearly fifty miles the day before we reached the Cat Head, it is provoking to be again stopped by the waves an hour after breakfast, and landed on a little sand-spit, backed by a marsh full of mosquitoes, where we must spend the remainder of the day ; nor comforting that night their might, for the wind is increasing rapidly, preventing our return before we go a mile, and necessitating a run of several miles before the wind ere we can gain a haven. Billy, always a dismal prophet, begins to exclaim at the large and increasing size of the waves between us and the

THE WINNIPEG STERN-WHEELER.

to hear the rain pattering on our tent, betokening a storm, and further delay. What is our pleasure to find, after breakfast, that our men think we may proceed ; that the traverse from Point Wigwam, where we are, to the nearest island in the bay, six miles distant, is decided on.

As we leave the little harbor, a tremendous splash beneath our very paddles startles us. "Nahmä !" cry the men, "ah ha, Nahmä," and we are introduced to the king of the northern waters.

We now try the sail, a rude affair enough — a square-sail hauled up over a forked pole in the front part of the canoe — but by means of which we make much more rapid progress than is our wont; yet not rapid enough for George, who sets the men at work paddling also with all

Sturgeon Islands, to which we are heading, asserting in short and decided phrase that we can never reach them. The waves grow larger and noisier, and we reckon with anxiety the space that still remains. We speed along as never before, the wave-crests occasionally dashing over our gunwales, the canoe bending and twisting as each wave rushes angrily from stern to bow, and the wind threatening to tear the mast from its frail lashings.

We are glad enough when the lee of one of the Sturgeon Islands is reached at the end of an hour — the most perilous experienced. Did we know that this island was to be our prison for three miserable days, we should have taken our arrival with less equanimity ! Hoping later in the day to be able to push forward, our canoe is not

[1] This article forms one of the chapters of a most entertaining volume just published by Cupples, Upham & Co., of Boston. The author made a journey from St. Paul, in Minnesota, to a point on the Saskatchewan River, in Canada, for the purpose of observing the eclipse of 1860. A part of the country which at that time was a wilderness contains, by the census of 1880, 70,000 souls, supporting 28 newspapers. We would like to find room for the whole book, for it is full of suggestive narrative.

THE START FROM THE STONE FORT.

ever watchful George, and though the waves are still high, and the traverse ahead a long one glad enough to venture it The men hastily arouse themselves, light their pipes, take two or three whiffs, and then, laying hold of the canoe with many interjections and "ughs," they turn it over, and, three men on each side, carry it, stern foremost, into the water, bringing it around as the stern floats, so that it lies broadside in water up to the men's knees. Steersman and bowsman then hold each his end, steadying the canoe, and directing the loading. Narcisse jumps in, and stows away, with the two Georges' help, the boxes and bags which the others bring, working always on the run. An open framework is placed on the floor in the middle, and on it oil-cloth, tent-bag, and blankets are thrown for the philosophers' seats; the men sit on narrow slats slung by thongs about six inches below the thwarts. The baggage

at first unloaded, but merely kept next the shore by small trees falling from the beach across the bow and stern. Landing is made in the pelting rain; and the tent-poles being at the bottom of the canoe, we three philosophers solace ourselves with one umbrella and one rubber blanket between us, until the men have made a sort of wigwam of poles, bent, twisted, and bound together, and on the windward-side have thrown over it the tent-cover; to this, and the comfort of a roaring fire in front, we then retreat and bemoan our fate. The days are gliding swiftly by. Ten have passed since leaving Fort Garry. Less than ten remain to the day of the eclipse, after we are at last freed from our prison; and half the journey is not made. It is true that winds will not detain us on the river, but there we will have to contend with the unfailing current.

The island which affords the philosophers at once a shelter and a prison is about a foot above the level of the lake, and about a hundred and fifty yards long by half as wide: so at least we estimate it; but with all our explorations, we are unable to penetrate to either extremity. It is made up of a bulrush muskeg, willow and alder chapperal, sand and boulders. We explore nearly half an acre of it with limited success, and have for an outlook fragments of similar islands of equal interest in the near distance.

We are glad to be called at three o'clock on the morning of the fourth day by the

A RISKY SHOOT.

all in, the philosophers are carried out in the same way, the men get in, and the canoe is off. After rounding Limestone Point, and crossing Portage Bay, we land on a little island for breakfast, which the men by this time have surely earned. Breakfast, dinner and supper are all one and the same thing. Pemmican, bannocks (simple flour, water, and salt), and hard biscuit are the staples, washed down with tea. Potatoes long since gave out, and the ham and salt beef are so strong that the saltless pemmican is soon preferred. This, too, is the genuine article, just as put up on the plains—now no longer to be had —and a vastly different thing from the material of that name put up in England for Arctic travelers.

The meat, cut in long flakes from the warm carcass of the buffalo, and dried in the sun, is afterwards beaten into shreds by flails upon a floor of buffalo-hide on the open prairie ; the hide is then sewn into a bag, the meat jammed in, the top sewed up, all but one corner, into which more meat is crowded ; and then the fat, which has meanwhile, been tried, is poured in scalding hot, filling every crevice. A species of cranberry is often added with the meat. The whole forms a bolster-shaped bag, as solid and as heavy as stone ; and in this condition it remains, perhaps for years, until it is eaten. Each bag weighs from a hundred to a hundred and twenty pounds. One who has tried it will not wonder that it was once used, in the turmoils of the contests between the Northwest and Hudson Bay Companies, to form a redoubt, armed with two swivel guns.

We have two ways of preparing this — one called "rub-a-boo," when it is boiled in a great deal of water, and makes a soup ; the other more favorite dish is "rousseau," when it is thrown into the frying-pan, fried in its own fat, with the addition, perhaps, of a little salt pork, and mixed with a small

amount of flour or broken biscuit. But sometimes, when our philosophers are hard put to it, and forced to take their meal in the canoe, the pemmican is eaten raw, chopped out of the bag with a hatchet, and accompanied simply by the biscuit, which has received the soubriquet of "Red-river

PADDLING.

granite." These wonderful objects, as large as sea-biscuit, are at least three-quarters of an inch in thickness, and against them the naturalist's geological hammer is always brought into requisition.

But the "infidel dish," as we termed rousseau, is by comparison with the others palatable, though it is even then impossible to so disguise it as to avoid the suggestion of tallow candles ; and this and the leathery, or india-rubbery, structure of the meat are its chief disqualifications. But even rousseau may lose its charms when taken as a steady diet three times a day for weeks ; especially when it is served in the frying-pan, and breakfast or dinner over, one sees the remnants with the beef or pork all hustled together into the boiling kettle ;

WILL PORTAGE FOR PEMMICAN.

cloth and table-cloth, thrown into the canoe to rest until the next meal, when at last Billy finds time to wash the dishes — the table-cloth, never.

We are able, indeed, to vary our diet a little now and then — but they are rare occasions — by barter with the Indians for fish, which they catch in the streams (not in the lake), by shooting a stray duck, goose, or gull (nothing coming amiss), or — shall we tell it to civilized ears? — by the eggs of sea-fowl, picked up on the sandy islands, where they can be found in every stage of incubation. Our first experience of this was only a few days out — the day we made the traverse from the west to the east coast. We passed an island where the men dashed ashore to get a gull they had shot, and brought it back with several dozen eggs besides. The gull measured fifty-six inches in spread of wings, and the eggs were as big as turkeys'. We ordered ham and eggs that night, but, when the meal was served, discovered that

the biscuit, broken bannocks, and un-washed cups placed in the bread-bag; the plates, knives, and forks tossed into the meat-dish, and all, combined in the ample folds of an old bit of gunny-cloth which has served daily at once as dish-

Billy had fried the ham indeed, but *boiled* the eggs. They were "fresh," however, Billy declared; for had he not tested them by a plunge in water? Not one, however, but had been under the mother for a week, and some were on the

THE SERIOUS WORK OF CANOEING.

point of hatching. We were a little hesitant at first, but four or five days of pemmican gave us less scruple ; and, the Rubicon once crossed, incipient feathers no longer alarm us, and half-hatched gulls' and terns' eggs are an eagerly sought diet. We are indeed fast lapsing into savagery.

We have now a long stretch of tame coast before us—low-lying forest land of tamarack and spruce, with occasional poplars and willows, edged by a muskeg, and that by a sand beach little indented. Here and there horizontal layers of limestone crop out a few feet only above the water ; and now and then the marshes appear to overflow, as some small stream seeks a dozen outlets for its murky flood.

FORT GARRY IN 1860.

Along this uninteresting shore we fortunately make steady progress. We are glad enough, however, as toward nightfall we espy some Indian lodges, to stop and exchange, with equal relish on both sides, pemmican and tobacco for fresh fish and ducks. As usual, the women come out to the canoe for the barter, wading nearly to their waists, regardless of their clothing, and among them a very pretty maiden of about seventeen with whom our boys pass many a merry word ; while the men squat on the beach, speechless, smoking, their faces half hidden behind their knees. This little diversion gives our boys new spirit ; and after paddling briskly twelve miles farther, making in all about sixty miles this day, we come to a cosy little harbor and a most welcome fish supper.

The following night proves the coldest we have experienced, the thermometer falling to forty-four degrees (July 10-11). The men awake stiff with their long day's pull and the chilly air, and it is sunrise or nearly four o'clock before we are off—an unwonted late hour for an auspicious day. But after a time, when at the end of our long uniform coast line we have begun to turn toward the east, to round Cape Kitchinashi, alias " Missineo," the Big Point," or " Detour," which stretches ten miles or more abruptly into the lake, the wind freshens, and we are forced to the lee of one of the Gull Islands, which we reach by dinner time and cannot leave until the

next morning, finding a bit of grass-land for our bed, but scarcely a stick of wood for a fire.

The next day we paddle from three o'clock in the morning until supper time, rounding the cape and camping perhaps ten miles north of where we started ; the wind being southerly and freshening with the day, we are fortunate in getting around the point to its northern lee shore in season; an hour later might have detained us another day.

Along this smooth coast we try for the first time a new style of progression — tracking. A long light line is attached to the canoe near the bow, while to the other end three men upon the beach fasten their tracking or portage straps — long pieces of rawhide, broad in the middle and ending in thongs ; the broad part is passed over the shoulder, the ends fastened to the rope, and thus harnessed, the men drag our canoe at a dog-trot, while George, with his sweep-paddle, keeps the bow from shore, and Boozie has an eye out for rocks. The water in this portion of Lake Winnipeg is much clearer ; and we judge its name, " dirty water," was given it by frequenters of the southern portion. The same difference was noted on the return voyage.

Billy announces " no more sugar ; " even the flour is getting low. The only article of food of which there appears to be an abundance is pemmican, and of this we have already cached a bag on the road, and now make a second cache.

We comfort ourselves, however, by a sight of the shores about and beyond the entrance to the Saskatchewan, which only a northerly or easterly storm can now prevent our reaching on the morrow. Still, we confess to much uneasiness. But five days remain to the eclipse, and George says, and all his men corroborate him, that five days is the least time in which the journey up the river can be made. Are we to miss it by the paltry distance that the eye can traverse? Cumberland House, a Hudson Bay Company's post, is our destination, and is most favorably situated in the very center of the belt of total eclipse; but the river below it runs in a very oblique course through the belt, so that if we can only reach the Pas, a mission-station some distance farther down the river, we shall still gain the desired belt, though only its edge, where the period of totality will be very brief. But we say nothing of this to our men.

WINNIPEG IN 1871.

26

A Montreal Winter Glimpse

JOHN C. MARTIN

A MONTREAL WINTER GLIMPSE.

BY JOHN C. MARTIN.

At Montreal there are ten clubs which have a joint interest in a common rendezvous over Mount Royal, in the hostelry of Host Lumpkins, a genial, broad-minded Englishman, who knows right well how to treat his guests and cater to their simple requirements. "The Snow-shoer's Retreat" is a low, two-story, expanded hotel, which straggles over a wide area, furnishing a plenty of floor-space, and, in its exterior lines, affording relief to the eye by its broken outline of Gothic crests and spires. The house nestles in the very bosom of the mountain which rises in a precipitous acclivity from the rear. Dining-rooms and also committee rooms occupy the nooks and corners, and the entire second floor is thrown into a grand hall, where the clubs assemble. A piano on a raised platform is perched in an angle of the room, and comfortable seats are placed around the walls. The floor is clean, and the polished surface irresistibly suggests dancing.

Having looked in at the retreat we will return and accompany a club on one of its regular weekly tramps. We drive up in a luxuriously appointed sleigh, buried in soft robes, and to the music of jingling bells are deposited at the honored gates of old McGill College. Our Jehu, who is dubbed "a carter" by some inscrutable application of the English language to his calling, informs us that we have reached our destination, and that a compensation in the shape of *une piastre* would be acceptable. He hesitates in the demand, and we know that he is laboring under the sense of showing great effrontery in extorting more than *un écu*, or half a dollar, for the three-mile ride. We leave him to the unmerciful berating of his own conscience, and we take observations.

The club-members have begun to arrive, and a score of blanketed forms are capering up and down the smoothly-beaten street. Some are seen stooping under the rays of a gas-lamp, tying on their shoes, or stretching the elastic buckskin thongs that attach the racquet to the foot. Animal spirits abound, and shivering, squeamish souls, contracted and warped by the keen air, cannot be discovered in the composition of the different groups. Caloric is superabundant, and the air resounds with shrill and hoarse exclamations, as the boys romp with kittenish glee, as if rejoicing in

MIXED PLEASURE.

the release from overheated rooms. Having already passed the neophyte stage, we are taken in hand. A pair of shoes are procured. With experienced fingers we don them and are allowed to join the ranks. This courtesy, by the way, is rarely extended, as a rigid observance of rules demands the absolute exclusion of outsiders. Presently the air parts with the rattling call, — an Iroquois war-whoop, which can only be expressed in type by o–o–o–o–o, modulated from a high key to a profound bass, a resonant, protracted and penetrating summons that is far-reaching in this dry atmosphere.

The president has arrived. The call is answered and repeated from all sides. The brethren center around their chief, and a few words serve to tell the nature of the trip. The clubs vie with each other in making the mountain passage in short time, and this evening, it happens that the wearers of the *tuque Verte* were to lower the record, if possible. A whipper-in is appointed.

"All ready?" exclaims the president.

Cheery responses immediately follow, and a dash is at once made. The president, who is elected by virtue of his performances as a runner, and his knowledge of the environment, strikes off in the lead. He goes at a swinging pace, with elbows close to his sides and arms well up. The street and branching roads are abandoned, the fields are entered, and the snowy crystals fly in a shower. In Indian file the members fall in, and soon a tortuous string stretches across the undulating hills. The leader may have covered a mile or more before the whipper-in takes his place. His duty is to remain in the rear and render assistance to the weak, weary, or disabled trampers. Like the leader, he is a veteran, and the polished framework of his shoes tells the story of long and arduous cross-country tramps. Drop him from the sky anywhere within a radius of fifty miles from home, and he will, after taking his bearings, unhesitatingly strike out in an air-line for the nearest road-house. He knows the country thoroughly, and was selected on that account. It must not be supposed that he relishes the office, and when appointed to act as whipper-in his soul is possessed with acerbity, and he grows jealous of the fleet-footed leaders. His commands are issued in incisive tones, and woe betide the youngster whose innocence or ignorance is prolific of delay. An amateur tumbles in a drift, breaks a shoe, loses his wind on the steep grades, or hangs behind from sheer stubbornness. Then the tact of the whipper-in is called into play, as his only pride is in bringing the club all in together at the finish.

Repairs may be made, and when the march is resumed the column is lost to sight. A hot pace is struck, and the last man is reached.

The line is pushed up closer, and order and regularity are restored. The office

THE MONTREAL CONVEYANCE.

of whipper-in is a responsible and onerous one. To wander from the line, or to be abandoned on the mountain on a cold night, would mean death to a tyro not conversant with the topographical features that would guide him to a hospitable shelter.

The captain's call passes down the line, and as the summit is reached the inquiry "All up?" is again handed down. "All up!" is repeated by the whipper-in, and like a *feu-de-joie*, a rattle of musketry, running the length of the column, the warning is affirmed. A momentary halt, under the low-hanging pines, with the whistling winds soughing mournfully overhead, and making an insidious search through the warmest clothing. Panting after the hard climb, and stiffened somewhat by tiresome scaling, which causes the perspiration to flow freely, it is dangerous to linger long in such an exposed locality when the thermometer probably registers 30° below the disappearing point. The group dissolves again, and the figures stream out into the night. A plunge headlong into Cimmerian darkness, down the hill they go, with head thrown back, shoulders firm, and eyes alert for obstacles in the shape of uneven surfaces and branches. Not the least, in the many causes for apprehension, is the man in front, who may stumble and take a header in the soft snow, from which extrication is a tedious task. Faster and faster, as the impetus of the decline is felt, the shoes rattle with incredible quickness, and the line becomes a tangle of flying feet shackled together like a centipede of strange growth. A fence, and with a warning exclamation, the leader leaps the half-buried obstruction and continues on his way. He seems never to weary or to care for his trained retinue, for he never glances back, but the musical patter behind him tells the whole story: A slow-up, for the laggards!

The line is re-formed, and now for the home-stretch! A wild burst of speed; every

through the serpentine drifts and avoiding the low, canopied bushes. As the cheerful lights of the club-house loom up, an aboriginal whoop is echoed over the hills, and, with a final dash, the door is reached and a haven of rest entered.

Shoes are kicked loose, outer garments discarded, sashes cast aside, and cool, refreshing drinks absorbed.

Look at them! Zero is discounted. These travelers are hot and thirsty, perspiration

BOUNCING THE REFRACTORY MEMBER.

man straining himself to the utmost; each muscle distended, and, with nerves rigidly set, they tear down a narrow lane, winding

rolls down their glittering faces and saturates even the gloves that cover the hands of the more effeminate members. Health

IN GOOD WIND.

and it is the baptism of the novice — the only penalty of initiation. Six stalwart fellows seize the victim, and with a peculiar movement he is rapidly thrown into a horizontal position, and, despite earnest struggles, is tossed to the ceiling. As he descends he is caught in outstretched arms and the operation thrice repeated, and at the conclusion the unfortunate selection is landed upright on the floor, inclined to feel more happy than reproachful.

In the dance the "lady" is distinguished by a handkerchief tied around his arm. This distinction

and firmness of flesh and muscle are shown in each ruddy countenance. With a bound they take the stairs leading to the assembly-room, three at a time, where fifteen minutes are quietly spent in club-chat before a comfortable warmth supersedes the torrid temperature of the body. A pianist is inducted, and, as he considers himself a victim, he refuses point-blank to manipulate the ivories. Resistance is worse than useless. Remonstrance being of no avail, corrective measures are adopted.

This mutinous spirit must be subdued; insubordination must be quelled. The unwilling musician is seized by his companions, and, despite his good-natured struggles, he is incontinently "bounced." The punishment is effective. He is no longer aggrieved. With an air of feigned resignation he seats himself, and presently waltz-music is energetically pounded forth, and the amateur athletes are again seen in graceful form, with flying feet, keeping time to the measures of the music.

A word for "bouncing." It is the most delectable of all the snow-shoers' delights,

is rendered very necessary in the cotillion, as the fair sex is sternly excluded on these occasions. The programme of music, etc., is conferred on a very masculine audience, which is not always chary of adverse and humorous criticism. When a man is nominated to sing, recite, or play, there can be no refusal. He simply must, and any churl who objects to the informality is quickly placed in "Coventry." The exclusiveness of these entertainments serves to stimulate the curiosity of lady friends, and, when the annual receptions to the favored public are given, the attendance is invariably large.

At eleven o'clock the order to return is given, and, with their racquets strung over their shoulders, the members step out in a body, ten deep, for the march home on the smooth road, which obviates the use of artificial supports. *En route*, voices are raised in song, and the residents of the hill-sides are made familiar with the grand chorus :

" Tramp, tramp, on snow-shoes tramping,
　All the day we marching go,
Till at night, by fires encamping,
　We find couches on the snow."

They reach home shortly after midnight, and a sound, refreshing sleep repays them for their journey of twelve miles.

The prescribed costume is made of white blankets, with fancy-colored borders, and consists of knee-breeches and coat, girdled with a silk sash of some pronounced color. A *tuque*, similar to an old-fashioned nightcap, but topped with a long knitted cord and tassel ; stockings of the same color, and soft moose moccasins completed the outfit. The undress uniform, worn in-doors, is a navy-blue jersey, with the club monogram embroidered on the breast, and was adopted to secure a uniform appearance after the outer coat had been cast off. Each club has a distinctive color for sash, stockings and *tuque*, and an old-timer can always call a man's club as soon as he glances at the shade of the knitted goods.

To an American the uniforms are picturesque, and objects of universal admiration among the ladies, who appreciate harmonious interminglings of color and such a departure from conventional clothes. The colors of some of the clubs may be given as follows : Montreal, blue and red ; Emerald, green and white St. George, purple and white ; Le Canadien, red, white and blue; Argyle, blue, and the Molly Bawn's, black and white. The last-named organization, although having less members than the other clubs, is an object of most profound interest, as the requirements of the constitution call for an equal number of ladies and gentlemen. The ladies look piquant—they are all pretty—in their blanket skirts, white moccasins, trimmed with colored porcupine quills, blanket sacques and the regular sash and *tuque*. The members

are brothers and sisters, and, when they take the road, the ladies are exchanged and the brothers assist some other fellow's sister. This disposition makes life more agreeable. They march in pairs, each gentleman supporting a lady, and no single member of either sex is tolerated. The rule is inflexible. This club had one steeple-chase across six miles of rough country, but, after the first experience, the experiment was abandoned. The prize-winners, it seemed, were in danger of losing, as they were second, with the first couple leading them some distance.

The lady was petite, and her cavalier tall and strong. A suggestion, a hurried consultation, and the next minute the gentleman was seen scudding through the darkness with his partner in his arms. He took a circuitous route to avoid detection in passing the leaders, and, when within one hundred yards of the goal, he deposited his partner on the ground, and linking arms, the two ran in together, winning the prize. The story leaked out through a confidence reposed by the lady in a friend of gentle nature. It was too good to keep, so the truth leaked out and the award was reconsidered. If their American cousins were one-half as fond of out-door pursuits, less would be heard of debility, weakness and nervous prostration. Lewiston, Me., has the honor of establishing the first snow-shoe club in the United States. It appears that several residents of that city attended the '83 winter carnival in Montreal, and after returning home endeavors were made to form a club, but action was deferred until last season, when an organization of fifty members was perfected, with Dr. Martel, of Lewiston, as president. The members are all naturalized Canadians, with a sprinkling of native Yankee blood; and the prospects of the infantile institution are fair for a hale old age. The climate and conditions of the country are analogous to Montreal surroundings, and at no distant day we may hear of international competition for suitable prizes.

27

The Story on the Factor's Book

VINGIE E. ROE

MARIE LE BAULT MET HIM SOMETIMES AT THE GREAT GATE AND WALKED OPENLY WITH HIM,
THROWING BACK HER SPARKLING LAUGH AT THE SMILES OF THE MEN
AND THE HINTS OF THE MATRONS

THE STORY ON THE FACTOR'S BOOK

BY VINGIE E. ROE

WITH A DRAWING BY GEORGE WRIGHT

THE books of the factor tell parts of many tales. Sometimes it is but the beginning, often it is snatches out of the middle, but seldom the ending, for that lies so frequently far in the gloom of the great woods where hangs eternal silence, or out among the pot-holes in the desolate stillness of the Ragged Lands. On a grimy, much-marred page of the great volume which never leaves the factor's desk at Fort Du Cerne (showing that the pages of many years have been filled since then) there lies the name " Polier Le Moyne," written in a bold hand, and opposite it an account with the Hudson Bay Company, an account bursting with bales of rich furs on the credit side and with a showing of riotous living on the other—but an account that was never closed.

There are many who could tell you of Polier Le Moyne, of his great height and mighty strength, of the breadth of his bulky shoulders, of his manly beauty of black eyes, rich blood-color, and gleaming teeth, of his wonderful skill at trapping and hunting, and of his absolute joy of living. Also many tales would be told of his love-affairs, for who among those that came from the far fastnesses into Fort Du Cerne stood so well with the bright-cheeked maids? But their stories would stop abruptly with his last going away into the un-tracked ways of the dim forest to the north. For the rest, there was only the open account on the factor's book.

All this was years ago, and no one ever knew that the end of the story, taken up from that last entry and carried down to a day in the still, spirit-haunted silence of the region beyond the Windage Flats, was locked forever in the uncon-scious breast of the old woman, Olee Bouyer—Olee Bouyer, vacant of eye and mind, withered of skin and with hair white as the snow that drifted against the old stockade in the long winters. And this was the ending of the untold chronicle, could Olee have remem-bered it.

There is nothing prettier at a certain period of her life than a French-Cana-dian girl, and the old trading-post, in the high days of the fur-trade, could boast as many beauties as the town of Henriette, farther back toward civiliza-tion. There was Marie Le Bault, who could show more gifts of the fine bead-work of the Crees, which her admirers brought her, than any other ; there was Aline Courrier, whose pretty face had caused more than one bloody fight ; and there was small, golden-haired Bertel Cardac, for whose sake the company had lost its best employee. When Father Tenau came up on certain times to hear confessions, he was burdened to the depths of his big heart with love-affairs from all save one, a tall and slender girl, silent, haughty, her head, with its shin-ing braids of purple-black, held with the conscious pride of beauty which knows itself to be unsurpassed. From a face which held men's hearts with a yearning, tense desire, there looked a pair of eyes somber, dark, unreadable as the dreary stretches of the wind-swept flats. As far beyond the beauty of all others as the flaming lilies above the small wood-trailer, she came and went with a pride of bearing which would have been inso-lence in any other. And this was Olee Bouyer, only daughter of old Pierre Bouyer, trapper.

Did a party of hunters or voyageurs

drift into Fort Du Cerne, what drew them into trouble and heart-break and sent them away with a sense of loss and sadness, every one? Not the liquor, which flowed freely in those days, but the scornful eyes under the bands of Olee's black hair. Not a man at the post who did not follow the tall figure and haughty, glorious face with a nameless yearning in his heart, a heavy pumping of blood in his veins. And no one, except his own soul, ever knew why Father Tenau did the deepest penance of his blameless life in the cold, stone cell at Henriette.

All men, did I say, fell under the spell of the girl's beauty? No, not all; there was one who sent his glances everywhere save on Olee Bouyer, who went his way as if she did not exist, too proud or stubborn to follow in the common current. And this fact was the sweet morsel under the tongue of every unmarried woman at the post. One man there was among the many that knew her who did not acknowledge the supremacy of the queen. This man was Polier Le Moyne. Nor was it unnatural that these two proud hearts should stand out against each other until both were broken in the conflict. For this girl, haughty of mien and soul, Polier was the one man who appealed to every atom of her intense nature, fired her with love, hatred, and jealousy, and, by his indifference, laid on her a whip of humiliation. But of such unyielding coldness and such unmoved disdain was her bearing that the living fire in her heart sent out no banner of betrayal to the eager eyes on watch.

For Marie Le Bault, Olee felt a hatred as fierce as the dying fury of the savage beast trapped in the dark reaches of the somber forest—Marie Le Bault, who met him sometimes at the great gate and walked openly with him, throwing back her sparkling laugh at the smiles of the men and the hints of the matrons. There was a gift of hard-bought candles with the stamp of the H. B. Co. in their sides on the altar of the little church, and Father Tenau, shrewdly guessing, burned them with an added prayer.

But there came at last a time when, in the dusk of a winter's evening, in a lonely forest-way beyond the palisade of Fort Du Cerne, the girl stood face to face with Polier Le Moyne—Le Moyne, the cold, the indifferent, the smiling. And it was only in accordance with the fate that held these two that the man, knowing the time had come, should reach out his great arms, and lift her, panting with sudden passion, to the height of his broad breast. This was a consummation—and a beginning. The surrender of both at once, and the flame that enwrapped them both from this time forth was indeed fire, as fierce, as wonderful, as appalling as the lights that shot across the black lakes on the windy nights when the trappers stayed in their cabins and the Cree runners crouched in their willow huts.

But no one knew that the water had found its level, for it was the whim of the girl that their love should be a secret, and this was a punishment for her lover's long pretense of indifference. She passed him in utter silence when they met under the eager eyes of the populace. Polier smiled as he watched her, his blood afire with the love that got no expression save in their lonely, infrequent meetings, when his eyes glowed above her head with the joy of the uncertain victor who is conquering a mighty force. She had promised to marry him in the fall, suddenly, without warning; and their secret love was to be her revenge upon Marie Le Bault and those who had smiled at her failure to win this man. In the meantime, a small cabin grew up secretly on the shore of the Black Lakes. It was two days distant, and its eerie solitude well fitted it for the part it was to play in the unfinished story on the factor's book. There was a riot of untempered joy in the strange, wild heart of Olee Bouyer, and the smoldering light in her eyes belied the cold smile on her lips.

II

IT was about this time that a painter came to Henriette, a stray genius, his courtly manners strangely out of place in that rough wilderness. He had come from France, bringing across seas his own unwritten tale, to bury, in the forests of the New World, one knew not what burning memories of high estate, of love, and, mayhap, of banishment. He had brought with him, too, his artist's skill. The very soul that looked out of a face looked out of it again beneath his magic brush. The rumor spread through Fort Du Cerne that this wonderful man was to come to the post for the sole purpose of painting the portrait of Marie Le Bault. But the strange part of it all was the fact that no one, not even Marie herself, so said the people, knew from whose traps were to come the furs for the fabulous price of the picture.

The painter came and began his work. A small man he was, and silent; the most adroit questioning elicited nothing. Speculation was rife. There was no living with Marie in those days, and the artist faithfully portrayed on the bit of ivory the self-complacence of her soul. If there was mystery, there was no lack of conclusions, and Olee heard a whisper that struck her dumb with a great, sickening horror of suspicion, a horror so vast, so overwhelming that she walked like one dazed through the days that followed. She never knew, nor would have cared had she known, that the watchful eyes of the painter gazed intently upon her, wherever she appeared, studying each curve, and hue, and outline, as if he would stamp her wondrous face indelibly in his memory. But at last the face of Marie was finished—an ivory miniature in a quaint gold frame—and hung in the factor's room, " awaiting further orders," as the man said who had made it ; and every one came to see its dainty beauty, until one day, after the painter had returned to Henriette, it disappeared, and the factor only smiled.

But what about the man whose name was on the lips of every one in connection with the picture? He had gone up the long trail for the first far trip of the early fall, leaving in Fort Du Cerne a woman behind whose haughty face the fires of hell were beginning to glow redly. The adder of suspicion stung her ever more and more sharply, and, in the days when she brooded with heavy eyes of agony, she looked into the future and beheld her tragedy. He had told her that he would go to Henriette and up to the cabin on the Black Lakes before he returned ; and what did that mean save the taking of furs to the painter and the hanging of the picture in the quaint gold frame on the walls of the house that he

had built for her? She paced wildly back and forth with clenched hands, and the look in her somber eyes was cruel and fierce as a tiger's. The climax to her suffering came, sharp, decisive, electric— the young Pierre Vernaise, posing in the general store, remarked :

" I met in Henriette M'sieu Le Moyne. He was there on some mysterious business concerning the silent painter."

Three days after Pierre had made his smiling speech, the sun rising over the eastern edge of the forest looked down on a strange sight. Before the cabin on the shore of the Black Lakes, his strong hands bound behind him and a bright silk scarf across his lips, lay Polier Le Moyne. A little way from him a girl, in whose still face there was no sign of life except the horrible light in the glinting eyes, knelt and drove into the ground with ringing strokes a strong stake. A gun leaned against her knee as she worked. She drove four stakes, their heads pointing outward. In silence she rolled the man between them and began attaching a rawhide thong to his moccasined feet above the ankle. In a flash he understood and made a mighty spring with the length of his whole body, but the girl was upon him like a panther, and he stumbled down with the chill of steel against his throat.

" Perhaps M'sieu Le Moyne, the traitor, would prefer the knife? " she said. With watching eyes and ready blade, she tied him hand and foot, then rose and looked down at him.

" So it was to have been Marie Le Bault who lived in the new cabin—Marie whose face in the gold frame cost M'sieu Le Moyne so many furs. A quaint conceit, *m'sieu,* and how the bride would have laughed at it on the walls of the house built—for me. But the bride will wait, and the factor will wait for the return of the trapper from the Windage Flats, and Father Tenau will wait for the gift of the ceremony."

The man's eyes begged wildly for speech, but with a bow and a cold smile Olee turned toward the forest. A dozen steps away she looked back.

" Pardon, *m'sieu,* but I will console Marie."

And so she left him, staked out beneath the hazy sky, in the silence of the great woods and the barren reaches of the Ragged Lands beyond.

III

FATHER TENAU had come up from Henriette for the confession. The trappers and half-breeds were gathering in for the remission of sins, before the long journeys into the wilderness, and there was much gaiety in Fort Du Cerne. Olee had been back two days, silent, triumphant, inscrutable, and none knew where she had been.

But the end of the story was nearer than she knew, and it came with the usual suddenness of such things. She had passed the laughing Marie before the house of the factor, and her fingers curled to the hilt of a knife in the folds of her skirt; but the long revenge was best, after all, when she should see the color fade from the bright cheeks and the light from the eyes with the shame of waiting for the lover who never came. It would be——

" My daughter," said the good father, and his gentle face was before her. She bowed her regal head for his blessing and dropped her burning eyes. Thoughts of her revenge ran through her mind, drowning out his soft voice. She waited, not knowing that he had blessed her, lost in her unholy dream. Suddenly, *mon dieu,* what was he saying? Through a maze of incomprehension came the words: " It is vanity, the painting of your face, my daughter, for the beauty must be of the soul; but there is nothing like a headstrong lover. And it is a good likeness, made, too, from the painter's memory of you, and Polier——"

The father stopped breathless with the impact of her body. She had sprung upon him, and clutched him with fingers that drew blood.

" I? I? " she gasped. " My face? "

At his answer, out upon the crisp air rang a cry that reached every corner of the post, a scream of anguish, the voice of a strong soul in hell. She stood one moment as stone, and a forecast of the vacant look of the old Olee came into the young eyes for whose sake so many men would have given their hearts' blood. One moment, and then she was away, running like a hound, low to

earth, guarding strength for the long trail. Father Tenau watched her go and wondered. But she was ever a strange, lawless being, eerie and not to be understood. The father sighed and went among his people.

With long, crouching strides Olee leaped like a panther through the dim woods, under the low-hanging branches. It was the impossible, men might say, that she accomplished that day. To the cabin on the Black Lakes and the thing she had left there it was a two days' journey, and she made it a matter of hours. At noon she might have been seen, had there been any to see, skirting the Windage Flats, and two hours later she was far among the pot-holes, running still with long, low leaps.

The sun was dropping toward the rim of the forest, sending over all the North Land great flaming bands of fire, turning to deepest red the waters of the still lakes, when she stood, wide-eyed and silent, at the edge of the small clearing. Her eyes, burning and flashing, traveled round the circle to the space before the door. Some lingering hope of the strength of the splendid arms of Polier Le Moyne, or of the unsoundness of the thongs, had sustained her and lent her speed in her race over the wild trail. With a savage snap of her beautiful teeth she sprang forward. A heaving cloud of vultures rose, spreading like the smoke when the Devil's Hole burns in the Red Hills. Down on her knees between the stakes, her body swaying drunkenly, she thrust her hands among the tattered rags. Over the side where his proud heart had beaten, she found it and brought it up—a bit of ivory in a quaint gold frame. She held it a moment in her hands, then turned it upward toward the fading light. Her own fair face, haughty, cold, insolent in its marvelous beauty, looked up at her with its dark, somber, inscrutable eyes.

A band of the Blackfeet came into Fort Du Cerne in the early spring, and brought a woman, tall, beautiful, silent, with a face like a queen of heaven, but with great eyes that saw not and long braids of snowy hair. But months before that the factor had married Marie Le Bault.

28

Sas-katch-e-wan

EMERSON HOUGH

SAS-KATCH-E-WAN

THE MISSOURI OF THE NORTH

BY EMERSON HOUGH

PERHAPS you may have heard of the celebrated divine who could move a congregation to tears simply by repeating the word "Mesopotamia." It was in the sound. Some words have individuality of their own. You cannot twist "Mesopotamia" to mean anything but a sleepy, sun-kissed land. You could not, for instance, endow those soft vowel sounds with the rugged quality of another unmistakable word—Saskatchewan!

Sas-katch-e-wan! Spoken as though it came always from the full ridged chest of a tall red-man, thin in the flank, hard in the leg—spoken as though with the exhalation of lungs full of rugged northern air. What word in the glossary of rivers surpasses this in the virility of its sheer sound? It reeks of kinnikinnick and dried white fish and smoked breasts of wild geese, and service berry and pemmican. You cannot avoid seeing dog sledges or help hearing the honk of wild fowl, or refrain from noting the blown breath of men running in the cold, when you hear the mere name, wild, mysterious, of this river, one of the trails of the young men.

A few rivers you and I may have seen, perhaps, yet not so many as we shall see. The Mississippi, two thousand miles of it, from the sea to the falls of that reverend liar Father Hennepin; three hundred miles north of that to the trickles among the wild rice fields; the yellow sea of its lower flood, where it breaks into wide swells beyond the many channels of the sea marshes of the Gulf—we have seen all that. We have seen perhaps four thousand miles of the Missouri, seen its source and its midwaters, and its eventual outlet in the Gulf; a strange stream and one full of romance. The Ohio, the Arkansas, the Red, the Platte—great American streams full of

history, full of destiny—all these we may have seen, beginning and end, front and back and all between. But these, our own ways, our old ways, are old indeed to-day, and the history which they write to-day is that of commerce and not of adventure. To-day they are paths of old men.

Let us have rivers for young men, men thin in the flank and hard of leg. All America to-day wheezes with fat. Lo! we cry, we of this America, behold our most amazing fat, our bulk, our immensity! —thinking of no better thing to boast than bigness. Yet this Saskatchewan, with the wilderness still in its legs, youth still in its eye, could tell us that bulk is not strength, but its opposite, that it spells coming weakness. Wherefore, let us who do not care for rose leaves, or turbots' tongues, or for the stealing of other people's millions, get us to Saskatchewan.

For there is still upon this continent another Missouri. It rises in the snow and ends in the ice, and in its crooked arms it holds an empire. Few men now know the Saskatchewan throughout all its length. Two hundred and thirty-six years ago it was that the Hudson's Bay Company began to know it, studying it in the speech of the wild tribes who came down with cargoes of furs. These red-men, the Salteurs, the Assiniboines, the Crees, the Piegans, the Slaves, told the white men of a vast, meandering waterway, leading deliberately out toward the west, running backward and forward, east and west, north and south, with the open and obvious purpose of showing all corners of a new empire to men in search of empire. That was the Missouri of the North, and from the first it has been competitor of our Missouri.

Once came a race between these rivers. When Lewis and Clark were crossing our

273

continent by way of the Missouri, the men of hard-legged Simon Fraser were racing up the Saskatchewan trying to beat us to the coast and take away from us that West, now so much richer than Thomas Jefferson dreamed. The Scotchman started a little late. In the winter, when our men were at the mouth of the Columbia, Fraser was more than a thousand miles northeast of them, snowbound far up in the mountains. He had gone up the Saskatchewan beyond Edmonton, and thence swung straight west toward the Peace River Pass—the same pass toward which four railroads are reaching to-day. It was next spring before he could cross this pass and seek for the west-bound waters.

Old Simon would have done far better could he have gone down the Wood River, or the Canoe River, and so struck the point of the Big Bend of the Columbia, where Steinhof and Barnes and myself last spring saw the mountain gorges opening out toward the heads of the Peace and Saskatchewan. But Simon went across by the Tête Jaune Cache and got upon a bold water which he thought was the Columbia, but which was not, being the stream later called after him, the Fraser. Rivers thereabout were not named in his day. The Indians warned him not to try to run the Fraser, but old Simon paid no heed to that, being bound to find the mouth of what he thought was the Columbia. And so he built Fort St. James and Fort Fraser and Fort George—the latter still there if you want to make a trip for giant moose—and deliberately fastened his grip upon that country. But it was spring of 1808 when he learned that he had long ago lost his race with the young Virginians, and lost the empire of the northwest coast. Lewis and Clark were by that time back home, and America was growing wild over her newly discovered empire on both sides of the Rockies. So now Fraser went back east again, ascended his wild rivers to the wild mountains, crossed the mountain pass which has lain for a hundred years unused, tramped east over the muskegs to the north arm of the Saskatchewan, and so followed it down to Lake Winnipeg. Then he came down that lake to the Portage of the Prairies, and so got down through the Rainy Lake waters to Lake Superior, and thence back to Fort William on the Great

Lakes, where he had first got word of the intention of these same young Virginians. That hard, historic journey of Simon Fraser over the country which Saskatchewan traverses, was one of the hero journeys of the world. It almost deserved to win. Verily I believe that since then the ghosts of Clark and Fraser have shaken hands in their graves and have said that neither was beaten, and that river equaled river, and that both were meant to be the pathways of the young men.

The story of Simon Fraser is but one of the many stories of Saskatchewan. Through many years it remained mysteriously unknown, highway only of the furs. Bull boats and flat boats, York boats and Northwest canoes laden with furs alone coming down, supplies going up, parted this flood, yellow far to the east in its fifteen hundred miles of length, blue toward the west, and green where it emerges from the ice. We did not yet concern ourselves with fields of wheat below this river, or with exhaustless forests for the maws of coming pulp mills north of it. Saskatchewan was still unexploited. The nets came up full of fish in all the lakes along it. Its plains were tenanted by the buffalo and antelope. The plover circled about the uplands; the painted wild fowl streamed across; and the wind blew always fresh and keen enough to wash away a strong man's sins. On the Saskatchewan a man did as he pleased. There were little churches with crosses at the mouths of the great rivers where the furs came down, and one might there confess and be absolved. So for a hundred years Saskatchewan lay at our doors, the very sign and symbol of a wilderness. No doubt its real discovery was due to the finding of gold far down on the Yukon. The movement toward Alaska by one or another way was the beginning of the end of all the mysteries of the far North. Of course the Hudson's Bay Company knew all about it, but the Hudson's Bay Company, finger on lip, was gum-shoeing around with a big secret on its soul for more than two centuries. "Whisper!" said the Hudson's Bay Company, and so all was done in whispers.

Speaking of its physical aspects, what does the average man to-day know about this historic river? Can you without studying a map tell offhand where it rises, or where it finds its mouth? How long is it? How big is it, this Missouri of the North? It is well enough to know some of these things of a river now so swiftly coming into notice. For twenty years you have been able to ride by rail to its source. For two years you have been able to take trains to a part of its lower waters. But even yet these lower waters are little known to most folk. A friend of mine, a man of average intelligence and education, told me the other day that of course the Saskatchewan River emptied into Lake Superior through the Rainy Lake region. Questioned closely, he was of the belief that its sources were somewhere in the musk-ox country of the arctics! The truth about the Saskatchewan is that it is a Missouri tilted up and running eastward instead of south. It is the backbone of the most wonderful waterway of all the world.

Strangely related, too, with our own backbone river, is this Missouri of the North—the Swift-flowing Water, as the red-man's name for it means. The Saskatchewan drains the whole of the upper Rockies, from the Athabascan waters to the Missouri, hence its head waters lead down to ours. The old voyageurs trafficked freely between the two. The two forks of the Saskatchewan resemble the upper sources of our river, the Yellowstone and the main Missouri. The south fork of the Saskatchewan is made by the Red Deer and the Bow, and again the Bow receives the Little Bow and the Belly Rivers from the southward, and so we come in direct touch with the St. Mary's waters on this side of the line, with the Swift Current, with the Milk River, which is ours for most of its course.

The Blackfeet knew no national line, and traded from the Yellowstone to the north arm of the Saskatchewan. I have often heard my friend, Joe Kipp, of the Blackfeet nation, tell of a starving march he once made in the winter from the Saskatchewan to the Milk River; how nearly they came to perishing; how they ate owls and eagles, and how at last they rejoiced when they found a half dead, starving bull out on the prairies. I have listened to old John Monroe, of the Piegans, tell how he killed grizzlies far out to the east on the plains of the Saskatchewan, with no better arms than the old Hudson's Bay fuque and

heavy knife—once with the bow and arrows, when he was on horseback and the bear pursuing him.

From John Monroe I heard of his father, Hugh Monroe, old Rising Wolf of the Blackfeet, a Hudson's Bay man from his youth. Hugh Monroe was the son of a British Army officer and of a daughter of the distinguished La Roche family of Montreal, émigrés, bankers, large landowners, aristocrats. When only fifteen years of age, Hugh Monroe harkened to the call of Saskatchewan, and followed the fur brigades far toward its source. It was he who was perhaps the first white man to cross from the Saskatchewan to the Missouri. He joined a great band of Blackfeet, who followed up the lower sources of the former river and went south along the eastern edge of the Rockies, sometimes close to the foothills, sometimes fifty miles out on the prairies, flat as a floor, and covered then with buffalo. Presently they came to the Sun River and the Musselshell, and the Judith, and the Marias, and the Missouri.

That party of Blackfeet numbered eight hundred lodges, or about eight thousand persons, a splendid savage cavalcade, in a splendid savage day, and one that has had few parallels. They were bound south to sample the trade of the white men then coming up the Missouri, and Hugh Monroe went along, though then but a boy, to learn their language, to dissuade them from the American trade, and to bring them back to the Saskatchewan with their furs in the coming season. It was again rivalry of river against river—Saskatchewan against Missouri; the Northwest Company against the American Fur Company; Canada against the United States. That was in 1813, and soon everybody of any consequence knew all about both of these great swift-flowing rivers which took hold upon the fur-bearing hills.

It was, by the way, this same Hugh Monroe who, in the opinion of a few men studious in early western history, was the first white man to set eyes on the Great Salt Lake of Utah. He left no written history, but once at least left his name on the country. At the head of the beautiful Two Medicine Valley of Montana, not far from the pass of the Great Northern railroad, there is a noble mountain called Rising Wolf Mountain—the mountain called Mah-quee-a-pah, or "Wolf-Gets-Up," after this early adventurer. When I talked with his son, John Monroe—who speaks five languages all at once—it was in his smoke-fragrant teepee, in sight of this noble mountain, and I digress now for sake of a little matter of justice which ought to be set right so far as possible. In one of its illustrated folders some years ago the Great Northern railroad printed a photograph of this noble mountain, with the subtitle of "Hough's Mountain." This is an inaccuracy that is little less than a sin. The members of the Blackfeet tribe who were with me on a winter hunt in that country some years previous had given names, now geographically accepted, for most of the peaks in that part of the Rockies, and because I killed a sheep on one mountain there they named it after me; but this is across the cañon from the mountain called Mah-quee-a-pah, or Rising Wolf. He would be a very poor sort of man who would wish to change nomenclature so old and just as that.

Old Hugh Monroe, who died some years since, after a life which could not now be duplicated on this globe, passed his later years in what is now Montana. His son John, old and gray and feeble when I last saw him, had wandered all over the country between these two great rivers. His last wife was a Cree woman, born north of the Saskatchewan. That river had led his father, his wife and himself down to our own mountains. There is no romance so keen as that of these great early water trails.

The southern arm of the Saskatchewan runs pretty much all over the pair of Canadian provinces and past several cities. It passes Calgary and Banff, and shows the railway the road up the mountains to a point opposite the wild Kicking Horse stairway on the west slope of the Rockies. You can see all this, a series of wonderful mountain pictures, by rail to-day on the Canadian Pacific railway. The northern arm remains more remote. The two streams diverge into a wide loop, and both so ramify and wander that literally there is Saskatchewan within touch almost anywhere you go west of Winnipeg Lake. And when you touch Saskatchewan you are within reach of all North America.

Knowledge of the wonderful extent and efficacy of the old waterways of the North has now almost passed out of mind, but there is no study more curious and interesting.

The false mouth of the Saskatchewan is in the northwestern corner of Lake Winnipeg, but the true mouth, in Hudson's Bay, is at about the fifty-seventh parallel of latitude. After passing through Lake Winnipeg it is called for a part of its length "Katchewan." Then, picking up more northern streams, it is called the Nelson River, which of course it is not, no matter what the geographies say. It is Saskatchewan, the Swift-flowing Water, the link between the Rockies and Hudson's Bay.

One of the many lakes strung on the lower thread of Saskatchewan is Sturgeon Lake, where was located the old Cumberland House, from which men departed both to the Missinnippian and Athabascan streams—the center of a tremendous geography. By means of a chain of lakes and connecting streams the voyageur got west to the Athabascan system, or east to Hudson's Bay. As Dr. Coues remarks: "We have brought our traveler from the Red River of the North by water up to Cumberland House; we could bring him down to this place from the Rocky Mountains. In fine, we are here in the focus of a vast network of waters whose strands radiate in every direction. A canoe could start from this house, and with no portage of more than a day's length, could be launched on the Arctic Ocean, Hudson's Bay, Gulf of St. Lawrence or Gulf of Mexico, and without much greater interruption, could be floated on the Pacific Ocean!"

We in America followed down the Ohio, up the Mississippi and the Missouri, the Platte, the Arkansas and the Red. Thus the men of Canada followed the rivers of the North, and most of all, the Saskatchewan. In those splendid unknown years, what adventurous keels plowed those upper floods! How many feet, red and white and brown, made the little tracking paths along these shores!

Many early men passed up the Missouri of the North at one time or another—Mackenzie, later knighted for his daring, who started west from Fort Chippewayan and reached the Pacific June 22, 1793, the

The fur brigade tracking up the Athabasca River.

first man to cross the American continent, and the first to trace an arctic river down; Fraser and Thompson, and both the Henrys, Alexander the uncle and Alexander the nephew; McDonald, Hearne, Harmon, Tanner—scores of those who wrote or who did not write, save as they helped to blazon over all the North the cabalistic letters H. B., or X. Y., or N. W., for one or other of the great companies which combed that country for its furs.

Mackenzie is not more useful to us than Fraser, and he not so good as the astronomer, map-maker, and naturalist, David Thompson; nor the latter so useful in some ways as the younger Alexander Henry, the coarsest, most literal and most matter-of-factly informing of all the "Northers." Henry is not very interesting, having no imagination and small conscience, but he kept a precise and literal diary day by day, which few of these others did; so he is useful as giving us both a general and a specific knowledge of the country along the Saskatchewan.

On Monday, August 8, 1808, Henry left the mouth of the Pembina River—he had been trading in all northern Minnesota, and knew the country west as far as the Missouri—and took boat to the foot of Lake Winnipeg, where he joined a brigade of canoes that had come from Fort William on Lake Superior via the old Rainy Lake water trail. A rough voyage brought them on August 20th to the mouth of the Saskatchewan. The Northwest men were the hustlers of the fur trade. They despised York boats, the heavy craft of the H. B. Company, and prided themselves on their own swifter canoes.

West of Lake Winnipeg our voyageurs note many wild pigeons, many wild fowl, many moose, elk and antelope, or "cabbrie," as Henry calls them. On August 29th they see tracks of the grizzly bear, as well as those of black bears. The grizzly once ranged almost as far to the east as the buffalo. Without doubt or question Henry knew bears, and he saw the grizzly often in Minnesota. By September 5th they were far to the west. "Now," says Henry, "we may be said to enter the Plains." Sandbars and willow patches appear; there are buffalo crossings, and now they see buffalo swimming the river.

A month out from the Red River they are near Battle River, in a splendid buffalo range, and in good grizzly country also. There are many "red deer," by which Henry means elk, and this is a fine beaver country. A to the Indians whom they have been meeting, they were to the east Salteurs and Assiniboines. Now they meet Crees and Sarcees, and many "Slaves," by which they mean the Blackfeet, Piegans, Bloods, etc., the latter not always very friendly. Their brigade reaches Fort Vermillion on September 14th, having been absent since May 10th, journeying to Fort William on Lake Superior, and back again. Henry wintered at Fort Vermillion, and in June of the next year was himself back at Fort William. It must have been a splendidly regular schedule after all, that of this tremendous, matter-of-fact voyaging, for in the next fall Henry arrived at Vermillion again on September 13th, precisely his date on the preceding year! The journey from Fort William to Vermillion required about two months.

But we are interested in Saskatchewan as part of the transcontinental trail, wherefore we may use this same man as well as any other in following it to the Rockies. He left Edmonton on September 29th, and on October 3d was within sight of the Rockies. Two days later he reached the already ancient trading post, the Rocky Mountain House, near the mouth of the Clearwater. Leaving here February 3d by dog sled it took him just a week to arrive at the lower end of that singular and beautiful mountain valley known as the Kootenai Plains, where the Saskatchewan rests gently for a time before sallying forth on its long journey east to Hudson's Bay. A great mountain wall came down close to one side of the valley; there were mountains ahead and all around, but our traveler set about crossing the Rockies in the dead of winter as though it were a matter of course, which indeed it was to those old timers. He passed up the Kootenai Plains to the place where the river forks, head of navigation for even the lightest canoe. Beyond that it meant snowshoes, and the voyageur followed the lower arm of the dwindled river and began to climb.

He gives us no very great story of his ascent of the mountains, but the pass does not seem to be very difficult. On February 9th, as he calmly remarks, he sees what he presumes to be "the highest source of the Saskatchewan"—there hidden beneath the snow. A half mile from its apparent end in a rock wall he leaves it and enters a pine-covered forest; and so, with very little ado about it, he makes the summit. "We went on about two hours through the thick woods," he says, "and at nine o'clock came to a small opening, where three small streams of the Columbian waters joined." So there he was at the crest of the Rockies. And I would rather have been Alexander Henry then than John D. Rockefeller now.

Henry reached the summit February 9th. We may therefore now figure the entire Saskatchewan schedule somewhat thus: Red River (from near Winnipeg) to Fort Vermillion, thirty-five days; to Edmonton, three days; to Rocky Mountain House, six days; to the summit, nine days —or say about fifty-three days in all, a trifle less than two months of travel by sail, paddle, pole, cordelle, horse, dog and snowshoe. It took hardy men to do that, but the journal figures it thus. The average must be over twenty miles per day at a low estimate.

On this trip our voyageur did not go down into the valley of the Columbia, although some of his Indians went on over the perfectly well-known trail which David Thompson had often used, that from Howse Pass down the Blaeberry Creek, which empties into the Columbia near Moberly on the C. P. R. to-day. This point is farther up the Columbia than Beavermouth, where my own bear-hunting party struck the Big Bend of the Columbia last May. For a time I tried to figure out the old localities by means of David Thompson's early maps. These maps show a river coming down from the Howse Pass into the Columbia River at a big lake or widening of the stream. There is no such lake on the Big Bend excepting Timbasket Lake, and there is no river that enters Timbasket Lake except the Middle River, which heads off somewhere toward the Howse Pass. When I first saw our secret valley up the Middle River, I thought we might be on the old Thompson trail, but there is no historical warrant for thinking that any of these old travelers crossed any summit and came down our valley. I do not know

where the Middle River heads, and cannot learn about it from any man or any map or any writing. Some day I am going to find out, and some time, perhaps, find the "highest source" of the Saskatchewan from that side of the Divide. The Howse Pass lies fair for the head of the Blaeberry, but that does not enter the Columbia anywhere near Timbasket Lake. Neither does the Wood River nor the Canoe River, which enter at the head of the Big Bend. It was above this point that the old voyageurs crossed west after coming through the old Peace River Pass, toward which four railroads are now crowding. So I suppose that our valley is about as virgin as most valleys in the Rockies to-day. It lies between the two main paths which lead from the heads of the Saskatchewan and the Peace, down to the Pacific Ocean, by way of the Columbia and the Fraser. It must run up to a glacier-topped range at its head, which not even Simon or David or Alexander of old found it necessary to tackle.

Those early men did not travel for sport or adventure so much as they did for business. Their story is always of fur. All Europe had its eyes on the furs of western America. La Valliére, Parabére, Pompadour—imperial mistresses for three generations, looked to Saskatchewan for their sables and their ermines and their otter robes. The nobles of Louis XIV. trafficked with the merchants of Canada for furs. The courtiers of the regent, the new-made nobility of John Law, looked to Canada for their winter finery. The young macaroni of old London wore a hat of beaver that grew on Saskatchewan. The Swift-flowing Water ran toward Europe, toward Paris, toward London, then as it does to-day.

The conquest of all this new land of furs was at first Gallic. The thin edge of the wedge of civilization west of Superior was French. Volatile, unstable, migratory, the Frenchman of that day was by all odds the best advance guard in the wilderness. Picards and Normans erected the early settlements of old France all along the Great Lakes—the fortress to repel invasion; the chapel to shrive one of one's sins; the little fields to keep the women busy. All around these swept the vast forests, full of fur, full of the sins of the flesh. The local commandant, smug, far from France, owner of a dozen wives, reared in peace his swarms of dusky offspring—"Bois Brulès" they were called, in tribute to their complexion—wielders of paddles later in their lives, perhaps, alongside the sons of some godly Father who had found no sin in learning a savage language in the most practical fashion, since the Pope was far away in Rome.

Back from all these little settlements—gay, insouciant centers of a gay, insouciant age, when perhaps they got more out of life than we do in our own anxious times—ranged always these new men, the Coureurs des Bois, runners of the forest, half-breeds or renegade French, able as Indians with paddle, or rifle, or trap, more able to endure large privations and hardships, more patient, more mercurial and merry than any savage, stronger to bear heavy burdens, less moody, more tenacious—more useful than any other breed for the subduing of the wilderness. These Coureurs des Bois were part white and part savage in their look and garb. They wore the breech cloth and the tunic, though the latter might be of cloth. Their caps were knitted of red worsted, their blanket coats were of many colors. Their moccasins were of hide, their leggings of buck, fringed *au sauvage*. In heavy weather they wore a hooded surtout of blue cloth—the capôte or "capoo" as it was called, with a belt of scarlet wool, carrying a heavy knife, the latter comprising axe, hammer, skinning knife, table knife, jack-knife and weapon all in one.

From these men, the gayest, most generous, most wasteful and most licentious gentry any part of this continent ever knew, came the later engagès or *mangeurs du lard* —"pork eaters"—of the later fur trade. It was these coureurs of Greysolon d'Lhut and his partner Grosseilliers who extended the fur trade west of Superior and founded Fort de la Reine, near where Winnipeg arose later. It was they who established New Albany and Post Nelson on Hudson's Bay, and in 1686 they had taken away from England all her fur posts in the North excepting that of Nelson.

It was the French who first learned of Saskatchewan; and it was the French who won in the West, until the English conquered in the East, and in 1763 by the Treaty of Paris exacted the cession of all that immense realm which had been won by La Salle and by the French fur traders beyond Superior.

Meantime the Hudson's Bay Company had its own serene way until 1766, when private traders pushed west beyond the Great Lakes. In 1783 these banded together as the Northwest Company, soon to prove more enterprising, more daring and more able than the old Hudson's Bay Company, and it is with these that the practical history of Saskatchewan begins. For now the Saskatchewan becomes a known and beaten trail, and one full of picturesque incident, whose total would make the most romantic history ever written in the world. The Northwest Company wore no gum shoes. Its boots were full of hobnails, and it cared not who heard where it trod.

The men of the Northwest Company used great canoes in their trade, birch bark craft thirty feet in length, four feet wide, two feet and a half deep, capable of carrying down stream or on the lakes at least three thousand pounds in cargo, or say sixty-five "pieces" of ninety pounds each. Similar boats carried all the trade goods up the rivers (thirty "pieces" or less, sometimes, to the load on Saskatchewan), as well as the supplies of the outlying posts—cloths, beads, prints, mirrors, weapons, powder and lead, and above all, whiskey. Only it was not whiskey, but high wine or alcohol, diluted after arrival on the spot where needed. As the years went on the dilution became less. The Salteurs, far to the east and accustomed to strong drink, rebelled at too much water. The more innocent Blackfeet, far to the northwest, would accept more dilution, and trade for this thin fire-water their furs, their horses, their robes, their women. The record of the fur trade of the Northwest Company is one of a continual debauch, and the voyageurs, the half-breeds and the natives were sometimes joined by their *bourgeois* in the universal *boisson*, or drinking match, which preceded and ended every trade.

But with the Hudson's Bay Company and the Northwest Company were many abler and more sober-minded men, leaders, resident traders, factors, and finally perhaps partners, such men as Donald Mac-Tavish, drowned with Alexander Henry in the Columbia finally. These strong characters were content to spend their lives in the wilderness, to take native women for their wives, to subsist on the hard fare of the country—meat, fresh or salted, pemmican, white fish, smoked meat of wild fowl. Gardens were rare on the Saskatchewan; a hen was a priceless thing; fruit was unknown, save as the service berries or thorn apples could be called fruit. Yet men of brains and commanding qualities lived thus and led in a brutal merchandising which was for years little better than thievery. They took a boat load of furs for a few kegs of diluted high wines—one hundred and twenty beaver, one record says, for two blankets, two gallons of watered whiskey, and one pocket mirror. Joe Kipp told me that in his time whiskey on the Saskatchewan brought sixty-five dollars for a little keg, and quicksilver—for the mysterious Saskatchewan is full of fine gold along its bars—cost ten to twenty dollars per pound.

Yet these resident traders, the kings of the Saskatchewan, were the aristocrats of their land and day. They curiously show the power of the wilderness over civilized man. I have remarked on the birth and breeding of old Hugh Monroe, one of the most remarkable, though one of the least-known discoverers of a century now passed. He was a gentleman bred, but the woods called him when he was still a boy, and he never came back. He took with him the old La Roche dueling pistols, which had defended the family honor many a time in France. Perhaps they defended life in some forgotten fight on the plains of Saskatchewan, but they never returned to Montreal. Others of the better bred men who went West came back from time to time, engaging in revelries at the settlements of the East, spending their money like water in prodigality and licentiousness, to make amends for their years of solitude and privations.

Such, then, were the leaders of the trading posts and the fur brigades who conquered the Saskatchewan; such, too, the voyageurs, the common canoemen, squat, short, brawny, sinewy, strong as wild asses and of small intellectuality. One can see them now, these hardy travelers, passing westward and northward in their great canoes, high in bow and stern, at each extremity a brown-faced, grizzled man for steersman. There are four paddlers or polesmen on each side when the current stiffens. When the wind comes fair astern a blanket sail is rigged. When a portage must be made, out go these voyageurs, waist deep, holding their thin-skinned craft off the rocks that it may not be injured. Laughing and singing, each slings on his back his "piece" of ninety pounds, more usually two of these pieces, and so off over the rocks, or knee-deep through the mud. At paddle or portage, the "pipe," or interval of rest, as long as it takes to smoke a pipe, is religion of the labor union of that day. The distance between pipes or pauses on a long portage was usually about a third of a mile.

Thus, paddling, poling, sailing, carrying, the voyageurs learned every bend and riffle of the Saskatchewan, and all its shores as well; for when, far out on the plains, the current became too strong and steady, each of the paddlers slung his pack strap across his shoulder, and fastened himself like a draft beast to the sixty-foot towing line. For more than a thousand miles along Saskatchewan they towed, slipping, stumbling, wet, weary, beset with all manner of pests, yet laughing and merry, going at a trot to the very head of the water where it comes out of the snow, across a continent of vast adventuring.

Once a voyageur, always one. A wife in every tribe, a little finery out of one's wages for each, a "debt" like an Indian, if one wished to trap for a season, a little trinket now and then for the purchase of the smiles of some new girl here or there—Susanne Duchesne of Mo'reaw' or Ah-ta-kà-pi of the Sarcees at Fort Augustus—it was a merry life, that of the voyageur. Sickness and rheumatism came at last, and finally the end. But when one was old was time enough for repentance, and meantime at every post along the water trail there were little chapels and priests to whom one might confess.

Such was a wild commerce which enriched many families—a commerce which presently was to purchase a large portion of Manhattan Island; for it was Astor who bought out the old Northwest Company south of the Canadian line, and began to turn brown furs into brown stone, and to found an aristocracy as proud, perhaps, as that once the aim and mark of all the belles of Mo'reaw' and old Quebec!

These men, who mapped the Mackenzie

and the Peace and the Athabasca, the Finlay and the Liard and all the arms of old Saskatchewan, saw all of a bold, brave life of which you and I to-day read covetously, wishing we had been young when they were young, when the world was but beginning, when Saskatchewan was a household phrase at every hearthstone of the East and every tepee fire in all the West. They waged not war, but commerce, They did not exterminate, but mingled their blood with the savage tribes. And after later days had come along the Saskatchewan, the larger and more just souls of these leaders, seeing that civilization had caught up with them, and brought a new code of morals, did what they could to set right what civilization now called wrong. They gave millions of acres of land scrip to the half-breed children of the old fur trade, descendants of the men who made the trails. And later white men came, shrewd trading Yankees or others, and got this half-breed scrip for a song, and robbed of their birthright the descendants of the men who really won Saskatchewan.

Yes, if you seek romance, or love adventure, scratch in the sands along Saskatchewan. Its story still is there. Saskatchewan to-day speaks of the wild rose, typical flower of the frontier—the same flower your mother gathered when she came to Iowa or Kansas, before you, my friend, went East to live in a Flatiron on Manhattan, and be ironed out to smoothness and nothingness. Saskatchewan shall speak to you to-day of vast, white mountains—oh, so beautiful are those mountains! It shall show you still its wild, wide plains—ah, so wonderful are these plains! It can show you still the passing harrow of the wild fowl high on the sky, and offer you the brilliant note of the curlew, and the splash of the beaver at its work, and the track of the great moose in the bog. If the smell of tepee smoke be now less, it will give you sod house fire and drying nets, and dog harness, and snowshoes, and ox gads and —ah, well, coal smoke now, and the reek of towns!

Not long ago a friend of mine rounded up a horse band in North Dakota, crossed the line and broke north to see what he could see. He turned up at Red Deer and then started westward to discover a continent for himself. He followed the north arm of the Saskatchewan, and at last traced it up and through the eastern front of the Rocky range. Here, to his surprise, he discovered a vast, wide, level valley, fenced all about by snow-capped mountains. Ah, it was the Kootenai Plains, as new to him as it was to Thompson and Henry a hundred years ago! He saw trees thick as his leg growing in the old trail at the Rocky Mountain House. The wanderer built him a little rail fence from the edge of the mountain to the edge of the river at the lower end of this valley, and so had a horse ranch made to order; and there he is to-day, in Paradise.

The white man has indeed come to the Saskatchewan. In 1906 these buffalo plains raised thirty million bushels of wheat, and each year now adds a half million or a whole million of acres under plow. Soon there will be ten million acres of wheat standing in the bull wallows along the Saskatchewan. Soon there will be two hundred million bushels of wheat to sell annually. Soon this Missouri of the North will be sending to Great Britain twenty times as much wheat as she can use to-day. Wheat has come to take the place of fur.

The old words of our treaties with the redman ran: "So long as the waters shall run or the grass shall grow." There is no more solemn phrase to be found in the measuring of time. We come to that same phrase in the measuring of the future. Where does the water come from—have you not asked your mother that?—have you not made inquiry of your father asking where it goes? As for this icy drop of Saskatchewan, it passes through a country still belonging to the young men. The story of a young world lies along its shores. And while we may be young—why not? If we may still run and exult, then why not? And even if we be old, will not the winds of Saskatchewan, as of yore, wash out a strong man's sins? Why should not our young men dream dreams?

For myself, who could never quite learn to love the boulevards, I most love to dream the dreams of the ghosts of Clark and Fraser, shaking hands on the shores of the Saskatchewan, and admitting that, river against river, one Missouri against the other, neither adventurer had the better of the other, but that both joined in winning a mighty victory for the world.

29

Snowshoeing in Canuckia

JAMES C. ALLAN

SNOWSHOEING IN CANUCKIA.

BY JAMES C. ALLAN.

THE CLUB HOUSE.

 NOWSHOEING is surely one of the most fascinating of sports. To the uninitiated it might appear strange that there should be any pleasure in ambling along over the snow in a manner somewhat resembling the ungraceful waddle of that unornamental bird, the domestic duck, and with feet hampered by the weight and the inconvenient form of a pair of ungainly snowshoes, so-called.

To a certain extent our captious critic would be right; the source of enjoyment is to be found in the accessories of the sport, and in the knowledge that under him are many feet of yielding snow, in which he would be helplessly floundering but for the aid of his trusty *raquettes*.

Then there is the peculiar indefinable charm of the winter scenery, the beautiful effects of the sunset on the dazzling expanse of snow, scenic effects perhaps even more entrancing when the pale moonlight casts ghostly shadows here and there, and brings into brilliant prominence some snow-crowned elevation in the landscape. I cannot do better than quote the glowing description which a noted American writer gives of the appearance of the country over which he tramped on one of his first excursions on "the merry snowshoe":

"The mountain rose up behind us, covered with snow. Away toward the declining sun the landscape spread as far as the eye could reach, with low white hills away off on the horizon. Between the hills and the foreground flowed the river under its cover of ice. The red, wintry sun now low in the heavens, touched the prominent points of the rolling, snow-covered country with crimson, while the far-off clouds that stood motionless in the sky were of all the hues of the rainbow, and these varied tints were in turn faintly reflected on the broad expanse of spotless snow."

The snow, let it be borne in mind, is not of the nature or consistency of that which falls in softer climes ; it is so fine, so dry and loose as much to resemble flour, only infinitely whiter, and of dazzling purity.

As many of my readers very probably have never seen a snowshoe, a short description of its form and construction may not be amiss. It consists, broadly speaking, of a framework composed of a long, narrow piece of hickory wood, over which is stretched a network of thongs, or cords, made sometimes of strips of deerskin dried and prepared in a peculiar manner, and sometimes made of the intestines of animals. This network is called the "gut." The hickory rod of which the frame is to be made, after having been steamed and steeped in boiling water, and so rendered pliable, is placed edgewise and then bent round somewhat in the shape of a tennis-bat, with an oval-shaped front, and the two ends joined together at one extremity and tapering off to a point corresponding to the handle of the tennis-bat. The total length of the shoe is about three feet, the extreme width from thirteen to sixteen inches. Across the oval and fitted into the inside of the framework by mortises, are two bars or battens of wood, each of them five or six inches clear of either end. In front of

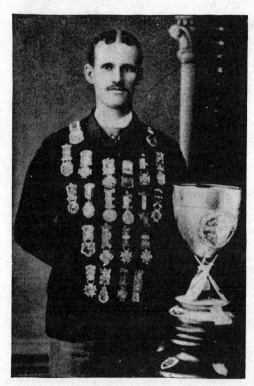

MR. J. G. ROSS, CHAMPION SNOWSHOE RUNNER, CANADA.

that cross-bar nearest the fore part of the shoe is an open space, and over the bar a deerskin thong is fastened, forming an aperture for the reception of the great toe. The thong is then crossed over the top of the foot, passed around the ankle once or twice and then tied. This leaves the heel free to move in any direction ; the toe works in and out of the opening in the shoe, and in lifting the shoe in making a step forward its weight rests on the toe. When placing the foot down again the toe touches the snow first. Occasionally the framework is adorned with tufts of many-colored wool.

The size and shape of the snowshoe varies according to the requirements or the taste of its owner. Some are nearly round and present a squat appearance ; others again are long and narrow, and resemble somewhat in shape the Norwegian *ski.*

For a tramp over untrodden or "virgin" snow, of course a large shoe of considerable area is desirable ; for racing purposes over a beaten track, a smaller shoe is used. The regulation width of a pair of racing shoes is not less than ten inches of gut ; the weight, including strings, must not be less than one and a half pounds.

The Indians and the half-breeds seem to enjoy a monopoly of the manufacture of snowshoes, and of toboggans as well.

The snowshoe enabled them, in former days, to traverse with ease, when in pursuit of game or on the warpath, leagues of wilderness otherwise impassable in the winter season ; the toboggan they used as a sledge on which to drag their provisions or to convey to camp their slaughtered game.

It is true that there is in use in Norway an implement somewhat similar to the American snowshoe, called a "*ski,*" and composed of a couple of long, narrow slabs of wood, one for each foot, painted and turned upward at both ends. The ski, however, is principally used for sliding down declivities and jumping crevasses ; it is ungainly and awkward to use on level ground. The aid of a staff, or alpenstock, is necessary in skieing, and a description of it hardly comes within our province.

"Raquettes" was the name originally given by the hardy Canadian *coureurs du bois* and the *voyageurs* of the Hudson Bay Company to the snowshoe, and we can easily imagine of what inestimable value it must have been to these adventurous individuals in their trips of almost incredible length, difficulty and peril. To the present day hardly a farmhouse in all broad Canada is without its pair of snowshoes, and they are generally of the sturdy, old-fashioned kind, long and broad and substantial.

In hunting the moose and the caribou, in the wilder parts of the Dominion, the snow-

all over Canada, and in those parts of the neighboring Republic favored with the slightest suspicion of the "beautiful," and of all these the premier, in point of seniority, is the Montreal Club, founded in 1840, and composed originally of twelve members.

HOMEWARD BOUND.

shoe plays an important part. The crust on top of the snow is insufficient to sustain the weight of these heavy animals; they break through it at every stride, its sharp edges lacerate their legs, and the hunter can follow their course guided by the blood-marks on the snow. Sustained by his trusty shoes, he soon overtakes the laboring game, and a well-directed shot puts it out of misery.

But it is in its aspect as a sport, as a means of healthful recreation, that we have principally to consider snowshoeing. Of late years many clubs have been formed

As Canada is the home of snowshoeing, so is Montreal, *par excellence*, the leading city of Canada in this branch of athletics, both on account of the severity and the long duration of its winters, the natural advantages possessed by the city as regards its situation, and the widespread devotion among its young men to sports in general.

And of all the hardy winter sports snowshoeing is easily the first. Tobogganing and skating rise in public estimation and decline, but snowshoeing, like Tennyson's "Brook," "goes on forever," and is continually gaining ground, as any one who

Old Time Rendezvous.

J. W. Fosdick

dalia, Royal Scots, etc., while other Canadian cities are not far behind.

Toronto, Ottawa, Quebec, St. Hyacinthe, Winnipeg, Brandor, Souris and Portage la Prairie have all sent their representatives to the Montreal Ice Carnivals, and now St. Paul and Minneapolis, those twin cities of the American Northwest, have caught the fever and are enthusiastic in their emulation of their Canadian brethren.

A snowshoe club is organized in much the same manner as other athletic associations. It has its president, vice-president, secretary, treasurer, and last, but by no means least, its entertainment committee, whose pleasing duty it is to provide amusement for their fellow-members at the club rendezvous when half the tramp is over and the "boys" are resting previous to their return home.

The costume of the snowshoer is at once comfortable, singularly well adapted

has been so fortunate as to witness one of those unique winter carnivals in Montreal, and to gaze upon the hosts of picturesquely clad athletic young "knights of the shoe" in their attack upon the marvelously beautiful ice castle may well believe.

In place of the one solitary club of twelve members in existence in 1840, Montreal may now boast of dozens. The old Tuque Bleue Club, *alias* the Montreal, has now a membership of 2,000. The St. George has, perhaps, half that number; other principal organizations are the Emerald, Argyle, Le Trappeur, Le Canadien, St. Charles, Maple Leaf, Wolseley, Vanto its purpose, and picturesque in the extreme. The head is protected by a gaudy knitted woolen cap, with brilliant tassel, and is called a *tuque*, in the Norman French of the Canadian habitant, who used it first of all. Then there is a coat with capote, and knickerbockers made usually of white blankets with many-hued border. Of late years, however, colored blankets have come into favor and bid fair to rival the white in popularity. Around the waist the coat is drawn together by a sash ; colored stockings and deerskin moccasins, and, of course, snowshoes, complete the costume. Each club is distinguished by some peculiarity in the uniform of its

rest, invest in buckskin hunting shirts and fringed leggings. They are made by Indians and half-breeds in Manitoba and the Northwest, and are, of course, more expensive than the blanket suits.

In Montreal it is usual for each club to tramp out on one evening in each week, and to take a more extended tour across country on Saturday afternoons.

On the evening appointed for the tramp the boys meet at their club-rooms ; shoes are strapped on, the president leads the way, the members follow in Indian file, and the whipper-in brings up the rear to give the novice or the lazy a lift, and off they go. Let us suppose we are taking the

Rendezvous of To-day

J. W. Fosdick

members ; for example, the Montreal club affects a blue *tuque*, red sash and red stockings ; the Knights of St. George, or the "Saints," as they somewhat arrogantly style themselves, a purple *tuque* with white stripes, purple sash, and stockings of Tyrian hue also. So with the other clubs.

An entire outfit, including complete costume and snowshoes, may be procured for less than twenty-five dollars, and the suit under ordinary circumstances will outlast several winters. Some of the boys who have plenty of cash, or better opportunities of obtaining the articles than the

route usual for evening tramps, partially around and up over a spur of Mount Royal, thence across country for about a mile and a half to our rendezvous. The pace increases, and, excepting an occasional nip at one's ears, Jack Frost is forgotten as we warm to our work. "Number off," cries the president. "No. 1, No. 2," and so on, until the whipper-in responds, "No. 60; all up."

What a pretty picture the long line of ghost-like shadows makes, as it silently winds in and out in the light of the moon! Now they disappear from view for a moment or so as they plunge through brushwood; they race down gullies, clamber over fences and mount hills, until at last the goal of their desire is reached at mine host Lumpkin's, or at the Athletic Club-house, where, after enjoying the programme provided by the committee, and perhaps refreshing the inner man, we take up our homeward march, and, our starting-point attained, separate for another week, or until the following Saturday afternoon.

It is a popular though erroneous idea among the uninitiated that snowshoeing in the night is done by torchlight. Torches are never used. This notion probably owes its birth to the fact that at the various carnivals snowshoers have used torches, purely, however, for effect, and rather against their will.

A new member of the club or a distinguished visitor is generally welcomed by his future comrades or his hosts by "bouncing" him. The victim is seized by as many as can lay hold of him and is unceremoniously flung skyward, or, more correctly, ceiling-ward, and on his descent from on high he is caught again and the ceremony repeated two or three times. He is not allowed to fall, however. He suffers only in his wind and perhaps his nerves.

In snowshoeing the fatigue and consequent stiffness are great at first, but with practice this soon wears off, and the motions become easy and rapid. Of course, it is hardly possible to travel on snowshoes as rapidly as afoot on dry ground, yet, nevertheless, the speed obtained is not inconsiderable, as the records of snowshoe racing will show. For the various distances these are as follows:

	Min.	Sec.			Min.	Sec.
100 yards,		12		1 mile,	5	42½
220 "		26		2 "	11	52¾
440 "	1	08		3 "	20	18½
½ mile,	2	33		5 "	33	43

Mount Royal Steeplechase, distance about 2 miles, 500 yards, 17m. 20s.

The last record, as well as others, is held by Mr. James G. Ross, perhaps the fastest all-round amateur who ever buckled on the "raquette."

It is not an uncommon thing, however, for clubs to traverse thirty, and even eighty, miles across country in a tramp. A tramp from Montreal to St. John's is a regular annual event with the Tuque Bleues.

I will conclude by quoting the words of a well-known litterateur, who had been induced by the genial president of a certain club to come out for a tramp with his club:

"Thus briefly was I brought to know that our winter sports are a means of health and good spirits to all who take part in them. They quicken the circulation, clear the brain and lighten the heart. No such good is got out of the formal drill of a gymnasium as there is out of a snowshoe tramp or a toboggan slide, under the broad sky with pleasant companionship. Men with kinky spines, sluggish livers and narrow chests—get blanket suits, moccasins and snowshoes, and use them soon and often. They will dispel your pains and aches and gloomy views of life."

30

The Truce

CHARLES G.D. ROBERTS

THE TRUCE

BY

CHARLES G. D. ROBERTS

AUTHOR OF "THE ALIEN OF THE WILD"

ILLUSTRATED BY ARTHUR HEMING

OO early, while yet the snow was thick and the food scarce, the big black bear had roused himself from his long winter sleep and forsaken his snug den under the roots of the pine tree. The thawing spring world he found an empty place—no rabbits to be captured, no roots to be dug from wet meadows ; and his appetite was sorely vexing him. He would have crept back into his hole for another nap ; but the air was too stimulatingly warm, too full of promise of life, to suffer him to resume the old, comfortable drowsiness. Moreover, having gone to bed thin the previous December, he had waked up hungry ; and hunger is a restless bedfellow. In three days he had had but one meal—a big trout clawed out

half dead from a rocky eddy below the falls ; and now, as he sniffed the soft, wet air with fiercely eager nostrils, he forgot his customary tolerance of mood and was ready to do battle with anything that walked in the wilderness.

It was a little past noon, and the shadows of the tree-tops fell blue on the rapidly shrinking snow. The air was full of faint, trickling noises and thin tinklings where the snow veiled the slopes of little rocky hollows. Under the snow and under the rotting patches of ice, innumerable small streams were everywhere hurrying to swell the still ice-fettered flood of the river, the Big Fork, whose roomy valley lay about a half a mile eastward through the woods. Every now and then, when a soft gust drew up from the

" roused himself from his long winter sleep "

south, it bore with it a heavy roar, a noise as of muffled and tremendous tramping—the voice of the Big Fork Falls thundering out from under their decaying lid of ice. The falls were the only thing which the black bear really feared. Often as he had visited them, to catch wounded fish in the black eddies at their foot, he never could look at their terrific plunge without a certain awed dilation of his eyes, a certain shrinking at his heart. Perhaps by reason of some association of his cubhood, some imminent peril and narrow escape at the age when his senses were most impressionable, in all his five years of life the falls had never become a commonplace to him. And even now, while questing noiselessly and restlessly for food, he rarely failed to pay the tribute of an instinctive, unconscious turn of head whenever that portentous voice came up upon the wind.

Prowling hither and thither among the great, ragged trunks, peering and sniffing and listening, the bear suddenly caught the sound of small claws on wood. The sound came, apparently, from within the trunk of a huge maple, close at hand. Leaning his head to one side he listened intently, his ears cocked, eager as a child listening to a watch. There was, indeed, something half childish in the attitude of the huge figure, strangely belying the ferocity in his heart. Yes, the sound came, unmistakably, from within the trunk. He nosed the bark warily. There was no opening ; and the bark was firm. He stole to the other side of the tree, his head craftily outstretched and reaching around far before him.

The situation was clear to him at once— and his hungry muzzle jammed itself into the entrance to a chipmunk's hole. The maple tree was dead, and partly decayed all up one side of the trunk. His craft forgotten on the instant, the bear sniffed and snorted and drew loud, fierce breaths, as if he thought to suck the little furry tenant forth by inhalation. The live, warm smell that came from the hole was deliciously tantalizing to his appetite. The hole, however, was barely big enough to admit the tip of his black snout, so he presently gave over his foolish sniffings and set himself to tear an entrance with his resistless claws. The bark and dead wood flew in showers under his efforts, and it was evident that the chipmunk's little home would speedily lie open to the foe. But the chipmunk, meanwhile, from the crotch of a limb overhead, was looking down in silent indignation. Little Stripe-sides had been wise enough to provide his dwelling with a sort of skylight exit.

Suddenly, in the midst of his task the bear stopped and lifted his muzzle to the wind. What was that new taint upon the air? It was one almost unknown to him, but one which he instinctively dreaded, though without any reason based directly upon experience of his own. At almost any other time, indeed, he would have taken the first whiff of that ominous man-smell as a signal to efface himself and make off noiselessly down the wind. But just now his first feeling was wrath at the thought of being hindered from his prospective meal. He would let no one, not even a man, rob him of that chipmunk. Then, as his wrath swelled rapidly, he decided to hunt the man himself. Perhaps, as the bear relishes practically everything edible under the sun except human flesh, he had no motive but a savage impulse to punish the intruder for such an untimely intrusion. However that may be, a red light came into his eyes and he swung away to meet this unknown trespasser upon his trails.

On that same day, after a breakfast before dawn in order that he might make an early start, a gaunt trapper had set out from the settlement on the return journey to his camp beyond the Big Fork. He had been in to the settlement with a pack of furs, and was now hurrying back as fast as he could because of the sudden thaw. He was afraid the ice might go out of the river and leave him cut off from his camp—for his canoe was on the other side. As the pelts were beginning to get poor, he had left his rifle at home and carried no weapon but his knife. He had grown so accustomed to counting all the furry wild folk as his prey that he never thought of them as possible adversaries—unless it might chance to be some such exception as a bull moose in rutting season. A rifle, therefore, when he was not after skins, seemed to him a useless burden; and he was carrying, moreover, a pack of camp supplies on his broad back. He was tall, lean, leather-faced and long-jawed, with calm, light blue eyes under heavy brows; and he wore a stout, yellow-brown home-spun shirt, squirrel-skin cap, long leggins of deerhide, and oiled cowhide moccasins. He walked rapidly with a slouching stride that was almost a lope, his toes pointing straight ahead like an Indian's.

When, suddenly, the bear lurched out into his trail and confronted him, the woodsman was in no way disturbed. The bear paused, swaying in surly fashion about ten paces in front of him, completely blocking the trail. But the woodsman kept right on. The only attention he paid to the big black stranger was to shout at him authoritatively—"Git out the way, thar!"

"to catch wounded fish in the black eddies"

To his unbounded astonishment, however, the beast, instead of getting out of the way, ran at him with a snarling growl. The woodsman's calm blue eyes flamed with anger; but the life of the woods teaches one to think quickly, or, rather, to act in advance of one's thoughts. He knew that with no weapon but his knife he was no match for such a foe, so, leaping aside as lightly as a panther, he darted around a tree, regained the trail beyond his assailant, and ran on at his best speed toward the river. He made sure that the bear had acted upon a mere spasm of ill-temper and would not take the trouble to follow far.

When, once in a long time, a hunter or trapper gets the worst of it in his contest with the wild kindreds, in the majority of cases it is because he had fancied he knew all about bears. The bear is strong in individuality and delights to set at naught the traditions of his kind. So it happens that every now and then a woodsman pays with his life for failing to recognize that the bear won't always play by rule.

To the trapper's disgusted amazement this particular bear followed him so vindictively that, before he realized the full extent of his peril, he was almost overtaken. He saw that he must deliver up his precious pack, the burden of which was effectively handicapping him in the race for life. When the bear was almost upon him he flung the bundle away, with angry violence, expecting that it would at once divert the pursuer's attention.

In about ninety-nine cases out of a hundred, perhaps, it would have done so, for it contained, among other things, bacon and sugar, dainties altogether delectable to a bear's palate. But as luck would have it, the bundle so bitterly hurled struck the beast full on the snout, making him grunt with pain and fresh fury. From that moment he was a veritable demon of vengeance. Well enough he knew it was not the bundle, but the man who had thrown it, upon whom he must wipe out the affront. His hunger was all forgotten in red rage.

Fortunate it was now for the tall woodsman that he had lived abstemiously and labored sanely all that winter, and could depend upon both wind and limb. Fortunate, too, that on the open trail, cut years before by the lumbermen of the Big Fork drive, the snow was already almost gone, so that it did not seriously impede his running. He ran almost like a caribou, with enough in reserve to be able to glance back over his shoulder from time to time. But seeing how implacable was the black hulk that pursued, he could not help thinking what would happen, there in the great, wet, shadow-mottled solitudes, if he should chance to trip upon a root, or if his wind should fail him ere he could reach the camp. At this thought, not fear but a certain disgust and impotent resentment swelled his heart; and with a challenging look at the ancient trunks, the familiar forest aisles, the high branch-fretted blue, bright with spring sunshine, he defied the wilderness, which he had so long loved and ruled, to turn upon him with such an unspeakable betrayal.

The wilderness loves a master; and the challenge was not accepted. No root tripped his feet, nor did his wind fail him; and so he came out, with the bear raging some ten paces behind his heels, upon the banks of the Big Fork. Once across that quarter mile of sloppy, rotting ice, he knew there was good clear running to his cabin and his gun. His heart rose, his resentment left him, and he grinned as he gave one more glance over his shoulder.

As he raced down the bank, the trampling of the falls, a mile away, roared up to him on a gust of wind. In spite of himself he could not but notice how treacherous the ice was looking. In spite of himself, he noticed it, having no choice but to trust it. The whole surface looked sick, with patches of sodden white and sickly lead-color; and down along the shore it was covered by a lane of shallow, yellowish water. It appeared placid and innocent enough; but the woodsman's practised eye perceived that it might break up, "go out," at any moment. The bear was at his heels, however, and that particular moment was not the one for indecision. The woodsman dashed knee deep through the margin water, and out upon the free ice; and he heard the bear, reckless of all admonitory signs, splash after him about three seconds later.

On the wide, sun-flooded expanse of ice, with the dark woods beyond and the soft blue sky above, the threat of imminent death seemed to the woodsman curiously out of place. Yet there death was, panting savagely at his heels, ready for the first misstep. And there too, a mile below, was death in another form, roaring heavily from the swollen falls. And, hidden under a face of peace, he knew that death lurked all about his feet, liable to rise in mad fury at any instant with the breaking of the ice. As he thought of all this besetting menace, the woodsman's nerves drew themselves to steel. He set his teeth grimly ; a light of elation came into his eyes, and he felt himself able to win the contest against whatever odds.

As this sense of new vigor and defiance spurred him to a fresh burst of speed, the woodsman took notice that he was just about half way across the ice. "Good," he muttered, counting the game now more than half won. Then, even as he spoke, a strange, terrifying sound ran all about him. Was it in the air or beneath the ice ? It came from everywhere at once—a straining grumble, ominous as the first growl of an earthquake. The woodsman understood that dreadful voice very well. He wavered for a second, then sprang forward desperately. And the bear pursuing understood also. His rage vanished in a breath. He stumbled, whimpered, cast one frightened glance at the too distant shore behind him, then followed the woodsman's flight—followed now, with no more heed to pursue.

For less than half a minute that straining grumble continued. Then it grew louder, mingled with sharp, ripping crashes ; and long black lanes opened suddenly in every direction. Right before the woodsman's flying feet one opened. He took it with a bound. But even as he sprang the ice went all to pieces. What he sprang to was no longer a solid surface, but a tossing fragment which promptly went down beneath the impact of his descent. Not for nothing, was it, however, that the woodsman had learned to "run the logs" in many a tangled boom and racing "drive." His foot barely touched the treacherous floe ere he leaped again, and yet again ; till he had gained, by a path which none but a river man could ever have dreamed of traversing, an ice-cake broad and firm enough to give him foothold. Beyond this refuge was a space of surging water, foam and ice-mush, too broad for the essay of any human leap.

The Big Fork from shore to shore was now a tossing, swishing, racing, whirling and grinding chaos of ice-cakes, churning in an angry flood and hurrying blindly to the falls. In the center of his own floe the woodsman sat down, the better to preserve his balance. He bit off a chew from his plug of "blackjack," and with calm eyes surveyed the doom toward which he was rushing. A mile is a very short distance when it lies above the inevitable. The woodsman saw clearly that there was nothing to be done but chew his " blackjack " and wait on fate. That point settled, he turned his head to see what the bear was doing.

To his surprise, the animal was now a good fifty yards further up stream, having evidently been delayed by some vagary of the struggling ice. He was now sitting up on his haunches on a floe, and staring silently at the volleying cloud which marked the falls. The woodsman was aware of a curious fellow-feeling for the great beast which, not five minutes ago, had been raging for his life. To the woodsman, with his long knowledge and understanding of the wild kindreds, that rage and that pursuit now appeared as lying more or less in the course of events, a part of the normal savagery of nature, and no matter of personal vindictiveness. Now that he and his enemy were involved in a common and appalling doom, the enmity was forgotten. "Got cl'ar grit, too !" he murmured to himself, as he took note of the quiet way the bear was eyeing the falls.

And now it seemed to him that the trampling roar grew louder every second, drowning into dumbness the crashing and grinding of the ice ; and the volleying mist-clouds seemed to race up stream to meet him. Then, with a sickening jump and turn of his heart, a hope came and shook him out of his stoicism. He saw that his ice-cake was sailing straight for a little rocky islet just above the falls. Two minutes more would decide his fate—at least for the time. He did not trouble to think what he would do on the island, if he got there. He rose cautiously and crouched, every sinew tense, to renew the battle for life.

Another minute fled away and the island was close ahead, wrapped in the roar and the mist-volleys. A cross current, seizing the racing ice-cake, dragged it aside—and the man clenched his fists in a fury of disappointment as he saw that he would miss the refuge after all. He made ready to plunge in and at least die battling, when fate took yet another whim, and a whirling mass of logs and ice, colliding with the floe, forced it back to its original course. Another moment and it grounded violently, breaking into four pieces which rolled off on either side toward the abyss. And the woodsman, splashing into turbulent shallows, made good his hold upon a rock and dragged himself ashore.

"'Git out the way, thar'"

Fairly landed, he shook himself, spat coolly into the flood, and turned to see what was happening to his fellow in distress. To the roaring vortex just below him—so close that it seemed as if it might at any moment drag down the little island and engulf it—he paid no heed whatever, but turned his back contemptuously upon the tumult and the mists. His late enemy, alive, strong, splendid, and speeding to a hideous destruction, was of the keener interest to his wilderness spirit.

The bear was now about twenty paces above the island ; but, caught by an inexorable current, he was nearly that distance beyond it. With a distinct regret, a pang of sympathy, the man saw that there was no chance of his adversary's escape. But the bear, like himself, seeing a refuge so near, was not of the temper to give up without a struggle. Suddenly, like a gigantic spring uncoiling, he launched himself forth with a violence that completely upended his ice-cake and carried him over a space of churned torrent to the edge of another floe. Gripping upon this with his mighty forearms till he pulled it half under, he succeeded in clawing out upon it. Scrambling across, he launched himself again desperately, sank almost out of sight, rose, and began swimming with all the energy of courage and despair combined.

But already he was opposite the head of the island. Could he make it ? The man's own muscles strained and heaved in unconscious sympathy with that struggle. The bear was a gallant swimmer and for a moment it looked as if there might be the ghost of a chance for him. But no ; the torrent had too deadly a grip upon his long-furred bulk. He would *just* miss that last safe ledge !

In his eagerness, and without any conscious thought of what he was doing, the man stepped down into the water knee-deep, bracing himself, and clinging with his left hand to a tough, projecting root. Closer came the bear, beating down the splintered refuse that obstructed him, his long black body laboring dauntlessly. Closer he came —but not quite close enough to get his strong paws on the rock. A foot more would have done it—but that paltry foot he was unable to make good.

The man could not stand it. It was quite too fine a beast to be dragged over the falls before his eyes, if he could help it. Reaching out swiftly with his right hand, he caught the swimmer by the long fur of his neck and heaved with all his strength.

For a moment he wondered if he could hold on. The great current drew and sucked almost irresistibly. But his grip was of steel, his muscles sound and tense. For a moment or two the situation hung in doubt. Then the swimmer, stroking desperately, began to gain. A moment more and that narrow, deadly foot of space was covered. The animal got first one paw upon the rock, then the other. With prompt discretion the woodsman dropped his hold and stepped back to the top of the island, suddenly grown doubtful of his own wisdom.

Drawing himself just clear of the torrent, the bear crouched, panting, for several minutes, exhausted from the tremendous struggle ; and the man, on the top of the rock, waited with his hand upon his knife hilt to see what would come of his reckless act. In reality, however, he did not look for trouble, knowing intuitively as he did the natures of the wild kindreds. He was merely holding himself on guard against the unexpected. But he soon saw that his caution was unnecessary. Recovering breath, the bear clambered around the very edge of the rocks to the further side of the island, as far as possible from his rescuer. There he seated himself on his haunches and devoted himself to gazing down, as if fascinated, at the caldron from which he had been snatched.

During the next half hour the woodsman began to think. For the present he knew that the bear was quite inoffensive, being both grateful and overawed. But there was no food on the island for either, except the other. So the fight was bound to be renewed at last. And after that, whoever might be the victor, what remained for him ? From that island, on the lip of the falls and walled about with wild rapids, there could be no escape. The situation was not satisfactory from any point of view. But that it was clear against his principles to knuckle down, under any conditions, to beast or man or fate, the woodsman might have permitted himself to wish that, after all, his ice-cake had missed the island. As it was, however, he took another bite from his plug of " blackjack " and set himself to whittling a stick.

With a backwoodsman's skill in the art

"In the common and appalling doom, the enmity was forgotten"

of whittling, he had made good progress toward the shaping of a toy hand-sled, when, looking up from his task, he saw something that mightily changed the face of affairs. He threw away the half-shaped toy, thrust the knife back into his belt, and rose to his feet. After a long, sagacious survey of the flood, he drew his knife again and proceeded to cut himself a stout staff, a sort of alpenstock. He saw that an ice-jam was forming just above the falls.

The falls of the Big Fork lie at a sharp elbow of the river, and cross the channel on a slant. Immediately above them the river shoals sharply, and though at ordinary seasons there is only one island visible, at times of low water huge rocks appear all along the brink. It chanced, at this particular time, that after the first run of the ice had passed, there came a second run that was mixed with logs. This ice, moreover, was less rotten than that which had formed near the falls, and it came down in larger cakes. When some of these big cakes, cemented with logs, grounded on the head of the island, the nucleus of a jam was promptly formed. At the same time some logs, deeply frozen into another floe, caught and hung on one of the unseen mid-stream ledges. An accumulation gathered in the crook of the elbow, over on the further shore; and then, as if by magic, the

rush stopped, the flood ran almost clear from the lip of the falls, and the river was closed from bank to bank.

The woodsman sat quietly watching, as if it were a mere idle spectacle, instead of the very bridge of life, that was shaping before his eyes. Little by little the structure welded itself, the masses of drift surging against the barrier, piling up and diving under, till it was compacted and knit to the very bottom—and the roar of the falls dwindled with the diminishing of the stream. This was the moment for which the man was waiting. Now, if ever, the jam was solid, and might hold so until he gained the further shore. But beyond this moment every second of delay only served to gather the forces that were straining to break the obstruction. He knew that in a very few minutes the rising weight of the flood must either sweep all before it or flow roaring over the top of the jam in a new cataract that would sweep the island bare. He sprang to his feet, grasped his stick, and scanned the tumbled, precarious surface, choosing his path. Then he turned and looked at the bear, wondering if that animal's woodcraft were subtler than his own to distinguish when the jam was secure. He found that the bear was eyeing him anxiously and not looking at the ice at all; so he chuckled, told himself that if he didn't know more than a bear he'd no business in

" Closer he came—but not quite close enough to get his strong paws on the rock "

the woods, and stepped resolutely forth upon the treacherous pack. Before he had gone ten paces the bear jumped up with a whimper and followed hastily, plainly conceding that the man knew more than he.

In the strange sudden quiet, the shrunken falls clamoring thinly and the broken ice swishing against the upper side of the jam, the man picked his way across the slippery, chaotic surface, expecting every moment that it would crumble with a roar from under his feet. About ten or a dozen yards behind him came the bear, stepping hurriedly, and trembling as he looked down at the diminished cataract. The miracle of the vanishing falls daunted his spirit most effectively, and he seemed to think that the whole mysterious phenomenon was of the man's creating. When the two reached shore the flood was already boiling far up the bank. Without so much as a thank you the bear scurried past his rescuer and made off through the timber like a scared cat. The man looked after him with a slow smile, then turned and scanned the perilous path he had just traversed. As he did so the jam seemed to melt away in mid-channel. Then a terrific, rending roar tortured the air. The mass of logs and ice, and all the incalculable weight of imprisoned waters, hurled themselves together over the brink with a stupefying crash, and throbbing volumes of spray leaped skyward. The woodsman's lean face never changed a muscle, but presently, giving a hitch to his breeches under the belt, he muttered thoughtfully :

"Blame good thing we came away when we did !"

Then, turning on his larriganed heels, he strode on up the trail till the great woods closed about him and the raving thunders gradually died into quiet.

31

The Last Stampede for Cheap Homes

EMERSON HOUGH

THE OUTING MAGAZINE

JANUARY, 1907

THE LAST STAMPEDE FOR CHEAP HOMES

I—THE GREAT TREK

BY EMERSON HOUGH

THE greatest story of the day is the story of the Canadian Northwest. Tales of new lands are always interesting; but this is the chronicle of the last great trek, the trek into the last of the new lands, at least of the North American continent. It is the greatest people movement the world ever saw; greater than the migration of the Aryans, the Cimri, the Goths. Silently, irresistibly, with an unparalleled rapidity, the people are moving forward and occupying new lands, even as they did the forests of Europe long ago, the forests of the Appalachians since then. This army of wayfarers bears no banners; few are its trumps and drums. Attila the Hun led his savage clans over an old empire and laid waste its cities, boasting that no blade of grass might grow behind his horse's feet. This army of peace has for its purpose the simple one of making two blades of grass grow where but one grew before. It is well-nigh the last army of home-seekers the world will ever see march into unconquered lands. Hereafter we must ravage and lay waste if we would occupy, must extirpate a people to make room for us, wipe clean a country in the Orient or elsewhere, and set on the law of might as between man and man. But this great trek to the Northwest is no battle march, other than the ever-joyous marching of man to do battle with the wilderness, with the out-of-doors. It lays waste no homes, but builds homes anew. It makes place for the strong, but there is no feud-tax to follow. It is the mightiest as well as the most peaceful conquest of the conquering Anglo-Saxon race. More than that, it is the swiftest.

When the world was young, peoples marched slowly, their flocks and herds with them, gaining a hundred miles a year in westward course perhaps; pausing to build, to breed, to till; slipping back, edging forward, feeding, like pigeon flocks, in waves. To-day the earth is winged with rapid wheels. The flocks and herds are swept forward as swiftly as their owners. Property, possessions, home, family, all go

Photograph by Mathers.

Loading boats after making the third portage on Slave River.

forward at once, and what was once a hundred miles is now a thousand, two thousand, more. A week spans a year to-day, a day measures indeed a century. In result, we have a splendid, fateful, somewhat awesome thing, one of no mere commercial significance.

This is the trek of humanity, the trek of the last chance, the trek of Magna Charta. It is not English, not Canadian, not American, but human. It leaves to those who fancy them the cocktails and *creme de menthe* of young men, the license and degeneracy of middle-aged men, the avarice and injustice of old men. It leaves illegal usurpations and outworn monarchies, and calls out to the red-blooded that here is the trek, and at its end fair play and a wide sky.

The nineteenth century belonged to the United States. We used it magnificently, even our high crimes and misdemeanors being large. There was still a feeling that the world was young. The twentieth century belongs to Canada. Yet between these two, Canada and the United States, I saw no line of demarkation. None of the trekkers could see that line. They only feel, as any man may feel who has ridden where the winds blow and read where the types tingle, that of late the true empire of the Anglo-Saxon was west of the Missouri, and that now it is northwest of the Missouri. From the sun to the ice, from the salt to the snow—these are terms of territory so big that to call it British or Canadian or American is folly. Call it the land of fair play, of new opportunity, and admit that the world is trekking thither; for that comes near to the full spelling of it.

Now, what is this new country regarding which most of us have lived in partial ignorance? If it has been there, why have we not heard of it? No seas divided us, no mountain barriers, yet the world has lived for two centuries as ignorant of this far Northwest as though a wall mountain high had separated it from all the rest of the world. That wall did exist, but it was a wall of mystery and misrepresentation. In truth, it was largely erected by that unique and picturesque monopoly, the Hudson's Bay Company, which wanted a wilderness and got it at a time of Homeric ignorance and apathy. The story of how

that wall was broken down, how its gates were thrown wide for the westbound, the real and human story of the Great Trek, is a peculiar and interesting one.

The Hudson's Bay Company saw to it that Prince Rupert's Land should always be construed as a land of ice and snow. There was its farm, and it reaped its harvest of fur where no man sowed or tilled. Sir John Franklin was lost. Very well. It might have been expected. Explorers came not back. What would you ask of a land where desolation ruled? All this was indefinite by four thousand miles or so; but none the less a vast, icy fiction enshrouded all this upper land for well-nigh two hundred years.

To show that this new empire does not of right belong either to England or France or America, we have only to examine the abstract of title. To begin with, England profited rather by her good luck than by any daring or desert. It was by no means an Englishman who discovered the great region west of Hudson's Bay, but a Frenchman, or rather two Frenchmen, Fierre Radisson and the Sieur des Grosseilliers. It was, moreover, not an English sailing master who first took the emissaries of the great Company of Adventurers into Hudson's Bay, but a mere Yankee, by name of Zachariah Gillam. England ran third, but none the less took the stakes.

Radisson and Grosseilliers, hardy men from the French settlements of the St. Lawrence, pushed west along the Great Lakes into the forests beyond Superior. They were free trappers, evading, as did du l' Hut and many others, the edict of the French monarch that only his chosen appointees might reap the harvest of the wilderness. When they came back from their voyaging into what is now Manitoba or Minnesota, perhaps much of what is now Ontario, plying the paddles of the first fur brigade from the far Northwest, the French governor fined them all they had, leaving them not a skin but their own hides. Angered, they crossed to France and made complaint to the king, but got no satisfaction, for the king needed the fur taxes to feed his own armies. Angered still more, they returned to Canada and went to Boston, where they got, for the most part, little encouragement about a West so far away. Here, however, or rather in New

Photograph by Mathers.

The ferry at Fort Saskatchewan.

York, they met Sir George Carteret, who asked them to take their story of the new land to King Charles II. of England. They were ready to take it anywhere; and so, after further grievous mishaps, they got audience of King Charles, good, easy soul, who was quite ready to give away anything in the world, even if he did not own it or know what or where it was. Those were fine days for kings!

The royal favor was the enabling act of "the Governor and Company of Adventurers trading into Hudson's Bay." Surely if ever title was accurate, then was this of "Adventurers." They paid in sums for stock—about as much as would float a third-rate coal mine or a new family steam laundry to-day—gave away a few shares to different distinguished persons, after the ancient Whittaker Wright method, and proceeded to fit out a couple of ships, the *Eaglet* and the *Nonsuch*, dispatching them for Hudson's Bay, the same which we usually miscall Hudson Bay. The English captain of the *Eaglet* got "cold feet" in this Arctic land, and saying that no man might win through, calmly returned to the Thames, where he knew the country better. Stout Zachariah of New England had sailed a schooner northward along Labrador in 1664, and he did not so easily abandon his undertaking. He took the *Nonsuch* through and reached the lower end of Hudson's Bay September 29, 1668. The crew wintered in that latitude and claimed the country for their own. That was the beginning of the great conquest story of the Hudson's Bay Company, and the beginning also, one might say, of the Great Trek to-day. Without stout Zachariah, England's flag had perhaps not floated where it does. To-day, two hundred and thirty-eight years later, descendants of Zachariah Gillam are trekking westward to take their share of the empire which their forefather helped to found, thanks to the grouch of Grosseilliers. On the face of the returns, neither Canada nor England ought to begrudge the Yankee his share of the new empire now rediscovering.

Now, what was it that King Charles blithely gave away to a few of his well-beloved friends? Charles himself did not know; and, indeed, no man from that day to this ever has known. Moreover, he gave no title. The fiction that the king owned the land was long ago dispelled. A century later, and Parliament, not the king, must have given the title. Another century, and the House of Commons, not the outworn House of Lords, would claim the essential right to own and give. There, indeed, you have the story of the Great Trek to-day. It covers the growth of the House of Commons, the growth of Democracy, of human equality all over the world. So, if it be treason to this flag or that, to the United States or to old England, to say that two flags blended may one day float where two now flutter in the western air—aye, over a better land than either of these two—then make the most of it. You cannot read the history of the last two centuries and call that an impossible thing. Those who cannot lift up their eyes upon the vast pageant of humanity may cast down their eyes and gnash plenteously their insular or industrial teeth.

In terms, what Charles gave away was this: "The whole trade of all those seas, streights, and bays, rivers, lakes, creeks, and sounds, in whatsoever latitude they shall be, that lie within the entrance of the streights commonly called Hudson's Streights, together with all the lands, countries, and territories upon the coasts and confines of the seas, streights, bays, lakes, rivers, creeks and sounds aforesaid, which are not now actually possessed by any of our subjects, or by the subjects of any other Christian prince or State."

The Governor and Company of Adventurers reconstrued their charter from year to year, as they saw opening up before them a splendid empire—how large they never yet have learned. It covered all the country draining Manitoba Lake, Rainy Lake, Lake Winnipeg, and Lake of the Woods, and most of what is now Ontario, almost down to Lake Superior. It covered the whole Valley of the Saskatchewan, the Mississippi of Canada, whose black lands to-day are repeating the story of our own Father of Waters. The charter even was stretched later to cover grants running to the Arctic and to the Pacific. Our country is an infant on the map alongside this empire, which was not thought worth while by any other Christian prince or State.

Let us remember the Company of Adven-

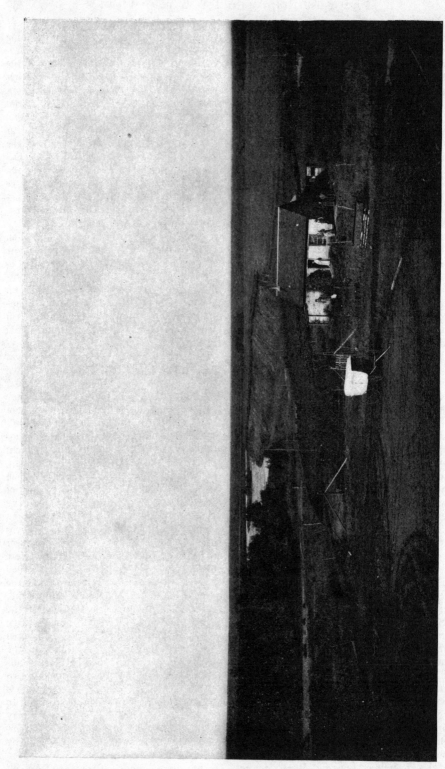

Photograph by Steele.

The limitless stretch of the prairie.

turers owned this empire all for their own. The king gave it in fee, "in full socage," with provisions that they might govern it, administer justice in it, even outfit armed expeditions to it. Never was such a charter given to any body in the world—transferring what never was owned or discovered to persons who never owned it or discovered it or paid for it. Those were fine days for kings and other adventurers as well. And not only did the Hudson's Bay Company own this country "in full socage," but owned it with a fence about it. England, the great free trader, gave her Adventurers "the whole, entire and only liberty of trade and traffick there"; and the Hudson's Bay Company was authorized to make peace or war with "any prince or people whatsoever that are not Christians." If you want a real, eighteen-carat corporation monopoly, read the early history of this ancient operation!

This splendid, if somewhat amazing, state of affairs went on for a long time, but could not forever continue. The claims of France as first discoverer of much of this country were calmly ignored; and the question of the illegality of these "absurd royal charters," which ran from some indefinite spot clear across to some unknown sea, was slurred over for a century or so. The Company of Adventurers held down its bluff, the most glittering four flush the world ever saw.

It had able men to guide it, some of England's greatest, for more than two centuries. Prince Rupert himself, eager cavalryman, was the first governor, and there were James of York and other royal men and big men of affairs, fit to rule even down to to-day. Lord Strathcona heads it now—Strathcona, not long since plain Donald Smith, until he and George Shepard, President of the Bank of Montreal, and now Lord Mount Stephen, and Duncan McIntyre, Director of the bank, and R. W. Angus, General Manager, very wisely took the funds of the Bank of Montreal—which they owned about as much as Prince Rupert ever owned Canada—and went into another adventuring, whose result was the second winning of this empire, a second rebuilding, making it ready for the third and final occupancy by the peoples of the earth; who really owned it all along. Title or no title, these men, able in affairs, ruled it

wisely and well at all the stages of the history of the Hudson's Bay Company; so well that they never had a serious Indian war in all their history; whereas, we of the United States have robbed our Indians so steadily and consistently that we have for the most part been obliged incidentally to kill them in order to keep them quiet.

But after the presumptuous Northwest Company had broken into the fur trade of the West, and after the expansion of America had placed restless folk close along the borders of the ancient empire of fur, the white or semi-white inhabitants of this land of mystery began to grow restless. They wanted to do a little trading of their own; wanted to get out of a salaried life and wide paternalism, and do a little individual living of their own. That was the beginning of a new but inevitable day. Thus were sown the seeds of the great people movement which is now in progress.

The Red River half-breeds began it by asking that they might be made good subjects, human beings indeed, to live and trade and lie and cheat as they pleased, like white folk on both sides of the border. That was more than fifty years ago. The father of the Louis Riel who was later hanged was one of the first agitators, one of the first to ask for the inevitable. How strange a thing, how calmly unjust, and how dramatically big is history at times!

Beside absolute ownership of the empire tributary to Hudson's Bay, the Company of Adventurers held under license other vast empires—Athabaska, British Columbia, etc.—and these lands were held under terms of twenty-one-year leases. In 1859 these leases will come up for renewal, and then for the first time the Company will have an encounter with advancing civilization. Canada has begun to covet this great empire to her west, has begun to talk about actual title, and that sort of thing. Great Britain sits up and rubs her eyes. Perhaps Canada as a colony is worth something, after all. She sends over Chief Justice Draper in 1857 to see what and where Canada is and why she is making all this disturbance. When the Chief Justice returns to answer the questions of the House of Commons—ah, how that House of Commons has grown in power since Prince Rupert's time!—he answers that in his belief Canada should be free to ex-

Bullock teams hauling hay wagons in the Northwest Territories.

tend to the Rockies, and that the people of that land should be free to belong to Great Britain and not to the Hudson's Bay Company.

Then began the giant battle between young Canada and the old monopoly. There was fear that the big Canadian West would go over to the United States. There was need of some better government out there. Wise and kindly and efficient as the government had been there for two hundred wilderness years, Governor Dallas, of Prince Rupert's Land, admits that while he can govern a wilderness, he cannot govern a country filling up with settlers. He thinks the territorial rights should now revert to the crown. In this pretty coil, the best adjustment of the ownership of an empire seems to be the purely commercial one of cash in hand. The "International Financial Association," a band of men enterprising in politics and commerce, actually buys out the entire lock, stock, and barrel of Prince Rupert's Land, paying one and a half million pounds for what was bought of Charles at the price of "two elks and two black beaver"; and paying rather too little for this usufruct of two great centuries. Upon this, much outcry from many scattered factors and traders far out in the icy West, who are, or think they are, partners of the old Company under certain of its widening policies inaugurated early in the past century. Indeed, much cry and little wool for Canada for another ten years! In 1867, two years after the reunion of the North and South in the United States, Canada federates her provinces peacefully. She wants more room to grow. The Homeric monopoly at last faces its day of fate. The wilderness must yield to the farms. The imperial government in England at length realizes that to-day is to-day and not yesterday; that the world has indeed moved. It presses the Company of Adventurers to cease its adventurings, pleading that these troubles along the Red River may grow; urging that the country ought to be civilized. So a second vast international *opera-bouffe* real estate transaction is concluded. England, which is to say Canada, buys back what once was given away by an Englishman who never owned it. The Hudson's Bay Company surrenders all its rights in Canada. Canada pays over three hundred thousand pounds; allowing the Company, however, a sub-empire of one-twentieth of all the arable land of the entire country claimed; also the privilege of trading as a regular commercial enterprise, but with no monopoly. In other words, competition is to reign henceforth and not monopoly, democracy and not absolutism, a fair chance for many instead of a lead-pipe cinch for a few. The House of Commons has grown. The days are not so good for kings.

This is how the land was prepared for this great trek from all countries where the House of Commons feels the restricting hands of absolutism or of oligarchy. This is how the Canadian West, the last West, was born. The names of Manitoba, Alberta, Saskatchewan, Athabaska, Assiniboia, become vaguely familiar terms on both sides of the border. Presently the term "Northwest Territories" disappears. Two vast provinces, no longer territories, but what we would call states in our governmental system, although they have nominal governors appointed instead of elected, are now to be seen on the map. Assiniboia has disappeared, and Manitoba, Saskatchewan, and Alberta occupy all of old Prince Rupert's land from the Rockies to the end of Superior. The mystery has gone. Winnipeg is Chicago now, and Calgary is Denver, and Edmonton is St. Paul, and vast lands of unknown extent are proving themselves fit to feed and support an actual civilization. So thither, silently at first, now with shuffle and murmur and dust-cloud of many feet, go the people of the world on the last Great Trek; and if this is not a great and significant thing, then you and I have never seen one. The trek leads to a new home for humanity, a new land of opportunity and fair play.

The longer one examines the history of the Canadian Northwest, the more does he discover that history to be a simple and continual record of misconceptions removed. There remain misconceptions yet to be removed. The extent, the resources, the climate and characteristics of this whole vast region are matters in part of future education. The trail of the Hudson's Bay Company is still over that country, and that of the succeeding range barons lies over it as well. The cowman of our trans-Missouri never wanted the farmer,

The beginning of the British colony at Lloydminster, 1904.

Photograph by Ernest Brown.

but the farmer came and ousted him. The Hudson's Bay Company did not want the free trader or the rancher, yet in turn these came. The farmer was kept out by deliberate propaganda, but he came.

Not even the Canadian Pacific Railway, biggest and shrewdest monopoly since the Hudson's Bay Company, knew what it was getting twenty years ago. It looked only at the map, and the map placed the apex of the Great American Desert about where Battleford is to-day. They raise as good wheat as ever grew from two hundred miles north of Battleford as far south as the high plains of Texas. The Canadian Pacific Railway got from an ignorant and sceptical government twenty-five millions in cash, twenty-five million acres of land, certain completed railway lines in the East and others upon the Pacific Slope. "Now," said the imperial and the colonial government to the Company of Adventurers of the Canadian Pacific Railway, "let us see you do it!" The Company of Adventurers did it, but they did it in ignorance. They built their first line through some of the poorest farming country, and, rebelling at this, asked for the privilege of selecting lands outside of the covenanted belt of twenty miles from the railway track. They got choice land all over the Northwest for nothing. They have sold it in rivers and seas at two, three, five, six, seven dollars an acre, take it or leave it, and would rather you left it, for next year it will go up and up again in price. To-day the Canadian Pacific Railway is building nineteen new branches, spending six million dollars for rails, seven and one-half millions for rolling stock. Once more the country has outgrown all prophecy. The crops threaten to swamp all transportation.

The next railroad that came along did not receive quite so good treatment at the hands of the government. Kings, and corporations also, are discounting, it seems. The Canadian Northern Railway got some lands and had its bonds guaranteed; yet the Canadian Northern Railway sweeps through a continual succession of fading misconceptions. It is taking thousands and thousands of settlers into regions not long ago thought icebound throughout the year. The truth is astounding. From the foot of the Winnipeg Lake, eight hundred and twenty-five miles northwest to Edmonton, lies absolutely the greatest continuous wheat belt of the entire world. Siberia does not equal it, nor New Zealand, nor Australia, nor our own West. It raises the hard Fyfe wheat, the "No. 1 Hard" of the miller's dream. The amounts? About twice as much as North Dakota at her best per acre.

What shall we do with facts like these? What is such land worth, this icy land rebought and salvaged out of mystery? No one knows. It is as much worth forty dollars as ten. Perhaps the latter figure is the average price to-day. It will be fifteen flat next year. Three years ago, two years ago, eighteen months ago, it was three dollars, two, one dollar an acre. How much has Prince Rupert's Land enhanced in value in the last five years? Tenfold? Once it fetched "two elks and two black beavers."

Far back eastward, but with transcontinental ambitions, comes the Intercolonial Railway, not oversubsidized, but getting good government jobs and a gladdish sort of hand. Now comes also the Grand Trunk Pacific, hurrying westward across the continent, seeing that what has happened in the trans-Missouri will happen again in the trans-Assiniboine. It puts out contracts for eight hundred miles of new line and crowds on all steam. More misconceptions have cleared away. The government has become more tight-fisted now. The Grand Trunk Pacific gets its bonds guaranteed, and should be glad of that; but it must submit to rate control by the government —and in Canada that means an actual and not a theoretical rate control. Comes also another great Canadian, the able *emigré*, James J. Hill, who has written history in transportation south of the Canadian border. Mr. Hill, for once beaten at the game of prophecy, sees his wildest ideas discounted by the swift growth of the Canadian Northwest. A while ago he sold his Winnipeg line; but he has spent more for new terminals in Winnipeg than he got for all the former railway outright. He lays before the Canadian government a simple proposition, that if they will let him in he will build a road across the continent on Canadian soil, without a foot of land, a dollar of subsidy, or a yard of ready-made line. He will build it so fast that he can carry freight for the other roads, he says, absolutely! And Canada will let him in. For one after another these great leaders' misconceptions regarding Prince Rupert's Land have cleared away. But even to-day they cannot dream big enough.

Since 1896, lands all through the American West have doubled, in many cases trebled, in value, in spite of the fact that great tracts are continually opening in the West for settlement, and in spite of the fact that only a small per cent. of our foreign immigrants go to farming. A million acres, ten million, amount to very little. It was about 1900 when it became obvious to many of our American home-seekers that our great West was getting a trifle small, according to their notions. In that year about twenty thousand Americans went over into Canada. Two years later, the army had reached fifty thousand in numbers. Last year, more than that many went across the line within three months of the spring. At least seventy-five thousand will this year leave the United States to go into Northwest Canada, not to mention more than a hundred thousand more from Europe. These figures are far within accuracy, for it is not claimed by the officials that they get the name and record of every man moving over the line in these packed columns of the Great Trek. The figures stagger, and, indeed, their ethical import might well cause a certain confusion to our own government; yet there is no use in attempting to blind ourselves to the meaning of it, even though it represents a certain hardship to the United States. One able objector out in Iowa complains in a widely circulated American periodical that this "wild land craze" is taking away from his commonwealth thousands of men and causing the local banks much hardship. He opines that folk presently will realize that Iowa land is better than wild land, and so will come back home, even as lost sheep return. What utter folly! The truth is that the population of Iowa is thirty thousand less than it was two years ago, most of this loss occasioned by the Great Trek. That is not because Iowa lands are no longer good, but because they are no longer cheap.

There is little sentiment in these matters.

I remember a magazine article which described the thrills experienced by a Russian Jew immigrant when he saw the top of the Statue of Liberty in New York Bay, so knowing that he was at last approaching America, the land of the free. The article struck me as excellent tommyrot. The immigrant may thrill a few thrills because he believes he is going to make more money here than where he came from, but his exultation ends thereabout. It is frankly the same way with Americans who are headed to the Northwest. They are going to a country where they think they can better themselves. The Anglo-Saxon is always land hungry. Show him where he can get good land for one-tenth what it costs at home, and he will trek, flag or no flag. The complaint of the Iowa writer that these outgoers will meet disaster is based upon no historical review, which would simply show that Alberta is to Iowa what lately Iowa was to New England. The only disaster to the farmer who leaves his one-hundred-dollar land in search of ten-dollar land will come through partial payments for land which he fails to buy outright; in other words, speculation instead of investment—the danger of any boom, any country, or any commercial system.

If pretty much all the earth could for two hundred years remain misinformed or uninformed regarding this great northwestern country, then surely we cannot within a few months or years have overcome all that ignorance and misconception. The day of details is following for the Canadian Northwest, and so perhaps a chapter dealing more with line and verse should follow in the story of that Northwest. Facts and figures having to do with the extension of Magna Charta, the widening of personal rights and personal opportunity have always held a human interest, from the Alleghanies to the Rockies; so that an assemblage of facts as against a mass of misconception may offer something less dry than a table of crop averages, immigrant reports, and meteorological tables; even though the barb of the story be thereabouts for the man who feels moved to set his face westward and go a-trek, even as his red-blooded father did before him.

THE
OUTING
MAGAZINE

FEBRUARY, 1907

THE LAST STAMPEDE FOR CHEAP HOMES

II—THE LOST FRONTIER

BY EMERSON HOUGH

OST of us know that there is a city of delights known as Paris, and a city of *frappé* real estate known as Winnipeg; but how many of us know that Winnipeg and Paris are on the same parallel of latitude, and hence not so far north as London? All Great Britain, most of Germany and France, lie north of the upper boundary of the United States; but most of us ignorantly believe that the climate is a matter of latitude, and think that everything north of the United States is uninhabitable country.

We do not stop to learn that although St. Paul is six hundred and fifty miles south of Edmonton, there is only one degree of average difference in the temperature the year round.

It is so much easier to suppose things than to know them, that it really is not surprising that we have lost a frontier which we supposed was a permanent institution. Edmonton remains to-day the gate city of civilization; but if you seek a frontier you must go farther than Edmonton. Yesterday her history was one of romantic adventure; to-day it is one of not less romantic industry. It is a trifle awkward to reflect that Edmonton was founded just two years after the French Revolution, at a time when George Washington was a much respected citizen of America; although no one at Edmonton had ever heard of George Washington. Up to 1891 she held the title of Queen of the Wilderness. Her new Canadian Pacific Railway even then concluded that it could not jump the deep Saskatchewan, and so halted at Strathcona, hoping that Edmonton would cross the river, which she did not. Then came the Canadian Northern Railway, and revolution began. Four railways trend toward Edmonton.

While you and I have been rubbing our

Mother and baby have just arrived from "the other side," while father has been in Alberta a year and is a leading citizen in labor circles.

Waiting to be claimed by kith and kin.

eyes about Edmonton, she has been rubbing her own eyes about her frontier. Far out beyond was the Peace River—you and I have read about wood-bison in there, and dreamed how one day we should go there. Did the frontier linger on the Peace? Let us go, you and I, and see what Edmonton sees to-day—wheat farms on the Peace River, the open valleys settling up, steamboats with electric lights plying up and down that stream, late sacred to the wild!

In 1901, this village at the edge of what we wrongly deem an icy world had 2,600 people. It has 15,000 to-day, even though it is still the pioneer, the town furthest west on the upper railways. Three years ago, it had a world of open lands; to-day there is not a homestead left open within fifty miles west of Edmonton city limits. Five years ago the assessed value of Edmonton property was a million and a third; to-day it is sixteen millions. Five years ago a few men very foolishly said they could raise wheat four hundred miles south of Edmonton. They are raising it and milling it four hundred miles *north* of Edmonton to-day! The men of Fort Vermilion, which was beyond our wildest travel dreams, are begging the government to survey their land for them and allow them to throw it open for settlement. They have mills and waterworks and electric-light plants up there, under birch-bark roofs. But there is no frontier. The arm of Edmonton, the gate city, is two thousand miles long, but where does it touch a frontier, when you may now make a perfectly safe and comfortable summer journey by steamer to the Arctic Circle and return? What about the frontier, when they now calmly mention the Peace River as the coming winter-wheat region of the world! Many eyes are now on the McLennan River Valley, west of the Rockies. If presently some one shall erect palace hotels on the Liard or the Porcupine, I for one shall evince no surprise.

The day in the Canadian Northwest is one of contrast. The tepee still stands beside the new mansion of the real-estate agent. The pony races of the Crees are held close to the splendid driving-park at the capital of what you and I thought was the frontier. Lacrosse survives, but with it polo. You see a bundle of silver-fox skins worth forty thousand dollars; but the merchant does not care for that; he wants to show you wheat and oat fields, the crops taller than your head. They tell you of hunting grounds to the far north full of appeal to the adventurers; but they add that a railway is building to Lac la Biche and another to Hudson's Bay; and they add casually that if the great Bay shall prove too icy for winter transportation of these millions of bushels of grain to England, then they will build a road from its east shore across Ungava and Labrador. And these things they will do! But where is the frontier? Among the green poplars which enfold what we thought was to remain forever the wind-swept capital of the fur trade show now many tents, scores of them. They are the tents not of Crees and Breeds, but of new settlers who have not had time to build their houses. Wild fowl still breed thereabout; but close to the wild lakes axe and billhook are cutting away the bush and opening up the rich black soil for farms.

But where is the frontier? They show you pictures of the old Hudson's Bay Company's stores of other days and tell you of low-roofed rooms, smoky and filled with a jumble of furs and dog harness and gaudy cloths for the native trade; yet when you find the Hudson's Bay Company's stores to-day, you discover windows filled with lingerie from Paris, picture hats and boots of dainty make as those of Broadway, gloves for gentle hands, silks, furs and fine linens. Alas! for the Hudson's Bay Company; it caters no more to Pie Face, the Esquimaux belle, but to Estelle and Angeline from Ontario, Katie and Bess from the "States," and Mary and Nora from over seas.

Where is the frontier? Perhaps it is in Chicago. That may well be; for there they are wrangling over municipal ownership and calling in all manner of doctors to argue about it. Edmonton did not argue about it, but merely did it, in her own quaint, fur-clad fashion. She owns her own waterworks, her own electric-lighting plant, her own telephone system, and, moreover, runs them all smoothly and honestly and well. Her schools and churches and residential houses are wholly adequate to the standards of any western American city. Her farm lands can and do average thirty bushels of wheat to the acre; oats to the tune of fifty-seven bushels average, which is almost freakish; and whereas in the United States oats need weigh but thirty-two pounds per bushel to be standard, around Edmonton they would throw such oats to the hogs, for there the average runs thirty - eight, forty-four, sometimes fifty pounds per bushel—this on what we thought was the fish-fed frontier!

There are some moose to be had from Edmonton. She is indifferent as to that. What she wants to show you are her cattle and hogs and sheep, fat and flourishing as any on the range lands or dairy regions of the "States." Once Edmonton lived in logs; but last year she cut twenty million feet of sawn lumber from logs floated down the Saskatchewan from somewhere out west where the frontier form-

The Russian peasant garb of sheepskin is a trifle warm of a Manitoba spring morning.

from the Saskatchewan opposite the city hall; and she has twelve flourishing banks, eighteen wholesale houses, and factories and mills, how many I do not know.

Not long ago, the sole and absorbing mission of Edmonton, in a commercial way, was to bilk ignorant Klondike adventurers—poor fellows who thought that Alaska was perhaps one hundred miles west of Winnipeg—into outfitting there for the land of gold. There were Englishmen bound for the Klondike who brought with them as far as Edmonton their own baled hay—a fact, though it seems impossible, even for an Englishman; and others who brought traction engines to carry them thence merrily over the Rockies to the Klondike; and yet others who had barrels rigged with axles and shafts for horse draft, which in tran-

erly was, but but is not. Lately, in our estimation, she shivered over fires of little sticks; but now she has coal mines within her city limits, and ships coals to those who have none. Commerce thereabout not long ago was on the basis of the made-beaver; but to-day Edmonton dredges gold sit nicely mingled nails, sugar, baking-powder and other goods into one homogeneous fabric; and many other similarly crazed and wholly idiotic men, who thought they knew where the frontier was and how it might be mastered—even as you and I in our ignorance have thought

Last Mountain Lake.

we knew where the frontier is to-day. Industriously bilking these to the best of her ability, and knowing that of course the frontier was a permanent and indestructible thing, Edmonton six years ago did not dream that presently she would be in touch with Winnipeg, Chicago, New York, Paris, London, all the world, and so within the scope of business honor. To-day, Edmonton does not refer to her past; she shows you her railway yards, and explains upon the map how her new transportation will bring the Peace River and Athabaska country into direct tribute.

I did not wonder when they told me that up to the end of May, 1906, five months in all, there had come into Edmonton district 5,000 Americans, 3,000 Canadians, 540 English, 230 Scotch, 200 Irish, 98 Germans, 170 Austrians, 140 Russians, 68 Swedes, 26 Danes, 8 Hollanders, 11 Finlanders, 75 Frenchmen, 120 Belgians, 18 New Zealanders. I was not jarred when they told me 25,000 settlers would move into Edmonton district this year— 10,000 more than came last year. But when they showed me that last year fifty families had removed from Riverside, Pasadena and Eureka, in the crack districts of California, and settled far to the north of Edmonton, I admit I gasped and sat down! But how much more than this have you known about the frontier to-day, and about climate and latitude, and many other things? Did you know that Edmonton has a much milder climate than Winnipeg; that any one who can live at all in New York may gain in comfort by going to Edmonton? Did you know that any one who can endure the climate of Chicago— But why multiply these revelations?

Edmonton is merely an instance. Winnipeg, Calgary, Moose Jaw, Saskatoon, a score of new cities of the Canadian Northwest, have records of similar sort; and all this drama of change and contrast has been a peaceful one, founded upon no greater conquest than that wrought by a simple plant with a bearded head, which will grow in some lands but not in others, and which seems to have a way of empire about it— the wheat plant, closely intermixed with war and famine, with ocean steamer lines and colonial policies, with Wall Street fluctuations and national bank reserves.

Wheat has been grown in Manitoba some thirty years, and it does better now than when its planting was first essayed. They marketed some fifty-six million bushels in 1905. But, after all, Manitoba is close to Minnesota, and we understand its terms. It is a trifle more difficult to understand that in the wild western regions of Alberta and Saskatchewan, hundreds of miles due north of the cow country of Montana and Wyoming, the horse and cattle barons are folding their tents and resignedly making way for the incoming farmers. Last spring I saw three trains a week going across the line, loaded to the windows with bronzed, silent men from the slopes of the Rockies, Colorado, Idaho, Wyoming, Montana, New Mexico; all of them calmly ignoring the promises of the government of the United States to throw open now and then a few million acres more of land. Three thousand of these choice settlers went through Coutts last year.

Canada naturally has strong English sentiment, but the actual leaders in affairs in the Canadian Northwest admit that the English immigrant neither made a past nor assured a future for their new empire. First came the typical English "remittance man," who lived on money from home and subsisted chiefly on whiskey. He was a cumberer of the earth, and spelled no progress whatever. Then came the English colonists from the cities, poor folk for the most part and eager to better themselves; willing to work, but in fitness generations behind the men who fought their course across the continent by way of the Appalachians and the Missouri and the Rockies. Later there arrived numbers of the agricultural classes of England, peaceable, hard-working and frugal, admirable settlers, albeit somewhat ignorant of the conditions of life in a new country. All these were welcomed in Canada; but, although the English immigration in numbers equals that of many other nations combined, it does not equal the American immigration alone in striking power, in foot-pound terms of potential civilization.

This moving out to the "colonies" is forever a holiday notion with the average Englishman, his knowledge of the colonies being founded mostly on sporting literature or pure fiction. It was of a typical English colony that a hard-headed Canadian railroad official recently made the following report to an inquiring superior officer: "Their golf is flourishing; their cricket is doing well; their four-o'clock tea is a success, and their polo all that could be asked —but God help such sod-breaking!"

With these *insouciant* recruits from the Old World mingles the leaven of East Canada and the American West, men with the American hat, the American chin and hand and eye, as developed in a century or so of American frontier-chasing. The Canadian government sends instructors for young Englishmen, and there are schools purporting to teach farming, just as we have schools of journalism in America. It was not in any such school that there was written the drama of the wheat. Canada and the United States did that. It was winter wheat that changed Calgary from a cow town to a city severely modern and contagiously alive.

Fifteen years ago, Calgary dreamed no wider than a wagon trade north and south of the Canadian Pacific. "Rawnch" interests supported the town. (If it is a "ranch" it pays, and if it does not pay it is a "rawnch"; so runneth the humor of speech thereabout, wotting that early Calgary "rawnches" sometimes chiefly produced money from Old England.) Then came the north and south railroad, which helped Calgary less than she had planned for, and built up small towns on both sides of her, which supplied the scanty population. But Calgary hustled. She began to bake and brew and sell. She put up elevators and factories and began to wholesale by rail where once she had trafficked by wagon. She accepted the Turkey Red wheat as greater than the white-faced cow and drew no indignant line at the industrious hen. In 1897 the Crow's Nest Pass road was built, and Calgary widened her sphere of influence. Then came the Canadian Pacific Railway's vast scheme for the benefit of Turkey Red, embracing nearly fifteen hundred miles of irrigation ditches; and Calgary calmly stepped into the place of the Canadian Denver, becoming the largest town between Winnipeg and Vancouver, a city having to-day about twenty thousand population, eight million dollars of assessed property, twelve banks, a dozen churches, nine public schools, a hospital, a sanatorium, a college, a land office, a division headquarters, sixty-four wholesale stores,

and thirty retail factories, a thousand telephones, scores of business blocks—it is difficult not to go madly into western boom figures. That would be risky, after all, for these western cities are jealous, and they change over night in their amazing totals.

What we are to remember is that Calgary once sold saddles, and now grinds wheat. It was Turkey Red that did this. If you seek a frontier, search not for it near Calgary. But Calgary will insist that you listen specifically to her for a time. She will tell you that she has three hundred sunshiny days in the year, and that sunshine is contagious. She will remark that she has nine million acres of Canadian Pacific Railway land yet to sell, and will put three million acres under irrigation— not because that is wholly necessary, but as a matter of crop insurance. Then, ere you may turn about, Calgary will lapse into swift, compelling figures, pointing out three great irrigation sections now under the watchguard of Divine Providence (which, in Canada is exemplified by the Canadian government and the Canadian Pacific Railway), each section comprising a million acres, more than half of which will presently be under irrigation. The first big ditch from the Bow River is eighteen miles long, and of three secondary ditches one is finished for sixty-five miles, with thirty-two miles of distributing ditches, some three hundred and fifty miles of which will be completed during this year. These are parts of a project which on the blue-prints shows a mileage of 1,318 miles, all to be built with real money and on no wild-cat bonds of individual enterprise; all putting actual water on actual land at fifty cents per actual acre per year; that land to cost not over twenty-five dollars, and in some districts much less. Calgary irrigates and is proud of it.

"But," you say, "taking Calgary as typical of the western portions of these provinces, as Edmonton is taken for the northern, surely the climate is very cold?" Calgary laughs aloud and points to baseball in shirt-sleeves in February as one of her annual pastimes. "You forget the Chinook," says Calgary. "Why, once a farmer was driving into town here in his sled, and the Chinook came up before he got in. He whipped up his horses and traveled as fast as he could, but, do his best,

Two Magyar maids at a Saskatchewan depot. Types of
the builders of this western empire.

A street scene in the Winnipeg of to-day.

the Chinook melted the snow so fast behind him that he drove into town on the gallop, with only his front bobs on the snow and the dry ground chasing him every jump!"

When one is in touch with histories like those of Edmonton and Calgary, the study of geography becomes an interesting pastime, and even columns of figures gain a graphic interest. Suppose we establish Edmonton as the gateway of the upper Northwest, and reckon with Calgary, on the east edge of the Rockies, as the capital of the winter-wheat district or Chinook belt. East of Calgary about four hundred and fifty miles is the outer edge of the Chinook belt, and hereabouts lie Moose Jaw and Regina, old-new towns, with real-estate records of surprising figures these last two years, and joint capitals of the approved spring-wheat belts. East again four hundred miles lies Winnipeg, capital as yet of all these capitals, and eastern point of the great triangle whose western extremities are Calgary and Edmonton.

No use attempting figures on Winnipeg, for long ago she ceased to be close to any edge of things, and is to-day only the capital of capitals, the commercial heart of the great Northwest. In 1870, she had a grand total of two hundred and fifteen population, and the dog teams fought in the stockade of old Fort Garry. To-day only the stone gate of old Fort Garry remains, and near it rises the mansion house of the Manitoba Club In 1874 there were eighteen hundred people in Winnipeg; in 1900 there were forty-eight thousand five hundred; in 1906 she had over one hundred thousand population; though what it may be at the present clock strike one may not say. No one particularly cares for statistics regarding a city like New York or Chicago or Montreal or Winnipeg, for they are a matter of course; but Winnipeg, plus the map and minus the last few rapid years, is full of interest for those who have lost a frontier.

Winnipeg is where they do things. This is really the place where the frontier was abolished by the real-estate regicides. A kingdom is sold daily in Winnipeg, an army is marched in by rail to occupy it over night. The yards of the Canadian Pacific Railway alone in Winnipeg have over one hundred and twenty miles of trackage, and they need it. The immigrants come by battalions—-Englishmen in caps, Scotchmen in bonnets, Breton French in blue coats, Germans, Swedes, Norwegians, Austrians, Mennonites, Galicians—all manner of furtive folk and wild. There are fifteen known languages in the Winnipeg schools, and a lot too late to classify. When you see a stranger, you cannot tell whether or not he is within the range of human speech. You bitterly reflect only that he is one of those who have wiped out the old frontier, lost it forever to those who love the wilderness.

They come in broods and flocks and colonies. Last year the Salvation Army brought out four thousand immigrants from England, and next year it plans for ten thousand more. Other English colonies are to rival the successful one at Lloydminster. Some thousands of Galicians have trekked hither, coming from a country which God forgot, and which is alternately trampled upon by Poland, Austria, Hungary, Russia — whenever a European nation gets angry over anything it licks Galicia. It is easy. The largest colony of Galicians lies northeast of Edmonton, and its people are making good citizens. When they reach Winnipeg they are half-wild, gypsy folk, the women barefoot or in heavy boots, some of them brutish, some of them comely, all of them picturesque. For a time the Galician men are disposed to set their women at pulling the plows when horses lack—much to the disgust of the long-suffering Northwest Mounted Police, who have to attend to everything and do all manner of work, from chasing a killer to taking the census or hanging out the family washing of the oppressed.

Near Lashburn town, on the Canadian Northern, there is a colony of negro porters, retired from active life at brush and broom. At Yorkton remains the famous colony of Doukhobors, known to the public by reason of their abandonment of their farms and their march *en masse* toward Winnipeg in search of Jesus—though why at Winnipeg no one may say. These people are now more content. They are good settlers, retaining in their domestic life many of the old Russian customs, the great oven-like stove, the raised platform around the large living room, where the beds are made down, the icon above the door. They are hard-working, and from late wild and hairy savages have become good citizens.

The Doukhobors use their women to the plow instead of horses.   Canada is stopping the practice.

Few of these foreigners ever wish to go back to the Old World. I talked with one Galician, a big, strapping fellow who had been in this country two years. "I am a man," said he, "a full-grown man, but in my time, back home, I have been whipped like a serf by my boss because I did not do my work as he wished; laid over a bench and whipped with a leather lash. They often whipped us there. They do not whip us here. Go back? Ah, what do you say? Here we are rich, rich!"

To all these many newcomers the Canadian government has offered free land for actual homesteading--not false and fraudulent homesteading, such as marked some of our Western States. As for the railways, they have simply ladled out land. It has been treated not as land but as a fluid, a figment, a fiction, one ladleful as good as another. The buyer does not know where his land is until he has paid down his first installment of two dollars an acre; then he goes out to find his land. The wonderful thing is that so little really cheap land, say at two or three dollars per acre, seems left in this old home of the frontier, where the acreage was so immense. It averages around ten dollars now, all the way out to Edmonton along the newest road, the Canadian Northern, which comes as near as any at this writing to having the frontier as its touch.

But what do you ask? How far will the farms go above this last railway? No one really knows. Perhaps a hundred miles, two hundred. We have seen that they raise wheat four hundred miles north of this road. New towns spring up over night—Kamsak, Battleford, Dauphin, Vermilion, a dozen more. Did you ever hear of these names? They are all railway division points. Last year some of them were prairie sod. The Carrot River Valley—did you ever hear of that? It is as good a district as the once vaunted Portage la Prairie, over which the fur brigades passed on their way eastbound to Montreal.

At the mouth of the ancient Rainy Lake, waterway of the fur brigades, sits Fort Francis, with three railways headed thither and a fourth hoped for. At Port Arthur, near by vast trout fishing, is the largest elevator in the world for the transhipment of wheat, wheat, wheat. At Fort Churchill, on the Hudson's Bay. whither the iron trails of the Canadian Northern are hurrying, there may be some emporium of the North, for all man may know. At Fort Simpson, or some other point upon the Pacific, whither the Grand Trunk Pacific and the "Jim Hill" road and all the others are hastening, there will arise new cities and great ones, and these will have touch with Halifax upon the east by transcontinental lines. They will be in touch with Hudson's Bay, in touch with the Arctic, in time in touch with the Klondike. Follow these lines with finger on the map and answer for yourself the question as to that frontier which you and I late thought would last forever.

In conditions such as these, vast things may happen, and that right swiftly. Canada, or more especially Great Britain, wants the Yankee farmer, but looks with none too friendly eye upon the American invasion. As for the Yankee himself, he seems little concerned. I asked scores of men how it felt to leave the old flag. Some said it was the flag of the corporations now. One said: "I was working for the Chicago packers, and not for myself, and so I left." Most said that if a man was law-abiding he felt no law in any land. All said the law was good in the new country, the government fair, the schools all that could be asked, the opportunities better than they had left at home.

I talked with many women, knowing them more conservative than men, and knowing that it is upon the women that there falls the real burden of all frontiers. Few of them were discontented. One grim-faced matron from Colorado was taking her son north to find some homestead lands. "He is homesick, but I reckon he'll stick," said she; "leastways, his dad did when he came to Colorado from Illinois, till land at sixty dollars got to be too high for sugar beets, and a feller had to git his gun out to hold his share of water. They say over here a man gits his share of water without no gun."

Although it is already well-nigh too late to secure homesteads within twenty or thirty miles of the existing lines of railway in Alberta and Saskatchewan, it must be remembered that new districts are swiftly opening each month, as the hurrying rails move westward, northward, netting the land with iron as our own country is netted. The rate of homesteading runs about thirty thousand claims per year; but millions of acres remain open for homesteading and more millions of land are still held by the railways. No reference is made here to the great empire west of the Rockies in the valleys of British Columbia, but only to the more or less open prairie lands or rolling country between the Rockies and Winnipeg Lake. This is a country easily accessible, and its swift occupation is simply a matter of removing the remnants of the old misconceptions regarding it—misconceptions regarding climate, soil, agricultural possibilities and the frontier.

Listen to this! There are over one hundred and seventy million acres of wheat land in the Canadian Northwest, and not three per cent. is yet farmed. The average wheat yield in the spring-wheat belt for seven years was twenty and ninety-six one-hundredths bushels, against eleven and eight-tenths for North Dakota and twelve and one-tenth bushels in Minnesota. The Province of Saskatchewan as first established contained two hundred and seventy-five thousand square miles. Since 1897 homestead entries have increased eighteen hundred per cent. in that province. Since 1902 twelve million acres have been homesteaded. Since 1885 the Canadian Pacific Railway alone has sold over five million acres to settlers. Three years ago, one real-estate concern bought seven million acres of land from the Canadian government at one dollar an acre. In these last two years they have sold every foot of that land, much of it at ten dollars per acre—the swiftest and largest real-estate transaction ever known in the world. Twenty-five years ago there was not a mile of railway in Alberta or Saskatchewan. The mileage to-day is changing too rapidly to be obtainable; it is perhaps around ten thousand miles. Four years ago, there was only one incorporated city in the Canadian Northwest. Land sells to-day at thirty dollars which five years ago was bought at one dollar an acre, one fifth paid down.

Over one hundred and fifty thousand settlers came into Northwestern Canada in the year 1904–05. There were fifty-four nationalities of Europe represented, with a government total, admittedly not comprehensive, of 146,266. In twelve months of that fiscal year there entered through the one port of Portal, on the Soo Line, 121,765 settlers, with 1,495 carloads of household goods. Last year there came also 33,700 travelers, classified not as settlers but as tourists, of these 28,000 males, of whom an unknown number bought lands or entered homesteads. In April, 1905, 26,600 settlers entered Northwest Canada, of these 6,750 being Americans. Last April, 42,700 crossed the line—11,000 of these were American settlers. The fall immigration runs about half as large as that of the spring. This of course, is the largest year to date. What next year's figures may be no one seems willing to guess.

Tempting as is the task, one dare not venture much more deeply into figures, and must summarize briefly by saying that during the current year 160,000 to 200,000 settlers will move into Western Canada. That does not seem very large as against a million immigrants landed at our own Ellis Island. But of these latter not ten per cent. go to the West to farm. Of the Canadian immigrants, more than ninety per cent. move to the West upon the farms. They are going to make a country there. How great that country will be is one of the swift stories of the immediate future.

I remember that as I looked out of the car window at the station where a well-wisher from Idaho left us, far out in Western Alberta, I saw a steam traction engine, with a vast gang of breaking plows, turning over the sod and exposing the fresh black soil. There were many buffalo wallows still visible in the sod, hundreds of them, and the giant plow was turning them under carelessly. Was that the frontier passing? Perhaps. Was the woman who hoped the traveler would "make a good selection of land" the mother of future rulers of the land which is supplanting the frontier? Perhaps. Lost, one frontier? Found, one real human democracy? Perhaps. Lost, the Canadian and the American West? Found, a new country better than either Canada or the United States? Perhaps. It is hard to say that; yet to the mind of any American who has noted our own industrial and political history for the last few years that shameful admission will arise perforce. He will be obliged to say, Perhaps.

32

The Ride of Waster Cavendish

W.A. FRASER

THE RIDE OF WASTER CAVENDISH

By W. A. FRASER

JACK CAVENDISH was a really Cavendish. This in England stands for something; a really Cavendish is a Brahman of the social caste. But in the valley of the Saskatchewan, in the great northland, all this stood for nothing; Hogan or Montmorency were at sixes as regards primogeniture label—the man was the thing.

Cavendish had lived in the teepees of the Crees and half-breeds; and had shoveled the gravel bars of the Saskatchewan River for flour-gold, homing in a hole in a clay bank. Half-yearly some sovereigns came from England to the Hudson Bay Company's fort, at Edmonton, to the credit of this socially elided one. The gold created a ripple in the stream of Jack's life that filled the old clapboarded hotel at Edmonton with noise of carouse while the Englishman sifted in his remittance. When the money was gone, Jack would mount Montana Gold, a chestnut mare of lineage, and ride back to Wenotah the Cree.

"Waster" Cavendish they called him because of these things; and he slumbered morally, until Louis Reil raised the flag of rebellion, and the half-breeds and Indians snapped and snarled like wolves at the British overlord. Then Waster woke up—the sluggish Cavendish blood ran hot and strong.

It was Wenotah who told him that Yellow Bear and his Indians had mas- sacred the whites at Frog Lake; and the next day would surprise Fort Andrew and kill the small force of redcoats.

"Wenotah," said Cavendish, "the gray-eyed people—who are my people —need me; I go to them. You, who are a Cree, do you choose the Cree trail?"

"Yes, Ogama. My people are my people; we hate the whites."

He took his rifle and a blanket; put in the Cree woman's hand a bottle of gold-dust, and an order on the factor at Edmonton for his first remittance, and said, "Good-by, Wenotah; all that is left is yours—the teepee, all." Then he swung to the back of Montana Gold, and the Cree woman, crouching in the slitted door of the teepee, watched him ride out of her life over the trail that led to Fort Andrew, with his warning of the advent of Yellow Bear.

All night Waster rode, and the red tide, the blood-athirst Crees, had not swept up to the stockaded wall of Fort Andrew when the tired mare loped to the square by the Hudson's Bay Company's store.

Major Woodcote, the superintendent of police, knew nothing of the Frog Lake disaster; he simply knew that the wires had been cut. He discredited Waster Cavendish's tale until ten o'clock. At that hour a police constable, as he dipped a pail in the brown waters of the Saskatchewan, dove into the river, a 45-90 Winchester bullet plowing down his

333

spine and cutting a pulpy canal beneath the skin. A puff of blue smoke, hanging like a gentle bit of lacework over a clump of wolf-willow on the opposite bank, was a convincing attestation of Waster's unbelieved message, and the subtle malignity that had come to hover over Fort Andrew.

The rebels had struck at the vital part first—the water; no man could go down that bare clay bank, a hundred feet from rim to river edge, and hope to return alive. No rebels had appeared on the fort side of the river as yet; and the major decided that he must send a message to Fort Carford before his communication was cut.

That night two constables rode forth; the log gate swung to behind them, as, their horses' hoofs muffled in bags, they melted silently into the night gloom. The dwellers in the fort strained their eyes and strained their ears till the murmur of their own hearts grew articulate; the minutes went by, and the black pall that was over the face of the valley held nothing but the weird cry of a loon, as, unseen, the harsh-voiced diver passed up the river.

"Thank God! the boys have got through," the major whispered, hoarsely. "I was afraid. This Yellow Bear is a bloodthirsty brute. My God! there they go!"

Over on the trail there was an eruption of noises as though lost souls issued from the doors of hell. Rifles crackled; there was the deeper bellow of shotguns; and the Cree battle-cry, caught up from point to point till it rang in a circle the full sweep of the compass. The watchers could see the red, serpent-like tongues of fire, vermilion letters of alarm on the black background of night.

In the morning, the two dead constables were brought out into the open, and then their hearts were stuck upon stakes, that the garrison might know of the method of Yellow Bear.

The rebels' ambush had been betrayed; and now the prairie, beaten by the moccasined feet of blooded Crees, who slipped stealthily from poplar bluff to poplar bluff, and the green ribbon of spruce and tamarack, through which

the gleam of Little Otter wove like a silver thread, held camp-fires that sent many shafts of purple smoke skyward. These seemed like monuments of constancy; they were shadows of evil against the blue heaven, writing the somber message that until the fort yielded the fires would burn.

Twice in the night, Yellow Bear's Indians wriggled, belly to earth, to the very wall of the fort. Each time the rebels were beaten off, with gifts of death handed out to them. And because of this, Yellow Bear's wolves said, in wisdom, "The throats of the gray-eyed thieves, who are white men, will close up, and they will die, if we keep the river."

On the fourth course of the sun, there fell upon the shingled roofs of the post a sputtering rain of fire-arrows—air-serpents, clothed in oakum that blazed with a resinous flame.

"The redcoats are cowards, they are dog-hearted," said the chief; "send them a wampum tied to an arrow—a wampum to come forth; then we will not kill——"

"Not kill the Company man," Duplisse, his lieutenant, added.

So the shaft of an arrow carried a message of literary kinship to the episode of the staked hearts, as barbarously malignant. Strange to say, the arrow clove, in influence, between two factions; it rested in the rift that was between the factor's authority and the major's.

Factor McNeil existed that the Hudson's Bay Company might acquire fine furs cheaply; and the rebel chief had promised to respect the Company's pelts —he would only take the provisions— if the police-soldiers would surrender. So the factor was for giving in.

With the major the British flag was trumps; and he said, to the factor's face, "Damn your furs! we're here, and here we stay."

"And here ye'll dee—yon deevils'll burn ye oot," retorted McNeil. "Send for relief to Fort Carford."

For answer, Major Woodcote said, "Send one of your own men, factor."

"I'll no' do that—we're no' in the war business. Yon's your bit task, Major."

Drawn by George Gibbs
"Her stride carried Cavendish into the wind, until it was like a brush against his face"

He marched out of the police barracks; but in ten minutes returned, saying, "Waster Cavendish says he can get through the rebel lines, Major."

"If he thinks that, we'll call him 'Mr.' Cavendish; ask him to come in. What's your plan, Mr. Cavendish?" the major asked, as Waster saluted.

"I want four horses, sir; and a service revolver in exchange for my Winchester."

"You've got one," the major clicked, nodding toward Waster's belt.

"I want two, sir. I'll have to ride like bally hell, and can't carry a rifle. I'm going to play breed—juice my skin —it's pretty dark now—it won't need much. I'll slip up the coulée from the fort with the horses, riding my own mare, and I want your men to cut loose with their carbines—sound the alarm, shout that the horses are stolen, and generally convey the impression that a breed has looted the broncos. There's a bit of a moon to-night, and they'll see one man riding into their lines with horses; they won't shoot. There are breeds from all over the country out there—they'll think I'm one of themselves. While they're busy with the broncos, I'll make a break on Montana Gold. Once on the trail, they'll never catch her, by Jove!"

"It looks a good plan—to get shot," Woodcote commented; "but it's a straight, plucky, English way of doing things. Come into my quarters; I want to give you the despatches." Inside, the major said, "Now, sir, what about the folks at home?"

"Here is an address; if I don't get through—the breeds'll show you in the morning—you might write that the blood hadn't turned to water; it'll wipe something off the score. If I have luck, and you're relieved, you can burn this slip."

It was ten o'clock before the valley of the Saskatchewan cradled enough of darkness to blur the trail-scored prairie to a dim field of mystery. Even then, a low-hanging half-moon wove the poplar shadows into a fretwork of chased silver. Behind the fort, from the bosom of the river, a ghostlike mist streamed through the valley, an attenuated cloud of vapor, as though a steamer had passed. The rebels, flitting from camp-fire to camp-fire, dark shadows, like rabbits in a muskeg, were suddenly stricken to silence by the defiant crack of a carbine on the fort walls. Immediately the imperious music of a bugle sounding the alarm came to the ears of the listening breeds. Then the somber stockade of the fort, a gloomy blotch in the gray transition of light, spurted patches of fire; the valley crackled as though it were a beaten tin pan.

From the human hedge of the rebel force a shrill cry of fighting rage went up; and the Indians, throwing themselves into the trenches they had steadily thrust toward the fort, and behind trees, waited for the sortie they fancied was coming. There was the rolling thunder of hoofs beating the sleepy prairie, and above this, that was like the deep melody of drums, a shrill voice rose, calling in Cree: "Ho, brothers! help me! I bring the police horses!"

Silent, grim-watching, half a thousand marksmen lay hidden, rifle in hand, waiting for the closer manifestation of the hoof thunder, and the voice claiming blood-kinship. Now the galloping shadows were close to the watchers; surely it was but one man and a handful of horses.

Now the rider reins his horse to his haunches, and calls again: "Ho, Louis Duplisse! Ho, Maskotic! Ho, brothers that did the brave battle at Frog Lake!"

"Hi-hi-yi-hi-ya-hi!" From a trench the shrill signal started a blare of wolf-like calls; from poplar bluff and prairie rose up the warriors to crowd about this one of the brotherhood who had done the brave deed.

"Ho, nichies," he was saying, "where is the teepee of the great chief Yellow Bear? Say to him that Buck Roland has brought a present of four horses."

"This way is the teepee of Yellow Bear; I am Louis Duplisse, an' frien' to any Roland," a rebel called in answer.

The horses, excited by the gallop— the flaring torches held by the breeds, and the rifle-fire, were ready to create the diversion that Waster Cavendish had meant for their part. On the toe of each boot he had fastened a big

Mexican spur; and as eager hands stretched forth to clutch the prizes, Waster, crying "Don't get kicked, my brothers," tickled the ribs of the horses with his spurs. All the time they were moving toward the chief's teepee. Now the stronger music of iron shoes against the gravel came up to Waster's ears, and he knew that they were on the beaten trail.

"Here, brave one, is Chief Yellow Bear's teepee," Duplisse said.

As he spoke, Cavendish ripped the flank of a horse with his toe-spur, let the leading-rein slip from his fingers, and as the startled brute plunged, his three mates broke away and stampeded. The wave of humans rolled back from beneath the fierce hoofs of the charging beasts; the torches twisted bewilderingly; clamorous uproar lent most delicious confusion to the scene.

"Off the trail, brothers!" Waster yelled. "I will round up the horses."

Not a rifle called halt to the fleeing man; the breeds ran here and there, chasing the stampeded horses. It was the swift runner, Big Moose, flying over the trail at the heels of Montana Gold, who suddenly sent back to his comrades an angry call that the one who rode was fleeing beyond the loosed horses. They had been tricked.

Yellow Bear's Indians unhobbled their ewe-necked, cow-hocked cayuses, and, rifle in hand, swinging to their bare backs, chased the one who had called to them with a forked tongue that he was of kinship.

Montana Gold had the long-reaching gallop of her thoroughbred sire. For half a mile the trail lay over a level prairie, and her stride carried Cavendish into the wind until it was like a brush against his face. As they dipped into the hollow of a creek-bed, he eased the mare to a walk. Up the other bank he stayed the mettlesome beast, until she clamped eagerly at the bit; then he let her swing along at a hand-gallop. Presently his ear caught, "Clickety-patter, clickety-patter, clickety-patter," the erratic beating of untrained hoofs that carried unwise riders. Then he let the mare go forward at a strong gallop.

Through the few hours of night, Cavendish rode the race of a long trail.

Three times Waster slipped from his saddle, and, hand in stirrup-leather, ran for a mile to ease the mare. When the light had come, Cavendish rested in a jack-pine clump, from which he could see a mile of the back trail. There he gave Montana Gold a little breakfast of oats from a bag bound to the horn of his saddle.

For the time they were as two humans. Waster talked to the mare, and from the tired head, low-drooping in restfulness, the beautiful big, full eyes, soft and gentle in their courage, looked at him in understanding, and said plainly enough, "Everything is all right—we can manage it."

Cavendish led the golden-chestnut down to a stream of ice-cold water that stole from a bronze-green blur on the horizon that was a spruce forest, and let the mare stand where the waters babbled over a gravel-studded crossing; and with his hands rubbed the fever of the night's gallop from her tendons; and with his neckcloth washed her nostrils and her lips and her eyes, and held the cloth between her ears. Then the loosened girth was cinched tight; each foot examined to see that no gravel-stone lurked in the frog; and on again the two, that were like comrades, raced on their mission.

Cavendish knew the trail well. He had passed Vermilion Creek—that was fifty miles from Fort Andrew; now he skirted Egg Lake, just an elongated pond, its waters, strangely blue, dotted by myriad ducks. At midday, he gave the mare an hour in the young blue-joint grass that clothed the little valley through which wandered Sturgeon River, watching the trail from the bank. At three o'clock, Waster came to a stack of hay in a muskeg which he remembered —it was John Whitford's, and his shack was just beyond. Whitford, being an English half-breed, was supposed to be loyal.

"I ought to jump the trail," Waster muttered; "a breed is a breed, and this duck may be a rebel." Then he looked at the mare; she stood low-drooped in the neck—her feet wide apart. "You're tired, old girl, and it's rough going off the trail. I'll take a chance; this pinto man may have information—and grub."

He slipped one revolver into his shirt, letting the other rest in its place in his belt. As he rode up to the turf-roofed, low-slouching shack, a colony of train-dogs charged out at him; and then a dozen breeds came forth, rifle in hand. Cavendish realized that he had popped his head into a dangling noose that the slightest mischance would draw tight.

"Every devilish one of that outfit is a rebel," Waster muttered. Then aloud, in answer to their greeting, he said: "Ho, boys, it's a hell of a long trail from here to de Beaver. Got any grub?"

As the breeds crowded around, eying Montana Gold from every point, Waster recognized one as Felix Monkman.

"Dat's pretty damn fine hoss, I t'ink me. Where you get bronco lak dat?" asked Monkman.

"Bought him from Buck Rolan' me."

"Who's Buck Rolan'? Where he get dat hoss?"

"I don' know me; he say a English-man is die, an' mak' him presen' dis hoss."

"Dat's Waster Cavendish cayuse."

"Dat's my hoss now; I don' know no Cavendish mans."

"You wan' for sell him?"

"An' be set afoot, wit' de redcoats poppin' der guns lak fools, an' swearin' for keel ever' fell' what's not white man?"

As he spoke, Waster uncinched the saddle, and threw it and the bridle in a careless heap on the sod. Then he swaggered nonchalantly into the shack.

As Waster ate the food Whitford set out for him, he developed a plan for getting away. The rebels in the shack would all be mounted; working from this datum, Waster's vocabulary became of a lurid sportiveness.

"By Goss! dat's hell of a fas' hoss," he swore, through a mouthful of bacon. "I never see me a bronco run lak dat mare. I t'ink me I don' sell dat yellow mare 'tall—jus' keep him for race."

"How you lak for try beat my olê hoss?" Monkman asked. "I got ole cayuse dat I drive all tam in Red River cart. By Goss! I'll mak' match wit' you' yellow mare."

"All right," Waster answered; "I'll race you' cayuse. How many skins you wan' bet—how far you wan' run?"

"Same's alway race in de ole tam—de man dat win tak' both hoss," Monk-man answered.

From the first, Cavendish felt that a huge breed, Baptiste Lefèvre, the leader of the party, was suspicious of him. Whenever he raised his head from his food, from beneath the half-breed's massive forehead a pair of piercing black eyes returned his look. The prospect of a race acted as a relieving distraction upon all the rebels except the yellow-red giant. The distance and form of the race led to an interminable wrangle. Waster affected a gentle indifference, saying: "Dat's new hoss for me, dat yellow mare; p'r'aps she's bloody fas' for half-mile, p'r'aps she can run down buffalo bull—I don' know me. I t'ink 'bout mile pretty fair for ever' fell'."

Then, the others jabbering in Cree, he would join in, and agree first with one and then with the other. Once he said to himself, "If I can make that long sweep of a Mephistopheles think I'm a bit of a fool, I may not have to plug him with lead to get away."

Finally, half a mile out along the trail, turn a dead poplar and gallop back, was agreed upon; and Waster thought sweetly of how he would gently leave the return journey with its victory to Monkman. But the leader, who had sat evilly silent, objected that the run with a turn was no good. "I will take Lynx Howes," he said in Cree, "and together we will go to Springcreek, which is a mile. There we will start these two swift runners, and they will gallop back here to the shack. That is a good way, is it not, brothers?"

Then the horses were saddled. Waster smiled to himself when Monkman's hope was brought up out of the creek-flat. He knew the horse well—a flea-bitten roan bronco named Kewatin, meaning "the North Wind"; he had seen him win at Fort Saskatchewan.

With an inward groan, Cavendish

Drawn by George Gibbs

"The oath died away in a scream of fright and rage, as the chestnut mare swerved and crashed into him"

ostentatiously placed his blanket and caribou-skin coat against the log wall of the shack; then he loosed his belt, and taking from it the revolver, carelessly threw it with his other goods, saying, "Dat's good-lookin' hoss what m'sieu got; goin' to be a damn hot race, I t'ink me. I don' wan' for carry no dead-weight."

He saw the black eyes that were always watching him clear a little at this evidence of his intention to return to the shack. But Lefèvre carried a rifle swung across his knees as they jogged out toward the starting-point of the race.

"Here is de start," Lefèvre said, wheeling his cayuse.

"All right," Waster answered; "we'll go fer de li'le run back, an' if he's fair start, you drop de hat, m'sieu."

"I don' drop no hat me; I jus' call 'Marse'—dat's bes' way."

"He's most determined to get shot," Waster muttered, regretfully.

Then Monkman and Cavendish went back; and as the latter wheeled Montana Gold behind Kewatin, he slipped his hand beneath his shirt. He could see the rebel leader's finger tickling the trigger of his rifle, which a little swing would bring into play.

"Go on!" Waster called to Monkman; and the two horses, familiar with the racing game, sprang forward like hounds slipped from the leash. With joyous eagerness, the breed stole a length of start. The mare's nose lapped on the roan's quarter; the chestnut mare, her mouth wide open, was straining at the reins that her rider had knotted short. Now they were within a stride of the starter, who sat grim and erect in his saddle, ready at the first suspicious movement to send a bullet through the heart of the man he distrusted. Ah! by the great Manitou, it was to be a race! Lefèvre's blood leaped hot to the beat of the mad hoofs that sounded a loved rhythm in his ears.

"Marse!" the swarthy chief yelled, a frenzy of delight blurring his eyes to all but the passionate reach of the eager animals. "Sacré—hell!"—the oath died away in a scream of fright and rage, as the chestnut mare swerved and crashed into him.

The big breed's startled cry had not ceased to vibrate, when it was echoed to silence by the cackle of Waster's long-necked Colt's, and a hot fragment of something like molten iron ripped at the breed's thigh—even at the base of his skull he could feel the mad thing tearing as though a serpent fanged him in a dozen places. Twice Waster's gun spat from its narrow mouth, its thin, hard lips, a vicious command, and Lynx Howes lay beside his chief, his thin fingers clutching at the short grass in animal rage.

Then the chestnut, plunging from the collision, and all but thrown, was wheeled, and her slim-pointed ears penciled the southern sky, which was the way of Fort Carford. Low to her neck, flat on the wither, leaned Waster; and there was need. Gather your loins and race, gallant mare! make small the mark, brave rider! Lefèvre seeks to rise; he cannot. Hate concentrates his mind; his Winchester—he reaches it. It is at his shoulder. Along the open trail he trains the sights; the hazard is cast; and the bullet, speeding in the groove of chance, flattens against the shoulder-blade of the brave messenger.

"Ugh! almost a cropper!" Waster's voice drove the mare faster. At the start Monkman had raked his Mexican rowels up the pepper-and-salt flank of the roan, yelling with joy because he had stolen the lead. Ten yards, and the imperious, harsh bark of the pistol came to him; then the cry of his chief. The breed drew the roan's head to his chest, swung him to a turn, and galloped back to where the two men lay. Curious dabs of red flecked their bodies—their own blood, cast back by the leaves as the wounded men writhed.

Howes clutched at the air, then at his shirt-collar; his legs twitched; he sat bolt upright—his eyes wide-staring, not seeing; and then—he was dead.

Lefèvre's gun, a sigh of smoke issuing from the muzzle, dropped from his hands. "Trail de moneas—tak' dat odder gun!" In fragments he gave the order.

Monkman was down; he had the

gun; then on the back of the speedy roan he raced, his hatchet-face of swarthy greasiness hung forward like a hawk's. It was a Hudson's Bay trade gun he carried, a muzzle-loader, and the only ammunition was the one charge it held. On they raced. Stretch her muscles as Montana Gold might, the roan could not be shaken off.

Waster's breeches were glued to his hips. "I'm bleeding," he muttered. "If I weaken, I'm a loser; that hound is waiting for a pot-shot."

Soon he rode unsteadily; he rolled in the saddle; he was growing weak. The mare, checked in her stride, changed her feet. "If I could plug that hole, to stop the blood, I might make it; if I could wing that breed—curse him!" he thought. He must—Waster must wing the breed, or the breed would creep up, and up, and at the last get his pot-shot.

Ahead, the tops of spruce showed, springing from the prairie as though the trees were buried; that meant a creek-bed. Waster rocked violently, pitched, clutched the horn, and let his body dangle to one side as though he would fall; and, as the mare drove into the coulée, he drew the rein, slipped to the trail, and struck her over the quarter with his heavy hat. Startled, she plunged forward through the little ford, and up the other bank.

Waster slipped into the undergrowth of dogwood, and crept back to the edge of the hill; there he hid behind a black poplar. He knew exactly what his pursuer would do. The breed would see that Cavendish was falling from the saddle; then the riderless mare, galloping in fright, would convince him that the white man was down. Monkman, with the caution of a Wood Cree, would dismount, and creep, cunning as a wolverene, to the brink of the hill for a shot at his victim.

As Waster listened, there was a slipping sound as though leaves scurried over dry grass. Again! It was from beside the trail—his side. The wounded man could see nothing; there was just that sound as of palms rubbed together,

and then silence, as the breed, creeping, searched the coulée for his mark.

Closer, closer came the whisper of the crushed grass and the troubled leaves, until it seemed as if Waster could stretch out his hand and grasp the creeper who sought his life. And then, as a little cloud of dust suddenly spirals up from a roadway, the head and shoulders of the murderous breed silently topped the gray-leaved wolf-willow ten feet from the black poplar. Monkman turned his head sharply at a sibilant whistle from Waster's lips, to look down an unsympathetic lane of steel, at the bottom of which lurked death.

"Hands up! That's right—walk toward me! There, turn the butt of that gun this way—so; pass it now! Marse! steady—just in front—so!" The white man's lips bit the words off.

Out on the prairie Waster spoke again. "I didn't kill you, because I needed you. Peel that shirt from your back, and tie up this shoulder good and tight. Plug the wound with this—wet it!" and Waster tossed the breed his wedge of tobacco. "If you make a break, I'll kill you."

Still covering Monkman with his gun, Waster made the breed lead the roan, that had been tied to a tree, over the coulée, and along the trail until they came to Montana Gold, who was quietly clipping the young grass, waiting for her master.

"Now, I'm going to confisticate your cayuse and gun, nichie," Waster said; "and you ought to be damn glad to get off with your life. Now, Marse! Hit the back trail."

Cavendish climbed wearily to Montana's back, and, leading the roan, once more took up the trail to Fort Carford, muttering, "I'm too weak to risk taking that skunk in as a prisoner."

It was midnight when the sentry challenged him. And when a regiment swung out of the fort gates in an hour, Waster, hearing the drums, said: "I've made good. Some one tell Major Woodcote to burn the address I gave him, and not blab."

33

Crossing the Rocky Mountains of the North

ROBERT DUNN

OUTING

MAY, 1903

CROSSING THE ROCKY MOUNTAINS
OF THE NORTH

By ROBERT DUNN

HOW I came on August 12, 1898, to be at Fort St. John, British Columbia, is a story beginning back East, in June, with spells of big-game longing, gold craze, and a boyish fervor to set foot in the heart of our northern wilderness; mostly the last—"horizon fever," we called it. It lured Jack and me from Edmonton, Alberta, on the Hudson Bay slope, to struggle 350 miles, driving pack horses, northwest across the muskegs of Athabasca; and then, with straps galling our shoulders, to drag Peterboro canoes 200 miles more up Peace River in flood time.

Fort St. John is a Hudson's Bay fur post in the least-known corner, probably, of North America; the triangular space that the eastern boundary of British Columbia, striking straight north from the west-trending Rockies, at latitude 54°, makes with the mountains and the south border of the Yukon district. It is the country of Peace River, the main head water of the Mackenzie; of the last herd of bison (which I never saw); of the deadly Liard parallel to it, a hundred miles north, whose fur posts were abandoned in the '50s, after voyageurs by the dozen were swept to death in its "Hell Gate" and "Devil's Portage."

In '98, swallowed in the vast Hudson's Bay country, were 1,000 gold-seekers bound for the Yukon, mostly city tenderfeet, "busted" ranchers, and prospectors, men least fitted in character and experience for sub-arctic life; men lured by the false dreams of gold fever, their ignorance of geography, and the lies of those at Edmonton who wanted their town boomed, to do the impossible, by crossing 2,000 miles of unexplored swamps, rivers, and mountains to the Yukon. How of these men, 200 by the lowest estimate died in the land, frozen, murdered for their grub, hung by their own hands, the Pacific Coast read when the survivors reached it next spring.

Ten minutes after we landed at St. John on the Peace, where the northern river scarp is .bowed about an aspen flat and the mud and logs of the factor's home and geranium garden, I found Jack excited by tales of bison and a grizzly then terrifying the Indians back of the fort. He was for hunting. I was n't. So long had I travelled west in this flat country, through the smoke of forest fires, that the fret for great heights and snow was in my blood.

By the post storehouse, which smelt of briny pork, smoked moose-hide, and the gutty underside of beaver pelts, I also walked. A black-haired man in a black sweater was boiling tea by the door. Six cayuses stood by, only one saddled, only three packed. That struck me. According to the free speech of the trail, I said:

"Pulling out to-night?"

"Right off," he answered, "for Graham."

Disheartened Gold-Seekers Tracking Homeward Up Parsnip River,
Head Water of the Mackenzie, to Escape Starvation, September, 1898.

To me, wearied with the talk of heart-broken argonauts, which meted death and starvation to all that had gone before them, Fort Graham, or B. L. O. (Bear Lake Outpost, officially to the H. B. C.), was remoter than the Barrens, though I knew it lay on the Finlay River, west across the Rockies, and that in all the North it was the remotest post from a grub base, and had twice been abandoned.

" Alone ? " I asked.

" Alone," the dark man answered. " There won't no one come with me. The trail has a bad name—if there is a trail," he added,

said Carter, as we rode through the young aspen groves and purple fire-weed of the prairie. " Some say two hundred miles and some four. A dozen outfits has struck out ahead of us to cross to Graham following Moodie. Those sorefeet at the post think they 're all lost or dead. Nothing 's been heard, except from Black Dan's outfit ; that got back a ways and lost itself again."

Every one knew that Major Moodie had been sent by the Canadian Government to get overland to Dawson in six months. At Edmonton they said he was " cutting wagon roads" ; and perhaps this lie was responsible

Argonauts' Pack Train Leaving Peace River for the Rocky Mountains, Where All That Had Preceded It Were Supposed To Be Lost.

eyeing me ; and I saw his eye was the right sort—nervous, piercing—the pioneer's. Perhaps I mumbled something.

" You mean you want to come along with me ? " he asked slowly. " Well, there 's two horses here that I ain't packing."

So I bought a rope bridle and saddle from the post missionary.

" All right," said Jack ; " take care of yourself," when he heard what I was up to. He had a look at Carter and knew that this year, in the North, to be free of one partner one minute and have another the next was the way of the land.

" No one knows how far it is to Graham,"

for more gold-seekers' deaths in the land than any other. The wilderness had swallowed him as Peace River closes over a pebble. Miles apart we had seen the triple notch of the police blaze on spruces, often far from any trail. Moodie had left Edmonton a year ago and no one had heard from him. Yet every gold-dreamer in the land was following Moodie, following Moodie.

" He got here in November," said Carter. " One man had died on his hands. But he was bound he 'd cross the mountains that winter, though Gunn, the factor, could n't find a Siwash that knew the pass, and said he 'd die in his tracks. So he set the squaws

Map Showing Author's Route.

at the post making mits and moccasins just the same, till the tents were like sweat shops, says Gunn; and he got the bucks bending birch for sledges. After a while they found a Siwash named Dick Eggs that said he'd been through the Rockies to Graham as a kid. Moodie left here with him, in December, with a ten-horse outfit drawing sleds, and six dog teams. They were to kill the horses to eat in the mountains. Well, Eggs faked he was sick and shook them this side of the pass, twenty-one days out. Provisions were low. The Siwashes they met would n't sell them moose.

"Moodie had the right stuff, eh? And he had it at fifty below zero. And after he'd killed the horses, he'd have food for men and dogs for only three weeks more.

"If he'd 'a waited at St. John, it would take him two years to fetch the Upper Yukon. He spelt failure to his orders, staying or going. I wonder how he felt, I do," Carter rambled on. "But I've a notion that sort of person can't get there unless he lays for the worst and bucks the worst odds he can find, and one in a thousand has that streak, and people call them fools and laugh at them; and that makes a choosing of the tough way all the harder, for a man does n't like to get the grin when he knows his chances are for ending him. I'd like to know that man. I believe he's got there."

And Carter was a piano drummer from Michigan, twenty-two years old, who had dreamed of gold, and left the wife of a year. No, all were not British "remittance men," Arizona "palousers," and bank clerks on the trail.

That night we overtook and camped with John and Hiram Burton, bearded Mormons, whose big hearts let them travel with, and feed "Mr. Doolittle," of New Jersey, a morose, black-haired carpenter and his one black horse with raw withers; and "Colorado Pete," white-haired and seventy, who held forth, like a stump orator, on Denver when it was where the trail forked. Mighty tales they told that night of grizzly fights in the Wasatch peaks.

We left them and traveled west, then northwest, three days. Now we slid down terraces to the Peace flats, where Indian fires shone through the sweet wood smoke like ropes of flame under the balsam groves; and we heard Amontio, the Beaver chief, and his sons in their scarlet caps, gallop across the glimmering prairie shouting, "O 'hé, O 'hé!" as their lithe bodies and beaded rifles swung madly in the saddle. And we slept under their blackened canvas, where the stringy moose meat hung over smouldering cotton-wood, where frowsy women scraped and scraped the pelts with sharp stones, and children beat the yelping, thieving huskies. One dawn, heavy with the scent of the North—balm o' Gilead, spruce smoke, dried grass, sun-baked clay, and all faint animal odors—we climbed the river hills, that rose like smoky exhalations, and plunged into the prairie beyond.

We were following Indian trails, by horse sense, on the lookout for Halfway River, which enters the Peace from the north; traveling twelve hours a day, often camping without water, beating the horses over burned windfalls, strewn thick as jackstraws; dragging them through muskegs, fighting mosquitoes. Forever we searched for the mountains. Once we "lay over" (rested), but there is no rest on such a venture as this in such a land. Once in the North, it is said, you must afterward travel forever from camp to camp across the face of the world. Carter would say at night: "I tell you, boy, once you've hit the trail, you can never leave it."

Then we would camp on a flat of lean grass. No whisky jack foraged our duffle. Under some constraint, all life had vanished from the country. But the fire lit, a sudden sense of intimacy would pervade the place, though no human ever had camped here before. This is the secret of the wanderer's at-homeness in the world: the memory of old camping places. Night forces you to stop in the purgatory of some muskeg, a moose head with bleached horns and rotting hair spiked on a tree above you—but once

"Mr. Doolittle," of New Jersey, Who Arrived at Wrangel Island in the Spring of 1899 With a Story of Frightful Suffering on the Edmonton Trail.

spread your bed, and the place is intimate as a meadow at home. Travel east, travel north and west, then pass this camp again. There the remotest memories in life return. It is as if you had reached home after years on far continents; and to have these camps scattered over the world is not to be a man without a country, but to have the world your door-yard.

That night, Sunday, we came upon the Halfway stretching north into the sun, an avenue of fretted gold. Long Jim, from California, tottered down into camp behind us with Nova Scotia Mack and the marvel of

Most of his sort were worse than a silk hat in the North. Mack and Jim were going ahead with his horses to find winter pasture. Typical of the best in the land they were, even in name, for most good prospectors are Macks and the rest Jims or Bobs, and born wanderers they were, as at bottom every gold-seeker on the trail was—cooks, noblemen, gamblers all, though in most their dreams had proved mightier than their manhood. Say what you will, it was not alone the thirst for gold that drove the hordes of '98 north; but unknown to each of them, perhaps, a spark in their hearts of the old

Gold-Seekers' Camp at Little Slave Lake, Athabasca Territory, July, 1898.

the country, a huge bay packhorse that was stone blind and had to be led. Many men had tried it, given up, and passed the beast on, though he could carry two hundred pounds; but Mack would n't sell him for $300. Mack could travel faster than we, leading him with a halter across the Rockies on the worst trail in North America. This tall, angular man with gentle eyes and a great beard like the Zeus in the school history was that sort.

Some Englishman had taken them both in his outfit to do the work, and Burnham, the Briton, was now a hundred miles behind.

love for the horizon Columbus and Raleigh felt.

The horse of some ribbon-counter Raleigh, anyway, lay very dead in the river near camp. We avoided it, but Mack and Jim lit their fire, browned their hard bannocks in the gold-pan and boiled their inky tea close by the carcass. Jim began to tell of the boiler shops he'd worked in in 'Frisco, and a ranch he had earned in the Napa Valley.

"Say, you, come closer here," Mack said to us. "This ain't nothin' but a horse. A man," he added tragically, "a human dead man, was drownded once in a Seattle water-main, and the folks down there kept on drinking water till they only found his bones. This here is only a horse. He won't hurt you."

So we rested a day there, Mack and Jim keeping on ahead. Then we traveled northwest two days along the Halfway, where wild roses, dank grass, and kinnikinnick flourished with astounding luxury.

" We ain't slep' much lately, have we ? " said Carter once. " Funny how we can make twenty miles a day and not tucker out. Say, I 've had all sorts of queer dreams since we came into this valley. Have n't you ? " Still

But the muskeg was two days long, the trail being plainly an abandoned winter one, for whenever it could it made for the wettest places, where black spruces stuck like hooded figures out of the reddish moss, or the laden horses floundered pitifully and tore their legs on wither-high windfalls. Such open places are closed in winter, and a dog trail is easily broken over them. When the horses could n't drag their legs from the mud and fell over exhausted, now and then wrenching their bodies to be free, we had to lash and lash them, and at last drag each out with a lariat tied to a free horse's sad-

Poling Up Parsnip River.

no mountains; but that night we camped in a grove of birches, and birches do not grow upon the prairie ; and we lit our pipes, as a pipe should be lit, with their oily bark.

The next noon, scrawled in charcoal on a dead cottonwood was—the first of many such warnings:

After five miles no horse feed for twenty-five. All muskeg. Black Dan.

At sunset we climbed north out of the valley into a burned country, whence for a moment we saw the mountains through the smoke in black silhouette against a sulphurous sky.

dle, weakened and quaking.   But no animal happened to fail us yet.

A day so spent hardens heart and soul. The stress of travel in the North can never be expressed.   Sometimes I marveled at the stoic cheerfulness of the desperate argonauts.

On Wednesday we veered west, and scratched on a saddle-crotch, read:

Hole of Hell, Sacred to the memory of Dollie, Bella, and Calgary Buck, Hic Jacet 400 pounds of flour, 2 of beans, and that damned Hall's compressible stove.

Don't ask how we crossed. I remember

Klondikers on the Peace River, Athabasca, Tracking Peterboro Canon With Eight Month's Grub Toward Fort St. John.

Carter ahead, dripping with mud, calling to me, dripping by the trembling cayuses, "River! river!" and we came out again upon the inexorable Halfway. This time we did ford it, and camped—our twelfth day on the trail—where we caught thirty-five pounds of rainbow trout with bacon fat in an hour, while the cleared sun lit up opalescent rock and snow toward the head of a western tributary. In the dawn we followed that stream, again across prairie, the uttermost corner of it in all America, tucked between mountain and barrens, but fairer and more silent in this month of the Golden Eagle than Iowa or Minnesota. Somewhere here bison roamed; northward, ducks chattered on lakes strewn like broken mirrors; but in the stillness here, only the faint polar wind edged glittering fields of ice-cloud across the sky; and our quest was the setting sun.

Once a horse ran whinnying to join us; a horse not lost, but left to die, for his hoofs were split, and his back eaten away by flies. Tenderfeet had left him there, for they have a strange short-sighted sympathy; the old prospector will kill his worn-out servant. It is only a short twinge for him, and in the North the mind broods on what is left behind. But we could not shoot him; he was not our horse.

We camped under an ochre dome reaching above tree line, the first mountain. That night water in the teapot froze hard. In the morning reddish peaks seemed to have sprung all about us—single, naked, sharp; though due west a way seemed

Amontio, Chief of the Beaver Indians, Believed to Have Pursued Six White Men to the Liard River and Murdered Them in the Early Spring of '98.

open. It was the entrance to the pass. We were packed and off at dawn.

At the end of the meadow the trail forked. One track was barred by a spruce trunk chopped flat, on which was scrawled:

Take the left-hand trail. Every one ahead of the bulls has gone wrong. Black Dan, August 2nd.

A bull outfit had left St. John, August 1; most of the gold-seekers in early spring. So the prophecy of the Indians to Moodie, the beliefs of the St. John sorefeet, the very menace of the vacant sky of the North, might be fulfilled. Many things are pleasanter to come on in the wilderness than words like those. Nearness to the lost, helplessness to aid them, gives you feelings to be wary of in the North. Unlike the sea, the forest never even gives up its dead. We said nothing. This day on which we were to triumph, entering the pass, was blighted.

And had Mack and Jim seen the warning?

Soon we plunged into one of the cañons that flank the Rockies all along the range; in the North small affairs, compared to the Royal Gorge and such; but, while in Colorado you climb 8,000 feet, before really entering peaks hardly 6,000 feet higher, the low sub-arctic plain is but 1,500 feet above the sea in the Peace Valley, and mountains of 7,000 or 8,000 feet rise sheer from it. So here you get an equal, or better, effect of height, as the Northern Rockies are far more pinnacled and slender.

Up out of a cañon our pack train wandered across meadows of bunch grass and white anemones, in a fierce rain that hid the peaks and the trend of the pass; but at sunset crooked elbows and haunches of rock started out of mists curdled by icy winds from ahead, and soon smooth peaks layered with crumpled brown strata, plain as in a boy's geology, seemed after our prairie life pressing forward to crush us. The next day, the trail followed under the northern summits, snowless still, though we could see the low line joining the brown upper moss from which the snow had just melted to the green below. Once we passed a pole like a well sweep, dangling a loop of babiche over a bark shelf atop four-lopped spruces, where skins long ago had been cached from wolverines. Far beyond lay the bare timbers of an old Siwash camp where the way suddenly mounted and narrowed, turning a little south between the mountains—to camp by a snaky meadow stream. Near thirty miles we had struggled up the pass, and still far ahead nameless, tented peaks of snow shone in the late light like windowed castles at sunset. And boiling beans on the fourteenth night from St. John over our willow fire, darkness rushed up the tottering gorges, stars came out overhead in the narrow fillet from east to west, and tendrils of the aurora rose and sank over the northern heights.

The next night we topped, as we thought, the summit of the pass—5,000 feet or more high—where a snowy pyramid, perhaps 3,000 feet higher, with a gray blue "incipient" glacier on its face was thrust out to narrow the way that pitched at once invisibly downward. That noon we had come to a maze of trails and a scrub spruce grove with all the lower branches lopped, where we found a pile of willow withes and broken travois with rusty clamps and runners clinging to the bleached wood; an empty can of evaporated potatoes; a heap of rotten thongs and moccasins, and a rusty horsebit. A winter camp!—Moodie's camp, of course, where he had killed his horses, though thanks to wolf and wolverine not a bone of them remained. Then all afternoon, as the ranges grew more saw-tooth and narrower, topping one another giddily far away north and south, our own beasts mounted through the reddish muskeg more and more wearily under the wintry sky, staggering with their loads. As we drove them up the last slope they stampeded, and the bay mare spread her legs, whinnied, and toppled over on her

right side. We ran to her. A horse that once "fails" like that is useless for days; and we could not delay, for the smell of snow was in the air, and snow kills all fodder, hides trails, may mean—never mind what.

"Leave her?" I said.

"I won't shoot," said Carter. We divided her load between the pinto and the buckskin. She got up and staggered behind one of the barked white spruces that lifted twisted arms like a living skeleton from the gray willows. Well, were we not tenderfeet ourselves?

We camped on the west slope of the pass, below an azure pond, filled by foamy cataracts from the glacier. After supper Carter saw a herd of goats above it, crossing the mountains like a line of gray insects; and all night the marmots whistled above the roar of torrents, and we woke in the morning under two inches of snow—with the "sponge" for yeast bread, which I had put in my blanket bag to raise, hard as a rock. But we ate it, for the tougher flour is the better it "stays" with you, and that's all you want of food in the North.

We shivered and slept in our blankets all day. Late, it suddenly grew light, and Carter ran down toward the V-shaped opening ahead, which surely, we thought, led to the Finlay Valley.

"Hey-a! Hey-a! Look, look at her clear!" he shouted.

Far away, across the valley, another range of peaks, higher and snowier, were struggling with mist and sunlight. Another range! What range? Why west of us, for had we not crossed the mountains? No; the Rockies we had not yet crossed. And this was not the Finlay Valley below, after all.

The Rocky Mountains, in this latitude, lie in three parallel ridges: the stream below us was a small tributary of the Peace, and beyond the range ahead—the middle and highest—should be the Ospica River, tributary to the Finlay near its mouth. The northern part of British Columbia is declared by George Dawson to be the most "persistently mountainous" region of North America.

By the next night we had crossed this desolate valley of burnt dwarf trees, with its umber mountains and steel-cold sky, and camped in a coulee in the shadow of a white peak, shaped like a titanic church, with long rock nave and tall spire—Cathedral Mountain, we called it. Its sharp rock edges burned overhead in the sunset, for we had come from a cheerless country of twisted yellow strata into a land of stark limestone color, snow, and cold, blue shadows.

At dawn the sound of unfamiliar horse bells came across the frosted clearing, and the Burton brothers' eight beasts—reduced from ten—tottered through the scrub, with old Pete, his two pintos, and Mr. Doolittle behind. The brothers, Hiram and John, each drove four horses separately to opposite ends of the clearing. Before they had driven the whole train together. Hiram's buckskin mare stampeded past John and

distances to understand. Monotony, exhaustion, something, aggravates man's tiny peculiarities, so that in the tension of travel nerves grate on nerves, till the best of partners hate one another. Strong seekers of the Pole, who fall to quarreling like children and excite the public mind about it, could tell of this—if they would: but this unique ailment, on reaching civilization, like nostalgia, vanishes, evil dream that it is, and all hands feel sorry and ashamed. Men whom the craving for sugar enrages are known through the North as "sugar-hogs."

"Part sugar-hogging," said Pete, stroking

Deserted Indian Cache, Upper Halfway River, Rocky Mountains, British Columbia.

mired herself in the stream. John didn't try to stop her, nor help when we all fell to and roped the poor thing out. Every one was silent and sullen. Plainly there had been a quarrel.

"What about was it?" asked Carter of Pete. "Who's been sugar-hogging?"

Why craving for certain foods—especially sugar—in the North becomes with many men such a passion that to see a partner's spoon go too often into the sack to sweeten one cup of tea may stir up ungovernable pangs of anger and jealousy, you must lead this lonely life of travel across imperious

his white beard, "but most that two of their horses failed top of the pass, and the scrap was which two—John's or Hiram's. They divided up equal, and they ain't spoke since." And the Burtons were brothers, alone on the Edmonton trail, traveling together. Of all the outfits we saw disband— and three out of five did so that year—the first to divide up were men of common blood. Brother to brother, there is less "human nature" to be worn down to fundamentals; their tragedies are generally deeper and swifter. But if six months of the trail had not drawn real blood between the Burtons, it could not now. And perhaps the brotherhood of Mormons is different.

"I'd have liked to shake them Burtons, the both of them. They're no good, anyhow. They used to talk me and them silly, and now they travel too darned slow," ended old Pete. But when John drew Carter aside, I heard him say:

"Pete and Doolittle has n't fifty pounds of grub left, and I'm still afeeding them. And they cry for soup—soup, every morning, man."

"Drop them," I heard Carter answer "Shake them." And I believe that was the cruelest thing that ever passed his lips.

John shook his head. He knew it is better to share your grub to the last bean with men alone with you in the wilderness, than to have them follow on starving, crawl under your tarpaulin to steal, and perhaps knife you. Starving men do not ask questions. Every man's life in the North that year was a race with starvation, and between a week's grub and a year's there was little difference, here on the way to the tragic Nowhere whither most trails led.

By their halters, we dragged the horses up Cathedral Mountain, and at noon reached the summit of the second pass. Past the ever-present dead horse, the trail pitched straight down a stream-bed, where our live animals cut their legs and lay down on the sharp stones, till we beat or dragged them on; and by night we camped again in burnt forests, under a spire sharp as the Matterhorn. Wednesday, the nineteenth day on the trail, the cañon curved southwest till we saw open country ahead, and traveled with the exciting certainty of coming out into some open. But suddenly we left the fast-growing stream, and struck north at right angles, by a sign which read:

Eight miles to Ospica River. Worst trail yet. Take all day resting your horses beforehand. Pack light and double anyhow.

Beneath, in another hand was written:

lotes of gotes Billy shot five.

But being packed light (and encouraged by Billy) we defied the warning, and hauled our horses up the 400-foot bank to make the Ospica, to which for weeks we had looked forward.

But we saw no "gotes," and that trail was the worst yet, the worst I have ever seen, or hope to see. I remember Doolittle and the Burtons far behind, struggling through that burned and plague-stricken forest, where not a blade of grass, not a twig of underbrush grew from the pounded floor of sepia clay, that shook everywhere with mud springs like running sores; at last coming to a big stream in the twilight, with dense forests beyond—a forest slashed with gullies of inky mud, in each of which lay a rotting carcass. I can feel now the smell and touch of that flesh, the frenzy of our horses scenting the dead white hair and bones in the darkness; how they whipped their legs before they fell, and we hauled them out, unpacked them, and scraped the mud from the food-sacks; hear the eloquence of Mormon oaths, and the echo of our cries. And then we came out by the river in the moonlight, the Ospica.

On two gnarled trees by the river, Carter made out another sign. It read, lit by match after match:

Place the eye on a level with the second limb of the blazed tree; look northwest by compass toward the notch in mountains, and follow down toward the tall spruce tree. You will see the corner of a cache. Follow up the shore till it is in line with the flat topped peak, and you will be at the ford. It is 70 miles to B. L. O.—Moodie.

"Poe's Gold Bug—The Death's Head and Bishop's Glass!" I exclaimed.

Carter turned to the white faces of Doolittle and the rest.

"Moodie, Moodie, did you see that?" he cried.

"So he got through, did he, to here?" drawled John Burton. "But cache, ford—what'd he mean by that, boys? Must have been all winter—six months till May, when the river broke—getting over the mountains."

"All winter," repeated Carter, "unless he cached part of his stuff here and came back after it."

This was first news of Moodie's having crossed the mountains, news for which all the disheartened, grubless argonauts lived on to hear. And how these men with us felt as we rode to the ford, their long silence told—and hid.

As our horses plowed in the dark through the swift water of the Ospica, we heard the roar and swish of other horses approaching us in midstream from the far side. We called, and a familiar voice answered. Jim, the Scotchman, Mack's partner, drew up beside us in the middle of the river. At least he and Mack had seen Black Dan's warning at the entrance of the first pass. But Jim was all alone now. Without parley, Jim said, and rather dazedly, I thought:

"Burnham, the bloated Britisher, he'll never get the rest of the outfit through the mountains alone before snowfall. One of us had ought to go back long ago to help him. Mack'll cut hay enough for two at B. L. O."

We said nothing. We knew snow had already fallen in the pass, and likely was still falling.

"Well," went on Jim, "I've got to be traveling nights. It'll be snowing in the pass before long, I guess, and no man's a right to hit those high places under the snow without company."

As we reached shore, we saw Mack's fire blaze out up under the old cache. He was sitting with his head buried in his hands. By his side were two whittled sticks, one two inches shorter than the other—the lots which they had drawn to see who should return across the mountains.

Three days later we reached Fort Graham, in the intramontaine valley, which from Montana north is occupied successively by the Columbia, Fraser, Parsnip, and Finlay rivers. Mack, blind horse and all, had counted his footsteps from St. John, like a Michigan timber-cruiser, and made the distance 346 miles. In the pass beyond the Ospica, a cubical rent in the range holding

Indian Chapel, Fort Graham, B. C.   In the Absence of Any Missionary Christian Songs Were Sung Here Every Morning, Native Ones Every Night.

What could we say? With a man's resolves in the North you dare not interfere, and the grub-stake man has sold himself; he is a slave of the wilderness. What use to tell Jim it was snowing there now? He would have gone just the same, for there are prospectors with appalling ideas of duty, and to plant apprehension in his heart would be to steal the land's own fire.

"Good-night, and good luck to you," said Carter, grasping his hand.

"Good-night," we all said; and my throat was thick.

Jim laughed a good-night and a good luck to us, and vanished in the dark with the roar of water.

two little ponds, Wanatla, chief of the Tsikani Indians, got fighting mad when I tossed, instead of handed him, a chunk of bannock: and he laughed when our horses slipped off one of his dog-bridges and were mired to their noses. Two Tsikani bucks, back-packing sixty-pound loads thirty-five miles a day—Tsikanis are the best travelers in the North—tramped out our fire the night we swung out of mountains, whispering "Tse! Tse!" (grizzly bear), for we were in the heart of their country. Horses they had never before seen, and ours they fingered from ears to frogs, murmuring, "Hwodsi, hwodsi" (caribou), which it seemed they most resembled.

At the two log huts of B. L. O., in the carmine garden of fire-weed, cleared in deep forest on the Finlay banks, about thirty Klondikers were waiting for Moodie. Many had taken the wrong trail where we saw Dan's warning. Of those who had not yet reached the Fort, they spoke sullenly, presupposing tragedies. Only one man was known yet to have died in the mountains, the partner of old Laundy, a stone-cutter, seventy years of age, whose head had been turned by his friend's agonies in inflammatory rheumatism. It was pitiful to hear old Laundy tell over and over how he had nursed the man up to death, and cut his epitaph in the rock with the tools of his trade which he had carried with him.

Moodie had reached B. L. O., starving, on January 18, and, having no horses to keep up his journey, traveled south for some to Quesnelle, in the Cariboo country—500 miles and back—and left Graham for the indefinite North on July 19. When Fox, the half-breed H. B. C. clerk, asked him when he expected to reach Pelly Banks (on the Upper Yukon), Moodie answered, "Oh, in two years, perhaps." Some prospectors had struck north ahead of him, some had followed.

Never shall I forget that night of September 12, when an Indian guide Fox had sent with Moodie burst into the post, half-starved and tattered, with two big salmon trout, or "sappi," slung upon his shoulder. The argonauts were playing penny ante—they that had mortgaged their homes with hot and certain promises to wives and children to return millionaires, and now for a dollar a day were roofing the Company's storehouse. The Indian had a letter from Moodie. Fox read it aloud, during a fearful silence; how Sylvester's outpost had been reached, 270 miles from Graham, in seventeen days, with only two bags of flour and forty pounds of bacon, and the "outlook pretty desperate"; how twice Moodie had nearly lost everything in forest fires.

Then the courier took one of the goldseekers by the shoulders, and made to press him down upon the floor. Fox asked in the man's tongue what the dumb show meant. The Indian clucked words in his throat and waved his arms. "He says he has found dead white men on the trail," said the clerk to the tense argonauts; "burned or starved, he could not say." And all that night, as I lay out under the big pelt press, their candles shone in moons through their tent walls, and their voices murmured on softly till dawn.

With all these men, who, with Moodie's failure to reach the gold fields, saw their blighted dreams finally wiped out, I soon started south. Nova Scotia Mack came, too; it was no business of mine why he should not. Ice caked our hands as we poled up Parsnip River; deep snow fell on the ninety-mile portage across the Pacific-Arctic watershed; and we were all but wrecked shooting the Nechaco River rapids. But we reached Quesnelle, on Fraser River, in mid-October. I am glad I did not winter in the North with Doolittle and the Burtons, to see enacted the wolfish dramas which we were yet to read of.

Some experiences make men no wiser and age you. Doolittle lived, and one of the worst narratives was his, when he reached Wrangel Island the next June. Of the Burtons or California Jim, I have never heard. Major Moodie somehow did cover the 500 remaining miles to Pelly Banks that year, running down to the forks of the Yukon with the mush ice and reaching the coast over Chilkoot; but the Klondike he did not see.

34

North of Fifty-three

REX E. BEACH

NORTH OF FIFTY-THREE

BY

REX E. BEACH

AUTHOR OF ''THE SHYNESS OF SHORTY,'' ETC.

ILLUSTRATED BY HARRY RALEIGH

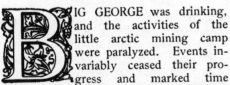

BIG GEORGE was drinking, and the activities of the little arctic mining camp were paralyzed. Events invariably ceased their progress and marked time when George became excessive, and now nothing of public consequence stirred except the quicksilver, which was retiring fearfully into its bulb at the song of the wind which came racing over the lonesome, bitter, northward waste of tundra.

He held the center of the floor at the Northern Club, and proclaimed his modest virtues in a voice as pleasant as the cough of a bull-walrus.

"Yes, me! Little Georgie! I did it. I've licked 'em all from Herschel Island to Dutch Harbor, big uns and little uns. When they didn't suit I made 'em over. I'm the boss carpenter of the arctic and I own this camp; don't I, Slim? Hey? Answer me!" he roared at the emaciated bearer of the title, whose attention seemed wandering from the inventory of George's startling traits toward a card game.

"Sure ye do," nervously smiled Slim, frightened out of a heart-solo as he returned to his surroundings.

361

"wrenched at the circling bands which wheezed the breath from his lungs"

"Well, then, listen to what I'm saying. I'm the big chief of the village, and when I'm stimulated and happy them fellers I don't like hides out and lets me and Nature operate things. Ain't that right?" He glared inquiringly at his friends.

Red, the proprietor, explained over the bar in a whisper to Captain, the new man from Dawson: "That's Big George, the whaler. He's a squaw-man and sort of a bully — see? When he's sober he's on the level strickly, an' we all likes him fine, but when he gets to fightin' the pain-killer, he ain't altogether a gentleman. Will he fight? Oh! Will he fight? Say! he's there with chimes, he is! Why, Doc Miller's made a grub-stake rebuildin' fellers that's had a lingerin' doubt cached away about that, an' now when he gets the booze up his nose them patched-up guys oozes away an' hibernates till the gas dies out in him. Afterwards he's sore on himself an' apologizes to everybody. Don't get into no trouble with him, 'cause he's two checks past the limit. They don't make 'em as bad as him any more. He busted the mold."

George turned, and spying the newcomer, approached, eyeing him with critical disfavor.

362

Captain saw a bear-like figure, clad cap-a-pie in native fashion : Reindeer pants, with the hair inside, clothed legs like rock pillars, while out of the loose squirrel parka a corded neck rose, brown and strong, above which darkly gleamed a rugged face seamed and scarred by the hate of arctic winters. He had kicked off his deer-skin socks, and stood bare-footed on the cold and draughty floor, while the poison he had imbibed showed only in his heated face. Silently he extended a cracked and hardened hand, which closed like the armored claw of a crustacean and tightened on the crunching fingers of the other. Captain's expression remained unchanged and, gradually slackening his grip, the sailor roughly inquired :

"Where'd you come from ?"

"Just got in from Dawson yesterday," politely responded the stranger.

"Well! what're you goin' to do now you're here ?" he demanded.

"Stake some claims and go to prospecting, I guess. You see, I wanted to get in early before the rush next spring."

"Oh! I 'spose you're goin' to jump some of our ground, hey? Well, you ain't! We don't want no claim jumpers here," disagreeably continued the seaman ; "we won't stand for it. This is my camp — see ? I own it, and these is my little children." Then, as the other refused to debate with him, he resumed, groping for a new ground of attack.

"Say! I'll bet you're one of them eddicated dudes, too, ain't you? You talk like a feller that had been to college," and, as the other assented, he scornfully called to his friends, saying : "Look here, fellers ! Pipe the jellyfish ! I never see one of these here animals that was worth a cuss. They plays football an' smokes cigareets at school ; then when they're weaned they come off up here an' jump our claims 'cause we can't write a location notice proper. They ain't no good. I guess I'll stop it."

Captain moved toward the door, but the whaler threw his bulky frame against it and scowlingly blocked the way.

"No, you don't. You ain't goin' to run away till I've had the next dance, Mister ! Eddication ! Humph ! I ain't begun to tell ye yet what a useless little barnacle you are."

Red interfered, saying : "Look 'ere, George ; this guy ain't no playmate of yourn. We'll all have a jolt of this disturbance promoter, an' call it off." Then, as the others approached, he winked at Captain, and jerked his head slightly toward the door.

The latter, heeding the signal, started out, but George leaped after him and, seizing an arm, whirled him back, roaring : "Well, of all the cussed impidence I ever see ! You're too high-toned to drink with us, are you? You don't get out of here now till you take a lickin' like a man."

He reached over his head and, grasping the hood of his fur shirt, with one movement he stripped it from him, exposing a massive naked body, whose muscles swelled and knotted beneath a skin as clear as a maiden's, while a map of angry scars strayed across the heavy chest.

As the shirt sailed through the air Red lightly vaulted to the bar and, diving at George's naked middle, tackled beautifully, crying to Captain : "Get out quick ; we'll hold him."

Others rushed forward and grasped the bulky sailor, but Captain's voice replied : "I sort of like this place, and I guess I'll stay a while. Turn him loose."

"Why, mon, he'll kill ye," excitedly cried Slim. "Get out !"

The captive hurled his peacemakers from him and, shaking off the clinging arms, drove furiously at the insolent stranger.

In the cramped limits of the corner where he stood, Captain was unable to avoid the big man, who swept him with a crash against the plank door at his back, grasping hungrily at his throat. As his shoulders struck, however, he dropped to his knees and, before the raging George could seize him, he avoided a blow which would have strained the rivets of a strength-tester and ducked under the other's arms, leaping to the cleared center of the floor.

Seldom had the big man's rush been avoided and, whirling, he swung a boom-like arm at the agile stranger. Before it landed, Captain stepped in to meet his adversary and, with the weight of his body behind the blow, drove a clenched and bony fist crashing into the other's face. The big head with its blazing shock of hair snapped backward and the whaler drooped to his knees at the other's feet.

The drunken flush of victory swept over Captain as he stood above the swaying figure ; then, suddenly, he felt the great bare arms close about his waist with a painful grip. He struck at the bleeding face below him and wrenched at the circling bands which wheezed the breath from his lungs, but the whaler squeezed him writhing to his breast and, rising, unsteadily wheeled across the floor and in a shiver of broken glass fell crashing against the bar and to the floor.

to the questions of the arrivals. "This feller tried to make a get-away, but George had to have his amusement."

A newcomer addressed the squaw-man in a voice as cold as the wind. "Cut this out, George! This is a friend of mine. You're making this camp a reg'lar hell for strangers, and now I'm goin' to tap your little snap. Cool off—see?"

"'Shut up, curse you, and get in!'"

As the struggling men writhed upon the planks the door opened at the hurried entrance of an excited group, which paused at the sight of the ruin, then, rushing forward, tore the men apart.

The panting Berserker strained at the arms about his glistening body, while Captain, with sobbing sighs, relieved his aching lungs and watched his enemy, who frothed at the interference,

"It was George's fault," explained Slim

Jones's reputation as a bad gun-man went hand in hand with his name as a good gambler, and his scanty remarks invariably evoked attentive answers, so George explained: "I don't like him, Jones, and I was jus' makin' him over to look like a man. I'll do it yet, too," he flashed wrathfully at his quiet antagonist.

"'Pears to me like he's took a hand in the remodeling himself," replied the gambler, "but if you're lookin' for something to do, here's your chance. Windy Jim just drove in and says Barton and Kid Sullivan are adrift on the ice."

"What's that?" questioned eager voices, and, forgetting the recent trouble at the news, the crowd pressed forward anxiously.

"They was crossin' the bay and got carried out by the off-shore gale," explained Jones. "Windy was follerin' 'em when the ice ahead parted and begun movin' out. He tried to yell to 'em, but they was too far away to hear in the storm. He managed to get back to the land and follered the shore ice around. He's over at Hunter's cabin now, most dead, face and hands froze pretty bad."

A torrent of questions followed and many suggestions as to the fate of the men. "They'll freeze before they can get ashore," said one.

"The ice-pack'll break up in this wind," added another, "and if they don't drown, they'll freeze before the floe comes in close enough for them to land."

From the first announcement of his friends' peril, Captain had been thinking rapidly. His body, sore from his long trip and aching from the hug of his recent encounter, cried woefully for rest, but his voice rose calm and clear: "We've got to get them off," he said. "Who will go with me? Three is enough."

The clamoring voices ceased, and the men wheeled at the sound, gazing incredulously at the speaker. "What!" — "In this storm?" — "You're crazy," many voices said.

He gazed appealingly at the faces before him. Brave and adventurous men he knew them to be, jesting with death, and tempered to perils in this land where hardship rises with the dawn, but they shook their ragged heads hopelessly.

"We *must* save them!" resumed Captain hotly. "Barton and I played as children together, and if there's not a man among you who's got the nerve to follow me — I'll go alone, by Heavens!"

In the silence of the room, he pulled the cap about his ears and, tying it snugly under his chin, drew on his huge fur mittens; then with a scornful laugh he turned toward the door.

He paused as his eye caught the swollen face of Big George. Blood had stiffened in the heavy creases of his face like rusted

stringers in a ledge, while his mashed and discolored lips protruded thickly. His hair gleamed red, and the sweat had dried upon his naked shoulders, streaked with dirt and flecked with spots of blood, yet the battered features shone with the unconquered, fearless light of a rough, strong man.

Captain strode to him with outstretched hand. "You're a man," he said. "You've got the nerve, George, and you'll go with me, won't you?"

"What! Me?" questioned the sailor vaguely. His wondering glance left Captain, and drifted 'round the circle of shamed and silent faces — then he straightened stiffly and cried: "Will I go with you? Certainly! I'll go to —— with you."

Ready hands harnessed the dogs, dragged from protected nooks where they sought cover from the storm which moaned and whistled round the low houses. Endless ragged folds of sleet whirled out of the north, then writhed and twisted past, vanishing into the gray veil which shrouded the landscape in a twilight gloom.

The fierce wind sank the cold into the aching flesh like a knife and stiffened the face to a whitening mask, while a fusillade of frozen ice-particles beat against the eye-balls with blinding fury.

As Captain emerged from his cabin, furred and hooded, he found a long train of crouching, whining animals harnessed and waiting, while muffled figures stocked the sled with robes and food and stimulants.

Big George approached through the whirling white, a great squat figure with fluttering squirrel-tails blowing from his parka, and at his heels there trailed a figure, skin-clad and dainty.

"It's my wife," he explained briefly to Captain. "She won't let me go alone."

They gravely bade farewell to all, and the little crowd cheered lustily against the whine of the blizzard as, with cracking whip and hoarse shouts, they were wrapped in the cloudy winding sheet of snow.

II

Arctic storms have an even sameness; the intense cold, the heartless wind which augments tenfold the chill of the temperature, the air thick and dark with stinging flakes rushing by in an endless cloud. A drifting, freezing, shifting eternity of snow, driven by a ravening gale which sweeps the desolate, bald wastes of the Northland.

The little party toiled through the smother till they reached the "egloos" under the breast of the tall coast bluffs, where coughing Eskimos drilled patiently at ivory tusks and gambled the furs from their backs at stud-horse poker.

To George's inquiries they answered that their largest canoe was the three-holed bidarka on the cache outside. Owing to the small circular openings in its deck, this was capable of holding but three passengers, and Captain said: "We'll have to make two trips, George."

"Two trips, eh?" answered the other. "We'll be doin' well if we last through one, I'm thinking."

Lashing the unwieldy burden upon the sled, they fought their way along the coast again till George declared they were opposite the point where their friends went adrift. They slid their light craft through the ragged wall of ice hummocks guarding the shore pack, and dimly saw, in the gray beyond them, a stretch of angry waters mottled by drifting cakes and floes.

George spoke earnestly to his wife, instructing her to keep the team in constant motion up and down the coast a rifle-shot in either direction, and to listen for a signal of the return. Then he picked her up as he would a babe, and she kissed his stormbeaten face.

"She's been a good squaw to me," he said, as they pushed their dancing craft out into the breath of the gale, "and I've always done the square thing by her; I s'pose she'll go back to her people now, though."

The wind hurried them out from land, while it drove the sea-water in freezing spray over their backs and changed their fur garments into scaly armor, as they worked through the ice cakes, peering with strained eyes for a sign of their friends.

The sailor, with deft strokes, steered them between the grinding bergs, raising his voice in long signals like the weird cry of a siren.

Twisting back and forth through the floes, they held to their quest, now floating with the wind, now paddling desperately in a race with some drifting mass which dimly towered above them and splintered hungrily against its neighbor close in their wake.

Captain emptied his six-shooter till his numbed fingers grew rigid as the trigger, and always at his back swelled the deep shouts of the sailor, who, with practised eye and mighty strokes, forced their way through the closing lanes between the jaws of the ice pack.

At last, beaten and tossed, they rested disheartened and hopeless. Then, as they drifted, a sound struggled to them against the wind — a faint cry, illusive and fleeting as a dream voice — and, still doubting, they heard it again.

"Thank God! We'll save 'em yet," cried Captain, and they drove the canoe boiling towards the sound.

Barton and Sullivan had fought the cold and wind stoutly hour after hour, till they found their great floe was breaking up in the heaving waters.

Then the horror of it had struck the Kid, till he raved and cursed up and down their little island, as it dwindled gradually to a small acre.

He had finally yielded to the weight of the cold which crushed resistance out of him, and settled, despairing and listless, upon the ice. Barton dragged him to his feet and forced him round their rocking prison, begging him to brace up, to fight it out like a man, till the other insisted on resting, and dropped to his seat again.

The older man struck deliberately at the whitening face of his freezing companion, who recognized the well-meant insult and refused to be roused into activity. Then to their ears had come the faint cries of George, and, in answer to their screams, through the gloom they beheld a long, covered, skin canoe, and the anxious faces of their friends.

Captain rose from his cramped seat, and, ripping his crackling garments from the boat where they had frozen, he wriggled out of the hole in the deck and grasped the weeping Barton.

"Come, come, old boy! It's all right now," he said.

"Oh, Charlie, Charlie!" cried the other. "I might have known you'd try to save us. You're just in time, though, for the Kid's about all in."

Sullivan apathetically nodded and sat down again.

"Hurry up there; this ain't no G. A. R. Encampment, and you ain't got no time to spare," said George, who had dragged the canoe out and, with a paddle, broke the sheets of ice which covered it. "It'll be

"He dreamed quaint dreams, broken by the chilling lash of spray"

too dark to see anything in half an hour."

The night, hastened by the storm, was closing rapidly, and they realized another need of haste, for, even as they spoke, a crack had crawled through the ice-floe where they stood, and, widening as it went, left but a heaving cake supporting them.

George spoke quietly to Captain, while Barton strove to animate the Kid. "You and Barton must take him ashore and hurry him down to the village. He's most gone now."

"But you?" questioned the other. "We'll have to come back for you, as soon as we put him ashore."

"Never mind me," roughly interrupted George. "It's too late to get back here. When you get ashore it'll be dark. Besides Sullivan's freezing, and you'll have to rush him through quick. I'll stay here."

"No! No! George!" cried the other, as the meaning of it bore in upon him. "I got you into this thing, and it's my place to stay here. You must go——"

But the big man had hurried to Sullivan, and, seizing him in his great hands, shook the drowsy man like a rat, cursing and beating a goodly share of warmth back into him. Then he dragged the listless burden to the canoe and forced him to a seat in the middie opening.

"Come, come," he cried to the others; "you can't spend all night here. If you want to save the Kid, you've got to hurry. You take the front seat there, Barton," and, as he did so, George turned to the protesting Captain: "Shut up, curse you, and get in!"

"I won't do it," rebelled the other. "I can't let you lay down your life this way, when I made you come."

George thrust a cold face within an inch of the other's and grimly said: "If they hadn't stopped me, I'd a beat you into dog-meat this morning, and if you don't quit this sniveling I'll do it yet. Now get in there and paddle to beat —— or you'll never make it back. Quick!"

"I'll come back for you then, George, if I live to the shore," Captain cried, while the other slid the burdened canoe into the icy waters.

As they drove the boat into the storm, Captain realized the difficulty of working their way against the gale. On him fell the added burden of holding their course into the wind and avoiding the churning ice cakes. The spray whipped into his face like shot, and froze as it clung to his features. He strained at his paddle till the sweat soaked out of him and the cold air filled his aching lungs.

Unceasingly the merciless frost cut his face like a keen blade, till he felt the numb paralysis which told him his features were hardening under the touch of the cold.

An arm's length ahead the shoulders of the Kid protruded from the deck hole where he had sunk again into the death sleep, while Barton, in the forward seat, leaned wearily on his ice-clogged paddle, moaning as he strove to shelter his face from the sting of the blizzard.

An endless time they battled with the storm, slowly gaining, foot by foot, till in the darkness ahead they saw the wall of shore ice and swung into its partial shelter.

Dragging the now unconscious Sullivan from the boat, Captain rolled and thrashed him, while Barton, too weak and exhausted to assist, feebly strove to warm his stiffened limbs.

In answer to their signals, the team appeared, maddened by the lash of the squaw. Then they wrapped Sullivan in warm robes, and forced scorching brandy down his throat, till he coughed weakly and begged them to let him rest.

"You must hurry him to the Indian village," directed Captain. "He'll only lose some fingers and toes now, maybe; but you've got to hurry!"

"Aren't you coming, too?" queried Barton. "We'll hire some Eskimos to go after George. I'll pay 'em anything."

"No, I'm going back to him now; he'd freeze before we could send help, and, besides, they wouldn't come out in the storm and the dark."

"But you can't work that big canoe alone. If you get out there and don't find him you'll never get back. Charlie! let me go, too," he said; then apologized. "I'm afraid I won't last, though; I'm too weak."

The squaw, who had questioned not at the absence of her lord, now touched Captain's arm. "Come," she said; "I go with you." Then addressing Barton, "You quick go Indian house; white man die, mebbe. Quick! I go Big George."

"Ah, Charlie, I'm afraid you'll never make it," cried Barton, and, wringing his friend's hand, he staggered into the darkness behind the sled wherein lay the fur-bundled Sullivan.

Captain felt a horror of the starving waters rise up in him and a panic shook him fiercely, till he saw the silent squaw waiting for him at the ice edge. He shivered as the wind searched through his dampened

parka and hardened the wet clothing next to his body; but he took his place and dug the paddle fiercely into the water, till the waves licked the hair of his gauntlets.

The memory of that scudding trip through the darkness was always cloudy and visioned. Periods of keen alertness alternated with moments when his weariness bore upon him till he stiffly bent to his work, wondering what it all meant.

It was the woman's sharpened ear which caught the first answering cry, and her hands which steered the intricate course to the heaving berg where the sailor crouched, for, at their approach, Captain had yielded to the drowse of weariness and, in his relief at the finding, the blade floated from his listless hands.

He dreamed quaint dreams, broken by the chilling lash of spray from the strokes of the others, as they drove the craft back against the wind, and he only partly awoke from his lethargy when George wrenched him from his seat and forced him down the rough trail toward warmth and safety.

Soon, however, the stagnant blood tingled through his veins, and under the shelter of the bluffs they reached the village, where they found the anxious men waiting.

Skilful natives had worked the frost from Sullivan's members, and the stimulants in the sled had put new life into Barton as well. So, as the three crawled wearily through the dog-filled tunnel of the egloo, they were met by two wet-eyed and thankful men, who silently wrung their hands or uttered broken words.

When they had been despoiled of their frozen furs, and the welcome heat of whisky and fire had met in their blood, Captain approached the whaler, who rested beside his mate.

"George, you're the bravest man I ever knew, and your woman is worthy of you," he said. He continued slowly, "I'm sorry about the fight this morning, too."

The big man rose and, crushing the extended palm in his grasp, said: "We'll just let that go double, partner. You're as game as I ever see." Then he added: "It *was* too bad them fellers interfered jest when they did—but we can finish it up whenever you say," and as the other, smiling, shook his head, he continued: "Well, I'm glad of it, 'cause you'd sure beat me the next time."

35

The Mysterious Awa-toose and the Strange Nebog-atis

ROBERT T. MORRIS

THE MYSTERIOUS AWA-TOOSE

AND

THE STRANGE NEBOG-ATIS

BY ROBERT T. MORRIS

NAT stepped into the bush and cut a pole. He put a piece of pork on the hook, tucked another piece of pork between his shirt and the waistband of his trousers for provision against sudden need, and sat down upon the wet bank of the river. The whole calm procedure was suggestive of confidence born of success on some former occasion. Nat was an Indian. Years ago he was in the Hudson Bay Company's service, and Wake and I considered ourselves fortunate in getting him to go along with us, to find portages between Flying Post and Moose, on our exploring trip.

We had found plenty of fish all along the way so far, but they were old friends—sturgeon, ling, doré, jackfish, whitefish, lake trout and others of less consequence. What we wanted was to find something new to tell about at the next Canadian Camp dinner in New York, and although our notebooks already described jackfish fully as large as any that we actually caught, and whitefish so toothsome that their deliciousness seemed to be peculiar to the region of our search, there was nevertheless a longing and an unsatisfied feeling that nothing short of a new fish could relieve.

Nat had filled us with expectation, for he had told us that when we reached a certain part of the Kokateesh River we would come upon a fish called the awa-toose, and that they would be caught all of the way from there down to Hudson Bay. The awa-toose, he said, was shaped and colored something like a sucker, but it had teeth and was "very good for heat." Furthermore, it would take almost any sort of lure. Now, there were three suckers in the river, the common gray one, that was round and

pudgy; the ember mullet with graceful outlines and golden-bronze in color, with a deep red band along the sides; and the brilliant silver mullet, with red fins and a compressed body. Repeated questioning had failed to draw from Nat a satisfactory description of which one of these fish his awa-toose resembled, and our imaginations were set to the hair trigger now that the looked-for place had been reached.

"How big is the awa-toose?" I asked.

"She weigh two pound. Guess some of it weigh one pounds," replied Nat.

"What is the best bait?"

Nat answered by picking up a handful of mud from just below the water's edge and handing it toward me. One who is not familiar with translating from the Indian might be surprised on being informed that a handful of mud was the best bait for a fish alert enough to take the trolling spoon, and perhaps the fly, but I recognized the sign language for crawfish, and proceeded to capture half a dozen of them at once. Nat fished with pork and a sinker. I used crawfish bait on light tackle, Wake chose a trolling spoon of such pretty and attractive model that it would almost draw land animals into the water to get at it; and we sent Alex and Sol out to set the collecting nets in likely places.

The red crossbills sang in jaunty camaraderie as they flew in joyous company amongst the pointed firs. White-throated sparrows called and answered each other in different octaves, and a water-wagtail sent his clear notes across the river to us every few minutes. We stood in the tracks of moose and bears on the bank, and awaited the coming of a wild fish, among wild surroundings. Did the awa-toose take

the fly? Did it leap when hooked? Did
it fight longer than any other known fish?
Was it a surprise for the palate at every
new mouthful? Had it ever been described
by a naturalist? These were the questions
that we asked while we waited until the
stars came out, and a horned owl called
with his minor screams, that are intended
to inform timid animals that the caller
does not carry legs like a lynx. It was not
the night for awa-toose, and Nat, antici-
pating a hard day's work on the morrow,
thought best to tell us that the awa-toose
did not bite after sundown.

For the next two or three days on our
way down river we camped early, and devoted most of our spare time to the awa-
toose, but without attracting its attention;
although Nat assured us that in former
days, when supplies for Flying Post all
came from England by way of Moose Post,
the canoemen caught awa-toose whenever
they stopped to camp at night. This was
not quite in accord with his statement that
the fish did not bite after sundown, for the
Hudson Bay people waste very little of the
daylight in traveling time.

Nat was a reliable Indian nevertheless;
and it was simply necessary to be well
enough acquainted with him to realize
when he was reliable. He was simple and
unassuming in manner. He looked at one
with a clear level eye when first speaking
and then dropped his eyes modestly before
finishing a sentence, but there was nothing
of deception in his manner. If he informed
us that there were no game animals and
few fish about the lake that he had chosen
for his permanent abode it was because
he spoke before he thought. If he had
stopped to think, he would have said nothing at all. Lakes and streams and special
hunting grounds are handed down from
father to son in his country, and Indians
recognize and respect each other's right
and title to such grounds. They would
expect to have Nat answer them as he did
me, that his chosen ground was a miserable
one for game and fish; but when I said
"Ki debwe," and gave a knowing wink, he
at once joined my other Indians in a hearty
shout of laughter. The idea of possession
is so well grounded that when I asked Nat
if he knew about a certain small river, he
replied, "Guess know it pretty well. Made
it myself," which on translation means

that he had cut all of the portages himself.

Nat was really a good and kindly old
soul, and during the two months that he
was with us we got to be very fond of him.
There was nothing in reason that he did
not want to do for us, and he was evidently
distressed because we could not find the
awa-toose. The evening of July 27, 1905,
was destined to be an eventful one, however. We were then pretty well down the
Mattagami River, and at the end of a hard
day's work in rain and wind we camped
late on the bank of a long, swirling eddy.
A good hot dinner of sturgeon, flapjacks
and chocolate, with a change to dry woolen
clothing, made one feel like a butterfly just
out of the chrysalis. I lighted a sweet old
pipe and stepped out on the rocks in front
of camp.

The wind had died down, and the clouds
had broken away enough to let one little
star peep through and watch the coming
scene. Our tired Indians were already
asleep in their tents, and Wake, with his
rare combination of industry and love of
luxury, was arranging the boughs in our
tent according to the formula of my old
guide Caribou Charley, who liked "a bed
boughed down with care." All was quiet,
with that vast, impressive quiet that settles
over the great, untraveled spruce forest of
the North at night, and I seemed to be
alone. The deep black river swept ma-
jestically by on its way to arctic seas, and
noiselessly, excepting for an occasional
swish of the inky current where it met the
return flow of the bank eddy. I listened.
It was easy to listen, on that quiet night.
Yes, it was another sound that I heard
above the swish of the current, and to a
fisherman's ears it meant that fish of some
sort or another were rising for ephemeras.
I knew the sound made by a rising trout,
a rising bass, a rising doré, a rising perch,
a rising smelt, a rising mullet, a rising
salmon. It was none of these. Oh, joy!
After days of seeking for a mysterious fish,
here, on this night for gnomes and goblins,
in the eerie current that came out of the
dark, passed silently and went into the
dark, there was some fish that I had never
heard rise before.

"Just wait a minute," said some one to
himself—and when the first fly rod out of
the case was mounted, I knew by the feel

that it was a lucky old split bamboo of seven ounces that had been made for me by Dr. Fowler in his best days, twenty-five years ago. It was a rod that had landed everything from grilse in Labrador to brown trout in Sweden and smelts in Maine. In the fly book all varieties were of the same color at this hour, but a loosely coiled cast that had been rather carelessly tucked into the book a day or two previously kept working itself into my hand, and insisting upon being first in at the contest, so it was looped to the line rather more because of its insistence than as a matter of choice. It carried a brown hackle for dropper and a Parmachenee Belle for stretcher.

In the hurry of getting ready, the landing net was not taken out of the case, but as my pipe had gone out it was necessary to start up the sweet puffs of Guard's mixture for luck, and that required a quarter of a minute of time that was more precious than first-water diamonds. Then, comfortable, contented and expectant, I sent the cast out into the gloom and knew that it had alighted true, at the margin of the eddy.

Instantly there came a ferocious tug at the fly, the reel sang *chir-r-r-r-r*, and through the darkness I saw the gleam of a white, glistening fish in the air. Here was my awa-toose after all, but what manner of fish could the awa-toose be? Nothing that I had ever caught before gave such peculiar fluttering leaps, and nothing before had ever shone in the dark. Out into the sullen current he ran, then back into the eddy. With the persistence of a bass he failed to know when he was beaten. Would the hook hold? It must hold. If that hook failed to hold I would write letters to the editor denouncing the manufacturer. With every rush of the fish into the current my heart stood still, but finally the uncaptured prize began to yield, and in a few minutes he came sliding toward the bank on his side. In the absence of a landing net I carefully found his gills and quickly tossed him out upon the grass. Then began more gymnastics, but with the aid of both hands and of both knees and of the friendly sedge grass I was able to grasp a fish shaped like a shad, with some of its large loosened scales sticking between my fingers.

Kneeling by the embers of the camp fire,

which responded to the addition of a few chips, I made out a fish that was clearly of the herring tribe; but of what sort? A herring living in rapid fresh water like a trout, independent, and feeding upon ephemeras! His open mouth was found to be armed with very sharp teeth, both on jaws and on tongue, and that again seemed strange for a herring. While I wondered there came to memory a lecture that I had heard twenty-eight years previously at college, in which Professor Wilder had spoken of the existence of a big-toothed herring which had a double pupil of the eye. Yes, this fish had a double pupil of the large, lustrous eye, and both pupils of the same size. Surely this was not Nat's awa-toose, but some other fish that he had neglected to tell us about. Carefully the fish was packed away in damp moss to await daylight inspection, and then I stepped out on the rocks again for the next one.

Two or three times the cast was sent out of sight in the darkness, and suddenly there was another pull at the fly, but the hard-headed pull at the outset and the quick giving up showed that my old acquaintance, the doré, had been hooked this time; and he is no sort of a hero. The star overhead had seen enough, the clouds were gathered over it again, and the tattoo of raindrops was the call to bed. Although we were all tired, and Wake had made the softest and springiest of fragrant beds, I slept uneasily and impatiently awaited the coming of daylight, that would reveal all of the features of my prize.

Nat was up early. It was not his awa-toose at all, but a fish that he called the "nebog-atis" (plural, add iwog), and one that was seldom captured by the Indians. The color was almost startling in its brilliancy of flashing silver, so bright that my negatives were all over-exposed. Over the silver was a scintillating iridescence of pea-green and lilac, and on the back a suggestion of transparent steel-blue and purple. It was fifteen inches in length, and nine and a half inches in girth. The outlines were those of a shad, but the body was compressed at the anal fin in a curious way, just as though somebody had pinched the fish between his thumb and forefinger at that point when it came hot out of the smelter. There were no scales on the opercles, but the body was smoothly covered with large, rounded scales which readily separated on handling. The double pupil of the eye had changed during the night, and the lower one was now the larger of the two. This changed again in the sunlight, and the upper pupil became so large that the lower one was a mere pin-hole opening in the iris. The stomach was filled with ephemeras.

We were too impatient about testing the table qualities to wait for a bed of hard-wood coals for broiling purposes, so the fish was carefully fried. It was delicious indeed. The flesh was remarkably white, firm and tender, with a streak of brown fat along the side, as in the shad. The herrings that I have eaten would be placed in about this order of classification for table quality: Shad, nebog-atis, Labrador herring, European red herring, hickory shad, common American herring, alewife, tarpon, menhaden.

We found that while the nebog-atis would take the fly at night, one could get it as well in the daytime. The favorite habitat was in deep, steady currents, but often enough it chose trout or salmon water. The one fly that was chosen in preference to a dozen others that we tried was the Par-machenee Belle, although casts resembling the ephemera upon which it was feeding were made up in various combinations. Like ourselves, the nebog-atis was out for new specimens, and cared little for its tried and true flies when a Parmachenee Belle was anywhere in sight. Nebog-atisiwog do

not travel in schools like most other herring but are found singly, although fifty may be in sight at one time when they are breaking water for ephemeras. On dark days the fish may be at the surface at almost any time of day, but as a rule they suddenly appear about four o'clock in the afternoon, and feed from that time until night.

On our trip we found only one more interesting fish than the nebog-atis to report, and while that was a great surprise, and something that will attract the immediate attention of every fly fisherman in the land when we get time to tell about it, we are nevertheless going down to the Mattagami River again for nebog-atisiwog alone, unless some one knows where they may be found at some nearer point.

As to the mysterious awa-toose, he is still uncaught. On our return trip I offered Nat ten dollars if he would get one four inches long, and finally offered in addition a hundred pounds of pork, with no further result than to leave the Indian with the impression that we were probably daft to make such an offer for any four-inch fish.

The autumn leaves are changing fast on the Mattagami River to-day, and perhaps there has been a snowstorm and a skim of ice on the still waters already. The great river roars in the rapids, bears swim across it, and moose and caribou browse upon its banks. In its waters somewhere there is a fish called awa-toose by the Indians, but what manner of fish it is, some one else must say.

36

Alone in the Arctic Wilderness

A.J. STONE

Alone in the Arctic Wilderness.

By A. J. Stone.

Illustrated from photographs by the Author.

An Experience with Renegade Indians in the Northwest Territory—Boat-Building under Difficulties—Down the Liard in a Canvas Boat.

EDITOR'S NOTE.—The results of Mr. Stone's Arctic explorations have already been exploited through the bulletins of the American Museum of Natural History, in whose interest he was working. The incidents here narrated took place in the vicinity of Fort Simpson, just before the author's researches along the Mackenzie River.

DURING the month of December, 1897, I transported my entire outfit, consisting of provisions and utensils necessary for my future expeditions, to a point on the Liard River just below Hell Gate Cañon. Here I stored them in a rude cache built of heavy logs. Below Hell Gate the Liard is navigable; and my object in selecting the place was to be in a position, as soon as the river should be clear of ice in the spring, to take my provisions down stream by boat without loss of time. The cache was completed in December. The river, I knew, would not be navigable before April. The intervening time I determined to employ in exploring the surrounding country. So, leaving two men to guard the cache during my absence, I set out at once with a sledge of provisions, and succeeded in reaching a point on a tributary of the Liard about a hundred miles from Hell Gate, where news reached me which made it necessary to retrace my steps in all possible haste. A band of murderous renegade Indians was reported encamped in the immediate vicinity of the cache where my outfit was stored.

During my absence in the late winter and early spring I gathered many facts concerning the history of these murderous renegades. They were, as I found, a thieving and vicious lot, composed of outlaws from various tribes, driven from among their own people for the crimes and deeds of violence they had committed there. The most brutal murders were laid to their charge—murders of feeble or troublesome members of their own tribe—

children, women, and cripples. Occasionally, too, a strong man would be suddenly despatched to the hunting grounds by an offended neighbor. In such cases nothing was ever said. There was no retribution. I only heard of one case in which the opposite of this held true. The blood-stained hands of one fellow had accomplished such slaughter among them that he had been forced to flee even from their vengeance, and, at the time of my visit, he had been living alone in hiding

AN ARCTIC HUNTER'S CACHE.

The cache of Arctic hunters is a rude shelter of logs built for the protection of their supplies and goods, and the Indians of the region being very superstitious regarding these structures, they are rarely meddled with.

for a period of three years. These Indians, called the "Hell Gates," always seek winter quarters away from the river, back in the mountains, but return to the stream early in the spring. When, therefore, news reached me late in March that a party of from seventy-five to a hundred of these dangerous customers had assembled on the river near my cache below Hell Gate, I naturally felt anxious for the safety of my outfit, and lost no time in hurrying to the spot.

When I arrived there, after a long and difficult return journey over the snow, I found the place, much to my astonishment, quite deserted. The men I had left in charge of the cache were nowhere to be found. My first thought was that they had been murdered, but, failing to find any trace of their bodies, and, on closer inspection, discovering that the contents of the cache had not been disturbed, I was forced to the conclusion that they had deserted of their own accord. Even Powder, an Indian medicine-man I brought back with me from the north, deserted me the morning after our arrival, so I was left alone, with only my faithful sledge-dog, Zilla, for a companion, to cope as best I might with my unwelcome and murderous neighbors. What became of Powder and the guards I never knew, nor did I much

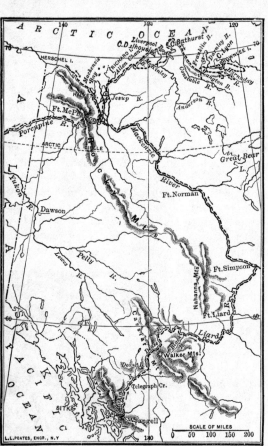

MAP OF NORTHWESTERN BRITISH AMERICA.

Showing Mr. Stone's route and his geographical discoveries.

care. In the dangerous position in which I was placed it was sufficient compensation to know that the outfit and provisions, upon which the success of future expeditions depended, were still intact.

The reason why the cache had not been disturbed was soon made clear. The Indians had not yet become aware of its existence. Upon my arrival, however, several of the renegades made bold to approach me, and, discovering the cache, to ask what it contained. I put them off as well as I could with evasive answers, which I could readily see were far from leaving upon them the desired impression. I was resolved, however, in case of attack, to risk my life, if necessary, in the protection of the cache and its contents.

On the supposition that in all probability there would be more danger by night than by day, my first idea was to arrange a safe and suitable place to sleep. Around the cache I had previously cleared a considerable space by cutting down trees for firewood. In the centre of this clearing two large spruce trees were still standing. Under these I determined to spread my blankets. In this way, by abandoning my tent altogether and sleeping in the open air, I should be enabled, I thought, by the light of a good fire, to command an uninterrupted view

LIARD RIVER INDIANS.

of from seventy-five to a hundred yards on all sides.

It seemed advisable, also, on account of having brought with me on the sledge sufficient provisions for present needs, to leave the cache unopened until I had done my best to rid myself of the Indians. Had it been necessary, I could have rolled the heavy logs from the top of my hoard without assistance, but I could not have put them back again unaided, and as the Indians are somewhat timid about breaking into a cache, I knew that it would be much easier to keep them from pilfering before I opened it than afterward.

Even so, my situation was a trying one. Here I was with an outfit weighing a ton, to be taken down the river, without a boat, and, worse still, with no one to help me build one. The three men I had counted on for this emergency had deserted. Nor was there assistance within available distance. The nearest settlement to which I might appeal was a Hudson Bay trading post on the Liard, one hundred and fifty miles down stream, which I could not reach without sacrificing my cache to the Indians. I resolved, therefore, to remain, and trust to diplomacy and my knowledge of local customs and superstitions to bring me safely out of my predicament. Among other things, I decided carefully to avoid any quarrel with my neighbors, to be firm, never to show fear, to refuse absolutely all demands, and always to be ready for self-defence. I slept under the two big trees in the clearing as I had planned, certain that no one could approach unseen. As an added precaution, however, I always tied Zilla on one side of my bed, and placed three loaded rifles with extra ammunition on the other.

For many days I kept my lonesome watch. I was beginning to feel worn out and very nervous, and had about concluded that, after all, I had over-estimated the possible dangers from the renegades. The snow had by this time quite disappeared from the little clearing, but was about eight inches deep in the timber. During the day it grew soft, but at night a hard crust formed over the top.

One night, having taken my usual precautions, I was awakened by a low growl from Zilla, and presently, just behind me, I heard footsteps in the snow at the edge of the timber. Raising myself on my blankets, at the same time keeping perfectly still, I listened. I could hear the steps plainly, a regular tramp, tramp, tramp, as though the prowler were moving slowly and cautiously along the edge of the clearing. The event I had been so long awaiting had at last come. Now that the rascals were surrounding me, preparing to seize upon my life and belongings, I was conscious that my heart was

THE AUTHOR'S CAMP IN THE FOREST.

OVERLOOKING THE LIARD FROM THE SUMMIT OF NAHANNA ROCK, FOUR THOUSAND FEET HIGH.

beating more rapidly, and felt my teeth gritting together. Carefully and noiselessly I lifted and cocked one of my rifles. I did not feel especially nervous or excited. It was high time to conclude this tiresome business, and if I thought of any one's death it was that of a Hell Gate Indian.

Tramp, tramp, tramp continued the steps.

Evidently my visitor was circling the clearing and trying to locate me by the dim light of the midnight stars. My fire was low, and gave little light.

The steps continued around the camp until they reached a point directly in front of me, where one of the trees of my camp stood between me and my unseen foe. Here was my chance. By crawling up close behind the tree I should gain a decided advantage. I feared an ambush, however, and realizing that my slightest movement might reveal my position, I laid low.

The footsteps ceased, and I could not discover whether the disturber of my rest was crawling toward me or standing still and listening. The suspense became unbearable. I called. If there was to be any shooting I wanted to get through with it.

No response. I called again. Not a sound. I was at a loss what to make of the situation. I still thought it advisable, however, to remain concealed, so there I sat on my blankets, waiting, until I was chilled through. At last, thoroughly disgusted, I lay down again and tried to persuade myself that I had been dreaming and had better go to sleep. But very soon I heard the steps again, and sat up rifle in hand.

This time I was *not* dreaming. Some one was coming directly toward me with the evident intention of keeping the tree between us. The steps drew nearer and nearer. I lifted my rifle, secretly rejoicing that there would soon be a dead Indian in the neighborhood. I held my breath, and just as I expected to see my enemy emerge, a big white dog stepped from behind the tree. Although my finger was on the trigger I did not shoot. I just laid down my rifle and crawled back into my blankets.

I never shall forget my feeling of mingled relief and disappointment. I rather wanted to complete the interesting little tragedy promised, but, on the whole, my relief was great. An Indian dog had scented some moose meat hanging in the tree above me, and had manœuvred to reach it undiscovered. Its step was most deceptive, and if I had not seen the animal I should always have believed that I had been visited by an Indian.

The Indians continued to harass me daily, and became more and more troublesome. To give them anything would, I knew, be like giving a tiger a taste of blood. Their pleas grew insistent, but I stubbornly refused them. The reader may wonder how I conversed with them. I knew a number of their words, beside something of Chinook, of which they also knew a little. Most helpful of all was my skill in the sign language, so necessary to travellers in this region, and only to be acquired by contact with the natives. One big fellow became so intolerably insulting one afternoon that I had to drive him out of camp with a club. This quarrel, which I had felt sure would bring trouble upon me, really put an end to my worries, for the Indians, like the cowards they really were, concluded that they could secure provisions elsewhere with less danger; and the very next day they began moving away to their hunting grounds. I was very glad to see them go. Besides their greedy longing for the contents of my cache, there was another reason why their presence endangered me. In one of their camps was a man nearly dead with consumption, and if he died while I was there, I knew that they would be sure to attribute his death to the white man. Undoubtedly either my life or my *ictas* (possessions) would have been required to make good the loss. I had seen the man and knew that he was near his end, and I should not have known how to avert the superstitious wrath of his friends. When all the Indians had departed except the consumptive and his family, I visited these with rice and fruit. A white man, I told them, always has a good heart, but he always does what he

chooses with his own *ictas*. Finding that they had plenty of moose meat, I bought some for Zilla.

When, after the torment I had gone through, the Indian cut-throats finally went away and left me in peace, I felt immensely happy and relieved. My courage seemed renewed, and I did not doubt that as I had proved my ability to withstand such a band, so I could also model and construct a boat single-handed, although I had never watched the building of one, and was scantily provided with suitable materials. I went down the river for several miles, and discovered that for about three miles the water was likely to be dangerous; but that one mile farther on there was an ideal spot for a camp, with all kinds of timber in abundance, and one magnificent grove of straight, slender young spruce, just what I was likely to need.

I set about moving at once, loading three hundred and fifty pounds on the sled at a time, which Zilla could easily draw over the four miles of smooth ice which lay between my camp and the spruce grove. By the time I had unloaded a cargo and hauled it up the bank, I was tired enough to get on the sled myself, and let Zilla carry me back after another load.

Thus, in three days, I moved my entire outfit, pitched my tent, and put everything in order.

My new camp was among the big timber on the river bank, and about twenty feet above the level of the ice. There was an abrupt bend in the river just above, and another about half a mile below. A belt of thick timber stretched behind me; and across the river; the country rose steeply from the water's edge. Thus I was completely shut in on all sides.

During my troubles with the Indians I had found time to plan my boat. I had heard that a man alone could cut boards from trees by placing a log in position, standing on the top of it with a hold on the upper end of the saw, and tying a bag of flour to the lower end. This feat seemed too difficult for me, so I hung my

MR. STONE STRIPPING BARK FROM A SPRUCE TREE WITH WHICH TO COVER THE RIBS OF HIS BOAT.

whip-saw in a tree and decided to try some more practical expedient. I considered skin boats and birch-bark canoes, but I had no skins for the one, and I could not make a bark canoe large enough or strong enough for the load. The only other kinds which occurred to me were canvas boats and log rafts. Evidently I must choose one of these for transport.

First of all, then, I decided on the size of boat necessary to carry my goods. I figured that it must be twenty-four feet long, five and a half feet in the beam, and twenty-one inches deep amidships. I brought out from my stores all the canvas I had, and decided, after careful examination, that by judicious piecing and patching I should be able to cover such a frame. So I promptly set to work and constructed a row of benches upon which I could bend and shape the frame of my craft.

Next I cut down a number of tall, slender young spruce, selecting, as I soon learned how to do, those that were straight-grained. These I trimmed, hewed, and planed; and then, bending them into shape, made them fast. Day after day I worked away until keelson, gunwales, bilge keels,

and ribs were all in place. This done, I was much pleased with the outlines; for, although I had not built boats, I had travelled in them enough to know that mine was shaped to ride the rough water it was likely to encounter.

When the frame of the boat was completed, it contained over forty pieces of timber, each from eight to twenty-five feet long, every one of which I had planed on top of a log, by walking alongside, back and forth, on my knees, since the log was too low to admit of my standing while using the plane. Next, I cut down two large trees, from which I peeled the bark in great strips twenty-five feet long, as I had learned to do by watching the Indians. With this bark I now covered the frame, fitting it down smoothly, with the sap side next to the canvas to give it a smooth support and prevent it from sagging between the ribs. Then I darned the holes in my canvas, sewed it together, and stretched and fastened it over the bark. The neighboring woods afforded me a large quantity of spruce gum, which I mixed with the fat from bacon, heating the two together until they blended. A rag, wound

THE FRAMEWORK OF MR. STONE'S BOAT.

THE BOAT FINISHED AND LOADED READY FOR ITS TRIP DOWN THE RIVER.

around the end of a stick, served as a swab with which I spread the hot pitch over the canvas until it was completely covered. I worked out some oars, and my boat was complete.

While I was still hard at work on my boat two heavy falls of snow almost buried my camp. Soon, however, the snow disappeared; and one beautiful Sunday morning, while still in my blankets, a robin near camp roused me with his bright, familiar song. I sprang up and dressed as quickly as I could, fearing that the little fellow would fly away before I could get a sight of him, but he continued to cheer me with his sweet notes all the morning.

While thus occupied, I observed very regular habits. I rose at five, breakfasted at six, and before going to work on my boat, prepared the skins of whatever small rodents my traps had captured during the night. I lunched at twelve, and, after a six o'clock dinner, took a run with Zilla, for our mutual good, which he seemed to enjoy quite as much as I. At one time I was threatened with pneumonia for nearly a week, but I tried to work on as though perfectly well, convinced that if I allowed myself to give way I should be seriously ill. At all times I used the greatest precautions while chopping, for the reason that, with my life depending entirely upon my own exertions, I could not afford to cripple myself.

My nights were somewhat restless. The awful strain of the long solitude was harder to bear than the dangerous presence of the Indians, and sometimes I wished for their return. In spite of my hard work I ate very little. I could not obtain much variety of food; and to cook the same thing over and over again, and eat it all alone, became very tedious. My isolation would have seemed less oppressive if I could have seen any prospect of a companion, but my anticipation of a lonely and difficult trip down the great unknown river,* in my untested, improvised, canvas boat, depressed my spirit. I had frequently heard the effects upon the mind of such loneliness

* The Mackenzie.

discussed, and many a tragic story came back to sadden me. Although I kept as busy as I could, and made a companion of Zilla, talking with him and running with him on the beach, my sensations during those solitary weeks were indescribable. I regard this period as the most trying ordeal of my life. In that one month of April I lived a lifetime.

On the fifth day of May, while at work, I heard a peculiar long-drawn swishing noise in the direction of the river, and, running to the bank, saw a tongue-like strip of water boring its way through the ice down the middle of the stream. Some distance below it stopped for a time, then began again. Sounds as though the mountains were tumbling down came from upstream. With mingled fear and joy I realized that the river ice was breaking, and that soon I should be released from the awful prison where I had been held for over thirty days. Was I freed only to find a watery grave in this mad, unknown river? The crushing, breaking ice roared louder and louder, until in front of me the ice of the whole river suddenly lifted and broke into huge, floating masses which began to move down stream. Then a great swell from above piled ice upon ice many feet high. So deafening was the battering of millions of tons of monster ice cakes that I could hardly control my nerves or my thoughts. For the three days during which this awful grinding continued, I obtained very little sleep. Then the ice began to move down stream, and at the end of five days most of it had disappeared, and I decided to launch my boat.

I crawled under it, knocked away the frame, and, lifting it from beneath with my shoulders, managed to work it forward inch by inch over the edge of the bank to the sand beach below. Once there, I found difficulty in extricating myself. If I lifted up one side, I could not get my body half-way out without finding myself held fast in such a position that I could not hold up the boat, which, with its heavy spruce bark, canvas, and pitch, probably weighed five hundred pounds. Luckily I

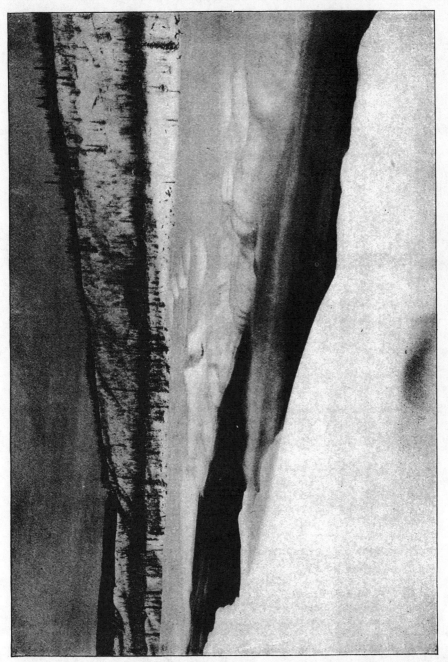

THE COMING OF SPRING IN THE FAR NORTH.

" . . . I heard a peculiar long-drawn swishing noise in the direction of the river, and, running to the bank, saw a tongue-like strip of water boring its way through the ice down the middle of the stream."

remembered seeing dogs scratch their way under fences, and in like manner I scratched my way out.

Once launched, my boat proved its capability to float a ton of cargo; and steering a difficult course among snags and rapids and fields of heavy ice, I made my way, with considerable difficulty, one hundred and fifty miles down stream to Fort Liard, a Hudson Bay trading post, where assistance for further navigation was procurable.

Once launched, my boat made its way with excessive difficulty. The river was very swift, and was shut in most of the time between high walls. I struck one rapid with a heavy swell a half mile long; and just as I did so I observed two enormous cakes of ice on either side, both of which seemed about to roll in on top of me and crush the boat each time we passed over the crest of a high wave. However, I took my oar and managed to ward them off, my boat turning sideways the while and tipping dangerously.

Farther down, the current had swept so strong against a high bank that this had been undermined, leaving the roots and ends of broken trees protruding from the water. Several times I just brushed them, but escaped without damage. Then, for many miles, the river spread out over a low, flat country.

It was nearly six o'clock before I saw a convenient place to land. I made for this, and, anchoring the boat, prepared my camp for the night. I had eaten nothing since five in the morning, and had been constantly exerting my strength, but I had no desire for food.

The next morning I was up early and well started down stream again by 5.40. The river, here, was everywhere separated into small streams by many islands, but was still very rapid. How I ever escaped getting caught irrevocably in a tangle of drift, has ever since been a perfect wonder to me. Then, again, side winds kept me busy fighting off shore, and from the time I broke camp until twelve o'clock I pulled at the oars without stopping.

About that time I saw an Indian settlement a mile ahead of me, on the opposite side of the river, and was so anxious to see a human being that I made up my mind to land. So I bent to my oars and crossed to the farther bank, where I was met by a motley crowd which I at once recognized as friendly. I was invited up by one of the Indians, to his cabin, and there was as royally feasted as I have ever been in my life. My host, who could speak a little English, told me that he and his boy would take me to Fort Liard the following morning. When I was ready to start several women had brought me moccasins as gifts, and all the settlement was at the boat to bid me good-by. The morning was perfect, the waters of the great river everywhere calm and mirror-like.

Thus, after having steered a difficult course among snags and rapids and fields of heavy ice, and having undergone much fatigue and danger, I was not sorry when, a little after noon, we reached Fort Liard, and I was welcomed once again by white men.

A GROUP OF RENEGADE INDIANS FROM THE LIARD REGION.

37

On the Snow

MAXIMILIAN FOSTER

ON THE SNOW.

By Maximilian Foster,

Illustrated by Carl Rungius.

NWARD led the track—a deep, unswerving trail—still pushing along the forest's snowy floor northward toward the upper reaches of the Kippewa. Beauchene now lay far in the rear, and through an interminable silence of unbroken winter woods the chase fared on, striking from the lower swamps upward along the open timber. Lemaire led, no longer stealing, cautious, with cat-like steps through the bush; but plunging on, determined to wear down the quarry by a sheer persistence. One day was gone, another dying, and the moose—a big bull—still was travelling, vigorous in his stride. Once lingering, curious and fearful to find whether the pursuit still held in his trail, he had shown himself among the trees. Then a futile bullet drove him on still faster. Verily, Lemaire was right. "Hunh—deer," said he, "deer run round and round." He leaned over and heaved his pack higher upon his shoulders, moving the tump-line band where it had cut deeply into his brow. "Deer go round an' round. Moose not like deer. Moose know a place far 'way—moose *go there!*" He beckoned me to follow, and took up the trail. In the beginning, his eye had glistened with a vivid passion of the chase, but now it pored dully upon the tangled covers. "Bimeby moose get mad. Then moose turn round fight." But now

the second day was ending, and the bull still postponed his temerarious last frenzy of fear.

The track dipped over the brow of a tall ridge, where, on the right, a thicket of black spruce turned its slender spires whispering toward the sky. Yet even this secret murmuring of the wind among the tops added to the utter quiet of the woods. Solitude was there, and a deep silence, too.

Lemaire paused and brushed away the matted hair hanging before his eyes. He swept the woods with an inquiring glance, hurried onward, halted, and then turning abruptly from the trail, pushed through the abattis of a windfall. Beyond lay an opening in the trees, a narrow intervale sheeted with snow, and at its head he stopped, transfixed.

Age had told lightly upon Lemaire. He carried the weight of his three-score years strongly as the bull moose swings his heavy yellow antlers in the rut. His blanket mackinaw hung squarely upon his broad, determined shoulders; his eyes gleamed keenly, almost with the fire of youth. He stood, drawn forward, peering beneath his uplifted hand. Had he seen the game—*quick*—where was it? Lemaire shook his head and breathed deeply. His hand stretched slowly out, pointing along the intervale. "Look —so," said he.

In the glade's centre was a cross, rude

"THE MOOSE—A BIG BULL—STILL WAS TRAVELLING, VIGOROUS IN HIS STRIDE."

and uncouth, a vivid emblem of the loneliness of death, shining there against the black background of spruce, solitary in this appalling stretch of solitude. Lemaire lifted the tump-line from his brow and made the holy sign. Silently, as before, he turned, then pushed on. Night was drawing down, and anew the evening wind stirred among the trees. Dark and dejected, Lemaire threaded the dusky closes of the wilderness, silent till he reached a hollow under the hill. "Camp now," he muttered brusquely. "Pretty soon dark—bimeby cold, sartin mighty cold."

Still in this dark humor he scraped away the snow and laid a fire. He hung over it, husbanding its first flickering blaze, and in the glow his face showed heavy and drawn. From under the rim of his sable cap he pored blankly upon the fire; then when it had burst into a cheerful flame, he put on the frying-pan, the bacon, the kettle, and the tea. "Tired out, Lemaire?" He turned stolidly, his expression unchanged, and slowly shook his head. "Hunh!" he answered, "tired to-morrow—nex' day— mebbe. Not tired now." Once more he bent over the fire, turning the bacon with his skinning-knife, and shaking the kettle of tea. But this done, he fell anew into his slow dejection, and sat, stolidly glooming upon the dark forest's flank until the bacon was in a fair way to burn.

"Hoh-tay-o!" he cried abruptly, in the tongue of his Algonquin mother. "Wee wuish a-shum-sun. Tea—I am hungry!" Leaping to his feet, he snatched off the bacon and the tea, laid out his cups and birchbark plates, and with a clattering knife fell to work at his food.

Overhead the stellar host burned with all their brilliance in the unclouded winter sky, and around the night-camp a swirl of pungent smoke wreathed among the trees. Lemaire drew his blanket about his knees, and a garrulous pipe came forth and added strong incense to the clear and frosty air. Once a fox barked shrilly in the distance, and in the north an owl screamed its affrighted note. Lemaire listened. The echo passed, and the dead forest regained its quiet.

"Over there," he said, waving his arm broadly toward the north, "are many graves of my people. Where shall you find them? Mujizowaja—Abittibe—the lost Kwingwishe —yes, in many places; from there to the big water on the edge of the high ground. There is where they sleep—many of them —yet I—I am here. Listen. Many winters ago—more snows than you have seen —the moose went eastward, and the caribou travelled far out there, far beyond this country—up there where there are no trees. Hunger then came to the tribes, and many died in the lodges. It struck the old people, and they were dead. It touched the little children, and they breathed no more. I myself saw it—for I was a young man then among my people—I and my brother."

He spoke, halting in his words, his language partly English, partly the patois of the French-Canadian, and here and there a hoarse guttural of Algonquin.

"There was no meat among my people, and the summer's dried fish was gone. Nor were there rabbits, for it was the year of their evil, and they died. 'Come,' said my brother, 'we will go south to the Temiscamingue, the Deep Water, to the company post where my father's money waits. Then we shall buy flour and fat meat, and our throats shall no longer parch for want of tea. Come.' Fear, then, was in my heart. Many winters before had my father lived here among these my mother's people. He was a white man—like you—from the place where there are many houses. Yes, I have seen him. I am a big man like him, and my blood is strong. I do not blame him. He went away; but many years, when the fur canoes came down from the north, there was money for us at the post. He did not forget, and twenty—yes, thirty snows—ago, when there was no money, I knew he was dead.

"My brother said these words, 'Let us go.' In my heart was fear. I looked about, and my mother's eye was on mine, as she lay weak among the rabbit blankets of fur. Down there—there at Temiscamingue—we should laugh in our hearts at death. But how should our mother find her way? Even now death had touched her, and her breath whistled as she breathed. My brother spoke again. 'I cannot stay,' he said, and my mother's eye turned from him to me. 'Go,' she whispered; 'you are strong, and for me, death scrapes his finger upon the lodge's door. I shall go the long journey.'

"'Why do you go?' I cried strongly, for he was my brother and I loved him. Another I should have pushed out into the snow, to go his way as he chose. But he was my brother. He did not speak, but turned away. Then I cried roughly to him. There was hot blood in our hearts, and he struck me on the mouth. No man had done that before, and my anger was great—mad like the she-bear in the spring. We fought —strongly, for we were big men. And as we fought there was a cry. We looked about. Our mother was dead. Then we fought no more. I heard the wailing of women in other lodges, and I longed to cry out too. But I was a man and must not. So I sat beside my mother, and took her hand, and my brother sat on the other side, and took her hand too. I saw his heart had softened, and I was glad, and I thought that the hunger, maybe, had made his heart bad before. But then I did not know.

"The good father at the post had taught me many good words, and I prayed. I prayed in my own tongue. I felt it was good. My brother heard, but did not understand. He knew only the rum-trader and the head man at the post; also only the fur-traders who go up to the big water along the water-trail. They say the words I spoke only in anger, and using them strangely. He heard my words, but did not know. 'Listen,' he said. 'You cannot wake our mother. She sleeps on the long journey. Come, we will bury our mother, and take the trail to the deep water. Let us go.'

"He went away in the darkness, but soon he was back. 'Look,' he said, 'I have food. Eat and we will go.' I looked at the food and wondered. It was the meat of the caribou, dried, and there had been no caribou since two snows had gone. 'What is this meat?' I asked, and my brother turned his face. 'Eat,' he said, and I ate, tearing the meat with my teeth, like the gray wolf at the moose's throat. Yet I wondered. 'Come, we will bury our mother now.' But we were too weak with the long hunger. We could not dig the snow, and how should we, then, break the hardened ground. 'Peace, mother,' said I. 'I shall return in the long days—peace and sleep.'

"My brother waited by the lodge. I saw that he stepped more strongly, and wondered. Had not the long hunger made me weak who was once so much stronger than my brother? But my thought was like a dream, and I was dizzy like one who has the hot-sickness and cries out strange things that have no meaning. I followed, but I knew that it was the upper trail—the long path leading to the big water—the *Kitci-gami*— at the edge of the high ground where there are no trees. 'This is not the trail,' said I; but he shook his head and bade me follow.

"There was light, for the night had gone. We went to the north, and by and by there was the trail of two people in the snow. I looked and saw that they led back and forth, and that one was a woman. My brother took my little bag of food from me, and threw it down at the door of the last lodge. It was the place of the chief's son, and he was wealthy. Many winters have passed since then, and I have forgotten his name—Muckwa, I think it was—Muckwa, the bear. He too died in the long hunger. But I cried out, knowing that he had much and we little for the journey. It was many camps beyond to the deep water, and I tried to seize the food. But my brother laughed, not like a man, but like the cackle of Kwingwishe, the meat-bird. 'Leave it. Peace! There is more and better, and I give him that. Go on.' I came away, for I walked still in a dream, and nothing was as it should be. Then we came to where the long *muskeg* touches on the pond of many moose, and we crossed upon the ice, following in the tracks that the man and woman had made. There my brother stepped from the trail sharply, as one turns from the moose track when the wind is blowing and the moose has turned to lie down where he can smell the foe on his trail. 'Come,' said my brother, but I kept on. He called again, but I kept on many steps. Before long I saw a man in the snow, and he was lying down. He slept, I thought, and there was the trail of a sledge in the snow and the tracks made by the feet of many huskies. 'Look,' I said, crying out, 'here is a man from the big water where the streams run the other way. Come, we will waken him.' I saw he was from the north, for he wore the high moccasins of fur made from the big otters without legs, that play on the rocks of the big water over there. Also, he still held in his hand a bone knife, such as there was not among our people. 'Hoh!' I cried, but he did not awaken. Then I saw that he was dead. He had been stabbed in the back, and there were the marks of the woman's feet beside him. 'Hoh!' I cried, 'he is dead!' But my brother did not come, but beckoned me on. I followed, and called out to him, but he gave no answer. Then I ran, falling this way and there, like my people when they have tasted the trader's rum. But my brother ran too, and we reach the edge of the bush. I heard then a dog bark, and another. In our people's keep were no dogs, for the last had been killed long before in our hunger. Then I looked and saw a sledge and dogs, and it was of the country where there are no trees. I knew, for the sledge runners were of bone, and lower than we use here where the snows are deeper than the reach of the biggest moose. But I saw no more, for I fell, and my mind turned from me. I was like the dead man in the trail; I knew nothing.

"When I awoke, I lay in a sledge and we were on the ice. We crossed there and went up into the bush. There I saw a woman waiting among the trees, and now she ran with the dogs. I covered my face, for still I was weak and did not know. 'Hoh!' I cried, 'it is our mother's spirit, and she walks beside us in the snow!' But a laugh answered, and it was not my mother's voice. I looked again, and the woman turned. I saw it was Pin-e-ah, Muckwa's wife, the stranger-woman who came from up there where there are no trees. She was smaller than our women, and her face was round, with eyes turned up—so. Nor could she speak our tongue when first she came among us. She ran now beside the dogs, and I said, 'Tell me, O Pin-e-ah, where is thy husband? Does he come with us? And this, no doubt, is his dog-sledge.' But she laughed, and ran beside the sledge. 'No,' she said, 'this is the sledge of good Maätuke, who rests up yonder a while. Peace to him.' I thought for a while, but did not understand. Then I knew. 'Hoh— it is Maätuke lying up there in the snow. He is dead, and, brother, thou hast slain the stranger.' My brother's heart was black, and he made no answer. But Pin-e-ah laughed, crying out, ''Twas I that did it,' she said, and I wondered at this woman of evil. She laughed, singing, like the hunter when he has killed the moose, and blood was on her hand.

"'Listen,' she said. 'He was my lover over there—in the land where there are no trees. Then Muckwa came, and he was stronger, so I went with him. He brought me here, into the land of the big sticks, and I was his. Now, in this the long hunger, Maätuke comes with his dogs to take me, for he has heard of the trouble among your people from the hunters that have gone into the north. Yet I do not go with Maätuke. He is waiting. He is lying in the snow to rest after his journey.' She laughed again.

"'Hoh!' I cried, stopping the dogs. I arose, walking beside the sledge. 'Tell me, O Pin-e-ah, why is thy husband Muckwa not with us? There is food and plenty here for all.' Again she laughed.

"'Also he is lying up there beyond. Let him lie and rest himself, for he will have a long journey if he follow, pot dog that he is.'

"I followed in the sledge trail, wondering, for I did not understand. 'Tell me, my brother,' I asked, 'why does this woman come with us?' He looked, and showed me his teeth, like huskies fighting over a rotten fish. 'Have done,' he spoke; 'she comes with me.'

"Three days we journeyed, and I grew strong. Boasting, this woman told me all. At the beginning of the long hunger, because she knew by the signs her people learn that it was there, she had saved largely of Muckwa's food. She had laid it where no hand but hers should take it, and Muckwa soon felt the grip of the hunger upon him. But she had not given him of her hidden store. She had fed herself and then my brother, bringing in her hand a piece each day. Thus they had lived, and our mother had died, for he was to keep up and have this woman for his own. 'And Muckwa?' I asked. 'What of Muckwa, O Pin-e-ah?' She looked and laughed.

"'Twice have I said it. Muckwa lies over yonder. He is gone on the long journey. He left nothing, yet good Maätuke brought us meat.'

"Then I knew that the bag of food my brother had cast before the door of Muckwa's lodge was but an offering to the dead. I cried out, for my heart was sad, 'Peace, O Muckwa, son of Kab-a-o-sis! Peace to thee.' For he, likewise, was dead— dead because of this woman that had come down from the land where there are no trees. 'O Pin-e-ah,' I said, and my heart was hot with anger that was for her, 'thou art a thing of evil. Was not Muckwa thy husband, for he ran beneath the blanket with thee?' And she laughed aloud, while her eyes shone as those of the wolf-devil when he sings outside the hunter's fire. 'Aye, he was my husband according to thy people; but am I a *kimuck*, a mangy sledge-dog, that is whipped among the traces, that he should beat me with his hand?

"Again I wondered, for this woman was not like the women of my tribe. 'Tell me,' I said, 'among thy women is not love taught with a hand that is strong?' She arose then, drawing her blanket about her. 'Many women are there who listen weakly while the dog-whip cracks, yet I am not one. I am the daughter of a chief, and my will is strong, like the mad-wolf that cannot be driven in the traces among the dogs. Over there'— and she waved her arm toward that country many camps beyond—'I am called in our tongue Amaroke, the She-Wolf, and so shalt thou know me.'

"My brother sat by the fire. He wound a thong about his gun-barrel, that was broken from the wood. He spoke not, but his eyes looked upon the woman strong with flame for her. Again my heart was troubled, and I looked at him sitting by the fire.

"'Hark!' I said, 'O my brother!' I arose and threw the blanket from my shoulder, for speech was on my lips. 'Hark! O my brother! This woman that thou hast taken to thy breast is a she-wolf, and if thou cling to her she will gnaw at thy heart. Turn this woman away, my brother, lest thou die as all have died who follow.'

"Then this woman looked at my brother in the eyes, and, seeing what they spoke, looked boldly at me and laughed. Nor did she look with hate, but as the young woman looks at her lover when he brings home plenty from the hunt. 'Have done, O Mus-kosi-Amik,' she cried, calling me by my Al-gonquin name; 'am I to be like the wounded caribou that is driven from the herd? Thou art a strong man, but I too am strong.'

"Then she wrapped the blanket about her head and lay beside the fire.

"Three times again we camped. Three times by the fire I cried out to my brother that this woman was a wolf. 'Let us turn our faces on the trail,' I said, 'and take back this woman to the place where Muckwa lies dead within his lodge.' But my brother made no answer, and Pin-e-ah laughed, looking at me with eyes that burned wetly, like the doe's when she licks her spotted fawn.

"Six camps we had come, breaking out the trail. Late the sun left its place among the trees, and early it lay down again, for it was the heart of winter. My brother went ahead, beating down the snow for the dogs, and the woman ran beside the sledge. I too went ahead when my brother's feet were tired, but it was not I that led upon the ice. One camp over there we came to a running water, and it was singing beneath the ice. 'Hoh, my brother,' I said, 'we shall go a little way before we cross this running water, lest we break through and drown.'

"But he laughed aloud, and there was anger and evil in his eyes. Maybe, then, he had seen the woman looking at me with eyes wet like the mother doe's; but I do not know. 'Come,' he said, 'is my brother a coward that he keeps the shore like Ginibig the wood-snake? Come.' And I said no more. Then my brother drove the whining huskies forward, and the woman fell behind, watching. 'Thou art a strong man,' she whispered, 'and no coward.' And I saw her eyes peer up into mine. 'Go!' I cried, striking her off, but she only laughed. My brother went on, three sledges from the shore, and I heard the ice speaking out. 'Come, O my brother!' I cried; but the ice spoke again. Then it broke across till I saw the river underneath. 'O my brother,' I cried, 'thou art gone, and this woman hath slain thee, too!' But again I saw him, fighting for his life among the dogs, and, forgetting all, I ran and drew him out. But as we came toward the shore, again the ice split across, and both were in the water. Then I heard the woman, and she was lying on the bank, and her hand was stretched toward me. 'Thy hand!' she cried, and it was to me she spoke. 'My brother drowns!' I cried; and again she spoke, but to me. 'Thy hand, and I will save thee.' And I took her hand, but held my brother by his hair, and she drew us both ashore. Then we sat on the bank and looked. Our sledge was gone, its dogs and all our meat. I only had saved my gun, for I had dropped it when I ran to my brother's help. So we sat on the bank till our clothes were stiff, like the fur of the beaver when it is dried upon the splints.

"'Come,' I said, 'the deep water lies over there more than seven camps away, for now we walk. But there is no meat, and we shall die!' Shaking, my brother arose, for the cold had touched his bones. One day we walked and camped. Half another day we walked, and my brother sang. He saw it was the spring and that the fur canoes came down from the north while the traders sat in the fort. But I, who was of clear mind, saw that it was still the winter, and that my brother went this way and there, like my people when they have tasted the trader's rum. 'Tell me, my brother, why do you sing?' I touched his skin, and it was hot, like the horns of the moose in the spring. I saw his eyes, and they were red and looked nowhere. Then I knew that my brother had the cold-sickness, and my throat with fear was so that I could not swallow. So I walked on, holding my brother by the waist, and the woman walked behind, saying nothing. We camped, and in the night my brother talked aloud, so that the forest was full of sound. But when the sun came from the trees, he was still breathing like the caribou before it dies. He will die without food, I thought. I will look in the forest. I took my gun and went into the bush, walking a short way. I walked a little further. Maybe I would see a rabbit. Then I looked back, and there was the woman. She was walking behind me. 'Come,' I said, 'you shall sit by my brother while he sleeps. You shall not follow me in the snow.' But she held up her hand, holding the palm outward. 'See,' she said, 'I have brought the food.' Food she had, indeed, of the dried flesh of the caribou. 'Tell me, O Pin-e-ah, where did you get this food?' And she laughed. 'Strong man, you would turn me away in the snow. So I have saved the meat of the caribou, and hid it within my breast. It was to keep me on the way, so that I could follow in the trail of the dog-sledge.'

"I took the food and held it in my hand. 'Why do you give me this?' She looked away, but I saw that her eyes were soft.

"Again I spoke to her. 'Why do you give me this meat of the caribou?' 'I know not,' she answered, 'lest it is that thou art strong and that I would have thee, O Muskosi-Amik"—calling me in my Algonquin name. Then I spat upon the meat, and threw it on the snow. 'Go!' I said, and walked among the trees. I came to a ridge, and there was a moose. He was a big bull. He yarded alone because he was big. 'Hoh!' I cried to myself, 'there is a big bull. I will kill him, and my brother shall live.' I raised my gun. Then I put it down again. I prayed, saying the good

words the father had taught me. Then I raised my gun, and fired. I saw him fall, and ran in shouting. But he got upon his feet, and went away. I looked, and there was blood upon the snow. I saw his hair where the bullet had cut it. I saw that it was yellow, and I knew I had hit him too low. I lifted the blood upon the snow, and it showed no froth. 'Never mind,' I said, 'I will follow. Maybe he will fall.' So I followed a long way till he came to the ice. There he ran fast, and I could not catch him. So I came up to the camp.

My brother lay by the fire. I heard his voice, and he talked with Muckwa—the dead Muckwa, who lay in his lodge over there. They talked as friends, for they had often taken the caribou together. But the woman spoke shrilly, bidding him be done. 'Peace!' I said, standing before the fire. She looked at me, and saw that there was blood on my hands, where I had lifted it from the snow. 'See,' she said, softly speaking that my brother should not hear, 'the strong man returns and there is moose meat. Come, we will go and skin the moose.'

"'Have done,' I said, 'I have not killed the moose.'

"I sat beside the fire. 'You have food,' I said; 'give it to me, so that my brother may eat.' She drew her blanket about her, and rose up. 'No,' she said, 'he is already starting on the long journey, and needs no food. I and you shall eat.' I thought a while, 'Shall I kill this woman?' Then I remembered the good words the father spoke, and I said, 'No, I cannot kill this woman.' So I said:

"'Pin-e-ah, give me food; I am hungry.' I said to myself, 'I will get this food, and give it to my brother.' So she gave me a part of the caribou meat, and I made a pot of birch-bark. I thought to myself, 'I will boil it for my brother.' She sat beside me, and put her hand upon my shoulder. 'Listen, O Muskosi-Amik,' she said, calling on me by my Algonquin name. 'Thou art a strong man and shall live. I will go with you.' She looked at me with her eyes wet like the eyes of the mother doe, and I trembled. For I was afraid of this woman, the She-Wolf, who came from the land where the streams run the other way; from the land where there are no trees.

"'Hoh!' cried my brother, rising up. He threw off the skins, and looked at the woman. Then he looked at me, and at the pot of birch-bark boiling on the fire. 'Hoh!' he cried; 'there is food, and yet I starve!' He reached for the pot, but the woman struck down his hand. 'Hoh!' he cried, 'am I Muckwa, to die like this?' He struck the woman on the face, and she fell. 'Peace, O my brother!' I said, and he turned, roaring strange words. 'Thou, too,' he said, and fell upon me. The fever-madness had made him strong, and I was a child in his arms. He threw me on the snow, holding one hand upon my throat. In his other he held the skinning-knife. 'Hoh!' he cried, putting it to my throat; 'thou, too, shalt die.' He raised his hand to thrust, and then I should have died. 'Peace, O brother!' I cried aloud. Then I heard a loud noise and my mouth was filled with smoke. My brother fell on my face, and his hand loosened upon my throat. My eyes were blinded, and my face was sticky wet as with sap when the trees run in the spring. 'Hoh!' I said to myself; 'I am dead.' But I was not hurt. I pushed my brother from me, and looked up. Pin-e-ah stood beside us, and my gun smoked in her hands. I looked about, and my brother lay upon his face. He was dead. 'You have killed my brother, O Pin-e-ah,' I said, and she shook her head. 'No—yes—and I have saved thy life.'

"'Thou hast saved my life, but look, thou woman of evil, thou hast slain my brother.'

"I sat by the fire and the night went away. I saw the sun come out of the trees. I wrapped my brother in his blanket and carried him into the bush. The woman sat by the fire and held my gun between her knees. I saw that it was loaded again. 'Give me my gun,' I said, but she shook her head. 'I will keep thy gun, O Muskosi-Amik,' she answered, 'and I shall go with you, following behind. Come, shall we go?' I looked at her and smiled, lying like the traders in those days when they took the fur of the tribes.

"'Yes, you shall go, and I shall carry the meat you have, because I am strong.' Then, too, she smiled, calling me a strong man, and handing me the meat. 'But I will walk behind.'

"'Give me the gun,' I said; 'I am strong, and will carry that too.'

"'No, I will walk behind, carrying your gun.'

"So I walked ahead, and when we got among the trees I ran. 'Do not run!' she cried, and I looked behind me. I saw her point the gun, and jumped behind a tree, like the deer when he is frightened. Then she fired, and I went back, unharmed, and plucked the gun from her hands before she could load again. I took the powder and the bullets, and she crouched at my feet like the husky when the whip cracks over him in the snow. 'Come,' I said, 'we will go. Come, chief's daughter, She-Wolf from the land where there are no trees.'

"I led her among the trees, and she wept —'Ay-I-ay-I! You will take me with you on the way?' I said, 'Yes,' but smiling no more. 'Yes, I will take you on the way, Pin-e-ah. It is a long journey we shall take.'

"It snowed then. I went a long way, camping twice, and we came into this country. It snowed again, and hid our tracks almost under our feet. 'It is good,' I thought, 'for this woman from the land where there are no trees cannot find her way among the bush. Good-by, O Pin-e-ah.'

I ran and she followed. But I was a strong man, and ran far ahead. Then I hid in the bushes, doubling on my track like the bull moose when he rests. I saw her run by, calling; she was calling me in my Algonquin name. But I let her go by. I knew she could not find me, nor could she find her way among the trees. So I laughed, for my heart was bad. I walked away and camped. I sat in the snow, with my blanket about my knees and a little fire between. She should not see my fire, I said. Once I heard her calling in the night. She called then three times, and after that she screamed like the cat-owl when he hunts. I smiled. When the sun came up from the trees, there was no snow in the sky. So I walked back a long way, and there were her tracks. I followed. Sometimes she ran, but not for long. But I was strong and soon caught up. She had fallen in the snow, yet she was not dead. I watched, and she arose from the snow. She looked around and ran. Sometimes she yelled, for when one has a fear among the trees and is lost, he runs and wastes his breath in screaming. So I watched her a long way, and then I went back to my brother, where he lay in the snow. 'Come,' I said, 'I will take you to the fort, and then you shall lie among your people. Come.' So I took him on my shoulders and—many days I walked—and brought him to the fort.

"'Father,' I said, 'here is my brother. He is dead, and I have left the woman from the land where there are no trees over there in the bush.'

"'You have done evil, my son,' he said. 'Go find the woman who was from the land where there are no trees.'

"So I went to find her. Many days I looked, for she had run far among the trees. It was when the sun shines longest that I saw where she fell. A bear had been there—Muckwa in his spirit. He had torn the woman from the north, for his rage, no doubt, was great. So I buried her, and this is her cross that stands in the bush."

Lemaire arose and threw a log upon the fire. The leaping flame lighted his face, and calmness lay upon it. He stood a moment staring into the snow. Then he waved his arm broadly.

"Many snows have passed since then," he said.

38

The Best Man out of Labrador

LAWRENCE MOTT

"'Keep him off fur God's sake!' he screamed."   Drawing for "The Best Man Out of Labrador," by N. C. Wyeth.

THE BEST MAN OUT OF LABRADOR

BY LAWRENCE MOTT

DRAWING BY N. C. WYETH

I

HEN Ellison moved from the mouth of the For- teau, Labrador, to Port Saunders, Newfound- land, in order to trap lobsters for the canning factory, he aroused en- mity among the lobster fishermen there.

"What t' devvil do un want acomin' to us's waters?" Mat Wheeler grumbled to a group of men that squatted on the rickety dock one Sunday afternoon.

"Might 'a stayed to cod haulin', 'stead o' tryin' to take us's money!" another answered.

They were silent then, these great rough men of Newfoundland, whose lives and existence depend on the whims and fancies of the ocean, whose money is made by gathering the crawling, great crabs from beneath its surface. In the warm sunlight they seemed more gaunt, more tired than ever, but their eyes were sharp and keen with that clear depth only found in eyes that have to see by night almost as well as by day, that have to look far outside and judge the weather, that have to be quick to note "signs."

Behind them the houses of the village shone in the soft lights, and the stench of decaying lobster bodies, uncovered in great heaps by the low tide, was wafted here and there in the faint breeze. But they were used to it.

To the east, straight down Ingarnachoix Bay, the waters, blue and scarcely rippling, stretched away towards the Labrador coast, one long interminable surface, unmarred by swell, because the sullen rolls of the Straits do not run inside. Some clouds drifted over the heavens, moving with almost un- noticeable motion. Anchored abreast of the dock were a score of fishing boats, and rising huge among their puny forms the hull and spars of a trading schooner. The scene, peaceful and quiet, seemed a sooth- ing draught to men who fight the elements year in, year out, adjusting themselves to its requirements, watching their chances, and taking many, always. The lighthouse on the point stuck up from the gray rocks like a white finger, the curtains drawn over the lenses shining by reflection.

Lobster cars, full of the succulent fish to be boiled, stripped from their shells and packed in tins, hung low to the water, their top gratings sousing when little ripples broke against them.

On both sides of the bay the wooded shores were green with the small growth of pine and fir; the hues dwindling to a cold gray beyond, where nothing but the rock and great shingle withstands the fury of autumnal gales and the fierce grinding of winter ice.

Wheeler got out his pipe slowly, one leg stretched out, that he might shove his big hand in his pocket for a plug of tobacco. He wrangled little hunks from it with a dull knife and crumbled them between his palms, scraped a match and puffed stolidly. The others waited.

"B' God, boys—" he smoked hard, the blue cloud issuing from his lips in dribbles, "—let us cut away his buoys!"

"Un'll lose all t' traps?" Ezekia Nelson mumbled suggestively.

"Ay, an' un'll go back to Forteau t' cod-haulin' an' leave us-s t' our lobsters then "

"T'ere's room fur all o' uns, Mat, on t' Bay."

Wheeler glowered at Nelson. "Ay, an' sp'osen t'ere be room? Ah'm no zayin' t'ere b'aint, but t' man has t' luck, an' gits more lobsters than any o' we."

"Iss t'at hiss fault or ourn?" Ezekia was a fair man, and saw things only in their best light.

"Don' know whose fault, but t' Boss sayz un catches more lobsters 'n we, 'n sayz un'll cut t' price on we ef we do-na git more lobsters 'n him."

Several heads nodded solemnly.

"Mat ha' right," Drisco announced "Ellison'll cut de prices on we, ʒure."

Wheeler stood up, knocking the ashes from his pipe on a weather-worn string piece. "Shall us-s run un out?"

A long pause.

"Un's got a woman an' bo'y t' feed, Mat," Nelson said gravely.

The other leered at him, "An' aint we uns got womin an' childer. t' feed, too? Yer a fool, 'Zeke, wi' a fambily o' seven t' talk 'bout odder men's womin."

Wheeler walked to the end of the dock, the old boards creaking under his weight, and spat angrily on the still water. He watched the tiny ripples tremble away.

"No," he shouted then, swinging on his heel, "I'll ha' no prices cut for me by Jack Ellison. We uns'll cut hiss buoys wance, an' t'at'll do it."

The crowd shuffled their feet. They did not like this forcing a man out by the loss of his entire set of traps, hired from the factory. One by one they gave in then, remembering their own families—all but Nelson. He jumped up, shook his fist at Wheeler.

"I'll ha' no hand i' thiss dirty bu'sness. T' man's got all t' right we uns have." He strode away up the dusty path to the village.

The men stared after him sulkily; then Mat followed, and caught up Nelson, grabbing him by the shoulder.

"Mind me what me be sayin', 'Zekia Nelson, ef you un 'fraid o' Jack Ellison, that be a'right, but do na tell un 'bout t' buoys, man, ye mind?"

Nelson's face changed with a suddenness that startled the other. He shook off Wheeler's hand roughly.

"You be a liar, Mat Wheeler, fur well y'

know I fear'd *no* man, but there's some'at y' do'n know, an' that's thiss—" he stuck his chin forward aggressively his eyes shining in the sunlight, "I wass borned honest, I've so lived honest, an' I haint 'goin' to hev' no mixin' wi' y' w'en y' go for to try ruinin' a honest man like Ellison. That's my word. As for tellin'; h'it aint no fishin' o' mine; I'll do as I well—damn —please."

Wheeler laughed sneeringly; he dared no more because he remembered a certain fight between Nelson and a big Swede from an American schooner; he had a vivid recollection also of what the short heavy man before him had done to the Swede on that occasion.

"Ye'll coome by a H—— of a lot 'bein' *honest*, hein?"

Nelson's characteristic good nature reasserted itself; he smiled—"Wall, la'ad, I haint so tur'ble bad these forty yearn bein' honest," and walked away.

Mat watched him turn into the trim little garden about the wee white-washed house on the hillside.

"We do no need y'," he growled, "an-ny-way—go to H——!"

He went back to the rest. For a long time they talked in whispers, while the sun sank, glowing and scarlet into a brilliant west. One by one the crowd dwindled till but a few were left. These too shuffled off in the gloaming and the old dock was deserted; still save for the lap-lap of tiny wavelets and the gentle sithing sound made by the lobsters in the nearest car as they crawled in and out of water over each other. The shadows were superb by East River Mountain, lengthening, ever lengthening till their long dark fingers crept on the water. The evening lights were of that peculiar cold purple haze of summer in the Northland, beautiful in their gauze-like texture, filmy and waving as the tinted clouds moved. A long streak of yellowed crimson bored its way into the night skies that rose out of the east, like a shaft of light in a mine. From across the bay came the vigorous *qua-ack* of sheldrakes, the harsh noise smoothed by distance. For a few minutes the houses stood out glowing-white against their dark background; then instantly they became vague blobs of gray on black as the sun disappeared in its nest of hot colors. The crimsons and scarlets changed to soft blues and violet; the bright yellow to amber and deep orange, the dainty greens of the north and south merged into blue-black; and they were all gone.

Flickering chill and far away the evening star cast its rays to earth. In groups of few, in masses, then in myriads, the suns of the night shone forth with mystic effect. From the windows of the houses yellow beams came warmly, and the noise of barking dogs, as they were fed, awoke the echoes that flung and re-flung themselves from the cliffs beyond. A glorious scene of peace and quiet.

When the moon rose in full crescent, both tips pointed upward, Nelson, from his doorstep turned to his wife, "'T'll be un dry month, Car'y." He shut the door after him.

Higher and higher till the houses cast no shadows, the moon climbed slowly, and everything was silent in the little village of Port Saunders, Newfoundland.

Figures stole carefully to the dock when the white crescent was on the wane.

"Sssht, man!" Wheeler hissed when Drisco dropped his oar on the dory bottom, the clatter seeming like small thunder in the stillness. Nine men got aboard their own boats anchored out, and cast off their moorings silently. Six boats vanished toward the outer bay, the faint creak of thole-pins becoming fainter till they were gone. Silence everywhere.

II

"'T'is a'goen' to be un foine da-y, Kyrie." Jack Ellison pulled on his long sea boots at the door of the shack, his temporary home on Ingarnachoix Bay.

"A', Jack, but may-b' t' wind'll blow?"

"'T'll no blow so's I can no haul de traps, Kyrie, my guess!" He laughed as he spoke, the same old Jack as of yore; huge, powerful and gay. "I's got mor' lobesters dan anny o' t' rest, Kyrie."

She stared across the waters, that were clearer and clearer in the growing daylight. "Me hope un'll allus do, Jack."

He kissed her, not roughly, but with the strong love of a nobleman of the sea.

"Tell un to To'mie I'll bring un back a bit'ty lobester to play wi'."

She watched him clamber into his boat,

hoist his single sail, and move away to the weak breeze, toward the outer bay.

"Un's de bessis man out o' Labrador," she whispered to herself, going in again.

It was a grand day, and Ellison whistled softly to the crinkling of water at the bows. "Un'll be just good o'tside ter haul de traps thiss eleven 'clock maybe. 'Mornin', Drisco," as he passed the fisherman tugging with slow lifts at a line.

"Mornin'," the man answered, and looked after Ellison curiously, then bent to his work again with a meaningless grunt.

The *Kyrie E.*—Jack named all his boats after his wife—swung cleanly on, passing the great bowldered shores with even glide and good speed; for the breeze was freshening. Into the East Bay and across it, round Big Point and out into the open Straits, Ellison held on, snuggled comfortably in the stern sheets, his feet resting on the stone ballast, arms leaning on the stout tiller.

"I do be have de luck, zure," he said aloud. "D'odders do-na git lobesters like me. I do-na knaw why 'tiss zo, but t' God must be a-glad wi' me."

His ranges—the big pine by the cliff and the peak of East Mountain—were coming into line. He stood up, easing away the sheet and shading his eyes, looking for his trap buoys.

The glare on the twinkling waters was great; a path of molten silver and very broad. He came about, ducking under the boom as it slathered over the boat. She careened, steadied, then filled away.

"T' outside bu-ooy mus' be 'bout here."

The pine and the peak were in line, and his Straits range was correct. He brought her into the wind, holding the boom away from him, and stared keenly over the depths that shone and rippled in the sunlight. No black speck of a trap buoy anywhere. Nothing but the expanse of sea, unbroken and rolling with a gentle ground swell from the north.

"Zure my eyes be bad, I guess."

He kept away and beat up and down for hours. Not a buoy could he find.

The sun reached its height, and began to recede from the upper heavens. Still he sought, tacking back and forth, searching every acre of his lobster grounds. His noonday meal lay untouched in the shadow of the middle thwart.

At last he knew what had been done, and sat down, his eyes aching from the strain of continual looking, his heart saddened.

"D.ey've cut my bu-ooys," he muttered apathetically.

The boat drifted and slatted; he, with head between his hands, heedless in the stern. Of a sudden he jumped up.

"I do-na knaw who done dis, but, by t' God, I'll settle wi' un."

He took his course for home.

"'T'll mean my work wi' t' factory," he muttered; "I ain't got no money fur to buy more traps. Kyrie, *Kyrie*—" he continued with a deep groan, "d'ey's done me, zure. But—" his voice trembled with anger—"I'll settle wi' 'em fust afore we hass to go back ter Forteau."

He reached the little shack by the shore just as the sun was setting, crimson-glorious in the west, and the clouds a melody of harmonious colors. Kyrie was waiting for him.

"Hass un done well thiss day?" she called before his boat struck the shingle.

He looked at her silently, and she saw the expression on his face.

"T'ere's some'at de matter, Jack?"

"Aye!" he sprang on the beach, "Aye— t'ere's much t' matter."

"Whut is't, man?"

"No matter, Kyrie, no matter whut 'tiss." He would not sadden *her* yet. "Give un some'at t' eat, girl."

She placed boiled cod and lobster before him, and a dipper of steaming tea. He ate and drank feverishly, gulping the food.

"I be goin' 'cross ter t' Port."

She, who knew him so well, felt the fury in his voice; was frightened by the look in his eyes.

"Whut for t'iss time o' night?"

"No matter, Kyrie—no matter."

He drew his rough sleeve over his mouth, stalked to the boat, pushed off and sailed toward Port Saunders. She watched him, as always, till his canvas was but a blur in the evening purple lights.

"T'ere's bad doin's, I know," she whispered brokenly.

III

The dock at Port Saunders held the same crowd of lobstermen as the night before, all but Mat Wheeler, and when darkness fell, shrouding the distances envaging the forests, he too came down, smoking, his great paws thrust in his pockets, cap akimbo, boots rattling loudly on the timbers.

"'Twass a good job, boys," he announced slowly, "sixty-wan buoys cut an' sixty-wan traps gone to H——." He puffed and puffed, then—"That'll do fur him thiss trip—I guess."

No one answered. The massive faces were expressionless in the gloom, appearing through it like white masks.

"Ain't ye glad we done it—now come— ans'er?" Wheeler squatted on a string piece.

No sound, not a word or a whisper from these simple fishermen. Those that had taken part in the cutting of Ellison's buoys were silent; the rest did not care to speak.

"Cod hooks!" Wheeler growled, "arter my given ye t' plan an' ye doin' of it, ye'r ashamed ter say ye'r glad!"

"Ay!" Nelson said with slow precision, "Ay, an' well they mought be ashamed!"

Wheeler sprang to his feet, moved over to where Nelson was sitting, "Ye coward, y' that dassent say y'r glad!"

Nelson, still sitting, looked up.

"Take it back, Mat Wheeler."

"I no take back nuthin'."

"I'll gie ye wan more chance; take—it —back!" Nelson stood up, pocketing his pipe as he spoke.

Murmurs came from the group.

"Take it back, Mat!" was to be heard here and there.

Wheeler was stung to the quick. He, the leader always at Port Saunders, to take back his word—no!

"I do-na take back what I said!"

How it was done not one man could tell. All they saw was a whirlwind of sledge-hammer blows from which Wheeler emerged staggering, bleeding from his mouth and nose.

"'Nough, 'Zeke, 'nough!" some one shouted.

Nelson was thoroughly aroused. "Not till I kills him!" he snarled, striking with all his great strength. No one dared interfere, and Wheeler, groggy, weakly tried to parry the blows that showered on his head and face.

"Keep him off fur God's sake!" he screamed.

No one moved. Nelson closed with him. A sharp wrestle, a heave and a loud splash.

"Thar'—curse ye, that'll do fur ye!" Panting, livid in the night light with fury, Nelson stood at the edge of the dock watching the struggles of the nearly unconscious Wheeler in the deep water below.

Drisco Beldon ran toward the dock side.

"Stan' back, Drisco! He's got it now, an' I 'low no man to undo my work!" 'Zeke's huge fists clenched with his words. His whole figure was one of enormous strength; standing there in the starlight, his massive shoulders loomed aggressively, and his breathing was plainly audible. Drisco fell back. Not a sound save for the gurgling and feeble splashing of the man in the water, broke the deep, chill silence. Nelson watched Wheeler grow weaker and weaker.

Then, as a wraith on the tiny breeze, a sail appeared close to. No one had seen it come.

Ellison heard the drowning man, jammed his tiller over and slid up to him.

"Keep away, thar'!" Nelson growled.

"Keep 'way, iss it?" Jack shouted back, his hand on Wheeler's coat collar—"Thiss man's a'drownin'! Don't y' know it?" He lifted Mat aboard.

"I'm dam'ed!" 'Zeke whispered.

The others crowded about as Ellison landed, the half-dead man in his arms.

"Ye be a foine lot, a-settin' thar' when thiss pore feller be a-drownin'!" he said contemptuously.

"Ij-jiot!" Nelson breathed in his ear, "'Tiss de man, Wheeler, dat set a lot o' 'em on ter cut y' bu-ooys, an' helped do ut! He wass dead ef y' had no comed along, ij-jiot!"

The gaunt Labradorian looked down at the white, bleeding face that rested in the crook of his arm.

"So *he* be un, hein? I knawed I'd find un."

The group waited, not knowing what to expect. Nelson, still shaking and trembling from the exertion of the fight, stood at Ellison's side.

From out of the horizon the full glory of the moon burst on the strange scene. Its first beams, reaching over the forests, lighted strongly on the Labradorian's face. He threw up his head suddenly.

"He did-no try fer to kill me, boys; I'll settle wi' un fur t' traps later."

A murmur of incredulous surprise came from hoarse throats as Ellison moved up the hill toward the village, carrying Wheeler. He took him to his house and laid him on the step.

"Tak' care o' un, Missus," he said to the woman that answered his thundering knock; "un be near drownded."

He went to the factory. The "Boss," Armstrong, was at his desk.

"Hello, Jack; what's your load to-day? Good as ever, I suppose?"

"Naw, Mister Armstrong, I's lost all my traps." He twirled his cap awkwardly, tumultuous thoughts racing through his brain.

"Lost your traps, man? How? There's been no storm!" Armstrong leaned back in his chair.

"Dey's—dey's—" the huge fisherman hesitated and stuttered—"I's lost un all, da's all!"

The "Boss" looked at him keenly for a moment.

"Another trick to get more traps without paying," he muttered to himself; then aloud, "that is too bad, Ellison; I'm afraid I can't let you have any more."

Jack staggered. "No more trap, Mister Armstrong? I'm finushed ef y' do-na trust me."

"Sorry, Jack—can't do it—good-night."

"'Night, zor."

Somehow he found his way out of the lobster-reeking cannery, into the pure night air, and walked, unseeing, unheedingly toward the dock. A hand grasped his arm. He stopped.

"I's was listenin', Jack, whut do it mean ter ye?"

Nelson's burly form seemed slight in the moonlight beside that of the giant Labradorian.

Ellison looked at him with such a world of sadness that tears came to the Newfoundlander's eyes.

"It means p'utty near starvation t'iss winter, 'Zeke—da's all!"

"'T'll no mean it, man, fur I axes y' now to trap along o' me an' un's'll go halfs."

Ellison whirled round. "Y'r a good man, 'Zeke, but I can-no take de bread an' money f'om ye dat-a-way."

"I's got money in de bank ter St.

John's, man. I's al—l right; do's I tells y'." The sincere eagerness in Nelson's voice thrilled Ellison through and through.

"An' ye w'ld 'a let un drownded, 'Zeke."

"Ay," the Newfoundlander growled, "an' glad o't."

"Fur my sake?"

Nelson saw his chance to equivocate without lying, and took it instantly.

"Naw, man, naw! Un called me fust a loiar, then a cow—ard; da's why."

Ellison drew a long breath. "I's knawed long since y' were friend to me, 'Zeke, but I could-no be wi' y' ef ye tried t' kill fur *me*."

"Wull ye go halfs?"

The Labradorian's eyes swept the dim far away till they rested on a tiny light across the Bay.

"Kyrie, *Kyrie* an' To'mie!" he muttered.

"Ay, Kyrie an' To'mie!" Nelson urged. "Will un?"

"Yiss, 'Zeke, an' t' God'll bless un fur thiss."

"An' y'll sattle wi' Wheeler?"

Jack drew himself up, his muscles working under his rough clothes. "I'll sattle wi' un fur t' traps, but I'll no kill un," he answered very softly.

"Da's right, Jack, ye be right. An' me'll help y' sattle."

They went to the dock together.

IV

For two weeks Ellison threw in his lot with 'Zeke, working hard. The days were longer at the traps, and because of summer calms, many miles had to be rowed back and forth. When he came to the shack, sometimes very late, he would throw himself on the bunk too tired to eat, but never too tired to kiss Kyrie and to have a minute's play with the boy.

"Aw', girl," he sighed one night, sitting on the door-sill, the cool night air moving caressingly over his hot forehead, "I be zure done, an' on'y four dollars thiss two week. I do-na know w'ere 'tiss goin' end. Them divvils!" he dashed to his feet— "T' G——"

"Sst, man, no t' say it." She had her hand over his mouth. "We uns 've lived happy an' well manny bit'ty year, an' 'tall coome right; no t' currse, man."

He pulled her hand away gently, looking at her from his great height, and a smile flitted over his face as he bent toward her.

"Y' be zure right, Kyrie, an' I'm sorry I thought o't." It was no effort for him to lift her in his arms. "I be on'y sad, Kyrie, 'cause ye an' t' boy've no much t' eat, or clo'es." He swallowed hard. She felt the quiver of his body.

"Da's a' fine, Jack; don't'y worrit. 'Tiss summer yit a time an' y'll h've more better luck soon."

He stood silent in the starlight, watching the slowly darting reflections of the night lights on the waters of the bay.

"I be goin' sleep." He pulled off his boots and curled up on the far side of the rough bed.

The woman looked out beyond, where the lights of Port Saunders blinked drowsily.

"Ye've tried fer to drive un out, an' would 'a but fer 'Zeke, bless un, an' my Jack'll show y' yit."

There was a fierce subdued anger in her low words; the emotion of a woman who knows that the man she loves has been unfairly treated. She shivered.

"'Tiss goin' t' blaw by mornin'," peering across the twinkling heavens.

She went in, shutting the rickety door securely.

"Up, girl, an' break'fus'." Ellison touched her.

"Wh't—wh't?" heavy with sleep, she stared at him standing over her in his oil-skins, sou'wester in hand.

"Dad?"

"A'—To'mie!"

"Be un goin' out thiss day?"

He laughed for an instant, then was silent. The woman roused herself, listening.

The wind hurled itself viciously at the shack, pulling in gusts at the door, sobbing under the thin eaves. She jumped up and ran to the little window. The bay was only ruffled by the powerful wind, but in the Straits great sheets of spray lathered into the air and were driven away instantly.

"Y' be no goin', Jack?"

"Ay, Kyrie; I told un 'Zeke I'd go-a thiss day. T' rest'll no dare go; mabbe I'll make some'at better prices."

"Do-na go, Jack, do-na, fur *my* sake—an' To'mie?"

"Naw, naw, Kyrie, do-na take on thiss a-way; 'tiss a'right! Manny a-time I be out i' wuss' nor thiss, an' ye knaw it." He picked the lad, in his coarse woolen night shirt, up in his great arms. "Zure, To'mie, y' be no afeared?"

The boy looked into his father's eyes with absolute confidence. "Naw, Dad, ef y' t'ink bestis."

He sat him in his long crib again.

"Thar', Kyrie—be no afeard. T' bo-oy knaws."

She said no more, placing cold fish and tea before him. He ate heartily.

"By—, Kyrie. 'Tiss day I make de money—*zure!*"

To'mie, the boy, clinging to her skirt, she saw Ellison double reef his sail, shove off and bear away toward the Straits, waving his hand to her.

"T' God be wi' un," she prayed softly.

Overhead a whirling, racing mass of wind, cloud and feathery drift, dashed on to a nor'-nor'-east wind that stung on the Labradorian's face and drove spray sharply over his boat as he held on outside. The shores of the bay seemed a duller gray and more bleak than ever; forbidding in their harshness when mists upon mists of spume flew over them. As a distant, furious roar the sound of the breakers on Long Point came to Ellison. He shifted his course a point.

"'Tiss un bad un, no misstake. T'ere'll be no un out thiss day but me."

Ahead of him, rearing their crests to enormous heights, the combers of the Straits raced by, dirty-green and frothing in the pale daylight.

Ellison hove to under the point and stood up, water dripping from his sleeves and hat. Long and keenly his eyes swept the tumbling stretches of seas, and he reckoned his chances.

"'F 'twere no fur Kyrie an' t' bo-oy, I'd no go," he muttered, "but t'ey need un money, an' ef I kin find dem traps—da's good thiss day to de factory."

He examined his halliards and sheet, noting also that the rudder was securely stepped, and steered out into the full strength of the wind. The boat scurried ahead, water just reaching the thole-pins to leeward, blowing back sharply. For a time he was in calm surface, then, as he flew along past the point, the heave of the long surges reached him, tossing the boat up and down with squirts of spray.

"Can-no git to de outsiders," he said aloud, "'ll have fer to haul by d'East Rocks."

Tumultuous and wild, the huge seas, but a little way beyond him, rose and hurried on, their sides white with sickly foam. He could faintly hear their hiss and curl as they broke over each other in the mad rush on the outside bar. Full daylight was on, but the salt haze and shifting veils of wave mist prevented his seeing far. He shivered with cold as a stinging crest dashed over him.

"'Tiss ba-ad!" wiping the water from his eyes.

"*Swsshle— swsshle— swis-s-s-s—t!*" was the sound of the waves, to a weird crying and whistling of the wind in his rigging.

He worked ahead carefully keeping her away and luffing as the gusts came more and more viciously. His hands were purple with chill and strain, but he dared not let go of either the tiller or sheet, and he sat tight, grimly holding on, spume and liquid dust flying over him.

"T'ere's bo-at!" he shouted loudly then, seeing a bit of sail outside of him, laboring badly in the seas. He got to his knees and watched it keenly each time he rose on the heights. Sometimes it, too, was on top of a sea, and he could distinguish a lobster boat, heavy loaded with traps, struggling for the inner bay.

"T'll niver live onless un t'rows de traps away," he muttered, heading more into the wind to slow his speed.

"'Tiss gon-ed," he yelled, as a monster curling sea rushed on the other.

"No-a," as he saw it slowly climb the next oncoming wave. He watched it several minutes.

"T' fool! I be goin' see whut ails un." He brought the *Kyrie E.* into the wind, waited his chance, and came about throwing himself to leeward as she took in the green badly. He beat his way to within a hundred yards of the other, then looked sharply.

"'Tiss Mat!" he said, gave a glance at the lone man who bailed with one hand, trying to steer with the other, and kept the *Kyrie E.* away.

"Un's got it now," he whispered, "an' t' be on'y fair." Some impulse of a powerful nature made him turn his head.

Wheeler, desperate, had hove his boat into the wind, and was standing up, waving a handkerchief. Ellison chuckled grimly.

"Ye've tried fer to sta-arve me an' Kyrie an' To'mie out. No-ow take it." He kept his boat to her course.

Suddenly his wife's face came before him, and he saw the look in her eyes at his leaving a man to such a death. He looked back again. Wheeler was bailing, the stern of his boat so heavy with lobster traps that the seas broke in over it every instant.

"T' fool, w'y do-na he t'row un out?"

A fight to the end went on in the Labradorian's mind. On one hand the great wrong the man had done him, on the other, his life, for well Jack knew he could save him. Against this sympathetic sensation, Ellison put the fact that Kyrie and the boy had had no clothes for a month, and very little to eat; his heart bittered at the thought, and he kept on. Then the vision cf Wheeler's family, destitute, with no one's hand to help them, a wife and five children, and a woman's chance in Newfoundland is a very slight one, rose up. He jammed his tiller over.

"I'll do my best—God!" he murmured apologetically, ashamed of his first desire. Carefully, with steady nerves, watching the combers as they hurled themselves by him, he drew alongside the other. Mat's boat was over half full, and soggering heavily in the seas.

"T'row out de traps," Jack shrieked, standing to his tiller.

"Can't do it. Tied fasst, an' I dassunt leg-go t' untie," Wheeler screamed back.

"Stan' by!" the Labradorian bellowed, seeing an awful breaker, its top beginning to furl, rushing down on them. Wheeler lost his head. He kept away instead of holding his bows into it, and the thing was done. Ellison took in some water, not much, and when the Kyrie E. slid into the long valley after the big wave, all he saw was Wheeler's upturned boat and the man swimming toward him. Jack got him aboard with a deft heave and a lurch.

"Da's twict ye ain't killed me w'en y' had t' chanct," Mat sobbed.

Ellison looked at him contemptuously, guiding his boat the while with innate skill.

"Pore fool ye!" he thundered. "God ain't made me t' kill t' likes o' ye."

Wheeler stared at him. The wind yelled and droned about them and the seas snarled hungrily. In a few moments Port Saunders came into sight and within an hour the Kyrie E. glided into the smooth waters of the bay. Ellison sat down in the stern sheets, moodily silent, Mat watching him furtively.

"Are ye glad or sorry un saved me?" he asked.

"I don-na know," the Labradorian answered gruffly.

The Newfoundlander was silent. They slid up to the dock at the port. Nelson and several others were clustered there.

"Don-na that beat all?" 'Zeke mumbled, seeing Wheeler in Ellison's boat.

Questions by the score poured on the two when they landed.

"Whut is't, Jack, lad?" Nelson whispered. Ellison drew away from him roughly.

"'Tiss now't, 'Zeke; I be sorry, but I did-no haul t' traps thiss day."

Nelson clung to his arm, "How be Mat Wheeler along o' ye?"

The Labradorian straightened in his wet clothes, shivering with cold. "'Tiss now't, I tell un, 'Zeke."

"Aye, it be some'at, boys."

The group turned as one man when Wheeler spoke. His face was gray-drawn and haggard.

"'Tiss Ellison ha' sav-ved me t'iss day an'—" he swallowed several times— "I war a' stealin' hiss trap an you'n, 'Zeke, w'en he did it, da's all."

Nelson sprang viciously at him, but a long burly arm thrust him back. Ellison towered between the two, grimly smiling. "T' traps be gone annyway, 'Zeke; t'aint no use growlin' now."

"Coome wid me," Wheeler grabbed Ellison by the arm, and led him to the Boss's desk in the factory.

"Mister Armstrong."

"Well, Mat," the Superintendent asked, flicking the ashes of his cigar to the floor.

"I done cut dis man Ellison's bu-oys t'ree week ago; me an'——"

"Sssht!" Jack gripped the Newfoundlander hard; "tell on yersel' cf ye like, but don-na **giv'** t'odders names, seein' ye coaxed 'm t' do it."

"I's got two hund'er dollar t' my **credit?**" Wheeler leaned forward impetuously.

"Yes, Mat, you have."

"I wants Jack ter be fitted out **wi' a** new set o' traps, an' I'll pay."

Ellison and Nelson stared in surprise. Wheeler was breathing hard in his excitement.

Armstrong pushed back his chair and stood up slowly.

"You are a dirty scoundrel and a thief, Mat Wheeler. Here I've been almost starving this man, because of your tricks. I'll not take your 'pay' as you call it. You have two hundred dollars to your credit, yes, but not one more lobster does this factory buy of you. And I'll fit out Ellison at our expense. He's a better man than ever came into Port Saunders, and I'm proud to have him trap for us. My apologies, Jack?"

Ellison shuffled awkwardly again.

"'T'ass a'right, Mister Armstrong, but —" he *was* sorry for the poor devil beside him, for he knew what the factory's boycott meant. "Wull ye not let Wheeler go on?"

"No," Armstrong shouted, "not for any amount of lobsters."

The Labradorian, his old grudges forgotten, thrust his face close to that of the Superintendent. "Ye'll let Wheeler go on, else me an' 'Zeke—eh, 'Zeke?" turning to the burly man. He nodded. "Else me an' 'Zeke an' Wheeler sell to Bonne Bay."

Silence in the dingy office, more dingy and dark than ever in the dull storm light. The wind yowled lustily down the little chimney, creating a vicious draught on the wood embers. Armstrong felt the power of Ellison's words.

"Go on, all of you then," he growled. The three stalked out. Wheeler seized the Labradorian's hand.

"Y've been too squar'," he muttered, "an' I'll gie ye quarters my haulin's a week fer two mont's to pay ye."

"Go on, go on home," Ellison answered shortly.

"Ye be a foine man, Jack," Nelson breathed deeply.

"Aw, 'Zeke, dere's odder things in life but chokin' a man out." The Labradorian hoisted his sail and fled across the bay toward the little shack, the group watching him all the way.

"Foine man!" Drisco said quietly.

"T' bessis dat iver coome out o' Labrador," and Nelson swung up the hill.

39

A Day's Work in the Mounted Police

LAWRENCE MOTT

A DAY'S WORK IN THE MOUNTED POLICE

BY LAWRENCE MOTT

"ANY complaints?"

One of the mounted policemen slid wearily from his saddle as he spoke.

A November sky spread the cold yellow hues of a stormy sunset over the endless prairies, and a chill, strong wind mourned its desolate way through the horses' tails, whistling around the corners of the squatter's shed with a doleful whine that rose and fell monotonously.

A woman had come to the low door in answer to their halloo and the two men looked at her disconsolately. She rubbed her work-worn hands together nervously.

"No ther hain't, leastways—" she hesitated and looked keenly past the horses, seeking to pierce the winter's gloom that lay heavy over the bare landscape, "leastways, none that I can tell on," she continued, with a catch in her voice. "Jim ain't ter hum; ye'd best stay the night; it's er goin' ter snow, I guess, by the feelin'. Yer kin stable yer critters down in th' shed an' welcome."

"I reckon we'd better, Fred; it's a long thirty mile to old Ned Blake's, and *I* think snow's a-comin,' too."

The other nodded and, still mounted, walked his horse toward the shed. The first speaker followed, leading his animal. The long, rickety building was down in a little roll of the prairie, and as the two approached it a forlorn old hen cackled harshly, and a pig, disturbed by the sound of the horses' feet, grunted and rustled in the straw.

"Who's the old gal, Bert?" Fred asked, as he undid his girths, the horse playfully nibbling his shoulder.

"Sho, forgot ye warn't over this route yet; she's widder Gleeson; a feller called Jim Stephens lives yere, kinder helps round the farm, y' know!" and they both chuckled.

Bert Saunders was an old member of the N. W. M. P.* The years had grown on his broad back in the service, and, as he said, "I hain't no good for nawthin' else."

With gray hair and deep-set eyes that were hardly to be seen behind fierce, bushy eyebrows, Saunders showed that if age brings experience, he must have his full share of it. The other was a young man; tall, well built, a good horseman, with a "good eye," but old Saunders would quietly suggest that "he was a leetle too quick."

"Th' widder seems to hev sum'n on her mind," Bert remarked as they went back to the house, "but 'tain't nawthin' excitin', I'll bet; mabbe she's lost a calf, or mabbe ol' Jim got some whiskey som'ere."

"Set ye down, boys, set right down near, till I gets ye some vittles." The old woman hurried about, pottering among the kitchen implements, or rather makeshifts for them, and rattling vigorously in a huge tin box that served as tea-bag, salt cellar, meat holder and bread basket.

"Queer old place," Fred muttered, looking about as they stood by the fire.

"Yes," Saunders answered in a whisper, "an' ther used to be some queer doin's too, when she—" he jerked his thumb toward the kitchen—"was a young 'oman."

The inside of the main room was dark and dingy with age and dirt. A huge four-poster bed stood in one corner, the blankets on it rolled up in a tangled heap, and the shabby, ragged pillows had evidently been used as footstools. Old cowhide boots stuck out from beneath the bed, and overalls with a strange assortment of clothes dangled ungracefully from pegs all about. The candles spluttered and flick-

* Northwest Mounted Police.

ered, giving out but faint, weak rays of light that scarce illumined the long, narrow room.

"Thar, ye kin eat!" Widow Gleeson drew up the dangerously tottering stools, and seated herself on the edge of the bed while the two men began their supper. For some minutes nothing was to be heard but the metallic clinking of the tinware, and the gurgling sips Saunders took of the hot tea.

"I'm d—n glad we're in here, instead of fightin' our way to Blake's; listen to that—" Fred said then.

"Gosh, yes!"

The threatened snow had come outside, brought by a gale of wind. The particles were hard frozen and battered viciously in their million numbers against the walls, while the wind screamed fitfully. When supper was over the men got out their pipes and smoked by the crackling fire, whose flames shot up the flue in straight, roaring lines, drawn by the fierce draught.

"No complaints, d'ye say, Widder?" Bert asked slowly, rubbing the tobacco fine between his palms. She fidgeted nervously, then hesitated again, seemingly listening for something.

"Nawthin' that I can tell on, but Jim he hain't been good ter me lately; hit me with th' axe handle two weeks 'go, an' cussed som'n arful becos I didn't have no whiskey; ye boys know thet since ye've ben so sharp a-watchin' them fellers 'cross the line it's purty hard to get whiskey, ain't it, now?" she finished appealingly.

"Yes, Widder, we're lookin' arter 'em purty close now, sure," and Saunders laughed; "it's tol'able hard ter run th' liquor over into Canady now! Wall, what about Jim? What's he done?" The chance question told, and the old woman was startled.

"How d'ye know?" she whispered.

"Don't, but I'm guessin'."

"Now, boys, I don't know nawthin', but since I comed back from Uncle Jack's—I went over thar when Jim got c'ntanker'us, ye know—I seed som'n funny 'bout h'ar; look ahere!"

She reached down and pulled out one of the cowhide boots. Saunders examined the rough, worn leather carefully; then he gave a short, sharp whistle. Any one that knew Bert's ways would have realized that something was wrong, and Fred did know the old fellow well, having made many a ride and route with him; therefore he leaned forward eagerly.

Saunders turned the boot over and over. "How long's Jim had these yer boots?"

"They bain't hisn!" the woman answered quickly.

"Oh, ho! so they ain't Jim's? Did ye ever see 'em afore?"

"Um—mm," and a strong negative shake of her head.

"Looks like blood, don't it, Bert?"

"Looks like blood an' es blood."

Saunders put the boot down. "We'll look round a mite, Widder."

With stolid eyes the woman watched them searching here and there, peering into dark corners, shaking old baggings while the dust rose in clouds.

"Here's something!" Fred called, and held up a red-stained block of wood that he had found under the mess of plow chains and old metal.

The older man examined it as carefully as he had the boot, and again whistled sharply to himself; the block he put by the boot.

"Look furder, Fred." They hunted and prodded in silence, then Saunders turned on his heel.

"Looky here, Widder, what you got 'gin Jim?"

The old woman seemed to shrivel and her eyes grew large and black.

"Nawthen' 'cept he's cross an' I'm sick o' him," she answered shortly.

"H'm," and they searched again.

"When'd Jim go 'way?"

"Three days ago, jus' afore the last snow."

"Where'd he go?"

"Dunno; said as he was goin' ter Rickson's, but he allus wuz a liar."

"H'm, Rickson's; that's eighty mile by the trail," Saunders said more to himself than for the benefit of the others.

"How'd he go—ride?"

"Yep, took th' horse, an' I kin stay here an' starve, or walk out, I s'pose!"

They found nothing more, though the search had been long and thorough.

"What do you think about it, Bert?"

"I hain't thought 'nuff yet; let ye know in th' mornin'; better turn in now!"

He pulled off the long service boots and

stretched his feet gratefully to the fire. The old woman watched them a while longer, then took a candle and crawled slowly up the shaky ladder that led to the small attic over one end of the long room.

"You boys kin hev the bed," she called down.

Saunders looked at the mess of clothes. "I guess not for mine, Fred; I'll roll up in the blankets right here."

"The same for me!" Fred got their blankets from their saddle rolls they had brought in, and unfolded them on the rough floor. They took off their coats, and these, with the long fur capotes, made excellent pillows.

When the candles were out, and the tiny glows at the ends of the wicks had vanished, the interior was dark save for the ember glow, and silent save for the storm sounds outside.

Gust on gust the fierce breaths shook the old timbers till they creaked, drone on drone came from the flue, and the bitter cold air found its way through the cracks in the floor, biting the men's faces as they lay rolled in the warm, blue wool blankets.

Just then the door blew inward, burst by a gust more powerful than the others.

"Damn, damn!" Fred grumbled, as he got up slowly to close it. He looked out first. It was a wild winter's night on the prairie. In the faint snow sheen the short distances were hazy and vague, laden with hurtling masses of white. Overhead the sky was dark, but the heavy cloud banks were black, and their dim shapes could faintly be seen tearing in great rent and split masses across the heavens. Fred shivered as he pushed the boards into the aperture and fastened it with a bar of wood.

"The horses 'll catch it t'night," he muttered as he curled up again. It seemed to him that he was hardly asleep when something moving caught his attention. He lay quiet, listening intently, trying to locate the sound. From his position he could just see the foot of the attic ladder as it was between him and the window; then a black something came between him and the faint white reflection. It moved aside.

"Th' old woman! What's she want?" he whispered, his lips scarcely moving. The dull scrape of a sulphur match came to him softly in answer, and he shut his

eyes to slits. The blue flame spluttered into life, then came the yellow shine, and he saw the widow carefully light a candle stub under cover of her hands. Its light came redly through the flesh of the fingers.

She looked a long time at the sleeping men, and the policeman felt his eyes twitch and jerk with the strain. Then she turned her back and moved noiselessly to the far end of the building. She stopped there, looking back, and Fred started at the ugly expression on her face. She shook her gnarled fist at the two, then leaned over and began pulling and tugging at some of the floor boards. Now wide awake and alert, Fred sat up carefully under cover of the blanket and watched. At last she got one of the boards well up and drew a long something from the bosom of her tattered dress. The policeman looked hard, but could only see that it seemed black, and a piece of cloth.

As slowly the woman dropped the thing in the hole, lowered the board, quietly replaced the things that had been on it and turned to come back. Quick as he was she saw Fred drop.

Instantly the candle went out and everything was quiet save for the weird sounds of the wind.

He felt for his revolver, and was about to call Saunders, when the bar at the door was violently pushed aside, the door itself flew open, and he caught a fleeting glimpse of a muffled figure sneaking out.

"Halt there!" he shouted, but the wind forced the sound of his voice into his throat.

"W's matter?" Saunders asked, sleepily.

"Wake up, man, quick! Something's wrong!"

As though to the bugle call the other was out of the blankets and on his feet, revolver in hand. The two stood still for an instant in the darkness, the snow piling coldly on the floor.

"The old woman's skedaddled," he called then, and hurried over to the corner where he had seen her mysterious actions.

In his haste he broke match after match trying to get a light.

"Take it easy, boy, take it easy!" Saunders followed him over.

"What's all this anyhow? What ye doin'?" as Fred hauled at the boards, tossing everything right and left. He got them up and the light showed a dark, long hole dug in the earth. He leaned over, lowering the candle.

"Holy tickets, Bert, look at that!"

The other craned his neck. "He hain't ben dead more'n two days neither!" he said slowly; "she's done it, an' tried fer to set us on this same pore feller, so's we'd go ter Rickson's ter-morrer an' give her a chanst ter git out. The ol' varmint didn't expec' us till next week. I tol' ye we were early on this route. Well, come on an' find her; she ain't far t'night; hidin' in the barn, mos' likely. Hell of a job to take her to the post, now, ain't it?" So talking quietly, with the coolness of long years at this sort of work, Saunders calmly pulled on his boots while the younger man chafed at the delay.

"Look out she don't shoot ye, Fred; may hev er gun," he advised, as the two with lowered heads went out into the fury of the night.

They reached the shed; the thatch door was wide open.

"She's in there all right," Saunders stood at the entrance. "Come out, ye ——, ——, ——, we've got ye, —— ye!" No answer.

Slowly Bert's anger grew, and he swore at the black interior.

His voice echoed each time very faintly in the straw-smelling place.

"Le's go in an' haul her out—come on!"

They went, and Fred struck a light.

"The horses!" he gasped. Saunders turned; the horses were gone!

"Out wi' ye quick, 'less ye want ter walk! Strike fer Blake's, she won't go agin' this wind for Rickson's, an' I don't believe she kin manage them horses, not both on 'em, anyhow!"

They floundered on to the trail, discernible only under the snow by its flatness, and hurried along it as fast as they could. The snow hindered them more and more, piling against their legs and creeping up under their trousers, where it clung freezingly.

"There's one of 'em!" Saunders shrieked, as a black object came in sight just off the track. They came up to it; one of the horses, and cleverly hobbled! The poor brute stood there helpless, its mane and tail heavily laden with ice particles, the nostrils' edges solid and eyes tight frozen. When the hobble was cut it moved stiffly.

Saunders started to mount. "Get out o' that," and Fred shoved him aside; "I'll go! Ye ain't fit to go on such a night as this; ye'r a better man for it, but I'm younger and you'll freeze 'thout your fur; go back and wait. I'll find her if she's between here and Blake's!" and he rode off, hearing Saunders' curses but for an instant. The latter turned against the flying snow sheets.

"He's a good un, jus' same," he muttered. "Gosh, it's d——n cold! I believe I must be gettin' old after all." He went back to the house and built up the dead fire.

Meanwhile Fred struggled on. Little by little the horse recovered its strength and moved faster, but the cold began to tell on the man's body, damp from the exertion of the run he had had. He got the horse into a gallop and swung his arms viciously.

"That's better," he whispered, as the flying scud showed brighter in the east. He kept on steadily and daylight grew: the snow drifted worse and worse. The little horse labored badly, sank into a trot, and from that to a walk, hanging its head and licking the snow.

Then far ahead the policeman saw a speck, and urged the horse to a trot again.

"That's her," he said aloud in a few moments.

The distance between them lessened. There, astride of the other stolen mount, was the old woman, her head and body wrapped in an Indian rabbit-skin blanket; the horse was walking steadily along, she huddled in the saddle. She heard nothing because of the noises of the wind till Fred reached her side.

"Halt!"

She stuck her face out, saw him, and before the man could move, grabbed her bridle, jerked the horse off the trail and galloped across the snow plains.

He drew his revolver.

"I'll shoot!" he yelled, but he might as well have thought it for all she heard.

"By God, I will shoot!" he swore, and took aim. "Great tickets, can't I catch her? I *will!*" and away he went, firing twice in the air to try to intimidate the fleeing figure, but without success. His horse stumbled, gathered itself and stumbled again, and he saw that she would get away from him.

"I'll have to shoot the horse. Poor old Bill, but I'll have that woman, so help me!"

He drew up, took aim and fired.

"Too low!" as a spit of snow rose behind the other horse.

Bang!

"Too far to the left!"

Bang!

"Got him!" as the brute staggered to and fro.

He moved on slowly and came up to the fugitive.

The ugly face peered at him through the blankets.

"I've got you now; get off that horse!" She did not move; he dismounted, grabbed the blankets and yanked her off.

Another shot and the wounded beast was dead. He patted the lifeless head as it lay on the snow.

"Poor old Bill—good horse!" he said huskily; "you died for the service." He turned savagely.

"Now you walk, d'y hear? Walk!" He waited. No move from the shape on the crust.

"I'll kill yer if you don't get up!"

"Ye dassent," she snarled then, speaking for the first time. He coaxed, threatened, promised—all to no end.

Then he picked her up, slung her over his saddle, fastened her there, stripped the dead horse of its saddle and bridle and fastened them on his own.

"I'll have to walk; the hoss can't carry both," and so they started, he leading, bridle rein over his arm. The exercise warmed him, as he was chilled through and through and his ears were frozen. He rubbed snow on them as he went on. They proceeded thus for some time.

"Funny I don't hit that trail!" He led the way to a snow rise. As far as he could see in the now full gray light were moving clouds of snow; no flat anywhere, nothing but hills or hollows that appeared and vanished between the squalls.

"Here, you," he shook the mass in the saddle roughly. "Where are we?"

"S'pose I'm goin' ter tell?" the cracked voice answered fiercely.

"But we'll die out here—I'm lost!"

"S'pose I care? They'll kill me at the Post fur killin' Jim—what's the dif'rence?"

"You admit murdering Jim?" he shouted.

She nodded, as he could tell by the shaking of the blankets.

"Here's a fine outfit," he said to himself. "A clear, good case; maybe stripes if I land her at the Post, and certain death if I don't find the way!"

He thought hard and an idea came.

He put the bridle rein over the horse's head again, patted it, stroked its ice-hung muzzle. Then he stood aside, and struck its back sharply with his hand.

The horse threw up its nose, hesitated, then swerved sharp to the right and started to trot. Fred ran behind, holding it lightly by the tail. On the animal went, its ears pricked forward, life in its movements where it had been sluggard and slow. Sometimes walking, then trotting again, but always moving decisively, the horse kept on. The man was tired and the snow chafed his ankles and legs badly. His body was warm, but his hands, feet and face pained severely. They came up over a rise, and the long-familiar house stood just beyond.

"Thank God!" he muttered incoherently, and kissed the poor frozen muzzle again and again. The animal seemed to understand and tried to nip his hand.

Saunders was waiting.

"Ye got her?" was the first question.

"Sure!"

"Where's my Bill?"

When Fred told the story the old sergeant's face quivered hard, but, "A good horse was Bill, an' many miles I've done wi' him!" was all he said.

He helped to undo the lashings, and the blanketed figure dropped into his arms.

"Here, none o' that—stand up!" He let go and it fell inert.

"Froze a mite, I guess."

Saunders pulled aside the blankets. The face he saw leered up at him white and lifeless, the eyes open and dull set. With a curse he drew the blankets back. A short knife was driven in over the heart, and the old, worn hand was still fast to the handle.

"D'ye know this?" he asked.

"God! no," Fred answered, "I saw nothing, 'cept when the horse started out right the blankets moved a trifle."

"That's it, then; she knowed the way, and when she seed you was a-comin' right she did this job; wouldn't that beat all? Wall," he continued with a sigh, "it's all in the day's work!"

40

To the Pacific Through Canada

ERNEST INGERSOLL

TO THE PACIFIC THROUGH CANADA.

BY ERNEST INGERSOLL.

PART I.

ONE hundred years ago, "through Canada to the Pacific" was first achieved by Sir Alexander Mackenzie. Making his way in a birch canoe from Montreal up the Ottawa and connecting rivers to Lake Huron, he came to the Sault Sainte Marie. Then followed hundreds of miles of paddling along the homeless shores of Lake Superior until civilization was seen again at Fort William on the northern shore. Yet that was only the real starting-point. Here Mackenzie began one of the most adventurous and productive explorations of that era, when the world was busy with exploration. Through rivers, ponds, and portages to Lake Winnipeg, across it and up the Saskatchewan, he pursued a well-defined route of the Hudson Bay Company's *voyageurs*. But finally he reached even the fur-trader's frontier, and pushed forward into a region never then penetrated by a white man. He came to the Peace River and began its ascent. It led him into, and guided him through, the mountains. At its sources he found water flowing westward, and through weeks of hardy adventure traced this river or that until he scented the salt breezes, and looked abroad upon the Pacific—the first man to cross Canada!

That is only a century ago; yet when you place Mackenzie's canoe beside our transcontinental railway train, the contrast is as wide as between the first and last page of history; but put the courage of the old fur-trader beside the pluck which built this railway, and the extremes meet again.

The transcontinental trip by the Canadian Pacific Railway, then, is the subject of this article. We shall not precisely follow Mackenzie's devious route, but shall touch it here and there, and see all the way the same kind of things that he saw.

Let us, first of all, have a clear understanding of what this journey is to be.

The Canadian Pacific is the largest railway system on the continent, yet there is none so little known to the general public in the United States, and none so widely misapprehended. It lies wholly in Canada. From Quebec it follows the St. Lawrence to Montreal, and then the Ottawa to the capital of the Dominion. From Ottawa it directs an almost straight course to the northernmost angle of Lake Superior, and skirting its shore for a hundred miles, strikes west to Winnipeg. Thence it crosses 900 miles of prairie, enters the Rocky Mountains 150 miles north of the United States boundary, and forcing its way through 250 miles of magnificent highlands, descends to the Pacific coast near the mouth of the Fraser River.

This main line is 3,070 miles in length, and reaches from ocean to ocean. Its through trains do not change their sleeping-cars all the way. An English family bound for China need make only two changes of conveyance between Liverpool and Hong-Kong—one at Montreal from the steamer to the cars, and another in reembarking at Vancouver, the Pacific terminus. This is a notable advantage over the pieced-up route through Europe or the United States.

Yet this main line is only the *stem* of the great system. One side-line goes to Boston. Two others communicate with railways in New York State, at Brockville and Prescott, on the St. Lawrence. Short branches reach a dozen towns in Quebec Westward, Montreal and Ottawa are connected with Toronto, whence branches ramify through all Ontario. Lake Huron is reached at Owen Sound, whence a line of ocean-like steamships on the Great Lakes is sustained. From Sudbury, a station 443 miles west of Montreal, a branch runs along the northern shore of Lake Huron to Sault Sainte Marie, where it is joined by a bridge over those historic rapids with two new American lines—one to Minneapolis, and another to Duluth. In Manitoba, branches penetrate all the corners of that rich wheat-growing province. Thus, the total length of its railways approaches 5,000 miles, and a year

of London, to the outskirts of the city, and into the quaint French villages named by pious founders after some Ste. Rose, Ste. Therése, or St. Phillipe, or other revered personages of the olden times.

We go to sleep, and do not know when Ottawa, Canada's pleasant capital and lumber market, is passed at midnight. We are oblivious to this and all the world besides until a cheery call of " Breakfast-time, sir ! " rouses our energies, and we peep out of our window to find ourselves rushing through a dense green forest, still glistening with the night's dew. Then the breadth of Lake Nipissing opens like a plain of azure amid the green woods, and we halt at North Bay, where a road from Niagara Falls and Toronto terminates and makes a junction with ours. We step out and take a run up and down the long platform. The sunlight seems unusually bright and clear, the breeze from the lake is " nipping and eager "—everything and everybody has an air of alertness and glee which is inspiriting. We have slept well—we are wide awake ; this balsamic odor of the woods is appetizing—we are hungry. The dining-car is therefore doubly inviting. Its furnishing is in elegant taste ; its linen white as the breaking of the lake-waves ; its silver glitters in the sunlight ; on every table is a bouquet of wild flowers, masking a basket of fruit. There are tables for two and tables for four. One of the latter holds a family party—father, mother and two young ladies, Vassar girls, perhaps. We seat ourselves opposite, and as the train moves smoothly on, eat and talk with a gusto forgotten since last summer's outing.

Our *vis-à-vis* at table proves to be an official of the company, who knows the whole line, as he says, " like the book." He is going clear through to attend to matters on the western coast. This is great luck, for he seems quite as willing to answer our eager questions as we are to ask them. He is intensely interested in this great achievement, as is everybody connected with it, and wants us to become equally enthusiastic.

" This ought to be a good region for fishing," we suggest, looking out upon the beautiful lake whose rocky shores we are skirting.

" Excellent," the official agrees, as he quarters his orange. " Lake Nipissing

"SMOKING IN A SNUG CORNER."

hence will be increased by a direct line to St. John, N. B., and Cape Breton, to connect with especially swift steamers, forming a new Atlantic ferry and carrying England's Oriental mails. Yet, as has been said, few Americans know or realize these important facts in Canadian progress.

The new station in Montreal, whence we take our departure for the transcontinental journey one summer evening, is a magnificent piece of architecture. It stands just at the corner of Dominion Square, where the first strains of the band concert are calling together the loitering, pleasure-making crowds which twice a week throng its gravel walks or lounge upon the turf of its green parterres.

Out from the station stretches a series of broad stone arches, carrying the tracks upon an elevated way that reminds one

abounds in big fish, and so does French River, its outlet into Lake Huron. I have had capital sport at the end of the steamboat pier at North Bay, ' whipping ' with a rod and spoon for pike, bass, pickerel, whitefish, etc. Sometimes muskallonge weighing forty or fifty pounds are caught by trolling from a boat."

" How about trout ? "

" Well, if you're bent upon trout, and don't want to go up to the Jackfish or Nepigon River (which we shall cross to-morrow morning), your best plan is to go to Trout Lake and down to the Mattawan. Trout Lake lies four or five miles inland, behind those hills, where the scenery is exceedingly beautiful and the fishing practically untouched. In the lake itself are huge bass, pickerel and muskallonge. I know of one caught there by a lady, which weighed thirty-five pounds. Down to the lake, through tortuous, shady ravines, come cataract-rivers filled with untroubled trout. You can get a boat at a settler's, or take your own and camp where you please, and fish in a new place every day all summer. Then from Trout Lake you can run a canoe down through a chain of lakes into the Mattawan River. Each of these lakes and streams has plenty of fish of several kinds, and charming camping places. The Mattawan carries you into the Ottawa, which you can descend in a boat—fishing all the way—to the St. Lawrence."

" That's an alluring story," we say.

" It's literally true ; and in the fall and winter, sport with the gun is equally good. Moose, caribou, and deer are plentiful, and the town of Mattawan forms an excellent outfitting place for a shooting trip. Indian and white guides can be got who know the country, and the many lumberers' roads and camps facilitate the sport. New Brunswick used to be the best place for that sport, but now this part of Canada is far more accessible and convenient."

At noon we come to Sudbury, where extensive mines of copper and gold are worked, and a brisk village is growing up, with some farming and a great deal of lumbering in the neighborhood. Here branches off the new "Soo" route to St. Paul.

All the afternoon we run through forested hills, the line bending hither and yon to avoid rocky ridges and crystalline lakes, cutting athwart promontories, and bridging ravines. Here and there are extensive tracts of arable land, but little agricultural settlement can be expected in these forests as long as the rich prairies westward, all ready for the plow, are only half-tenanted. Yet the cabins of settlers, who are part farmers, part lumbermen, part trappers, and part "Injun," are scattered all along the line ; and every hundred miles or so we encounter a railway "divisional" station, where there are engine-houses, repairing shops, and the homes of the men employed on that section of the line.

In the evening, groups gathered in our brilliantly-lighted palaces — for every one had become acquainted, like a cozy ship's company at sea — and whiled away the time with books, story-telling and whist. The Vassar girls, the Official and the Editorial *We* had a grand game, closing with a tie at eleven o'clock. Just then we were at Missanabie, where you might launch a canoe—"that frail vehicle of an amphibious navigation," as Sir George Simpson styled it—and run down to the fur-famed—

" Beware of puns ! " cried Miss Dimity Vassar.

—Michipicoten, in Lake Superior ; or, with a few portages, glide northward to Hudson's Bay.

Bidden to be awake early, at six next morning we were astir, and, lo ! there was Lake Superior. All day we ran along its shores, here taking advantage of a natural terrace or ledge, there rolling with thunderous roar along some gallery blasted out of the face of the gigantic cliffs whose granite bases were beaten by the waves ; next darting through a tunnel or safely overriding a long and lofty bridge, beneath which poured some wine-colored torrent. This is daring and costly engineering.

Always high above the water, which sometimes dashes at the very foot of the trackway, and sometimes is separated from us by barriers of vine-clad rock, the eye overlooks a wide and radiant scene. A line of distant and hilly islands cuts off this interior part (Nepigon Bay) from the open lake ; and as we swerve hither and yon in our rapid advance, these islands group themselves into ever changing combinations, opening and closing lanes of blue water, displaying and hiding the silvery horizon, letting passing vessels appear and disappear, and taking some new charm of color with each new position.

Nor was this all. Cliffs and shore are grandly picturesque in form, brilliant in color, and constantly varied. After we had reached Jackfish River—a famous fishing-place—and the gaudy overhanging

INDIAN TEPEES.

cliffs had been left behind, the lake began to be hidden by a line of trap-buttes, masked in dense foliage ; and these beautiful table-lands lasted all the way to the crossing of the Nepigon, where again we were face to face with Nepigon Bay. You may say later that the scenery of the Rocky Mountains is better than this morning ride along Lake Superior ; but you will not forget, nor be willing to omit it, all the same.

Nepigon River, up which we have a long view, is the prince of trout-rivers, and at the railway station canoes, camping supplies and Indian crews are always obtainable. Think of brook-trout weighing five or six pounds, to be caught, and bass and whitefish and what not in plenty besides !

That afternoon we passed Port Arthur, a town of 3,500 population, on Thunder Bay, and the port for the fine Canadian Pacific steamers, which present an alternative summer route between the East and West by way of the lakes, Owen Sound and Toronto. Five miles farther on we came to old Fort William, now a growing village and grain port. Here, on the fertile flats of the Kaministiquia, more than two hundred years ago, was planted an Indian trading-post, which a century later became the headquarters of the great Northwest Fur Company, and then an important post of the Hudson's Bay Company, to which, after years of warfare, the Northwest corporation finally capitulated. Some of the storied old buildings, to which a whole magazine article might easily be devoted, still stand, but they are overshadowed by the railway shops and warehouses, the huge elevators and coal-bins, which here, as at Port Arthur, testify to an enormous shipping traffic.

For four hundred miles west of Fort William, where we bid good-bye to Lake Superior, the road passes through a wild, rough region of rocks and forest, reticulated with

lakes and rivers. It is the most unattractive piece of country on the whole line, but it abounds in minerals, and supplies the treeless region beyond with lumber. Near its eastern border, at Rabbit Mountain, exceedingly rich silver mines are worked. The Lake of the Woods, in the centre of this tract, is a very beautiful spot, and one whose water-power supplies many large mills.

Morning found us among open groves and thickets—the fringed-out western edge of that almost continental forest which sweeps behind us to the Atlantic, and northward until it half envelops Hudson's Bay. Finally even this disappeared in an expanse of verdant turf—the prairie of Manitoba, —its perfectly level horizon broken only by the tall buildings and steeples of the city of Winnipeg.

Winnipeg stands at the point where Red River receives its largest western tributary, the Assiniboine. It has been the site of an Indian trading post, and the centre of the "Red River settlements" for almost a century ; but until ten years ago it was nothing more. Then it sprung at one bound, amid an ecstasy of speculation, into a city. It had a hard time after this injudicious exuberance began to subside ; but it survived, and now Winnipeg is as well founded, and growing as healthfully, as is Denver or Omaha. The town has ridiculously wide streets, which it cost a fortune to pave with cedar blocks, and which make the really tall and fine business buildings look dwarfed. There are several expensive churches, hundreds of elegant residences, and some stately public buildings. The width of the streets ; the great number of vacant lots, due to the large expectations of the "boom" period, which spread the town beyond all reason ; and the use of cream-colored brick and light paint in the buildings, give to Winnipeg a singularly pale and scattered appearance, likely to diminish in the eyes of a casual visitor the city's real wealth and importance.

"While you would find here in Winnipeg," says our *cicerone*, as we sat smoking in a snug corner, "if you studied the matter a little, the key to much that you will see beyond, you must look beyond for the key to much you will see in Winnipeg. Situated just where the forests end and the vast prairies begin, with thousands of miles of river navigation to the north, south and west, and with railways radiating in every direction into the wheat lands of all Manitoba, like spokes in a wheel,

THE VIEW FROM THE HOT SPRINGS, BANFF, LOOKING DOWN THE BOW.

Winnipeg has become, what it must always be, the commercial focus of the Canadian Northwest. Looking at these long lines of warehouses filled with goods, and these twenty miles or more of railway side-tracks all crowded with cars, you begin to realize the vastness of the country we are about to enter. From here the wants of the people in the west are supplied, and this way come the products of their fields, while from the far north are brought furs in great variety and number."

The surrounding prairie is absolutely flat, and was the bed of a prehistoric lake— the last remnant of the waters that once

region lighter in soil and formerly held at a cheaper price than the speculative tracts near the city, whose owners have seen settlers go steadily past them.

The centre of this is the far-scattered town of Portage la Prairie, an old landing-place of the *voyageurs*, who here loaded their boat-cargoes into carts and carried them across to Lake Manitoba, there to be re-embarked for the long canoe voyage inland. Here are now great wheat elevators and mills, and hence a railway has pushed 250 miles northwestward, to continue nobody knows how much farther. Brandon, seventy-five miles

NEARING THE ROCKY MOUNTAINS.

covered the whole interior ; and as we race across it we can picture how the wavelets rose and fell before the ancient wind by noticing the olive-and-gray ripples that flow over the long grass under this noonday breeze. Here and there cattle are standing up to their bellies in the lush meadow. Far off to the southward a dark line indicates the fringe of trees along the Assiniboine. Nothing else breaks the verdant flats that sweep around us save the track and the telegraph poles, straight as a ray of light behind and ahead to their vanishing points on each horizon. After a while habitations and farms grow more numerous, for we have imperceptibly risen to a

beyond, is a wide-awake, handsomely built young city on the Assiniboine, sustained by an immense agricultural environment. In regard to this let me quote somewhat from a standard work on the prairies : " Leaving Brandon, we have fairly reached the first of the great prairie steppes, that rise one after the other at long intervals to the Rocky Mountains ; and now we are on the real prairie, not the monotonous, uninteresting plain your imagination has pictured, but a great billowy ocean of grass and flowers, now swelling into low hills, again dropping into broad basins with gleaming ponds, and broken here and there by valleys and by irregular lines of trees marking the watercourses. The horizon only limits the view ; and, as far as the eye can reach, the prairie is dotted with newly made farms, with great black squares where the sod has just been turned by the plow, and with herds of cattle. The short, sweet grass, studded with brilliant flowers, covers the land as with a carpet, ever changing in color as the flowers of the different seasons and places give to it their predominating hue. . . . Here is produced, in the greatest perfection, the most famous of all varieties of wheat—that known as the 'hard Fyfe wheat of Manitoba'—and oats as well, and rye, barley and flax, and gigantic potatoes, and almost everything that can be grown in a temperate climate. . . . Three hundred miles from Winnipeg we pass through the famous Bell Farm, embracing one hundred square miles of land. This is a veritable manufactory of wheat, where the work is done with almost military organization—plowing by brigades and reaping by divisions. Think of a farm where the furrows are ordinarily four miles long, and of a country where such a thing is possible ! There are neat stone cottages and ample barns for miles around, and the collection of buildings about the headquarters near the railway station makes a respectable village, there being among them a church, an hotel, a flour mill, and, of course, a grain elevator, for in this country these elevators appear wherever there is wheat to be handled or stored."

The fertile, pleasantly habitable region of the Canadian West is a triangular region with a base 800 miles in width east and west, and a northern limit marked by the forests beyond the Saskatchewan. Between these forests and the Rocky Mountains the arable country extends almost to the borders of Alaska, and through it are scattered trading stations and small settlements among a peaceful and semi-industrious Indian population. The climate is dry, yet the rainfall (except in the southwestern part) is quite sufficient for agriculture. The winters are rigorous, but not so long as those of Quebec, and the snowfall is light. Wheat, oats, barley and vegetables grow to perfection even farther north than the Peace River valley, in latitude 56° to 57°—the parallel which in the east passes just north of Labrador. Settlement on these fine prairies (which are often bushy, and show no sage-brush and little alkali) is only a decade old, yet last year there was produced a surplus for export of twelve million bushels of wheat alone.

Not far beyond the Regina wheat plain, which is about 1,800 feet above the sea, the altitude is abruptly increased by a rise to the top of the *Coteau de Missouri*, where the average of elevation is 3,000 feet. Here the climate is drier, and grazing becomes the principal industry, especially toward the foothills, where enormous herds of horses, cattle and sheep are pastured. Of this great and growing business Calgary is headquarters.

Only ten years ago this was the home of millions of buffalo, whose trails and wallows mark the surface in every direction ; but not a bison is now to be seen within a long distance northward. The prairies from Regina westward are dotted with lakes, generally of fresh water, are well grassed, and broken by wooded eminences. The elk and mule-deer are still common, and in the autumn immense herds of antelope, migrating southward, are still to be seen from the car windows. Around the lakes crowd countless wild fowl at all seasons, while flocks of prairie chickens whirl away on each side at our approach. In the seasons of migration geese and ducks are here in myriads.

We cross the South Saskatchewan near some extensive coal mines, and toward evening of Friday (we left Montreal on Monday night and Winnipeg on Thursday morning) we catch our first brief glimpse of the Rockies—a serrated white line notching the sunset horizon. To-morrow morning we shall awake within their glorious gates.

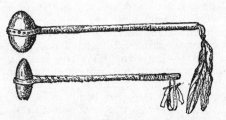

STONE POGAMOGGANS OF THE CANADIAN SIOUX.

TO THE PACIFIC THROUGH CANADA.

BY ERNEST INGERSOLL.

PART II.

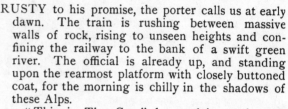

TRUSTY to his promise, the porter calls us at early dawn. The train is rushing between massive walls of rock, rising to unseen heights and confining the railway to the bank of a swift green river. The official is already up, and standing upon the rearmost platform with closely buttoned coat, for the morning is chilly in the shadows of these Alps.

"This is The Gap," he explains, "through which Bow River comes out. We follow it almost to its sources, before we come to Kicking-horse Pass, through the central range, or Main Divide. Better have the ladies called. We shall be at Banff in an hour, and they ought not to miss any of this."

He touches an electric button, directs the responding porter to summon the Vassar family, and we return to the platform.

The Gap has now been traversed, and we can see the great mountains on each side of it. Then we turn northward and run along the river between gigantic upheavals. Their tops are half hidden in the lingering night-mists; but rifts now and then reveal bristling, snow-crested peaks, rosy with premonitions of sunrise, and tiers upon tiers of cliffs bounded by long lines of snow resting upon narrow ledges, and broken by gorges of unmeasured depth filled with blue shadows and swirling fog. It is a wonderful, inspiring, never-to-be-forgotten sight. Awakened and driven out by the skirmish line of the hosts of the morning, the clouds reluctantly forsake their rocky fastnesses, and more and more of the rugged grandeur and height of the bordering ranges, right and left, come out. Soon far-away peaks show daintily, "like kisses on the morning sky," as one of the ladies expressed it, in imagery chaste, no doubt, but rather cold; and finally, as we sweep toward the face of the gigantic precipices of Cascade Mountain (which seem to rise courteously and advance to welcome us), even the valley shakes off its blanket of haze, and sunshine pours over the crystal heights to sparkle upon dewy leaves and glistening river.

Under these brilliant auspices we step out of the car and into a carriage at Banff, and are whirled away to a great hotel, built upon the grandest site in Canada.

"This hotel is the Company's property, and here you are to be my guests for the day," was the command of our genial official, as he registered the names of the party. "It is too early for breakfast. Let us go to the upper balconies and have a look at the mountains. This is Canada's National Park, you know, and she is proud of it."

What a picture that north-western balcony opened to us ! In the foreground green rolling woodland dotted with turfed openings and the red roofs of cottages or white dots of tents. Then the tortuous and shining course of the Bow River, sweeping gracefully to the right. On the left, steep and wooded slopes; ahead, high mountains —some with their splintered spires towering above rugged and darkly forested foothills, others more distant and breaking into jagged outlines, gashed by blue gulfs and piled with snow, others still farther away, filmy and white upon the western horizon, where the water-shed of the continent rises supreme and superb. Nearer is the cliff-fronted mass of Cascade Mountain, 5,000 feet high, its slender waterfall trembling like a loose ribbon down its broad breast — the badge of its identity. Past it, through a rocky gap, our eyes follow the lower Bow, sparkling with ripples, parted by islets, shadowed by leaning spruces and cottonwoods, to the green ridges where the railway runs, and on to where the white wall of the Fair-holme range, a massive rank of heights, upholds wide spaces of stainless snow.

"Just behind that mighty wall, whose tallest peak—Mt. Peechee—is over 10,000 feet in altitude," our friend tells us, "there is an immense cañon, occupied by a narrow and very deep lake. The Indians believe it to be haunted by malignant demons, and I don't wonder at it. Cliffs thousands of feet in height rise straight from its mar-gin, and its waters are shadowed by the Devil's Head and other peaks, that can be seen for a hundred miles out on the plains. To cruise upon its surface in a canoe and catch the monstrous trout that lurk in its coves, while the echoes of your talk and paddling wander from scaur to scaur, and wild goats come to the edge of the crags to look down upon you, is an experience not to be duplicated easily anywhere else in the world."

"What is this lake called?"

"Devil's or Devil's Head Lake. We will drive over there this afternoon, if you like. I think the views you get from that road are the best of the whole park scenery, unless, perhaps, you except the view of Mount Massive and the Main Divide from a boat on the Vermilion Lakes. Now let us go to the other end of the building."

"Here," he continued, when we were gathered upon the south-eastern balcony, "you are looking *down* the line of the Rockies, instead of up their length, as you were before. This is the valley of the Spray, which joins the Bow just below the hotel."

We could not see the river, but we could hear its rushing, and readily believed our friend's stories of the trout in its pools. On the left of the valley long slopes of whitish limestone rose bare and glistening with dew far above the forest, until they termi-nated in two sharply cut peaks, from which fell suddenly away, for many hundreds of feet, the precipices that we had half seen earlier that morning. This was Mount Rundle—an excellent type of the moun-tains of stratified limestone, shaped like wedges laid upon their sides, in parallel rows north and south, which constitute the eastern half of the Rocky Mountain sys-tem in this part of the world. The eastern aspect of all these ranges, therefore, is a rank of precipices—tier upon tier of nearly or quite level ledges of limestone, strongly indicated by banks of snow and lines of trees — broken into separate headlands, and bordered at their base by bush-covered

slopes of débris. Here and there a great gap allows you to pass to the rear of these headlands, when you find them sloping back with much regularity into the forest-covered valley, beyond which another rank of cliff-faced promontories again confronts you, and so on until the central water-shed is reached.

"Why does that curious little cloud stay so persistently on the slope of that hill?" asked one of the ladies, pointing to the right.

"That is the steam from the hot springs," was the reply, "and after breakfast we will walk up there."

The hot mineral springs at Banff lie along the base of Sulphur Mountain, where they flow from exits round which great masses of tufa have been built up. The up-per spring, some 700 feet above the river, commands a wonderful view of "peak o'er-topping peak," with green vales and broken crags between. From this spring a large stream of sulphurous water, at a warmth of 120° F., is conducted down to the hotel, to supply the luxurious bath-houses. More plebeian arrangements exist at the spring itself for bathing and drinking the waters, which have proved wonderfully efficacious in curing a great variety of diseases, espe-cially obstinate cases of rheumatism and dyspepsia. Two miles distant, up the Bow, are two other prominent springs—one an open basin, and the other a large pool, occupying a dome-shaped cavern built out of its own depositions when it was more copious, and this is now a most curious place. Originally, the only way of reach-ing the water was by squeezing one's self through the chimney at the top of the dome and sliding down a slippery ladder, like entering a Tchuckchi house in Siberia. Now a tunnel has been bored through the side of the dome, level with the surface of the diminished water, and you go straight in from your dressing-room in the rustic cottage at the entrance. Another pretty cottage admits to the open pool. In both the pool and the cave the water is pleas-antly warm, clear and almost tasteless, though highly impregnated with salts, giving it a close resemblance to the Ar-kansas Hot Springs. These improvements of the springs, and the good roads through-out the Park, are the work of the Govern-ment, which is making easily accessible all the most interesting localities and best points of view.

We could have spent a week in this most delightful spot—rambling, climbing, sketch-

MOUNT STEPHEN FROM THE WEST.

Between the two, right in the foreground, stands Castle Mountain, isolated, lofty, brown and yellow, vividly contrasting with the remainder of the land-scape, and terminating in a ruinous round tower from whose top pennants of mist are waving more than a mile above our heads. As we roll past its base it gradually changes from a lone castle tower to an escarpment of enor-mous cliffs. These can be climbed, and the ex-pectation of what the out-look would be is more than realized.

But we must not forget in the grandeur of the Castle the splendid peaks fronting the valley on the left—Pilot, a leaning pyr-amid poised high upon a pedestal of square-cut ledges; next to it the more massive summit of Copper Mountain, to which you may almost ride on horseback along an old road cut to the copper mines near its apex; then the green gap of Vermil-ion Pass (into the Kooten-ay Valley), through whose opening we catch allur-ing glimpses of many a haughty spire and brist-ling ice-crown along the Continental Divide. To the north of this gap stretches Mount Temple's rugged wall, and beyond it, supreme over all, Lefroy's lonely peak—loftiest and most majestic of them all.

When Castle Mountain and the steel-pointed sierra behind it have swerved to the right, we see northward the great glacier that nourishes the childhood of the Bow with milky meltings, and in the midst of a galaxy of hoary peaks the noble form of Mount Hector—a monument to the first ex-plorer of Kickinghorse Pass. Then, leav-ing the Bow, we climb the gorge of a little creek and enter the jaws of a narrow gap through the central range. Upon either hand rise rugged walls crowned with Al-pine peaks, framing a chaos of snow-fields,

ing, shooting (outside the Park limits), fishing and boating. The beautiful river and lakes, and the falls, have hardly been mentioned, even. But time presses, and next morning sees us reluctantly resuming our journey.

From Banff we pushed straight westward through wooded defiles into the upper val-ley of the Bow, where the scenery is upon an even grander scale. On the left runs a line of magnificent promontories—prodig-ious piles of ledges studded with square bastions and peaked towers. On the right is a gray sloping wall, 5,000 feet high, of slaty strata tilted on edge, and notched into numberless sharp points and splin-ters, like the teeth of a badly hacked saw.

THE SELKIRK PEAKS.

glaciers, and sharp black summits westward—some close by, and showing the scars of ages of battle with eternal winter; others calm and blue in the far distance. Yet here in the pass it is warm and pleasant: trees flourish, flowers bloom, cataracts leap and flash in the sunlight. Backward we review in profile the line of mountains we have passed; beside us are the crumbling terraces and turrets of the Cathedral, thousands of feet straight upward; ahead, reflected in a lake whose waters flow east to the Atlantic and west to the Pacific, the stately head of Mount Stephen, brandishing cloud standards and carrying with royal dignity its ermine mantle of snow and gleaming coronet of ice.

We have pierced the Rockies and are looking down the Pacific slope. Range after range of blue-and-white crests, rising from valleys of forest and prairie, burst upon our awed vision. The scene is past adequate description; we do not say much about it to one another, but only look; and when the descent has been accomplished, and some hours later we halt on the bank of the Columbia (only 100 miles from its source), we are almost stunned with the sublime panorama that has been unrolled so rapidly before our eyes, each scene more astonishing in its magnitude and beauty than the last.

Yet we have crossed only one of the three great subdivisions of the Canadian Rockies. Just ahead lie the Selkirks, and beyond that is the Gold Range. Then we shall cross a wide, hilly plateau region. Finally we must follow the Fraser River in its profound cutting through the Cascades range, before we see the coast of the Pacific. The whole distance from the eastern base of the Rockies to the coast— Banff to Vancouver—is done in thirty-six hours, and the night travel comes where there is little loss of fine scenery; but it is too much to take in at once. Our stop of only one day at Banff was not only a rest, but allowed us to become acquainted with the mountains and prepared us for what we should see ahead; and we mean to stop again at the summit of the Selkirks.

The ascent of the Selkirk range from the east is begun in a regular gateway, where the Beaver River pitches down some rocky stairs at the bottom of a chasm, and is continued along the forested side of its valley, gradually ascending until the track is a thousand feet above the stream. Here the splendor of the Selkirks is manifest in the west, where a rank of stately mountains, side by side and loaded with snow, are grandly outlined. Then we turn up a branch cañon and enter Roger's Pass through the terrific cleft between Mount Carroll and The Hermit.

In another place * the present writer has described his first impressions of these singularly impressive heights—the climax of the transcontinental trip.

At the western extremity of Roger's Pass lies the Great Glacier, where the Company has built a beautiful little hotel, within twenty minutes' walk of the ice. It would have been nothing short of criminal to have gone past this point without stopping.

The path through the forest, the huge size of whose trees, and the redundancy of whose mossy undergrowth, bespeak our nearness to the warm coast, is along a brawling river gushing from underneath the glacier. Presently the vast slope of creeping ice is before us, completely filling the head of the gorge. All the glaciers we have hitherto seen were near the very crest of the range, but this one comes far down into the forest, so that flowers and shrubbery are sprouting all around its lower margin, whence a dozen rivulets gurgle out to feed the river. The rounded forefoot is broken, where blocks of loosened ice have been sloughed off, and seamed with numberless cracks, the commencement of further sloughings. These cracks and the freshly exposed faces are vividly blue, while liquid turquoise fills all the cavities and deepens to ultramarine in the shadows; but the general tone of the glacier, as it slopes steeply upward in billowy undulations toward the head of the ravine, is grayish white. Curving crevasses cross from flank to flank, and longitudinal rifts gash the surface as if cut with a sharp knife in an elastic substance. These crevasses

* "Mountaineering in British Columbia." A lecture delivered before the American Geographical Society, in Chickering Hall, January, 1886.

may be as blue as the clearest sky, or sometimes green as young grass, according to the light; and between are often pure-white patches of fresh snow. Toward the top (where the breadth is nearly two miles) the slope is still steeper and the surface smoother; but along the very crest, jagged and hard against the sky, thousands of fractures appear, indicating how the mass of ice breaks, rather than bends, as it is pushed over the cliffs. These breaks then reunite, and the chaos becomes the smoothly congealed and undulating surface we see below.

"This glacier," the official remarks, "is only one of several overflows from a *mer de glace* occupying a plateau on the summit, scores and perhaps hundreds of square miles in extent. It is continually crowded

A CAÑON ON THE ILLICILLIWAET.

over the edge through breaks in the rim of cliffs, and thus room is made for the new deposits of snow annually heaped upon its frigid wastes."

For several hours we scrambled about the edges of the ice. On its right is a huge moraine, which we climbed for a few hundred feet and thence ventured out upon the glacier itself, but could go only a few steps, for we had no spiked shoes, alpenstocks, ropes, or other appliances for safety. Greater in size than any of the Swiss glaciers, its exploration needs at least equal precautions. On one side a cave in the ice remains to mark the former exit of some now diverted stream ; and when we entered it we found ourselves in an azure grotto, where the very air was saturated with blue and we expected to be turned into petrifactions of sapphire.

All the morning there rests upon the ice-slope the huge triangular shadow of Sir Donald—a superb pyramidal pile of cliffs, shooting its slender apex far above all its royal mates—Ross, Dawson, Carroll, The Hermit, and Cheops — and cleaving clouds that have swept unhindered over their heads. It is imperial in its grandeur and separation from the rest, and nowhere shows more magnificently than when we look back from a point far down the pass, and can see how royally this richly colored, elegantly poised spire soars exceedingly sharp and lofty above the group of lesser mountains—themselves monarchs of the range—grouped sublimely about it. These were the pictures we saw as, refreshed by a night's slumber in the balsamic air of the spruce-clothed mountains, we renewed our journey next morning, and from the foot of Ross Peak gazed back with amazement at the tortuous descent our train had made around the loops and trestles that had "eased" us down from Roger's Pass and Glacier Station to the bank of the Illicilliwaet.

This river, fed by unmeasured stores of snow and ice kept in a circle of heaven-piercing peaks, rushes away down a series of densely wooded and rocky gorges. With much ingenuity the railway follows it to the Columbia, which has made a long detour around the northern end of the Selkirks since we last saw it. Here is Revelstoke, a railway headquarters, the limit of steamboat navigation, and the supplying centre of many mines. Behind it are lifted the western outliers of the Selkirks ; before it, beyond the Columbia, is the Gold Range, some

of whose glacier-studded peaks constitute a grand view.

The Gold Range is easily crossed. Eight miles beyond the Columbia bridge, we have risen into Eagle Pass, which is only 1,900 feet above the sea, and are gliding past lake after lake nestling between magnificent headlands. Trees 200 feet tall fill the pass and encircle the lakes in a close and continuous forest, and wherever a ledge or bit of easy slope allows soil to cling, the rocky crag-sides are clothed with luxuriant foliage. It is the White Mountains, or the Blue Ridge, doubled and trebled in scale. Each of these deep, still lakes is filled with fish, and along the Eagle River, which leads us westward out of the pass through a darkly shaded ravine, are many camps of sleepy Indians fishing for salmon.

As evening approaches we escape from the hills and run along a connected series of long, narrow and very deep bodies of water, penetrating between hills and ridges covered with unbroken forest. This polypus-like lake is called the Great Shushwap, and is as large as Cayuga, Seneca, and all the other lakes in Western New York would be were they connected by navigable straits. Fed by several strong rivers, it forms the reservoir which guarantees a steady supply to Thompson River, by whose side our train will run all night.

" These lakes are wonderful places for sport," says the official. " Salmon and several other fish are numerous, and every kind of game abounds. It is an almost untouched field, too, although facilities for getting over an immense region of wild country, by steamboat, sloop or canoe, are exceedingly good."

" What are we missing in the night ? " asked Miss Vassar, as darkness blotted out the landscape and the cheery lamps were lighted for the last of so many jolly evenings together in this overland voyage.

" You don't miss much until toward morning ; and that you may get a fair idea of by moonlight if you sleep on the right-hand side of the car. We are getting entirely past and away from the mountains now, into a plateau country of grassy hills where farming (except by irrigation) has small success, but grazing is a great industry. At midnight we go through the important town of Kamloops, the headquarters of this grazing region, which extends for hundreds of miles southward, and is interspersed with many gold and silver mining localities. Then we pass. Kamloops Lake and get into the cañons of the Lower Thompson River. There the scenery is very curious. This is a dry country — looks like California — and the rocks and earthen river-banks have been carved by wind and occasional deluges into the most fantastic and gayly colored of monumental forms, through which the waters of the racing Thompson mark a sinuous line as green as the purest emerald. It's a very extraordinary, grotesque landscape, but having seen it once in daylight, I, for one, am satisfied to go through henceforth by night. After we leave the mouth of the Thompson at Lytton, however, and begin to descend Fraser River, the scenery becomes very grand and beautiful ; so you must get up early once more."

How shall I tell in a few words what those Fraser cañons are like ? They are not like the thin, abysmal clefts of Colorado, nor the weird corridor through which the Missouri makes its way.

The Fraser is the main water-course of British Columbia, and comes from the far northern interior. It is a broad, heavy, rapid stream, flowing between steep banks sloping ruggedly back to the mountains, whose white and shapely peaks stand in splendid array before us at Lytton. The railway is at first on the eastern bank, and high above the turbulent yellow river, which is soon compressed into a narrow trough, where the hampered water rushes and roars with frightful velocity. Cliffs rise for hundreds of feet with out-jutting buttresses that almost bar the passage. Huge rocks, long ago precipitated into the water, have been worn "into forms like towers, castles, and rows of bridge-piers, with the swift current eddying around them."

Near Cisco advantage is taken of a particularly narrow strait to cross the river upon a huge cantilever bridge, the farther end of which rests in a tunnel. The scenery here is savage, but the air is soft and the sky clearest blue. As we proceed, the cañon rapidly becomes narrower, deeper, and more terrific ; the river, a series of whirlpools among knife-edged rocks. The railway pierces projecting headlands in short tunnels, springs across side-chasms, and is supported along sharp acclivities by abutments of natural rock or careful masonry. Finally the constantly heightening wall on the opposite side culminates in the crag of Jackass Mountain, which rises 2,000 feet in a well-nigh perpendicular mass — a second Cape Eternity. Nearly

1,000 feet above the boiling torrent, and often overhanging it, the wagon-road built years ago to connect the Fraser River gold mines with the coast creeps about its brow ; and the little party of Indians trotting along this airy pathway look like pygmies or gnomes who have come out of some stony crevice to see us pass. Yet four-horse stages were driven here for many a year, and before the road was built men traveled afoot over the trail which preceded it, passing places like these on swinging pole-bridges, something like the foot-ropes under a ship's yard-arm. Thrilling stories of that trail and road in the fierce old mining days of '58 and '64 are recorded in books and told by the "mossbacks" one meets up and down the coast. But since the building of the railway the wagon-road is little traveled, though the Cariboo district northward, and other districts south of the line, still yield gold and silver bountifully under systematic mining.

As we roll steadily onward through long shadows projected across the gulf by the rising sun the cañon alternately expands and contracts, but never loses its grandeur. The queer little figures of Chinese gold-washers dot the gravel-bars here and

ON THE BROAD WATERS OF THE FRASER.

there (we can't help wondering how they got down there !), and on almost every convenient rock near the river's edge are perched Indians with large dip-nets, industriously scooping in an eddy after loitering salmon. Their rude bivouacs are scattered about the rocks ; and their fish-drying

TYPES OF WESTERN STEAMBOATS.

SCENERY OF THE FRASER CAÑON.

the important old town of Boston Bar (now abandoned to the Indians) and over the bridge above Skuzzy Falls, which come sliding down fern-strewn rocks in cataracts of lambent emerald. Gradually the cañon walls grow high again, and encroach more and more upon the channels. The railway passes from tunnel to bridge and bridge to tunnel in quick succession, always curving and costly. It is one long gallery of wonders. Ponderous masses of rock, fallen from the cliffs and long ago polished like black glass, obstruct the current, which roars through narrow flumes between them and hurls showers of spray far up their sides. This is the Black Cañon of old settlers; and an idea of its tortuous narrowness may be got from the fact that in freshets the choked-up water will rise a hundred feet above the ordinary level.

At the foot of this cañon is Yale, an old trading post and frontier town, ensconced in sombre mountains. As the head of navigation on the lower Fraser, it was once the leading town of the Province, and still has some 12,000 inhabitants. A few miles farther on is another similar village, Fort Hope, which is at the limit of steamboating, and is charmingly placed in front of a cluster of brilliant Cascade peaks. At times the figure of a colossal anchor is marked in snow-banks upon one of these summits; whence the name of the village—for is not the anchor the emblem of hope? In these mountains rich silver lodes await development.

Gradually the cañons and cliffs are left behind, and we gather speed on a level track through woods of prodigious growth. The river becomes a broad and placid stream, "backing up" here and there into lagoons, and making prairies utilized for herds of cattle. Beautiful mountains show themselves in every direction—last and finest of all, Mount Baker, fifty miles away.

At Agassiz many passengers leave the train to visit the Harrison Hot Springs,

frames, festooned with the red flakes of salmon-flesh, among which the curing smoke curls as lazily as Siwash smoke might be expected to do, add the last . touch of artistic color to the picture.

But a painter will be attracted constantly by the form and color of the bronze-brown chaotic rocks, the tawny, foam-laced river, the gaunt, desperately rooted trees, and the brilliant azure of the sky. And everywhere he will find handy a foreground-bit of "life"—gold-diggers, mule-trains, Chinese red-labeled cabins, Siwash "wik-kiups" and barbarically adorned graves, or some trim railway structure—to lighten the composition with a sympathetic human touch.

At North Bend we get breakfast in a charming hotel, and then go on again, past

at the foot of Harrison Lake, five miles northward. This is one of the pleasantest watering-places on the coast, and a most interesting spot for sport and amusement. Harrison Lake and its outlet into the Fraser, with other lakes and portages, formed the foremost route to the northern interior twenty-five years ago. Its waters were then alive with steamboats, and the roads with wagons and pack-horses; but now the route is quite abandoned, and its wayside habitations have fallen into decay.

At noon we scent the saline odor of the ocean, and presently come with eager curiosity to the shore of Burrard Inlet. Half an hour later we are at Vancouver, and our transcontinental trip has reached its western terminus.

Two years ago a saw-mill represented civilization, and a dense forest covered the peninsula between Coal Harbor (a widening of Burrard Inlet) and English Bay (an offshoot of the Gulf of Georgia), where now a city of 5,000 people is established. The town is crescent-shaped, rising with gentle ascent to the ridge overlooking the open gulf, the heights of Vancouver Island and the Olympic and Cascade ranges in Washington Territory. Upon this high ground a group of residences has already arisen, whose windows command a wonderfully beautiful view of water and mountains.

The town has been built with great rapidity, but the wooden houses first thrown up are fast giving place to substantial buildings of brick and stone. All the improvements of modern civilization have been introduced; business and agriculture flourish; mining and the fisheries are engaging more and more capital, and the foundations of a great and beautiful seaport have been laid.

Thus the Canadian Pacific Railway is, in fact, a new way round the world!

41

The Winged Snowshoer of the North Land

CASPAR WHITNEY

THE WINGED SNOWSHOER OF THE NORTH LAND

By CASPAR WHITNEY

HOW I happened to be setting out for ptarmigan, eight hundred miles from the railroad, where, nearby, the birds could be found without forsaking all the comforts of home, is a matter of little moment to any one but me. It is enough, for the purpose of this tale, to say that the immediate impelling force was hunger; for I had recently come from Fort Smith, where starvation rules for nine months of the twelve, and had exhausted the beggarly three days' rations, which were all I got to carry me a full five days' journey, running thirty-five miles every day of the five. It was with great difficulty I squeezed even so scanty a stock from the Company store; and the big heart of "Mc," its presiding genius, gave me, I am sure, out of his own treasured little horde of sugar, put aside to later hush his crying children when lack of nourishing food made them fretful.

And now I had come to the end of the supply, and we were yet about eighty miles from my destination, for storms of unusual severity had slowed our daily average of travel. There was the frozen whitefish we carried for dog feed—but I would not permit it to be eaten; the life of a dog was of greater consequence, under the circumstances, than that of an Indian. Had it been a rabbit year, we could have set snares, and over night replenished our empty larder; but, worse luck, it was the bad season, which comes every seven years, when the rabbits are strangely stricken and die in great numbers. 'Tis a curious disease, which smites without warning. Indians say it overtakes the running rabbit and lays it low as suddenly and as mysteriously as would a bolt of lightning. In one of these years it was that I found myself journeying northward. All along the Great Slave River I met starvation among the straggling Indians. They sat huddled around the tepee-fire, barely keeping life in their bodies with an occasional fox, or lynx, or rabbit, or ptarmigan, that chanced into their traps and snares—one trapped fox, cringing in its miserably cold captivity, I had killed the day before and left for its lucky owner—while back from the river one hundred miles were moose and bear: and caribou, another hundred miles. Yet there they sat starving, lacking resolution to secure the comparative plenty that was to be had for the seeking. God Almighty modeled these Indians with strange mental warp; though

"Fort Smith, where starvation rules for nine months of the twelve."

fin, fur, and feather abound sufficiently to keep the scattered inhabitants of this vast area well fed, yet always there is feast or famine among them. In the autumn preceding my visit, one party of hunters, two hundred miles from where I stood, had killed 25 moose, 7 woodland caribou, 4 bears, 90 marten, 26 beaver, and 3 otter. In the summer the lakes teem with whitefish—a provision which makes the country inhabitable, for overland travel, because of its swampy character, is, for the greater part of the year, all but impossible.

We had tried to get food of the only In-

leave the river in the hope of getting ptarmigan to relieve our pressing needs. I could see that my proposition was distinctly unpopular, and I felt sure trouble with the Indians was coming. Such had been my impression, indeed, even when engaging them, for both had been very reluctant to undertake the trip, and neither inspired me with confidence. Each wanted an order to the Company for a sack of flour to leave with the "starving" family during his absence, a rifle, and many other presents, before they would even discuss the question of daily wage. Denying those demands, I was obliged to

Photograph by the Author.

" A party of eight was preparing to feast upon its last morsel—the hind leg of a lynx."

dians we met, but they were as badly off as we; worse, for we had plenty of tea and tobacco—the traveler's solace, in this silent white land. One party of eight we passed, camped at the river's edge, was preparing to feast upon its last morsel—the hind leg of a lynx; another, a tepee, we overtook emptied itself—men, women, children, and dogs—to beg food of us, the beggars.

I could not discuss the situation at length with my Indians, for my vocabulary in their tongue was limited to about a dozen words—signifying hurry, stop, fire, good, yes, no, meat, fish, tea, smoke, sleep—but with signs I made them understand that I wished to

furnish them with moccasins, duffel (the Northland sock), strouds (leggings), babiche (caribou thongs for snowshoe stringing), and mittens. Had the men proved willing travelers and good tempered once we were on the road I should have enjoyed the involuntary rôle of Santa Claus, but from almost the first fire they had been halting and grumpy. Besides, they annoyed me by repeated stops under pretense of disarranged shoes or sledge, which were really excuses to boil tea and further reduce our dwindling rations. An Indian cannot resist the temptation to eat so long as anything to eat remains. True, we encountered severe weather

Photograph by the Author.

" Frequent stops * * * to boil tea and further reduce our dwindling rations."

with storms driving into our faces practically all the time, and the thermometer ranging from 40° to 47° below zero.

Checked in their raids upon our slender supply, they grew sulky. At each of the two Indian camps we passed I had much difficulty to get them going again, and at the last camp had been obliged to defend the dog fish, of which they were bent on making a feast for themselves and the other Indians. The row that resulted was tempestuous while it lasted; but they did not get the fish. It was only after a demonstration of force —as it is put, I believe, in diplomatic parlance— not to mention some picturesque American talk, unintelligible to their ear, but obviously impressive, that I persuaded my Indians to leave this camp. They wanted to stop by the fire, where, even though food was no more plentiful than with us, was at least more comfort than facing a head wind on an empty stomach. I sympathized with their feelings, but did not propose to starve either in camp or out of it if I could help it. So we renewed our course down the river, battling a head wind of great strength and stumbling over hummocky ice, with now and then a gaping crack, which in the dusk of a snow-driven wind invited broken legs at every encounter. Mean while, as we traveled, I watched for a clearing of the timber along the river bank that suggested open country beyond, and possible ptarmigan. Early in the afternoon I turned off into what seemed to be promising land, and before we had gone inland a mile we came directly upon as squalid a cabin as I ever beheld. It had no

"I sent the Indians to gather firewood."

Drawing by
Henry S. Watson.

window; it was cold and dark, and a worn piece of blanket served as door. In one corner flamed a tiny fire, and around it crouched three children, the oldest surely not over eight; while on the side wall, laced into its moss bag, hung a baby. As we entered, one of the children was tearing the last meat shreds from a rabbit's leg, that caught the eye of my Indians and started an animated dialogue, in which I could distinguish frequent use of the word I knew stood for rabbit or meat. While the parley was at its height an Indian woman lifted the door blanket and stood before us with three rabbits over her arm. Eager attention was at once given her by the Indians, and I could read in their actions and tones a demand for one of the rabbits she now held tightly. They were all talking and gesticulating in the center of the little hut. The children turned about from the fire and stared mutely. Suddenly an Indian grabbed a rabbit; and then I interfered in behalf of the woman —for though we were three hungry men, here was a woman with four children, all, I made sure, in at least as much need as we were.

My men now flatly refused to continue the journey, and it was only through threatening them with my rifle, which I got from the sledge for the purpose, that they resumed travel; in what state of mind may readily be imagined.

After this experience, I thought best to carry my rifle, for although I did not really expect an attempt to do me bodily harm, yet I thought it wise to be prepared; and I knew they were in ugly mood.

"One tepee we overtook emptied itself—men, women, children, and dogs—to beg food of us, the beggars."

It was bitter going, even in the more or less sheltered woods, and we tramped on slowly, making our way into country which seemed to me likely for ptarmigan, until dusk, when I decided to camp. As was my custom, I sent the Indians to gather firewood, while I cleared the ground with my snowshoe and cut pine twigs for bedding. Once or twice while I worked, it occurred to me the Indians were taking an unusually long time, and once or twice I called on them to hurry. That no response came to my shouts did not especially impress me, for I thought perhaps the wind carried away the sound of my voice, or that they were too sulky to reply. So I kept on working, making camp more elaborate than ordinarily I would, in order to keep busy — and warm. When, however, after completing a camp fit to shelter even a tenderfoot, and there were still no signs of the Indians or a fire, I became suspicious, and raising my voice I yelled lustily; but there was no response save the howling wind.

Taking my rifle, I sought their tracks, and found they went into the woods for a few hundred yards, and then bore directly toward our sledge trail. This I followed back for about three miles, until I became convinced that the Indians had deserted me for the woman's cabin, which we had left fully twelve miles in the rear.

The thought of being deserted in a pathless country, without guide and without food, was not precisely cheering; but it was not my first venture in the wilderness, and I faced the situation determined to make the best of it—philosophy which reflected no especial credit on me for there was nothing else to be done. I could, of course, have gone back to the cabin, but that would have availed me nothing. The Indians, in their mood, were

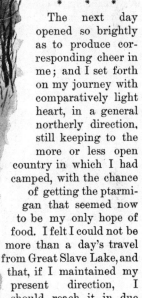

"I pursued my way slowly and laboriously."

Drawing by Henry S. Watson.

worse than helpless; to retrace my steps was getting farther from my objective point, and there was no greater prospect of food behind than lay immediately before me. I returned to the sledge and sought comfort in a roaring fire and a kettle of tea. I was afraid to unharness the dogs lest they follow the example of the Indians, and to lose them would have turned me back; so I fed them in harness their ration of thawed whitefish.

As I rolled in my blankets for the night, it was a consoling thought that the Indian woman and her children would have disposed of the rabbits long before my Indians reached the cabin to rob her.

* * *

The next day opened so brightly as to produce corresponding cheer in me; and I set forth on my journey with comparatively light heart, in a general northerly direction, still keeping to the more or less open country in which I had camped, with the chance of getting the ptarmigan that seemed now to be my only hope of food. I felt I could not be more than a day's travel from Great Slave Lake, and that, if I maintained my present direction, I should reach it in due course.

Driving Indian dogs, with all the noise incidental thereto, are not likely conditions under which to stalk birds, especially when the dogs are as unfriendly and require as much urging as I found to be now the case. Having turned the sledge on its side, therefore, to keep the dogs from running away, I would go ahead for a distance, looking for ptarmigan, and then return to the sledge and bring up the dogs to the end of the trail I had made. Thus, I pursued my way slowly and laboriously, for, toughened as I was, the trail-breaking was severe on ankle and instep muscles. The snow was much deeper than it had been on the river, and on narrow tripping shoes I sunk to my knees, while the snow piled on the toe of my shoe, making necessary, as a preliminary to every step, the lifting of the heavily laden shoe to knock off the accumulated snow. It is such kind of going that brings on the terrible *mal de raquette*, the most fearsome affliction with which the lone snowshoer can be overtaken.

Searching every bit of snow which seemed likely to cover ptarmigan, I was tramping through a kind of open swale, when, shortly after noon, a streak of dark, skimming slowly over the snow, arrested my attention—and as suddenly disappeared. I stopped short and surveyed the surroundings very carefully, realizing, of course, that the white bird on the white snow would not be easy to find; but, though I scrutinized every inch of snow, it was minutes before I discovered a black thing, shining like a bead; even when I had made out this black bead to be the eye of a bird it was some time before I could outline the bird itself. Then I counted nine of the beautiful white things with black-tipped tails, sitting quietly on the snow not more than thirty feet in front of me. After I had shot, I realized why, perhaps, earlier in the day I had not found them, for they disappeared like a cloud of smoke, and in the glistening snow, which made seeing difficult under the best conditions, it was, for me, at least, after seven continuous weeks' travel in the glare, impossible to follow their flight. There were remnants only of the single ptarmigan I shot, for the ball had hit its body, and a 45-90 is not an ideal gun for bird-shooting. Yet it provided a mouthful or two of shattered meat, and put new heart in me.

I saw several other small packs during the remainder of the afternoon, but was not again successful, although I shot at them sitting near and far, and, in desperation, even at them flying. Time and again, as I caught fleeting glimpses, they so instantly disappeared that I sometimes wondered if, after all, it was not a delusion. They seemed to be suddenly swallowed up by the snow. And that is practically what did happen. They do actually fly *into* the snow without alighting, so that no track is left by which a four-footed enemy can trail them. When it cares to do so, this winged snowshoer can run over the lightest snow without sinking, because of the feathered

feet its Creator has provided. Nature generously safeguards this bird against enemies, summer as well as winter, for in the former season its plumage of mottled brown blends almost completely with its surroundings.

Mean time, I was making slow progress, and the sun, which all day had shone so brilliantly, toward the end of the afternoon went under heavy storm clouds that had come up suddenly. Believing the lake could not now be far off, I pushed on harder, and with darkness falling came out upon its bank just as the storm broke. I could see, practically no distance ahead, but knew I had gone almost due west when leaving the river originally, and that I must now, therefore, bear sharply to the northeast. I had been traveling in storms so continuously that the present one did not impress me so much as it should have done; nor, although it was severe and looked black and threatening, did I doubt I could reach the other side of the lake that night. The sensible plan would have been to camp on the bank until morning, or until the weather cleared, but I was so hungry and so jaded in mind and body that a few more difficulties of one kind or another seemed immaterial. Under such conditions, I have found the desire always to push on and get it over.

Taking my bearings, as well as I could by my compass (the needle pointing twenty-five degrees east of the true north), I drove my dogs down the bank onto the lake, which I estimated was about seven or eight miles wide to the point I sought to reach. For about three miles, I made my way fairly well, the storm holding with unchanged severity; but suddenly, and when I was well out into the open, it burst with terrific force upon us and with a suddenness that swept me off my feet, and doubled the dogs in confusion. I thought it merely a flurry, perhaps, and, straightening the dogs, urged them on with my whip, but I could scarcely keep the dogs going or stand on my feet. How long we groped about blindly I do not know. It seemed hours, and the storm to increase every minute. I cut the hand line from the sledge and tied one end to the foregoer and the other to my sash, that, in the confusion of the shrieking wind and the blinding snow which swept upon us, we should not become separated.

I found it impossible to maintain any course. I could not see my compass without a light; I did not dare to open my capote in

Drawing by Henry S. Watson.

" It seemed as if we were in the center of a furious crystal maelstrom."

that hurricane; and no light would have lived, could I have made one. As fast as I untangled the dogs, they doubled on one another in frantic search of protection.

I might have made my way back to land, remembering the direction from which the storm was coming when we set out on the lake, but the storm had changed its direction; indeed, it seemed now to have none in particular. It came apparently from every direction; swirling around us on all sides, wrapping us in its furious whirl, and driving the fine frozen snow on the surface of the lake with cutting force into our faces. It seemed as if we were in the very center of a furious crystal maelstrom; it was absolutely blinding, suffocating, bewildering; and after buffeting and struggling for some time I knew that the only thing to do was to stop, lest we wander farther away from land—for Great Slave Lake is about three hundred miles long and of not much smaller area than Lake Michigan.

So I turned the sledge over and laid down behind it, while the dogs crowded beside and on top of me, and the drifting snow soon made us one with the landscape. Here we lay buried until the screech of the storm had lowered, and my watch read four o'clock. Then I dug the dogs and sledge out of the drift, but it was a long time before I could induce the miserable half-frozen brutes to face the storm, which had lessened considerably, but was still blowing furiously and making travel extremely arduous. However, as I could read my compass I felt sure of myself and kept on, the storm abating all the time. Gradually daylight came to make the situation a little more hopeful, though it still stormed so that I could not see very far; but at last, to my great joy, I distinguished a ragged-looking bank looming darkly on my left hand.

In half an hour I had given my dogs a well-earned feed, and was myself inside the tepee of an Indian hunter eating a caribou rib before a warming fire.

I never did get another ptarmigan.

Drawing by Henry S. Watson.

Drawing by Charles Livingston Bull

"One trapped fox, cringing in its miserably cold captivity,
I had killed the day before and left for its lucky owner."

42

The Way of a Half-breed

W.A. FRASER

"I'M DE BES' BULLY STEERSMAN ON DE RIBBER!"

OUTING

APRIL, 1900.

THE WAY OF A HALF-BREED.

By W. A. Fraser.

THE Canadian Government doesn't feed an Indian at Stony Mountain jail for seven years for nothing. He must have done something serious to be fed well, decorated with the iron jewelry, have a trained chaperon, and become really the exclusive ward of the nation.

If he get seven years in all probability he should have been hanged, for the Queen's agents are tolerant of these half-tamed children of the forest.

Maxepeto, a Blackfoot half-breed, had been sent to Stony Mountain for seven years. According to this tale, a white man in his place would have been hanged.

Maxepeto was always bad. Those who knew him best said he was exclusively bad.

When an evil Indian dies—too evil to get into the Happy Hunting Ground—he comes back reincarnated as a half-breed, and Maxepeto was unholy even for a "breed."

It was at Trapper's Landing that the thing happened. Trapper's Landing was within seven miles of the northwest boundary line of the Canadian Territories. Beyond that was a wilderness of spruce, and muskeg, and fierce-running rivers stretching away to the Arctic. In the wilderness were fur animals, Indians, a few white traders, and a deficiency of law and holy writ.

The clay feet of Trapper's Landing rested in the waters of the Saska River, and a box tossed on its current at the Landing would fetch up on the shores of Athabasca, or Great Slave Lakes, over a thousand miles away; in pieces, of course, for the hell-gate of Grand Rapids would batter it into smithereens, as a coffee bean is smashed in the mill.

Maxepeto knew that water roadway well, clean through to the home of the Musk Ox, in the land that had been cursed by the Gods, and left bare of everything but moss, away to the north and east of Great Slave Lake.

Once he had gone there with a mad Englishman who had a long purse and wondrous rifles of unique make. The half-breed had returned with money enough to develop a highly embellished season of delirium tremens, and some classical Oxford oaths, which he had adapted from the Englishman's vocabulary. Mexepeto's "By Jove! I get me bully squiffy, don't you know!" was a revelation to his coffee-colored brethren. "Oh, he had a *bally* bad time," he assured them.

And as for the Britisher, he had acquired no Musk Ox heads, but had left an ear, three fingers of his right hand, and several toes to bear witness to the "bloody awful climate, don't you know."

If the sporting rifles could have shot through two hundred miles of atmosphere, almost frozen solid, without a stick of wood the size of a pen handle in the whole expanse of it, he might have bagged a bull's head. But together he and Maxepeto tracked their Peterboro canoe up the muddy side of the Athabasca, and he sailed back to England, while the half-breed industriously labored at the propagation of an ecstatic drunk.

Trapper's Landing was the whiskey limit. No man might take the fire-water beyond the territories' borders, and to that end two preventive police abode at this jumping-off place.

With extreme diligence that liquor law was enforced, so that the Landing's soil was more or less always soaked in corn juice. A keg stopped was a keg broached, and liquor drunk was liquor destroyed.

Life at the Landing in conse-quence was one long jubilee of hilarious precaution; it would have been a sin to let the fire-water go out amongst the benighted redmen of the North.

The Trading Company's Factor was king of this Bac-chanalian vale. He was magistrate in the face of the law, and arbiter of all things, in the belief of the Indians. Sometimes when a petty case was on in his court room, which was the store, and it dragged a bit, he would say, with drunken gravity, "Oh. Shoo! Give him three years."

Then court would stand ad-journed for a week, and the policeman would bring the case up again at the end of

"OH, SHOO! GIVE HIM THREE YEARS."

that time; the magistrate would have forgotten all about it, and probably put the culprit on to work for the company at a dollar-and-a-half a day, under the impression that the man was a victim of somebody's malice.

There were no Courts of Appeal, noth-ing only the varying moods of the Factor Magistrate to average out justice. Some offenders got ten times the possible

sentence, while others got nothing who should have been hanged.

It was because of this climatic atmos-phere that Maxepeto selected Trapper's Landing as his place of abode.

One morning the Factor called Maxe-peto into the store and said : "Go and get Nonokasi, and bring her here ; I'll marry you."

There was nothing very startling in this sudden command, because they were all at Trap-per's Land-ing. If the Factor had said,"Here's a pair of new boots for you, *Nichie*," the half - breed would have been more surprised. That he had never thought of marrying Nonokasi, or for the matter of that any other woman, did not matter in the slightest ; the Fac-tor had not consulted his wishes in the affair — didn't care a mink-skin whether Maxe-peto would like to have Nonokasi for squaw or not. Also what the Indian maiden might think about it was of small moment ; Hudson's Bay Factors are supposed to do the thinking for the people in these districts. So he sim-ply said : " Marsh ! (Go) bring her soon."

Maxepeto rummaged among the te-pees until he found Nonokasi.

" The Ookimous wanting you, I think me," he said in his crook-limbed patois.

The girl brushed her black, glistening hair smooth ; tied a bilious-yellow silk handkerchief, with impossible blue de-signs in the corners, about her neck ; threw a Scotch plaid shawl over her shoulders, and silently followed the big half-breed to the company's store. Per-haps the Factor wanted to give her a pound of tea, or an order for silk-worked moccasins.

The Factor had been enforcing the law by patriotically destroying much overproof whiskey, so he was enthusiastically primed for the work in hand.

"Stand up there together," he said with maudlin dignity. "Hold on a bit!" and he fumbled in a drawer where much jewelry of unique design and unheard-of metal was kept in disorderly abandon. He fished out a ring with an olive-colored diamond, half the size of the Koh-i-noor, and handing it to Maxepeto said : "Now we'll go ahead. When I shout put it on her finger."

The marriage was more or less legally consummated, with the store assistant as witness.

as he would a pack horse, with tea, sugar, biscuit, tinned jams, fat pork and some household furniture, consisting of a looking-glass, comb, a frying-pan and several yards of gaudy print. He threw a bag of flour on his own broad shoulders, and stolidly led the way over the hill, behind which nestled the smoke-tanned canvas tepees of his red-skinned friends.

"He's a damn bad lot," muttered the Factor, leaning groggily against the door-jamb, as he watched the two figures slouch along the winding trail. "He's a bad lot, but she'll steady him, and it'll take her out of the way."

"By Goss !" muttered the breed, as he labored along under his hundred weight of flour. "What the debbil I want

"WHAT THE DEBBIL I WANT GET SQUAW ME FOR?"

"How old are you ?" the Factor asked Maxepeto, the census routine becoming indefinitely mixed up with the other rite in his mind.

"Fifty summers," answered the breed.

"And you ?"

"Twenty," lisped Nonokasi, covering her face with the red-checked shawl, bashfully.

The Factor pulled a big sheet of brown wrapping paper towards him, made an exhaustive calculation with his pencil and said : "That averages thirty-five. Write them down as thirty-five years old," he added to the clerk.

Then Maxepeto's reward materialized immediately.

"Give them debt for a good outfit," the Factor commanded the clerk.

The bridegroom loaded up the bride

get squaw me for ? S'pose the Factor got some game make me marry dat gal."

Then he thought cheerfully of the pork, and the sugar, and the many plugs of black tobacco, and they rose like a barrier between him and the inconvenience of having a wife. Also there was no doubt he had made a friend of the man in charge of the commissariat, the Ookimous. That was as good as a pension. He even might hope to take part in some of the whiskey-destroying bouts.

The marriage was the making of Maxepeto from a worldly point of view. From that time forth he was like the lilies of the field : he toiled not, yet still had raiment—not gorgeous, but shop-made and of wondrous cut—still it was raiment.

Of a free choice work is never included in the curriculum of an Indian. Maxepeto was a specific redman in his abhorrence of labor. There were many things he could do, but best of all could he steer a six-ton flat-boat, carrying a hundred pieces of goods, down through the treacherous rapids of the Saska River.

And this was the one thing he *would* do. When well loaded with liquor of unquestioned vileness his constant boast was, " I'm de bes' bully steersman on de ribber !"

No man on all that boiling turbulent stream, with its rock-blocked rapids, could handle a boat like the huge half-breed. He liked the danger of it, and the pay was big. There was little manual labor, which was the saving grace of the thing in his eyes.

Two months after his marriage he went down with the first boat of the season ; he was gone three moons. The boats never came up the river again— they couldn't ; so the pilots always walked back.

Maxepeto tramped up the river bank day after day, and when he was near home cut across the hillside and appeared unannounced in his tepee home.

He should not have come as a leopard stalks a deer. But he was a big, blundering breed, with a thousand-year heritage of savagery in his blood.

That night he came to the store and asked for a bottle of Jamaica ginger for Nonokasi ; she was ill, he said.

The next day he came again, and fumbled among the limited stock of patent medicines, and went off with a bottle of fruit salts and a tin of mustard plasters—his wife was worse.

Next day he came back and said she was dead.

The clerk went over to the tepee and had a look at Nonokasi. She was dead, of a surety.

Maxepeto got a few rough pine boards from the Factor, made a rude coffin, and in that she was brought down to the Mission House, so that Father Le Farge might perform the last rites before she was laid away in the little clay cell up on the hillside.

There was no inquest, no bother of any sort ; doctors and lawyers, and undertakers and coroners, and the others who make such a serious business of dying, were hundreds of miles away. Trapper's Landing had no time for that sort of thing. When people wanted to die in peace they just died; and nobody bothered them or the friends who were left behind.

There was the body in its rough pine case, down at the Mission House, if anybody wished to look at it. Father Le Farge would return that night, and Nonokasi would be buried next morning, as became a good Catholic.

In the morning, after the simple service, they were carrying the coffin outside to fasten on the cover. Some one tripped on the step and the case fell. The good Father started back with a cry of horror, for the head of the dead girl had rolled to one side.

The slender neck had been completely severed by a sharp knife, and that while she was still alive.

The glazed eyes stared with horrible grotesqueness into the face of the evil Maxepeto as he stood beside the coffin and glared down at his dead victim.

Why he only got seven years no one can say, for he never denied it—but that was his sentence.

43

Amid Birch and Balsam

EDWIN C. KENT

Down the crooked trail to the cabin in the clearing.

AMID BIRCH AND BALSAM

A NEW BRUNSWICK MOOSE

By EDWIN C. KENT

PHOTOGRAPHS BY THE AUTHOR

DURING the past decade the men of the north countries have slowly realized the fact that in the wild denizens of their streams and woods, the salmon, the moose, the caribou and the bear, they are possessed of an asset of far greater money value than any crop which the land with its sterile soil and inhospitable winter climate can produce, a crop which needs no sowing or care, but to be let alone, to yield a bountiful harvest.

Year by year the game laws are increasing in stringency and also, what is of far greater importance, they are being more and more supported by popular opinion, for in this land of ours no statute was ever yet enacted which practically was worth the paper upon which it was written, unless it had the support of public opinion.

Twenty years ago, thanks to the exertions of the hide hunter and the game butcher, the moose had almost ceased to exist south of the St. Lawrence River; but a fair amount of protection has had its due effect, and to-day any one taking a two or three weeks' trip into the wilds of Maine or New Brunswick is reasonably certain of at least seeing game. Whether he will succeed in securing a trophy is quite another matter, and will depend upon a combination of the experience of his guide as a woodsman, the sportsman's own personal qualities and willingness to work, and last, but by no means least, good luck.

While the number of moose is undoubtedly increasing and the absolute protection given to cows and calves warrants the belief that they will continue to do so, really good heads are rare. Eight or ten years must pass before the antlers reach their highest pitch of perfection, and, owing to the number of sportsmen who yearly make a pilgrimage into the wilds of New Brunswick (most of whom are anxious to kill a moose upon any terms), the life of any bull

moose for ten years is not a good insurable risk. The life of the New Brunswick moose, except from the 15th of September to the 1st of January, is of more interest to the naturalist than to the sportsman, but during this time the sport can be divided into three distinct phases, although they shade into each other so that it becomes impossible to say with any exactness when one ends and the other begins. When the season opens on the 15th of September the moose are still to be found living and feeding on the shores of the lakes and ponds. The rutting season has hardly arrived, and the moose still seek the protection of the water from the persecution of the flies and mosquitoes, although they are becoming restless and are moving about continually. At this time the sportsman's best chance is had by stealing up the creeks and dead waters in the early morning and about sunset, when the moose are often found standing shoulder deep in the soft mud and feeding on the long, juicy roots of the water-lily. Calling is at first not used, or only used as an experiment, but this time is short, for the last week of September is generally considered the rutting season proper, which lasts about a month, the cream of the season being reached during the full of the "hunter's" moon. The snow begins to fly during the latter part of October in that high north land, and with the snow comes the season of still hunting, when the white carpet covers the crackling twig and rustling beech leaf, and shows, as on a printed page where all may read, the movements and doings of the wild-wood dwellers.

The shooting ground is generally reached either by way of Fredericton, or *via* Perth up the Tobique River; the latter is perhaps the most popular, as the hunting grounds are rather more easily reached from the railroad terminal. I chose that route on my way to the woods to try that most fascinating but uncertain sport, calling the moose, and met my guide at Riley Brook, some twenty-four miles from the end of the railway at Plaster Rock.

Among woodsmen the idea is generally received that the cow stays with the bull about three days, then, watching an opportunity, steals away and hides, while the bull, after vainly pursuing her, looks for a new mate. The hope of every woodsman is that he may happen upon a bull recently deserted, as at that time he seems fairly distraught and loses much of his cunning and caution. He seems to think that any and every noise is worth following and investigating. As his disappointment has made him extremely irritable and as he absolutely refuses to trust to the evidence of his eyes and ears, he at times makes it extremely interesting to the unarmed "timber-cruiser" or logger who has happened to attract his attention. However, in his wildest moments he never loses his instinctive dread of man, nor does he ever doubt the warning which his nose gives him, and should the wind bring the man scent to him he at once loses all interest in further investigation.

It seems to be almost a superstition among writers that only an Indian can ever successfully acquire the art of calling a moose. Doubtless, a few years ago only Indians ever practiced it and they were the only guides procurable. Lately however, the red man has been declining in favor and the white man has been taking his place. Of course it is far more poetical and romantic to have Indians as guides and it is also generally cheaper. But the red man is dirty and very lazy, besides being subject to fits of the sulks; and now that taking parties into the woods has been systemized into a business and the men are obliged before taking charge of a party to take out a license, a better class of men than were to be found in the old days are engaged in the work. Certainly a hundred or more bull moose are each season called up and shot in New Brunswick alone, and there are more white than red guides engaged in the work.

Although it is the custom to call only in the early morning and late in the afternoon (the law forbids calling after nightfall), the cows can be heard calling at any hour of the day or night, and at the latter time the call is almost continuous—a long, wild bellow not unlike, in its general character, the lowing of the domestic cow.

This call, the most common and the one most often heard, is easily learned and imitated by any one whose ears are attuned to the sounds of the woods and is able to remember the notes. This call is given by every guide, and will bring a moose if he happens to have recently lost his mate or, blind with rage and desire, is looking for one. It will start any bull who happens to be within ear shot with a desire to investigate the origin of the sound. A bull coming under the latter circumstances will probably be intensely suspicious. When he first starts he may or may not grunt an answer, but he will move silently. It is one of the many marvels of the woods how that great deer will put his hoofs down on the dry beech leaves without a rustle, while to your feet, although shod with rubber or buckskin, they are absolutely explosive. The moose manages it, however, and moreover will keep those antlers with their five feet spread of points, from tapping against the trees and bushes, that would scrape and rasp on your clothes and ring on your rifle barrel in spite of your best efforts. At such times the bull will circle to get the wind, and will utilize the densest thickets as points of observation, and it is then that the man who can put that bull's suspicions to sleep and persuade him to show himself in the open is indeed an artist; but such an artist, either white or red, is not common.

No one who has passed much time in the woods, or has given much thought or attention to the ways and movements of the wild folk, can doubt for a moment that they have an articulate method of communication. Listen to that wild-goose flock as they swing on the wind, or better still, listen to the stand of tamed wild geese, as they honk and croak and soothe and plead and argue with their wild brethren to forget their wildness and come within reach of the concealed gunner; then say if you dare that animals have no spoken language, and that each sound does not convey some definite and distinct idea to the listener.

Our trouble when we seek to imitate is that we cannot associate sound with sense, and when speaking are perpetually giving

With the bows pointed down toward civilization.

the wrong intonation, using the wrong sound and simply talking nonsense, which naturally must make the hearer suspicious and so defeat our object.

As a natural effect when two bulls come to the call of the same cow one or the other must give way. This cannot generally be settled without a fight, and should the bulls be equally matched the struggle must be Homeric indeed. Every now and then when hunting you come upon such a battle-ground, and the manner in which the ground is torn up, the deep impressions of widespread feet, and the uprooted bushes and smashed young trees show the power which is exerted. Occasionally the antlers become locked; then both animals perish miserably. This, although a matter of frequent occurrence with deer, happens but rarely with the moose owing to the palmation of the antlers.

Many of the woodsmen claim that the young bulls are generally victorious over the older ones, and there are good reasons for thinking that this is so. A moose gets its full growth and strength long years before the antlers gain their full size. The small, narrow, sharp-tined antlers must be more effective weapons and more easily handled in the woods, and youthful agility must be a considerable factor. An old bull, one who carries a magnificent set of antlers, is always most careful and cautious in answering the call of the cow. Perhaps this is owing to having more than once detected the cheat, but also perhaps it is due to unhappy memories of recent defeats and a desire, pardonable enough on his part, not to put himself in the way of another thrashing.

When the shooting trip is over and one looks back, the every-day occurrences, interesting enough in themselves, become blurred and indistinct with the lapse of time; but every now and then some scene, some incident, seems to have photographed itself upon the memory, and stands out clearly and distinctly against the hazy background. Such a scene was the night of the October full moon. The night was cloudless and breathless, and I was tempted to leave the seductions of the bright camp fire to drift about the lake in a canoe, and if possible see or hear what the wild things were doing.

Near the camp was a so-called lake; in

reality it was a long, narrow slough with a foot of water over two or more feet of mud, stretching east and west through a wide marsh; the clear water was only a few yards wide. The moon hung in the eastern sky, a globe of silver light, and the slough and marsh were abundantly illuminated; but the light in the open only served to accentuate the intense blackness of the shadows cast by the fir and spruce woods on either bank.

The silence was intense, so intense that it could almost be felt. There was no sound of insect or bird, not even the splash of a fish or of a feeding musk-rat, and sitting there in the canoe the same feeling came over me which one feels when in some vast, empty cathedral, or when wandering through the great silent woods of the Pacific coast.

Lindsay, my guide, wished to try the effect of a call, but I objected; it seemed almost profanation to rudely break in upon that profound calm. In a short time, however, a cow moose came down to the edge of the marsh, and without showing herself outside of the black shadow, began to call. The wild, savage, but half-pleading wail floated over the marsh in perfect accord with the wildness of the scene.

After some half hour of continuous calling, during which time we could hear her splashing restlessly about in the shallow water, far, far off on a hardwood ridge we heard the fierce grunt of an answering bull. Nearer and nearer came the grunting, low, savage, but perfectly audible, and then the call of the cow changed to a low, whining note with varying inflections impossible to imitate or describe. The bull answered with low roaring moans, then the cow left the water, and we could hear the two wild lovers meet, and silence once more settled over the lake.

At last the end of the outing had come, and it was time to pack up and go back to civilization, after a trip barren of results in the way of game trophies, but rich in the "pleasure of the pathless woods." We had been out in the woods early and late, had worked hard and faithfully without having seen a single bull, save one, an enormous youngster with a very small. head, who came trotting up to us one morning in all the rashness of youth and inexperience, and stood for some minutes calmly contemplating us,—I presume much disgusted at seeing two men, instead of an expectant and lonely cow.

The weather for the last week of the trip had been cold and rainy and my guide had contracted a severe cold, which, settling in his bronchial tubes, made calling or still hunting impossible; the poor fellow could do nothing but cough.

We had returned to the main camp, which we had some ten days before deserted, because two other parties had come into the woods and camped upon what we considered our lake. Six sportsmen in all, with guides, a full complement of attendants and cooks—surely no one tract of country was big enough to provide sport for such a crowd.

We reached camp about ten A.M., and after lunch I told my guide to stay there, and employ the afternoon packing up and getting ready to pull out next morning; while I, with Andy, the cook and camp-boy, would take a walk on the hardwood ridges lying to the south of our camp and away from the other camps. I did not expect to see anything, because we had repeatedly hunted over that country when we first arrived. Judging from the signs seen we believed that the young bull spoken of above, and one or two cows which were drifting about, were all the moose in that piece of woods; besides, we thought that the country had been thoroughly hunted by the other parties.

It had been wet and rainy for a couple of days. The dead leaves and dried sticks were soft and soggy, so that still hunting was possible.

All through the afternoon we rambled on until, shortly before sunset, we found ourselves some four miles from camp, having seen absolutely nothing, not even fresh signs. We were then on the top of a hardwood ridge, and as the evening was perfectly still Andy proposed to try the effect of a call. He had only called up one bull before this, and had not seen that one, but like every other boy and man in the back settlements, had practiced calling assiduously, and was longing for an opportunity to put his knowledge into practice. In that country of birches a horn is soon made, and we hid ourselves in the center of a little thicket of young spruces. In orthodox fashion Andy gave the first call in a

It is not often the hunter comes face to face with a moose, giant of the deer family.

The calves are tame enough in their innocence.

low tone in case any moose should be close by. The call had hardly died away in the wood when sudden and fierce came the answer, the harsh, savage grunt of a running bull, apparently not three hundred yards away. And he was coming—we could hear the crash and splinter of the dead wood and the click-clickety-click of the boughs as they brushed against the antlers.

Then a cow, angry and jealous at the thought of a rival, began to plead and moan back, down in the lower swamp. Instantly the bull stopped and evidently stood irresolute for a moment. Again the cow moaned and whined, and the bull slowly obeyed her, grumbling as if discontented. Andy tried to call again, but through excitement the sound he uttered was anything but an accurate imitation. Nevertheless the bull answered and started toward us again, and again the cow began to plead and again he stopped. He was evidently more than ready to be off with his old love, but lacked the moral courage or brutality to say so, while as for the cow, no matter what may have been the family bickerings which had occurred before this, she had no intention of allowing any other cow to take her bull away. This went on for some time; the bull answered every call

which Andy gave, but apparently had returned permanently to his allegiance, and while discussing the matter they were making a great to-do down in the dark recesses of the swamp. The trouble was evidently settled, for we heard nothing for some minutes, when suddenly Andy, with his face simply blazing with excitement, whispered, "He is coming up over there on your left." His ears were better than mine, for I could not hear a sound.

A few moments of breathless tension, a few notes of the horn and then an agonized "He has stopped, he won't come." Then the noise in the valley recommenced, and Andy's language as whispered became both red-hot and sulphurous. He managed to gasp, "Slip over the hill quick and see if you can see him," then, "Don't make a noise," in a perfect agony, as a twig caught and snapped on my coat. I doubt if the tiny snap could have been heard ten feet away, but just then to our tense organs it sounded like the crack of doom.

Once out of the dense spruce thicket it was a simple matter to move slowly from tree to tree over the wet, soggy leaves, stopping at each shelter to carefully examine everything in sight. I had gone in this manner for a few hundred yards when my eyes fell on a pair of magnificent antlers protruding from a spruce thicket, and immediately below and between them a huge gray nose. The light was now fading, and peer as I would I could not make out the animal, not even the loom of his body. To approach any nearer was impossible, for the trees were wide apart and the cover low and thin between us. I dared not wait, for at any instant some vagrant air current might bring clear and certain information to that enormous nose. It was too far for a head shot and something must be risked. I sighted the point of the nose, drawing the bead well down in the notch, and then sinking the muzzle, pulled! The great horns pitched forward on the ground with the crack of the rifle.

Then followed a ridiculous sight, for Andy, wild with delight and excitement, came through the wood bounding over the logs and crashing through the bushes, yelling, "Shoot, shoot, don't let him get away!" and my answer that the bull was dead had no effect on him. Together we went up to the fallen game, and as we approached, the poor brute made a desperate but abortive attempt to rise; so stepping round so that I could see his back, I broke his neck between the shoulders, killing him at once.

On seeing the size of the head Andy's delight was unbounded. He threw handsprings around the body, ending by jumping on the moose and dancing a Highland-fling. When he had somewhat calmed down we examined the prize. It was well worth the winning. The moose was very small and almost jet black. Of course in the woods any estimate of weight is purely guesswork, but he probably did not weigh more than six hundred pounds at most. The head, however, atoned for the size, for while not by any means a record head, it was one such as is rarely seen nowadays in New Brunswick—fifty-nine and one-half inches spread, twenty-three points with a thirteen and one-half inch palmation, the whole head being very level and perfectly balanced. To complete the beauty of the specimen, the bull was decorated with a twenty-inch bell in perfect condition.

44

For the Under Dog

RILEY H. ALLEN

FOR THE UNDER DOG

BY

RILEY H. ALLEN

ILLUSTRATED BY F. RICHARDSON

IT was in December, '97, that a half-dead Tahkheena River Indian, his frozen feet showing through worn caribou-skin moccasins, came into the Police Post at Lake Linderman with a letter for the captain. It said:

Chambers has turned up here and there'll be the deuce to pay. For Heaven's sake, send McWilliams. POWELL, Tahkheena Road House.

The captain swore and called McWilliams. To the latter he said: "I want you to go to Powell's Roadhouse. Chambers is there. When can you start?"

"An hour," said McWilliams, and an hour later he was *mushing* his dog-team toward the Tahkheena River, two hundred miles away across the frozen snow-fields.

McWilliams was a sergeant in the Canadian Mounted Police, a dour old Scotchman, with a pair of steady gray eyes and a big chin under his close-cropped, grizzly beard; six foot one of bone and sinew on his moose-hide snow-shoes—and the silence of Alaskan snow-fields clothed him like a mantle. He had been in the service of the Queen for twenty years, and they said of him in the North that he had never failed to get his man, dead or alive. It was McWilliams that faced three hundred raging miners at Miles Canyon and saved the horse thief, Dixon, from hanging to the nearest mountain pine. It was McWilliams who brought "Nigger" Sloan back to Haines Mission on a dog sled, after a running fight of twenty

miles. It was McWilliams who was known from Skagway to Dawson as the grimmest machine of a man that ever carried justice into a lawless country.

McWilliams traveled light, for he had to go far and fast. An average Eskimo "husky" can cover fifty miles a day on good going, and McWilliams's dogs were malamoots —great, savage brutes, thin and hungry, but trained like race-horses. On the sled were twelve days' provisions, a coffee-pot, and a sleeping-bag. There was also a bundle of wood, chopped fine, and dry as three months' seasoning under shelter could make it, for in winter the Yukon mercury crawls down to forty or fifty below and ten feet of ice grips the rivers. Then the sled driver is glad of a tiny, chip-fed fire to thaw his freezing fingers, and sleeps on hard snow six inches from the glowing embers.

The low-running dogs headed up the ice-packed trail toward the Tahkheena River, and McWilliams smiled grimly under his gray-shot beard when he thought of Chambers.

Chambers! Outlaw and thief, gambler and murderer; under sentence of death three times and each time escaping; "Bad-man" Chambers—sworn to kill McWilliams on sight and to die rather than be taken; and yet in his desperate heart a fierce pride of manhood that made him scorn to strike the under dog. McWilliams smiled grimly that night as he *cached* two days' provisions at Lake Argell, sixty miles out from Linderman, for use on his return trip with

Chambers; and after he had fed the dogs on dried salmon, he threw the empty paper sack into the air and drew a revolver. There were three quick reports and the sack fell to the ground with three holes neatly drilled within the round of a dollar. The revolver was not a dainty pearl-handled one such as ladies use. The barrels were of blued-steel and the caliber was forty-four. And as McWilliams crawled into his sleeping-bag he smiled, and smiled grimly as he slept, with the dogs howling about him.

McWilliams bent forward a little and looked into the window of Powell's Roadhouse, blinking as the light fell upon his eyes. Back on the trail stood the dog-team, a patch of gray against the star-lit snow.

The room was full of men, gambling and drinking—great, rough, heavy-bearded fellows, and boisterous with whisky. Behind the bar stood Powell; his ruddy face was troubled and his eyes glanced continually toward a table near the door.

There were three men at the table, playing poker. One of the men was a dark-browed miner, his companion a tenderfoot—a mere boy—and both were excited. The third man lolled back in his chair with easy grace, dealing the cards with swift, sure flips of his wrist and white fingers. His eyes were slow and languid, but there was alertness in the poise of his blond head and audacity in his clean-cut features. When he moved, the muscles flowed under his skin like those of a panther. Altogether, a handsome, mocking devil, and a slow smile touched his face as he added the miner's chips to the stack before him.

McWilliams knew enough about poker to see that the miner and the boy were losing heavily. The third man played carelessly and smiled at the flushed faces and trembling hands of his companions. He reached for a stack of chips and, as he did so, from the sleeve of his woolen jacket a card dropped and lay face upward on the table.

There was a loud oath from the miner and the tenderfoot sprang to his feet, his hands clenched. The slow smile deepened on the gambler's face and, with an easy, almost a careless motion, he drew his revolver. McWilliams turned from the window and flung himself into the room.

Yet in that time many things had happened. On the floor, beside the overturned table, lay the tenderfoot—shot through the head, and blood spurted over a scattered stack of poker chips just in front of his face. The miner lay in a shapeless heap, all knees and elbows; his limbs jerked spasmodically, and then stiffened. Back to the wall, the third man covered the room with his revolver. Powder smoke, biting and pungent, eddied out the open door.

McWilliams stepped forward and his voice stung the silence like the lash of a whip. "Chambers, drop that gun !"

Chambers whirled. "McWilliams !" he said ; both revolvers spoke, and the crowd of miners surged forward with a yell. The light went out with a crash of broken glass, and the room was filled with human tigers.

Out of the thick of it staggered McWilliams, his right arm limp and twisted, but with him came Chambers, handcuffed, and the sergeant's steel fingers were sunk deep in his shoulder.

McWilliams knew the Alaska miner when his blood is up as a child knows its book. He turned to the trail, flung Chambers upon the ten-foot sled, and called to the dogs. There was a tightening of leather traces, a leap against collar, and the malamoots settled into their stride—the stride that eats up the miles like fire. The roadhouse sank behind them and they headed for Lake Argell.

"I sure reckon," said Chambers, "there'd been some fun if you hadn't got me. Guess I'd been there yet."

"Aye," grunted McWilliams, and he lashed Chambers more securely—a slow proceeding with a broken arm; but it was done at last, and Chambers lay helpless on the sled and cursed McWilliams reprovingly.

That night, twenty miles out, the gambler slept in the wadded canvas bag, while McWilliams, among the dogs for warmth, kept back the groans when his crushed arm bit and tortured. His face was hard the next morning after breakfast, as he motioned Chambers to the sled. The gambler threw back his head and laughed.

"Curse you, McWilliams," he said pleasantly; "can't you talk once in a while ?"

There was a sudden flush in the sergeant's gray eyes, and with one sound arm he threw Chambers across the sled. And still Chambers laughed.

So into the south McWilliams drove the malamoots. By day the air glistened with

"'Curse you, McWilliams; can't you talk once in a while?'"

millions of diamond atoms, and great orange sun-dogs flashed and played around them. The cold drove straight to the heart like a pang, and the reflection of sunlight across miles of snow was blinding. Sometimes a puff of wind spat the powdered ice of the trail against their faces, lightly, yet with the cut of steel. At night the strange northern fires flickered redly on the far horizon, streaming across the sky in ribbons of crimson, and the stars were cold and merciless.

McWilliams never spoke save to the dogs, but the man going to his death down at Linderman hummed airily the songs of Klondike dance-halls, or sometimes broke into oaths and beat his steel wrist-bands against the sled, till the sergeant would raise his revolver with a look in his steady eyes that killed the words on Chambers's lips.

Two days of watchfulness and pain for McWilliams, and latterly a weariness of body and mind that was worse than pain. And on the third night the gaunt dog-team stopped in front of the cabin on frozen Argell, where McWilliams had *cached* provisions on the way out.

The sergeant staggered as he unbound the rope from Chambers's feet and built a fire on the cabin floor. There were two rude bunks and a table, and to one of these bunks McWilliams fastened the gambler with buckskin thongs from the sled harness. The wolf-dogs howled outside, and the northern lights wavered on the far horizon, while within the sergeant turned restlessly on his narrow bed of pine boards, muttering brokenly. The gambler, tied to his bunk, looked on and hummed a gay little song under his breath.

In the early morning light the sergeant's gray eyes were set in deep, dusky circles, but they looked steadily out from a resolute white face and the fever was quite gone. Chambers, lashed to his bunk, smiled at the trembling fingers of the other and his smile was not good to see.

McWilliams crossed the room and unfastened the ropes around the gambler's feet— it was a long job, for the fingers continued to tremble, but it was finished. Then he slipped a hand underneath his deerskin *parka* and brought forth a small key. There was no comprehension in Chambers's eyes, but he smiled lightly. McWilliams fitted the key to the gambler's handcuffs and turned the lock. Chambers shook off the manacles. The

sergeant sank back upon the bunk, panting and white.

Chambers rose to his feet and stretched himself, just as a wintry sun shot redly through a chink in the wall. He threw open the door, and the sunlight, straight over a thousand miles of virgin snow, leaped into the room and filled it with a merry gleam. Outside the lean wolf-dogs were stretching themselves, and they crowded around him for the breakfast of dried salmon.

Far to the southeast the trail ran, till it dwindled to a darker streak on the snow and disappeared. Straight down to Linderman, or, if you choose, swing to the left at Tornado Creek and on to Skagway, then——

Chambers turned back into the cabin and seated himself on the table; he looked at McWilliams, lying white and weak in the bunk, at the sergeant's shattered arm and at the handcuffs on the floor with the key still in the lock, at the buckskin thongs beside them.

There were four days' provisions in the cabin; outside stood a sled, and even now a ring of impatient, wistful canine faces filled the doorway. Turn off at Tornado Creek, and on to Skagway and the States. This man—who would know? A lonely trail— perhaps in the spring—surely not for weeks. By that time—the fight at Powell's Roadhouse? Well, he could have got out without McWilliams's help—at least, he could have made it hot for those devils. After all, what would it matter, back in the States, with gold, plenty of gold, and no one need know—could know. Ten days to Seattle— he was safe there—ten days. And at Linderman? What chance of escape there? Linderman, sixty miles away, and McWilliams, dying from exposure, had saved his life. McWilliams had got him out of the roadhouse—McWilliams—with one arm broken; right arm, too. Tornado Creek at noon, four days to Skagway—Seattle——

McWilliams watched the murderer's pale face without a word, but in his eyes was the look of a trapped wildcat as he dies unconquered. Then Chambers's head went up, inch by inch; on his lower lip burned a red line, but his eyes were glad.

McWilliams turned his face away to hide its emotion.

"Curse you, McWilliams," said Chambers; "I sure reckon I've got to take you down to Linderman."

45

When the June Rise is On

EMERSON HOUGH

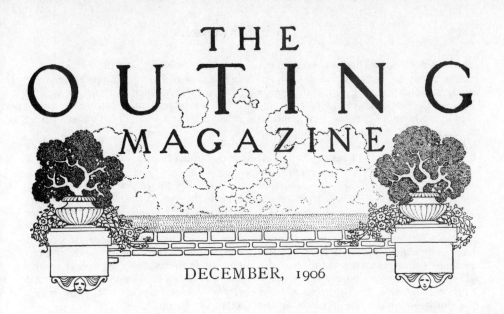

THE
OUTING
MAGAZINE

DECEMBER, 1906

WHEN THE JUNE RISE IS ON

DOWN THE COLUMBIA AFTER GRIZZLIES

BY EMERSON HOUGH

PHOTOGRAPHS BY THE AUTHOR

WE Americans exult in the history of our early West, the history of Lewis and Clark, of Ashley and Fitzpatrick and Sublette and all the bold crew of adventurers who found our Rockies for us; yet the deeds of Alexander McKenzie and Simon Fraser, of David Thompson and Samuel Hearne, and Harmon and Henry and Pallisser and a score of others in the vast country north of us were in some instances quite as bold, and perhaps more full of danger and hardship than those of our own captains. We esteem our western mountains the biggest and most beautiful and most dangerous, our rivers the most wild and alluring, our plains the widest and most fascinating; yet these northern plains are riper and richer than our own, these northern rivers are wilder than ours; and when McKenzie and Thompson did their work they crossed a mountain region where certainly none but

men belonged. To be first in the northern Rockies, first in the white Selkirks, first on a score of waters where even to-day the beaver swarm and the foot of tourist has never trod—that, my countrymen, was real life!

We are accustomed to think of the Columbia River in terms of canned salmon, and to consider it a river wholly American, with a source somewhere near the Yellowstone Park, *via* the Snake River. As a matter of fact the true Columbia does not head on our soil, but north of the international line. It is up in the mountains of lower British Columbia that the great river first trickles down out of the glaciers and snow-banks. I know how it starts, for I have photographed some of the absolute heads of it, a pace wide, up in the clouds. At first it does not run west or southwest, but heads northward, until presently it strikes what is now the line of the Canadian Pacific Railway, running between what is now called the Kicking Horse Pass over the Rockies and what is called the Rogers Pass over the Selkirks. Thence the Columbia makes north for another hundred miles, dropping down a steep green stair, a gorge between the Selkirks and the Rockies, cutting through one of the most noble mountain regions of the world. Reaching far up into the ancient beaver wilderness, the Columbia at the head of this great but almost unknown Big Bend sweeps around toward the south, a mighty panorama lying at every space along its cañons on the west slope of the Selkirks, running parallel to its northbound course at the opposite or eastern side; and so breaks down through more gorges until at last it broadens and expands and Americanizes and becomes commercial and flows gently into salmon cans; through sale of which men go to see the European Alps. The Big Bend of the Columbia is not commercial. It belongs to the wilderness.

There are a few, a very few, men of to-day who have run all of the Big Bend. There are Walt Steinhof and Jack Bogardus—trapping partners, who took a month to get from the railroad last fall, *via* part of the Big Bend, and the Canoe, and the McLennan, and so down the Fraser into a land of much marten and herds of giant moose; Kid Price, an old-timer, and one Evans; and Bob McCurdy, whom the Columbia would once have got had not Steinhof swam out and caught his boat rope as it swept past; and Leo Davis, a Shuswap Indian, who will drown there before long; and McBean, a good cruiser, and Old Joe Lemacknamee, who warps up river with a block and tackle, and who will die in his cabin out there some day; and Douglas Allison, ex-Boer War-English sergeant and now good game warden. This spring two new men ran it, one of whom never will want to run it again—Elliott C. Barnes of Banff, one of our party that went in search of Ephraim; and myself, reported by Steinhof, who has been in that country eleven years, to be the first tourist, pilgrim, tenderfoot or infernal fool that he ever heard of making that trip when he didn't have to. It is only ignorant and foolish men who unnecessarily trouble the Big Bend. A few of these men named above would say the river is sometimes fairly safe. When the June rise comes down, and the four foot rise of a night on the broads means twenty feet in the cañons, and the flood goes from icy

green to roily brown, and the water howls—friend, take it if you like; you also may be foolish. But neither you nor the best of these wilderness men will ever speak lightly of the Columbia after seeing it at such a time.

The country around the Big Bend is one of the greatest pieces of wilderness now left on this continent. It was from one certain valley thereabout that Fred Hussey brought out seven bear hides three years ago, three of them grizzlies, and that after missing several shots, and seeing twenty-nine bear on one hunt—the world's record so far as I know. Tell any lover of Ephraim these things, and the green and white stairway of the Big Bend seems at the time tame. All he says is, "Let us march against Ephraim!"

We made quite a flotilla when we left the railroad at Beavermouth, B. C., where lies the bottom of the gap between the Rockies and the Selkirks. Our men had made a couple of weird boats out of thin, unplaned boards—the *Yellow Peril* we called ours, because its nose was crooked and it did dangerous things betimes and was saffron of complexion. Jack Bogardus, Walt's partner, was to take on Curtis Hussey, Fred Hussey's brother, who had the family zeal bearwards. Fred Hussey and Jimmy Brewster were to go along as aids in getting the two bear camps placed. My party, Steinhof and Barnes, were to pack farther back into the mountains, into the valley of Ephraimistic delights where Fred had seen them in flocks. We had two canoes, mostly worthless. One of them, *Mabel*, wiser but pensive, remains. The *Echo* is matchwood somewhere, but we do not know where.

The first rapid below Beavermouth is Brinkman's Terror, so called for one Brinkman, who was unable to touch bottom with the naked leg after carefully trying it for a quarter of a mile. He was scared so badly that he has never since then been able to tell the truth, and has been installed by the Canadian Pacific road as official liar, with quarters at Golden.

"There's lots of bears down where you're going," Brinkman said. "I killed one thousand seven hundred and sixty-three there one year—exactly three carloads of them. I loaded them cars, so I know. I was mad—I couldn't get the last three

THE CHARGE OF DESTRUCTION

Looking up Little River Valley.

hides in the last car to save my life—had to let the car go with them three left on my hands. Only thing is, look out for the rapids."

Yet we swam down the Brinkman Rapids with our *Yellow Peril* and all the rest of our fleet with only that rising of blood which makes one feel gay in good water. The rollers were not more than five or six feet in height, and the way through was easy and obvious. We camped the first night at the head of Surprise Rapids, meeting there Tom Ogborn, who had trapped there all winter, and one Hamilton, who had been back in the wilderness somewhere, and had not seen a human face for over six months. We portaged our supplies over three miles of fairish trail here, Walt and Jack taking the boats through light, of course lining over the worst chutes. We left *Mabel* above the rapids. Jimmy and Fred got ambitious and started down with the *Echo*, our fourteen foot canoe, but this was insult to the Columbia, and she wrapped the *Echo* around a rock a few hundred yards below the starting point, the boys being then, by great good fortune, only waist deep in the water and near shore, lining down the canoe into the head of a bad chute. They got out on the far side of the river, and walked up to the head of the rapids, where we rescued them, very glad it was no worse.

There are several bad pieces of water in the twenty-odd miles from the foot of Surprise to the head of Timbasket Lake (Kinbasket on the maps), where the big river expands into as lovely a mountain mere as one could ask. It is enough to say we got through whole, running even the Double Eddy with little discomfort, though sometimes this is a bad place. As all river men know, it is not straight white water that is most dangerous, but backsets along shores, and cross-currents and boils. There is no formula for the Columbia. It is never twice alike even in the same place.

Curtis Hussey and Fred Hussey and Bogardus now went up a pathless stream which our guides called Windy River—the maps are shamelessly ignorant of all this region—while the rest of us crossed the lake, made a headquarters camp and the next day set out up what they called Middle River,—a day and a half of the bitterest sort of a march, under packs of sixty to one hundred and ten pounds, and over the hardest of

hard mountain countries. We had our reward, however, and at last reached Canaan, our shut-in mountain panorama widening out into a grand flat valley ten miles long, a mile or so broad in places. This wide opening in the mountains was hemmed in with eternal white snow-fields and deep, blue-fronted glaciers, unknown and unnamed. These ragged peaks not ten men ever saw, and none has ever christened. Their lower slopes were all shrouded in black forests, with strips torn through them by the awful might of the spring snow-slides. It was on these slides, now covered with faint green, that we were to do our hunting. The bears come out on these open places to feed on the first vegetation of the spring, and, as I believe, to escape the oppressiveness of the eternal gloom of these dense forests. At any rate, our own hearts expanded when we saw the light of the open valley lying before us, without a smoke or a footprint visible, and apparently as wild and sweet as on the day of creation.

The river here wanders and splits, as we could see evidenced in the dark threads crossing the white snow; and this division into channels made it fordable. We did not mind the river, into which we plunged, accoutered as we were, hip deep and better; and we tried not to mind the chilling wade in the deep snow with our wet clothing afterward, although it came very near to freezing our feet, and we had to stop and strip and wring out. A great joy possessed us all. Surely it is an unapproachable, not to be equaled, feeling, this joy that you have a valley, a new one, all for your own. Not a dozen other men had ever seen this valley—only three parties so far as we know. No Indians live anywhere within a hundred miles or more of it. No one has ever trapped here—the rapids of the Big Bend are the fence for all that country, high enough to keep out most trappers. It is off the old fur companies' trails altogether. Horses, of course, cannot get into this country.

"I believe I've got to the edge," said I to Jimmy. "You have," said he, "or I can't get you there. This is the hardest trip we can show any tourist." I let the term "tourist" go unrebuked, being much pleased with life at that time.

We went into camp four miles up the valley and fell happily to work exploring

The Author.

Portaging around Surprise Rapids.

the country. But alas! for seventeen whole days we explored and I for one saw not a bear nor a sign of one. Barnes made the frightful trip down to the lake and brought up another awful backload of grub; for men eat, and eat. We could not have a tent, of course, but we had enough blankets, and so made good camping of it. Walt went off over a wild high divide, prospecting for Ephraim. Barnes worked out both sides of our valley patiently and thoroughly, seeking Ephraim. I waited for Ephraim to come out on the slides; waited wet and cold and mad clear through. But Ephraim came not.

Each day, as we made our five or six miles hunt up the valley to inspect the many different slides, we had to wade the boiling river channels from five to a dozen times. This meant wet clothes all the time—we never got to camp dry. At times the mountain storms were very cold. We had no fresh meat. We all began to lose weight and temper, for the conditions were very trying; but still Ephraim came not. Walt was hopeful for a long time— so hopeful that he saw divers and sundry things in the bear line, for the most part wearing quills or pine needles, porcupines or stumps, or shadows; but none of them was Ephraim with the silver-golden hide. At last, much to the chagrin of both the boys, I ordered the beds rolled and we turned our backs on the valley, the most

disappointed seekers for Ephraim that ever packed a rifle. And lo! just as we reached the lower end of the valley, there was the trail of Ephraim—his foot-mark, ten inches long, or better, in the wet sand, and fresh.

My boys put down their packs and gazed. We had worked hard enough to kill a dozen bears. Should we stop and go back? Was Ephraim moving in to stay, or was he crossing over into the unknown country of the interior beyond us? We had to guess. We guessed wrong. Ephraim was moving in, but we did not know it or believe it; so we decided to go on down to the headquarters and see what we could find below.

We found that Jimmy and Fred had gone back on foot up to the railroad; that Curtis Hussey was just down, and stopping at Allison's tent; that he and Jack had seen seven bears, all black, and had shot at three, but missed. So there we were. Hussey was going on up the river with Jack, and cordially quit-claimed his valley full of black bears. Wherefore, having worked hard thus far without seeing even a despised black bear, I took Walt and we set out up the Windy River.

Barnes, a six-foot athlete, hard as nails, killer of two dozen grizzlies in his Wyoming hunting days when he was a rancher, looked wistful. "I don't like to leave that valley up there," he said, "maybe something has moved in." So it was decided to let him risk the very dangerous trip back up the trail alone, and have one more look into what ought to have been a good bear country but had not proved such. I consider the man who would willingly take that trip alone, pack on back, to be a sportsman of as clean grit as any in the world. The trail is certainly the worst I ever traveled. I was a little uneasy at seeing Barnes go out alone; but we arranged to meet at Allison's camp one week from that day.

Walt and I made it up to the Hussey camp the first night out, under good packs, and as it had taken the other party two days to get in, we thought we had done very well. At six that evening I saw my first bear—across the Windy River cañon, perhaps five hundred yards away. It was not a sporting shot, but I was getting ugly in temper by now, and must shoot. Walt said the bear was a grizzly, but I do not know. It was sitting in the green bush scratching its ear with its hind foot. I missed the first time, and could not mark the shot, but saw the bear look down, so elevated the front sight all sorts the next time, and heard the bullet chuck into him. He ended over into the bush, and I later fired two more shots at a dim, dark object which I took to be the bear. Walt said he was not killed. I rather

thought he was, simply from the sound of the bullet, which, as any hunter knows, can be heard at a great distance and is not easily to be mistaken. We found we could not ford the river for six days, and then it was too late; so we must leave the question of this bear a mystery.

I lost one bear on what might have been a better chance had I waited. He also showed up across the river, but ran into the willows on the shore. Walt ran below to see if he could get sight of him, and the bear broke back on the jump, giving me a snap-shot. Walt said I should have waited, and that the bear would have come out to see what we were. Bears in that country are not afraid of a man as yet, for they have been very little hunted. This was only a black bear. Perhaps it had a hind leg broken—I hope not. Walt forded the river here, and his little dog, Rod, swam with him. The dog stopped this bear three times, and had he been of more experience would no doubt have held it till Walt could have reached him. This was baddish luck. Walt thought I should have killed this bear.

The little dog, a half spaniel, got us a couple of bear a few days later in a peculiar way. We were packing down the mountain after breaking camp for our return to the rendezvous, when the little fellow

Walt Steinhof   E. C. Barnes

Old *Ironsides* and her crew.

Lining down the Columbia River.

began to sniff and whine. Lo! a few feet up the trail, rose up Mrs. Bear, also sniffing and whining, an easy shot. And while we were skinning her out, we heard some more sniffing and whining, and saw a little shiny black fellow up a tree, from which he very quickly tumbled. This bear and the first one killed offered proof of the hitting quality of the modern high-power rifle, my .405 bullet fairly taking off the shoulder.

Our first bear was also a black bear, and as it was killed under circumstances showing how they hunt bears on the slides in that country, I may mention it, although personally I no longer care to kill black bear, as they offer no sort of sport unless with a pack of good dogs and in a riding country. We were moving slowly up the river valley, examining the slides, when at about dusk we saw the bear, a fair-sized one, show far up at the top of the slides, perhaps three-quarters of a mile of a climb. We stalked him fast as we could, but when we got up he had disappeared. We went on, and after we had nearly given it up, he arose ahead of us, sitting up within sixty yards. Then I did a bad bit of sportsmanship, as it seemed to me—hastily shot with my sights elevated for the long shot which I had anticipated! The bear did not start, and the next guess I made at it caught him through the hind leg—which so disgusted me I stopped and arranged the sight before I chucked another into him, as he rolled. This bear was badly cut up, Walt firing into him also, just as I did the last time. These high-power bullets cut entirely through a black bear, of course.

I had no special pleasure killing these black bear, and did not care to hunt for any more. Walt insisted that he saw three or four others that I did not. I saw the four that I killed, or thought I killed, and the one that was perhaps crippled, but which escaped. Certainly I was never in my life where black bear were so numerous. Only the extreme density of the timber kept us from making a great raid there. In one march we saw seventeen fresh "signs"; and there was a deep bear trail on each side of the river, with innumerable logs, trees, etc., torn up with their workings. I presume there were at least thirty bear on that ten miles of valley, possibly more, though I could not satisfy myself any were grizzly, in spite of some certainly gigantic foot-

marks. Ephraim was not at home here any more than on Middle River. Possibly somewhere very high up on the bare basins among these snowy peaks he may have been, but by all rules he belonged at that date down on the fresh grass and green bulbs.

Walt and I had three robes, or more accurately, about two and a half; but were only half happy when we rounded up at Allison's, that worthy cooking for us beans, and again beans, of which we ate very many dishes at his hospitable fireside. Allison went with us to our camp across the lake. A big windstorm was raging and the lake was bad, the mountains very stormy. And lo! that night, as we sat by our fire, who should come in out of the storm but Barnes, worn and haggard and thin and brown, with a vast pack on his back, bigger than he had taken away. Walt sprang to his feet. "By the Lord!" he cried, "he's got him!"

It was even so. The plucky sportsman had won the reward, the chief trophy of this continent. He had marched up to our old valley the first day, and seen Ephraim on a slide a half mile away. Calmly he stalked him within sixty yards, and smashed a bullet through back of the shoulders. Ephraim let out a vast amazed bawl and dropped for the count. Barnes sent another ball into him, that lodged between the shoulder blades, and it was all over. The robe was eight feet in the raw, a very good one; but the story of the successful hunter was brief and modest.

After killing this bear and curing the hide, Barnes had gone out hunting again on the valley, and one evening saw no less than four grizzlies on one snow slide at one and the same time; which again is a record, so far as I know, for that country of grizzly records. Two of these bears were very large, much larger than the one he had killed. I asked Barnes why he had not tried for them, and he said he did not doubt he could have killed two or perhaps three of them before they could have got away; but that he wanted me to get a shot, and so he had come down after me, in the hope that we might see the bears in company again, and kill the whole bunch.

Both men now asked me what we ought to do, and the problem was a hard one. It certainly seemed that Ephraim was now coming out, and that we had at least a fair chance to get him. On the other hand, it would have been the fifth day after these bear were seen before we could possibly 'have got up there; moreover time was growing short, and it would require the best part of a week to get back up the river after we had finished our hunt. It would take us scarcely more time to run the whole Big Bend downstream, a trip no sportsman had done so far as Walt knew; and there was to be found, somewhere eighty miles downstream, a somewhat fabulous stream known as End Creek, where Walt said we would have just as good a chance to get a grizzly as we would back up Middle River. Barnes and I were keen to make this river trip, although Walt, who had made it, was by no means so keen. As we debated this a night and a day, we had a chance to reach a mature decision. During the evening we made a mad race in the white caps across the big lake after a bear which we saw on a snow slide some three miles away, and which Allison's glasses made out to be a grizzly according to some of the party, although to me it looked like only a big black bear. We did not get across in time for a shot, for the old fellow had retired to the cover; and our return in the growing storm was even more dangerous and difficult, keeping us out far into the night. It was on this long, hard pull that Walt concluded Barnes was a good enough substitute for his partner Jack; and that night he said he was willing to make the run down the river if we were willing to chance it. It was thus concluded; and here was where we lost what was no doubt our best chance to get a grizzly—minor matter as that subsequently appeared to us.

We wheeled good-natured Douglas Allison out of old *Ironsides*, his twenty-four foot double-ended, flat-bottomed batteau —far better for our voyage than the *Yellow Peril*; and on the next morning traversed our dunnage from camp to the mouth of Middle River and set out. That was as beautiful a morning as I ever saw in the mountains, the cloud effects being simply superb; and we lingered for a time trying to secure some sort of photographic records, inadequate as these must always be of such grand spectacles of the wilderness. Then we paddled down four or five miles to the

end of Timbasket Lake, opened up a narrow gap in the black forest wall that seemed to shut it in, and—dropped.

At the lower end of this lake a deep rock wall runs from the Rocky side to that of the Selkirks. Above this ancient rock dam stretches back the resultant lake; below, the water plunges down to make up for the descent it has lost in the eight miles above, the river here being called the Twenty-six Mile Rapids. It was wicked water from the start, and we had not run three hundred yards before Walt, stern paddle and commander-in-chief, called out for the first landing, and Barnes got his first ice bath for the day. He took the flying leap when we rounded to, nose up stream, along the rocky shore where a narrow beach offered footing. As landing-man, he carried in his hand the fifty-foot knotted rope on which our lives were to depend for some ensuing days. The water caught him midbody, but his feet held and he checked the boat.

This in effect was epitome of our progress. We got out, lined *Ironsides* down over the white water we could not run, jumped in when the water looked passable below, rode as far as we dared, and then reconnoitered again. Just before noon Barnes made his first and only mistake, one which nearly cost us our outfit if not our lives. He mistook an order Walt gave while in the very clamorous middle of a bad drop, heading the boat in shore instead of out, and so throwing us broadside into the middle of the rollers. We wallowed through however, the white crests some eight or ten feet above us, and not over-comfortable to look upon. We made good progress all day, running the bellowing chute at the mouth of Cummins Creek, nine miles down the rapids, about six o'clock, and so making camp in a little flat where the mountain foot stood back from the water. All night we could hear the din of the grinding waters in our ears, and I doubt if any of us slept very well, tired as we were, for there was some anxiety as to what was ahead. We had by this time learned that the Columbia in this part of its course is no place for little boats or inexperienced men.

In this handling of a heavy river boat the paddles are three inches thick in the shaft—they must not break. The blade is also heavy and strong, the entire paddle about seven feet in length. The boat is worked in precisely the opposite way to that familiar to most canoeists. With a small canoe you go to starboard by paddling on the opposite side, and hold her straight by the wrist turn, all on one side the boat. That would mean destruction on the Columbia with the heavy boats necessary and in smashing, mixed currents. For instance, you wish to get over to the right, and do it quick; bow paddle reaches over to the right and claws with all his might and all his paddle, his blade slanted slightly so that the current helps draw the boat over. Meantime, stern paddle perhaps shoves his paddle deep down on the same side and pries her over to the left at the stern; or if the case be not so urgent, paddles strongly out on the left; or steers with the paddle far behind as the case may be. "It's not here as it is in East Canada," said Walt, who is East Canadian and a riverman of old. "There's no water like the Columbia. She has more power in her than any river in all this Northwest, she's so deep and strong. Besides, there's devils in her."

That expresses the feeling—it has devils in it. It is not like any other water. Along its shores, as I learned when I scrambled along at the foot of the mountain walls while the boys were lining the boat, there are mica-shot bowlders running from the size of Trinity Church down to the size of your head. These must also fall far out midstream, so that no one can gauge the nature of the bottom. There may be cones that run down a hundred feet or more, rocks that thrust up a hundred feet or more under the water, not to mention the visible ones over which the water breaks in deadly surges in shore— the dangers which forced us to the line so often. The water has extraordinarily curious qualities. Sometimes the paddle sweeps back lightly with no resistance; again, the water seems thick and hard, not fluid, but compressed unspeakably where a boil or a cross current halts the sweep of the boat forward. There is very much noise in this water all the time, and of a sort I never heard elsewhere. At times the compression is such that the water seems shivered, and it grinds on itself like thin ice or like crunching glass. Often in the nights I would waken and think the ice

was coming down, but it was only the grinding of the water on itself, never twice alike. That was the fearsome thing of it. The river would run silent for minutes at a time, then, with no reason in the world, it would unheave and fling out waves from midstream, and wail, and grind and crash, as though something were down in there. It was our feeling all the time we were on the Columbia that it was a real creature, and was after us, laughing and threatening, and mocking and chasing. "She's after us, fellows," was a common expression as we would find ourselves grinning at the foot of some steep pitch. It is a devil's water. Those who like it may have it. Not again for me, I think; or at best, not on the June rise.

At the end of our first day we set a watermark, so that we could test the rise or fall. Walt was glad when he saw that there was but a trifling difference. It was now May 28th, and the snow was melted in all the valleys. The great snow fields up high, from which come the June rise of all great mountain rivers, might turn loose any day of warm sun; and if the June rise caught us we were trapped for fair, for now there was no getting back up river. It was run through or lose our numbers. I could see that Walt was uneasy, though better river work than his I never saw. But for him we would be in the wet somewhere to-day. Barnes claimed less experience, but a more gallant soul never went into the hills. I would want no better companions than these two. Our second day continued to be of a certain interest to the life-insurance companies. We were getting more tired now, and less cautious, and so took swifter and swifter pitches. I cannot say just how heavy were some of the swells, but I should say a third to half the length of our boat, which was twenty-four feet. She proved quite a ship, and we gained confidence. At the fast runs down midstream on the white water we could not help yelling, no matter how hard we tried to be serious—it was such fun after all.

At about noon on this day, at Walt's order, we hauled out to bail and take stock. Walt was looking troubled. "There's a trail up there a half mile," said he, pointing to the black mountain side, "and if you follow it five miles, you can strike the river at what we call the Boat Encampment.

Reconnoitering Methodist Cañon.

You can tell it when you see a tree and a burned flat;" etc., etc.

"Me for the trail," said I to Walt, misdoubting something was up.

"Below us is the worst thing we've struck yet," he admitted. "There's a piece of cañon there, a mile or so, where we can't get out, and have to go through. If we get off the comb of the river, we're in the eddies—and then it's all off. But it'll only take ten minutes to go through, while it'll take you several hours to get around, and we'll have to wait. And maybe you won't get around at that; or if you do, maybe we won't get through; and if we didn't, where'd you be? I don't want to waste any time hunting you up, for if she starts to booming while we're in here, we're up against it sure. Still, you're the boss."

"I've got a hunch not to run this cañon," said I, after reflection.

"I've got a hunch you're scared," said Walt, also after reflection.

"You can just bet I'm scared, said I; scared deep and lasting, and I don't care who knows it. But now, since you don't know the difference between being scared and being a coward, I'm just going to run through with you, as far as you go." So saying, I stepped hastily toward the boat —and sprained my ankle on a rock, to prove there is something in hunches.

We embarked, after careful explanation by Walt of precisely what must be the plan of action when once we were in this cañon, the one known as Rocky Cañon sometimes, although we named it the Upper Death Cañon, by reason of its character. It was the comb of the river we must run, the midrib of white water, flung up high in the center by the confining walls of the cañon. This rib was high and definite, rolling ten or twelve feet high in breaking white crests, all moving forward and down. We struck square for the middle of it; and then I saw a sight I would not have missed for very much, now that I am through with it.

We swung around a sharp bend, madly hugging this white, high water in the middle, old *Ironsides* plunging into the crests game as a pebble, and winning our admiration. Then there opened up a sharp, double bend in the narrow, rocky cañon, a big Z, two right angles almost, in the rock wall. We ran down into this, clinging as best we could by fast paddling to our white

comb of the river, which suddenly grew higher and narrower. We were riding ten feet higher midstream than the level of the water on either shore. On the left, at the end of the first leg of the Z, the water flowed backward, upstream, in a steady green sheet, unrippling, in a curve like the bent glass of a vast show-case. Upon the right-hand side the current also was upstream and very rapid, but the water here was white and broken. The downstream current was out in mid-river on the comb; and ahead of that a ledge, with plenty of water, but with fifteen or twenty degrees of drop it seemed, ran almost across the river. Below this ledge was a wide scooped-out basin of water where the river turned into the second leg of the Z, and on the farther edge of this the water ran high and swirled around, flung up by the force of the fall against the side of the amphitheater, as a bicycle is swung by its speed on a walled track.

All this I saw unfold before us in a swift picture, one not to be forgotten, as we raced on down where no boat belonged. We held to our comb, however, and kept out of the side currents and the white-topped boils which come up out of the mysterious depths of this mad river. Even so, we had the nearest of squeaks to get through, an event happening for which no one could have been prepared. Out of the stiff rib of the river's mid-current, somewhere in the white crest that raced with us and above us, there opened up a deep hole, a white edged, cyclonic looking cone, so deep one could have dropped a church into it had one had a church; and this twisting thing came down and followed us, racing after us as though it wanted nothing so much as to get hold of us—one of the most dangerous pitfalls of this wicked river, inhabited of devils. I saw this hole open and follow on, and run alongside for a few yards, dropping quickly astern as we swept past. It missed us hardly a dozen feet. I could look down straight into it. I heard Walt call out, and saw the paddles claw and scoop; and then came the derisive scream of the water as we swept on down over the ledge, into the basin, around its bicycle track, and around the next bend; where Mother Columbia, relenting, smiled at us treacherously, as who should say, "Never mind, my children, I'll get you next time." A few moments later we were in a wide, beautiful, gentle bend, and so pulled up at the beach known as the Boat Encampment. Walt wiped the sweat from his face.

"Did you see that hole open up alongside back there?" he asked. I nodded.

"Maybe that was your hunch," he said soberly. "If the stern of the boat had slid back over the edge of that hole, she'd have filled behind and stood straight up on end. That whirl would stand a small saw-log up, and pull it down." After which no one seemed to think the incident of special interest.

"This is better sport than hunting grizzlies," I ventured, as we were eating lunch.

"A thousand times better," agreed Walt. "The old Columbia's worse than a thousand grizzlies, I'll tell you that;" and Barnes nodded also. "I take off my hat to her every time I run her," said Walt.

From the Boat Encampment to the head of the Big Bend is brisk, but not very dangerous water. The scenery here is magnificent, two splendid valleys opening back into a vast white solitude of untracked mountains. First came the Wood River—part of old David Thompson's trail from the head of the Saskatchewan to the Kootenais, and just beyond that, at the spot where the Columbia swings around for the south, the Canoe River, a rapid water leading up toward the Tête Jaune Cache, and so northward and Fraserward, world without end. We had little joy of even so grand a panorama as this little-known one at the head of the Big Bend, for our souls were troubled. Walt gave a muttered exclamation of disgust as we reached the current of the Canoe River. Both it and the Wood were stained yellow, very yellow. The June rise was on!

We had no great pleasure after that. We swept down another twenty miles, southward, before dark, and camped at the mouth of End Creek, Nagle Creek, or whatever it is; but we exulted not at all that now and again we were near the home of Ephraim, as indeed we were at any one of these many tumbling creeks that came down from the high basins. Walt confessed he had never been up this creek to the slides. He thought it might be eight or ten miles, which might mean a couple of days before we got our upper camp es-

tablished. Our supplies were very low, only a little flour, very little baking-powder, a very few pounds of bacon. If we could not run the river, we would be a hundred miles from the railroad, and three-fourths of this would be over country almost impassable. This sort of walk on flour and water and a sore ankle is not inviting. Barnes and I, however, were for the hunt, thinking it wrong to come so far and then to back out. Walt, who knew more of the river than we did, set out his water-mark that night with a very sober face, and in the morning he was still more sober. I was much of the mind to tell him I thought he was scared; as indeed he had license to be. We held a council after breakfast, and resolved that, as there would have been more anxiety than sport in a bear hunt when the river was coming up so fast, each foot here meaning perhaps a dozen feet in the wild cañons below, it was better wisdom to quit the hunt and get out while we could; and if we could.

We were off early, and had nothing of special interest for part of the day, as the river for forty miles below the bend has little current in many of its longer reaches. We paddled against a head wind part of the time. In the afternoon we got some rough water, and we were all ready to camp when evening found us near an accessible place, this being, as near as Walt could remember, about ten miles above the dreaded Death Rapids, and the equally dreaded Big Eddy, which was esteemed by Walt as the worst thing on the whole river, and a place over which we should line if we lined nowhere else. We were still some sixty miles above Revelstoke as near as we could tell—no one knows what the distances are in a boat running at such varying speeds; and we were in no mood now to walk out. We decided to run on down. We were glad we had not lingered after Ephraim when we noted the rapid rise of the river, and saw its flood turn from green to chocolate, and heard new groans, wails and mockings come up from the depths as we lay at the river's brink that night listening to the tortured things that live below that always heaving floor. I noted again the strange grindings, like crashing glass or grating ice sheets, a sound I had never heard on any other river in the summer time.

The Columbia does not merely threaten, but performs. No one can tell how many men have been lost on the Big Bend. The Surprise Rapids, far up at the head of the bend, are about as bad as any. Seventeen men are known to have drowned here. Leo Davis was capsized on these rapids while we were at Timbasket Lake. We found his boat crushed and flung ashore a hundred miles down stream, and twenty miles below the head of the bend, and so thought Leo was gone. Later we learned that he got out alive, though losing all his supplies. I saw another broken boat on the Twenty-six Mile Rapids, whose owner we never knew, nor what became of its owner. We saw on a big bowlder near shore the name of a Swede who was drowned a few years back, whose body, of course, was not recovered: for the Columbia never gives up its dead. Now below us were the bloodiest of all these waters, the Death Rapids, where, in the mining stampedes soon after the California gold rushes, so many miners were drowned—some say one hundred and sixty-three, in what was called the Frenchmen's stampede. These men were mostly drowned from rafts, in which they foolishly tried to get down river to avoid the awful walking. Seven Chinamen once started down on a raft. One got through alive, hanging fast by a rope, and he was so scared he left America without ever saying a word. One man was cast up a few feet from shore on a rock from which he did not dare jump. His companion was swept down in their boat for a mile before he could get ashore and come back to rescue him. Three men went over in a boat, and only one, a duffer who could not swim a stroke, got out. Further down the river, in the Revelstoke cañon, was where Tom Horne, as good a river man as there was in the Northwest, was drowned with Jack Boyd, the mail carrier, a man who was in deadly terror of the Columbia, and who would not even go on the ice in the winter, preferring to wallow through the snow-piled trails up on the mountains. Yet the Columbia got him. There is little virtue in swimming when you get out in the Columbia Rapids; the boils and sucks pull down the stoutest swimmer. Walt said that an oar under the chin helps, and that without it one cannot last long. He ought to know; he was in the middle of the Surprise Rapids

with that equipment once. To fight the current is fatal. A couple of hundred yards was as far as Tom Horne got. From the top of the cañon they saw the boat go over. Boyd, fearing trouble, had lashed his wrist fast to the line, and so was found. Horne's body never was found.

We always lashed our guns fast to the gunwale of the boat, though Walt said that was taking thought for others after us rather than ourselves; yet he never liked to see me have a rope coiled by my side, saying it was bad luck to take such precautions and that in any case it would do no good if we went over. Such were a few of the cheerful reflections in which we indulged as we dropped down near Death Rapids.

The river was now much changed from the appearance it had when Walt went through in low water. Our first five miles the next morning were like shooting the chutes at a park. The water acted very strangely part of the time, sometimes coming up in a great boil and striking the bottom of the boat as though a big arm had swung a heavy hammer against it. Sometimes the boat was wrenched as though with opposing giant hands—places where the upstream and downstream currents caught her. Sometimes a big swell would fall down out of the white mid comb and seem to turn our boat almost over in spite of all we could do to keep her up. I confess that I never saw water with such power or with so many inexplicable freaks. I think some of this worst water must have been in the dreaded Big Eddy; for, to our own surprise, the water was such that we ran clean across the Big Eddy and did not line an inch. I doubt if Walt knew it until after we were over.

Below this eddy there was a short cañon, which he said was not very dangerous; but it was fortunate we got out and reconnoitered here, for the rise of the river had made this cañon a raging chasm, where no boat could have run, and where at one point we could not even line down, having to take old *Ironsides* out and around for a hundred yards, inch by inch, up along the side of the slanting rock wall, from which bowlders big as houses had rolled down. We were hours going two miles here.

While the men were lining down below this place, which we called the Methodist

Cañon, I walked on below, and so saw far off on the left, some hundreds of yards away, the dreaded Death Rapids, a ridge of white water, then perhaps twenty-five feet high, in which no boat could have lived, a bad trap to any man not knowing this river; for on the opposite shore the entrance to the chute looked inviting and easy. Once below the end of the Methodist Cañon, one could not escape on that side of the river. The men got *Ironsides* through on the relatively safer right-hand shore, only after a long, hard strain with the line. Meantime I was two miles down stream, and had found another nasty water, through which it seemed to me they could not line—the Priest Rapids, as I afterward learned. Below this I built a fire, to show the others where I was. I saw them come out and reconnoiter, and then go back. The next thing I knew, I saw the boat shoot out on the far side of the river, where the water did not look so bad; and down they came, and through, like a race horse—a fine sight. They were not able to make landing for a long distance below where I was waiting. Barnes was full of glee, and said that was about the best run he had had. The waves were about twelve feet, they thought. From the shore they did not look the half of that, but no rapid can be gauged until you get into it. They had to cross, for the Priest Rapids were as bad on the right-hand side as Death Rapids on its left.

The Gordon Rapids we had side-stepped practically, the high water opening up a harmless chute of which we availed ourselves; so at the foot of the Priest we began to think that the worst of our troubles was over. We took it easy for a few miles of fast but steady water. Toward evening we got a shot at a lynx which came out on the narrow beach. Walt picked up the first rifle he could get loose, which happened to be Barnes' .35, and missed a couple of shots. I got hold of Walt's rifle, a .33, and killed the cat at the second shot. We thought it sixty yards, but it was over a hundred and sixty. When we finally got ashore, after rescuing our foolish little dog, who thought he could retrieve a lynx in the Columbia, and who came very near getting drowned, we went back after our lynx, and I was surprised to see that it was full grown, about five feet long, and

would weigh perhaps forty pounds. The distance across the water had been most deceptive. I presume the river here was three hundred and fifty yards wide. In some of the cañons it was not over a hundred yards wide; in some of the very worst, not over seventy-five yards. How deep it is there no one knows. Its power would light New York, or grind for Chicago. St. Anthony's Falls of the Mississippi are weak beside it.

The June rise was now on full, but we cared not that the river rose four feet the next night, for we now were safe. One night more we spent in camp, listening to the wailing and gnashing of the river, and so dropped down to the farm cut out of the wilderness years ago by poor Jack Boyd. We had no excitement after that. We met a steamboat captain who tied up above the Revelstoke Cañon, stopped by the June rise. He travels some of these safer lower waters.

"I wouldn't come through what you've run in that boat for five thousand dollars," said he, "and I wouldn't go a foot farther in it for all the money you could stack up in front of me. The Columbia's no place for little boats, my sons."

For one I am willing to take his word for that. But this is what a look at the Big Bend may cost; and this is what the pursuit of Ephraim sometimes means.

Meantime, as showing what a difference in luck may mean, I might state that two weeks before we struck Revelstoke, a resident sportsman, Dr M——, started out on a little hunt with a guide and a single pack horse, taking only four days' grub along. The second day from the railroad they found an eight-foot grizzly, methodically shot him up, took his hide and came home again that evening. I was thirty-five days in the mountains, and did not see a grizzly that I was sure was a grizzly. Last spring a young Englishman dropped off at Revelstoke and said calmly that he had come to kill a grizzly, you know. And, you know, he got a barber or somebody for a guide, and went out a little way, far enough to satisfy the guide's conscience for taking away his money, and in a week they were back. The Englishman had killed a splendid nine-foot grizzly. That is part of the pleasure in the search for Ephraim. You never can tell.

46

The Last of the Indian Treaties

DUNCAN CAMPBELL SCOTT

An Indian family travelling.

THE LAST OF THE INDIAN TREATIES

By Duncan Campbell Scott

ILLUSTRATIONS FROM PHOTOGRAPHS BY THE AUTHOR

THE Indian policy of the Canadian Government was inherited from the British procedure in the American colonies, which still survives with additions and modifications. The reserve system appeared at the earliest, and there was but little difference between the policy of the French and British in Canada with the exception that in the French design evangelization was an important feature. So that in 1867, when the Dominion of Canada took over the administration of Indian affairs, the Government found a certain well-established condition. The Indians of the old provinces of Nova Scotia and New Brunswick had been given lands; in Quebec the grants of the French king had been respected and confirmed; in Ontario the Indian titles had been surrendered by treaty for a consideration in land and money, as between sovereign powers. The first of the treaties was made by Governor Haldimand in 1784.

In the early days the Indians were a real menace to the colonization of Canada. At that time there was a league between the Indians east and west of the River St. Clair, and a concerted movement upon the new settlements would have obliterated them as easily as a child wipes pictures from his slate. The Indian nature now seems like a fire that is waning, that is smouldering and dying away in ashes; then it was full of force and heat. It was ready to break out at any moment in savage dances, in wild and desperate orgies in which ancient superstitions were involved with European ideas but dimly understood and intensified by cunning imaginations inflamed with rum. So all the Indian diplomacy of that day was exercised to keep the tomahawk on the wall and the scalping knife in the belt. It was a rude diplomacy at best, the gross diplomacy of the rum bottle and the material appeal of gaudy presents, webs of scarlet cloth, silver medals, and armlets.

Yet there was at the heart of these puerile negotiations, this control that seemed to be founded on debauchery and license, this alliance that was based on a childish system of presents, a principle that has been carried on without cessation and with increased vigilance to the present day—the principle

495

of the sacredness of treaty promises. Whatever has been written down and signed by king and chief both will be bound by so long as "the sun shines and the water runs." The policy, where we can see its outcome, has not been ineffectual, and where in 1790 stood clustered the wigwams and rude shelters of Brant's people now stretch the opulent fields of the township of Tuscarora; and all down the valley of the Grand River there is no visible line of demarcation between the farms tilled by the ancient allies in foray and ambush who have become confederates throughout a peaceful year in seed-time and harvest.

The treaty policy so well established when the confederation of the provinces of British North America took place has since been continued and nearly all civilized Canada is covered with these Indian treaties and surrenders. A map colored to define their boundaries would show the province of Ontario clouted with them like a patch-work blanket; as far north as the confines of the new provinces of Saskatchewan and Alberta the patches lie edge to edge. Until lately, however, the map would have shown a large portion of the province of Ontario uncovered by the treaty blanket. Extending north of the watershed that divides the streams flowing into Lakes Huron and Superior from those flowing into Hudson Bay, it reached James Bay on the north and the long curled ribbon of the Albany River, and comprised an area of 90,000 square miles, nearly twice as large as the State of New York.

This territory contains much arable land, many million feet of pulpwood, untold wealth of minerals, and unharnessed water-powers sufficient to do the work of half the continent. Through the map of this unregarded region Sir Wilfrid Laurier, Premier of Canada, had drawn a long line, sweeping up from Quebec and curving down upon Winnipeg, marking the course of the eastern section of the new

Jimmy Swain, head guide, Albany River.

Transcontinental Railway. The aboriginal owners of this vast tract, aware of the activity of prospectors for timber and minerals, had asked the Dominion Government to treat for their ancient domain, and the plans for such a huge public work as the new railway made a cession of the territory imperative.

In June, 1905, the writer was appointed one of three commissioners to visit the Indian tribes and negotiate a treaty. Our route lay inland from Dinorwic, a small station on the Canadian Pacific Railway two hundred miles east of Winnipeg, to reach the Lac Seul water system, to cross the height of land, to reach Lake St. Joseph, the first great reservoir of the Albany River. Our flotilla consisted of three canoes, two large Peterboroughs and one birch-bark thirty-two feet long which could easily hold eleven or twelve men and 2,500 pounds of baggage and supplies, as well as the treasure-chest which was heavy with thirty thousand dollars in small notes. Our party included three commissioners, a physician, an officer of the Hudson's Bay Company who managed all the details of transport and commissariat, and two constables of the Dominion police force.* I am bound to say the latter outshone the members of the commission itself in the observance of the Indians. The glory of their uniforms and the wholesome fear of the white man's law which they inspired spread down the river in advance and reached James Bay before the commission. I presume they were used as a bogey by the Indian mothers, for no children appeared anywhere until the novelty had somewhat decreased and opinion weakened that the magnificent proportions and manly vigor of our protectors were nourished upon a diet of babies.

Our crew of half-breeds and Indians

* Messrs. S. Stewart and D. G. MacMartin, Commissioners; A. G. Meindl, M. D.; T. C. Rae, Esq., Chief Trader, Hudson's Bay Co.; P. C.'s Parkinson and Vanasse, with the writer, made up the party.

The blind chief Missabay making a speech.

numbered not less than twelve and sometimes seventeen, so that the strength of the party never fell below nineteen and was often twenty-four.

New men were engaged at Albany and at Moose Factory and experience was had of many different types. The Scriptures had seemingly been searched to furnish names for our men and we had in service at one time or another the prophets, the apostles, and a goodly number of the saints, even to such minor worthies as Caleb who went to spy out the land for the children of Israel! A word or two of the chronicle must be given up to the chief members of the crew—to David Sugarhead, who had only one lung and worked as if he had four; to Oombash, the dandy of the party, a knowing bowsman who wore a magenta and blue sweater and always paddled in

a pair of black woollen gloves; to Simon Smallboy, a hard man to traffic with, but a past master of poling; of Daniel Wascowin, who cooked for the crew, and who was a merry man; and lastly, of Jimmy Swain, the old Albany River guide, sixty-seven years old, who ran to and fro over the longest portage carrying the heaviest pack.

He is a fine type of the old half-breed race of packers and voyageurs which is fast disappearing; loyal and disinterested, cautious but fearless, full of that joy of life which consists in doing and possessed by that other joy of life which dwells in retrospect, in the telling of old tales, the playing of old tunes, and the footing of old dance steps. Jimmy was enjoying a mighty old age after a mighty youth. He had been able to carry 600 pounds over a portage nearly a quarter of a mile long. He had run on snow-shoes with the mail from Moose Factory to Michipicoten, a distance of 500 miles, in six days, carrying only one blanket, a little hardtack, and a handful of tea. Now in his sixty-seventh year he was the equal of the best of the young fellows. He took all the portages at a tremendous speed and barefooted, for there was a thick layer of callous flesh on

in it. But what matter! When Jimmy closed the flap of his tent and drew it forth out of its blue pine box, I doubt whether any artist in the world had ever enjoyed a sweeter pang of affection and desire.

We touched water first at Big Sandy Lake and in three days had reached Frenchman's Head (Ishquahka portage), one of the reserves set apart by an earlier treaty. James

Chief Moonias.

An Indian, Albany River.

the soles of his feet. He was conscious of his virtues, for in reply to the question, "Well, Jimmy, is there anything left at the other end of the portage?" he would always say, "I was there last myself, surr." That was conclusive. Moreover, Jimmy was an artist. How he could play the violin at all with his huge callous fingers was a matter for wonder, but play he did; all the jigs popular on the Albany for the last fifty years, curious versions of hymn-tunes, "Abide with Me" and "Lead, Kindly Light," a pathetic variation of "Home, Sweet Home," the name of which tune he did not know, but called it after a day or two "The tune the bosses like; it makes them feel bad!" Every night after supper Jimmy withdrew into his tent, closed the flap, and took out his violin. The instrument was as curious as the art employed to play it. "Oh, it's a fine fiddle!" Jimmy would say. "It's an *expensive* fiddle. Dr. Scovil gave it to me, and it must have cost ten dollars." He had scraped the belly and rubbed it with castor-oil, and the G string had two knots

Bunting, the chief of the band, when he learned our business sent twelve of his stalwart Indians to help us over the long and difficult portage; as it was the occasion of a lifetime they brought their wives, children, and dogs and made a social event of it. But they doubled our working force and saved us a half-day on the portage. Once again we were to meet with such kindness, at New Post on the Abitibi River, when Chief Esau and five of his men, adherents of the new treaty, gave us an offering of their help for two days. "We do not expect any money, and no food for this. We will feed ourselves. You have brought us much; we have little to give, but that we freely give."

After Osnaburgh, Fort Hope was to come, then Marten's Falls, then English River, then Fort Albany and the salt water, then Moose Factory and New Post, But Osnaburgh had all the importance of a beginning.

It was about two o'clock one afternoon that we sighted Osnaburgh, a group of Hudson Bay buildings clustered on the lake shore, and upon higher ground the little wooden

Group of Indians, Fort Hope.

church of the Anglican mission. Everyone expected the usual welcome, for the advent of a paymaster is always announced by a fusillade, yells, and the barking of dogs. But even the dogs of Osnaburgh gave no sound. The Indians stood in line outside the palisades, the old blind chief, Missabay, with his son and a few of the chief men in the centre, the young fellows on the outskirts, and the women by themselves, separated as they are always. A solemn hand-shaking ensued; never once did the stoicism of the race betray any interest in the preparations as we pitched our tents and displayed a camp equipage, simple enough, but to them the matter of the highest novelty; and all our negotiations were conducted under like conditions—intense alertness and curiosity with no outward manifestation of the slightest interest. Everything that was said and done, our personal appearance, our dress and manners, were being written down as if in a book; matter which would be rehearsed at many a campfire for generations until the making of the treaty had gathered a lore of its own; but no one could have divined it from visible signs.

Nothing else is so characteristic of the Indian, because this mental constitution is rooted in physical conditions. A rude patience has been developed through long ages of his contact with nature which respects him no more than it does the beaver. He enriches the fur-traders and incidentally gains a bare sustenance by his cunning and a few gins and pitfalls for wild animals. When all the arguments against this view are exhausted it is still evident that he is but a slave, used by all traders alike as a tool to provide wealth, and therefore to be kept in good condition as cheaply as possible.

To individuals whose transactions had been heretofore limited to computation with sticks and skins our errand must indeed have been dark.

They were to make certain promises and we were to make certain promises, but our purpose and our reasons were alike unknowable. What could they grasp of the pronouncement on the Indian tenure which had been delivered by the law lords of the Crown, what of the elaborate negotiations between a dominion and a province which had made the treaty possible. what of the sense of traditional policy which brooded over the whole? Nothing. So there was no basis for argument. The simpler facts had to be stated, and the parental idea developed that the King is the great father of the Indians, watchful over their interests, and ever compassionate. After gifts of tobacco, as we were seated in a circle in a big room of the Hudson's Bay Company's House, the interpreter delivered this message to Missabay and the other chiefs, who listened unmoved to the recital of what the Government would give them for their lands.

Eight dollars to be paid at once to every man, woman and child; and forever afterward, each year, "so long as the grass grows and the water runs" four dollars each; and reserves of one square mile to every family of five or in like proportion; and schools for their children; and a flag for the chief.

"Well for all this," replied Missabay, "we will have to give up our hunting and live on the land you give us, and how can we live without hunting?" So they were assured that they were not expected to give up their hunting-grounds, that they might hunt and fish throughout all the country just as they had done in the past, but they were to be good subjects of the King, their great father, whose messengers we were. That was sat-

Indian mother and children, Fort Hope.

isfying, and we always found that the idea of a reserve became pleasant to them when they learned that so far as that piece of land was concerned they were the masters of the white man, could say to him, "You have no right here; take your traps, pull down your shanty and begone."

At Fort Hope, Chief Moonias was perplexed by the fact that he seemed to be getting something for nothing; he had his suspicions maybe that there was something concealed in a bargain where all the benefit seemed to be on one side. "Ever since I was a little boy," he said, "I have had to pay well for everything, even if it was only a few pins or a bit of braid, and now you come with money and I have to give nothing in exchange." He was mightily pleased when he understood that he was giving something that his great father the King would value highly.

Missabay asked for time to consider, and in their tents there was great deliberation all night. But in the morning the chiefs appeared, headed by Missabay, led by Thomas, his son, who attended the blind old man with the greatest care and solicitude. (In the picture of Missabay speaking you may see Thomas behind his father's staff on his left side [page 575].) Their decision was favorable. "Yes," said Missabay, "we know now that you are good men sent by our great father the King to bring us help and strength in our weakness. All that we have comes from the white man and we are willing to join with you and make promises which will last as long as the air is above the water, as long as our children remain who come after us."

After the payment, which followed the signing of the treaty, the Hudson's Bay

An Indian feast, Fort Hope.

store was filled with an eager crowd of traders. The majority of the Indians had touched paper money for the first time; all their trading had been done heretofore with small sticks of different lengths. They had been paid in Dominion notes of the value of one dollar and two dollars, and several times the paymasters had received deputations of honest Indians who thought they had received more in eight ones than some of their fellows had in four twos. But they showed some shrewdness in calculation when they understood the difference, and soon the camp was brightened by new white blanket coats, gay handkerchiefs and shawls, new hats and boots, which latter they wore as if doing a great penance.

Meantime, the physician who accom-panied the party, had visited the tents. He found the conditions that exist everywhere among Indians—the effects of unsanitary habits and surroundings, which are to some extent neutralized by constant changes of camping-ground, by fresh air and pure water; the prevalence of tuberculosis in all forms, a percentage of cases which at one time might have been relieved by surgical treatment, but which have long passed that stage.

It had become known that a mysterious operation called vaccination was to be per-formed upon the women and children, but not upon the men, whose usefulness as workers might be impaired by sore arms. Indians are peculiarly fond of medicine, and at least as open to the pleasure of making

Poling up rapids, Abitibi River.

experiments with drugs as their white neighbors, but operations they dread; and what was this mysterious vaccination? Jenner and his followers had time to carry on a propaganda, but here at Osnaburgh our physician had to conquer superstitious fear and prejudice in a few short hours. I have known a whole tribe take to the woods upon the mere suggestion of vaccination. But this very superstition, aided by the desire to be in the fashion, gained the day. The statement that something rubbed into a little scratch on the arm would have such powerful results savored of magic and "big medicine," but the question was solved by one of the society leaders, Madame Mooniahwinini! She was one of three sisters, all wives of Mooniahwinini, and she appeared with those of his thirteen children for whom she was partly responsible. That settled the matter and children were pulled from their hiding-places and dragged to the place of sacrifice, some howling with fear, others giggling with nervousness. Never in the history of the region had there been such an attempt at personal cleanliness as at Osnaburgh that day, and at the other posts upon like occasions. To be sure the cleansing extended to only three or four square inches of arm surface, but it was revolutionary in its tendencies.

As soon as the treaty had been signed a feast had been promised by the commis-

sioners and the comestibles had been issued by the Hudson's Bay Company. They consisted of the staples, pork and flour, tea and tobacco; with the luxuries, raisins, sugar, baking-powder, and lard. The best cooks in the camp had been engaged for hours upon the preparation of these materials. Bannocks had been kneaded and baked, one kind plain, another shortened with lard and mixed with raisins; the pork, heavy with fat, had been cut into chunks and boiled; the tea had been drawn (or overdrawn) in great tin kettles.

There is a rigid etiquette at these feasts; the food is piled in the centre of the surrounding Indians, the men in the inner circle, the women and children in the outer. When everyone is assembled the food is divided as fairly as possible and until each person is served no one takes a mouthful, the tea grows cold, the hot pork rigid, and half the merit of the warm food vanishes, but no one breaks the rule. They still wait patiently until the chiefs address them. At Osnaburgh while Missabay walked to and fro striking his long staff on the ground and haranguing them in short reiterant sentences —the same idea expressed over and over, the power and goodness of the white man, the weakness of the Indian, the kindness of the King, their great father—there they sat and stoically watched the food turn clammy! With us the cloth is cleared and the speeches

502

follow; with the Albany River Indians every formality precedes the true purpose of the feast, the eating of it.

The proceedings at Osnaburgh were repeated at the river posts, but when we reached Fort Albany we seemed in a different world. The salutation on the upper river is "Bow jou," the "Beau jour" of the early French voyageur; on the coast it is "Wat che," the "What cheer" of the English.

Marten's Falls was the last post at which we heard Ojibway spoken; at Fort Albany we met the Crees. In our journey we had been borne by the waters of the Albany through a country where essential solitude abides. Occasionally the sound of a conjurer's drum far away pervaded the day like an aërial pulse; sometimes we heard the clash of iron-shod poles against the stones where a crew was struggling up-stream with a York boat laden with supplies. For days we would travel without seeing a living thing, then a mile away a huge black bear would swim the river, slip into the underbrush through a glowing patch of fire-weed, then a lemming would spring across the portage path into the thick growth of Labrador tea; no birds were to be seen, but a whitethroat sparrow seemed to have been stationed at intervals of a hundred miles or so to give us cheer with his bright voice. But at Marten's Falls the blithe sentinel disappeared and "the rest was silence."

When one has heard even a few of the stories of Indian cruelty and superstition which haunt the river, of the Crane Indians who tied a man and his wife together, back to back, and sent them over the falls because they were sorcerers, of the terrible wendigo of Marten's Falls, the lonely spirit of the stream becomes an obsession. It is ever-present, but at night it grows in power. Something is heard and yet not heard: it rises, and dwells, and passes mysteriously, like a suspiration immense and mournful, like the sound of wings, dim and enormous, folded down with weariness.

Below Marten's Falls the Albany flows in one broad stream for three hundred and fifty miles through banks, in some places, eighty feet high, unimpeded by rapids or falls, rushing gloriously to the sea. One night the canoes were lashed together and floated on under the stars until daybreak. Above Marten's Falls the river is broken by

great rapids and cataracts and interrupted by long lake stretches, such as Makokobatan and Miminiska. The shores are flat and the land seems merely an incident in a world of water. Wherever a tent is pitched it is amid flowers; wild roses are inclosed within your canvas house, all about are myriads of twin-flowers, dwarf cornel, and pyrola blossoms. At James Bay the casual effect of the land is yet more apparent. Can these be called shores that are but a few feet high? The bay is vast and shallow; ten miles away the fringes of red willow look like dusky sprays brushed in against the intense steel-gray of the sky-line, and the canoe paddles will reach the sandy bottom! No language can convey the effect of loneliness and desolation which hangs over this far-stretching plain of water, treacherous with shifting sands and sudden passionate storms, unfurrowed by any keels but those of the few small boats of the fur-traders.

At the upper river posts the Indians had been stoical, even taciturn, but at Fort Albany and Moose Factory the welcome was literally with prayer and songs of praise and sounds of thanksgiving. The Hudson's Bay Company's property at Fort Albany separates the buildings of the Roman Catholic mission from those of the Anglican mission. Moose Factory was until lately the seat of the Anglican Bishop of Moonsonee, but that glory and part of the trading glory has departed; the bishop has gone to "the line," as the Canadian Pacific Railway is called, and the Hudson's Bay Company has removed its distributing warehouse to Charlton Island, fifty miles out in the Bay.

The Indians are adherents of either one faith or the other. Casuists they are, too, and very brilliant at a theological argument; so the religious element was largely mingled with the business, and here they thanked God as well as the King. The feasts at Moose Factory and New Post seemed like savage and debased "tea-meetings."

An address written in Cree, in the syllabic character, was presented at Albany; and at Moose Factory the proceedings opened with prayer and were enlivened by hymn singing. The use of the syllabic character is common on the river. Here and there messages from one group of Indians to another were met with, written upon birch bark and fixed to a stick driven into the ground in some prominent position—announcements that the fishing was poor and that they had gone to Winisk; that if Cheena's boy was met with, tell him his father was building canoes two days' journey up the Chepy River.

This method of writing the Indian languages was invented by Rev. James Evans, a Methodist missionary about the middle of the last century. He was then living at

Indians were better dressed, and although the fur trade is a sort of slavery, a greater self-reliance was apparent. The crew that took the commission from Moose Factory to Abitibi were constant in their vespers and every evening recited a litany, sang a hymn and made a prayer. There was something primitive and touching in their devotion, and it marks an advance, but these Indians are capable of leaving a party of travellers

Part of the Albany address in Cree syllabic.

From our hearts we thank thee, O Great Chief, as thou hast pitied us and given us temporal help. We are very poor and weak. He (the Great Chief) has taken us over, here in our country, through you (his servants).
Therefore, from our hearts we thank thee very much, and we pray for thee to our Father in Heaven.
Thou hast helped us in our poverty.
Every day we pray, trusting that we may be saved through a righteous life; and for thee we shall ever pray that thou mayst be strong in God's strength and by His assistance.
And we trust that it may ever be with us as it is now; we and our children will in the Church of God now and ever thank Jesus.

Norway House, north of Lake Winnipeg, where he had come from Upper Canada. As the Crees of Norway House are hunting Indians he found it difficult to make any headway with the work of evangelization. It was almost impossible to teach them to read by the English alphabet, and during the greater part of the year they were on their hunting-grounds, virtually inaccessible. So he invented the characters in which each sign represents a syllable modified by terminals and prefixes. He made his first type from the lead in which tea was packed, moulded in clay; his first press was a Hudson's Bay Company's fur-press, his first paper fine sheets of birch-bark. An intelligent Indian can readily learn to read by the aid of the syllabic character and the system is used by the missionaries of all sects to disseminate their teachings.

The effect of education and of contact with a few of the better elements of our civilization were noticeable at Albany and Moose Factory. There was a certain degree of cleanliness in the preparation of food, the

suddenly, returning to Moose Factory in dudgeon if anything displeases them, and the leader of the prayers got very much the better of one of the party in an affair of peltries. But any forecast of Indian civilization which looks for final results in one generation or two is doomed to disappointment. Final results may be attained, say, in four centuries by the merging of the Indian race with the whites, and all these four things —treaties, teachers, missionaries, and traders—with whatever benefits or injuries they bring in their train, aid in making an end.

The James Bay treaty will always be associated in my mind with the figure of an Indian who came in from Attawapiskat to Albany just as we were ready to leave. The pay-lists and the cash had been securely packed for an early start next morning, when this wild fellow drifted into the camp. Père Fafard, he said, thought we might have some money for him. He did not ask for anything, he stood, smiling slightly. He seemed about twenty years of age, with a face of great beauty and intelligence, and eyes that were wild with a sort of surprise—shy at his novel position and proud that he was of some importance. His name was Charles Wabinoo. We found it on the list and gave him his eight dollars. When he felt the new crisp notes he took a crucifix from his breast, kissed it swiftly, and made a fugitive sign of the cross. "From my heart I thank you." he said. There was the Indian at the best point of a transitional state, still wild as a lynx, with all the lore and instinct of his race undimmed, and possessed wholly by the simplest rule of the Christian life, as yet unspoiled by the arts of sly lying, paltry cunning, and the lower vices which come from contact with such of our debased manners and customs as come to him in the wilderness.